Abbreviations

Biblical Texts and Versions

ESV	English Standard Version
GNB	Good News Bible
HCSB	Holman Christian Standard Bible
KJV	King James Version
LXX	Septuagint
NAB	New American Bible
NASB	New American Standard Bible
NET	New English Translation
NIV	New International Version
NJB	New Jerusalem Bible
NLB	New Living Bible
NRSV	New Revised Standard Version
NT	New Testament
OT	Old Testament
RSV	Revised Standard Version
TNIV	Today's New International Version

Other Ancient Texts

ʾAbot R. Nat.	ʾAbot de Rabbi Nathan
ʾAbot	ʾAbot
1 Macc	1 Maccabees
1 Clem.	1 Clement
1 En.	1 Enoch
1QH^a	1QHodayot^a
1QM	1QWar Scroll
1QS	1QRule of the Community
2 Macc	2 Maccabees
2 Bar.	2 Baruch
2 En.	2 Enoch
2 Esd	2 Esdras
3 Macc	3 Maccabees

4Q174	*4QFlorilegium*
4Q175	*4QTestimonia*
4Q521	*4QMessianic Apocalypse*
4Q525	*4QBeatitudes*
4QMMT	*4QHalakhic Letter*
11Q19	*11QTempleᵃ*
Ant.	Josephus, *Jewish Antiquities*
As. Mos.	*Assumption of Moses*
b.	Babylonian Talmud
Bar	Baruch
CD-A	*Damascus Documentᵃ*
Deut. Rab.	*Deuteronomy Rabbah*
Embassy	Philo, *On the Embassy to Gaius*
Gen. Rab.	*Genesis Rabbah*
Ḥag.	*Ḥagigah*
Hist. eccl.	Eusebius, *Historia ecclesiastica*
Ign. Phld.	Ignatius, *To The Philadelphians*
J.W.	Josephus, *Jewish War*
Jub.	*Jubilees*
L.A.E.	*Life of Adam and Eve*
Lev. Rab.	*Leviticus Rabbah*
Life	Josephus, *The Life*
m.	Mishnah
Mart. Ascen. Isa.	*Martyrdom and Ascension of Isaiah*
Num. Rab.	*Numbers Rabbah*
Pss. Sol.	*Psalms of Solomon*
Šabb.	*Šabbat*
Sanh.	*Sanhedrin*
Sib. Or.	*Sibylline Oracles*
Sir	Sirach
T. Benj.	*Testament of Benjamin*
T. Dan	*Testament of Dan*
T. Gad	*Testament of Gad*
T. Levi	*Testament of Levi*
T. Mos.	*Testament of Moses*
T. Naph.	*Testament of Naphtali*
T. Reu.	*Testament of Reuben*
T. Sol.	*Testament of Solomon*
Taʿan.	*Taʿanit*
Wis	Wisdom of Solomon

Aji

(Iowa)

www.valleychurchia.com.

THE
WITNESS OF JESUS,
PAUL AND JOHN

An Exploration in Biblical Theology

LARRY R. HELYER

IVP Academic

An imprint of InterVarsity Press
Downers Grove, Illinois

InterVarsity Press
P.O. Box 1400, Downers Grove, IL 60515-1426
World Wide Web: www.ivpress.com
E-mail: email@ivpress.com

InterVarsity Press® is the book-publishing division of InterVarsity Christian Fellowship/USA®,
a student movement active on campus at hundreds of universities, colleges and schools of nursing
in the United States of America, and a member movement of the International Fellowship of
Evangelical Students. For information about local and regional activities, write Public Relations
Dept., InterVarsity Christian Fellowship/USA, 6400 Schroeder Rd., P.O. Box 7895, Madison, WI
53707-7895, or visit the IVCF website at <www.intervarsity.org>.

Scripture quotations, unless otherwise noted, are from the New Revised Standard Version of the Bible,
copyright 1989 by the Division of Christian Education of the National Council of the Churches of
Christ in the USA. Used by permission. All rights reserved.

Design: Cindy Kiple

Images: St. Paul: Scala/Art Resource, NY
        Six apostles: Cameraphoto Arte, Venice/Art Resource, NY

ISBN 978-0-8308-2888-3

Printed in the United States of America ∞

Library of Congress Cataloging-in-Publication Data

Helyer, Larry R.
  The witness of Jesus, Paul, and John: an exploration in biblical
theology / Larry R. Helyer.
    p. cm.
  Includes bibliographical references and index.
  ISBN 978-0-8308-2888-3 (casebound/cloth: alk. paper)
  1. Bible—Theology. 2. Bible. N.T.—Theology. I. Title.
BS543.H435 2008
230'.041—dc22
         2008022673

P	18	17	16	15	14	13	12	11	10	9	8	7	6	5	4	3	2	1
Y	23	22	21	20	19	18	17	16	15	14	13	12	11	10	09	08		

Contents

Secondary Sources

ABD	*Anchor Bible Dictionary.* Edited by D. N. Freedman. 6 vols. New York: Doubleday, 1992.
BAGD	*Greek-English Lexicon of the New Testament and Other Early Christian Literature.* By W. Bauer, W. F. Arndt, F. W. Gingrich and F. W. Danker. 2nd ed. Chicago: University of Chicago Press, 1979.
BAR	*Biblical Archaeology Review*
BBR	*Bulletin for Biblical Research*
BDAG	*Greek-English Lexicon of the New Testament and Other Early Christian Literature.* By W. Bauer, F. W. Danker, W. F. Arndt and F. W. Gingrich. 3rd ed. Chicago: University of Chicago Press, 1999.
BJRL	*Bulletin of the John Rylands University Library of Manchester*
BSac	*Bibliotheca sacra*
BZNW	Beihefte zur Zeitschrift für die neutestamentliche Wissenschaft
CBQ	*Catholic Biblical Quarterly*
DJG	*Dictionary of Jesus and the Gospels.* Edited by J. B. Green and S. McKnight. Downers Grove, IL: InterVarsity Press, 1992.
DLNTD	*Dictionary of the Later New Testament and Its Developments.* Edited by R. P. Martin and P. H. Davids. Downers Grove, IL: InterVarsity Press, 1997.
DNTB	*Dictionary of New Testament Background.* Edited by Craig A. Evans and Stanley E. Porter. Downers Grove, IL: InterVarsity Press, 2000.
DPL	*Dictionary of Paul and His Letters.* Edited by G. F. Hawthorne and R. P. Martin. Downers Grove, IL: InterVarsity Press, 1993.
DTIB	*Dictionary for Theological Interpretation of the Bible.* Edited by Kevin J. Vanhoozer. Grand Rapids: Baker, 2005.
EBC	Expositor's Bible Commentary
EC	*Encyclopedia of Christianity.* Edited by Edwin H. Palmer. 4 vols. Marshallton, DE: National Foundation for Christian Education, 1964-1972.
EDBT	*Evangelical Dictionary of Biblical Theology.* Edited by Walter A. Elwell. Grand Rapids: Baker, 1996.
EDNT	*Exegetical Dictionary of the New Testament.* Edited by

H. Balz and G. Schneider. 3 vols. Grand Rapids: Eerdmans, 1990-1993.

EDSS   *Encyclopedia of the Dead Sea Scrolls.* Edited by Lawrence H. Schiffman and James C. VanderKam. 2 vols. Oxford: Oxford University Press, 2000.

EGGNT   Exegetical Guide to the Greek New Testament

EvT   *Evangelische Theologie*

ExpTim   *Expository Times*

GTJ   *Grace Theological Journal*

IDB   *The Interpreter's Dictionary of the Bible.* Edited by G. A. Buttrick. 4 vols. Nashville: Abingdon, 1962.

IDBSup   *The Interpreter's Dictionary of the Bible: Supplementary Volume.* Edited by K. Crim. Nashville: Abingdon, 1976.

Int   *Interpretation*

ISBE   *International Standard Bible Encyclopedia.* Edited by G. W. Bromiley. 4 vols. Grand Rapids: Eerdmans, 1979-1988.

JBL   *Journal of Biblical Literature*

JETS   *Journal of the Evangelical Theological Society*

JSNT   *Journal for the Study of the New Testament*

JSJSup   Journal for the Study of Judaism Supplement Series

JSNTSup   Journal for Study of the New Testament: Supplement Series

JTS   *Journal of Theological Studies*

KD   *Kerygma und Dogma*

LRC   Library of Religion and Culture

LW   *Luther's Works.* Edited by Jaroslav Pelikan. 55 vols. St. Louis: Concordia, 1955-1986.

NCBC   New Century Bible Commentary

NDBT   *New Dictionary of Biblical Theology.* Edited by T. Desmond Alexander and Brian Rosner. Downers Grove, IL: InterVarsity Press, 2000.

NDT   *New Dictionary of Theology.* Edited by Sinclair B. Ferguson and David F. Wright. Downers Grove, IL: InterVarsity Press, 1988.

NICNT   New International Commentary on the New Testament

NIDNTT   *New International Dictionary of New Testament Theology.* Edited by C. Brown. 4 vols. Grand Rapids: Zondervan, 1975-1985.

NIDOTTE   *New International Dictionary of Old Testament Theology and Exegesis.* Edited by W. A. VanGemeren. 5 vols. Grand Rapids: Zondervan, 1997.

NIVAC	NIV Application Commentary
NovTSup	Supplements to Novum Testamentum
NSBT	New Studies in Biblical Theology
NTS	*New Testament Studies*
OCD	*Oxford Classical Dictionary.* Edited by S. Hornblower and A. Spawforth. 3rd ed. Oxford: Oxford University Press, 1996.
OTL	Old Testament Library
PS	Pauline Studies
PTMS	Princeton Theological Monograph Series
RSG	Regent's Study Guides
SBT	Studies in Biblical Theology
SJTOP	Scottish Journal of Theology Occasional Papers
TDNT	*Theological Dictionary of the New Testament.* Edited by G. Kittel and G. Friedrich. Translated by G. W. Bromiley. 10 vols. Grand Rapids: Eerdmans, 1964-1976.
TLNT	*Theological Lexicon of the New Testament.* By Ceslas Spicq. Translated and edited by J. D. Ernest. 3 vols. Peabody, MA: Hendrickson, 1994.
TWOT	*Theological Wordbook of the Old Testament.* Edited by R. L. Harris and G. L. Archer. 2 vols. Chicago: Moody Press, 1980.
WBC	Word Biblical Commentary
WTJ	*Westminster Theological Journal*
WUNT	Wissenschaftliche Untersuchungen zum Neuen Testament
ZPEB	*Zondervan Pictorial Encyclopedia of the Bible.* Edited by M. C. Tenney. 5 vols. Grand Rapids: Zondervan, 1975.

Preface

ONE OF THE HARDEST THINGS TO DO, after laboring on a book for a number of years, is to sit down and explain to the reader what you've attempted to do and why. In the beginning, of course, I had an idea and an outline of what I wanted to accomplish. And my editor, Dan Reid, at least thought the proposal worth pursuing. So here is my attempt to say what this book is all about.

The impetus, like the other books I've written, comes from the classroom. For about twenty-five years, I've taught a course for undergraduates at Taylor University called "Biblical Theology." It's a required course for Biblical Studies and Christian Educational Ministries majors, usually taken their senior year. The course has undergone numerous modifications; not surprisingly, so has this book! The material has been field-tested, so to speak, at point blank range, by bright, inquiring minds.

This book expounds the essential message of the New Testament. In order to do this, I first address perhaps the single most important question in biblical studies: Is there a genuine unity organically connecting the Old and New Testaments? I devote two chapters to this crucial question. I survey various non-evangelical options, outline an evangelical consensus and examine two competing evangelical systems of biblical theology. I conclude by proposing a mediating position combining the strengths of both.

The rest of the book takes up the theology of Jesus, Paul and John. The reader may well wonder why only these three? My first response is that to consider all the witnesses would make a rather lengthy book even more so! But beyond practical considerations is this: if you have a basic understanding of Jesus, Paul, and John, you have the heart of the New Testament message. In fact, Jesus is the most important witness. Paul and John are fundamentally indebted to the Master for their theology. This assertion requires support, and I attempt to provide precisely that both in the exposition of their respective theologies and in a summary chapter detailing the unity of their testimony.

My objective is to summarize the essential teaching of the New Testament. To that end, my book is introductory and foundational. It doesn't provide a comprehensive theology of the New Testament. For that purpose, there are a number of excellent works written by evangelicals (see the bibliography for chapter one).

My intended audience is undergraduates reared in, adhering to, or at least open to considering, evangelical Christianity. But I hope the contents won't be too difficult for general readers interested in knowing better what the New Testament teaches. I'm especially desirous that seminary students and pastors find it helpful in both their personal lives and their teaching ministries. There are many excellent books written from an evangelical perspective dealing with biblical theology, whether of the entire Bible or the Old and New Testaments considered separately. We're truly witnessing the coming of age of evangelical biblical scholarship. But more than a few of these are simply too intimidating for busy pastors and laypersons (and, truth be told, seminarians). I hope this book helps fill a gap.

So what makes this book different from the many others devoted to the same general topic? I've already suggested the first distinction: I think it's more accessible for the average reader. But beyond that, I want to accomplish five primary objectives:

1. To introduce evangelical college and seminary students and general readers to the discipline of biblical theology: its definition, presuppositions, basis, task and methodology.

2. To demonstrate the importance of biblical theology for spiritual maturity, both individually and corporately.

3. To help evangelical Christians locate themselves and the way they approach the Bible within the larger enterprize of biblical studies as practiced across the theological spectrum and to provide them with a clear demonstration of the Bible's unity.

4. To provide a summary understanding of the essential message of three key witnesses: Jesus, Paul and John. This core message is primarily focused on Christology (the person of Christ), soteriology (the doctrine of salvation) and eschatology (the study of last things, i.e., second coming, final judgment, heaven and hell), with brief forays into Christian discipleship, ethics and ecclesiology (the nature and function of the church).

If the message of these three witnesses is grasped and incorporated into one's life, nothing short of a spiritual revolution will occur. I'm convinced of it.

5. To argue that the overarching theme of the Bible is the coming of the kingdom of God. This theme, more than any other, organically ties together the many features that unfold within the basic storyline and plot. In short, there is a grand, overarching narrative (a metanarrative in modern literary terms) running from Genesis to Revelation. In my experience, this insight does more to help the average Bible reader understand the Bible than anything else.

So, where do I position myself theologically? Evangelicals are usually aware there's more to theology than simply identifying oneself as an evangelical. There are a number of pigeon holes into which one might fit. I'll not disguise my theological heritage or preferences. In college and seminary, I was trained in dispensational, moderately Calvinistic, Baptist theology. For my doctorate, I studied at Fuller Theological Seminary under Ralph P. Martin and David A. Hubbard. I now consider myself a "Calminian" (I'm still trying to figure out the mystery of election), a historic premillennialist (though not without some misgivings), a noncharismatic (but certainly not anti-charismatic!) and an egalitarian. I've found that I can be comfortable in a number of denominational settings. I've served as a Baptist pastor, interim pastor in the Christian Church, stated supply pastor in the Presbyterian Church (USA), and pulpit supply in Friends, United Methodist, Presbyterian Church of America and various independent churches. I'm currently a member of a church belonging to the Fellowship of Evangelical Churches, formerly the Evangelical Mennonite Church. The bottom line is this: I'm committed to the historic Christian faith based upon the Bible and summarized in the Apostles' Creed and the Nicene Creed. "Here I take my stand."

All books are collaborative efforts. So many have influenced my theological pilgrimage. A succession of pastors (which included two women) in a small, community church in Kent, Oregon (the only church in town), initially grounded me in the Scriptures. I went on to study at Biola University and Talbot Theological Seminary in La Mirada, California, and Western Seminary in Portland, Oregon. To this was added a year abroad in the land of the Bible, at what is today called Jerusalem University College. This was a life-changing experience that continues to shape my understanding of Scripture. The capstone was my doctoral studies at Fuller Theological Seminary. The influence of George E. Ladd and his emphasis on the kingdom of

God is readily apparent in this book. May his memory be blessed!

A special word of thanks goes to Taylor University's Department of Biblical Studies, Christian Educational Ministries, and Philosophy, and to the former provost and vice president for academic affairs, Dr. Dwight Jessup, for granting me a sabbatical leave in the fall of 2002. Some of that time was spent in the library of Regents Park College of Oxford, England, researching and writing. I have fond memories of the excellent tea shared in the Senior Common Room. It's always special to return to the land of one's roots. There'll always be an England!

This is now my second book published by IVP. In both instances, the editor has been Dan Reid, senior editor of reference and academic books. His expertise and encouragement along the way made this book possible. Dan saw the silver in the dross of the first draft and helped me refine the latter in order to expose the former. No doubt it could use more refining, but I'm grateful for his input and that of two external readers he enlisted. I take full responsibility for the dross that remains. The expertise of my copyeditor, Robert G. Maccini, is greatly appreciated.

Finally, a word of thanks to the many students who sat through a semester of biblical theology and discussed the ideas found in this book. Their input and interaction was invaluable. I must single out one student in particular. Nathan Brooks, a 2005 Taylor graduate in biblical studies and M.Div. from Asbury Theological Seminary, proofread a number of chapters and supplied discussion questions. The congregation that sits under this young man's ministry will be greatly blessed.

This project comes to completion on the day the church commemorates St. Paul's conversion. How reassuring to hear his words: "I want you to know brothers and sisters, that the gospel I preached is not of human origin. I did not receive it from any human source, nor was I taught it; rather, I received it by revelation from Jesus Christ" (Gal 1:11-12 TNIV). Thanks be to God!

Larry R. Helyer
Kershner Commons
Upland, Indiana
January 25, 2008

PART ONE

THE DISCIPLINE OF BIBLICAL THEOLOGY

1

What Is Biblical Theology?

BIBLICAL THEOLOGY IS THE CULMINATION of an intensive, systematic study of the Christian canon, Holy Scripture. It summarizes the message of the Bible and articulates its leading themes and ideas in a coherent, organized manner. Stated this way, its importance is self-evident for those who are members of the believing community. A recurring question in the community of faith is "What does Scripture say?" This almost instinctive question posed by believers grows out of a shared conviction: Scripture is God's Word. As such, Scripture provides guidance and direction for what should be believed and how one should behave. It functions, according to church terminology, as the "rule of faith and practice."

In many respects, most believers in Jesus Christ do a rudimentary form of biblical theology. That is, they seek to understand what the Bible teaches concerning God and his relationship to creation, especially human beings. They want to know why there is evil in the world and what God intends to do about it. Of utmost importance, they want to know how to be right with God and enjoy everlasting life in his presence. In short, they want to know how it all turns out in the end. These are the truly "big" questions of life.

However, Christians typically seek the Scriptures for much more than that. They also want to know what the Scriptures say about the mundane issues of life, such as vocation and career, the choice of a life mate, behavior to be avoided and behavior to be imitated. What kinds of advice do the Scriptures offer concerning relationships, stewardship of time, talent, and money, acceptable types of leisure and lifestyle, and literally thousands of other issues?

Frankly, many of these questions are not directly addressed in Scripture. One must draw inferences from truths and principles that are clearly stated, but this is not always a straightforward, unambiguous undertaking. Furthermore, a merely ad hoc reading of Scripture—searching Scripture with a particular issue in mind while failing to grasp the overarching themes and ideas—obscures the essential message of the Bible. To put it another way, "One loses the forest in all the trees."[1] The overall context in which the many individual directives of Scripture are found is only vaguely comprehended, with the result that many facets and implications of the gospel are overlooked. This lack of perspective tends to impoverish the spiritual life both on individual and corporate levels. The discipline of biblical theology seeks to remedy this defect for the community of faith.

In this chapter I want to define biblical theology and offer a methodology for practicing it in order to discover the message of the Bible. Such an endeavor already presupposes some important convictions that need to be recognized. I also locate biblical theology within the larger arena of theological studies. As in so many endeavors, I stand on the shoulders of those who have preceded me. Doing biblical theology is not a solo effort; it is always done best within the context of a community of faith, consisting of those who are contemporary, fellow pilgrims on the way to Zion and those who have gone on before.[2]

DEFINITION OF BIBLICAL THEOLOGY

Here are six definitions offered by evangelical practitioners of biblical theology. The definitions are arranged chronologically from 1948 to 2000.

- "Biblical Theology is that branch of Exegetical Theology which deals with the process of the self-revelation of God deposited in the Bible."[3]

---

[1]"One real danger in Bible study is to get lost in the single phrases and verses of a Bible passage and never really understand the entire message the author was trying to communicate" (Oletta Wald, *The Joy of Discovery in Bible Study* [rev. ed.; Minneapolis: Augsburg, 1975], p. 23).

[2]Many biblical theologies devote an introductory section to the history of the discipline of biblical theology. This has been rehearsed numerous times, so I opt to forgo it. The reader may profitably consult a number of works for such a history. I recommend the following: Otto Betz, "Biblical Theology, History of," *IDB* 1:432-37; J. Barr, "Biblical Theology," *IDBSup* 104-11; W. Taylor, "Biblical Theology," *ZPEB* 1:593-97; James D. Smart, *The Past, Present, and Future of Biblical Theology* (Philadelphia: Westminster Press, 1979); George Eldon Ladd, "Biblical Theology, History of," *ISBE* 1:498-505; idem, *A Theology of the New Testament*, ed. Donald A. Hagner (rev. ed.; Grand Rapids: Eerdmans, 1993), pp. 1-20; Brevard S. Childs, *Biblical Theology of the Old and New Testaments: Theological Reflection on the Christian Bible* (Minneapolis: Fortress, 1993), pp. 3-51; C. H. H. Scobie, "History of Biblical Theology," *NDBT* 11-20.

[3]Gerhardus Vos, *Biblical Theology: Old and New Testaments* (Grand Rapids: Eerdmans, 1948), p. 13.

- "Biblical theology is that branch of theological science which deals systematically with the historically conditioned progress of the self-revelation of God as deposited in the Bible."[4]

- "Biblical theology is that exercise in which an attempt is made to state systematically the faith affirmations of the Bible."[5]

- "Biblical Theology is first of all a descriptive discipline. Its purpose is to set forth in its own historical and religious categories the teaching of the several parts of the Bible about God, man, redemption, ethics, and eternal destiny."[6]

- Biblical theology is that "study of the Bible that seeks to discover what the biblical writers, under divine guidance, believed, described, and taught in the context of their own times."[7]

- "Biblical theology may be defined as theological interpretation of Scripture in and for the church. It proceeds with historical and literary sensitivity and seeks to analyze and synthesize the Bible's teaching about God and his relations to the world on its own terms, maintaining sight of the Bible's overarching narrative and Christocentric focus."[8]

Evangelical biblical theologians have a fairly consistent understanding of what biblical theology entails. This is decidedly not the case when one turns to nonevangelical understandings of biblical theology.[9] Evangelical definitions incorporate the following elements:

- Biblical theology confines itself to the Bible. Thus, it is *canonical* in scope.

- Biblical theology seeks to trace the progressive unfolding of God's revelation through time and space. Thus, it is *descriptive and historical* in method.

---

[4]Charles C. Ryrie, *Biblical Theology of the New Testament* (Chicago: Moody Press, 1959), p. 12.

[5]W. Taylor, "Biblical Theology," *ZPEB* 1:593.

[6]G. E. Ladd, "Biblical Theology, Nature of," *ISBE* 1:505.

[7]Robert W. Yarbrough, "Biblical Theology," *EDBT* 61.

[8]Brian S. Rosner, "Biblical Theology," *NDBT* 10.

[9]For an overview of the various approaches in nonevangelical biblical theology, see James Barr, *The Concept of Biblical Theology: An Old Testament Perspective* (Minneapolis: Fortress, 1999); Scobie, "History of Biblical Theology," *NDBT* 2-20. For an overview of recent trends in scholarly work in OT biblical theology, see R. W. L. Moberly, "Theology of the Old Testament," in *The Face of Old Testament Studies: A Survey of Contemporary Approaches*, ed. David W. Baker and Bill T. Arnold (Grand Rapids: Baker, 1999), pp. 452-78. For the NT, see I. Howard Marshall, *Jesus the Saviour: Studies in New Testament Theology* (Downers Grove, Ill.: InterVarsity Press, 1990), pp. 16-34.

- Biblical theology seeks to summarize the basic teachings of the Bible in regard to its theological content (i.e., what it teaches concerning God, human beings, sin, salvation, ethics and final destiny). Thus, its task is *theological* in nature.

- Biblical theology seeks to present these teachings in the categories that are actually used by the biblical writers themselves. Thus, it is foundationally *exegetical*.

- Biblical theology seeks to organize and state these teachings, themes, and ideas in a coherent manner. Very often, this involves central or controlling ideas that give coherence to all the other ideas. Thus, it is *synthetic and systematic* in organization.

Evangelical biblical theology also assumes certain, basic presuppositions. These may be stated as follows:

- God exists and has revealed himself in human language in the canonical Scriptures.

- The inspired, canonical Scriptures possess an inherent authority and are trustworthy.

- The message of Scripture is coherent and exhibits an essential unity.

- The message of Scripture functions as a rule of faith and practice. Biblical theology is thus not merely descriptive but rather is normative as well.

Biblical theology, carried out in an evangelical context, is not concerned to validate these presuppositions. That is the province of another theological discipline: systematic theology. Rather, the aforementioned presuppositions form the starting point for constructing a biblical theology because the Bible itself does not defend them; it assumes them as self-evident.

BIBLICAL THEOLOGY WITHIN THEOLOGICAL STUDY

Where does biblical theology fit into the larger scheme of theological studies? Traditionally, theology has been divided into four major areas: exegetical theology, historical theology, systematic theology and practical theology.

Exegetical theology specializes in the interpretation of the Bible. This includes a wide range of subdisciplines such as textual criticism, historical criticism, literary criticism, hermeneutics (principles of interpretation) and theological criticism. Typically, in Bible colleges, college and university religion departments, and seminaries students begin with survey courses (Old Testament, New Testament). They then progress to corpora (Pentateuch,

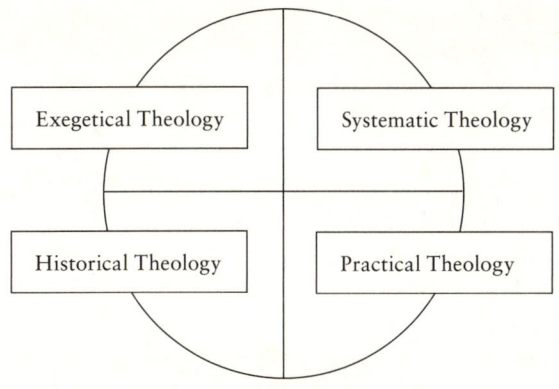

Figure 1.1. Traditional branches of theological study

Historical Books, Wisdom and Poetic Books, Prophets, Synoptic Gospels, Pauline Epistles, General Epistles) and then individual book studies (Gospel of John, Acts, Romans, etc.). Students are encouraged to undertake linguistic preparation involving the study of Hebrew, Aramaic and Greek, the original languages in which the Bible was written. Courses stressing the background of the Bible, such as the archaeology, history, religion, sociology, and literature of the ancient and Hellenistic Near East, are also deemed essential for understanding the world of the Bible.

The culmination of exegetical theology is biblical theology. In the words of Gerhard Hasel, "Biblical theology takes its place as the crown of biblical studies."[10] After one has read and interpreted the Bible, the ultimate question is "What is its message?" Biblical theology summarizes the teaching of the Bible. As such, it renders an extremely important service for believers and provides theological truths for the other three disciplines. This precedence reflects the fact that theology is possible only if God truly reveals himself, and the Bible claims to be precisely such a self-revelation (Rom 3:2; 2 Tim 3:16).

Historical theology deals with the growth and development of Christian thought and doctrine, focusing upon leading theologians, creeds, confessions, and traditions that have shaped the church from the earliest period of the church to the present day.[11] This is helpful because it informs us con-

---

[10]Gerhard Hasel, "The Future of Biblical Theology," in *Perspectives on Evangelical Theology: Papers from the Thirtieth Annual Meeting of the Evangelical Theological Society*, ed. Kenneth S. Kantzer and Stanley N. Gundry (Grand Rapids: Baker, 1979), p. 180.

[11]For a helpful overview of Christian thought, see Geoffrey W. Bromiley, *Historical Theology: An Introduction* (Grand Rapids: Eerdmans, 1978); Ted M. Dorman, *A Faith for All*

cerning various exegetical options. We learn from the masters who preceded us, and we leave ourselves vulnerable if we fail to check our results against theirs.[12] A completely novel interpretation or doctrine calls for caution.

Historical theology also makes interpreters of Scripture aware of their inherited traditions, traditions with the potential to blur the actual authorial intention of a particular text.[13] One must constantly take off blinders and really see what is in the text. David Allan Hubbard, one of my mentors at Fuller Theological Seminary, was fond of a golfing metaphor. He frequently reminded us, "You must play the ball where it lies." How tempting it is to move the ball back onto the green when we encounter the rough!

Practical theology seeks to apply the truths of Christianity to the outreach and maintenance of the church. Accordingly, in this division, one deals with Christian education, evangelism, missions, and pastoral ministry. This is where "the rubber meets the road" in theology. If it is to justify its existence, theological reflection must be communicated with the person in the pew and in the public square. The Scriptures are intended to testify to Jesus Christ and to provide believers with steadfastness and hope (Jn 5:39; Rom 1:1-6; 15:4). Practical theology seeks to implement these intentions. A special burden of mine is that pastors will incorporate biblical theology into their preaching and pastoral duties.

Systematic theology has the enormous task of articulating the truths of Christianity both for the church and over against the competing worldviews and non-Christian theologies of the contemporary world. Therefore, it is both didactic (intended to teach and instruct) and apologetic (giving defense and proof). Systematic theology is the grand climax of theological study and, as such, deserves the accolade "queen of the sciences."

Here is the distinction between systematic and biblical theology. Biblical theology is primarily historical in approach; systematic theology is primar-

---

Seasons: Historic Christian Belief in Its Classical Expression (2nd ed.; Nashville: Broadman & Holman, 2001). For a comprehensive survey of historical theology, see also John Haddon Leith, *Creeds of the Churches: A Reader in Christian Doctrine, from the Bible to the Present* (3rd ed.; Louisville: John Knox Press, 1983); Alister E. McGrath, *Historical Theology: An Introduction to the History of Christian Thought* (Oxford: Blackwell, 1998); idem, *Christian Theology: An Introduction* (3rd ed.; Oxford: Blackwell, 2001); idem, ed., *The Christian Theology Reader* (2nd ed.; Oxford: Blackwell, 2001).

[12]For a detailed examination of selected biblical exegetes from the early church to modern times, see Donald K. McKim, ed., *Dictionary of Major Biblical Interpreters* (Downers Grove, Ill.: InterVarsity Press, 2007).

[13]Trevor Hart reminds us that even historical theology needs to be revised (i.e., our understanding of what older theologians held is not always accurate). Nonetheless, we can never just dispense with it. See Trevor A. Hart, *Faith Thinking: The Dynamics of Christian Theology* (Downers Grove, Ill.: InterVarsity Press, 1996; reprint, Eugene, Ore.: Wipf & Stock, 2005).

ily logical. This does not mean that biblical theology is illogical or that systematic theology is ahistorical. Rather, biblical theology seeks to set forth the progressive unfolding of God's redemptive self-revelation, taking note of the chronological development of God's revelation in Scripture. It is thus methodologically diachronic (i.e., considers phenomena as they develop through time).[14] Systematic theology, on the other hand, is topical and encyclopedic in method. It processes the revelation in Scripture as a completed whole and thus is synchronic (i.e., considers phenomena without consideration of historical development). It then correlates this data with reason, tradition (historical theology), and experience, as well as the empirical and social sciences and liberal arts.[15] This correlation is formulated according to logical principles and in terms of a philosophical worldview, whether clearly articulated or not (e.g., Platonism, Aristotelianism, idealism, common sense philosophy, process philosophy, foundationalism, postmodernism, etc.).[16] A good way to grasp the essential differences between systematic and biblical theology is to compare the table of contents of an evangelical systematic theology with that of an evangelical biblical theology. The organizational pattern and method is quite different in the respective disciplines.[17]

The goal of systematic theology is the articulation of a grand edifice of Christian truth. This body of knowledge is laid out in a well-organized system, hence its name, and is couched in terms of the culture in which the

---

[14]Fred H. Klooster offers a helpful discussion on the historical character of biblical theology in "How Reformed Theologians 'Do Theology' in Today's World," in *Doing Theology in Today's World: Essays in Honor of Kenneth S. Kantzer*, ed. John D. Woodbridge and Thomas E. McComiskey (Grand Rapids: Zondervan, 1991), pp. 242-44.

[15]Willard Taylor says in this connection: "Systematic theology to be vital to the church's life and ministry must engage in a constructive presentation of the meaning of the Christian faith with full usage of any information beyond the Bible which will elucidate the faith to the current situation. The insights of secular history, psychology, sociology, philosophy, and science can aid in creating a viable view of Christian truth which will speak to men of the particular day in which it is composed" ("Biblical Theology," *ZPEB* 1:598).

[16]For a concise definition and exposition of each of these philosophical systems, see *NDT* 517-19, 43-45, 326-27, 152, 534-36, respectively.

[17]For some examples of recent evangelical OT biblical theologies, see Paul R. House, *Old Testament Theology* (Downers Grove, Ill.: InterVarsity Press, 1998); John Goldingay, *Old Testament Theology: Israel's Gospel* (Downers Grove, Ill.: InterVarsity Press, 2003). For evangelical NT biblical theologies, see I. Howard Marshall, *New Testament Theology* (Downers Grove, Ill.: InterVarsity Press, 2004); Frank Thielman, *Theology of the New Testament: A Canonical and Synthetic Approach* (Grand Rapids: Zondervan, 2005). Compare these approaches with the recent evangelical systematic theologies by Donald Bloesch's Christian Foundations series (7 vols.; Downers Grove, Ill.: InterVarsity Press, 1992-2004); Millard Erickson, *Christian Theology* (2nd ed.; Grand Rapids: Baker, 1998). For a comparison with a work on historical theology, see Roger E. Olson, *The Mosaic of Christian Belief: Twenty Centuries of Unity and Diversity* (Downers Grove, Ill.: InterVarsity Press, 2002).

systematic theologian lives. A comprehensive system of theological truths and their warrants comprises the essence of systematic theology. Often, this system is defended over against alternate worldviews and even alternative Christian systems of thought. Thus apologetics—the defense of Christian faith—often is viewed as a subdivision of systematic theology.[18]

The Bible itself does not read like systematic theology. Narratives predominate, but many other literary genres are included. From these various genres, each of which needs to be read with sensitivity within its own frame of reference, one may legitimately infer a theological understanding of reality. Biblical theology seeks to state what that theological reality is. It does not, however, formulate that reality in terms of our contemporary culture; rather, it simply allows the biblical writers to speak for themselves. Krister Stendahl says, "Our only concern [in biblical theology] is to find out what these words meant when uttered or written by the prophet, the priest, the evangelist, or the apostle, and regardless of their meaning in later stages of religious history, our own included."[19] Although I do not share Stendahl's insistence that discovering "what it meant" is our only task in biblical theology, I agree that biblical theology should seek to recover that meaning.[20] As such, biblical theology provides data for the systematic theologian who can then reformulate this material in terms of logical, philosophical, and contemporary categories and concerns. Biblical theology thus serves as a bridge between both systematic and practical theology. Good preaching should reflect the fruit of biblical theology.

THE BASIS OF EVANGELICAL BIBLICAL THEOLOGY: THE CANON

Evangelical biblical theology differs from mainline Protestant liberalism in its commitment to the Christian canon as the sole basis for biblical theology. Liberal Protestantism typically isolates a "canon within a canon" (i.e.,

---

[18]See Donald A. Carson, "Systematic Theology and Biblical Theology," *NDBT* 89-104, esp. 102-3.

[19]K. Stendahl, "Biblical Theology," *IDB* 1:422. J. P. Gabler, considered by many as the father of modern biblical theology, distinguished between biblical theology and systematic theology this way: "Biblical theology is historical in character and sets forth what the sacred writers thought about divine matters; dogmatic theology [akin to systematic theology], on the contrary, is didactic in character, and teaches what a particular theologian philosophically and rationally decides about divine matters, in accordance with his character, time, age, place, sect or school, and other similar influences" (*Oratio de justo discrimine theologiae et dogmaticae regundisque recte utriusque finibus* [1787], cited in Taylor, "Biblical Theology," *ZPEB* 1:594).

[20]Taylor criticizes Stendahl's sharp distinction between "what it meant" and "what it means": "This dichotomy can be unmanageable and distorting. What of the universal and authoritative nature of the Bible? 'What it means' is a form of 'translation' of 'what it meant' and need not therefore be far removed from the latter" ("Biblical Theology," *ZPEB* 1:598).

it evaluates the significance of biblical material by some external criterion, such as "educated mentality," or by a biblical idea, theme or concept, such as "justification by faith," that determines what is normative) or essentially ignores the boundaries of the canon when developing a biblical theology. In keeping with historic Christianity, whether Protestant, Catholic or Orthodox, evangelicalism seeks to explicate divine revelation as it lies before us in the text of the canon.

Of course, the definition and limits of the canon vary within Christendom. Evangelicalism follows the Reformers in accepting the canon of the OT as that which was demarcated by the Palestinian rabbis. It also distinguishes itself from a denomination such as the Mormons, who bring alongside Scripture authoritative, interpretive supplements, such as the *Book of Mormon, Doctrines and Covenants,* and *Pearl of Great Price.* In Mormon theology these books too are considered to be inspired and normative for faith and practice. Other sects, such as Jehovah's Witnesses and Christian Scientists, have additional writings or spokespersons that provide authoritative interpretations of Scripture.[21]

Evangelical biblical theology holds that God has granted special revelation of his person, attributes, will, and purpose for all creation, especially human beings, in Scripture. Scripture alone is inspired, authoritative, trustworthy and normative. This conviction is enshrined in the Reformation phrase *sola scriptura* ("Scripture alone"). In addition to superintending the composition of this authoritative collection, the Holy Spirit assists believers to understand and embrace what is contained therein. This ministry is called illumination and should not be confused with inspiration. Nor should illumination be appealed to as a guarantee for correct interpretation of Scripture. Human interpretations of Scripture, though often correct and edifying, can never claim to be infallible.[22]

Commitment to the canon of Scripture carries with it several implications and requires several qualifications.

1. A genuine theology may be extracted from sacred Scripture. One may do more than simply engage in a history of Israelite religion or of early Christianity. There is a real, divine self-disclosure in Scripture demanding a response on the part of the reader and not just a dispassionate analysis of its ideas and rituals.[23]

2. Since the canon is a Spirit-inspired production, it exhibits a fundamental

---

[21]See J. Stafford Wright, "Sects," *NDT* 633-34.
[22]See Carl R. Trueman, "Illumination," *DTIB* 316-18.
[23]This point is made emphatically by Th. C. Vriezen, *An Outline of Old Testament Theology* (Oxford: Blackwell, 1966), pp. 118-26.

unity. God does not speak out of both sides of his mouth. An authoritative, coherent message is found throughout the pages of the sacred canon.

3. Evangelicals recognize, however, that whereas the entire Bible is authoritative, given its divine inspiration, not all the Bible is normative for faith and practice. This requires explanation. For example, believers today are not bound by the dietary and ritual purity laws of the OT. Whereas an OT Israelite who violated those laws incurred ritual impurity and possible expulsion from the community, NT revelation makes clear that those regulations are no longer binding on the community of faith in terms of religious obligation (Mark 7:18-20; Acts 10:9-16; Rom 14:14; Gal 2:11-14). Furthermore, it is evident that the entire sacrificial system of the old covenant has been fulfilled and thus abolished for the Christian (Heb 9:6-14, 23-28; 10:1-14). Going further, evangelicals recognize that certain passages of Scripture are not addressed directly to the reader and thus are not obligatory. To take an obvious case, no one senses an obligation to carry out Paul's request in 2 Timothy 4:9, 13 to come as soon as possible and bring the cloak and parchments!

There are instances, however, when it is difficult to determine whether imperatives in the NT are contextually and culturally conditioned and thus not binding on the conscience or whether they transcend culture and are binding. The issue of the role of women in the church and society, for example, is hotly debated. Without entering that discussion, I would simply point out again that acknowledging the entire Bible as authoritative does not entail that the *entire* Bible is now normative for faith and practice.[24]

4. Another qualification recognizes that the canon, not its sources, constitutes the basis of biblical theology. That is, within the canon of Scripture are numerous quotations, paraphrases, and allusions to nonbiblical sources. Examples include the book of Jashar (Josh 10:12-13; 2 Sam 1:19-27; LXX of 1 Kings 8:12-13), the book of the Wars of the Lord (Num 21:14), the book of the Acts of Solomon (1 Kings 11:41), the book of the Annals of the Kings of Judah (e.g., 1 Kings 14:29; 15:7, 23; 22:45), the

---

[24]For general guidance in this difficult area see, Gordon Fee and Douglas Stuart, *How to Read the Bible for All Its Worth* (2nd ed.; Grand Rapids: Zondervan, 1993), pp. 70-77; Donald A. Hagner, "Biblical Theology and Preaching," *ExpTim* 96, no. 5 (1985): 138-39; Grant R. Osborne, *The Hermeneutical Spiral: A Comprehensive Introduction to Biblical Interpretation* (Downers Grove, Ill.: InterVarsity Press, 1991), pp. 318-38, William J. Webb, *Slaves, Women and Homosexuals: Exploring the Hermeneutics of Cultural Analysis* (Downers Grove, Ill.: InterVarsity Press, 2001); Elizabeth Yao-Hwa Sung, "Culture and Hermeneutics," *DTIB* 150-55.

book of the Annals of the Kings of Israel (e.g., 1 Kings 14:19; 15:31; 16:5, 14), Aratus, *Phaenomena 5*, or Cleanthes, *Hymn to Zeus* (Acts 17:28), Epimenides, *De oraculis* (Tit 1:12), Menander, *Thais* 218 (1 Cor 15:33), *1 Enoch* 1:9 (Jude 14-15), and *Assumption of Moses* (Jude 9). What are we to say about these other sources? In short, they are not inspired and authoritative simply by virtue of quotation, allusion or intertexuality ("the phenomenon that all texts are involved in an interplay with other texts"[25]). In other words, an inspired writing can incorporate elements from a noninspired writing without imparting to the latter an inspired and authoritative status.

This is not to say, however, that extrabiblical sources have no bearing on the exegetical process. On the contrary, much light is shed on the biblical text by extracanonical material. Indeed, numerous passages of Scripture can be fully understood only against the backdrop of the larger culture in which Scripture was written.[26] Both artifacts and literary remains illuminate the thought world presupposed by the Bible. This material does not, however, by virtue of its explanatory power, partake of inspiration and thus assume authoritative status.

5. By making the canon the basis of biblical theology, evangelicals investigate the actual text of Scripture, not events to which it may refer. God indeed revealed himself in historical events referred to in Scripture (e.g., the call of Abram, the exodus from Egypt), but interpreters have access to those revelatory events only through the inspired text. The meaning of those events is determined by the meaning intended by the inspired spokesperson in the text of Scripture. This means that the written text in its final form, not the putative prehistory of the text or the sources behind the text, is the focal point of biblical theology. Nor should exegetes confuse later interpretations of a particular text, even later biblical interpretations, with the text as it now stands in its own context. In short, the "meaning of the text remains that of the original author and not the interpretation of later generations."[27]

---

[25]Arthur G. Patzia and Anthony J. Petrotta, *Pocket Dictionary of Biblical Studies* (Downers Grove, Ill.: InterVarsity Press, 2002), p. 63.

[26]For the importance of Jewish literature of the Second Temple period, see Larry R. Helyer, *Exploring Jewish Literature of the Second Temple Period: A Guide for New Testament Students* (Downers Grove, Ill.: InterVarsity Press, 2002). For a book showing how Greco-Roman culture left its mark on NT literature, see Mark Strom, *Reframing Paul: Conversations in Grace and Community* (Downers Grove, Ill.: InterVarsity Press, 2000).

[27]John H. Sailhammer, *Introduction to Old Testament Theology* (Grand Rapids: Zondervan, 1995), p. 84. Sailhammer's entire discussion of "text or event" is worthy of close study (pp. 36-85).

6. A further qualification is necessary. Most evangelical biblical theologians acknowledge that the canonical text, not the *ipsissima verba*
("very words") of an inspired spokesperson, forms the content of biblical theology. For example, one cannot claim that the Gospels in Greek
always preserve the exact words spoken by Jesus; rather, we have a faithful representation of what he originally said in Aramaic or Hebrew. We
are, therefore, at least two steps removed linguistically from the original
language of Jesus' discourses.

This raises the question of whether a reconstructed Aramaic or Hebrew text might in fact be more authoritative than our canonical Greek
text.[28] Such reconstructions may well throw welcome light on certain
sayings of Jesus, but they are entirely hypothetical. Language is much
too complex, even for a gifted linguist, to accurately recover the supposed Aramaic/Hebrew original on the basis of the existing Greek text.
The possible permutations and variations are considerable. In any case,
the early church has already made the call for us in this matter: the Gospels in Greek stand as the inspired, canonical text. Evangelicals affirm
that, whether in the Greek text or English translation, one still hears the
vox Jesu ("voice of Jesus").

7. Evangelicals also take into account the fact that the canonical text gives
evidence of editorial activity. For example, the Pentateuch displays a
number of glosses updating the text for readers at a much later time
than the events narrated (e.g., Gen 12:6; 14:14 [cf. Judg 18:29]; 36:31;
Ex 16:35; Num 12:3; 21:14-15; 32:34-42; Deut 2:12; 34:1-12). The prophetic books appear to be anthologies bearing the earmarks of editorial
work throughout (e.g., Amos 1:1; 7:10-17). Both Psalms and Proverbs
show by traits of their structure that they have undergone a long process of collection and shaping before attaining their present canonical
form (e.g., Ps 41:13; 72:18-19; 89:52; 106:48; 150:1-6; Prov 1:1; 10:1;
22:17; 24:23; 25:1; 30:1; 31:1). The Gospels clearly evidence significant
selection, shaping and framing of traditional material. Even the Greek
texts of the same pericopae (self-contained literary units) offer variations in wording. Attempts to harmonize and combine are unconvincing
and unnecessary. These variations, in part, reflect the editorial shaping
of the evangelists. In fact, one can profitably study the theology of the
respective evangelists as inferred by their selectivity and redaction of the

---

[28]This has been the objective of the Jerusalem School of Synoptic Research, founded in 1985,
for recovering the Jewish backgrounds of Jesus' sayings in the Synoptic Gospels. See their
website (http://www.js.org).

Jesus traditions. The Epistles probably include preformed pieces all having their own prehistory (e.g., Eph 5:14; Phil 2:6-11; Col 1:15-20).

The process of writing, editing, and final canonical shaping is very complex, in many cases quite beyond our ability to reconstruct with any certainty. In this connection, the account of Jeremiah's writing a scroll and then dictating a new one, with additions, after Jehoiakim burned the original one, is instructive (Jer 36). All of this to say that canonical Scripture has a very complex compositional history, and the interpreter must be aware of this reality.

METHODOLOGY OF BIBLICAL THEOLOGY

At the risk of oversimplifying a rather complex task, I see the process of biblical theology involving two distinct phases, each of which consists of several steps. The two phases involve quite different intellectual skills: analysis and synthesis.[29] In actual practice, of course, the discrete steps in each phase do not march in lock step, but for pedagogical purposes, I list them in the following order.

1. Exegetical analysis. Biblical theology begins with exegesis. Individual passages are interpreted using the grammatical-historical-theological method.[30] This clumsy title embodies an approach to Scripture best suited to discern the original author's intention.[31] Because of the conviction that the human author's intended meaning takes priority in determining the Holy Spirit's meaning, biblical theology begins here.

I am wary of impressionist approaches in which readers equate what they think the passage means at first glance with what it really means. I confess that this method prevails in small-group Bible studies. Although

---

[29]Rosner says, "Biblical Theology is characterized by two distinct but related activities which may be broadly described as analysis and synthesis" ("Biblical Theology," *NDBT* 6). Already, Robert A. Traina had emphasized that "observation should be both analytical and synthetical. In fact, analytical observations should have as its objective synthetical observation. It is for this reason that the observational process should always culminate with a view of the whole" (*Methodical Bible Study: A New Approach to Hermeneutics* [New York: Biblical Seminary in New York, 1952]), p. 72).

[30]For a helpful overview of this process, see Douglas Stuart, *Old Testament Exegesis: A Primer for Students and Pastors* (2nd ed.; Philadelphia: Westminster Press, 1984); Ralph P. Martin, "Approaches to New Testament Exegesis," in *New Testament Interpretation: Essays on Principles and Methods*, ed. I. Howard Marshall (Grand Rapids: Eerdmans, 1977), pp. 220-51.

[31]Fred Klooster adds to an already cumbersome title further appellatives in order to bring out the multiplicity of perspectives one needs to interpret the Bible. He calls it the grammatical-literary-historical-theological-canonical method of exegesis ("Reformed Theologians," p. 245).

first impressions are not always wrong, and there can be some profit in such sessions, one needs a more reliable method when dealing with literature originating at such a great distance in time and place. Too much is at stake to allow first impressions to dictate what the Word of God is saying to us; more objective controls and checks are essential.

I also deem inadequate the venerable dogmatic approach. This approach dominated during the medieval era and is characterized by the search for proof texts (dicta probantia). That is, the Bible is ransacked for texts that can reasonably (and sometimes not so reasonably) support teaching (dogma) already held to be biblical by the church. The problem is that patristic and medieval theologians tended to import Christian doctrine indiscriminately into the OT. Furthermore, in our own era so much more has been learned about the world in which the Scriptures were originally written that was unavailable to the church fathers and scholars of previous times. This new information throws welcome light on both familiar and obscure passages. These insights are available through the grammatical-historical method.

I also resist the attempt of various hermeneutical approaches, such as reader response, deconstruction and political/social agendas (liberation theology, gay theology, feminist theology, etc.), to dismiss or ignore authorial intention. This is not to deny that social agendas are important, or that the Bible should be interrogated concerning them. Rather, I am concerned that "political correctness" not be allowed to hijack the message of the biblical witnesses and mute their authentic voices. I reject the notion that texts mean only what readers take them to mean, although I readily admit that readers do in fact bring prior understandings to the text. This is precisely why the historical-grammatical approach to Scripture is so important: it helps readers to distance themselves from the text and hear it on its own terms. The objective is to discover the original authors' intended meaning.[32] Amazingly, when this is done, Scripture offers insight into many of the complex issues of our postmodern world.

The exegetical process necessarily involves a number of disciplines previously mentioned, such as textual criticism, historical criticism and literary criticism.

1.1. Textual criticism makes judgments concerning the original wording

---

[32]This is not the place to go into the complicated issues related to the so-called intentional fallacy. Suffice it to say that in the majority of instances, when one discovers the intention of the human author, one also discerns the divine intention. See Nicholas P. Wolterstorff, "Authorial Discourse Interpretation," *DTIB* 78-80; Kevin J. Vanhoozer, "Intention/Intentional Fallacy," *DTIB* 327-30.

of the text. Sometimes variant readings must be evaluated because there is a significant difference in meaning. Most exegetes are dependent upon specialists for this aspect of exegesis. Several handbooks are available for the nonspecialist, and one may receive guidance from full-scale, critical commentaries.[33]

1.2. Historical criticism seeks to answer fundamental questions such as these: Who wrote the text? What was the purpose of the writing? When was it written? What is its presumed life setting? What historical events are mentioned in or presupposed by the writing? These are important questions, the answers to which throw light on the theological message of the text itself.[34]

A major preoccupation for biblical theologians, whether conservative or liberal, often has been determining the historicity of events mentioned in the Bible. Not surprisingly, the two camps arrive at significantly different conclusions in this regard. Historicity is a very important question because Christian faith rests squarely upon historical events (1 Cor 15:3-8). If these saving events should turn out to be fictitious inventions, the entire system of Christian belief appears in danger of collapse. No wonder attacks upon the essential historicity of salvation history, especially the resurrection of Jesus, have generated such impassioned responses by conservative scholars. On the other hand, conservative exegetes need to be more open to the possibility, perhaps even probability, that some ostensibly historical narratives are in fact fictional.[35] Faith and fiction are not necessarily antithetical (one

---

[33]For the OT, see Ernst Würthwein, *The Text of the Old Testament: An Introduction to Kittel-Kahle's Biblia Hebraica*, trans. Peter R. Ackroyd (Oxford: Blackwell, 1957); Bruce K. Waltke, "Textual Criticism of the Old Testament and Its Relation to Exegesis and Theology," *NIDOTTE* 1:51-67. For the NT, see Bruce M. Metzger, *A Textual Commentary on the Greek New Testament* (London and New York: United Bible Societies, 1971); J. Harold Greenlee, *An Introduction to New Testament Textual Criticism* (rev. ed.; Peabody, Mass.: Hendrickson, 1995); Bart D. Ehrman, "Textual Criticism of the New Testament," in *Hearing the New Testament: Strategies for Interpretation*, ed. Joel B. Green (Grand Rapids: Eerdmans; Carlisle: Paternoster, 1995), pp. 127-45.

[34]See Eugene H. Merrill, "Old Testament History: A Theological Perspective," *NIDOTTE* 1:68-85; V. Philips Long, "Old Testament History: A Hermeneutical Perspective," *NIDOTTE* 1:86-102; idem, "Historiography of the Old Testament," in *The Face of Old Testament Studies: A Survey of Contemporary Approaches*, ed. David W. Baker and Bill T. Arnold (Grand Rapids: Baker, 1999), pp. 145-75; I. Howard Marshall, "Historical Criticism," in *New Testament Interpretation: Essays on Principles and Methods* (Grand Rapids: Eerdmans, 1977), pp. 126-38; D. A. Hagner, "The New Testament, History, and the Historical-Critical Method," in *New Testament Criticism and Interpretation*, ed. David Alan Black and David S. Dockery (Grand Rapids: Zondervan, 1991), pp. 73-96.

[35]Ray Dillard and Tremper Longman III make this observation: "Conservatives must guard against the tendency to over historicize the Bible. Legitimate genre questions must be addressed in the interpretation of certain books" (*An Introduction to the Old Testament* [Grand Rapids: Zondervan, 1994], p. 23).

thinks immediately of parables). One thus needs to be careful not to create false dilemmas, such as seeing faith/history issues where in fact we are dealing with genre questions. Nor should ancient historians be judged by the standards of modern historiography. Rather, one must be sensitive to the patterns, structures, techniques and concerns of the biblical storytellers.

1.3. Literary criticism focuses on the shape and form in which the text stands before us. Linguistic communication occurs over a wide range of different types or genres, each of which carries its own "code." Understanding the code is essential if we want to understand the author. Narratives operate differently than do parables, psalms, proverbs, letters, sermons and apocalypses. For example, think of the many reading skills that one has acquired in order to read a newspaper. Familiarity with the various genres of news reporting, editorials, classified ads (with a host of abbreviations), obituaries, the sports page (with its own specialized jargon), and the financial section with its many technical terms, acronyms and abbreviations are all required for adequate comprehension. The Bible is no different. One simply cannot read the Bible as if it were of a uniform genre. Each type of literature makes it own contribution to the theological message found in Scripture.[36]

I pause to address what is probably a growing concern in the mind of the general reader. How in the world can the average reader do justice to this kind of in-depth study? There is no point in avoiding the fact that it takes many years of study to become truly proficient in biblical theology. The general reader of the Bible should not, however, lose heart and abandon the quest for working out one's own biblical theology. The fact is that resources are at hand to enable the general reader to do an adequate job. Let me make a few suggestions and set the anxious student's mind at ease.

When one installs various kinds of software on a computer, often several options are available. One might, for example, download an entire program on to the hard drive. This is the "full installation." Alternatively, one might prefer to place on the hard drive only those files that are likely to be used frequently. This is the "custom installation." Finally, one might,

---

[36]For tips on reading the various genres in the Bible, see Fee and Stuart, *How to Read the Bible for All Its Worth*; Leland Ryken, *Words of Delight: A Literary Introduction to the Bible* (Grand Rapids: Baker, 1993); Daniel M. Doriani, *Getting the Message: A Plan for Intepreting the Bible* (Phillipsburg, N.J.: P & R Publishing, 1996), pp. 222-27; Tremper Longman III, *Reading the Bible with Heart and Mind* (Colorado Springs: NavPress, 1997); Aida Besançon Spencer, "Literary Criticism," in *New Testament Criticism and Interpretation*, ed. David Alan Black and David S. Dockery (Grand Rapids: Zondervan, 1991), pp. 227-51; Dan McCartney and Charles Clayton, *Let the Reader Understand: A Guide to Interpreting and Applying the Bible* (2nd ed.; Phillipsburg, N.J.: P & R Publishing, 2002), pp. 223-42.

because of limited hard drive space, opt to download only some of the most basic files—the "minimal installation." In light of this analogy, I encourage every serious Christian Bible reader to at least plan on the minimal installation. This includes a good one-volume Bible commentary (even better, a multivolume commentary series), a large one-volume Bible dictionary or multivolume Bible encyclopedia, and a one-volume dictionary on biblical theology.

If every serious Christian Bible reader would regularly use the resources of a minimal installation, the spiritual life of the church would be greatly enhanced.[37] Even if pastors would commit to prepare sermons consistently using only the minimal resources, there would be a manifold increase in biblical knowledge and spirituality among parishioners. One of the lamentable ironies of our day is that in spite of unparalleled resources available, an appalling ignorance of the Bible and biblical theology generally prevails among Christians. Pastors must resist the temptation to preach "relevant" and "practical" sermons that amount to little more than "hot topics" with Bible verses thrown in for good measure. They should proclaim the great themes and teachings of the Bible because these are always practical and relevant. Biblical theology will "build [the] church, and the gates of Hades will not prevail against it" (Mt 16:18). Of course, I hope that a number of Christians will advance beyond the minimal installation, and that pastors in particular will set their sights on an even more ambitious level.

Please do not think that I advocate a hierarchical level of spirituality based on how many academic resources one possesses. I am well aware of the subtle sin of pride that can creep into even the most noble of ambitions. My concern is for those who lead Bible study groups and Sunday school classes and who preach sermons. While there is no substitute for sincere piety, there is no excuse for lack of knowledge. Surely, to whom much is given, much is required (Lk 12:48).

1.4. The last step of exegetical analysis consists in theological criticism, whereby the exegete isolates the discrete theological affirmations, whether explicit or implicit, found within the text. Here one looks for truths that relate to the nature, character, and will of God and his dealings with fallen human beings. Included within this search are human responses to divine

---

[37]For other suggested sources for a minimal Christian library devoted to biblical studies, see Doriani, *Getting the Message*, pp. 244-47; McCartney and Clayton, *Let the Reader Understand*, pp. 196-99. Those wishing to pursue a "full installation" may profitably consult Cyril J. Barber and Robert M. Krauss Jr., *An Introduction to Theological Research: A Guide for College and Seminary Students* (2nd ed.; Lanham, Md.: University Press of America, 2000); Donald A. Hagner, *New Testament Exegesis and Research: A Guide for Seminarians* (Pasadena, Calif.: Fuller Theological Seminary, 1992).

revelation, since these too may convey important theological affirmations. What does God require of me (Amos 5:4, 6, 14-15; Hos 12:6; Mic 6:8)? In this regard, one must be aware that particular texts, especially narratives, may not provide obvious theological content. If, however, one delves carefully into the substratum of a text, more often than not profound theological truths are found to underlay the narrative, argument or specific genre (i.e., lament, proverb, doxology, benediction, prayer request, confession, creed, etc.). Questions put to the text, whether at the level of paragraph, section or chapter, help to tease out embedded theological truths.

Discourse analysis provides invaluable help in tracing the flow of an author's thought and in detecting the real "burden" of the communicative act.[38] Does the text assume as part of its argument certain attributes or purposes of God? Does the text indicate how a holy and righteous God can be approached and on what terms? Does the text assume, state or imply any standards of behavior expected of believers? What motivation stands behind such standards? In the NT the focus falls on the person and work of Jesus Christ. How does Christ reveal God the Father and his kingdom? What does Christ accomplish by his life, ministry, death, resurrection and heavenly session? What does the Holy Spirit desire to accomplish in the life of believers, and in what ways does he enable and empower them? The traditional categories of systematic theology may prove helpful in formulating theological truths, although one must be careful not to read into texts the precise formulations of later developments. For example, Paul's letter to the Colossians does not directly address later christological debates in the postapostolic church (e.g., the nature of the hypostatic union).[39] Rather, one must try to assess Paul's understanding of the person of Christ as he develops it in his pastoral letter.

Over time, as one studies entire books and corpora, a large number of theological truths are collected and distilled. Many of these are redundant, but even this is helpful because they point to larger themes that dominate Scripture. Some may even be unique or seem to be at odds with other truths. These become grist for our next phase of biblical theology.

2. Theological synthesis. According to Donald Hagner, "Theological synthesis is the capstone of exegesis."[40] I agree. Biblical theology assumes that one has first done the necessary exegetical homework. Exegesis might

---

[38]For a helpful treatment of discourse analysis, with examples, see Doriani, *Getting the Message*, pp. 77-93.

[39]For a salutary caution in this matter, see G. B. Caird, *New Testament Theology*, compl. and ed. L. D. Hurst (Oxford: Clarendon, 1994), p. 6.

[40]Hagner, *New Testament Exegesis and Research*, p. 20.

be at the level of paragraph, section, chapter or entire book. For the sake of illustration, let us assume that we have worked our way exegetically through an entire book—say, Jonah, in the OT, or Colossians, in the NT. We have made a good number of observations and culled a significant number of theological truths from the text itself. Now it is time to turn to the next intellectual enterprise and synthesize the material.

2.1. The focus now shifts from the flow of a narrative or the argument of a letter to the theological affirmations that inform the discourse, whether explicitly or implicitly. This stage in the process requires careful reflection. Out of all the theological truths observed or inferred, is there a larger, overarching theological principle? For example, in Jonah the narrator clearly implies that God is omnipresent, omniscient and omnipotent simply by means of the story line. We see this in the fact that Yahweh is quite aware of Jonah's intentions and whereabouts and is always one step ahead of him. Thus Yahweh "hurled a great wind upon the sea," "provided a large fish to swallow up Jonah," "appointed a bush, and made it come up over Jonah," "appointed a worm that attacked the bush," and "prepared a sultry wind." These truths are important, but probably the truth that the narrator wants most to impress upon the reader, memorably portrayed in chapter 4, is Yahweh's love and compassion for those who are outside the boundaries of national Israel (Jn 4:11). God's love is not conditioned by ethnicity. There is a "wideness in God's mercy."

This is a profound theological truth, standing in stark contrast to the prevailing theology of neighboring peoples and most Israelites. Furthermore, it desperately needs implementation in our contemporary world of ethnic cleansing, genocide, racism and jingoistic nationalism. In other words, biblical theology seeks to discover those theological truths that were the burden of the inspired author. Too many sermons on Jonah focus on the trivial (the whale or the gourd) or sermonize on theological truths that, though important in their own right, were not the compelling issue of a particular composition.

In Colossians a rich repository of theological ideas and themes awaits the exegete, each one of which could easily become the main subject of a study or message. Yet, there seems to be an overarching "big idea" in Paul's letter to this congregation. By carefully analyzing the flow of the argument, especially Paul's counterargument against the false teaching, one realizes that his primary theological point is the unrivaled supremacy of Christ in the cosmos. I have created a series of messages on Colossians called "The Cosmic Christ," proclaiming Christ's role in creation and redemption. The relevance of this teaching for today is obvious: spiritual experiences that move Christ to the periphery are dangerous. Christians must be Christ-centered; otherwise, they will manifest lopsided tendencies. Perusing relevant articles in Bible dictionaries and encyclopedias and consulting commentaries on Colossians will open a whole vista of insights into the theology of this splendid letter. Of course, I hope that you will not deprive yourself of the joy of discovery by your own diligent reading and pondering of the biblical text.

This procedure, if faithfully carried out on the individual books of both Testaments, will lead to an ever-increasing grasp of the Bible's message and major theological truths. As one steadily gains a more comprehensive understanding of biblical thought, one also becomes aware of the rich diversity within this unified teaching. This diversity should not be submerged or ignored but rather appreciated and communicated.

But what about prior commitments to theological systems, acquired as the result of belonging to a particular religious community? The temptation is strong to harmonize one's findings with inherited interpretations. There is in fact much to be said for such a procedure. It would be arrogant on my part to think that all I need is the Holy Spirit to interpret correctly the Word of God.[41] I am indebted to previous generations for their careful interpretation of Scripture. Consequently, I need to acquire the habit of checking my interpretations against that of acknowledged masters. Whereas the Holy Spirit is the ultimate author of Scripture, the selfsame Spirit works corporately to guide the church in understanding revealed truth (Jn 16:12-15). Individual Christians do not have a monopoly on the truth.

A problem arises, however, if I decide that there is no need for independent exegesis and can save valuable time by accepting the verdict of previous scholars or my inherited system of interpretation and doctrine. I need to have the willingness to subject all such human traditions to the scrutiny of sacred Scripture. Acknowledging the lordship of Christ and relying on the illumination of the Spirit, I must have the courage of my convictions when it comes to interpreting the details of the Bible's theology, even if that means going against my received theological tradition.[42] I am referring not to major creedal statements that orthodox Christians have always confessed (i.e., the deity of Christ, his substitutionary atonement, his bodily

---

[41]On this point, see Daniel P. Fuller, "The Holy Spirit's Role in Biblical Interpretation," in *Scripture, Tradition, and Interpretation: Essays Presented to Everett F. Harrison by His Students and Colleagues in Honor of His Seventy-fifth Birthday*, ed. W. Ward Gasque and William Sanford LaSor (Grand Rapids: Eerdmans, 1978), pp. 189-98.

[42]See Daniel P. Fuller, "Biblical Theology and the Analogy of Faith," in *Unity and Diversity in New Testament Theology: Essays in Honor of George E. Ladd*, ed. Robert A. Guelich (Grand Rapids: Eerdmans, 1978), pp. 195-213.

resurrection, his second advent, etc.) but rather to peripheral theological truths wherein Christians of good faith differ (i.e., gifts of the Spirit, role of women in the church, timing of the rapture, millennialism, etc.).

2.2. The next level of theological synthesis operates on the level of an entire corpus of writings (e.g., the Pentateuch, the Historical Books [Former Prophets in the Hebrew Bible], the Prophets [Latter Prophets in the Hebrew Bible], the Psalter, the Synoptic Gospels, the Pauline letters, the Petrine letters, the Johannine writings). The objective here is to become thoroughly familiar with the thought of a particular inspired author or authors (whether known or anonymous). Once again, however, care must be taken first to interpret each document in its own context without assuming that all the writings reflect precisely the same occasion and purpose. This is especially critical in the case of Paul where passages dealing with the law of Moses, for example, seemingly stand in contradiction to one another. Without trying to minimize the tension, we must patiently sort out the varying audiences and agendas of each separate piece. Only then may we try to synthesize what he has to say on the topic of the law. (We will explore more on this later when we delve into the theology of Paul.)

2.3. If one wishes to pursue a full-scale biblical theology, the next step works at the testamentary level. Whether OT or NT, the varied voices of the respective witnesses are brought together in one choir, with an awareness that each Testament has it own distinct "sound." The material of each testament is incredibly rich—a lifetime could be spent just trying to synthesize the message of each by itself. The beginner should not be daunted by the magnitude of the task; the aim is to give a reasonably good account of the message of both Testaments. As one's grasp of the message of each Testament comes into greater clarity, there is invariably an incremental effectiveness in the ministry of the Word.

2.4. Finally, we arrive at the last stage of theological synthesis, in which we step back from the two major covenants of Scripture and look at the canon in its entirety, the Christian Bible. What are the great theological affirmations and themes that are common to the canon as one coherent book possessing a divinely inspired unity? Picking up the caution issued regarding the earlier level of book and corpus, one must resist the temptation to gloss over the obvious diversity. Clearly, there is progress in the history of redemption. Furthermore, in the OT there are some theological truths that do not continue across the sweep of the canon, and that stand in tension with later NT affirmations. These observations should be allowed to stand. They constitute challenges as we seek a canonical synthesis.

This last step brings us to perhaps the central problem of biblical theology: How do the two Testaments relate to one another? This problem is so crucial that it requires a separate chapter for an adequate discussion.

Before doing that, however, I address two further methodological questions. Neither of these questions requires a firm answer by pastors, Sunday school teachers, Bible study leaders and interested lay readers. In other words, biblical theology can be carried on without having first provided a definite answer. I think that one's grasp of Scripture will benefit if the effort is made, but it is not essential for effective teaching.

2.4.1. The first question is this: Can we discern in this diverse collection of religious writings a "center," a unifying idea that gives the entire collection coherence? This has long been a debated issue in biblical theology with no clear consensus yet emerging. Suggestions have been many: covenant, promise, salvation, God, God and humankind, God in community, election, monotheism, Jesus Christ, mystical union with God, God's elusive presence, and the love of God, to mention but a few. A growing number of interpreters opt for a multiplex approach in which several essential ideas provide coherence.[43] Some have sought a center in redemptive history and particularly in the notion of the kingdom of God. I think that this has merit. I readily admit that not everything fits comfortably under this rubric; nonetheless, I feel that from Genesis 3 to Revelation 22, the "big idea" is the irruption (breaking in or coming) of the kingdom of God. Thus, in Jesus' model prayer for disciples we have the first petition nicely summarizing the hope of redemptive history: "Your kingdom come!" The OT traces the unfolding of this kingdom idea, and the NT proclaims its mysterious appearance in the life, death and resurrection of Jesus Christ with its glorious consummation at the end of the age when Christ returns victorious over all opposition. (I defend this thesis in the next chapter.)

2.4.2. The second methodological question has to do with presentation. Having identified the leading themes and ideas of the Bible, how do I present the findings in an organized and systematic manner? This has proved to be another contentious point in methodology. Should one borrow the traditional categories of systematic theology (i.e., God, humankind, sin, salvation, etc.)? As already noted, most biblical theologians feel that one ought to let the categories emerge from the text itself rather than impose a scheme upon it. So what are these categories? In some cases, it seems to me, exegetes employ a scheme reflecting more their own cultural milieu than that of the Bible. I think that the answer becomes clearer as one carefully

---

[43]See Gerhard Hasel, *Old Testament Theology: Basic Issues in the Current Debate* (3rd ed.; Grand Rapids: Eerdmans, 1982), pp. 117-43; idem, *New Testament Theology: Basic Issues in the Current Debate* (Grand Rapids: Eerdmans, 1978), pp. 140-70.

Table 1.1. Methodology of Biblical Theology

1.	**Exegetical Analysis**: determination of what text actually says
1.1.	*Textual Criticism*: determination of original wording of text
1.2.	*Historical Criticism*: determination of background and setting of text
1.3.	*Literary Criticism*: determination of the genre and rhetoric of text
1.4.	*Theological Criticism*: determination of theological affirmations and presuppositions
2.	**Theological Synthesis**: determination of theology of text
2.1.	*Synthesis at paragraph, section, and chapter level*: evaluation of theological truths discovered and comparison with other portions of Scripture
2.2.	*Synthesis at book or corpus level*: discovery of main ideas and themes with a view to determining the essential theological understanding of a particular inspired witness or block of writings
2.3.	*Synthesis at canonical level*: determination of relationship between Testaments by means of leading themes and motifs common to both
2.4.	*Synthesis of entire canon*: essential message of entire Bible
2.4.1.	Center(s) of biblical theology: what central idea or ideas provide coherence for message
2.4.2.	Categories drawn from systematic theology, major themes, or philosophical-cultural ideas generated by interpreter: how best to organize the disparate theological affirmations
2.4.3.	Synchronic and diachronic presentations: how best to display essential message

notes the leading ideas and themes that have been uncovered. Surely, these must provide the primary categories. Not surprisingly, however, there will be some overlap with the traditional categories of systematic theology.[44] After all, generations of biblical exegetes and theologians cannot have been that far removed from the real pulse of Scripture. If the nature of God and his relationship to his creation, especially human beings, and the notions of sin and salvation nowhere appear in one's biblical theology, there are grounds to suppose that one has not really read the Bible.

2.4.3. The final methodological question is whether one should adopt a synchronic or diachronic method. The former seeks to distill the faith content of the documents considered as a finished product synthetically, and the latter attempts to display the temporal unfolding and chronological development of theological thought.[45] Good arguments can be made for

---

[44]See James Barr's response to the frequent criticism of borrowing so-called Christian dogmatic schemes (*Concept of Biblical Theology*, p. 39).

[45]See further discussion in Sailhammer, *Introduction to Old Testament Theology*, pp. 184-94. In OT theology, L. Köhler's method is synchronic, W. Eichrodt's is a combina-

both approaches, and surely there is room for both. I opt for a diachronic approach in order to bring out more clearly the progressive nature of God's revelation in Scripture. Systematic theology can then take these results and incorporate them into a synchronic presentation.

See my summary of the discussion of methodology, with a chart outlining the two chief phases of biblical theology and the individual steps within each, in table 1.1.

THE GOAL OF BIBLICAL THEOLOGY

I conclude this chapter with a few comments about the goal of biblical theology. As already indicated, biblical theology needs to be communicated. First, the individual interpreter must truly hear the message of Scripture and respond obediently to its summons to discipleship. Biblical theology, properly understood, is not merely an academic enterprise; it is a deeply spiritual exercise. This is so because the Bible proclaims itself as a divine revelation. As Peter Stuhlmacher insists, the Bible wants to be read in precisely this way.[46] Just as Moses' personal obedience took precedence over his mission to proclaim Yahweh's deliverance of Israel (Ex 4:24-26), so each Christian must, like Samuel, say, "Speak, for your servant is listening" (1 Sam 3:10), and seek to implement the teachings of Scripture (Mt 7:13-27; Gal 5:6, 6:7-10; Jas 1:22). Thus, an immediate goal of biblical theology relates to the obedience and spiritual growth of the individual reader. God is looking for lives that embody faith, hope and love (1 Cor 13:13).

Second, the goal of biblical theology has a corporate dimension. That is, it contributes to building up the body of Christ, the church (Eph 4:7-16). Not all are gifted to be teachers (1 Cor 12:29), but all can share out of their own personal interaction with Scripture what the Spirit of God has imparted (1 Cor 14:26; Col 3:16; 1 Pet 4:10-11).[47] Pastors and teachers,

---

tion of synchronic and diachronic, and G. von Rad's is clearly diachronic. In NT theology, owing to the relatively short period of revelation, this is less of an issue for some theologians (see Ryrie, *Biblical Theology*, p. 19). However, for a scholar such as R. Bultmann, a practitioner of the history of religions school (*religionsgeschictliche Schule*), developmental hypotheses abound, and his approach is decidedly diachronic. (We will examine his highly influential [and controversial] thought later.) For a whole biblical theology that is primarily synchronic, see W. T. Purkiser, Richard S. Taylor and Willard H. Taylor, *God, Man, and Salvation: A Biblical Theology* (Kansas City, Mo.: Beacon Hill Press, 1977).

[46]Peter Stuhlmacher, *How to Do Biblical Theology* (PTMS 38; Allison Park, Penn.: Pickwick, 1995), pp. 1-14.

[47]"In the last analysis, every Christian must become a theologian. . . . That is, every Christian must be learning to bring every thought into captivity to Christ; learning, in short, to relate every dimension of life to God's grace in the Christ event" (Hagner, "Biblical Theology and Preaching," p. 141).

on the other hand, have a solemn responsibility to feed the flock that God has entrusted to them (Acts 20:28; 1 Pet 5:1-5).[48] Whether on the level of a Bible study group, Sunday school class or congregation, teaching the Word of God carries with it accountability (Jas 3:1-2). The teaching ministry involves communicating the message of Scripture to the faithful and proclaiming the gospel to those who stand outside the community of faith. Ultimately, biblical theology addresses all human beings, for all stand under the judgment of the Word of God (Rom 2:12-16; 3:4, 19).

The gospel in all its ramifications is the subject matter of biblical theology, because this is the essential message of the Bible. There is much more to the message than John 3:16, though it must quickly be said that this is hardly a simple text. One might spend a lifetime probing the explicit and implicit theology of this one text. The point is that the task of biblical theology is to provide the people of God with "the whole purpose of God" (Acts 20:20-21, 26).

My plea to pastors and teachers in the churches is that they would become proficient in biblical theology. It is the lifeblood of the church. There is a correlation between the pastor's grasp of biblical theology and the spiritual vitality of the parishioners.[49] A number of helpful guides exist for pastors wishing to incorporate rigorous biblical theology into their preaching.[50]

Finally, the goal of biblical theology, in keeping with the source of the message itself, is the glory of God. God's self-revelation in Scripture calls for a wholehearted response of thanksgiving and praise by those who bear his image and are being transformed into the image of his beloved Son (Eph

---

[48]"The preacher must build bridges between the definitive past and the existential present. He or she is therefore called to be a competent biblical theologian who, through the proclaimed word in sermon (as well as sacrament), teaches and equips others to think theologically" (Hagner, "Biblical Theology and Preaching," p. 141). Osborne offers this conviction: "It is my contention that the final goal of hermeneutics is not systematic theology but the sermon. The actual purpose of Scripture is not explanation but exposition, not description but proclamation" (*The Hermeneutical Spiral*, p. 12).

[49]John Albert Bengel observed, "And thus it happens, that the outward form of Scripture and that of the Church, usually seem to exhibit simultaneously either health or else sickness; and as a rule the way in which Scripture is being treated is in exact correspondence with the condition of the Church" (*Gnomon of the New Testament*, ed. Andrew R. Fausset [5 vols.; Edinburgh: T & T Clark, 1857-1858], cited in Walter C. Kaiser Jr., *Toward an Exegetical Theology: Biblical Exegesis for Preaching and Teaching* [Grand Rapids: Baker, 1981], p. 7).

[50]For the OT, see Kaiser, *Toward an Exegetical Theology*. For the NT, see John Goldingay, "Expounding the New Testament," in *New Testament Interpretation: Essays on Principles and Methods*, ed. I. Howard Marshall (Grand Rapids: Eerdmans, 1977), pp. 351-65, 387-88; C. Richard Wells, "New Testament Interpretation and Preaching," in *New Testament Criticism and Interpretation*, ed. David Alan Black and David S. Dockery (Grand Rapids: Zondervan, 1991), pp. 563-85.

1:6, 11-12, 14; Phil 1:9-11; Col 3:17; 1 Pet 4:11; 2 Cor 3:18; Rom 8:29; Eph 4:13). *Soli Deo gloria!*

FOR FURTHER DISCUSSION

1. What is the aim of biblical theology?

2. What assumptions do evangelicals make when approaching biblical theology?

3. How is biblical theology like and yet different from systematic theology?

4. How are the findings of biblical theology typically organized?

5. How does that compare to systematic theology?

6. What are the characteristics of canonical Scripture?

7. Describe the process of exegesis.

8. How does the process of theological synthesis work?

9. How is sound biblical theology related to the health of the church?

FOR FURTHER READING

Of the many valuable treatments on the definition and importance of biblical theology, I recommend the following:

Anderson, Francis I. "Biblical Theology." *EC* 2:63-70.

Baker, D. L. "Biblical Theology." *NDT* 98-99.

Barr, J. "Biblical Theology." *IDBSup* 104-11. [An article written by a former evangelical that is more a critique of the biblical theology movement than of biblical theology per se.]

———. *The Concept of Biblical Theology: An Old Testament Perspective*, pp. 1-17. Minneapolis: Fortress, 1999. [A more positive assessment of biblical theology by Barr.]

Bartholomew, Craig G. "Biblical Theology," *DTIB* 84-90.

Guthrie, Donald. *New Testament Theology*, pp. 21-74. Downers Grove, Ill.: InterVarsity Press, 1981.

Hafemann, Scott J., ed. *Biblical Theology: Retrospect and Prospect*. Downers Grove, Ill.: InterVarsity Press, 2002.

Hasel, Gerhard F. "The Future of Biblical Theology." In *Perspectives on Evangelical Theology*, edited by Kenneth S. Kantzer and Stanley N. Gundry, pp. 79-94. Grand Rapids: Baker, 1979.

Ladd, G. E. "Biblical Theology, Nature of." *ISBE* 1:505-9.

———. *A Theology of the New Testament*, edited by Donald A. Hagner, pp. 20-28. Rev. ed. Grand Rapids: Eerdmans, 1993.

Marshall, I. Howard. *New Testament Theology*, pp. 17-48. Downers Grove, Ill.: InterVarsity Press, 2004.

Matera, Frank J. "New Testament Theology: History, Method, and Identity." *CBQ* 67 (2005): 1-21.

Osborne, Grant R. *The Hermeneutical Spiral: A Comprehensive Introduction to Biblical Interpretation*, pp. 263-77. Downers Grove, Ill.: InterVarsity Press, 1991.

Rosner, B. S. "Biblical Theology." *NDBT* 3-11.

Ryrie, Charles C. *Biblical Theology of the New Testament*, pp. 11-24. Chicago: Moody Press, 1959.

The following items helpfully discuss the methodology of biblical theology:

Caird, G. B. *New Testament Theology*, completed and edited by L. D. Hurst, pp. 4-26. Oxford: Clarendon, 1994.

Childs, Brevard S. *Biblical Theology of the Old and New Testaments: Theological Reflection on the Christian Bible*, pp. 80-88. Minneapolis: Fortress, 1993.

Doriani, Daniel M. *Getting the Message: A Plan for Interpreting and Applying the Bible*, pp. 107-21, 170-86. Phillipsburg, N.J.: P & R Publishing, 1996.

Eichrodt, Walther. *Theology of the Old Testament*, vol. 1, translated by J. A. Baker, pp. 25-35. Philadelphia: Westminster Press, 1961.

House, Paul H. *Old Testament Theology*, pp. 53-57. Downers Grove, Ill.: InterVarsity Press, 1998.

Marshall, I. Howard. *New Testament Theology*, pp. 17-48. Downers Grove, Ill.: InterVarsity Press, 2004.

McCartney, Dan, and Charles Clayton. *Let the Reader Understand: A Guide to Interpreting and Applying the Bible*. 2nd ed. Phillipsburg, N.J.: P & R Publishing, 2002.

Osborne, Grant R. *The Hermeneutical Spiral: A Comprehensive Introduction to Biblical Interpretation*, pp. 277-85. Downers Grove, Ill.: InterVarsity Press, 1991.

Rosner, B. "Biblical Theology as Construction Site." *NDBT* 5-10.

Sailhammer, John. *Introduction to Old Testament Theology: A Canonical Approach*. Grand Rapids: Zondervan, 1995. [An erudite and penetrating analysis of methodology and approach.]

Schultz, Richard. "Integrating Old Testament Theology and Exegesis: Literary, Thematic, and Canonical Issues." *NIDOTTE* 1:185-205.

Stendahl, K. "Biblical Theology." *IDB* 1:418-32. [A classic article written by a Lutheran with moderately liberal leanings.]

Stuhlmacher, Peter. *How to Do Biblical Theology*, pp. 1-14. PTMS 38. Allison Park, Penn.: Pickwick, 1995.

Taylor, W. "Biblical Theology." *ZPEB* 1:593-600.

Watson, F. *Text and Truth: Redefining Biblical Theology*. Grand Rapids: Eerdmans, 1997.

2

The Problem of
the Unity of the Bible

THIS CHAPTER FOCUSES ON WHAT MANY consider the central problem of biblical theology: Does the Bible possess a fundamental unity? This is primarily a question of the relationship of the OT to the NT.[1] Here I briefly survey historical theology in order to gain perspective and evaluate how Christians in the past and in modern times have answered this question.

APOSTOLIC ERA

The earliest Christians read their Bible, the Greek translation of the OT (Septuagint), as an inspired collection of writings all testifying to the reality of the Christ event (Rom 1:1-4; 3:1; 10:5-21; 15:3-4; 1 Cor 9:10; 10:11; Gal 3:6—4:7; 2 Tim 3:16; 2 Pet 1:19-21). In this, they were simply following the lead of Jesus, who taught his apostles to read the OT christologically (Lk 24:25-27; cf. Lk 9:44-45; 14:31-34; Acts 2:25-36; 4:11, 25-30; 8:32-35; 13:32-39). As the letters of Paul and the accounts of Jesus' life, death, and resurrection (the Gospels) circulated among the churches, these too were un-

---

[1]James Smart writes, "Of all the problems that arise in interpretation, perhaps none is more basic than that of the unity of the Testaments" (*The Interpretation of Scripture* [Philadelphia: Westminster Press, 1961], p. 65). Daniel Fuller voices a similar conviction: "As I began to teach the Bible book by book, it became increasingly clear to me that I would never really grasp the Bible until I understood the overall framework of redemptive history" ("Unity of the Bible" course syllabus [Pasadena, Calif.: Fuller Theological Seminary, 1965], p. 1). N. H. Ridderbos said, "The relationship between the Old and New Testaments: that is just about the whole story; the whole of theology is involved in that" (cited in G. Goldsworthy, "Relationship of Old Testament and New Testament," *NDBT* 81, from H. Graf Reventlow, *Problems of Biblical Theology in the Twentieth Century*, trans. J. Bowden [Philadelphia: Fortress, 1986], p. 11).

derstood as authoritative writings, and gradually they took their place along-side the sacred Scriptures of Israel. Two NT documents already reflect this process: in 2 Peter 3:16 Paul's letters apparently are included in "the other scriptures," and 1 Timothy 5:18 cites Luke 10:7 as "the scripture says."

The precise stages in the creation of the NT are unrecoverable, but the autographs and their copies possessed inherent authority eventuating in canonical status. This may be seen in, for example, the earliest Christian writings, the Thessalonian correspondence (ca. A.D. 50/51). Paul's pastoral admonitions are not mere suggestions; they are binding rules for acceptable behavior in the new community of faith (1 Thess 5:27; 2 Thess 3:6, 14). Furthermore, Paul's letters were read aloud in the congregations just as the OT Scriptures were (Col 4:16). Thus, Paul's letters already functioned as canonical literature, even though it would not be until the fourth century A.D. that a final, definitive statement demarcated the precise boundaries of the Christian canon.[2]

Perhaps by the end of the first Christian century, and certainly early on in the second century, house churches all across the Roman Empire acknowledged a collection of sacred writings consisting of the Scriptures of Israel and apostolic writings testifying to the saving events of Jesus Christ.[3] Both were referred to as "the Scriptures." By the second and early third centuries, these two blocks of writings bore the respective names "Old Testament" and "New Testament." The two Testaments, however, were read as one book, the Christian Bible. In debates with the synagogue, Christians argued that the Jewish Scriptures, the OT, were incomplete. Only as we read both Testaments together do we have a unified, complete, divine revelation of God's will and purpose.

Thus the earliest Christians universally proclaimed that the Bible, both Testaments, centered on Jesus Christ. A key to understanding the Bible was the rubric of "promise and fulfillment." The early Christians believed that what prophets foretold was now unfolding in the saving events of Jesus' life and in the life of the new covenant community. The last days had begun (cf. Acts 2:14-36; 3:17-26). NT writers single out selected proof texts from the OT with an introductory formula such as "This is what was spoken . . . ," "All this took place to fulfill what was spoken by . . . ," "So/as/for it is written . . . ," "Then was fulfilled . . . ," or a similarly worded

---

[2]On the history of the canon, see Lee M. McDonald, *The Formation of the Christian Biblical Canon* (2nd ed.; Peabody, Mass.: Hendrickson, 1995); John McRay, "Bible, Canon of the," *EDBT* 58-60; R. T. Beckwith, "The Canon of Scripture," *NDBT* 27-34.

[3]Justin Martyr's description of an early Christian worship service in which apostolic memoirs (i.e., Gospels) were read out to the assembled congregation is fascinating (*First Apology of Justin*, chapter 67, "Weekly Worship of the Christians").

catchphrase. Formally, this approach is similar to that employed by the Qumran community and is called "pesher."[4] Materially, however, there is an important difference: Christians held that the fulfillment of all that the prophets proclaimed was realized in Jesus of Nazareth, not the Teacher of Righteousness or a soon-expected messianic tandem (a Davidic scion and an Aaronic high priest).

NT writers also see connections between the OT and the gospel message through typology—that is, instances where persons, events, things, and institutions in Israel's salvation history prefigure or anticipate the saving events of Jesus Christ and his church. "Typology is employed by the biblical authors to show continuity in God's plan, the 'pattern in the carpet' of redemptive history."[5] This method is especially prominent in the book of Hebrews, where the tabernacle and its furniture and rituals are treated as types of the high priestly ministry of Christ. However, the Gospels of Matthew and John also incorporate significant instances of typological interpretation into their accounts of Jesus' ministry. In fact, typological interpretation of the OT is found throughout the NT corpus.

In short, the Bible possessed a christological unity, anchored in salvation history and manifested through promise/fulfillment and typology. There is no indication that the early Christians sensed a problem trying to explain or defend this unity. That, however, would change.

MARCION

In the second century Marcion, a professing Christian, sought to jettison the OT Scriptures and confine the church's Scripture to the NT, albeit a greatly reduced NT. Marcion's Bible contained ten highly edited Pauline letters, minus the Pastoral Epistles (and Hebrews), and a digest of Luke's Gospel. To this collection he added his own work, the *Antitheses*.

What prompted him to adopt such a drastic step? A bit of background is necessary for the answer. According to Hippolytus, Marcion was born to a bishop of Sinope in the region of Pontus (northern Turkey), and Justin Martyr adds that he was a wealthy ship owner. Marcion propagated his gospel

---

[4]The Hebrew word *pesher* means "interpretation." For further discussion of pesher, see George J. Brooke, "Pesharim," *DNTB* 778-82; E. Earle Ellis, "How the New Testament Uses the Old," in *New Testament Interpretation: Essays on Principles and Methods*, ed. I. Howard Marshall (Grand Rapids: Eerdmans, 1977), pp. 199-208; Larry R. Helyer, *Exploring Jewish Literature of the Second Temple Period: A Guide for New Testament Students* (Downers Grove, Ill.: InterVarsity Press, 2002), pp. 227-48; Richard Longenecker, *Biblical Exegesis in the Apostolic Period* (2nd ed.; Grand Rapids: Eerdmans, 1999).

[5]Arthur G. Patzia and Anthony J. Petrotta, *Pocket Dictionary of Biblical Studies* (Downers Grove, Ill.: InterVarsity Press, 2002), p. 119.

in a number of port cities in Asia Minor, most notably Ephesus. Sometime in the first half of the second century he engaged in a teaching ministry in Rome and rose to the rank of bishop. His radical ideas, however, stirred controversy and the Roman presbyters excommunicated him in A.D. 144.[6]

What did Marcion teach that elicited such stern punishment? He manifested pronounced anti-Judaic views leading to the conviction that the God of the OT was distinct from and inferior to the God of Jesus Christ revealed in the NT. Underlying Marcion's theology was a fundamental dualism, showing the influence of Hellenistic philosophy (Tertullian claims that he was a Stoic) or perhaps Gnosticism. Thus the Creator God of the OT was likened to a demiurge and stood opposed to the loving God and Father of Jesus Christ who dwelt in pure light.

For Marcion, Paul was the only apostle preserving the authentic gospel of Jesus, a gospel standing in stark antithesis (hence the name of his own composition) to the message of the OT. Marcion came to suspect that the other apostles and early Christian leaders had willfully or ignorantly distorted Paul's gospel or at least accommodated it to the OT. This led Marcion to scrutinize carefully Paul's letters in the attempt to peel off the accretions and rediscover the pristine gospel. The result was an edited version of Paul's letters that he called the *Apostolicon*. In this regard, Paul's polemic against the Judaizers in Galatians 1—2 became programmatic for Marcion's treatment of the NT documents. That is, Paul's law-gospel contrast served as a platform for a more sweeping OT-NT dichotomy. This virtually amounted to a Judaism/Christianity antithesis so characteristic of some early church fathers.

Ironically, Marcion made a significant contribution to the early church by virtue of creating his own individualistic canon of sacred Scripture. This forced the church to address the question of the boundaries of the canon. The importance of Marcion for our study is this: Marcion's truncated canon, which excluded the entire OT, was unacceptable and unorthodox. Any solution to the problem of the precise relationship between the Testaments must not discard the OT. As we will see, Marcion is not the only professing Christian to advocate an excision of the OT from the NT. Indeed, it might be said that Marcion prefigured some forms of modern liberalism, with its "canon within the canon." Finally, Marcion illustrates the perennial danger of reading the biblical text through the lens of an alien philosophy and thereby distorting its message.

---

[6]See A. G. Padgett, "Marcion," *DLNTD* 705-8; John J. Clabeaux, "Marcion," *ABD* 4:514-16.

IRENAEUS AND SALVATION HISTORY

The mainstream church resisted Marcion's attempt to sunder the OT from the NT. So how did orthodoxy propose that the relationship between the Testaments be grasped? Irenaeus's work *Against Heresies (Adversus haereses)* points the way. Irenaeus (ca. A.D. 130-200), a native of Smyrna and later bishop of Lyons, a Roman colony in Gaul (modern France), views both Testaments as one progressively unfolding history of redemption. Irenaeus deserves the accolade of being called one of the first biblical theologians.[7] He strongly objects to Marcion's attempt to dissociate the God of the OT from the God of the NT. For Irenaeus, the Bible possesses a theocentric unity. Brevard Childs concisely captures the essence of Irenaeus's solution to the question of the unity of the Bible: "Because of the unity of God's salvation, it was absolutely essential to the faith that the two testaments of the Christian Bible be seen as a harmonious witness to the one redemptive purpose in history. Through his use of 'types' and prophecy Irenaeus sought to demonstrate that the two covenants were of the selfsame substance and of the one divine author."[8]

THE ALLEGORICAL METHOD

Alongside Irenaeus's insistence upon redemptive history with its promise/ fulfillment, typology, and covenantal structure, another interpretive technique came to the fore that dominated biblical interpretation until the Reformation and, in a modified form, still survives. That approach is the allegorical method.

The allegorical method is not a Christian innovation. On the contrary, it already had a venerable prehistory when the Jesus movement first emerged; indeed, its roots go back to the Classical Age of Greece. The emergence of the various schools of Greek philosophy, beginning already in the sixth century B.C., raised an acute problem for religious thought of the classical Greek world. The problem, in short, was how to salvage the religiomythical worldview embodied in Homer and Hesiod with the new approach of the philosophers in which they attempt to explain reality in rational and naturalistic terms.[9]

---

[7]Brevard S. Childs, *Biblical Theology of the Old and New Testaments: Theological Reflection on the Christian Bible* (Minneapolis: Fortress, 1992), p. 30, citing J. Lawson, *The Biblical Theology of Saint Irenaeus* (London: Epworth, 1948), p. 35, and Bengt Høgglund, *History of Theology*, trans. Gene J. Lund (St. Louis: Concordia, 1968), p. 44.

[8]Childs, *Biblical Theology*, p. 31.

[9]As Michael Burney Trapp puts it, "The underlying motive force was (and would continue to be) the cultural need to maintain the authority of the revered classics in the face of new (philosophical) traditions of thought" ("Allegory, Greek," *OCD* 64).

The resolution was an exercise in human ingenuity. Basically, the canon of Homer was read employing a two-level hermeneutic. On the surface of the text lay the literal meaning. At this level, which surely was the intention of the original writer(s), we move in the world of Greek mythology. A pantheon of gods headed up by Zeus determined reality and decreed destiny, although even the gods themselves were subject to fate, the ultimate arbiter of destiny. On the other hand, so the argument went, a deeper level of meaning existed just below the surface of the text. The literal meaning contained a sort of code that, when translated, yielded a meaning in consonance with the thought of the Greek philosophers. One might cynically characterize such an approach as "having your cake and eating it too." That is to say, by such a hermeneutic, one could affirm a belief in the mythological world of Homer while at the same time giving him credit for penetrating to the "scientific" explanation for the universe. It was this reconciliation or harmonization of Greek religion and Greek materialism that made the allegorical method so attractive to many intellectuals. Of course, not all intellectuals bought into this approach; some opted to be thoroughgoing naturalists. Plato, for example, while believing in a creator god and the immortality of the soul, viewed allegorical interpretation "as either trivial or pernicious."[10]

What does all this have to do with Christianity? The short answer is that the tradition of allegorizing ancient texts to conform to "modern thought" was a legacy bequeathed the church by a Jewish scholar, confronting a problem similar to one faced by the Greek thinkers of the Classical Age. This scholar was Philo Judaeus, a native of Alexandria, Egypt, and a contemporary of the apostle Paul. Philo drank deeply from the wells of Greek philosophy and sought to reconcile it with his revered tradition of Judaism rooted in the Hebrew Bible. Philo himself read the Bible in Greek, the Septuagint version. This harmonization was carried out, to his satisfaction, in a voluminous literary corpus utilizing the allegorical method. He was thus able to claim that Moses was in fact the taproot of Greek philosophical thought. Beneath the text of Genesis, for example, lay the truths of Greek philosophy. Philo provides the reader with a number of commentaries that decode the text and "unlock" these truths. The procedure has clear affinities to the earlier allegorical method of the Greeks. A compelling motive for Philo, living in a city notorious for its anti-Jewish attitudes, was to provide a rejoinder to Gentile slanders and an apologetic for Judaism in the larger Greco-Roman world.

---

[10]Ibid.

As the Jesus movement spread throughout the Hellenistic world and became increasingly Hellenized, it is not surprising that Christians, especially those possessing a good Hellenistic education, seized upon the allegorical method as a useful tool, both for apologetics and for evangelism. The allegorical method already makes its literary appearance in Christian literature in the postapostolic fathers.[11] Thus a work such as *Epistle of Barnabas* adapts the allegorical method in order to read the OT as an essentially Christian book.[12] In commenting on Numbers 19 (the passage dealing with the ritual of the red heifer), *Epistle of Barnabas* goes well beyond typology by deducing meanings not at all obvious or historically connected with salvation history in the NT. Thus the three "boys" (Barnabas's term for the three priests who take part in the ritual) suddenly "correspond" to Abraham, Isaac, and Jacob. The calf is Jesus, the wood foreshadows the cross, and the hyssop speaks of Christ's cleansing from sins. This presumed correspondence derives from the fertile mind of Barnabas or the exegetical tradition that he learned rather than from the NT.

Origen (A.D. 185-254) of Alexandria, Egypt, was a learned and devout church father, perhaps the most versatile and brilliant theologian in the church until Augustine. He perceives beneath the literal or surface meaning of the text a "spiritual" meaning. One immediately senses a similarity to Philo, and we should note that Origen too lived and was schooled in Alexandria. For Origen, this spiritual or deeper meaning concerns Christian doctrine and morals. Origen's approach is determined by his firm conviction that the Holy Spirit authored Scripture. Readers, in order to understand Scripture, must have their minds renewed and illumined by the Holy Spirit. Christ is mediated to believers through the mystery of Scripture and its multilayered levels of meaning. The three levels of meaning may have derived from Origen's notion that a person is composed of three aspects: body, soul, and spirit. In actual practice, however, he usually mentions two meanings: literal and spiritual. One must begin with the literal, which Origen did not despise, and then proceed to the deeper things of Christian faith and life. Origen's interpretation of Hebrews 5:12—6:1 illustrates his approach. What the author of Hebrews called "the basic elements of the oracles of God," or "milk," Origen assigns to the literal meaning of the text. On the other hand, for Origen, "solid food," or "perfection," refers to the spiritual meaning of the text. It is at this latter level that one enters deeply into communion with Christ.

---

[11]See E. Ferguson, "Old Testament in Apostolic Fathers," *DLNTD* 827-34.
[12]See W. M. Holmes, "Barnabas, Epistle of," *DLNTD* 125-27; Helyer, *Exploring Jewish Literature*, pp. 488-90.

Exegetes trained in the modern historical-critical disciplines have not been kind to Origen. "They are typically disdainful of an approach judged quite inadequate, if not harmful. Much of this criticism is misguided and has not really understood Origen's hermeneutic."[13] Nevertheless, there are some genuine shortcomings. It would be silly to fault him for the many times he fails to understand the text simply because he lacked the requisite linguistic, literary, historical, and sociological background. Perceived problems in the text often owe more to his own failure to understand the culture in which the Bible was written. Beyond that, however, he struggles to reconcile immoral, unseemly, or trivial accounts in the sacred text with the tenets of Christianity. His solution, like that of his Alexandrian predecessor Philo, lay in a hermeneutic in which a deeper, hidden meaning "redeems" the plain, literal meaning. Although the resolution of difficulties was certainly not the raison d'être for Origen's hermeneutic, as it seems to have been for Philo, it did prove handy in dealing with any seeming irrelevancy, inconsistency, or contradiction. Most of these "spiritual" meanings seem contrived and fail to convince modern readers.

The most serious objection to Origen's allegorizing, however, resides in his failure to respect the integrity of the OT writings. Origen's hermeneutic tends to dissolve the boundary between the OT and the NT. What we wind up with is really one Testament. Christian doctrine and teaching is read back into the OT without adequate recognition of the OT context. Any sense of historical development is nearly effaced by the allegorizing method. Progressive revelation disappears behind a timeless revelation. We must, however, qualify this criticism as pertaining more to his homilies than his apologetic work. In fact, in Origen's debate with Celsus, the notion of prophecy and fulfillment does indeed play a key role in his argument that Scripture is divine. So it is not as if he had no awareness of salvation history, because clearly he did.

We give credit to Origen for maintaining a bulwark against Marcionite tendencies in the church. His central conviction that Scripture, both Testaments, is a divine composition through the work of the Holy Spirit and that one needs the assistance of the selfsame Spirit in reading it has remained a staple of orthodox Christian faith. He also insists that the purpose of inspired Scripture is to lead believers upward to a higher spiritual level.

---

[13]Henri Crouzel, "Origen," *The Oxford Companion to Christian Thought*, ed. Adrian Hastings, Alistair Mason and Hugh Pyper (Oxford: Oxford University Press, 2000), p. 502. See also Crouzel's comments in *Origen*, trans. A. S. Worrall (Edinburgh: T & T Clark, 1989), pp. 61-84. Childs observes, "Origen has generally served as the 'whipping boy' of critical exegesis and judged to have led the church astray for over a thousand years" (*Biblical Theology*, p. 33).

We should not carp at his constant focus on the mystery of this divine revelation of the heart of God. Finally, we applaud his insistence upon the christological center of Scripture, for that has been, without doubt, the single most important way Christians have stated the relationship between the OT and the NT. Christ meets us in the OT; Origen championed this conviction and historic Christianity has never abandoned it.

If Origen's synthesis shaped the church's understanding of the unity of the Bible until the Reformation and Enlightenment, then the most notable exponent of Origen's allegorical method was the North African Christian luminary Augustine.[14] In his discussion of the principles of interpretation "he insists that allegory should be based on the historic sense," but in actual practice his exegesis floats "high above the world of mere historical reality."[15] In fact, Augustine devotes much attention to the different levels of meaning in Scripture, even ascribing four levels, not three. Our disquiet about Origen's hermeneutic applies equally to Augustine. This is especially so when he seeks to instruct readers when a text should be interpreted literally and when figuratively (i.e., allegorically or spiritually): "Whatever there is in the word of God that cannot, when taken literally, be referred either to purity of life or soundness of doctrine, you may set down as figurative" (*On Christian Doctrine* 3.10.14).

Note how similar this is to a sophisticated Greek reader trying to make sense of Homer, to Philo harmonizing Plato and Moses, and to Origen trying to account for moral difficulties in the OT. Difficulties in the text were cues that one must resort to allegorical or spiritual exegesis. Still, we do Augustine an injustice if we fail to appreciate his holistic view of Scripture and its ultimate goal: love of God and neighbor. With this we should not quarrel.

Augustine embraces Origen's christological unity of the Testaments. This unity is achieved through a generous employment of typology. At numerous points in the OT narratives Augustine sees prefigurations of Christ. Just one example among many is the prayer of Hannah in 1 Samuel 2:1-10. Augustine interprets this passage as a prophecy of Jesus Christ and expends several pages showing point by point how Jesus fulfills the affirmations of this prayer (*The City of God* 17.4). Most modern interpreters agree that Augustine resorts excessively to typology. Many would even question the

---

[14]See D. F. Wright, "Augustine," "Augustinianism," *NDT* 58-63.
[15]F. van der Meer, "The Servant of the Word," in *Augustine the Bishop: The Life and Work of a Father of the Church*, trans. Brian Battershaw and G. R. Lamb (London: Sheed & Ward, 1961), p. 445.

hermeneutical appropriateness of typology.[16] In my opinion, however, typology is a valid approach for disclosing the inner unity of the Bible and at least some of Augustine's typological expositions still carry conviction.

Furthermore, I call attention to an important contribution of Augustine to the question of the unity of the Bible. He clearly recognizes in Scripture an unfolding kingdom of God. He depicts this reality under the figure of two cities representing the redeemed and the lost, a story that begins with Cain and Abel (*The City of God* 15.1). This divine reality lies behind all that transpires in time and space. God builds his kingdom, and Scripture testifies to its onward march. Augustine thus draws our attention to a story line that links the Testaments together. We have, then, the rudiments of a salvation history approach to the Bible.[17]

MARTIN LUTHER: THE CHRISTOLOGICAL PRINCIPLE

One can hardly overestimate the importance of Martin Luther (1483-1546) for church history and Western civilization. This Augustinian monk became the point man for the Protestant Reformation.

Our interest, however, lies in his view of the Bible and how it should be interpreted. Luther rejects the allegorical method in the forthright language for which he is well known. "He calls allegorical interpretation 'dirt', 'scum', 'obsolete loose rags', and likens allegorizing to a harlot and to a monkey game."[18] For example, in his commentary on Genesis he is unsparing in his criticism of Origen: "Such twaddle is unworthy of theologians, though for a mirthful poet they might perhaps be appropriate."[19] On the other hand, Luther himself is not above using allegory to embellish the plain meaning of a text or, for that matter, to pillory the pope! His interpretation of Genesis and Psalms, for example, clearly involves allegorical elements in which specific items are understood to convey spiritual truths of the gospel. In fact, it is clear that Luther does not break completely with

---

[16]"But for the sake of scientific veracity, typological and Christological interpretation today is an anachronism which cannot be permitted" (Friedrich Baumgärtel, "The Hermeneutical Problem of the Old Testament," in *Essays on Old Testament Hermeneutics*, ed. Claus Westermann and James Luther Mays [Richmond: John Knox Press, 1963], p. 150).

[17]Frederic W. Farrar says, "[Augustine] perceived that there is in revelation a progressive element, and that there is an inferiority in the degree of revelation furnished by the Old Testament" (*History of Interpretation* [London: Macmillan, 1886], p. 234). Farrar adds in a footnote that Augustine's "system of 'periods' was seized by the later Reformed Theology . . . where he speaks of seven periods, of which the creative week was a type. This is the first attempt to treat Old Testament theology." See also Wright, "Augustine," *NDT* 60-61.

[18]Bernard Ramm, *Protestant Biblical Interpretation: A Textbook of Hermeneutics* (3rd ed.; Grand Rapids: Baker, 1970), p. 54.

[19]*LW* 1:90.

a "spiritual" reading of the Bible. Still, one finds in Luther's expositions abundant evidence that he champions the primacy of the literal meaning of Scripture.[20]

Luther insists that Scripture is the sole authority for the church. Donald McKim emphasizes that for Luther, "every office and activity in the church falls under the judgment of Scripture. All of theology is contained in Scripture. God has revealed all that we need to know about God in Christ. Theology must be biblical theology; any other kind is human invention."[21]

Several of Luther's hermeneutical principles deserve mention. First, he vigorously defends the sufficiency principle; that is, the essential meaning of Scripture is clear and accessible to the average reader. Thus, practically speaking, there is no need for the official guidance of Rome to explain the meaning of the Bible. For Luther, the Scriptures are perspicuous—plain in meaning and not obscure or ambiguous. "To Luther the *perspicuity* of the Bible was coupled with the *priesthood of believers*, so that the Bible became the property of all Christians."[22] His prodigious effort in translating the Scriptures into vernacular German is one of his enduring legacies, and it reflects his confidence in the clarity of Scripture.

Another principle, closely related to the first, is the analogy of faith *(analogia fidei)*. Simply stated, the general sense of Scripture, derived from clear and unambiguous passages, should be the basis for interpreting unclear or ambiguous texts. This assumes that a basic understanding of the theological message of the Bible is possible for the reader. For Luther, the very heart of what is taught in the Bible is the great principle of justification by faith. This is an overarching principle whereby one makes sense of the entire Bible and by which each text is scrutinized. This needs further explanation.

A central feature of Luther's hermeneutic is his distinction between law and gospel. The gospel is the good news of salvation in Jesus Christ. The law is God's demand for perfect obedience; the gospel is God's gracious

---

[20]Hilton Oswald, in his introduction to Luther's commentaries, observes, "In general, Luther here still follows the traditional manner of his day, presenting a fourfold interpretation of a passage and labeling these interpretations as literal (or historical), allegorical, tropological, or anagogical" (*LW* 10:7). In Luther's own words: "The Christian reader should make it his first task to seek out the literal sense, as they call it. For it alone is the whole substance of faith and Christian theology. . . . Allegory, however, is too often uncertain, and is unreliable and by no means safe for supporting faith" (*LW* 9:24).

[21]Donald K. McKim, ed., *Dictionary of Major Biblical Interpreters* (Downers Grove, Ill.: InterVarsity Press, 2007), p. 690. Childs cites with approval David W. Lotz: "The Lutheran Reformation was . . . the work of a professor of biblical theology" ("Sola Scriptura: Luther on Biblical Authority," *Interpretation* 35 [1981]: 258, cited in Childs, *Biblical Theology*, p. 43).

[22]Ramm, *Protestant Biblical Interpretation*, p. 55.

gift of forgiveness and life. Law and gospel confront the reader throughout
the whole of Scripture, hence the necessity of determining which mode of
existence before God a particular text conveys. In Genesis 15:6 Abraham
responded by faith to God's gracious words in the gospel and was justified. The gospel is thus present in the OT promises of God. The Sinaitic
legislation, on the other hand, is pure law. As such, it represents God's just
demand for perfect obedience. Since such obedience is impossible for sinners, one obtains salvation only by casting oneself on the grace and mercy
of God as found in the gospel. This distinction between law and gospel is
foundational to Luther's approach to the Bible and functions as a major
hermeneutical tool. Every text is either one or the other. Errors creep in
when one confuses these two distinct modes of existence.[23] As we will see
later, Luther held that the Beatitudes were also law in the sense that they
call for perfect obedience, something impossible for sinners to render. The
law thus functions to drive sinners to despair so that they may grasp hold
of the promises of God in the gospel. In such a scheme the law is a means to
the end and thus serves the gospel by convicting sinners of their great need.
Thus, for Luther, justification by faith is the first article in the analogy of
faith. All scriptural texts should be read in light of this truth. No wonder
Luther had difficulties with the book of James and its seeming contradiction with Luther's great hero, the apostle Paul. His assessment of James is
well known: "an epistle of straw."

Equally crucial for understanding Luther's concept of the unity of the
Bible is the christological principle.[24] According to Luther, the aim of all
biblical interpretation is to discover what it teaches about Christ. In his
words, "The correct criterion for evaluating all books [of the Bible] is
whether or not they urge [i.e., promote or preach] Christ."[25] As is clear
from his comments on the book of Psalms, the fourfold interpretation of
Scripture is governed by the ruling principle of Christ. "In this way all four
interpretations of Scripture come together to one magnificent stream"; "All

---

[23]Willem Jan Kooiman says that for Luther, "the supreme art of the theologian, 'the treasure
of the true scribe' consists . . . in his ability to distinguish correctly between Law and Gospel, between God's demand and his promise. He repeats this constantly, so that at the end
of his life he could say to his students, 'By this time you should understand this'" (*Luther
and the Bible*, trans. John Schmidt [Philadelphia: Mulhlenberg, 1961], p. 213).

[24]"For Luther, both in his earliest and later periods, the one centre of scripture is Jesus
Christ. *Solus Christus* provides the key to all his exposition. . . . This understanding af-
fects his exposition at every point" (Childs, *Biblical Theology*, p. 44). See also R. D. Preus,
"Lutheranism and Lutheran Theology," *NDT* 404-6.

[25]Here is a famous statement of Luther's: "Whatever does not teach Christ is not apostolic
even though St Peter or St Paul does the teaching. Again, whatever preaches Christ would
be apostolic, even if Judas, Annas, Pilate, and Herod were doing it" (*LW* 35:396).

of these are Christ at the same time."[26] As Bernard Ramm notes, "This is Luther's method of making the entire Bible a Christian book. The Fathers did it with their allegorical method. Luther does it with his christological principle."[27]

Luther's law/gospel dialectic and his christological principle *(sensus principalis)* have contributed to disagreement over his view of Scripture. Because some biblical books do not obviously "urge Christ," Luther tends to relegate them to a place of relative unimportance. Since he generally avoids using the allegorical method by which to find Christ after the fashion of an Origen, the upshot was a tendency to devalue texts not easily yielding to a christological interpretation.[28]

Some in the liberal tradition view Luther as a forerunner for their own approach to Scripture: rejection of biblical infallibility and a theological criticism that dismisses various strands of biblical teaching for failing to adhere to certain standards, whether justification by faith, what urges Christ, or modern educated mentality. Conservative scholars, on the other hand, cite passages from Luther in which he affirms his belief in the inspiration and infallibility of Scripture and consequently deny that he employed his principles to determine a "canon within the canon."[29] Perhaps both liberals and conservatives can agree that Luther, like so many of us, was not always consistent. To portray Luther, however, as the fountainhead of modern theological liberalism seems anachronistic, for he was still very much a part of the medieval worldview.

JOHN CALVIN: COVENANT THEOLOGY

John Calvin (1509-1564), who wrote commentaries on most of the Bible,

---

[26]*LW* 10:52; 9:312.

[27]Ramm, *Protestant Biblical Interpretation*, p. 56.

[28]See Emil G. Kraeling, *The Old Testament Since the Reformation* (1955; reprint, New York: Schocken, 1969), pp. 16-17.

[29]Kooiman insists that Luther did not hold to the doctrine of plenary, verbal inspiration (*Luther and the Bible*, pp. 236-39). Kraeling thinks Luther's view of Scripture changed during his career (*Old Testament Since the Reformation*, pp. 9-20). On the other hand, both John Warwick Montgomery and A. Skevington Wood cite Luther as a champion of inerrancy (John Warwick Montgomery, "Lessons from Luther on the Inerrancy of Holy Writ," in *God's Inerrant Word: An International Symposium on the Trustworthiness of Scripture*, ed. John Warwick Montgomery [Minneapolis: Bethany Fellowship, 1974], pp. 63-94; A. Skevington Wood, *Captive to the Word: Martin Luther, Doctor of Sacred Scripture* [Grand Rapids: Eerdmans, 1969]). Even liberal theologian Paul Althaus admits that "[Luther] nonetheless followed the tradition of his time and basically accepted it as an essentially infallible book, inspired in its entire content by the Holy Spirit" (*The Theology of Martin Luther* [trans. Robert C. Schultz; Philadelphia: Fortress, 1966], pp. 50-51).

was a remarkable exegete.[30] Calvin, with Luther, rejected the allegorical method. Like Luther, he advocated the literal meaning of Scripture and insisted that "Scripture interprets Scripture." He takes to task Origen and others who "torture Scripture in every possible manner."[31] His advice to exegetes is still worth quoting: "It is the first business of an interpreter to let his author say what he does, instead of attributing to him what we think he ought to say." Furthermore, Calvin followed Luther in stressing the christological center of Scripture, the importance of the doctrine of justification by faith, and the correlation between the Word and the Spirit. He also recognized typology as a useful way of understanding the unity of the two Testaments.

A seminal contribution by Calvin regarding the question of the unity of the Bible lay in his understanding of the covenant concept.[32] For Calvin, there is one covenant uniting all the people of God in both Testaments. This one covenant, however, was differently administered in the OT. In his *Institutes* Calvin devotes two chapters to a discussion of the relationship between the Testaments (*Institutes* 2.10-11). In chapter ten he carefully notes the similarities between the Testaments, and in chapter eleven the differences. The similarities, says Calvin, are basically three:

1. Both Testaments teach that God offers sinners the hope of eternal life.

2. Both Testaments teach that this offer of salvation depends entirely upon God's undeserved mercy and grace.

3. Both Testaments teach that this gracious salvation is mediated to sinners in and through Jesus Christ. He is thus the instrumental means of salvation and was known by and present to OT believers.[33]

On the other hand, Calvin indicates that there are significant differences between the OT and the NT. These he summarizes as consisting of five points:

1. The OT teaches about spiritual blessings under the figure of temporal

---

[30]G. E. Wright pays tribute to Calvin's exegetical skills: "The more one studies these commentaries, the more astonished he becomes at their scholarship, lucid profundity, and freshness of insight. Although biblical studies have moved a long way since the sixteenth century, there is still little which can be held to be their equal" ("The Christian Interpreter as a Biblical Critic: The Relevance of Valid Criticism," *Interpretation* 1 [1947]: 133 n. 3).

[31]In his commentary on Galatians (note on Gal 4:22), cited in Thomas D. Parker, "The Interpretation of Scripture: I. A Comparison of Calvin and Luther on Galatians," *Int* 17 (1963): 69.

[32]P. A. Lillback summarizes Calvin's exposition of the covenant idea: "Calvin is in many ways the forerunner of Reformed federal theology. Calvin makes extensive use of the covenant idea in his *Institutes* (1559) and other writings" ("Covenant," *NDT* 175).

[33]John Calvin, *Institutes* 2.10.

blessings (i.e., land, fruitful seasons, posterity, etc.). The NT does not resort to this mode of instruction, since it concerns not the shadow but rather the substance of the good things to come (Heb 8:5; 10:1).

2. The OT uses types and ceremonies in order to teach of the spiritual realities found in Christ. In this regard, Calvin appeals to the book of Hebrews, where typology is especially prominent.

3. The OT is literal; the NT is spiritual. Here Calvin, showing indebtedness to Luther, employs a letter/spirit antithesis. The OT is literal (i.e., it was promulgated without the Spirit; the NT involves the quickening power of the Spirit), temporal (the types and ceremonies give way to their fulfillment in Christ) and deadly (the law can only condemn; it cannot provide motive power or save). The NT, on the contrary, is spiritual, eternal and life-giving.

4. The OT speaks of bondage; the NT speaks of liberty. Here Calvin cites the account of the giving of the law at Mount Sinai, the book of Hebrews (an exposition of this episode) and Galatians 4 (allegory of Hagar and Sarah), in which the response of the people was fear and trembling. In contrast to this (Calvin cites Rom 8 and Gal 4 [the Jerusalem that is above]), the NT elicits confidence and security and gladness.

5. The OT belongs to one people only, the Jews; the NT belongs to all peoples in Christ.[34]

What is striking in Calvin's approach is his conclusion that the two Testaments are really one in substance. They differ only in the mode of administration. "The covenant made with all the fathers is so far from differing from ours in reality and substance, that it is altogether one and the same: still the administration differs."[35] An application of this principle is Calvin's justification of infant baptism on the grounds of the unity of the Testaments. Christian baptism in the NT corresponds to circumcision in the OT, the latter, of course, administered on the eighth day. Since the efficacy of a sacrament need not depend on the exact moment of its administration, infants, though not yet able to exercise saving faith, could properly be baptized into the community of faith.

Calvin thus distinguishes between two dispensations of the selfsame covenant found in both Testaments.[36] This approach is quite different from

---

[34]Ibid., 2.11.

[35]Ibid., 2.10.2.

[36]Kraeling finds fault with Calvin's approach: "The plain fact is that Calvin has Christianized the Old Testament and Judaized the New Testament in his effort to make the two appear as one" (*Old Testament Since the Reformation*, p. 32).

Luther's, in which the law=gospel dialectic tends to locate more law than gospel in the OT, though Luther did find the gospel in the OT, especially in Psalms. In short, Calvin saw much more continuity between the OT and the NT than did Luther.

Calvin's successors went beyond his exposition and devised a threefold scheme of covenants: the covenant of redemption, the covenant of works, and the covenant of grace. I will take this up further in the next chapter, but at this point we should note that Calvin anchors the unity of the Bible in soteriology and Christology. That is, there is essentially one plan of salvation, signified by one covenant uniting both Testaments, and made effective by one savior, Jesus Christ. OT believers were not saved in a fundamentally different way than are NT believers. Calvin's covenantal perspective, somewhat like Augustine's city of God, locates the unity of the Bible in a particular understanding of redemptive history.

THE ENLIGHTENMENT AND MODERNITY: THE AUTONOMY OF REASON

It would unnecessarily lengthen this book to rehearse the monumental changes that transpired in the Enlightenment and its aftermath. Suffice it to say, Scripture increasingly was stripped of its authority and uniqueness. The venerable doctrine of the plenary verbal inspiration of Scripture was either jettisoned or redefined in vague terms of Scripture's ability to elicit religious sentiment or the faith community's role in valuing and privileging these documents. Reason became autonomous, and educated mentality the criterion for assessing what was authoritative and of timeless significance. The historical-critical method, operating with antisupernatural presuppositions, challenged the historicity of ostensibly historical narratives in both Testaments. As a consequence, liberal theology, an attempt to wed modernity with timeless religious ideas and ethics, made inroads in both church and academy. By the twentieth century, liberal theology dominated mainline denominations and university religion departments. The Bible was reduced to a merely human work having all the attendant errors that accompany such literature, and the history found in the Bible was radically reconstructed. A mere kernel from OT and NT narratives survived as a "critically assured" minimum. Those interested in the history of biblical exegesis and theology from the Enlightenment to our own postmodern age may consult any number of works.[37]

I jump forward and select several twentieth-century exegetes and bibli-

---

[37]Helpful here are Roy A. Harrisville and Walter Sundberg, *The Bible in Modern Culture: Baruch Spinoza to Brevard Childs* (2nd ed.; Grand Rapids: Eerdmans, 2002); McKim, *Dictionary of Major Biblical Interpreters*, part 1.

cal theologians in order to sketch out their respective solutions to the question of the relationship between the Testaments. Against that backdrop, I make my own suggestions for addressing this question.

RUDOLF BULTMANN: THE EXISTENTIAL MESSAGE OF THE BIBLE

Rudolf Bultmann (1884-1976) probably has exercised more influence on twentieth-century theology than any other single figure.[38] For this reason alone, he merits careful study. Born near Oldenburg in northern Germany, he held a chair at the University of Marburg from 1921 to 1951, after which he retired. Bringing to the study of the NT a mind trained in the classic liberalism of the nineteenth century, Bultmann was convinced of its abject failure to capture the hearts and minds of the new generation. But he was even more convinced that Protestant orthodoxy or fundamentalism was a dead end. He was a pioneer in the discipline of form criticism in Gospel research and a practitioner of the "history of religions" school,[39] making significant contributions to NT study. For example, he wrote numerous articles in the classic work *Theological Dictionary of the New Testament*.

For Bultmann, the master key to the NT derives from the thought of a colleague at Marburg, an atheistic philosopher of existentialism, Martin Heidegger.[40] Bultmann believes that existentialism, without a commitment to atheism, enables one to grasp what the NT writers were really trying to communicate.

Existentialism is not easy to understand or explain. "Existentialism is to be experienced directly rather than taught."[41] It bypasses the traditional metaphysical questions of philosophy; in fact, it eschews all formal systems or schools of philosophy and focuses upon human existence, being and nonbeing. Its frame of reference is the individual and one's attempt to live an authentic life. Authentic living is defined as making "choices in the present in light of the past and open to the future." Choices are made against the backdrop of human existence, an existence characterized by feelings of

---

[38]For a convenient survey of Bultmann's thought, see Robert Morgan, "Rudolf Bultmann," in *The Modern Theologians: An Introduction to Christian Theology in the Twentieth Century*, ed. David F. Ford (2nd ed.; Cambridge, Mass.: Blackwell, 1997), pp. 68-86; D. Fergusson, "Bultmann, Rudolf," in *Dictionary of Major Biblical Interpreters*, ed. Donald K. McKim (Downers Grove, Ill.: InterVarsity Press, 2007), pp. 261-67.

[39]For definitions of these two disciplines, see the respective entries in Patzia and Petrotta, *Pocket Dictionary of Biblical Studies*, pp. 47, 59.

[40]But according to Robert Morgan, "The true father of Bultmann's existentialist theology . . . is Herrmann, who (like Kierkegaard) responded to the collapse of classical metaphysics with new philosophical reflections on human existence . . . the locus of faith, genuine religion, and human meaning ("Rudolf Bultmann," p. 74).

[41]E. D. Cook, "Existentialism," *NDT* 243.

anxiety, dread and the absurdity of life. In a Christian context, coming to grips with human existence involves a new self-understanding, the essence of faith. Jesus was the perfect example of one who lived the authentic life, and his call for discipleship was a crisis of decision for the hearers. Saying yes to the kingdom constitutes a conscious choice to be open to the future. An unconditional surrender to God's gracious overture in Christ is the way one lives authentically. The NT gospel, stripped of its first-century trappings, is a summons to live authentically.

According to Bultmann, the NT writers, being people of the first century, not the twentieth, necessarily resorted to the language of mythology in order to express the spiritual reality of authentic living. Since the mythological framework is totally unbelievable and unacceptable to moderns, the interpreter must "demythologize"—that is, reinterpret—the trappings with which the NT kerygma (the content and act of preaching) encounters us.[42] The intent of demythologizing is to recover the kerygma's existential message. Bultmann's famous program of demythologization aimed at "enabling modern thought simply to know once again what Christian faith involves."[43] In the NT itself, the two writers who really explicated faith's self-understanding are the apostle Paul and John (not the apostle, but rather the author of the Gospel and Epistles of John, and not John of Patmos, the author of Revelation). The bulk of Bultmann's work focuses on them. In fact, the other NT writers fail to qualify as theologians, in Bultmann's judgment, because they did not grasp the existential dimensions of human experience.[44]

When Bultmann's writings were published, they set off a firestorm in the church and the academy on both sides of the Altlantic.[45] It is not an exag-

---

[42]Bultmann asks his readers, "Can Christian preaching expect modern man to accept the mythical view of the world as true? To do so would be both senseless and impossible" ("New Testament and Mythology," in *Kerygma and Myth: A Theological Debate*, ed. Hans Werner Bartsch [1953; reprint, New York: Harper & Row, 1961], p. 3).

[43]Friedrich Gogarten, *Demythologizing and History*, trans. Neville Horton Smith (New York: Scribner, 1955), p. 10. For Bultmann's own rationale for demythologization, see "New Testament and Mythology," pp. 1-16.

[44]See Morgan, "Rudolf Bultmann," p. 74. For an evangelical response to Bultmann's existential interpretation, see Clark Pinnock, *The Scripture Principle* (San Francisco: Harper & Row, 1984), p. 94.

[45]Much of Bultmann's work was originally published in German in the 1920s and 1930s. Because of Word War II, most was not translated into English until the 1950s and 1960s, so that, outside scholarly circles, there was a delayed response in the English-speaking world. Harrisville and Sundberg indicate that prior to his essay "New Testament and Mythology," delivered in 1941, Bultmann generated little name recognition. Their description of what happened afterward is worth reading ("Rudolf Bultmann: Biblical Scholarship in Crisis and Renewal," in *The Bible in Modern Culture*, p. 228).

geration to say that in order to make sense of theology in the second half of the twentieth century, one must be aware of Bultmann's thought.

Several factors are paramount for understanding Bultmann's treatment of the relationship between the Testaments.

1. He vigorously objects to any approach to the OT that assumes the stance of a neutral observer—that is, someone outside the circle of existential faith in God. To attempt to do so fails because the OT wants to be taken as a Word summoning us and calling for response and dialogue. In his view, both liberals and conservatives are misguided because they adopt a posture outside existential faith. Liberals resort to the historical-critical method, with its supposed scientific objectivity, and conservatives come to the text with the presuppositions of plenary verbal inspiration and infallibility, intent on defending the complete accuracy and historicity of the OT narratives. Both, ironically, seek to ground faith in "what really happened." For Bultmann, this simply will not do. The attempt to find an objective basis for existential faith must be abandoned. Bultmann is passionate about this.

2. As to the function of the OT, Bultmann insists that it makes understandable the kerygma, the apostolic preaching of the cross. How so? By depicting the underlying dilemma afflicting all humanity: the prideful attempt to declare independence from God and rely on one's own righteousness. The OT thus prepares the sinner to hear God's summons to decision. This, of course, reminds us of Luther, and the connection is not accidental. Bultmann was the eldest son of a Lutheran pastor, and his view of the OT is very much like that of classic Lutheranism, with its law-gospel dialectic. Thus for Luther, as for Paul, the OT as a whole appears under the concept of law—that is, as an expression of the demanding will of God. Whereas in the OT people stand under the divine demand, in the NT people stand under the divine grace that accepts them as sinners.[46]

At best, the OT can only usefully serve as a propaedeutic (preparatory instruction) for Christian faith. That is, it serves to articulate God's demand for obedience and expose human inability to respond. With its preponderance of narratives, the OT is well suited to portray Christian existence implicit in the kerygma: the failure under the law of Moses to be right with God. Bultmann went so far as to characterize the OT as a history of "failure" *(scheitern)*. This depiction, however, admirably mirrors our own failure to be open to the future and trust in the living God.

---

[46]Rudolf Bultmann, "The Significance of the Old Testament for the Christian Faith," in *The Old Testament and Christian Faith: A Theological Discussion*, ed. Bernhard W. Anderson (New York: Herder & Herder, 1969), p. 14.

Can one move beyond this rather negative use of the OT? Can one appropriate from the OT anything that strengthens Christian faith by providing objective evidence of God's working in and through history, especially the sending of his Son, the Messiah of Israel? Can we appeal to a typological connection between the Testaments, an approach so esteemed in the church? Bultmann is emphatic: he will not countenance salvation history, prophecy and fulfillment, or typology—concepts so important to the early church and modern evangelicalism.[47] His reason is simple: existential faith simply cannot rest on any objective grounds. Appeal to an historical basis of Christianity is not an option. The NT kerygma requires an exercise of faith that has no objective, historical, empirical foundation; it is a "leap of faith" into the arms of God.[48]

3. Bultmann programmatically reinterprets the Bible in such a way as to sever any connection between saving faith and redemptive history. Existential faith is not tied to a sequence of saving deeds performed by the God of Israel and culminating in the death of his beloved Son. He thus breaks with a long-established Christian tradition on this question. Ironically, Bultmann comes close to the agenda of Marcion, with whom we began our inquiry. "Bultmann, having identified revelation with the eschatological event of the preaching of Christ, is unable to find a parallel to such an event in the Old Testament and is driven to the Marcionite conclusion that 'for the Christian faith the Old Testament is not in the true sense God's Word.'"[49] More than a few researchers have even labeled Bultmann's thought as gnostic.[50]

In the end, Bultmann rejects unity in the Bible by means of the well-trodden paths of redemptive history, promise and fulfillment, Christology (traditionally understood), and typology. Rather, the existential plight of humanity and the profound, new self-understanding that occurs in a decision for the Christ of faith proclaimed in the kerygma become the focal point of the Bible. Some readers of Bultmann have concluded that, on his presuppositions, one can only speak of an anthropological unity to the Bible.[51]

---

[47]See Rudolf Bultmann, "Prophecy and Fulfillment," in *Essays on Old Testament Hermeneutics*, ed. Claus Westermann and James Luther Mays (Richmond: John Knox Press, 1963), pp. 50-75.

[48]Bultmann, "Significance of the Old Testament," p. 33.

[49]Alan Richardson, "Is the Old Testament the Propaedeutic to Christian Faith?" in *The Old Testament and Christian Faith: A Theological Discussion*, ed. Bernhard W. Anderson (New York: Herder & Herder, 1969), pp. 43-44.

[50]See, for example, Eric Voegelin, "History and Gnosis," in *Kerygma and Myth: A Theological Debate*, ed. Hans Werner Bartsch (1953; reprint, New York: Harper & Row, 1961), pp. 64-89.

[51]Kraeling, *The Old Testament Since the Reformation*, p. 227.

This seems hard to deny, given Bultmann's assessment of, for example, the apostle Paul's thought: "Pauline theology (is) at the same time anthropology," since for Paul, "every statement about God is also a statement about man, and vice versa."[52] Some of Bultmann's successors in the existentialist tradition even more narrowly truncated NT theology.[53] One unintended consequence of the Bultmannian agenda was the "death of God" fad during the 1960s made popular by such figures as Bishop John A. T. Robinson, Paul Altizer, and Paul van Buren, among others.

GERHARD VON RAD: TRADITION HISTORY

Gerhard von Rad (1901-1975) was born into a Lutheran family at Nüremberg, Germany, and trained at Erlangen and Tübingen. His teaching career began as a privatdozent at Leipzig followed by professorships at Jena (1934-1945), Göttingen (1945-1949) and Heidelberg (1949-1971).[54]

In many ways, von Rad's approach to the unity of the Bible is the antithesis of Bultmann's. That is, whereas Bultmann refuses to accord any salvific status whatsoever to redemptive history, von Rad insists that saving faith rests squarely on redemptive history: "Israel's faith is grounded in a theology of history."[55] For von Rad, the essential message of the Bible is indeed redemptive history, not existential self-understanding.

Von Rad's analysis of the Bible leads him to affirm that it contains a distinctive view of history, and this particular view makes the Bible unique in

---

[52]Rudolf Bultmann, *Theology of the New Testament*, trans. Kendrick Grobel (2 vols.; New York: Scribner, 1951), 1:191. Morgan observes, "There is surely more to theology than anthropology. . . . Reducing everything to this Procrustean bed is likely to eliminate much that is essential to Christianity. That is the main criticism of Bultmann which surfaced in the demythologizing controversy" ("Rudolf Bultmann," p. 77).

[53]As H. Graf Reventlow observes, "H. Braun radicalized Bultmann's anthropological approach in single-minded fashion, pushing the anthropological approach to the extreme (1961). For Braun, theology is nearly identical with anthropology, because God can be encountered nowhere other than in interhuman relations" ("Theology [Biblical], History of," *ABD* 6:495, citing H. Braun, "Die Problematik einer Theologie des Neuen Testaments," *Zeitschrift für Theologie und Kirche* 2 [1961]: 3-18).

[54]For a more complete discussion and evaluation of von Rad's contribution to OT theology, see G. Henton Davies, "Gerhard von Rad: Old Testament Theology," in *Contemporary Old Testament Theologians*, ed. Robert Laurin (Valley Forge, Penn.: Judson, 1970), pp. 63-89; Ben C. Ollenburger, Elmer A. Martens and Gerhard F. Hasel, eds., *The Flowering of Old Testament Theology: A Reader in Twentieth-Century Old Testament Theology, 1930-1990* (Winona Lake, Ind.: Eisenbrauns, 1992), pp. 120-44; J. L. Crenshaw, "Von Rad, Gerhard," in *Dictionary of Major Biblical Interpreters*, ed. Donald K. McKim (Downers Grove, Ill.: InterVarsity Press, 2007), pp. 843-48; Walter Brueggemann, *Theology of the Old Testament*, pp. 31-38.

[55]Gerhard von Rad, *Old Testament Theology* (2 vols.; New York: Oliver & Boyd, 1962), 1:106. See also 1:355.

its ancient Near Eastern setting. He discerns a dialectic operating throughout the various eras of redemptive history, a dialectic involving a tension
between the divine promises and their fulfillments in history. Redemptive
history moves forward along a line of Spirit-inspired prophecy and its subsequent fulfillment, albeit never on the same scale as the prophetic oracles
stated or implied. "Oddly enough," says von Rad, "there was . . . never
any satisfactory historical fulfillment and consummation"[56] This tension
between promise and fulfillment is the bedrock in Israel's way of viewing
history. I will explain this further.

1. Israel's linear conception of history stands in decided contrast to the
characteristic thought pattern of their pagan neighbors. Paganism operates
on a cyclical view of history, a *que sera sera* approach to reality in which
we have a return to primal origins, the myth of the eternal return. Quite
the contrary, Israel understands history as teleological—that is, moving inexorably toward a goal. This goal is divinely ordained, not impersonally determined, and stands under the benevolent guidance of a sovereign, loving
God. The nature of the goal is variously stated by prophetic spokespersons
and steadily enlarges in scope as one proceeds through redemptive history.
The ultimate goal, ushered in by the Day of the Lord, involves a new city
of God. For von Rad, the Christ event of the NT is the culmination of OT
redemptive history.

The biblical story line portrays Israel as always being driven forward in
spite of their failure and judgment. Von Rad describes this process: "We see
the people continually driven, moved about, shaped, reshaped, destroyed,
and resurrected through the divine Word that ever and again came to it."[57]
Invariably, failure and judgment are followed by new revelations of ever more
grand promises. The OT is thus a book of ever-increasing anticipation.

According to von Rad, "radical openness to the future" is the chief characteristic of Israel's understanding of their history. One can scarcely fail
to hear in this formulation echos of Bultmann.[58] Despite a fundamental
disagreement over the role of redemptive history in saving faith, both share
a conviction about the existential nature of faith: it rests on an assurance
that God holds the future, whatever that might be.

2. How, then, does von Rad understand the unity of the Bible? His
point of departure is a refrain throughout his *Old Testament Theology:*

---

[56]Ibid., 2:319.

[57]Gerhard von Rad, "Typological Interpretation of the Old Testament," in *Essays on Old
Testament Hermeneutics*, ed. Claus Westermann and James Luther Mays (Richmond: John
Knox Press, 1963), pp. 25-26.

[58]Indeed, von Rad footnotes Bultmann's *Primitive Christianity*, pp. 180ff., at this very point
in his discussion (*Old Testament Theology*, 2:361).

the OT is essentially history. For von Rad, the particular kind of history contained therein is a saving history *(Heilsgeschichte),* and it characterizes the NT as well. Thus, the story of salvation, begun in the OT with creation, culminates, in the NT, in a transcendent salvation accomplished through Jesus Christ.

Von Rad is at pains, however, to distance himself from earlier, conservative theologians who championed salvation history. Accepting the findings of historical-critical and tradition-critical research, he disavows any attempt to describe a "divine plan of salvation, an 'economy,' whose connectedness could be demonstrated down to the last detail . . . an 'organic evolution of salvation.'"[59] In fact, he denies that one can even discover a true focal point in the OT. The most that can be said is that "the situation in the Old Testament does correspond to the view variously expressed in the New that the true goal of God's relationship with Israel is the coming of Jesus Christ."[60]

Von Rad argues that a structural analogy exists between the saving events of both Testaments. This analogy consists in the indissoluble connection between a particular saving event and its inspired interpretation, a characteristic common to both Testaments. These interconnections between the Testaments are a species of typological interpretation, an approach that von Rad is compelled both to qualify and defend against detractors. In the final analysis, von Rad holds that typology is a valuable way to view the two Testaments as long as one fastens on the one event that provides the key: the coming of Christ. "Only in this event is there any point in looking for what is analogous and comparable. And it is only in this way of looking at the Old and New Testaments that the correspondences and analogies between the two appear in their proper light."[61] Clearly, the unity of the Bible, for von Rad, resides in the Christ event, an event that both climaxes salvation history and yet, in keeping with the OT pattern, points forward to a final and complete salvation. The relationship between the Testaments is thus a reciprocal one in that each Testament legitimates the other.

3. Von Rad believes that the redemptive history, found before us in the pages of the OT, consists of saving deeds that have been reinterpreted by charismatic spokespersons. These inspired spokespersons, however, exercised considerable freedom in reshaping earlier revelation. The reshaping follows no set hermeneutical rules but rather is fundamentally dictated by the impulse of the Holy Spirit. Von Rad has to admit that what actually

---

[59]Ibid., 2:362, especially n. 4.
[60]Ibid., 2:363.
[61]Ibid., 2:369.

happened *(Historie)* does not always correspond to the charismatic version of redemptive history lying before us in the OT. In other words, redemptive history *(Heilsgeschichte)* is really a reinterpretation imposed on earlier material by later redactors. This he admits is a fundamental problem of OT theology and must be faced head on.

The question then becomes this: Which version of Israel's history should be the basis for constructing a theology of the OT? Von Rad's answer is clear: the charismatic version. This is so because it is precisely the testimonies of the OT that comprise the subject matter of OT theology. Of course, von Rad's position has not gone unchallenged. F. Hesse replied that "it was not Israel's conceptions about her history but the actual course of that history, as revealed by historical-critical research, that is theologically important, since, if Yahweh really did act in history, only the facts could be of interest."[62] Hesse was not alone in his dissatisfaction with von Rad's handling of this dichotomy between Israel's salvation history *(Heilsgeschichte,* a charismatically interpreted maximum), and what really happened *(Historie,* the critically assured minimum). We turn next to a post-Bultmannian scholar who followed up on Hesse's contention about which version of history should be the basis of biblical theology.

JAMES ROBINSON: THE NEW HERMENEUTIC AND THE HISTORICALITY OF LANGUAGE

James Robinson (1924-), a former student of Bultmann's, was for some years director of the Institute of Antiquity and Christianity at the Claremont Graduate School and is now professor emeritus at that institution. Robinson is well known in NT circles because of his work in editing and interpreting the Nag Hammadi archives. The latter are an important cache of Coptic documents, dating to the second century A.D., that display pronounced gnostic tendencies. Included in the collection is the famous *Gospel of Thomas*, containing sayings of Jesus, a few of which may be authentic. We will look at this in more detail later in the discussion of the theology of Jesus.

My interest in Robinson centers on his criticism of von Rad's insistence that OT theology and Christian faith should be based squarely upon Israel's recital of redemptive history. Robinson's main criticism is simply this: von Rad's structure of promise and fulfillment is unhistorical. The result, says, Robinson, is a faith based on fiction, not history. Evangelicals agree! Robinson urges a counterproposal, a better foundation upon which to base redemptive history.

---

[62]F. Hesse, "Die Erforschung der Geschichte Israels als theologische Aufgabe," *KD* 4 (1958): 1-20, cited in H. Graf Reventlow, "Theology (Biblical), History of," *ABD* 6:492.

The proper starting point, for Robinson, lies in an understanding of the nature of human language. Robinson is heavily influenced by linguistic philosophy, prevalent in many North American university philosophy departments. He is a good representative of what became known as the "New Hermeneutic," as articulated by Gerhard Ebeling and Ernst Fuchs. The New Hermeneutic goes well beyond Bultmann and is really a school of philosophy, complete with its own epistemology (theory of knowledge). Essentially, it understands language as the way in which an individual makes sense of his or her world. Hermeneutics in the more narrow sense of interpreting texts is but a subdivision of a larger human enterprise of trying to interpret existence and finding meaning in that existence. According to Robinson, language is the basic "stuff" of historical events and not something belonging to a different category. Language acts (or events) must be probed in order to understand and reconstruct reality.

How, then, does this relate to biblical interpretation? Robinson fastens on an example of a language event: the blessing formula found in different layers of biblical tradition, indeed, throughout the entire Bible.[63] One frequently runs across Hebrew expressions such as "Blessed be the God of Israel!" and "I praise you, O God!" These formulaic expressions, called *berakot* and *hodayot*, respectively, also occur in Greek translation in the NT. They point to historical moments when individuals or communities encounter God and spontaneously recognize that God has acted on their behalf and shown favor. The blessing formulas, then, represent immediate and spontaneous responses to specific historical happenings. Furthermore, they are bound up with historicity (what really happened) and its historicness (what really mattered).

Robinson goes on, however, to assert that one must distinguish between what is primary and secondary in the biblical text. That which is primary is historical; that which is secondary is fictional. For example, in Ruth 2:20 the anonymous author places a blessing formula in the mouth of Naomi: "Blessed be he by the LORD!" But, according to Robinson, the question is this: Does the blessing formula occur in a fictional narrative or a historical one? As it turns out, Robinson is convinced that the story of Ruth is fictional. In spite of this, however, the blessing formula reflects actual life situations of the original storytellers themselves, life situations in which actual things happened that elicited language praising God. Thus, the life situation is the primary setting; the interpretations conveyed in the specific

---

[63]James Robinson, "The Historicality of Biblical Language," in *The Old Testament and Christian Faith: A Theological Discussion*, ed. Bernhard W. Anderson (New York: Herder & Herder, 1969), p. 133.

stories, in this case the story of Ruth, are secondary. According to Robinson, the great saving deeds of Israel, celebrated in their creeds, belong to the secondary setting; they are not historical. This highlights a crucial difference between von Rad and Robinson with regard to redemptive history:

Table 2.1. Faith and History in von Rad and Robinson

Gerhard von Rad	James Robinson
The words expressing the faith of Israel are later, charismatic reinterpretations imposed on earlier *events*.	The words expressing the faith of Israel (and the church) reflect an *experience* that actually happened to someone in the past.

The shadow of Bultmann's existential flight from history casts a pall over the thought of Robinson. When applied to the Gospels, this means that there were situations in Jesus' life and the life of the early church that elicited blessings and praises. Some of these, as found in the NT, ascribe to Jesus majestic titles. He is hailed as Son of God, image of God, firstborn over all creation, Lord, and so on. These ascriptions, says Robinson, cannot be taken at face value as historical facts. They are secondary, not primary. What is primary, what actually happened, is that men and women experienced God in their lives and blessed him in response. What is essential in post-Easter faith is rendering blessing to God for his benefits just as Jesus did during his earthly ministry.

The upshot of Robinson's approach is that the great preponderance of biblical history, whether OT or NT, is relegated to what is secondary and, as such, is not historical. Included in this category of secondary are such central events as the cross and resurrection. The best that can be said for secondary items is that they point to historicality[64] by virtue of the fact that men and women really did experience God in encounter with the Word of God.

Unfortunately, Robinson's attempt to unite faith and history (what really happened) results in a virtual disappearance of those things that the earliest Christians believed actually happened in their midst (Luke 24:18, 21-24). It was precisely those events that early Christians confessed as the basis of saving faith (1 Cor 15:3-5). As was the case with Bultmann, redemptive history is not necessary for Robinson's faith. What is left is an encounter with God in continuity with similar experiences of believers down through the

---

[64]This word is not found in the *Oxford English Dictionary*. He seems to mean by it that which has some connection to what is historical, though not itself necessarily historical. The connection is existential or experiential. A language event gives expression to an experience that is similar to one that actually happened to someone, somewhere, sometime.

ages—hence its historicality. Once again we see the enthronement of religious experience in place of objective, historical facts as the basis of saving faith. The legacy of Friedrich Schleiermacher lives on.[65]

OSCAR CULLMANN: REDEMPTIVE HISTORY

Oscar Cullmann (1902-1999) was born in Strasbourg, Germany (after World War I it became part of France). His gymnasium training (high school in Europe) was under liberal mentors with the result that as a young man he opposed orthodox Christianity. This changed, however, after World War I and after reading Albert Schweitzer, Karl Barth and Rudolf Bultmann.[66] These theologians convinced him that classic German liberalism had fallen prey to philosophical idealism rather than truly understanding and explicating the biblical worldview. He was appointed professor of NT at the University of Strasbourg, where he served from 1930 to 1938, after which he accepted the chair of NT and patristic studies at the University of Basel, Switzerland. At the same time, he held a NT chair at the Sorbonne, the most renowned of the thirteen colleges in the University of Paris. He taught until his retirement in 1972.

Cullmann, though agreeing with both Barth and Bultmann in their rejection of German liberalism, nonetheless found fault with aspects of their respective approaches to Scripture. He criticized Barth's lack of concern for historical exegesis as a vital and informing part of the theological enterprise and Bultmann's concentration on the anthropological dimension of faith to the exclusion of divine revelation in history.

In contrast to Bultmann and the New Hermeneutic (e.g., Robinson), Cullmann, in company with von Rad, regards faith as based on something objective: redemptive history as set forth in Scripture. Cullmann vigorously opposed Bultmann and his disciples. On the other hand, Cullmann agreed with Robinson, against von Rad, that redemptive history narrated in the Bible is inextricably tied to what really happened. This was in contrast to von Rad, who was willing to base faith on the kerygmatic version of Israel's

---

[65]For the importance of Schleiermacher as the fountainhead of modern theological liberalism, see H. Harris, "Liberalism, German," *NDT* 386-87. Harris says of Schleiermacher that he "drastically reinterpreted the fundamental doctrines of Christianity from an anthropocentric viewpoint. . . . Man's own feelings constituted his ground of reality, with Jesus as the man in whom these feelings of God-consciousness attained their highest perfection" (p. 386).

[66]For the impact of Schweitzer's 1906 book *Von Reimarus zu Wrede* (ET, *The Quest of the Historical Jesus* [1910]) on Oscar Cullmann as a young university student, see Theodore Martin Dorman, *The Hermeneutics of Oscar Cullmann* (San Francisco: Mellen Research University Press, 1991), p. 10.

(and the early church's) history. I hasten to add, however, that Cullmann championed the historicity of redemptive history as opposed to Robinson's mere historicality. For Cullmann, redemptive history is the essence of what the Bible is all about and is one story, not many stories. The unity of the Bible consists in the fact that a single redemptive history progressively unfolds from Genesis to Revelation. This story is God's self-revelation to human beings and clearly indicates his purpose and goal for all creation. Cullmann thus recovers the important insights of Irenaeus, Augustine and Calvin.

In the preface to one of his best-known books, *Christ and Time*, Cullmann announces his purpose: "to determine what is central in the Christian proclamation"; he is convinced of its utmost importance: "the endeavor to determine this central element must be designated the one great task of New Testament scholarship, and perhaps of all Christian theology."[67] For Cullmann, redemptive history is the primary content of the Bible, a history that exhibits unity in a progressive self-revelation of God and his purposes for creation. Redemptive history, though but a small slice of universal history, impacts forever all that transpires on the stage of world history. Redemptive history consists of a selection of particular events, occurring in the midst of secular, universal history and standing in a specific connection with one another. The nature of this connection between selected events in redemptive history may best be likened to a deed/word complex, instances in which God intervenes or reveals himself in history accompanied by an explanatory word by means of an inspired spokesperson—a prophet or apostle. We may diagram this relationship as event/word complexes comprising the progressive unfolding of redemptive history (see figure 2.1).

A distinctive view of history characterizes primitive Christianity, one that "concentrates primarily upon a definite number of events of a quite particular sort, of which some happened before while others will happen after Christ; and its chief aim is to set these quite definite occurrences in relation to the central event which took place in Palestine about the year one."[68] Cullmann insists that *"all Christian theology in its innermost essence is Biblical history."* [69] The similarities to the stance of von Rad are readily apparent. Unlike Bultmann and Robinson, who regard the most significant thing about the historical Jesus to be his example of living in complete dependence on God, Cullmann says that it is Jesus' work of dying on the cross for the sins of the world. Cullmann takes the

---

[67]Oscar Cullmann, *Christ and Time: The Primitive Christian Conception of Time and History*, trans. Floyd V. Filson (rev. ed.; Philadelphia: Westminster Press, 1964), p. xi.
[68]Ibid., p. 20.
[69]Ibid., p. 23.

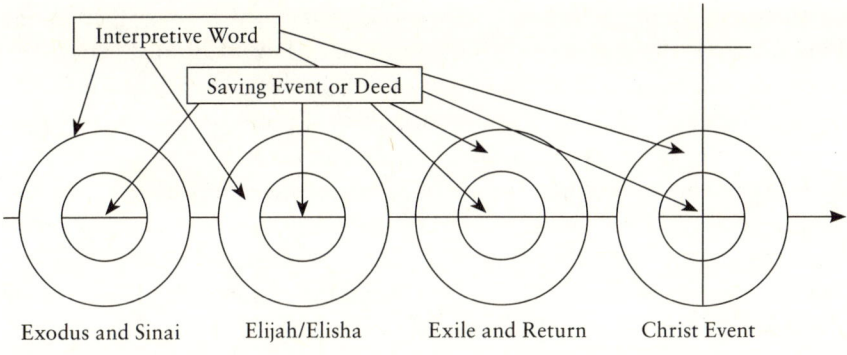

Exodus and Sinai   Elijah/Elisha   Exile and Return   Christ Event

Figure 2.1. Event and Word in redemptive history

cross and resurrection as objective, historical events.

Cullmann criticizes Bultmann for "remythologizing" (i.e., substituting one mythology for another). Bultmann's "myth" is his Heideggerian existentialism, which he supposes is the real point of the first-century mythology of the biblical writers. Cullmann insists that only an approach preserving intact the event character of myth should properly be called demythologizing. Cullmann thus claims that he, rather than Bultmann, demythologizes Scripture! In this regard, Cullmann acknowledges the presence of myth in the Bible, in the sense that there are narrated events incapable of verifiability by means of historical investigation. Cullmann draws a distinction between historically controllable events and historically noncontrollable events. The latter refer to events best described as "sagas" or "myths." These sagas and myths, however, still possess a certain "event-character."[70] According to Cullmann, we find myth in the Bible primarily in two locations: the primeval history in Genesis 1–11 and the canonical finale, the book of Revelation. Seen in this perspective, redemptive history is bounded by *die Urzeit und die Endzeit* (primal history and eschatological history), both of which are necessarily cast in mythological garb owing to the limited worldview of the biblical writers.[71] Cullmann justifies the event-character of the myths in the primeval history because the OT historicizes them; that is, the OT writers connect them with the history of Israel.

---

[70]For a brief discussion of this slippery term in biblical and theological studies, see "Myth," in Patzia and Petrotta, *Pocket Dictionary of Biblical Studies*, pp. 82-83. For further study, see W. Baird, "Myth in the NT," *IDBSup* 612; J. D. G. Dunn, "Myth," *DJG* 566-69; I. H. Marshall, "Myth," *NDT* 449-51.

[71]Cullmann, *Christ and Time*, p. 94.

Furthermore, in the NT Christ is identified as the mediator of all creation. This ties everything together around the central event of all history: the cross and resurrection. This midpoint of redemptive history binds together what precedes and follows it under the rubric of prophecy.[72]

This causes many evangelicals to pause and question whether redemptive history can be so construed. Can it be suspended at both ends by the nonhistorical and yet retain its credibility? One must concede that problems abound in the interpretation of both the Genesis primeval history and Revelation, so dogmatism is unwarranted. The admission, however, of some nonhistorical events in the middle section of redemptive history—for example, the virgin birth—is more problematic and troubling. Cullmann also frankly acknowledges that interpretations of redemptive events by biblical writers can occasionally diverge from what is historically verifiable.[73] He thus speaks of occasional "distortions," "deformations" and "human weaknesses."

Evangelicalism, in keeping with its faithful adherence to the authority and inspiration of Scripture, is extremely reluctant to admit that biblical interpretations of redemptive events stand in need of correction or modification. So although there is considerable appreciation for the work of Cullmann, most evangelicals have some reservations about his concessions to historical-critical scholarship. Nonetheless, his impact on evangelical scholarship has been significant. Two leading evangelical scholars in NT theology, Herman Ridderbos and George Eldon Ladd, clearly reveal their indebtedness to Cullmann in their highly respected works on NT theology. In fact, many evangelical scholars have adopted the general scheme of salvation history championed by Cullmann.[74]

NARRATIVE THEOLOGY

Under the influence of literary criticism, "narrative theology" has revamped the salvation history approach, drawing upon the insights of "narrative criticism." This latter discipline analyzes the complex ways in which stories are composed and function in the Bible. Matters such as plot, characterization and setting, with real and implied authors and readers, mediated by narrators and narrates, all figure into the equation, often with startlingly

---

[72]Ibid., p. 97.

[73]See Dorman, *The Hermeneutics of Oscar Cullmann*, pp. 166-69.

[74]Dorman remarks, "The influence of the Basel New Testament scholar's *heilgeschichtliche* perspective has been pervasive, in particular among North American evangelical Protestants. . . . And Fuller Theological Seminary . . . has had three professors who earned their doctorates under Cullmann's tutelage at Basel" (*The Hermeneutics of Oscar Cullmann*, p. 1).

new understandings and packing significant theological implications.[75] This approach takes seriously the fact that much of the Bible comes to us in the form of narratives, and many nonnarrative portions assume a basic story line as an unstated presupposition. Furthermore, it is precisely in the stories that theological convictions emerge. In short, the storytellers are also theologians of the first order who see God's purposes at work in these stories. Even in the NT numerous passages contain "echoes" of stories from the OT. These embedded stories resonate in the Gospel stories of Jesus and serve as the substratum of particular arguments in NT letters and treatises. Going even further, a number of literary critics believe that behind Paul's letters, for example, lies a narrative world created by him in order to achieve his pastoral purpose. This essentially fictive story, though perhaps loosely based on an OT story, serves as the narrative world or symbolic universe into which the reader enters through the process of reading the letter.

Narrative theology eschews extracting abstract propositional statements about God from the biblical text without regard to what actually happens in the story itself. That is, the constituent parts of the various stories and how they actually "work" in the narrative story line is the vehicle by which the dynamic nature of God and his interactions with and purposes for his people comes to light. Furthermore, the various discrete stories must be understood within the framework of an overarching story, a metanarrative, giving essential context and meaning to the numerous substories. The biblical metanarrative is the story of God's original creation, the Fall and the ensuing divine activity aimed at rescuing and recreating humanity and the cosmos. The central act in the metanarrative, of course, is the cross of Christ; the climactic act is the creation of a new heaven and new earth. In short, "the Bible is nothing less than the record of the actualization (and ongoing promise) of this purpose of God in the history of the cosmos."[76] The compatibility of this approach with the older salvation history seems obvious, and a number of evangelical scholars have incorporated its insights into their work.[77]

---

[75]See S. S. Bartchy, "Narrative Criticism," *DLNTD* 787-92; Robin Parry, "Narrative Criticism," *DTIB* 528-31.

[76]Joel B. Green, "Narrative Theology," *DTIB* 532.

[77]See, for example, Richard B. Hays, *Echoes of Scripture in the Letters of Paul* (New Haven: Yale University Press, 1989); Ben Witherington III, *The Christology of Jesus* (Minneapolis: Fortress, 1990); idem, "Christology," *DJG* 100-115; N. T. Wright, *The Climax of the Covenant: Christ and the Law in Pauline Theology* (Minneapolis: Fortress, 1992). However, for some potential pitfalls of narrative criticism, see G. R. Osborne, "Hermeneutics/Interpreting Paul," *DPL* 395.

CANONICAL CRITICISM

One last practitioner deserves mention. Brevard Childs (1923-2007) is well known for advocacy of what is often called "canonical criticism," although he was not entirely happy with this designation.[78] Trained in historical-critical methodology, after a fairly conservative upbringing, Childs spent most of his adult life recalling the church to its confession of the Bible as the rule of faith and practice and, at the same time, providing academic and scholarly justification for such a stance.[79] To this end, he insists that the final or canonical form of Scripture in two Testaments is the context within which the believing community of faith does its theological reflection. Even the ordering and shape of the canonical text is not without theological significance. Thus the Pentateuch forms an indispensable foundation for the later prophetic and poetic books, and the Gospels contain the bedrock events upon which the apostolic letters theologize.

For Childs, the Bible is authoritative and calls out to be read theologically. Precisely here much historical-critical scholarship is found wanting. Atomizing approaches eviscerate the inherent authority and theological message of Scripture by focusing on sources and traditions behind the text rather than on the received text. They discover competing, contradictory theologies rather than a theological unity. The dire consequences for the spiritual life of the church are obvious. This does not mean that Childs jettisons historical-critical approaches to Scripture; rather, he wants "to do justice to the final, received form of the two testaments in the light of their traditio-historical trajectories."[80] While recognizing that each Testament has its own historical context, which must be taken seriously, he insists that there is a theological unity that binds the two Testaments together. This unity is "their witness to the selfsame divine reality . . . the reality of God."[81] The focal point and norm for all theological reflection on this reality is Jesus Christ. According to Childs, "If Jesus Christ is not the norm, but various cultural criteria are, the result for Biblical Theology is an unmitigated disaster."[82]

---

[78]For further discussion and evaluation of this approach, see Mikeal C. Parson, "Canonical Criticism," in *New Testament Criticism and Interpretation*, ed. David Alan Black and David S. Dockery (Grand Rapids: Zondervan, 1991), pp. 255-94; Christopher Seitz, "Canonical Approach," *DTIB* 100-102.

[79]See G. T. Shephard, "Brevard Childs," in *Dictionary of Major Biblical Interpreters*, ed. Donald K. McKim (Downers Grove, Ill.: InterVarsity Press, 2007), pp. 301-10.

[80]Brevard S. Childs, *Biblical Theology of the Old and New Testaments: Theological Reflection on the Christian Bible* (Minneapolis: Fortress, 1993), p. 719.

[81]Ibid., p. 721.

[82]Ibid.

Evangelicals generally welcome Child's staunch defense of the canonical text as the locus for theological reflection. His commitment to the central affirmation of historic Christianity breathes new life into the academy. Although many have misgivings about his attempt to wed historical-critical methodology to his theological endeavor and wish for an expanded content of the theological unity that he finds, others have found in Childs a "safe house" in the often wild and wooly neighborhood of postmodern biblical and theological study.

AN EVANGELICAL APPROACH TO THE UNITY OF THE BIBLE

An evangelical approach presupposes the inspiration and authority of Scripture. A necessary corollary is the consequent unity of the entire Bible. The same Holy Spirit superintended the process of inscripturation for both Testaments, so it follows that the result is a unified, coherent message. God does not speak out of both sides of his mouth. Diversity per se is not incompatible with such a view; only outright contradiction falls outside the parameters of the control stipulated by the doctrine of inspiration (see 2 Tim 3:15-16; 2 Pet 1:20-21).

Still, one must articulate how this unity of message confronts us in the pages of sacred writ. There is a consensus among evangelicals that no single category or concept is adequate to describe and summarize the unity of the Bible. One must resort to several different ways of expressing this unity. This admission should not be viewed as inherently self-defeating; many analogies from nature instruct us that underlying the rich diversity of life processes are some profound unifying features. On the macrolevel, for example, physicists speak of four fundamental forces that determine our universe (the strong force [attraction within the nucleus of an atom], the weak force [attraction between protons and electrons], electromagnetism, and gravity). Why should it surprise us if the same is true of God's self-revelation in Scripture? In what follows, I list some of the primary ways in which evangelicals, following the lead of the historic Christian church, have described the unity of the Bible.

1. *Theology proper.* The nature and purpose of God provide a unifying factor in redemptive history. Patient exegesis of Scripture reveals that the attributes of God and his revealed intentions for the universe remain remarkably constant in both Testaments. It is true that some have demurred and drawn attention to alleged contradictions and inconsistencies. Marcion and the Gnostics led the assault in the second century A.D., and theological liberalism followed suit after the Enlightenment. When, however, one takes into account the progressive nature of redemptive history and the culturally conditioned backdrop against which God's saving activity unfolded, there remains a remarkable and reassuring coherence and consistency.

2. *Christology.* This too provides a unifying link between the Testaments. The doctrine of the person and mission of the Messiah unfolds over the vast sweep of redemptive history covered in the OT. A large area of agreement exists within Christendom that the OT witnesses to the hope of a coming deliverer. After all, Jesus himself said that all three sections of the Hebrew Scriptures testified concerning him: Law, Prophets, Writings (Lk 24:27; Jn 5:39). Not only is there a witness to the coming Messiah in the OT, but also there are good grounds for affirming that the preincarnate Christ actually participated in redemptive history and revealed himself to leading actors in the unfolding drama. Many think that the mysterious angel of the Lord, who occasionally appears in OT narratives, was none other than the preincarnate Christ. In a fascinating comment in 1 Corinthians 10:4 Paul says that Christ accompanied the wilderness generation. With whom did Jacob wrestle, and before whom did Joshua bow (Gen 32:22-32; Josh 5:13-15)? The actual presence of Christ in OT redemptive history does not seem fanciful and forced.

3. *Typology.* A very useful way of conceiving of the unity of the Bible is in terms of typology. This way of conceptualizing the unity of the Testaments has, to be sure, suffered from its friends as well as its foes. Too often imagination has run riot, with connections being "discovered" that have little basis in the Scriptural text itself. Excesses aside, there is a surprising degree of agreement among scholars across a wide swath of theological opinion that a circumspect use of typology is a valid way of stating how the Testaments relate one to another. A divine mind is at work behind the fabric of biblical writings.

4. *Promise/prophecy and fulfillment.* Another approach to discovering unity in the Bible, finding broad acceptance across the theological spectrum, is the notion of promise/fulfillment. This rubric draws attention to the way NT authors employ the OT in their writings. The story line of the Bible is punctuated by prophetic announcements of God's saving intentions. These announcements are taken up and elaborated in the progress of revelation. There seems to be an inexorable kind of movement forward, involving a taking up and reshaping of earlier promises into promises ever more glowing. In the OT fulfillment is never of the same magnitude as the promise—much is yet desired. That is where the NT revelation shines out with its note of ultimate fulfillment. In Christ all the promises of God are "yes," says the apostle Paul (2 Cor 1:20). The NT itself looks forward to a climactic fulfillment at the eschaton—the new earth crowned by the new

Jerusalem. This, then, is a helpful way of appreciating the progressive revelation of God's saving purposes in the Bible.

5. *Redemptive history.* Items 1-4 touch on a common feature. In each case, there is an assumed plot or story line running through the material. This plot is of utmost importance and becomes a significant way of stating how the two Testaments relate. Read as a connected story, Genesis through Revelation contains a profound story, a story of redemption. The best way to explicate this is to say that the Bible is primarily composed of a unique history, the history of redemption. In German scholarship the term *Heilsgeschichte* is used; in English a term such as *salvation history* or *redemptive history* conveys the same idea. I have already suggested that the leading theme of this redemptive history is the coming of the kingdom of God or, to put it another way, the struggle to reestablish the uncontested rule of God over the earth.

6. *Continuity/discontinuity.* Although items 1-5 indissolubly link the Testaments together, even a superficial reading of both makes clear that each one possesses distinctive features. The two are not, after all, the same. The postapostolic church left us the legacy of referring to the Testaments as the *Old* Testament and the *New* Testament. These temporal designations imply a priority residing with the NT. We may not roll back the clock of redemptive history and reassert the priority of the OT, nor may we even upgrade the OT to the level of independent witness without further qualification.[83] The predominant note of fulfillment ringing throughout the NT requires that a Christian read the Bible from the vantage point of this fulfillment in the Christ event. What this means, in terms of faith and practice, is that one recognizes a continuity/discontinuity polarity characterizing the two Testaments. There are ideas, themes, practices and concepts common to both Testaments, thus displaying continuity. On the other hand, some normative practices themes and features of the OT are discontinued and replaced in the New. The recognition and identification of the continuous and discontinuous elements remains one of the most challenging and contentious aspects of evangelical theology.

7. *Unresolved problems.* One of the problem areas in this regard is sorting out the relevance and normative status of the Mosaic law for the Christian church. Evangelical theologians are sharply divided over this issue. The next chapter examines two major systems of evangelical biblical theology—

---

[83]For misguided attempts to do precisely this, see Arnold van Ruler, *The Christian Church and the Old Testament*, trans. Geoffrey W. Bromiley (Grand Rapids: Eerdmans, 1971); Kornelius Miskotte, *When the Gods Are Silent*, trans. John W. Doberstein (New York: Harper & Row, 1967).

covenant theology and dispensationalism—that have been at odds over the resolution of this problem for over 150 years. Another problem area relates to the ultimate purposes of God. Does God have one, all-encompassing salvific plan, or are there multiple plans? For example, does Israel have a distinct national future, or has the church assumed the role of a new Israel and fulfilled those prophetic promises in the OT? The debate is highly charged and continues to elicit contrasting responses from the respective systems. Closely allied to this problem is the attempt to analyze and set forth the structure of redemptive history. Can one discern a clear pattern of organization by which God accomplishes his purposes? Is the covenant idea fundamental for structuring salvation history, or is there another pattern—the notion of dispensations, for example—that is more crucial in recognizing God's unfolding plan of redemption? Again, covenant theology and dispensationalism offer different structuring schemes.

We are now poised to look more closely at the history and stance of these two competing biblical theology systems, both based on an evangelical understanding of Scripture.

FOR FURTHER DISCUSSION

1. Is the approach of the early church fathers in understanding the relationship between the OT and the NT still valid and useful?

2. Why is Marcion's view of the OT still an important issue?

3. Does the allegorical method have any validity? Why or why not?

5. What value may still be found in Augustine's view of Scripture?

6. What are the strengths and weaknesses of Luther's view of Scripture?

7. How does Calvin relate the two Testaments, and how does this differ from Luther?

8. How did the Enlightenment completely transform the interpretation of the Bible?

9. Why is Rudolf Bultmann still an important figure for modern NT study?

10. Whose approach better upholds the unity of the Bible: von Rad's or Robinson's? Why?

11. What contribution does narrative theology make to the unity of the Bible?

12. Why is Brevard Childs's approach compatible with that of evangelicals?

13. Are there other valid ways of stating the unity of the Bible?

FOR FURTHER READING

Anderson, Bernhard W., ed. *The Old Testament and Christian Faith: A Theological Discussion.* New York: Herder & Herder, 1969.

Baker, David. L. *Two Testaments, One Bible: A Study of the Theological Relationship between the Old and New Testaments.* 2nd ed. Downers Grove, Ill.: InterVarsity Press, 1992.

Bartsch, Hans Werner, ed. *Kerygma and Myth: A Theological Debate.* 1953. Repr., New York: Harper & Row, 1961.

Childs, Brevard S. *Biblical Theology of the Old and New Testaments: Theological Reflections on the Christian Bible,* pp. 63-79, 196-207, 211-18, 717-27. Minneapolis: Fortress, 1993.

Cullman, Oscar. *Christ and Time: The Primitive Christian Conception of Time and History,* translated by Floyd V. Filson. Rev. ed. Philadelphia: Westminster Press, 1964.

————. *Salvation in History,* translated by Sidney G. Sowers et al. London: SCM Press, 1967.

France, R. T. France. "Relationship Between the Testaments." *DTIB* 666-72.

Fuller, Daniel P. *The Unity of the Bible: Unfolding God's Plan for Humanity.* Grand Rapids: Zondervan, 1992.

Goldsworthy, G. "Relationship of Old Testament and New Testament." *NDBT* 81-89.

Grant, Robert M. *A Short History of the Interpretation of the Bible.* 2nd ed. New York: Macmillan, 1963.

Hauser, Alan J., and Duane F. Watson, eds. *A History of Biblical Interpretation.* Vol. 1, *The Ancient Period.* Grand Rapids: Eerdmans, 2003.

Kraeling, Emil G. *The Old Testament since the Reformation.* 1955. Repr., New York: Schocken, 1969.

McKim, Donald K., ed. *Dictionary of Major Biblical Interpreters.* Downers Grove, Ill.: InterVarsity Press, 2007.

Ramm, Bernard. *Protestant Biblical Interpretation: A Textbook of Hermeneutics,* pp. 22-92. Grand Rapids: Baker, 1970.

Treier, Daniel J. "Scripture, Unity of." *DTIB* 731-34.

Verhoef, Pieter. "The Relationship Between the Old and New Testaments." In *New Perspectives on the Old Testament,* ed. J. Barton Payne, pp. 280-303. Waco, Tex.: Word, 1970.

Westermann, Claus, and James Luther Mays, eds. *Essays on Old Testament Hermeneutics.* Richmond: John Knox Press, 1963.

3

Two Evangelical Systems
of Biblical Theology

THIS CHAPTER INTRODUCES TWO INFLUENTIAL systems developed by evangelical biblical theologians. As we saw in the survey of various options for explaining the unity of the Bible, evangelicals are agreed on some essential links between the Testaments. They do not, however, agree precisely on how the Bible is structured and what concept or concepts best demonstrate its overarching unity. Covenant theology and dispensationalism share a common commitment to the inspiration and authority of Scripture, and yet they differ significantly on how to articulate its unity.[1]

First, I provide a historical sketch of the two systems, beginning with covenant theology, since it is the older of the two, and briefly outline the distinctive features of each system. Next, I compare and contrast the two systems, especially noting how each, in debate and dialogue with the other, has modified its stance over the years. Finally, I offer a critique of both and suggest a mediating approach.

HISTORY OF COVENANT THEOLOGY
All parties in the debate agree that covenant theology is a post-Reformation

---

[1]Paul Feinberg puts it this way: "It is difficult to think of any problem that is more important or fundamental than the relationship between the Testaments. There are two Testaments; no one questions that. How do they form one Bible? In evangelical, fundamental circles traditionally two answers have dominated the scene: Covenant Theology and Dispensationalism. Regardless of what one thinks of these approaches, they should be seen as serious attempts to answer this question" ("Hermeneutics of Discontinuity," in *Continuity and Discontinuity: Perspectives on the Relationship between the Old and New Testaments; Essays in Honor of S. Lewis Johnson Jr.*, ed. John S. Feinberg [Westchester, Ill.: Crossway, 1988], p. 110).

development. Of course, the concept of covenant—God graciously enters into mutual relationships with certain individuals or groups—derives from Scripture, and the early church fathers make repeated mention of the term and concept. The manner in which the expression functions in later covenant theology, however, does not appear in the fathers or medieval ecclesiastics.[2] As John Murray points out, "Covenant theology is . . . a distinguishing feature of the Reformed tradition because *the idea of covenant came to be an organizing principle* in terms of which the relations of God to men were construed."[3]

As we noted in the preceding chapter, Calvin frequently mentions the covenants, and for him the covenant idea is an important category for understanding the unity of the Bible, salvation and the Christian life. In short, God's relationship with humanity conforms to the notion of a gracious covenant.[4] Calvin's theology, however, is fundamentally structured not around the concept of covenant, but rather the Trinity. Covenant theology, or "federal theology," as it is sometimes called, is really a post-Calvin development.[5]

The earliest attempt by a Reformed theologian to deal extensively with the concept of covenant was the Swiss Heinrich Bullinger (1504-1575). He was the leading theologian of Zürich after the death of the father of the Reformation in German Switzerland, Ulrich Zwingli (1484-1531). Bullinger followed the lead of his mentor "in seeing in the Bible and the church's history as one long story of God's covenant relationship with humankind."[6] Bullinger, essentially a pastor at heart, built his theology on the premise that salvation history was the essence of the Bible, and the covenant, called a covenant of grace, was "the chief principle for interpreting the Bible and understanding God's rule in history."[7]

Two of Calvin's students, Zacharias Ursinus (1534-1583)[8] and Caspar

---

[2]P. A. Lillback, "Covenant," *NDT* 174-75. Dewey D. Wallace Jr. observes, "God's covenant . . . occasionally . . . appeared as a theme in patristic exegesis. Some late-medieval theologians, especially Nominalists, thought in convenantal terms, arguing that God's absolute power was constrained by God's ordaining to act in certain stipulated ways with respect to creation" ("Federal Theology," in *Encyclopedia of the Reformed Faith*, ed. Donald K. McKim [Louisville: Westminster/John Knox, 1992], p. 136).

[3]John Murray, "Covenant Theology," *EC* 3:200 (my italics).

[4]Lillback, "Covenant," p. 175.

[5]Some covenant theologians would take strong exception to this statement. See, for example, Mark Karlberg, "Covenant Theology and the Westminster Tradition," *WTJ* 54 (1992): 136-53 (review of David A. Weir, *The Origins of Federal Theology in Sixteenth-Century Reformation Thought* [Oxford: Clarendon, 1990]).

[6]Wallace, "Federal Theology," p. 136.

[7]Ibid.

[8]Ursinus, a German theologian, was born at Breslau and educated at Wittenberg (where

(Kaspar or Gaspar) Olevianus (1536-1587),[9] advanced beyond their mentor and postulated a prefall covenant of works and a pretemporal covenant of redemption. Thereafter, covenant theology typically structured salvation history around these three covenants: redemption, works, grace. Olevianus and Ursinus drafted the final revision of the Heidelberg Catechism, the official creed of the German Reformed churches.

At this point, I need to define each of these covenants. Calvin already saw the unity of Scripture consisting of one, all-embracing covenant of grace administered under two different dispensations, the OT and the NT. The covenant of grace is that gracious agreement between the offended God and the offending but elect sinner in which God promises salvation through faith in Christ, and the sinner accepts this believingly, promising a life of faith and obedience. Ursinus, in 1562, apparently first introduced a prefall covenant, the covenant of works. Adam was constituted, by God's sovereign appointment, the representative of the whole human race. With Adam as their representative, God entered into covenant, agreeing to bestow upon them eternal life on condition of Adam's obedience, but making the penalty of his disobedience to be the corruption and death of all his posterity. Finally, Olevianus, in 1585, spoke of a pretemporal covenant that was eventually called the "covenant of redemption" or sometimes "the counsel of peace." This is the agreement between the Father giving the Son as head and redeemer of the elect, and the Son placing himself voluntarily in their stead as their surety. It should be noted that this covenant "pushed the covenant pattern back into the inner life of the Trinity."[10]

Two English theologians also contributed to the development of covenant theology. William Ames (1576-1633) and Robert Rollock (1555[?]-1599) worked on the covenant of works. This covenant had also been occasionally called "the covenant of nature," but after Ames and Rollock the rubric "covenant of works" became a staple of covenant theology. The idea is that God promises to humankind eternal life on the condition of good works performed in the strength of nature, a condition that humankind in turn accepts. Even after the fall, this covenant is present throughout salvation history until the coming of Christ. Covenant theologians speak of its repetition throughout salvation history, the most notable instance being the

Luther had taught) under Philip Melancthon, Geneva under Calvin, and Paris under Jean Mercier. From 1561 to 1568 he was professor of dogmatics at Heidelberg University.

[9]Olevianus, an early German reformer, was born at Treves. He studied law at Paris, Orleans and Bourges, where he encountered Reformation thought. In 1558 he went to Geneva to study theology under Calvin and became well acquainted with Calvin, Beza, Farel and Bullinger.

[10]Wallace, "Federal Theology," p. 137.

Sinai covenant, in which Israel pledged itself to entire obedience of the covenant stipulations (Ex 19:8; 24:3). The outcome is always failure, owing to human inability. The intention of this covenant is that the sinner, being convicted of sin and the impossibility of good works in the strength of nature, takes refuge in the covenant of grace. An affinity with Luther's law-gospel dialectic is clear.

The leading systematizer of covenant theology was Johannes Cocceius (John Koch [1603-1669]).[11] He has been styled "the father of federal theology." Cocceius felt that Calvin was too rigid in his view of predestination. God did not cause the fall of humankind; each individual is responsible for his or her sin. In order to soften "high Calvinism," Cocceius introduced the idea of federal headship. He wanted to show how God graciously abrogated the covenant of works with its federal head, Adam—and its inevitable curse—by providing in the covenant of grace a new relationship with a new federal head, Jesus Christ. Louis Praamsma highlights a significant aspect of Cocceius's theology that is relevant for our study of biblical theology: "Through his federal theology, he wanted to avoid all speculations about and deductions from God's eternal decrees and to develop only the historical way of salvation in which these decrees were realized. This historical way was, according to Cocceius, a way of several covenantal dispensations that succeeded each other in such a manner that the new one meant the abrogation of the preceding one."[12] It was his move toward a historical ordering and arrangement of all the doctrines of the Christian faith under the two covenants of nature (works) and grace that gained for him the further appellation "the father of biblical theology." The upshot was a more practical theology than had previously obtained and more attention given to the successive periods of sacred history.[13]

The development of the covenant concept and federal theology as a way of explaining God's relationship to sinners did not come "out of the blue." This was the era when the dogma of the divine right of kings was increasingly being challenged. Parliaments and legal instruments curbed the power of absolute monarchs. Dissenters from state churches were clamoring for rights and guarantees of basic freedoms. Reformed theology developed in

---

[11]Cocceius was a Dutch Protestant Hebrew scholar, theologian and biblical exegete. He was born at Bremen and educated at the universities of Hamburg and Franeker. He accepted the chair of theology at the University of Leiden in 1650 and held that post until his death.

[12]Louis Praamsma, "Cocceius, Johannes," *EC* 3:25.

[13]See C. P. Wing, "Federal Theology," of *Cyclopedia of Biblical, Theological, and Ecclesiastical Literature*, ed. John McClintock and James Strong (New York: Harper, 1883), 3:515-20. Cocceius's concern to map out salvation history in its successive periods even led some dispensationalists to claim him as the fountainhead of dispensationalism.

this environment of political and ecclesiastical innovation.

Earlier debates within Calvinism about the *ordo salutis* ("order of salvation") fostered rancorous disputes. Did God decree to elect some sinners before he decreed the fall (supralapsarianism), or did he first decree (or permit) the fall and then elect some to be saved (infralapsarianism or sublapsariansim)? The whole discussion tended to distance God from believers and portray him as arbitrary, like an absolute monarch accountable to no one. In federal theology God condescends to enter an agreement with sinners. God is brought close in terms of a mutual agreement whereby he pledges his love and mercy on condition of faith and repentance. Vernon Ruland analyzes this development:

> Covenant theologians epitomize one phase of the late Renaissance transition from feudalism to constitutional monarchy, from fixed status to contract. They had to fit an omnipotent voluntarist God into a universe daily proving more rationally tractable, reconcile irresistible grace with man's natural rights, and develop a church polity blending elements of Old Testament theocracy with contemporary theories of voluntary social origins. In the light of current social contract theory, they reexamined the Biblical covenants of Yahweh with Noe, Abraham, and Moses, later renewed in the person of Christ, and discovered contractual relationships by which God freely imposed rational constitutional limitations on His whirlwind caprice, offered Himself as ready contractual partner to each believer, prescribed moral duties not brutally and irrationally but only with each Christian's reasonable and willing consent.[14]

This is a reminder that theology is never done in a vacuum. Ideas "in the air" often find their way into theological discussion and systems. Consequently, biblical theologians must be vigilant lest alien ideas force biblical teaching into a straitjacket. As we will see, contemporary covenant theologians recognize the need to modify their system in light of this awareness.

Two more figures after Cocceius add further refinements to covenant theology. Francis Turretin (1623-1687) was responsible for developing new aspects of the covenant of works. Adam was viewed as a contracting party, and his relationship to God was a bond joining him and all his posterity. This bond with all humanity was twofold: it was natural in that he was the physical father of all, and forensic in that he was the duly appointed repre-

---

[14]Vernon Ruland, "Covenant Theology," in *New Catholic Encyclopedia* (New York: McGraw Hill, 1967), 4:405. Many covenant theologians would have a different take on this. See, for example, Wallace, "Federal Theology," p. 137.

sentative of all. Note, however, that Turretin puts more weight on the gracious character of the prefall covenant than was previously the case. God is not obligated, owing to any natural right or merit of humankind, to make this offer of everlasting life contingent on perfect, personal obedience. Even if such obedience could be rendered, it is never worthy of so disproportionate a reward. The accent, then, falls on the voluntary condescension of God to allow such an arrangement. This more gracious construal of the covenant of works is reflected in the Westminster Confession of Faith (drafted 1643-1649).

Turretin's theology lived on in the great Princeton divines of the nineteenth century: Archibald Alexander (1772-1851), Charles Hodge (1797-1878), Archibald Alexander Hodge (1823-1886) and Benjamin Warfield (1851-1921). For sixty years, Turretin's theology (in Latin!) was used as a textbook at Princeton Seminary. The heritage of the "old Princeton" theology lives on today. Institutions such as Westminster Theological Seminary (Philadelphia), Covenant Theological Seminary (St. Louis), Reformed Theological Seminary (Jackson, Mississippi, with other campuses at Orlando, Florida, and Charlotte, North Carolina), and Knox Theological Seminary (Fort Lauderdale, Florida), to name several of the most prominent, perpetuate covenant theology. In addition, many teaching and administrative positions in other colleges, universities, and seminaries are held by individuals adhering to covenant theology, to say nothing of numerous pastors, missionaries, and lay leaders trained in this theological tradition. Denominations exclusively or predominantly committed to Reformed covenant theology are the Orthodox Presbyterian Church, the Presbyterian Church of America, the Christian Reformed Church, and the Reformed Church of America, among others. A significant number of covenant theologians were founding fathers of the Evangelical Theological Society (organized in 1949).

DISTINCTIVES OF COVENANT THEOLOGY

1. The covenant idea as the major organizing principle. As we have already noted, the covenant concept is the major organizing principle of covenant theology. In its fully developed form, covenant theology conceives of three covenants. Two covenants, the covenant of works and the covenant of grace, structure the whole of Scripture, from paradise lost to paradise regained. The covenant of works (or life) was instituted in Genesis 2 and broken in Genesis 3. The covenant of grace is intimated already in Genesis 3 but first comes to clear expression in the covenant with Abraham (Gen 12; 15; 17). All other covenants in the OT are elaborations of the one covenant of grace, climaxing in the new covenant prophesied in Jeremiah 31:31-34 and inaugurated by Jesus' death (Mark 14:23-25; Heb 9:11—10:18). The third covenant, the covenant of redemption, takes us back into the eternal council of the triune God in that the entire plan of redemption unfolds according to an eternal decree (Eph 1:4-6; 1 Pet 1:20). Clearly, then, the basis of covenant theology is the covenant concept. The following chart outlines the three covenants in terms of their primary components.

Table 3.1. The Covenants of Covenant Theology

Covenant of Redemption	Covenant of Works	Covenant of Grace
Parties: God the Father and God the Son	Parties: God and Adam	Parties: God the Father and believers
Proviso: The Son's perfect obedience even to his suffering the penalty of humanity's disobedience, death	Proviso: Perfect obedience by Adam on the basis of his original righteousness	Proviso: Faith in Jesus Christ as the only "work" required of the believer (Jn 6:29)
Promise: Salvation of all believers	Promise: Eternal life	Promise: Eternal life
	Penalty: Death, both physical and spiritual	
	Sign/Seal: tree of life, tree of good and evil, paradise, sabbath	Sign/Seal: Circumcision and Passover for the OT, and baptism and Lord's Supper for the NT

A classic expression of the three covenants is set forth in the Westminster Confession of Faith (1643-1646) and the Shorter Catechism (1648).[15]

2. The hermeneutics of covenant theology. Another feature of covenant theology relates to its method of interpretation. For the most part, covenant theologians, in keeping with Calvin's insistence, interpret the Bible literally; that is, they seek the author's intended meaning by understanding the author's words in the sense that they bear in ordinary discourse. This includes figurative and metaphorical meanings, where such are clearly implied by the context. The historical narratives about Israel are interpreted literally, although it is understood that within the larger empirical Israel of the OT exists the elect people of God, who are equated with the church. This calls for special mention. Since there is but one redeemed people of God in the two Testaments, no real distinction obtains between Israel and the church. The NT church is the new Israel, and the true Israel of the OT (the elect) is

---

[15]*The Book of Confessions* (2nd ed.: New York: Office of the General Assembly the United Presbyterian Church in the United States of America, 1970), 6.037-6.048.

the church; Israel and the church comprise essentially one people of God.[16] So when covenant theologians interpret prophetic passages dealing with the future of Israel, they understand "Israel" to refer to the church.

Justification for such an exegetical move is based primarily upon the manner in which the NT authors quote or apply passages from the OT. Employing a grammatical-historical method, one finds numerous instances in which an OT text, referring to historic Israel, is quoted in reference to a spiritual reality obtaining within the church.[17] In 1 Peter 2:9-10 we see a good example: "But you are a chosen race, a royal priesthood, a holy nation, God's own people, in order that you may proclaim the mighty acts of him who called you out of darkness into his marvelous light. Once you were not a people, but now you are God's people; once you had not received mercy, but now you have received mercy." A check of this passage shows that Peter cites Exodus 19:6; Isaiah 43:20-21; Hosea 1:9; 2:23, all of which speak about historic Israel in their respective contexts, but now they are reapplied to the primarily Gentile church.

Whether the NT application of OT texts to the church amounts to an identification of Israel and the church, however, constitutes a major sticking point in the debate between covenant theology and dispensationalism. Dispensationalists traditionally have dubbed covenant theology's method of interpretation as a "dual hermeneutic"—that is, a "literal nonliteral" or "literal spiritualizing" hermeneutic—though, in my opinion, this is not entirely accurate. Dispensationalism distinguishes itself from covenant theology by its insistence on a "consistently literal" hermeneutic. This will become clearer in my discussion of dispensationalism.

3. Eschatological variations within covenant theology. Within covenant theology there are at least three different eschatological stances, each of which is compatible with the overarching framework of covenant theology.[18]

3.1. The predominant eschatological view among covenant theologians is amillennialism. As the prefix *a-* indicates, this view holds that there is no millennium, or thousand-year reign on earth, after the second coming of Jesus Christ. Oswald T. Allis, a leading evangelical OT scholar of a for-

---

[16]Ibid., 3.16.

[17]Robert L. Saucy, a progressive dispensationalist, recognizes this (*The Case for Progressive Dispensationalism: The Interface Between Dispensational and Non-Dispensational Theology* [Grand Rapids: Zondervan, 1993], p. 20).

[18]For a concise overview of the various millennial options, see R. J. Bauckham, "Millennium," *NDT* 428-30. For more extended treatments, see Robert G. Clouse, ed., *The Meaning of the Millennium: Four Views* (Downers Grove, Ill.: InterVarsity Press, 1977); Stanley J. Grenz, *The Millennial Maze: Sorting Out Evangelical Options* (Downers Grove, Ill.: InterVarsity Press, 1992); Darrell L. Bock, ed., *Three Views on the Millennium and Beyond* (Grand Rapids: Zondervan, 1999).

mer generation and a prominent spokesperson for amillennialism, defines it this way: "This is the teaching that the only visible coming of Christ to this earth which the Church is to expect will be for judgment and will be followed by the final state. It is anti-chiliastic or amillennial, because it rejects the doctrine that there are to be two resurrections with an interval of a thousand years (the millennial reign of Christ with His saints on earth) between them."[19]

Amillennial eschatology generally holds the following tenets:

- The millennium of Revelation 20 refers to the present era of the gospel dispensation or the reign of deceased saints in heaven (or a combination).[20]

- The course of this age is characterized by a parallel development of good and evil.

- The end of this age is marked by the appearance of a personal antichrist.

- Some amillennialists, based on Romans 11:26, hold to a mass conversion of Jews at the end of the age.[21] Most interpret "all Israel" in Romans 11:26 to mean all believers, whether Jewish or Gentile. This is in keeping with covenant theology's equation of Israel and the church.

- This age is climaxed by the rapture of the church at the return of Jesus. The rapture is generally viewed as posttribulational (i.e., occurring after a brief period of intense persecution by the antichrist and divine judgments upon the earth).

- Accompanying the rapture is the general resurrection of the righteous and wicked.

- All humankind stands at the judgment seat of Christ. The righteous enter everlasting felicity, and the wicked experience everlasting punishment.

- A new creation supplants the old and ushers in the eternal state.

---

[19]Oswald T. Allis, *Prophecy and the Church: An Examination of the Claim of Dispensationalists That the Christian Church Is a Mystery Parenthesis Which Interrupts the Fulfilment to Israel of the Kingdom Prophecies of the Old Testament* (Philadelphia: P & R Publishing, 1945), p. 2.

[20]Interestingly, the Reformers "took the millennium to be an actual period of 1,000 years in the past (variously dated), during which the gospel flourished. Satan's release at the end of this period (Rev. 10:7) marked the rise of the medieval papacy. For the future, the Reformers expected the imminent coming of Christ, leading at once to the last judgment and the dissolution of this world" (Bauckham, "Millennium," p. 428).

[21]See, for example, John Murray, *The Epistle to the Romans* (2 vols.; New International Commentary on the New Testament; Grand Rapids: Eerdmans, 1959-1965), 2:96-101.

In terms of eschatology, amillennialism and dispensationalism differ primarily in their exegesis of Revelation 20:1-10 and their understanding of the nature of the millennium. This difference, however, is rooted in the more fundamental question concerning the identity of Israel and the church. This difference surfaces most clearly in the respective handling of OT prophecies dealing with the restoration of Israel. Amillennialists interpret them in one of three ways or a combination thereof:

- already fulfilled in the postexilic period

- relating to the present dispensation of the church

- describing the future glories of the eternal state

Dispensationalists, on the other hand, consistently interpret them as referring to national, ethnic Israel during the millennial kingdom on earth. Thus amillennial and dispensational exegeses of OT prophecy are markedly different.

3.2. A second branch of covenant theology espouses postmillennialism.[22] This view holds that Jesus Christ will return to earth after the gospel has been preached to all nations, resulting in the conversion of a majority of the world's population. The present gospel dispensation *is* the millennium, understood as a symbolic number for an extended period of time. This view appeared at the advent of the eigtheenth century in the writings of Daniel Whitby (1638-1726). He consciously articulates his view in opposition to both premillennialism (Christ returns before his thousand-year reign with his saints on the earth) and amillennialism. Postmillennialism dominated Protestant theology during the eighteenth century in North America (Jonathan Edwards adhered to postmillennialism) and continued through the nineteenth century as reflected in hymns such as "We've a Story to Tell to the Nations." Loraine Boettner defines postmillennialism this way: "Postmillennialism is that view of the last things which holds that the Kingdom of God is now being extended in the world through the preaching of the Gospel and the saving work of the Holy Spirit, that the world eventually will be Christianized, and that the return of Christ will occur at the close of a long period of righteousness and peace commonly called the Millennium."[23]

The salient features of postmillennialism are as follows:

- Like amillennialism, it understands prophetic passages dealing with the restoration of Israel as referring to the church.

---

[22]See Loraine Boettner, *The Millennium* (Philadelphia: P & R Publishing, 1957).
[23]Ibid., p. 4.

- It identifies the kingdom of God with the church and insists that the kingdom is spiritual and invisible rather than material and political.

- Through the preaching of the gospel, the kingdom of God increases dramatically and eventually Christianizes the world.

- There are many "comings" of Christ in world history, identified as clearly providential events (e.g., the Reformation, the rise of the modern missionary movement, the American Civil War) and the death of saints (cf. Jn 14:3: "And if I go and prepare a place for you, *I will come again* and will take you to myself, so that where I am, there you may be also" [my italics]). There will be a final coming of Christ, however, at the end of the age, viewed as still remote.

- Christ returns after the millennium, an indefinite period, not a literal one thousand years.

- A general resurrection and final judgment of the righteous and wicked, as well as the angels, follow the return of Christ.

- The eternal state concludes redemptive history.

A formidable obstacle for this view is the necessity of viewing history through rose-colored glasses. World history from the apostolic age to the present affords little optimism for a future "golden age" brought about by the gospel. Although it is, thankfully, true that civilization has made immense strides in technology, science, and quality of life for many, the unprecedented scale of misery, suffering, and unmitigated evil in the twentieth century offers little hope for dramatic improvement in the twenty-first century and beyond. Technology has failed to be a savior.

Of course, postmillennialists agree. They counter that the gospel is what offers hope. I applaud the confidence expressed in the power of the gospel (cf. Rom 1:16), but this question remains: Does Scripture teach that the majority of the world's population come to faith before Christ returns (cf. Lk 18:8)? Here is the primary problem with the view: it stands in opposition to clearly stated texts implying a deepening of evil at the end of the age. One need only peruse the Olivet discourse (Mk 13; Mt 24; Lk 21), Paul's "little apocalypse" (2 Thess 2:1-12), and the book of Revelation (Rev 6—19) in a straightforward manner to realize that postmillennialism goes "against the grain" of end-time scriptural texts. Postmillennialism has a number of scholarly defenders, but it is a decidedly minority position because of the aforementioned reasons.[24]

[24]See Keith Mathison, *Postmillennialism: An Eschatology of Hope* (Phillipsburg, N.J.: P & R Publishing, 1999); Kenneth L. Gentry Jr., *He Shall Have Dominion: A Postmillennial Es-*

3.3. Another minority position within the parameters of covenantal eschatology is premillennialism. As the word indicates, this is the notion that Christ returns at the end of the age and reigns with his saints for one thousand years, or at least for an extended period of time. Since premillennialism is essential to dispensationalism, one is surprised that some covenant theologians incorporate it within their system.[25]

Covenantal millennialism is characterized by the following tenets:

- In keeping with standard Reformed theology, the covenant of works and covenant of grace structure biblical theology.

- No distinction is made between Israel and the church. The future of ethnic Jews who respond to Christ is within the pale of the Christian church.

- Following the rapture of the church, the righteous stand at the judgment seat of Christ to determine rewards. Most hold to a posttribulation rapture occurring after a brief period of persecution by the antichrist and divine judgments on the earth, the so-called great tribulation, but some hold to a midtribulation view, and a very few even hold a pretribulation view.

- Jesus Christ reigns on this earth with his saints during the millennium.

- A resurrection and judgment of the wicked follows the millennial reign.

- The eternal state ensues.

Needless to say, both amillennialists and dispensationalists criticize adherents of this scheme for being inconsistent.[26]

CONTEMPORARY COVENANT THEOLOGY

The foregoing discussion has summarized classical covenant theology. Like all human theological endeavor, it has been developed and modified, reflecting new understandings of Scripture and, especially, new cultural contexts in which theological reflection takes place. Particularly in controversy and dialogue with Karl Barth and dispensationalism, one detects refine-

---

chatology (Tyler, Tex.: Institute for Christian Economics, 1992).

[25]See, for example, Diedrich Kromminga, *The Millennium in the Church: Studies in the History of Christian Chiliasm* (Grand Rapids: Eerdmans, 1945), pp. 5-6. See also idem, *The Millennium, Its Nature, Function and Relation to the Consummation of the World* (Grand Rapids: Eerdmans, 1948).

[26]For example, Loraine Boettner maintains, "There is a logical connection between Premillennialism and Dispensationalism. . . . But, conversely, we believe that most of those who become convinced of the errors of Dispensationalism proceed to throw Premillennialism overboard too" (*The Millennium*, p. 158).

ments and modifications in covenant theology as it is championed today at the beginning of the twenty-first century.

One area of modification has to do with the covenant of works. Several contemporary covenant theologians freely admit that the covenant of works is not as securely grounded exegetically or theologically as has usually been assumed.[27] Dispensationalists frequently have raised this criticism.[28] Karl Barth preferred to speak of one, all-embracing covenant of grace beginning at creation. In Barth's theology grace overwhelms law; there is no classic Protestant law/gospel antithesis.[29] Several theologians in the Reformed tradition have tended toward a Barthian perspective, most notably T. F. Torrance. Although resisting Barth's approach, John Murray nonetheless expresses discontent with the traditional rubric "covenant of works" and prefers to speak of an Adamic economy or administration.[30]

Thomas McComiskey shares Murray's misgivings, averring that the so-called covenant of works never offered eternal life on the basis of perfect obedience. Instead, he argues, it functions as a means of maintaining an already existing relationship. The stipulation that Adam not eat of the tree of the knowledge of good and evil threatened death for disobedience but did not offer life for obedience.[31] McComiskey suggests that a better designation for the relationship between God and Adam in the garden is "covenant of creation." In this way, one can view Adam as the federal representative of humanity and link it to Paul's discussion of the Adam/Christ typology of Romans 5:12-21. Going even further, McComiskey concedes that "there seems to be no absolute demand to designate this relationship a covenant

---

[27]See John Murray, *The Covenant of Grace: A Biblico-Theological Study* (London: Tyndale, 1953); idem, "The Adamic Administration," in *Collected Writings of John Murray* (4 vols.; Edinburgh and Carlisle, Penn.: Banner of Truth Trust, 1976), 2:49-50; Norman Shephard, "Life in Covenant with God" (sound recording; Philadelphia: Westminster Media, 1981 [series of lectures given during the French Creek Bible Conference at Sandy Cove, Maryland, 1981]); Thomas E. McComiskey, *The Covenants of Promise: A Theology of the Old Testament Covenants* (Grand Rapids: Baker, 1985), pp. 213-21. But already in the work of Charles Hodge one finds the admission that the doctrine is an inference and not an explicit teaching of Scripture (*Systematic Theology* [1923; 3 vols.; reprint, Grand Rapids: Eerdmans, 1979], 2:117).

[28]See Charles C. Ryrie, *Dispensationalism Today* (Chicago: Moody Press, 1965), pp. 183-87.

[29]Karl Barth, "Gospel and Law," in *God, Grace, and Gospel*, trans. James S. McNab (SJTOP 8; Edinburgh: Oliver & Boyd, 1959), pp. 1-28.

[30]Murray, *Collected Writings*, 2:49-50. This is interesting because the terms *economy, administration, disposition* and *dispensation* are virtually synonymous in this context, and dispensationalists prefer the term *dispensation*. At least, claim dispensationalists, the term *dispensation* occurs in the Bible, whereas the terms *covenant of works* and *covenant of grace* never do (Ryrie, *Dispensationalism Today*, p. 184).

[31]McComiskey, *The Covenants of Promise*, p. 219.

(the federal function of Adam is not diminished if the relationship is designated an administration), yet the relationship falls within the general category of *bĕrît*. Covenant theology should not be rejected on this basis."[32]

McComiskey's new tack carries with it a significant shift in understanding how the various covenants function in Scripture. He sees redemptive history as being structured by two distinct but related kinds of covenants: the promissary covenants, which are the promise to Abraham and the promise to David, and administrative covenants that govern human obedience, which are the Sinai covenant and the new covenant. This fresh approach to covenant theology reflects new insights gained as a result of studying ancient Near Eastern covenants and treaties and comparing them with biblical covenants.[33] It also implicitly acknowledges that seventeenth- and eighteenth-century covenant theologians read into the OT more than could be sustained exegetically and did not fully grasp how covenants functioned in the biblical times.

Palmer Robertson, another contemporary covenant theologian, also faults both traditional designations "covenant of works" and "covenant of grace":

> The terminology traditionally associated with this scheme has significant limitations . . . the nomenclature chosen to designate these two epochs suffers from a lack of preciseness. To speak of a covenant of "works" in contrast with a covenant of "grace" appears to suggest that grace was not operative in the covenant of works. As a matter of fact, the totality of God's relationship with man is a matter of grace. . . . This terminology further suggests that works have no place in the covenant of grace. But from the biblical perspective, works play a most essential role in the covenant of grace . . . those redeemed in Christ certainly must work. . . . While salvation is by faith, judgment is by works.[34]

This discussion of the covenant of works inevitably spills over into the doctrine of justification and precipitated an acrimonious debate and eventual dismissal of a faculty member at Westminster Theological Seminary. Norman Shephard, John Murray's successor as professor of systematic

---

[32]Ibid.

[33]In this regard, the work of Meredith Kline has been influential in covenant theology: *Treaty of the Great King: The Covenant Structure of Deuteronomy* (Grand Rapids: Eerdmans, 1963); *By Oath Consigned: A Reinterpretation of the Covenant Signs of Circumcision and Baptism* (Grand Rapids: Eerdmans, 1968).

[34]O. Palmer Robertson, *The Christ of the Covenants* (Phillipsburg, N.J.: P & R Publishing, 1980), pp. 55-56.

theology at Westminster (Philadelphia campus), taught that God never relates to humanity on the basis of works. The so-called covenant of works,
according to Shepherd, undermines the real heart of Reformation faith.
All God's dealings with mankind, whether prefall or postfall, are gracious
initiatives not depending on good works. On the other hand, saving faith
necessarily involves nonmeritorious good deeds, "the obedience of faith"
(Rom 1:5).[35] The notion that justification involves nonmeritorious good
deeds was viewed by some as a direct assault upon the Reformation doctrine of *sola fide* ("faith alone") and spurred a blistering attack by defenders of traditional covenant theology.[36] This is not the place to go into all the
nuances and subtleties of this theological controversy, but it does indicate
ongoing tensions and developments within covenant theology.

Was the Mosaic covenant one of works or grace? Classical covenant
theology views it as a restatement or reiteration of the covenant of works,
as can be seen in the Westminster Confession of Faith. Reformed theology,
however, also views the Mosaic covenant as part of the one, all-embracing
covenant of grace.[37] This tension leads to more than a few statements that,
if taken at face value, give the impression that salvation is possible on the
basis of works. Dispensationalists, reacting to Reformed attacks on dispensationalism for allegedly teaching two ways of salvation, have been quick
to point this out.[38] One senses the difficulty for covenant theology by reading Charles Hodge's exposition of the "Third Dispensation" (the period
from Moses to Christ). Hodge insists that the Mosaic covenant is at once
a covenant of grace—a national, legal covenant with the Hebrew people—
and a "renewed proclamation of the original covenant of works."[39] Contemporary covenant theologians have sensed the need to clarify the issue.
Meredith Kline argues that the Mosaic covenant has a dual aspect: with
regard to justification it functions as a covenant of grace; with regard to
Israel's tenure in the land, however, it functions as a covenant of works.[40]
But Palmer Robertson is still concerned about possible confusion:

---

[35]For this summary, I am indebted to Mark Karlberg, *The Changing of the Guard: Westminster Theological Seminary in Philadelphia* (Unicoi, Tenn.: Trinity Foundation, 2001).
[36]Ibid.
[37]For an in-depth study of this question, see Mark W. Karlberg, "The Mosaic Covenant
and the Concept of Works in Reformed Hermeneutics: A Historical-Critical Analysis with
Particular Attention to Early Covenant Eschatology" (Th.D. diss., Westminster Theological Seminary, 1980); idem, "Reformed Interpretation of the Mosaic Covenant," *WTJ* 43
(1980): 1-37.
[38]For citations from covenant theologians that are misleading, see Ryrie, *Dispensationalism
Today*, pp. 189-91.
[39]Hodge, *Systematic Theology*, 2:375.
[40]Kline, *By Oath Consigned*.

This phrase "covenant of law" [the Mosaic covenant] must not be confused with the traditional terminology which speaks of a "covenant of works." The phrase "covenant of works" customarily refers to the situation at creation in which man was required to obey God perfectly in order to enter into a state of eternal blessedness. Contrary to this relation established with man in innocence, the Mosaic covenant of law clearly addresses itself to man in sin. This latter covenant never intended to suggest that man by perfect moral obedience could enter into a state of guaranteed covenantal blessedness.[41]

This discussion demonstrates the difficulty of trying to integrate the Mosaic covenant into God's redemptive plan. Robertson does not exaggerate when he says, "The precise relationship of the Mosaic covenant to the promise that preceded it and to the fulfillments that followed has proven to be one of the most persistent problems of biblical interpretation."[42] This question will resurface in our examination of Jesus, Paul, and John.

The argument being made here is not that covenant theology as a system is now discredited; rather, covenant theology, like all theological enterprises, is a human undertaking, and as such it reflects progression and development. As new understandings of Scripture emerge, older formulations need revision and restatement. Contemporary covenant theology, in spite of intramural debate and dissension, still argues forcefully for one covenant of grace and one people of God, the church. Most still defend a nuanced version of the covenant of works. The great majority of covenant theologians do not see a distinct future for ethnic Israel in national, political terms. The hope for Jews today and the future is found in the church, the Israel of God. Finally, covenant theology still stoutly maintains, "The covenants are explicit scriptural indicators of divine initiatives that structure redemptive history. The dispensations instead represent arbitrary impositions on the biblical order. In the end it is not human design but divine initiative that structures Scripture."[43]

CLASSICAL (TRADITIONAL) DISPENSATIONALISM: ITS HISTORY

When did dispensationalism begin? This is a debated question, but the majority view holds that, strictly speaking, dispensationalism had its begin-

---

[41]Robertson, *The Christ of the Covenants*, p. 173.

[42]Ibid., p. 167. Daniel Fuller argues that both dispensationalism and covenant theology try, unsuccessfully in his opinion, to deal with the problem of law and grace (*Gospel and Law: Contrast or Continuum? The Hermeneutics of Dispensationalism and Covenant Theology* [Grand Rapids: Eerdmans, 1980], pp. 18-64).

[43]Robertson, *The Christ of the Covenants*, p. 227.

nings in the nineteenth century among the Plymouth Brethren in Great Britain through the teaching and writings of John Nelson Darby (1880-1882).[44] To be sure, a few staunch dispensationalists argue that it is older than the apostles themselves![45] Most, however, concede that, at the very least, Darby systematized it.[46] The question is how much earlier than that distinctive features of dispensationalism may be detected.

Arnold Ehlert and Charles Ryrie both argue that one finds dispensational elements long before the Brethren and Darby. Ryrie claims that premillennialism was the faith of the apostolic and postapostolic church, since he virtually equates premillennialism with dispensationalism.[47] Ehlert attempts an even more ambitious enterprise. He traces the roots of dispensationalism back to Jewish Cabalists who inferred from the creation narrative of Genesis 1 that human history would last six thousand years because the letter *aleph* is found six times in the Hebrew text of Genesis 1:1, and *aleph* = 1,000 in the Hebrew language. Coupled with this is Psalm 90:4: "For a thousand years in your sight are like yesterday when it is past, or like a watch in the night." Since the sabbath follows the six creative days, the sabbath in similar fashion represents a millennial era of rest and peace. Ehlert apparently holds, however, that the Cabalists were not the originators of this sexta- and septamillenary tradition. He cites D. T. Taylor, who sets out evidence that such a theory of earth history goes back to the Chaldeans, Zoroastrians, Tuscans, Egyptians, and Etruscans.[48] Among Jewish scholars, Ehlert adduces Rabbi Elias (ca. second century B.C.), Rabbi Gedaliah,

---

[44]"Dispensationalism, as a system of theological interpretation, dates from the nineteenth century and . . . was not known before in the history of Christian thought. . . . Dispensationalism can be traced to the theology and practice of John Nelson Darby, which was formulated in an atmosphere of theological controversy" (Clarence B. Bass, *Backgrounds to Dispensationalism: Its Historical Genesis and Ecclesiastical Implications* [Grand Rapids: Eerdmans, 1960], p. 7).

[45]Arnold D. Ehlert tries to distinguish between ancient and modern dispensationalism. The former he traces back to Genesis 1. "It seems likely that the roots of the whole doctrine of ages and dispensations will have to be traced back to the six creative days, and the seventh day of rest, of Genesis" (*A Bibliographic History of Dispensationalism* [Grand Rapids: Baker, 1965], p. 8). He admits, however, that "modern dispensationalism" is usually dated from Darby and the Plymouth Brethren of England (ibid., p. 5).

[46]Charles Ryrie admits, "There is no question that the Plymouth Brethren of which John Nelson Darby (1800-1882) was a leader, had much to do with the systematizing and promoting of dispensationalism" (*Dispensationalism Today*, p. 74). He goes on, however, to claim, "But neither Darby nor the Brethren originated the concepts involved in the system, and even if they had that would not make them wrong if they can be shown to be Biblical" (ibid.).

[47]Charles C. Ryrie, *The Basis of the Premillennial Faith* (New York: Loizeaux, 1953), p. 17.

[48]D. T. Taylor, *The Voice of the Church on the Coming and Kingdom of the Redeemer*, rev. and ed. H. L. Hastings (8th ed.; Boston: Scriptural Tract Repository, 1886), pp. 25-27.

the Midrash, and several rabbis of the Middle Ages who also subscribed to the theory.[49] The upshot of Ehlert's discussion is his contention that "the roots or foundations of [dispensationalism] reach far back into antiquity."[50] Needless to say, covenant theologians roundly reject the conclusion that he draws from such evidence.[51] Dispensationalists sometimes insist that, in actuality, all Bible-believing Christians are dispensationalists but just do not own up to it! Nondispensationalists, however, are quick to reply that recognizing periodization or even millennial schemes in redemptive history is hardly the essence of dispensationalism.

A major plank in Ehlert's argument is the claim that from the time of Clement of Alexandria (ca. A.D. 150-220) onward, many Christian theologians divided redemptive history into periods or dispensations.[52] He argues that an early form of dispensationalism long predated Darby, Pierre Poiret (1646-1719) being especially singled out. Ryrie essentially follows the evidence compiled by Ehlert.[53]

Since virtually all investigators agree that Darby was the systematizer of modern dispensationalism, we will look briefly at his life and thought.[54] Darby (1800-1882) was born into a well-to-do Irish family, the son of a landowner and merchant. He was an excellent student, receiving the Classical Gold Medalist award from Trinity College, Dublin, in 1819. Although inducted as an Irish barrister, he forsook a career in law for the Anglican Church, where he was ordained as a priest and served as a curate from 1825 to 1827. The experience disillusioned Darby. He left the established church and joined a free church in Dublin called the "Brethren." The Brethren sought to live under the authority of Scripture without the encumbrance of ecclesiastical tradition. By 1830 Darby had emerged as a leading figure within this movement and attracted many followers to his teaching. Among those of note were the Hebraist Samuel Prideaux Tregelles.

In 1838 Darby traveled to French-speaking Switzerland, where he established many congregations adhering to his doctrinal beliefs, and not only there but also in France, Germany and Italy. When he returned to England, doctrinal disputes were creating dissension among the Brethren. To address this he restricted the "circle of fellowship" to those agreeing with his particular doctrinal position. This group became known as the Exclusive Brethren.

---

[49]Ehlert, *Bibliographic History of Dispensationalism*, pp. 10-11.
[50]Ibid., p. 99.
[51]See Bass, *Backgrounds to Dispensationalism*, pp. 13-18.
[52]Ehlert, *Bibliographic History of Dispensationalism*, pp. 25-46.
[53]Ryrie, *Dispensationalism Today*, pp. 67-74.
[54]See Bass, *Backgrounds to Dispensationalism*, pp. 48-63.

Darby spread his system of biblical theology to North America and New Zealand, to which he made repeated trips, lecturing and preaching. Especially in North America his teaching found a ready response. Probably the single most important convert to Darbyism was the lawyer Cyrus Ingersoll Scofield. Darby was a prolific writer who covered a wide range of religious and theological topics as well as devotional materials and hymns.[55]

C. I. Scofield (1843-1921) was, more than any other person, responsible for propagating and popularizing dispensationalism in North America and the English-speaking world.[56] The greatest single avenue for this was through his well-known *Scofield Reference Bible*, first published in 1909,[57] a work that has sold over ten million copies.[58]

At the age of thirty-six Scofield was converted and embraced the teachings of Darby as mediated by James L. Brookes (1830-1897), a Presbyterian pastor and prominent American dispensationalist in the St. Louis area. Scofield also became acquainted with D. L. Moody and Arno Gaebelein (1861-1945), well-known spokespersons for dispensationalism. In 1882 the Congregationalist Church ordained Scofield to the ministry, after which he served in three pastorates: the First Church of Dallas, Texas (1882-1895); the Moody Church of Northfield, Massachusetts (1895-1902); and once again the First Church of Dallas (1902-1905). Among several organizations and institutions, he founded Central American Mission (1890) and Philadelphia College of the Bible (1913), now known as Philadelphia Biblical University. He was associated with fundamentalism and vigorously opposed the inroads of liberalism in American church life. Besides his famous reference Bible, he published *Rightly Dividing the Word of Truth* (1888) and the *Scofield Bible Correspondence Course* (begun in 1890; revised in 1907), both of which had a wide readership. His later years were devoted to preaching and lecturing in Bible and prophecy conferences in North America and Europe.

One other person should be mentioned as instrumental in disseminating dispensationalism, not only in North America but worldwide, and that

---

[55]See *The Collected Writings of J. N. Darby*, ed. William Kelly (32 vols.; London: G. Morrish, 1867-1883).

[56]See Charles G. Trumball, *The Life Story of C. I. Scofield* (New York: Oxford University Press, 1920).

[57]C. I. Scofield, *The Scofield Reference Bible* (New York: Oxford University Press, 1909).

[58]Ernest Sandeen designates this work as "perhaps the most influential single publication in millenarian and Fundamentalist historiography" (*The Roots of Fundamentalism: British and American Millenarianism, 1800-1930* [1970; reprint, Grand Rapids: Baker, 1978], p. 222). Like so many others, I remember the pleasure of receiving a new red-leather edition of the *Scofield Reference Bible* (1917 edition) as a Christmas present when I was a teenager. I still have it and refer to it affectionately as "Holy Scoly."

is Lewis Sperry Chafer (1871-1951).[59] Founder and president of Dallas Theological Seminary and prolific writer, Chafer influenced the thought of thousands of pastors and teachers who did their work in churches, the mission fields, Bible colleges, and seminaries literally all across the world.

Chafer was the son of a Congregational pastor and educated at Oberlin College, where he graduated in 1892. Ordained to the Presbyterian ministry, he achieved a reputation as an evangelist and Gospel singer (he studied at the Oberlin Conservatory of Music for three semesters). A move to Northfield, Massachusetts, in 1901 brought him into contact with Scofield, who mentored him in dispensationalism. Chafer was associated with Scofield for two decades in the Bible Conference movement. He assisted Scofield in the founding of Philadelphia College of the Bible in 1913 and apparently wrote most of the curriculum. From 1914 until 1924, when he founded Dallas Theological Seminary (originally called the Evangelical Theological College), he traveled as a renowned Bible lecturer. He served as president of Dallas Seminary and professor of systematic theology until his death in 1952. Chafer's magnum opus was his eight-volume systematic theology.[60] Whereas Scofield brought dispensationalism to the lay reader, Chafer elevated it to a higher level. It was the first major attempt to present premillennial dispensationalism in the framework of systematic theology, and thus it became, for many years, the definitive statement of dispensationalism.

DISTINCTIVES OF CLASSICAL (TRADITIONAL) DISPENSATIONALISM

In what follows, "classical dispensationalism" refers to that system of biblical interpretation set forth by Scofield in his three major works, *Rightly Dividing the Word of Truth*, *Scofield Bible Correspondence Course*, and the *Scofield Reference Bible*, and by Chafer in his many published works, but principally his *Systematic Theology*.

1. Classical dispensationalism makes a sharp distinction between Israel and the church and thus stands in stark contrast to covenant theology. According to Scofield, "Comparing . . . what is said in Scripture concerning Israel and the Church, [the student] finds that in origin, calling, promise, worship, principles of conduct, and future destiny . . . all is contrast."[61]

---

[59]On Chafer's life, see John Hannah, "Lewis Sperry Chafer," in *Dictionary of Premillennial Theology*, ed. Mal Couch (Grand Rapids: Kregel, 1996), pp. 67-70.

[60]Lewis Sperry Chafer, *Systematic Theology* (8 vols.; Dallas: Dallas Seminary Press, 1947).

[61]C. I. Scofield, *Rightly Dividing the Word of Truth (2 Timothy 2:15): Being Ten Outline Studies of the More Important Divisions of Scripture* (New York: Bible Truth Press, n.d.), pp. 12-14.

Darby, Scofield, and Chafer agree that confusion of these two distinct programs and peoples of God lay at the root of many errors and troubles in the church. In Scofield's words, "It may safely be said that the Judaizing of the Church has done more to hinder her progress, pervert her mission, and destroy her spirituality, than all other causes combined."[62] In fact, according to classical dispensationalists, there are multiple programs involved in redemptive history. Besides the two key components, Israel and the church, God also has distinctive programs for unbelieving Gentiles, angelic beings, and the cosmos. This multiplex divine program contrasts with the unitary soteriological scheme of covenant theology.

2. Dispensationalists insist on a consistently literal interpretation of prophecy. The distinction between Israel and the church is supported by the hermeneutical principle of literal interpretation of prophetic passages. Hermeneutically, dispensationalism shares with covenant theology a commitment to the historical-grammatical interpretation of Scripture. But, as we noted above, covenant theology also employs a nonliteral or spiritual interpretation in much of prophecy, particularly passages dealing with the future of Israel. Dispensationalism, on the other hand, insists that one must be consistently literal in the interpretation of prophecy dealing with Israel. Scofield states, "Here we reach the ground of absolute literalness. Figures are often found in the prophecies, but the figure invariably has a literal fulfillment. Not one instance exists of a 'spiritual' or figurative fulfillment of prophecy. . . . Histories may be reverently spiritualized, but are always literal."[63] If one does this, as covenant theologians admit, the result is an eschatological scheme featuring the restoration of Israel in an earthly, theocratic kingdom. The church, on the other hand, is a nonethnic, spiritual organism that inherits a heavenly kingdom. As we will see below, its program has little if any connection with that of Israel.

3. Dispensationalists draw a sharp distinction between law and grace. In *Rightly Dividing the Word of Truth*, Scofield succinctly sets out his understanding of these two contrasting principles. In his view, "Everywhere the Scriptures present law and grace in sharply contrasted spheres. The mingling of them in much of the current teaching of the day spoils both, for law is robbed of its terror, and grace of its freeness."[64] In some respects, one is reminded of Luther's law-grace dialectic. For dispensationalists, however, these two contrasting principles characterize the two main dispensations:

---

[62]Ibid., p. 18.

[63]C. I Scofield, *Scofield Bible Correspondence Course* (3 vols.; rev. ed.; Chicago: Moody Bible Institute, 1934), 1:46.

[64]Scofield, *Rightly Dividing the Word of Truth*, p. 52.

the Jewish dispensation of the law of Moses and the Christian dispensation of grace. For Scofield, John 1:17 encapsulates this fundamental difference: "The law indeed was given through Moses; grace and truth came through Jesus Christ." Two footnotes, however, from the *Scofield Reference Bible* raised the ire of covenantal critics:

> Grace . . . is, therefore, constantly set in contrast to law, under which God *demands righteousness* from man, as, under grace he *gives righteousness* to man. Law is connected with Moses and works; grace with Christ and faith.
>
> As a dispensation grace begins with the death and resurrection of Christ. *The point of testing is no longer legal obedience*, but acceptance or rejection of Christ.[65]

The italicized portions led to repeated charges, most recently by John Gerstner, that dispensationalism, despite what it may say to the contrary, really teaches two different ways of salvation.[66] As we will see below, revised and progressive dispensationalism vigorously deny this accusation.

4. Dispensationalists compartmentalize redemptive history into dispensations. In addition to the recognition that God has at least two distinct programs for Israel and the church (with additional programs for Gentiles, angelic beings, and the cosmos), dispensationalism arranges redemptive history into seven dispensations. As we have already observed, dividing redemptive history into distinct periods or eras is not unique to dispensationalism. Dispensationalism, however, is original in its definition and rationale for these distinct epochs. Scofield defines a dispensation as "a period of time during which man is tested in respect of obedience to some specific revelation of the will of God."[67] Furthermore, "These periods are marked off in Scripture by some change in God's method of dealing with mankind, in respect to two questions: of sin, and of man's responsibility. Each of the dispensations may be regarded as a new test of the natural man, and each ends in judgment—marking his utter failure in every dispensation."[68] Below is a representative chart of the seven dispensations.

The utility and appeal of a system so neatly outlining the flow of redemptive history undoubtedly accounts for the popularity of this system for many Bible readers.[69] Dispensationalism is also a philosophy of history

---

[65]Scofield, *Scofield Reference Bible*, p. 1115 nn. 1, 2 (my italics).
[66]John Gerstner and Don Kistler, *Wrongly Dividing the Word of Truth: A Critique of Dispensationalism* (2nd ed.; Morgan, Penn.: Soli Deo Gloria Ministries, 2000).
[67]Scofield, *Scofield Reference Bible*, p. 5 n. 4.
[68]Scofield, *Rightly Dividing the Word of Truth*, p. 18.
[69]For an appreciative evaluation of dispensationalism by a nondispensationalist, see Richard J.

Table 3.2. The Seven Dispensations of Dispensationalism

	Innocence	Conscience	Human Government	Promise	Law	Grace	Millennium
Personage	Adam	Cain	Noah	Abraham	Moses	Paul	Christ
Scripture	Gen 1:26—3:6	Gen 3:7—8:19	Gen 8:20—11:19	Gen 11:10—Ex 19:4	Ex 19:4—Acts 1:26	Acts 2:1—Rev 3:22	OT prophecies Rev 19:1—22:5
Termini	Creation to fall	Fall to flood	Flood to Babel	Abraham to Sinai	Sinai to Pentecost	Pentecost to rapture	Second Coming to White Throne
Responsibility	Not eat forbidden fruit	Do well	Govern earth and replenish it	Stay in land	Do all of the law	Believe on Christ	Submit to King and believe him
Failure	Ate of fruit	Degeneration	Defied God's command	Went to Egypt	Broke covenant	Rejection of truth	Join Satanic rebellion
Judgment	Sin nature Death Explusion	Worldwide destruction by deluge	Confusion of tongues and dispersion	Bondage in Egypt	Exile and dispersion	Great tribulation	Fire from heaven
Grace intervenes	New chance and promised redemption	Noah and family saved to replenish the earth	Abraham chosen and covenant established	Redeemer in Moses	Savior and restoration promised	Personal reign of Christ	Tests complete

with a decided apocalyptic coloring—short-term pessimism and long-term optimism about the future of earth. Dispensational eschatology asserts that the course of this age is characterized by increasing wickedness, culmi-nating in the great tribulation (Rev 6—19), Daniel's seventieth week. The church is raptured to heaven just before the great tribulation begins. After a violent reign of evil and terror for three and a half years under the anti-christ, Jesus Christ personally returns with his saints. He triumphs over all his enemies and reigns over the entire earth for one thousand years before renewing all things in a climactic act of judgment and new creation, usher-ing in the eternal state.

5. The church in dispensationalism is a parenthesis (Scofield) or an inter-calation (Chafer), beginning at Pentecost (Acts 2) and consummated at the rapture (1 Thess 4:13-17). Following on the recognition that Israel and the church are distinct, dispensationalism insists that the church does not fulfill the promises to Israel and was not foreseen by the OT prophets. As such, it is the "mystery" mentioned by Paul (Eph 3:5-6). During the church age there is no distinction between Jew and Gentile, and both become part of the spiritual body of Christ. As we noted above, the church is raptured out of the world just before the great tribulation, during which time God again turns his attention to Israel. For this reason, Scofield calls the church a "pa-renthesis," and Chafer uses the term "intercalation." During the church age the OT prophecies of Israel's return and restoration are "on hold." During the millennium, however, these prophecies are fulfilled literally by con-verted Israel while the church reigns with Christ over the world from the new Jerusalem, almost like a satellite hovering over the planet. (For Darby and Chafer, even in the eternal state the distinction between Israel and the church is maintained.)

Some think that the real catalyst for dispensationalism was Darby's view of the church. Discouraged about the worldliness of the established church in his day, Darby formulated a view of the church as a purely spiritual fel-lowship characterized by a new birth and indwelt by the Holy Spirit. The institutional church was largely apostate in Darby's view. This conception may well have generated the other distinctives.[70] Whether this correctly analyzes the development of Darby's theology or not, it does provide a help-ful window into the ethos of dispensationalism. The concern for doctrinal

---

Mouw, "What Old Dispensationalists Taught Me," *Christianity Today*, March 6, 1995, p. 34.

[70]See, for example, M. James Sawyer, "Dispensationalism," in *The Blackwell Encyclope-dia of Modern Christian Thought*, ed. Alister E. McGrath (Oxford: Blackwell, 1993), pp. 107-8; Bass, *Backgrounds to Dispensationalism*, p. 27.

purity and scriptural "correctness" is a hallmark of the system in all its
varied expressions.

6. Another hallmark of classical dispensationalism is its insistence that
the "kingdom of God" and the "kingdom of heaven" must be distinguished;
they are not synonymous. The former is broader in conception and corresponds to the spiritual realm. That is, all who are truly born again are part
of this mystical fellowship sealed with the Holy Spirit. The latter term,
on the other hand, is more limited and corresponds to the outward, visible realm of profession. In other words, it includes those not genuinely
born again. Primarily, it denotes the Davidic, theocratic kingdom offered
by Jesus to the Jewish people during his ministry and realized during the
millennium. Its rejection by the majority of Jews led to the creation of the
"parenthesis" church. The great majority of Jewish people living during the
great tribulation accept Jesus as the Messiah and enter the theocratic kingdom, reigning with Christ over the earth during the millennium.[71]

7. Dispensationalism is exclusively premillennial as dictated by its mode
of biblical interpretation for prophecy and the dictum that Israel and the
church are utterly distinct. The only place for a literal fulfillment of the
OT prophecies of Israel's restoration is the millennium. Postmillennialism could possibly fit this requirement, but dispensationalism's pessimistic
stance about the present age precludes it.

8. Darby's apparently unique contribution to Christian eschatology is
the notion of the pretribulational rapture of the church. The actual origin
of this doctrine remains obscure, first appearing as a coherent doctrine
in the writings of Darby.[72] Scofield, Chafer, and a host of other dispensationalists incorporated it into their system so that today many view this as
the hallmark teaching of dispensationalism.[73] The doctrine maintains that

---

[71]Scofield, *Scofield Reference Bible*, pp. 996 n. 1, 1003 n. 1.

[72]See Bass, *Backgrounds to Dispensationalism*, pp. 38-41. For the view that a fifteen-year-
old Scottish girl, Margaret Macdonald, was the source of this teaching, see Dave MacPher-
son, *The Great Rapture Hoax* (Fletcher, N.C.; New Puritan Library, 1983). However, for
arguments that this was not the case, see Thomas D. Ice, "Why the Doctrine of the Pretribulational Rapture Did Not Begin with Margaret Macdonald," *BSac* 147 (1990): 155-68;
John L. Bray, *The Origin of the Pre-Tribulational Rapture Teaching* (Lakeland, Fla.: John
L. Bray Ministry, 1982), pp. 31-32; William E. Bell, "A Critical Evaluation of the Pretribulation Rapture Doctrine in Christian Eschatology" (Ph.D. diss., New York University,
1967); Timothy Denny and Thomas Ice, "The Rapture and an Early Medieval Citation,"
BSac 152 (1995): 300-311; Grant R. Jeffrey, "A Pretribulational Rapture Statement in the
Early Medieval Church," in *When the Trumpet Sounds: Today's Foremost Authorities
Speak Out on End-Time Controversies* (Eugene, Ore.: Harvest House, 1995).

[73]Hal Lindsey's books in the 1970s and 1980s, *The Late Great Planet Earth* (Grand Rapids:
Zondervan, 1970) and *There's a New World Coming: An In-depth Analysis of the Book
of Revelation* (Eugene, Ore.: Harvest House, 1984) and Tim LaHaye's Left Behind series

just before the last seven years of the earth's history, the great tribulation or Daniel's seventieth week (Rev 6—19; Dan 9:24-27; cf. Dan 7:25), the church is raptured to heaven.

During the great tribulation God's attention turns to Israel. This period features the rise of the antichrist, the conversion of Israel, persecution of believers on an unprecedented scale (these include Gentile believers, called "tribulation saints" to distinguish them from the church converted by Jewish evangelists during this era), and terrifying judgments poured out on the "Beast" (antichrist) and his followers. The battle of Armageddon and the return of Christ in glory mark its termination (Rev 15—19).

Note that in this scheme Christ returns twice. The first is a secret, invisible return in which the church is raptured to heaven just before the great tribulation. The second, right at the end of the great tribulation, is a public, glorious, triumphant return accompanied by the resurrected and glorified members of the body of Christ, the church. These two returns are distinguished by the terms *rapture* and *revelation*. The latter involves the reestablishment of a theocratic kingdom in the land of Israel, though greatly increased in dimensions (Ezek 47:13—48:35), a new and enlarged temple complete with priesthood, sacrifices, and festivals (Ezek 40—44), and, of course, regathered and regenerated Jewish people who believe in Jesus as the Messiah.

So much for classical or traditional dispensationalism. In the 1950s, 1960s, and 1970s this system underwent important modifications, primarily from leading teachers at the citadel of dispensational theology, Dallas Theological Seminary.

REVISED DISPENSATIONALISM

Probably the most significant modification was the quiet dropping of an eternal distinction between Israel, the earthly people of God, and the church, the heavenly people of God.[74] Revised dispensationalists see an eventual unification of the two after the millennium in the eternal state, the new Jerusalem. On the other hand, they are still distinguishable; that is, Israel is always Israel, and the church is always the church, even in the eternal state. Even though these two peoples of God share the same salvation

---

(Wheaton, Ill.: Tyndale, 2001-2007) have made the "pretrib rapture" a household term. On this, see Timothy P. Weber, *On the Road to Armageddon: How Evangelicals Became Israel's Best Friend* (Grand Rapids: Baker, 2004), pp. 192-96.

[74]"The most important revision introduced by the dispensationalists of the '50s and '60s was their abandonment of the *eternal* dualism of heavenly and earthly peoples" (Craig A. Blaising and Darrell L. Bock, *Progressive Dispensationalism* [Wheaton, Ill.: Victor, 1993], p. 31).

experience in the eternal state, they do not lose their separate identities.

Another interesting modification emerged in regard to the eternal state. Some revised dispensationalists, such as John Walvoord and Charles Ryrie, held that in the eternal state all the redeemed, whether Israel or the church, reside in heaven. Others, such as Alva J. McClain, J. Dwight Pentecost, and Herman Hoyt, argued persuasively that the redeemed inhabit a new earth.

Revised dispensationalists, such as Ryrie, insist that a consistently literal interpretation of the Bible is a *sine qua non* of dispensationalism.[75] Significantly, there is less attention given to typology by revised dispensationalists, in contrast to classical dispensationalism. They apparently sense that a typological approach to Scripture leaves the door open for "spiritualizing" OT prophecy.

Reflection on the nature of the church has led to new emphases. The classical dispensational view of the church as a highly privatized, strictly spiritual entity now takes on a more corporate and societal dimension in revised dispensationalism. Craig Blaising and Darrell Bock attribute this to the "Body Life" movement of the 1970s spearheaded by Ray Stedman and Gene Getz.[76] This also reflects a cultural change in that evangelicals generally moved back into the mainstream of American life and politics during this era as opposed to the pronounced separatist tendencies of earlier fundamentalism.[77] Once again historical and cultural influences on theology manifest themselves.

Revised dispensationalism dropped the classical distinction between the kingdom of heaven and kingdom of God. In fact, most now admit that the expressions are virtually synonymous. Nonetheless, in a few instances, it is claimed, the context requires that one acknowledge a difference consonant with the traditional Scofieldian view. I bypass the finer points in this discussion and simply note that most revised dispensationalists now acknowledge at least three aspects to the kingdom of God: a universal reign of God over all things, a spiritual kingdom now present in and virtually identical with the church, and a national, political, Davidic kingdom to be fully realized on earth during the millennium. This latter aspect of the kingdom fulfills the land promise of the Abrahamic covenant (e.g., Gen 12:7) and the OT

---

[75]Ryrie, *Dispensationalism Today*, pp. 86-87. Earl Radmacher takes Ryrie to task for not clearly stating that a consistently literal interpretation of the Bible is the *basic* hermeneutical tenet of dispensationalism. ("The Current Status of Dispensationalism and Its Eschatology," in *Perspectives on Evangelical Theology*, ed. Kenneth S. Kantzer and Stanley N. Gundry [Grand Rapids: Baker, 1979], pp. 164-71.)

[76]Blaising and Bock, *Progressive Dispensationalism*, p. 33.

[77]See Charles Ryrie, *What You Should Know about Social Responsibility* (Chicago: Moody Press, 1982).

prophecies about the restoration of Israel (e.g., Amos 9:11-15).[78]

Finally, revised dispensationalism does not insist upon adhering to Scofield's scheme of seven dispensations. These writers stress that all Christians recognize at least two dispensations, and most recognize four or five. Nonnegotiable, of course, are the dispensations of the law, the church, and the millennium. At any rate, adherence to seven is no longer considered a *sine qua non* of dispensationalism.[79]

Progressive Dispensationalism (1970s-Present)

The most significant modification in progressive dispensationalism is its recognition that the church age inaugurates the messianic kingdom of God on earth, which will be culminated during the millennium. The church is not a parenthesis, intercalation, or interregnum but rather a vital phase in the overall kingdom program.[80] Some kingdom prophecies in the OT are in fact being realized now in the church age. This marks a radical departure from classic dispensationalism and creates tension with revised dispensationalism. However, in contrast to covenant theology, progressive dispensationalists do not see the entire set of new covenant promises found in Isaiah, Jeremiah, and Ezekiel fulfilled in the church; rather, there is a partial fulfillment, with a complete fulfillment awaiting the millennial kingdom.

Progressive dispensationalism has a significantly different take on how the dispensations function. They are now seen as successive arrangements in one grand outworking of redemption rather than as discrete, different arrangements, each one of which entails a specific test of human beings in their relationship to God. Progressive dispensationalism does, however, differ from covenant theology in that the dispensations are not merely different expressions of the one, all-encompassing covenant of grace. In progressive dispensationalism the content of saving faith and the experience of grace is not uniform, as it tends to be in covenant theology. There is a qualitative increase in the manifestation of grace in the successive dispensations such that a believer in the new covenant era has a greater experience of grace than in earlier dispensations.

Much of the change evidenced in progressive dispensationalism arises from a more sophisticated approach to hermeneutics. Grammatical-

---

[78]Blaising and Bock, *Progressive Dispensationalism*, pp. 39-45.

[79]"It would follow that the number of dispensations in a dispensational scheme and even the names of the dispensations are relatively minor matters. Presumably one could have four, five, seven, or eight dispensations and be a consistent dispensationalist as long as the scheme is true to the three essentials of dispensationalism" (Ryrie, *Dispensationalism Today*, p. 48).

[80]Blaising and Bock, *Progressive Dispensationalism*, p. 47.

historical exegesis is now understood in light of new insights stemming from philosophical, psychological, social, and literary approaches to hermeneutics. Things are not quite so straightforward as classic and revised dispensationalists thought. In short, "Progressive dispensationalists are themselves revised dispensationalists who through more developed historical-literary interpretation have come to what they believe is a more accurate understanding of certain biblical issues."[81]

Robert Saucy puts his finger on the decisive issue that separates covenant theology from dispensationalism: "The basic issue is the way we understand the historical plan and the goal of that plan through which God will bring eternal glory to himself. More specifically, it is the question of the purpose and plan of God *within* human history. . . . We must understand not only what God intends to do, but how he accomplishes it."[82] Progressive dispensationalists see the "pervasive mediatorial kingdom program, ultimately fulfilled through the reign of Christ, [as] the theme of Scripture and the unifying principle of all aspects of God's work in history."[83] Included in this kingdom program is a significant future for Israel in spiritual, national, and political terms.[84] This latter point, of course, sets it in opposition to the nearly unanimous view of covenant theology.

Finally, in regard to the question of which category structures redemptive history, progressive dispensationalism responds, "Our study of the history of the covenants shows them to be the structure by which the history of redemption is carried out. That history unfolds in a progression of divine dispensations."[85] This statement is remarkably similar to one found in Hodge's *Systematic Theology*. Note, however, that there is no mention of a covenant of works or a covenant of grace. Furthermore, there is no doubt about which idea—covenant or dispensation—plays the major role.

> God's relationship with human beings consists of a history of successive dispensations. These dispensations can be described as *ways of relating to biblical covenants*. They can also be seen as progressive stages of salvation history, which finds its fulfillment in the revelation of the eschatological kingdom of God. As a result, understanding these biblical dispensations is crucial to understanding the history and theology of the Bible.[86]

---

[81]Ibid., p. 52.
[82]Saucy, *The Case for Progressive Dispensationalism*, pp. 20-21.
[83]Ibid., p. 28.
[84]Ibid., pp. 221-323.
[85]Blaising and Bock, *Progressive Dispensationalism*, p. 199.
[86]Ibid., p. 127 (my italics).

In short, dispensations are still the more important category for understanding the structure of redemptive history.

A Comparison of Covenant Theology and Dispensationalism

The chart on pages 114-15 attempts to summarize the major points of contrast among the various positions.

An Evaluation and Critique of Covenant Theology and Dispensationalism

Robert Saucy correctly notes that one of the major factors in the modification of both systems has been the discipline of biblical theology.[87] The way forward entails a better job of hearing the original authors and seeking to explicate their theological understandings, not imposing our own theological categories and schemes. Both systems have been guilty to some degree of doing precisely that. Surely this highlights the importance of becoming proficient in biblical theology and the prospect of more agreement among evangelicals in the future. There is, of course, no guarantee of unanimity—that remains for the new Jerusalem!

I am personally indebted to dispensationalism for my earliest theological training. I have also profited from the insights of covenant theology. But I think that my most significant advance in theological understanding resulted from the approach to biblical theology taught by George Ladd. My misgivings about both classical evangelical systems arise from the conviction that neither produces a completely satisfactory biblical theology. To convinced partisans, this sounds condescending and dismissive. I can only reply that, in light of more recent scholarship, both systems have undergone modification, pointing to shortcomings in earlier formulations. Theologians candidly admit that theology is a human enterprise never claiming infallibility for its formulations.[88] Theologians are shaped and influenced by their particular culture and socioreligious background, with its inevitable biases and shortcomings. On the one hand, I want to guard against the notion that newer is always better; on the other hand, our current generation has the advantage of new information and historical perspective. Unfortunately, the earlier clash between covenant theology and dispensationalism

---

[87]"The rise of the discipline of biblical theology with its emphasis on interpreting the Scriptures in their historical environment has contributed to a greater appreciation of the development within the historical redemptive plan and the resultant differences entailed on the part of many non-dispensationalists" (Saucy, *Case for Progressive Dispensationalism*, p. 13).

[88]Consider the sage remarks of Geoffrey W. Bromiley, *Historical Theology: An Introduction* (Grand Rapids: Eerdmans, 1978), pp. 451-55.

Table 3.3. Varieties of Dispensationalism

Issue	Covenant Theology	Classic Dispensationalism	Revised Dispensationalism	Progressive Dispensationalism
Method of Intepretation	Literal-nonliteral (esp. in prophecy).	Consistently literal in prophecy, although there is room for allegorical or spiritual interpretation elsewhere if used with caution. Considerable emphasis on typology.	Consistent employment of literal or normal interpretation with no room for allegorical or spiritual interpretation. Typology is less emphasized than in classic dispensationalism.	Literal with recognition of some NT "spiritualizing" of the OT. A much more nuanced understanding of what is entailed in grammatical-historical interpretation.
Role of the NT for interpreting the OT	The OT must be interpreted by the NT.	Dual relationship: the two Testaments interpret one another.	Same as classic dispensationalism.	Dual but agrees with covenant theology that priority must be given to the NT.
Unifying principle of redemptive history	One, all-encompassing salvific covenant of grace structures redemptive history.	The glory of God displayed in several distinct purposes and plans for different groups of beings. A doxological principle.	Same as classic dispensationalism.	The unfolding kingdom of God in which successive dispensations progressively reveal the various covenantal structures.
How is redemptive history structured?	By the covenant concept: the various administrations of the one covenant of grace (covenant controls dispensations)	By the dispensations: differing economies of the divine administration (dispensations control covenants).	Same as classic dispensationalism. The essence of dispensationalism, however, is not tied to any specific number or nomenclature.	Same as revised dispensationalism.
How are law and grace distinguished?	Continuity-reiteration: covenant of works continues in force alongside the covenant of grace. Restated in the Mosaic covenant. Law demands perfect obedience; grace bestows Christ's perfect obedience.	Contrast-compartmentalization: the law/works system is placed in the dispensation of law.	Essentially the same as classic dispensationalism, but with greater emphasis on the presence of grace in the dispensation of law.	Even greater recognition of continuity of law/grace dialectic throughout redemptive history. There is now virtual agreement with covenant theology on this point.

Table 3.3. Varieties of Dispensationalism (continued)

Issue	Covenant Theology	Classic Dispensationalism	Revised Dispensationalism	Progressive Dispensationalism
How do we understand the church?	The church is the new Israel and fulfills the OT promises of Israel's restoration.	A parenthesis or intercalation: the bride of Christ exists from Pentecost to rapture and is a mystery not revealed in the OT.	Prefer to speak of the church as an interregnum or as the mystery form of the kingdom during the present dispensation. The separation and contrast between Israel and the church, however, ceases in the eternal state.	Greater awareness of the unity of the people of God. The church is an integral part of God's redemptive plan. Still, there are distinct features of the church that should not be overlooked. The church is not Israel.
What is the kingdom of heaven?	The same as the kingdom of God: the rule of God displayed in the church.	The Davidic theocratic kingdom promised to Israel and postponed when the Jews rejected Jesus' offer during his ministry.	Several nuances: The Davidic or mediatorial kingdom (during the past dispensation(s) and during the millennium) plus the proffered Davidic kingdom during Christ's earthly ministry; the mystery form of the kingdom, i.e., the church or the interregnum kingdom during the present dispensation.	Agrees with covenant theology that it is the same as the kingdom of God. It is already inaugurated during Jesus' ministry, but it will be consummated in the millennium.
How do we understand the Sermon on the Mount?	It sets forth the way of life expected of the believer in the church.	It sets forth the way of life in the millennial kingdom and is closely related to the Mosaic law. There is only a moral application to the NT believer.	Same as classic dispensationalism.	It sets forth the way of life for the believer now and will be fully realized in the millennium.
How do we interpret the restoration of Israel prophecies in the OT?	(1) They had a partial or complete fulfillment in the return from exile. (2) They were typologically fulfilled in the church. (3) They will be spiritually fulfilled in the eternal state. (4) They were conditioned upon faith.	They will be literally fulfilled in the theocratic, millennial kingdom.	Same as classic dispensationalism.	There is a *partial* fulfillment of these prophecies now in the church, with the complete fulfillment occurring during the millennial kingdom. The church age *inaugurates* the messianic kingdom.

was often, and sometimes still is, carried on in a sharply polemical manner, resulting in distortion and overstatement by both sides. Perhaps contemporary covenant theology and progressive dispensationalism may yet overcome the impasse. I certainly hope so.

It seems to me that rather than structuring redemptive history using the categories of "covenant of redemption," "covenant of works," "covenant of grace," or of various "dispensations," we do better to see the unifying theme of Scripture as the unfolding kingdom of God.[89] Underneath this overarching concept there is room for some of the major concerns of both covenant theology and dispensationalism.

Dispensationalists acknowledge that the concept of covenant is a major category in the kingdom program, and that one can helpfully trace its unfolding in terms of covenantal relationships. A dispensationalist agrees that all who seek to justify themselves by meritorious deeds stand condemned, and that salvation is always by grace through faith. A covenant theologian confesses that God progressively unfolds his saving plan through several "dispensations" or "economies." Progressive dispensationalists now acknowledge the fundamental unity of God's people. Although both systems are committed to historical-grammatical exegesis, increasingly they recognize that exegetical traditions and techniques of Second Temple Judaism must also be taken into account.[90] Indeed, most progressive dispensationalists now agree with covenant theologians that there are instances in which NT authors "spiritualize" OT texts. Both systems recognize a progressive unfolding of revelation during the various "economies," or "dispensations." Both speak of development and elaboration evident throughout redemptive history. Both confess certain distinctives and privileges accorded the NT church. And certainly, both agree that the ultimate purpose of redemptive

---

[89]Erich Sauer's statement is still worth quoting: "The 'kingdom' is the real basic theme of the Bible" (*Eternity to Eternity: An Outline of the Divine Purposes*, trans. G. H. Lang [Grand Rapids: Eerdmans, 1954], p. 89). I have written a survey of the OT in which the kingdom of God serves as the primary theme (Larry R. Helyer, *Yesterday, Today and Forever: The Continuing Relevance of the Old Testament* [2nd ed.; Salem, Wis.: Sheffield Publishing, 2004]). Willem VanGemeren, a covenant theologian, agrees: "The Bible unfolds the *development* of God's kingdom from creation to the new creation" ("Systems of Continuity," in *Continuity and Discontinuity: Perspectives on the Relationship Between the Old and New Testaments; Essays in Honor of S. Lewis Johnson Jr.*, ed. John S. Feinberg [Westchester, Ill.: Crossway, 1988], p. 58).

[90]For examples, see Larry R. Helyer, *Exploring Jewish Literature of the Second Temple Period: A Guide for New Testament Students* (Downers Grove, Ill.: InterVarsity Press, 2002), pp. 129-34; idem, "The Necessity, Problems, and Promise of Second Temple Judaism for Discussion of New Testament Eschatology," *JETS* 47 (2004): 597-615. See also Peter Enns, *Inspiration and Incarnation: Evangelicals and the Problem of the Old Testament* (Grand Rapids: Baker, 2005), pp. 113-65.

history is the glory of God. This unanimity is welcome indeed.

The real sticking point centers on the future of ethnic Israel. How one answers that question, however, should neither be accorded the status of a cardinal doctrine nor determine fellowship and cordiality. Both sides need to be less dogmatic about what God's future for the Jewish people might be. Dialogue must continue on this important issue.[91] We still "see in a mirror, dimly" (1 Cor 13:12).

I am encouraged by the convergence of evangelical opinion, resulting from a conscious effort to employ a more rigorous biblical theology methodology.[92] This greater sense of agreement stands in stark contrast to the multiplicity of voices heard in mainline liberal theology. Whereas the latter take pride in a cacophony of voices, the championing of familiar landmarks by evangelical theologians is reassuring in that it validates the Reformers' confidence in the perspicacity of Scripture.

This concludes my introductory comments on the discipline of biblical theology. Now it is time to "get to the heart of it." The next stop is with the Master himself. No question is more important to a Christian than this: What did Jesus actually believe and teach?

FOR FURTHER DISCUSSION

1. Why is John Calvin important for understanding covenant theology?

2. How do the three essential covenants of covenant theology relate to each other?

3. What is the relationship between Israel and the church in covenant theology?

4. Why do most covenant theologians tend to be amillennialists?

5. What are the primary distinctives of dispensationalism?

6. Why has dispensationalism become so popular among evangelical Christians?

7. What accounts for the variations that now exist in dispensationalism?

---

[91]VanGemeren exhorts his constituency: "Reformed Theology must remain in *dialogue*. . . . Dialogue also involves Israel. I have asked and am still asking that the exegetical case of Israel in the plan of God be reopened" ("Systems of Continuity," p. 60).

[92]John S. Feinberg comments on the modifications in both systems. "These modifications suggest something very encouraging to me. It is quite evident that members of both sides in this discussion are listening seriously to what scholars on the other side of the issue are saying" (epilogue in *Continuity and Discontinuity: Perspectives on the Relationship Between the Old and New Testaments; Essays in Honor of S. Lewis Johnson Jr.*, ed. John S. Feinberg [Westchester, Ill.: Crossway, 1988], p. 309).

8. What sticking points still distinguish covenant theology from dispensationalism?

9. What can we learn about doing theology from studying these evangelical systems?

FOR FURTHER READING

History and Distinctives of Covenant Theology

Heron, Alasdair I. C. "Covenant: Dogmatic Aspects." In vol. 1 of *The Encyclopedia of Christianity*, edited by Erwin Fahlbusch et al., trans. Geoffrey W. Bromiley, pp. 173-74. Grand Rapids: Eerdmans, 1999.

Lillback, P. A. "Covenant," *NDT* 173-76.

Murray, John. "Covenant Theology." *EC* 3:199-216.

Peterson, R. L. "Bullinger, Heinrich." In *Dictionary of Major Biblical Interpreters*, edited by Donald K. McKim, pp. 254-61. Downers Grove, Ill.: InterVarsity Press, 2007.

Robertson, O. Palmer. *The Christ of the Covenants*. Phillipsburg, N.J.: P & R Publishing, 1980.

Ruland, Vernon. "Covenant Theology." In vol. 4 of *New Catholic Encyclopedia*, p. 405. New York: McGraw Hill, 1967.

VanGemeren, Willem. "Systems of Continuity." In *Continuity and Discontinuity: Perspectives on the Relationship Between the Old and New Testaments; Essays in Honor of S. Lewis Johnson Jr.*, edited by John S. Feinberg, pp. 37-62. Westchester, Ill.: Crossway, 1988.

Van Til, Cornelius. "Covenant Theology." In *Twentieth Century Encyclopedia of Religious Knowledge*, edited by Lefferts A. Loetscher, pp. 306-7. Grand Rapids: Baker, 1955.

Vos, Gerhardus. "The Doctrine of the Covenant in Reformed Theology." in *Redemptive History and Biblical Interpretation: The Shorter Writings of Gerhardus Vos*, edited by Richard B. Gaffin Jr., pp. 234-67. Phillipsburg, N.J.: P & R Publishing, 1980.

Wallace, Dewey D., Jr. "Federal Theology." In *Encyclopedia of the Reformed Faith*, edited by Donald K. McKim, pp. 136-38. Louisville: Westminster/John Knox, 1992.

History of Classical Dispensationalism

Bass, Clarence B. *Backgrounds to Dispensationalism: Its Historical Genesis and Ecclesiastical Implications*, pp. 48-99. Grand Rapids: Eerdmans, 1960.

Blaising, Craig A. "Dispensationalism: The Search for Definition." In *Dispensationalism, Israel and the Church: The Search for Definition, edited by Craig A. Blaising and Darrell L. Bock, pp. 13-34. Grand Rapids: Zondervan, 1992.

Ehlert, Arnold D. *A Bibliographic History of Dispensationalism*. Grand Rapids: Baker, 1965.

Hannah, John. "Lewis Sperry Chafer." In *Dictionary of Premillennial Theology*, edited by Mal Couch, pp. 67-70. Grand Rapids: Kregel, 1996.

Hughes, Philip E. "Darby, John Nelson (1880-1882)." *EC* 3:301.

Ryrie, Charles C. *Dispensationalism Today*, pp. 65-85. Chicago: Moody Press, 1965.

Spencer, S. R. "Scofield, C(yrus) I. (1845-1921)." In *Dictionary of Major Biblical Interpreters*, edited by Donald K. McKim, pp. 906-10. Downers Grove, Ill.: InterVarsity Press, 2007.

Distinctives of Classical Dispensationalism

Chafer, Lewis Sperry. *Major Bible Themes*. Chicago: Moody Press, 1944.

———. *Systematic Theology*. 8 vols. Dallas: Dallas Seminary Press, 1948.

Darby, John Nelson. *The Collected Writings of J. N. Darby*, edited by William Kelly. 32 vols. London: G. Morrish, 1867-1883.

Scofield, C. I. *Rightly Dividing the Word of Truth*. Philadelphia: Philadelphia School of the Bible, 1888.

———. *Scofield Bible Correspondence Course*. Chicago: Moody Bible Institute, 1907.

———. *Scofield Reference Bible*. 2nd ed. New York: Oxford Press, 1917.

Distinctives of Revised Dispensationalism

Blaising, Craig A., and Darrell L. Bock. *Progressive Dispensationalism*, pp. 31-46. Wheaton, Ill.: Victor, 1993.

Hoyt, Herman Arthur. *The End Times*. Chicago: Moody Press, 1969.

McClain, Alva J. *The Greatness of the Kingdom: An Inductive Study of the Kingdom of God*. 1959. Repr., Grand Rapids: BMH Books, 2001.

Pentecost, J. Dwight. *Things to Come: A Study in Biblical Eschatology*. Findlay, Ohio: Dunham, 1958.

Radmacher, Earl D. "The Current Status of Dispensationalism and Its Eschatology." In *Perspectives on Evangelical Theology*, edited by Kenneth S. Kantzer and Stanley N. Gundry, pp. 163-76. Grand Rapids: Baker, 1979.

Ryrie, Charles C. *Dispensationalism Today*. Chicago: Moody Press, 1965.

Walvoord, John F. *The Millennial Kingdom*. Findlay, Ohio: Dunham, 1959.

Distinctives of Progressive Dispensationalism

Bateman, Herbert W. *Three Central Issues in Contemporary Dispensationalism: A Comparison of Traditional and Progressive Views.* Grand Rapids: Kregel, 1999.

Blaising, Craig A., and Darrell L. Bock, eds., *Dispensationalism, Israel and the Church: The Search for Definition.* Grand Rapids: Zondervan, 1992.

———. *Progressive Dispensationalism*, pp. 46-55. 1993. Repr., Grand Rapids: Baker, 2000.

Crenshaw, Curtis I., and Grover E. Gunn III. *Dispensationalism Today, Yesterday, and Tomorrow.* Memphis: Footstool, 1985.

Saucy, Robert L. *The Case for Progressive Dispensationalism: The Interface between Dispensational and Non-Dispensational Theology.* Grand Rapids: Zondervan, 1993.

A Comparison of Covenant Theology and Dispensationalism

Belcher, Richard P. *A Comparison of Dispensationalism and Covenant Theology.* Columbus, S.C.: Richbarry, 1986.

Feinberg, John S., ed. *Continuity and Discontinuity: Perspectives on the Relationship Between the Old and New Testaments; Essays in Honor of S. Lewis Johnson Jr.* Westchester, Ill.: Crossway, 1988.

House, H. Wayne. *Charts of Christian Theology and Doctrine*, pp. 15-16. Grand Rapids: Zondervan, 1992.

Karleen, Paul S. "Understanding Covenant Theologians: A Study in Presuppositions." *GTJ* 10 (1989): 125-39.

Poythress, Vern S. "Response to Paul S. Karleen's Paper 'Understanding Covenant Theologians.'" *GTJ* 10 (1989): 147-61.

———. *Understanding Dispensationalists.* 2nd ed. Phillipsburg, N.J.: P & R Publishing, 1993.

Saucy, Robert L. "Response to *Understanding Dispensationalists* by Vern Poythress." *GTJ* 10 (1989): 139-47.

Showers, Renald. *There Really Is a Difference: A Comparison of Covenant and Dispensational Theology.* Bellmawr, N.J.: Friends of Israel Gospel Ministry, 1990.

PART TWO

THE THEOLOGY OF JESUS

4

Jesus and the Kingdom

Ye know how each evangelist that tells us of the pain of Jesus Christ writes not in all things as the others do; yet none the less, all of their tales are true, and as to meaning, all of them agree, though in detail they show diversity. For when they tell the piteous pain He bore some will write less, and some of them write more—Matthew, I mean, and Mark and Luke and John—yet doubtless in their meaning they are one.

Geoffrey Chaucer, "The Tale of Sir Thopas,"
Canterbury Tales

A CRITICAL PROBLEM MUST BE SQUARELY FACED before any investigation of the teaching of Jesus can be undertaken. Can a "theology of Jesus" be extracted from the Synoptic Gospels (Matthew, Mark, Luke)? Many modern scholars cast doubt upon such an enterprise. Their skepticism centers on the nature of the Gospels. Are the Gospels reliable accounts of what Jesus really did and said? Up until the Enlightenment, few voices challenged the prevailing view that they were. What happened to change that consensus? Essentially, an entirely new view of reality and of knowing gradually emerged and shattered the confidence that had previously existed. In the wake of the Enlightenment, naturalism sought to relegate supernaturalism to the dustbin. Biblical history was subjected to the straitjacket of rigorous historicism with its axioms of probability, analogy and correlation (i.e., everything is explained by what "actually happens" in a cause-effect, closed universe).[1] Miracles were no longer credible; theological claims were labeled as myth, legend or pious invention. The very notion of revelation itself came under assault. Some redefined it as the immanent workings of the divine spirit in history. Others tried to reconstruct Christianity without reference to revelation at all. Skepticism became the prevailing mood in the face of all truth claims not based on rationalism or firmly anchored in a scientific method.

In such an environment the Gospels were now seen as instruments of Christian propaganda, reflecting what later Christians believed about Jesus rather than what Jesus himself actually believed. Still, most NT scholars believed that some historical information could be extracted from the Gospels. The problem, however, lay in devising a method that could extract this historical core from the layers of later, generally unreliable tradition. Therein lay the task. The Gospels, in their canonical form, consist of three layers or strands of tradition: old tradition, ideas produced in and by the church, and editorial work of the evangelists.[2] How does one recover the earliest tradition? The answer, simply put, is that you peel off the later traditions, somewhat like you peel an onion. NT specialists energetically set about peeling away the accretions, employing various criteria by which the material in the Gospels supposedly could be sifted for traditions going back to the "historical Jesus." The story of the so-called quest for the historical Jesus and of the various methodologies and criteria devised for the quest has been recounted many times. Since space prevents a full discussion, I refer the reader to helpful discussions.[3]

On a positive note, there are in fact substantial grounds for believing in the reliability and historicity of the Gospel traditions as we have them in our canonical Gospels. I direct the reader to resources that will prove helpful in making this case.[4] My own approach to the Gospels echoes that of Leon Morris:

---

[1]See Roy A. Harrisville and Walter Sundberg, *The Bible in Modern Culture: Baruch Spinoza to Brevard Childs* (2nd ed.; Grand Rapids: Eerdmans, 2002), pp. 155-57.

[2]Rudolf Bultmann, *Theology of the New Testament*, trans. Kendrick Grobel (2 vols.; New York: Scribner, 1951-1955), 1:3.

[3]See Colin Brown, "Historical Jesus, Quest of," *DJG* 326-41; Craig L. Blomberg, "Form Criticism," *DJG* 243-50; P. H. Davids, "Tradition Criticism," *DJG* 831-34; Stanley E. Porter, *The Criteria for Authenticity in Historical-Jesus Research: Previous Discussion and New Proposals* (JSNTSup 191; Sheffield: Sheffield Academic Press, 2000). For a more positive assessment of traditio-historical criticism, though acknowledging faults in early attempts, see Bruce Chilton, "Traditio-Historical Criticism and Study of Jesus," in *Hearing the New Testament: Strategies for Interpretation*, ed. Joel B. Green (Grand Rapids: Eerdmans, 1995), pp. 37-60.

[4]Craig L. Blomberg, "Gospels (Historical Reliability)," *DJG* 291-97. Also helpful are the treatments by Donald A. Hagner, "The New Testament, History, and the Historical-Critical Method," in *New Testament Criticism and Interpretation*, ed. David Alan Black

I propose to take the Gospels as giving us essentially what Jesus said and did. The part played by the prophets is unknown and I do not care to speculate. The part played by the church is shrouded in the mists of time, and I see no way of penetrating those mists. I am, of course, aware that there is much discussion concerning the authenticity of the sayings and deeds attributed to Jesus in all four Gospels and that scholars have evolved a variety of techniques to grapple with the problems. Even so, the scholars are a long way from being in agreement. Pursuant to the aim of surveying briefly the theology of the canonical New Testament, I do not propose to go into such discussions. To do so would lengthen the book beyond endurance and would in fact produce a different kind of book. My concern is with the theology of the Gospels as they stand, not with the hypothetical steps by which they reached their present form.[5]

Still, I am not naïve about the problems. One cannot simply use a "words of Jesus in red" edition of the NT. Evangelical biblical theology must take into account the complexity that clearly exists in our canonical Gospels, remembering, as pointed out in chapter 1, that they provide the voice of Jesus and only rarely the very words themselves.[6]

JESUS' PROCLAMATION OF THE KINGDOM OF GOD

There is a consensus across the theological spectrum that Jesus' message centered on the kingdom of God. The linguistic evidence speaks for itself. On page 126 is a chart showing three different expressions used for this idea in the Gospels and their occurrence in each gospel.[7]

As can readily be seen, the Synoptic Gospels differ markedly from John's Gospel in the frequency of basic expressions (103 compared to 5). John prefers to recast the idea of the kingdom of God in terms of eternal life, as our examination of Johannine theology in chapter 9 will demonstrate. No-

---

and David S. Dockery (Grand Rapids: Zondervan, 1991), pp. 77-83; Birger Gerhardson, *The Reliability of the Gospel Tradition* (Peabody, Mass.: Hendrickson, 2001); Samuel Byrskog, *Story as History—History as Story: The Gospel Tradition in the Context of Ancient Oral History* (WUNT 123; Tübingen: Mohr Siebeck, 2000; reprint, Leiden: Brill, 2002); Richard Bauckham, *Jesus and the Eyewitnesses: The Gospels as Eyewitness Testimony* (Grand Rapids: Eerdmans, 2006).

[5]Leon Morris, *New Testament Theology* (Grand Rapids: Zondervan, 1986), p. 92.

[6]David R. Catchpole concedes that "in looking to the gospels as sources for the sayings and actions of Jesus we can hardly avoid attributing to the later Post-Easter stage both the redaction of material, and, on occasion, its creation" ("Tradition History," in *New Testament Interpretation: Essays on Principles and Methods*, ed. I. Howard Marshall (Grand Rapids: Eerdmans, 1977), p. 168. The last phrase may concede too much.

[7]From C. C. Caragounis, "Kingdom of God/Heaven," *DJG* 426.

tice that Matthew alone uses the expression "kingdom of heaven." In the preceding chapter I discussed how classical dispensationalism insisted that the kingdom of heaven refers to the Davidic theocratic kingdom realized during the millennial reign of Christ on earth. The kingdom of God, on the other hand, is God's universal rule, chiefly inward and spiritual in nature, and is the sphere in which the church existed. Such a distinction is unlikely.

Table 4.1. Kingdom Terminology in the Gospels

Term	Matthew	Mark	Luke	John
Kingdom of God	5	14	32	2
Kingdom of Heaven	32	—	—	—
Kingdom	13	—	7	3
Totals	50	14	39	5

A comparison of usage in the Synoptics strongly suggests that the terms are interchangeable (cf., e.g., Mt 4:17 // Mk 1:14-15; Mt 5:3 // Lk 6:20; Mt 8:11 // Lk 13:28; Mt 13:31 // Mk 4:30-31). Matthew is simply showing sensitivity to Jewish conventions. Pious Jews avoided saying the name of God by (1) substituting the title *Adonai* ("Lord") for the sacred name "Yahweh," (2) employing circumlocutions such as "heaven," "the Majestic Glory," "the angels of God," "the Blessed One" (NIV), "the Mighty One" (NIV), "the Most High," (see, respectively, Lk 15:18, 21; 2 Pet 1:17; Lk 12:8-9; Mk 14:61-62; Lk 6:35), and (3) using the "divine passive," adopting the passive voice as a way of indicating that God was the actor without actually mentioning him by name (see Mt 5:4; 7:1, 7; 10:30; Mk 4:25; 10:40).[8] Thus the expression "kingdom of heaven" appears to be a circumlocution for "kingdom of God."

The content of the Synoptic Gospels reinforces the linguistic data. They indicate that John the Baptist preached repentance and baptism in preparation for the imminent appearance of the kingdom of God. Jesus himself commenced his public ministry announcing, "The time is fulfilled, and the kingdom of God has come near; repent and believe in the good news" (Mk 1:15; cf. Mt 4:17; Lk 4:43). Many of Jesus' parables begin with the phrase "the kingdom of heaven/God is like." The Sermon on the Mount is essentially an exposition of life in the kingdom (Mt 5—7). The second petition of the Lord's Prayer, a model prayer for disciples, requests that God's

---

[8]See Joachim Jeremias, *New Testament Theology: The Proclamation of Jesus*, trans. John Bowden (New York: Scribner, 1971), pp. 9-14.

kingdom would come (Mt 6:10). As Jesus approached Jerusalem for his last fateful visit, there was an expectation among his followers that "the kingdom of God was to appear immediately" (Lk 19:11). As Jesus descended the Mount of Olives, his disciples sang out, "Blessed is the king who comes in the name of the Lord!" (Lk 19:38). To this spontaneous demonstration he offered no objection (Lk 19:40). At the Last Supper Jesus promised his disciples that he would drink the cup of blessing with them in the Father's kingdom (Mt 26:29). The repentant thief on the cross entreated Jesus, "Remember me when you come into your kingdom" (Lk 23:42). Clearly, the kingdom was the focal point of Jesus' message.[9]

DEFINITION OF THE KINGDOM OF GOD

But what was the kingdom of God? Absence of a precise definition in the sayings of Jesus is striking. Understanding precisely what Jesus meant by the expression "kingdom of God/heaven" is crucial. There is widespread agreement that the Hebrew *(malkût)*, Aramaic *(malkû)* and Greek *(basileia)* nouns underlying the English word *kingdom* refer primarily to an activity. "Kingdom" denotes the exercise of sovereignty and power. Thus the expression "kingdom of God" can best be rendered into English by "the rule of God," or "the reign of God. This rendering correctly highlights the dynamic dimension of the expression rather than the more static sense of "realm" or "territory" that English speakers may first associate with the word "kingdom." It is not as if there is no reference to territory; it is just that this is secondary to the predominant idea of reign and rule.[10] Many Jewish prayers begin "Blessed art thou, O Lord our God, king of the universe." This captures nicely the fundamental notion of the biblical expression "kingdom of God": God's sovereign rule over all creation.

---

[9]"With Jesus everything is subordinated to the one essential declaration: God's reign is coming. It is as direct and unadorned as that, and Mark has captured its directness in 1:15" (Hugh Anderson, *The Gospel of Mark* [NCBC; London: Marshall, Morgan & Scott, 1981], p. 85).

[10]G. E. Ladd, "The Kingdom of God—Reign or Realm?" *JBL* 81 (1962): 230-38. Johannes Louw and Eugene Nida maintain, "It is generally a serious mistake to translate the phrase ἡ βασιλεία τοῦ θεοῦ 'the kingdom of God' as referring to a particular area in which God rules. The meaning of this phrase in the NT involves not a particular place or special period of time but the fact of ruling. An expression such as 'to enter the kingdom of God' thus does not refer to 'going to heaven' but should be understood as 'accepting God's rule' or 'welcoming God to rule over' (*Greek-English Lexicon of the New Testament Based on Semantic Domains* [2nd ed.; 2 vols.; New York: United Bible Societies, 1988-1989], 1:480 [§37.64]).

BACKGROUND OF THE KINGDOM OF GOD

Since Jesus did not bother to define his terms, his audience must have shared a common understanding. This common ground was the OT teaching on the kingdom of God and its development in Second Temple Judaism. The kingdom idea first appears in the creation narratives (Gen 1—2). God entrusts the government of earth to his vice-regents created in his image. Men and women are to rule planet Earth in his name and as his stewards (Gen 1:26-28). The story of the temptation and fall depicts how our first parents, at the instigation of the serpent, became rebels and fell under the curse of sin and death (Gen 3; Rom 5:12). The rest of Scripture unfolds the story of redemption whereby God's kingdom rule is reestablished over earth. Human beings are invited to switch their innate allegiance from the "Dark Lord" to the true king of heaven and earth. Remarkably, this counteroffensive against the kingdom of darkness begins in earnest with but one man and his barren wife, Abraham and Sarah (Gen 12—25). From them God raises up a "priestly kingdom" for his name, Israel in the old covenant and its continuation in the church of the new covenant (Ex 19:6; 1 Pet 2:5, 9; Rev 1:6).

The first explicit mention of kingdom terminology occurs at the Red Sea in the Song of the Sea. There the Israelites celebrate their glorious liberation by confessing, "The LORD will reign forever and ever" (Ex 15:18). At Mount Sinai the Israelites enter into a covenant with Yahweh as his vassal nation. They become the visible sign and instrument of his kingdom (Ex 19:8; 24:3-8; Deut 10:12—11:32). The Davidic covenant represents a high point in the OT kingdom idea. The Lord promises David an everlasting dynasty and throne (2 Sam 14:14-17; Ps 2:7; 89:26-27). Tragically, Israel is unfaithful to the covenant obligations, and the threatened curses for disobedience befall them (Deut 28:15-68). At the conclusion of the OT story the Davidic dynasty is crushed, and Israel and Judah languish in exile (2 Kings 25; Lamentations). Nonetheless, the righteous remnant clings to this great truth: "But you, O LORD, reign forever; your throne endures to all generations" (Lam 5:19). The kingdom of God frames the story of Israel.

The prophets, however, insist that God is not finished with Israel. They proclaim a future, national restoration and spiritual renewal (Ezek 34; 36). One of the latest OT prophets, Zechariah, describes the climactic intervention of Yahweh at the great Day of the Lord in these terms: "And the LORD will become king over all the earth; on that day the LORD will be one and his name one" (Zech 14:9). "Day of the Lord" is a key temporal expression for this climactic moment (e.g., Is 11:10; Joel 3:1-3, 16-21). Unfortunately, many misconstrued what it meant. For them, it was simply a matter of what was due them as Yahweh's elect people: the Day of the Lord was essentially setting the record straight in favor of Israel. The prophets disabuse their listeners of such self-deception: that day will involve a great reversal of fortunes (see Amos 5:18-24; cf. Joel 2:1-11; Zeph 1:14-18). Kingdom blessings accrue only to those who truly repent and walk humbly with their God (Hos 14:1-2; Joel 2:12-14; Amos 5:14-15; Mic 6:8).

Prophetic oracles of future salvation were of two distinct types. Many passages reflect the belief that the Davidic dynasty will be reestablished and a vibrant, prosperous, secure nation will arise (e.g., Amos 9:11-15; Is 2:1-4; 11). The oracles speak in very concrete, this-worldly terms. A few passages, however, seem to transcend the earthly and depict a transcendental order ushered in by Yahweh's cosmic judgment on evil. These passages tend to occur toward the end of the OT period and display characteristics that distinguish later apocalyptic thought (Is 65:17; Zech 14:6-7; Dan 12:1-3). Essential to the fulfillment of both types of eschatological blessing, however, is an indispensable prerequisite: a spiritual transformation. This may be pictured as a new heart, a cleansing by water, an outpouring of the Holy Spirit, or the implanting of a new disposition (Jer 31:31-34; Ezek 36:25-27). Regardless of its portrayal, it constitutes the *sine qua non* for experiencing the grand triumph of the kingdom and is attributable entirely to Yahweh's grace and mercy. Deeds of justice, righteousness, mercy and faithfulness flow forth as a consequence of inward renewal; knowledge of the Lord covers the whole earth (Is 11:9; Hab 2:14), and a great hallelujah chorus of praise rises to the heavenly throne. Unfortunately, the spiritual dimension of the kingdom tended to get lost in the desire for political freedom and material blessings.

During the Second Temple period hopes for the glorious kingdom of God were kept alive, especially in apocalyptic circles. Seers and visionaries depicted the final manifestation of Yahweh's kingdom on earth. As was the case with the OT prophets before them, two quite different scenarios emerged: some envisaged a restoration of what had been; others, because of the enormity of evil, could only conceive of a total transformation at the end of days. For example, *Psalms of Solomon* 17–18 and Tobit 13:9-17 sound much like Amos 9:13-15 and Isaiah 11:1-5, with the restoration of the Davidic dynasty and return to Eden-like conditions. On the other hand, *1 Enoch* 37–71 describes a radical transformation of nature at the climax of the kingdom, akin to Isaiah 65:17, in which the "wise shall shine like the brightness of the sky, and those who lead many to righteousness, like the stars forever and ever" (cf. Dan 12:3). Whereas visionaries dreamed and exhorted the faithful, religious nationalists, such as the Hasmoneans, sought to realize these dreams by force of arms and violence (167 B.C.). Eventually, however, the Hasmonean dynasty collapsed, and Judea came under the heavy boot of Rome (63 B.C.). Terrorist groups sprang up in a desperate bid to restore national sovereignty.

Jesus of Nazareth appeared in this politically charged atmosphere and proclaimed the imminent appearing of the kingdom of God. Needless to say, his "good news" fueled the fires of nationalistic aspirations (see Jn 6:15). Perhaps two of Jesus' disciples, Simon the Zealot and Judas Iscariot, initially pinned their hopes for liberation on Jesus, with his remarkable, charismatic powers. In fact, Judas's bitter disappointment over Jesus' real intentions may account for his betrayal. Many of Jesus' parables and teachings reimage the kingdom of God for his disciples. The Gospel of John makes explicit what is implicit in the Synoptics when Jesus replies to Pilate's question as to whether he is "the King of the Jews": "My kingship is not from this world" (Jn 18:33, 36; cf. Lk 22:47-53). This was a bitter pill for the disciples to swallow, but hopes for an imminent, political deliverance lingered (see Acts 1:6).

The Synoptic Gospels, John's Gospel, and the rest of the NT proclaim that Jesus Christ, the unique Son of God, plays a leading role in this drama of redemption, the coming of the kingdom of God (e.g., Mk 10:45; 14:24; Jn 1:29; Rom 3:25; Heb 9:11-14; 1 Pet 1:18-20; 1 Jn 2:2). He is the mediator who, by his atoning death on the cross, reconciles rebels to their heavenly King and Father (Rom 3:24-26; 5:1-11; 1 Tim 2:5-6). The Father graciously transfers them from the kingdom of darkness into the kingdom of light (Col 1:13). The Holy Spirit applies the saving work of Christ to the hearts of believers and empowers them to advance and enlarge the kingdom through their witness to the gospel (Rom 8:1-11). In the end, the kingdom of Christ will triumph over all hostile forces and be turned over to God the Father— the temporal gives way to the eternal (Eph 1:9-10, 22; 1 Cor 15:20-28). The book of Revelation concludes with the King of kings and Lord of lords returning as a divine warrior to defeat the forces of evil (Rev 19:11-21). He sits enthroned, alongside the Father, as the Lamb in the new Jerusalem, where he rules with his saints over a new earth (Rev 21). In short, the idea of the kingdom of God frames the entire corpus of Scripture.

INTERPRETATIONS OF THE KINGDOM OF GOD

God's old covenant people, Israel, have not been the only ones to struggle with the meaning of the kingdom. Christian theologians have offered widely differing views as to its nature. For some, it is an entirely spiritual concept, either the church, as the body of Christ, or heaven, the place to which believers go at death. Others have preferred a nonspiritual interpretation, identifying it with a utopian social order, a classless society. Still others have restricted it to the millennial reign of Christ on earth. A variation of this latter suggestion, as was discussed in chapter 3, is classic dispensationalism. In that system the kingdom of heaven is the theocratic, Davidic kingdom, entirely Jewish in scope and character. What follows here is a brief survey of some significant interpretations of the kingdom of God.

The medieval period and the reformation. Before the modern era, Christian theology was dominated by the views of Augustine of Hippo (A.D. 354-430). He argued that kingdom and church were identical. To enter one was to enter the other. This understanding provided a powerful theological foundation for the Roman Catholic Church throughout the medieval period and was not seriously threatened from within Western culture until the Reformation and Enlightenment.

The Reformers continued the medieval equation; they emphatically denied, however, that the Roman Catholic Church was that kingdom. In fact, they went so far as to identify the pope as the antichrist. Rather, the catholic (i.e., universal), spiritual church was the kingdom. The church was conceived of as having two main parts: the church militant, living members of the community of faith, and the church triumphant, the faithful who had died and were now reigning with Christ in heaven (Second Helvetic Confession XVII). Thus the notion of the kingdom of God could refer to either division. Following the lead of the apostolic fathers and the ante-Nicene theologians, the Reformers also maintained that the church was the new or true Israel supplanting the old covenant people of God.

In chapter three I have already discussed the differing stances of classical covenant theology and dispensationalism on the meaning of the kingdom of God, so here I move on to examine developments in modern theology. For the sake of convenience, I group the various responses into three main interpretations.[11]

Modern theology.

The Noneschatological School. During the heyday of classical liberalism, at the end of the nineteenth century and the beginning of the twentieth, the kingdom of God underwent a radical revision. According to Adolf von Harnack (1851-1930), a widely influential liberal theologian of this era, Jesus' message can be reduced to three essentials: (1) the coming of the kingdom of God, (2) the fatherhood of God and the infinite value of the hu-

---

[11]For what follows, I am indebted to Robert H. Stein, *The Method and Message of Jesus' Teachings* (Philadelphia: Westminster Press, 1978), pp. 65-79.

man soul, and (3) the higher righteousness and the commandment of love.[12] The kingdom of God is the reign of God in the human heart, an internal phenomenon, focusing primarily on the ethics of Jesus.

How should one treat the rather frequent appearance of eschatological material in the teaching of Jesus, such as references to the end of the age, cosmic cataclysms, angelic conflict, the coming of the Son of Man and final judgment? According to Harnack, the modern exegete must simply sift out this material because it fails to meet the test of modernity. He often uses the analogy of husks and kernel. The "husks," such as Jesus' eschatological beliefs, are to be discarded, whereas the "kernel," teachings in agreement with the lowest common denominator of liberal values and ideas, is retained.

This exposition of Jesus' understanding of the kingdom of God was extremely influential in liberal circles in Europe and North America. Luminaries such as Walter Rauschenbusch, pastor and professor of church history at Rochester Theological Seminary,[13] and Harry Emerson Fosdick, pastor of New York City's Riverside Church from 1929 to 1946,[14] crafted American versions of this stance, extending the idea to the realm of the social and political, in which industrial exploitation and governmental indifference were roundly condemned. This formulation became known as the "social gospel."[15] Unfortunately, among most liberal proponents of the social gospel, one of the discarded "husks" of Jesus' teaching was human depravity. Two world wars demolished liberal theology's sanguine assessment of the human condition.[16] But even before this shockwave, two European

---

[12]See Adolf von Harnack, *What Is Christianity? Sixteen Lectures Delivered in the Univeristy of Berlin during the Winter Term, 1899-1900*, trans. Thomas Bailey Saunders (New York: Putnam, 1908). See also H. M. Rumscheidt, "Harnack, Adolf von," in *Dictionary of Major Biblical Interpreters*, ed. Donald K. McKim (Downers Grove, Ill.: InterVarsity Press, 2007), pp. 504-7.

[13]Rauschenbusch's writings include *Christianity and the Social Crisis* (New York: Hodder & Stoughton, 1907); *Christianizing the Social Order* (New York: Macmillan, 1912); *The Social Principles of Jesus* (New York: Association Press, 1916); *A Theology for the Social Gospel* (New York: Macmillan, 1917); *The Righteousness of the Kingdom*, ed. Max L. Stackhouse (Nashville: Abingdon, 1968).

[14]See especially Fosdick's *A Guide to Understanding the Bible: The Development of Ideas Within the Old and New Testaments* (New York: Harper & Row, 1938); *The Man from Nazareth as His Contemporaries Saw Him* (New York: Harper, 1949). He also wrote a number of well-known hymns, such as "God of Grace and God of Glory" (1930).

[15]See M. A. Knoll, "Social Gospel," *NDT* 646-47.

[16]The casualties from the two world wars were horrific. In WW I there were 8.5 million killed and 21.2 million wounded. The number killed in WW II has been estimated at between forty and fifty million, making it the bloodiest conflict in human history. Neo-orthodoxy made its appearance in the aftermath of this slaughter, returning to some of the familiar themes of the Reformation. It never did, however, let go of its inherited distaste for the Reformed view of Scripture.

scholars already undermined the foundations of the liberal superstructure. They were Johannes Weiss and Albert Schweitzer, leading figures of an entirely different approach.

The Consistent Eschatology School. In 1892 Johannes Weiss (1863-1914), son-in-law of Albrect Ritschl (a well-known systematic theologian and exponent of the classical, liberal view of the kingdom), wrote a book that turned Ritschl's and Harnack's view on its head.[17] Albert Schweitzer (1875-1965) authored a book in 1906 that struck a similar note.[18] Both men denied that eschatology was merely the "husk" of Jesus' teaching; it was in fact the very "kernel." In order to understand Jesus, one must place him in the context of Jewish apocalyptic expectations.[19] Weiss's and Schweitzer's criticism of the noneschatological view amounts to this: it transforms Jesus into a nineteenth-twentieth century liberal!

For Weiss and Schweitzer, Jesus' understanding of the kingdom of God fundamentally was not about the moral transformation of the individual or society but rather involved a very concrete political reality ushered in by a supernatural display of God's power. Jesus was proclaiming nothing less than the end of human history as we know it and the irruption of a new age inaugurated by a resurrection, transforming believers into angels (Mt 22:30), and a destruction of the forces of evil. Jesus and his followers would rule over a restored land of Israel. Schweitzer labeled his view "consistent eschatology" in order to stress that, first and foremost, Jesus was an apocalyptic Jew and endorsed the mindset associated with Jewish apocalyptic as manifest in works such as *1-2 Enoch, Jubilees, Assumption of Moses, 4 Ezra* and *2 Baruch.* This, not an inner reign of God in the human heart, lay at the heart of Jesus' message.

Schweitzer, in particular, stressed the notion of imminence in Jesus' teaching on the kingdom. A couple of texts became programmatic for Schweitzer's understanding: "Truly I tell you, there are some standing here who will not taste death before they see the Son of Man coming in his kingdom" (Mt 16:28 [cf. Mk 9:1; Lk 9:27]); "For truly I tell you, you will not

---

[17]Johannes Weiss, *Die Predigt Jesu vom Reiche Gottes* (Göttingen: Vandenhoeck & Ruprecht, 1892). This has been translated into English as *Jesus' Proclamation of the Kingdom of God,* trans. and ed. Richard Hyde Hiers and David Larrimore Holland (Philadelphia: Fortress, 1971). Hiers and Holland observe, "Probably no book was more significant for twentieth-century study of Jesus than Johannes Weiss's *Jesus' Proclamation of the Kingdom of God*" (pp. viii-ix).

[18]Albert Schweitzer, *Von Reimarus zu Wrede: Eine Geschichte der Leben-Jesu-Forschung* ["From Reimarus to Wrede: A History of Jesus Research"] (Tübingen: J. C. B. Mohr, 1906). This was translated into English as *The Quest of the Historical Jesus: A Critical Study of Its Progress from Reimarus to Wrede* (New York: Macmillan, 1910).

[19]Weiss, *Jesus' Proclamation,* p. 114.

have gone through all the towns of Israel before the Son of Man comes" (Mt 10:23). This latter text was in many ways the linchpin of Schweitzer's interpretation of Jesus' view of the imminence of the kingdom. By themselves, these two texts do indeed seem to indicate that Jesus believed that the kingdom was imminent. Both Weiss and Schweitzer held that Jesus did not view himself, during his earthly ministry, as the Danielic Son of Man (Dan 7:13-14). Furthermore, both held that Jesus believed he was the Messiah of Israel, though transcending the traditional Jewish Son of David, and would soon come on the clouds of heaven as the exalted Son of Man.[20] Thus, as God's authorized spokesperson, Jesus often spoke as if the kingdom had already arrived (a proleptic [anticipatory] presence). According to Schweitzer, one could say that the kingdom was present in Jesus' ministry, even though its actual arrival was yet future.

Both Weiss and Schweitzer, however, remained liberals in the sense that neither accepted Jesus' own understanding of the kingdom as normative.[21] Rather, one must, like Harnack and Ritschl, sift Jesus' teachings for those abiding values that can still be meaningful in the modern world. Schweitzer is particularly fascinating in this regard. He believed that Jesus tried to force God's hand by his own death and thus precipitate the advent of the kingdom. According to Schweitzer, however, Jesus died a disillusioned man, as is reflected in the cry of dereliction: "My God, my God, why have you forsaken me?" (Mk 15:34).

Still, Schweitzer found in Jesus' heroic death something of abiding value. Sacrificing oneself for the good of humanity serves as a powerful paradigm for modern Christians. "Out of the depths of my feeling of happiness, there gradually grew up within me an understanding of the saying of Jesus that we must not treat our lives as being for ourselves alone."[22] Schweitzer sought to actualize this concept in his own life. He left Europe, where he was a first-rate organist, medical doctor, philosopher, and NT scholar, to minister to sick and underprivileged Africans at Lambaréné (Gabon, Africa), where he established (in 1913) and operated a hospital and leper colony.[23] There he lived out his days, with only occasional visits elsewhere,

---

[20]Ibid, p. 82.

[21]"The real difference between our modern Protestant world-view and that of primitive Christianity is, therefore, that we do not share the eschatological attitude" (ibid., p. 135).

[22]This was taken from some autobiographical notes written shortly before his death and edited by Roland Gammond, September 4, 1965, at Lambarene, Gabon. It was widely published by newspapers in America.

[23]"Albert Schweitzer was one of the truly incredible and wide-ranging minds of the twentieth century" (C. R. Mercer, "Schweitzer, Albert," in *Dictionary of Major Biblical Interpreters*, ed. Donald K. McKim [Downers Grove, Ill.: InterVarsity Press, 2007], p. 899).

eschewing the comforts and conveniences of modern society. He eventually formulated what for him encapsulated the truly ethical life: "a reverence for life."

Not all, of course, accepted the view of Weiss and Schweitzer, but in time it dominated scholarly circles. The influential "history of religions" school lent its support to the contention that Jesus must be placed against the backdrop of apocalyptic Judaism. The most famous student of Johannes Weiss, Rudolf Bultmann, agreed with his teacher on this point. As we have already seen, however, he adopted a quite different strategy in order to salvage the teaching of Jesus for modernity.

The Realized Eschatology School. The pendulum suddenly swung in the opposite direction in the work of C. H. Dodd (1884-1973), probably the most influential figure in British NT scholarship during the middle decades of the twentieth century. Dodd's work resulted in what is called "realized eschatology." In short, this view holds that in the ministry of Jesus the kingdom came. Furthermore, this was what Jesus himself believed.[24]

According to Dodd, the futuristic, eschatological material that one encounters in the teachings of Jesus must be interpreted as purely symbolic description of spiritual realities, quite beyond human comprehension. By resorting to this mode of description, Jesus was simply trying to depict the absolute character of the kingdom rather than its future dimension and literal character. As to the nature of the kingdom, Dodd seems to identify it with the person of Jesus himself and thus a timeless reality. As Dodd puts it, "The Absolute, the 'wholly other,' has entered into time and space."[25] In one sense, Dodd moves us back to the noneschatological view of the kingdom of God as a present reality. Clearly, "Dodd had a distaste for apocalyptic and future eschatology, which he regarded as a falling away from the teaching of Jesus."[26] Although greatly influenced by Harnack,[27] he did not accept whole cloth the classic liberal interpretation of the kingdom; rather, he connected the kingdom with the atoning death, resurrection, ascension, and parousia of Jesus—items consigned to the dustbin of

---

[24]Dodd makes his case in *The Parables of the Kingdom* (London: Nisbet, 1935). The book has been republished several times.

[25]Dodd, *The Parables of the Kingdom* (New York: Scribner, 1961), p. 81. One hears in this phraseology the echoes of neoorthodox theologians such as Karl Barth and Emil Bruner, contemporaries of Dodd.

[26]Donald Hagner, "Dodd, C. H.," in *Dictionary of Major Biblical Interpreters*, ed. Donald K. McKim (Downers Grove, Ill.: InterVarsity Press, 2007), p. 382.

[27]"From the outset, Dodd's reflections were strongly influenced by Harnack" (Richard H. Hiers, "Pivotal Reactions to the Eschatological Interpretations: Rudolf Bultmann and C. H. Dodd," in *The Kingdom of God in 20th-Century Interpretation*, ed. Wendell Willis [Peabody, Mass.: Hendrickson, 1987], p. 18).

"husk" by Harnack. In the end, Dodd did not ditch eschatology entirely. As he said, "There remains a residue of eschatology which is not exhausted in the 'realized eschatology' of the Gospel, namely, the element of sheer finality."[28]

INAUGURATED ESCHATOLOGY

So, which is it? Is the kingdom a present or future reality? The pendulum has swung back and forth in NT scholarship. A major reason for such vacillation has to do with the nature of the evidence itself. An inductive study of the Gospel tradition yields this conclusion: there is evidence for both views. Here we will evaluate the evidence for both.

The kingdom of God as a present reality. We begin with a saying from Q (a putative source of Jesus' sayings shared by Luke and Matthew), Luke 11:20 = Matthew 12:28, occurring in a pericope dealing with the charge that Jesus cast out demons by the aid of Beelzebul. Jesus replies, "But if it is by the finger of God that I cast out the demons, then the kingdom of God has come to you." Matthew replaces the expression "finger of God" with "the Spirit of God." Robert Stein suggests that Matthew is thereby stressing the renewed activity of the Holy Spirit in Israel, signaling the arrival of the messianic era (cf. Joel 2:28-29).[29] Special significance attaches to the aorist tense verb "has come" *(ephthasen)*. Dodd made this text a keystone in his "realized eschatology" agenda, and many others followed suit.[30] Does this text, however, demonstrate that Jesus believed that the kingdom had actually arrived with his ministry? Evangelical scholar Chrys Caragounis does not think so. He maintains that "the *ephthasen* saying makes excellent sense if understood according to a well-attested but little-known and generally misunderstood Greek idiom. The aorist tense is sometimes used to emphasize the certainty and immediacy of an action that properly belongs in the future by describing it as though it had already transpired."[31] In other words, for Caragounis, the kingdom is imminent, not present.

Caragounis's objection to realized eschatology is also based on a theological issue. If one assumes that the kingdom of God had actually arrived

---

[28]C. H. Dodd, *The Apostolic Preaching and Its Developments* (London: Hodder & Stoughton, 1936), p. 231, cited in Hagner, "Dodd, C. H.," p. 382.

[29]Stein, *Method and Message*, p. 68.

[30]See Werner G. Kümmel, *Promise and Fulfillment: The Eschatological Message of Jesus* (2nd ed.; Studies in Biblical Theology 23; Naperville, Ill.: Allenson, 1961); Herman Ridderbos, *The Coming of the Kingdom*, trans. H. de Jongste, ed. Raymond O. Zorn (Philadelphia: P & R Publishing, 1962); George E. Ladd, *The Presence of the Future: The Eschatology of Biblical Realism* (Grand Rapids: Eerdmans, 1974).

[31]Caragounis, "Kingdom of God/Heaven," *DJG* 423.

in Jesus' ministry of exorcism and preaching, then what role do the cross, resurrection, ascension and descent of the Holy Spirit at Pentecost play? Are they not relegated to a footnote? Does it not better fit NT thought, especially the Pauline letters, to see the kingdom as actually arriving when this foundational moment in redemptive history transpired? Perhaps it would be more precise to say that during Jesus' ministry the kingdom of God was imminent but not yet inaugurated.

Against Caragounis's position, however, is the generally agreed upon fact that in four out of the five other NT instances where the Greek verb *phthanō* is used it means "has arrived" or something very close to that (Rom 9:31; 2 Cor 10:14; 1 Thess 2:16; Phil 3:16). Furthermore, an appeal to the proleptic use of the aorist tense, while possible, is debatable.[32]

Weightier is his concern about minimizing the centrality of the cross and resurrection that looms so large in the rest of the NT. This deserves careful consideration. Does one marginalize the cross and resurrection by affirming that the kingdom was already present in Jesus' ministry? All parties are agreed that the kingdom of God is deeply rooted in the OT. Because redemptive history unfolds in real time and space, the cross can occur but once (Heb 9:25-28). This unique event is the basis and foundation upon which all redemptive history rests.[33] Those who responded to Jesus' preaching of the good news of the kingdom were saved by Jesus' death on the cross, just like all believers throughout redemptive history, even if they did not yet understand the role of the cross in their salvation. What they did know and experience was God's forgiving and reconciling grace as mediated through Jesus (Mt 9:2-8 = Lk 5:21-26; Mt 9:10-13; 11:25-30; Lk 7:36-50; 15:11-32; 19:1-10). Regardless of whether we hold to a present or imminent kingdom in Jesus' ministry, we can at least agree that the consistent eschatology of Weiss and Schweitzer was unbalanced; clearly, the kingdom appeared before the end of the age. For example, in Luke 17:21 Jesus says, "For, in fact, the kingdom of God is among you." The NRSV has a footnote with an alternative translation, "within" instead of "among." The Greek preposition is *entos*. Lexically, we have options such as "inside," "within," "within the limits of." When used in conjunction with the pronoun *hymōn* (second-person genitive plural, "you"), it allows us to render the phrase "within you" (i.e., your hearts) or "within your midst." Harnack favored the first, whereas Dodd preferred the second. In either case, the point was that Jesus

---

[32]Daniel Wallace cites this as a possible but debatable example of the proleptic (futuristic) aorist (*Greek Grammar Beyond the Basics* [Grand Rapids: Zondervan, 1996], p. 564).

[33]See Oscar Cullmann, *Christ and Time: The Primitive Christian Conception of Time and History*, trans. Floyd V. Filson (rev. ed.; Philadelphia: Westminster Press, 1964).

believed the kingdom was present at that moment. Or did he? BAGD offers
as a possible translation "among you, in your midst" (either now or *suddenly in the near future*).[34] The latter temporal nuance suggests that the
kingdom was merely imminent. Once again, we have an ambivalent expression, and personal preference tends to dictate the precise nuance.

Another tack in the attempt to resolve this problem focuses upon the note
of prophetic fulfillment. The evangelists draw attention to Jesus' fulfillment
of messianic texts during the course of his healing and teaching ministry.
In Jesus' day, certain OT prophetic texts were already given a messianic
interpretation in Jewish circles. Among them were Isaiah 35:5-6; 61:1-2. A
remarkable text from Qumran, 4Q521, closely parallels Matthew 11:2-6
= Lk 7:18-23. According to the passages, the Messiah is expected to cure
disease, heal the blind and lame, cleanse lepers and preach the good news
to the poor. Thus the Qumran community and early Christians, though
differing in their identification of who the Messiah was, shared a common
messianic expectation anchored in OT prophecy.[35] Both communities connected a Messiah who healed and preached good news with the appearance
of the long-expected kingdom of God.

Several OT prophetic texts speak of Gentiles being included in the blessings of the Day of the Lord (e.g., Amos 9:12; Is 2:2; 11:10; 42:6-7; 49:6;
Zech 14:16; Mal 1:11). Significantly, during Jesus' ministry a few Gentiles
do respond favorably to his preaching (Mk 7:24-30 = Mt 15:21-28; Mt
8:5-13 = Lk 7:1-10). Even Matthew's birth narrative already anticipates
the inclusion of Gentiles in the kingdom (i.e., the magi from the east [Mt
2:1-12]). Jesus viewed the temple as "a house of prayer for all the nations"
(Mk 11:17; cf. Is 56:7), and in response to a Capernaum centurion's faith,
Jesus assures his listeners that "many will come from east and west and
will eat with Abraham and Isaac and Jacob in the kingdom of heaven" (Mt
8:11). Although in Matthew's Gospel Jesus restricts his own public ministry to Jews (Mt 10:5), after his resurrection he commissions his disciples to
preach the gospel to all nations (Mt 24:14; 28:19-20). Of course, it could be
argued that all these references to Gentiles being in the kingdom are future
and thus do not really support the notion of a present kingdom. On bal-

---

[34]See BAGD, p. 340 (my italics). "The sense *within you, in your hearts* has linguistic support
in Ps 38:4; 102:1; 108:22, all *entos mou*; s. also Jos., *Ant.* 5, 107, but Lk generally avoids ref.
to God's reign as a psychological reality. The passage has invited much debate" (BAGD,
pp. 340-41).

[35]For further discussion, see Craig Evans, "Jesus and the Dead Sea Scrolls from Qumran
Cave 4," in *Eschatology, Messianism, and the Dead Sea Scrolls*, ed. Craig A. Evans and
Peter W. Flint (Grand Rapids: Eerdmans, 1997), pp. 96-97; Edward P. Meadors, *Jesus, the
Messianic Herald of Salvation* (Peabody, Mass.: Hendrickson, 1997).

ance, however, I think that Matthew intends for the reader to conclude that an important facet of the kingdom had at least begun with Jesus' ministry.

Finally, I draw attention to a couple of texts that suggest a new phase of redemptive history was inaugurated in the earthly ministry of Jesus. Luke is the theologian of salvation history par excellence. In Luke 16:16 Jesus locates John the Baptist at the apex of an age now superseded: "The law and the prophets were in effect until John came; since then the good news of the kingdom of God is proclaimed, and everyone tries to enter it by force." One could argue that the kingdom is still imminent from Jesus' perspective, but this saying fits most comfortably into an understanding in which the kingdom is, in some sense, actually present.[36] With this may be compared the Markan pericope of the wineskins (Mk 2:21-22 = Mt 9:16-17). The new wine and fresh wineskins, representing Jesus' preaching of the kingdom, comport well with the notion that the kingdom was already present.

All things considered, it seems best to conclude that the Synoptic Gospels depict an unprecedented and present manifestation of the kingdom of God during the earthly ministry of Jesus.[37] This becomes even clearer when several of Jesus' parables are examined in more detail. The entire story has not yet been told, however. There is evidence for a yet future manifestation of the kingdom to be considered.

The kingdom of God as a future reality. The evidence for a future manifestation of the kingdom of God is even more abundant than for the present dimension. Several different aspects of the yet-to-be-consummated kingdom vie for consideration. The best-known text to which I could appeal occurs in the most renowned prayer in history, the Lord's Prayer, which is better described as the Disciples' Prayer (Mt 6:9-13; cf. Lk 11:2-4). The first three petitions concern God and his kingdom (similar to the first four of the Ten Commandments). The first petition asks that God be treated with utmost reverence and devotion. The second petition, "Your kingdom come," entreats God to bring his kingdom in all its fullness upon the earth. That the earth is the location of this kingdom is made explicit by the third petition, really an expansion of the second: "Your will be done, on earth as it is in heaven." There can be little doubt that we are not talking here about an inner reign of God's love in our hearts, as in Harnack's view, or a realized presence, as in Dodd's view. It is thoroughly eschatological in orientation,

---

[36]Weiss argues that similar passages, such as Matthew 11:11; 21:31, do not demand a present understanding of the kingdom (*Jesus' Proclamation*, pp. 67-74).

[37]For a defense of the presence of the kingdom in Jesus' ministry, see Darrell L. Bock, "The Reign of the Lord Christ," in *Dispensationalism, Israel and the Church: The Search for Definition*, ed. Craig A. Blaising and Darrell L. Bock (Grand Rapids: Zondervan, 1992), pp. 38-44.

as may be seen in its similarity to a contemporary Jewish prayer, the *Kaddish*, which entreats God for the speedy establishment of God's kingdom on earth.[38] Jesus taught his disciples to pray this petition and then put feet on their prayers by living out kingdom principles (I will say more about this in my comments on the Sermon on the Mount). Only when Jesus returns in glory, however, will this request be fully realized. For now, it remains a longed for hope.

In the teaching of Jesus there are unmistakable instances where the kingdom of God is associated with final judgment at the end of the age. For example, in the Sermon on the Mount Jesus concludes with this warning: "Not everyone who says to me, 'Lord, Lord,' will enter the kingdom of heaven, but only the one who does the will of my Father in heaven. *On that day* many will say to me. . . . Then I will declare to them, 'I never knew you; go away from me, you evildoers'" (Mt 7:21-23 [my italics]). There can be little doubt that "on that day" refers to the Day of the Lord. Of similar import is Luke 13:22-30, where Jesus says of those excluded from the kingdom, "There will be weeping and gnashing of teeth when you see Abraham and Isaac and Jacob and all the prophets *in the kingdom of God,* and you yourselves thrown out" (Lk 13:28 [my italics]).

Out of several parables emphasizing a yet future dimension to the kingdom, I select the following. The first, to be more fully examined later, likens the kingdom to a field sown with wheat in which enemies surreptitiously sow weeds. The owner of the field is asked what should be done. His response is instructive: "Let both of them grow together until the harvest; and at harvest time I will tell the reapers, Collect the weeds first and bind them in bundles to be burned, but gather the wheat into my barn" (Mt 13:30). The eschatological thrust of the parable is apparent. Similarly, three parables in Matthew 25 depict an eschatological consummation of the kingdom of God. Whether the imagery is that of bridesmaids expecting the return of the bridegroom, an estate owner entrusting assets to household slaves or a shepherd separating sheep from goats, each makes the point that every person experiences eschatological judgment. Furthermore, this judgment transpires at the consummation of the kingdom: "When the Son of Man comes in his glory, and all the angels with him, then he will sit on the throne of his glory" (Mt 25:31).

---

[38]See J. D. G. Dunn, "Prayer," *DJG* 619-25. The *Kaddish* begins in a remarkably similar way to the Lord's Prayer: "Glorified and sanctified be God's great name throughout the world which He has created according to His will. May He establish His kingdom in your lifetime and during your days, and within the life of the entire house of Israel, speedily and soon; and say, Amen."

Finally, I draw attention to the accounts of the Lord's Supper. This communal meal, placed in a Passover setting by all four Gospels, unmistakably conveys an eschatological dimension. In Mark's account we read the climactic words of institution, "Truly I tell you, I will never again drink of the fruit of the vine until that day when I drink it new in the kingdom of God" (Mk 14:25 // Mt 26:29; Lk 22:18).

I conclude that the kingdom of God possesses a future dimension. This dimension is associated with the coming of the Son of Man—that is, the Lord Jesus Christ. The kingdom comes in its fullness when the Son of Man comes.

Now but Not Yet

Earlier scholars erred in taking one dimension as authentic and minimizing or denying the other. This imbalance was rectified by scholars who realized that what we have is a "both and" phenomenon. The kingdom was both present in the ministry of Jesus and yet to be consummated at his return in glory. This view has often been dubbed "inaugurated eschatology."

Oscar Cullmann was among the first to argue persuasively for a mediating or "both and" approach.[39] Others who followed in his wake were Werner Kümmel, G. R. Beasley-Murray, and George Eldon Ladd, to name but a few.[40] Methodologically, this view has much to commend it. Rather than dismiss part of the biblical evidence, one attempts to harmonize the data. As we already noted in chapter 1, this is a hallmark of evangelical theology and is a sound approach, if judiciously used, in all historical disciplines. Linguistically, inaugurated eschatology makes sense once past the misconception that "kingdom" in the NT refers basically to territory or realm. Instead, as we noted above, the primary force of this term is the dynamic idea of reign or rule. When we understand the kingdom in this way, we can easily see how a "now but not yet" dimension can exist without contradiction. The kingdom of God unfolds progressively and decisively in key moments. The incarnation, ministry, death and resurrection of Jesus stand at the very midpoint of this series of events, all of which are connected to the unfolding kingdom. The rule of God in the hearts of an ever-growing number of followers climaxes in the glorious return of the Son of Man. The powers of darkness are defeated once for all, and the planet is truly liber-

---

[39]Cullmann, *Christ and Time*.

[40]Kümmel, *Promise and Fulfillment*; G. R. Beasley Murray, *Jesus and the Future: An Examination of the Criticism of the Eschatological Discourse, Mark 13, with Special Reference to the Little Apocalypse Theory* (London: Macmillan, 1954); Ladd, *The Presence of the Future*.

ated from the throes of sin and death (1 Cor 15:24-28). The old Jerusalem gives way at last to the new Jerusalem (Rev 21:1-8; cf. Mt 19:28; Gal 4:26; Phil 3:20-21; Col 3:1-3).

Such an inaugurated eschatology has important implications for reading the NT. Indeed, an essential key to unlocking the NT resides precisely in the catchphrase "now but not yet." Jesus, Paul and John cannot be fully understood until one has a handle on this central idea. For example, we have a satisfying answer to the question of what Jesus meant by the "secrets [or 'mysteries'] of the kingdom" (Mt 13:11; cf. Mt 11:25). Foundational to the "secrets" is the twofold aspect of the kingdom. The kingdom appeared in a new and unexpected way in the ministry of Jesus, centered on Jesus' death and resurrection, the midpoint of redemptive history, and launched into a final, decisive phase, climaxed by Jesus' glorious return and everlasting reign. There is a breathtaking sweep to this whole connected story.

Seeing where we are in this metanarrative brings the realization that we are "between the times." That is, we are in a certain sense already projected into the age to come. We have an assurance that we are justified, even though we have not yet stood before God's tribunal. We already experience the forgiveness of sins, the gifts and graces of the Holy Spirit, the fellowship of the saints, and the powers of the age to come, all the while yet living in this present evil age, under the baneful influence of the world, the flesh and the devil. We know that we already have eternal life, yet we remain in our mortal bodies, burdened down by their limitations and succumbing all too often to the allurements of the sinful nature. We long to come into our final inheritance (Rom 8:23). NT believers thus live in a kind of tension: we are people with one foot in this age and the other foot in the age to come. Understanding who we are and where we are shapes our priorities. Kingdom values always take precedence (Mt 6:33).

The tension arising from this dual existence helps us understand NT parenesis (ethical and moral exhortation). The Pauline shift from indicative to imperative moods reflects the actual situation of believers who live between the times. Paul essentially urges his converts to act on the basis of who and what they really are in Christ. Act the part! Live now on the basis of spiritual realities. This tension is sometimes referred to as positional truth as opposed to experiential truth. I think that we better preserve the dynamic nature of NT thought by employing the temporal distinction "now but not yet." I will elaborate on this important concept in discussing Pauline and Johannine theologies.

Many of the sayings of Jesus teach a "realized eschatology." What is realized, however, is not yet complete; perfection awaits the consummation.

Whereas Jesus pointed John the Baptist to his present healing ministry, in which the blind received their sight, the lame walked, the lepers were cleansed, the deaf heard and the dead were raised (Mt 11:4-6), not all were healed (Mk 6:5), and none received their resurrection body. Jairus's daughter and Lazarus died again. We patiently await the "not yet," when the devil is sentenced (Rev 20:10), death and Hades are abolished (Rev 20:14), and all creation is liberated from its bondage (Rom 8:18-25).

Jesus himself expected an interval between his ministry and the consummation of the kingdom. This becomes clear in several pericopae. When criticized by Pharisees for not observing the twice-weekly fasts enjoined by oral tradition, Jesus responds with an illustration of a wedding (Mk 2:18-19). How inappropriate it is to fast at a wedding! The wedding feast represents Jesus' present ministry, but a time of fasting will come. "The days will come when the bridegroom is taken away from them, and then they will fast on that day" (Mk 2:20). As becomes clear in Mark's Gospel, the day of fasting is the cross and, probably, its aftermath. Fasting played an important role in the life of the early church (see Acts 13:2-3; 14:23). Jesus was thus aware that the final phase of the kingdom would not appear immediately. In common with Second Temple Judaism generally, Jesus looked beyond the present age of suffering and tribulation to a grand feast at the end of days, the final triumph of the kingdom of God (Mt 8:11; 22:1-10; 25:1-13). In Mark 10:35-40 we have the episode in which James and John request positions of prominence when Jesus' comes into his glorious kingdom power. Jesus grants only that they share his cup and baptism—that is, the experience of martyrdom. This saying assumes an interval between his death and glorious reign. He inaugurates his reign on a cross; he consummates his reign on a glorious throne. That there is an unspecified interval between these two events is made clear in the Olivet discourse, in which Jesus cautions that "the end is still to come" (Mk 13:7) and that "the good news must first be proclaimed to all nations" (Mk 13:10). His return in glory does not occur until some time afterward. Finally, Jesus' words at the Last Supper, "until that day," imply an interval before the consummation of the kingdom (Mt 26:29; Mk 14:25; cf. Lk 22:18).

Oscar Cullmann, who championed the "now but not yet" concept as a master key for NT interpretation, offered a compelling illustration from his own time. Military historians agree that the Allied invasion of Normandy, popularly called D-Day, was the decisive turning point in World War II (June 6, 1944). Once the allies secured a beachhead, it was just a matter of time before ultimate victory, or VE-Day (victory in Europe), would come (May 8, 1945). In like manner, said Cullmann, the decisive move in redemptive history was the cross. Christ's victory there assured ultimate and complete victory for the kingdom of God. But just as the Nazi war machine bitterly resisted and there was a bloody struggle from D-Day to VE-Day, so also Satan resists to the bitter but inevitable end. Unfortunately, there will be many casualties before we get to VE-Day (victory on Earth) in the kingdom of God. But victory is certain!

WINDOWS INTO THE KINGDOM OF GOD

In order to understand better Jesus' view of the kingdom, I focus on the parables found in Matthew 13. Here the evangelist culls from the Master's teaching eight parables that help us peer into the wonderful world of the kingdom.

Parable research has undergone considerable revision of late. The literature is extensive, and lack of space prevents a detailed discussion. Parables in rabbinic literature provide the closest and most helpful parallels for understanding Jesus' parables.[41] Scholars frequently divide parables into four subcategories: similitudes, example story, parable and allegory. Klyne Snodgrass, while not entirely rejecting this scheme, prefers to define parables "as stories with two levels of meaning: the story level provides a mirror by which reality is perceived and understood. In effect, parables are imaginary gardens with real toads in them."[42] For the sake of convenience, I will simply use the term *parable* as a cover term for the various subtypes. To me, the parables reflect the genius of Jesus' teaching. On the one hand, they are windows into the "magical kingdom"; on the other hand, they are weapons that parry his opponents' blows.

The supreme worth of the kingdom. I begin with the fifth and sixth parables, in the form of similitudes: the hidden treasure and the pearl of great price (Mt 13:44-46). A similitude is an extended simile (using "like" or "as") in which a comparison is drawn between an aspect of real life and something unknown, in this case, the kingdom of God.[43] There is something strikingly similar in discovering, apparently unexpectedly, a hidden treasure in a field and discovering the reality of the kingdom of God. It is also like a person who, after a long and deliberate search, finds an exceedingly valuable pearl. Everything else is liquidated in order to purchase this

---

[41]See K. R. Snodgrass, "Parable," *DJG* 591-601; Craig L. Blomberg, *Interpreting the Parables* (Downers Grove, Ill.: InterVarsity Press, 1990); Brad H. Young, *Jesus and His Jewish Parables: Rediscovering the Roots of Jesus' Teaching* (New York: Paulist Press, 1989).

[42]Snodgrass, "Parable," *DJG* 594.

[43]See F. B. Huey Jr. and Bruce Corley, *A Student's Dictionary for Biblical and Theological Studies* (Grand Rapids: Zondervan, 1983), p. 175.

one pearl. Both parables share this common conviction: nothing in this world compares to being in the kingdom of God. One should sell everything, if need be, to acquire an interest in the kingdom.

One misses the point by quibbling over the ethics of discovering a field containing hidden treasure and purchasing it without informing the current owner. The parable is true to life in that it reflects a region visited by repeated invasions and deportations. In such circumstances, people buried their valuables in hopes of surviving the crisis and later retrieving them. Sometimes they did, sometimes they did not. Modern archaeologists (but usually and unfortunately, modern treasure hunters and looters) occasionally have uncovered these burials and restored them to the admiring gaze of museum goers. One should look for the main idea, not try to "milk meaning" out of the secondary details. The main point is clear and compelling: nothing in life is as important as the kingdom of God. These two parables demand a verdict now. Indescribable joy rides on the decision.[44]

The varied responses to the kingdom. Despite the fact that exegetes such as Augustine had a "field day" allegorizing the details of the parable of the sower (Mt 13:1-8, 18-23), only a few key points seem intended by Jesus. Fortunately, Jesus himself provides an interpretation, identifying the features that have importance. This parable is not really a similitude, having but one primary point, nor is it an example story; it is best categorized as an allegory. This does not, however, mean that we resort to the allegorical method of an Origen or Augustine and find spiritual significance in each specific detail. The Master himself lays bare the meaning of the allegory.

Several features of the story line are important for its interpretation. The seed is equated with the "word of the kingdom" (Mt 13:3, 19). Although Jesus does not explicitly state it, one might reasonably infer that he himself is the sower, since he is so identified in the following parable of the weeds and wheat (Mt 13:37). The focus of the parable, however, falls on the varying responses. It is not likely that Jesus was predicting a precise ratio of response (i.e., 25 percent). Rather, I infer from the parable that a majority will not embrace the message. However, there will be a substantial response, one that varies in terms of fruitfulness.

Jesus offers several basic reasons why people turn a deaf ear to the word of the kingdom. First, the birds that eat up the seeds on the path represent the "evil one," a reference to Satan (Mt 13:4, 19). Jesus takes seriously the actual existence and persistent opposition of Satan to the kingdom program, as do other NT writers (cf. 2 Cor 4:4; Eph 6:12, 16; Heb 2:14-15; Jas

---

[44]See Donald A. Hagner, *Matthew 1-13* (WBC 33A; Dallas: Word, 1993), pp. 396-97.

2:19; 4:7; 1 Pet 5:8; 1 Jn 3:8-10; Rev 12:17). Paul states it most forthrightly when he says, "The god of this world has blinded the minds of unbelievers, to keep them from seeing the light of the gospel" (2 Cor 4:4). Second, trouble and persecution as a result of accepting the message of the kingdom cause some to turn back. They lack deep soil—that is, a firm commitment to the kingdom. A third reason, the thorns, lies in the allure of this present world. The message of the kingdom entails a set of priorities and values entirely different from those operating in the world. Some who start for the kingdom decide that it is not worth it. Pleasure now trumps "pleasures forevermore" (Ps 16:11). The reason(s) for the varying degrees of fruitfulness among those who commit to the kingdom is not stated in this parable. Other sayings of Jesus suggest, however, that the primary criterion for fruitfulness is simply being faithful in the exercise of God-given gifts and abilities (Mt 25:14-30; Lk 19:11-27).

Discouragements and difficulties in the kingdom. Three parables address potential discouragement and difficulty for kingdom citizens. The parable of the weeds and wheat (Mt 13:24-30), like that of the sower, receives an interpretation, perhaps indicating the importance that these two parables hold for an overall understanding of the kingdom. It is important to know that there are false professors within the kingdom who work at counterpurposes. This cautions us against strictly identifying the church and the kingdom. In this regard, note that Jesus explicitly identifies the field with the world, not the church (Mt 13:38). In the NT the church, the mystical body of Christ, consists only of the elect, whereas the larger sphere of God's rule includes unbelievers. Of course, the empirical church is also a "mixed bag" and has many "spots, wrinkles and blemishes" (see Eph 5:27; cf. 1 Cor).[45] The true-to-life nature of the parable is highlighted by the weeds (darnel), which bear such close resemblance to wheat in the early stages as to be almost unrecognizable. These false professors function as agents of Satan, whether wittingly or not. The fact that Satan does this "while everybody was asleep" (Mt 13:25) probably points not so much to a lack of vigilance on the part of the "good seed" as to the stealthy nature of Satan's activity. According to the story, angels do not purge these false professors until the final judgment, at the climax of the kingdom. The rationale for the delay is the difficulty in separating the weeds from the wheat without destroying some of the wheat in the process. The difficulty, on the human level, of passing judgment infallibly in such cases seems reflected in the NT caution about church discipline (see Mt 18:15-17; 1 Tim 5:19-22).

---

[45]See the Westminster Confession of Faith XXV:3-4.

In short, the history of the kingdom is marked by internal hindrance and conflict. Anyone only generally aware of church history recognizes how prophetic the parable is. And those actively serving in local churches almost certainly have firsthand experience with this sad reality. Jesus forewarns his followers about inevitable disappointments. None are more disheartening than those emanating from supposed fellow travelers who foster disharmony and division. At the same time, Jesus gives his disciples confidence that, ultimately, only the righteous experience the glories of the kingdom. Kingdom citizens need to know that up front.

I treat the next two parables together because essentially they make the same point. The parables of the mustard seed and of the yeast (Mt 13:31-33) offer, at least in the long run, a more encouraging prospect for kingdom citizens. They speak of remarkable growth in spite of inauspicious beginnings. Among Palestinian garden seeds, the mustard seed is the smallest one known. Yet, when fully grown, the shrub stands majestically taller than any other. In a similar vein, it takes but a small portion of yeast to leaven a large basket of dough (about fifty pounds of flour, yielding over one hundred loaves of bread).

Classical dispensationalism interpreted the yeast in a negative sense, as representing false teaching. To be sure, in one instance Jesus does liken Pharisaic teaching to leaven—that is, yeast (Mt 16:6, 11)—and so does Paul (1 Cor 5:6-8). But only a wooden approach to language insists that a gifted teacher such as Jesus always uses an image in the same way. Context dictates meaning, and the parable seems paired with that of the mustard seed. Furthermore, in rabbinic literature yeast is used as a positive image. This leads most interpreters to conclude that yeast here functions positively to represent explosive growth.[46] The statistics compiled by mission specialists are quite astonishing.[47] The growth of the kingdom has indeed been cause for amazement.

Both parables involve mystery: how can something so small and insignificant accomplish such far-reaching results? The parables do not explain; they simply proclaim. For Jesus' immediate followers, the point seems to be this: one should not be discouraged by small beginnings, for in the end, the kingdom will be extensive and effective. The image of birds coming to rest

---

[46]See Brad H. Young, *Jesus the Jewish Theologian* (Peabody, Mass.: Hendrickson, 1995), pp. 77-83.

[47]According to the U.S. Center for World Mission, in 2000 about 2.04 billion people identified themselves as Christians (http://www.religioustolerance.org/worldrel.htm). This constitutes 33 percent of the world's population. In the upper room, on the day of Pentecost, A.D. 30, there were about 120 believers gathered (Acts 1:15). This truly is phenomenal growth from such small beginnings.

in the branches of the mustard shrub highlights the majestic climax of the kingdom (cf. Dan 4:10-12).

The mixed character of the kingdom. The seventh parable, the dragnet,[48] is similar to the parable of the weeds and wheat. The main difference is the absence of any mention of the evil one; the bad fish (unbelievers, false professors, or both) are such by nature. The reason for their rejection lies in their own character and choice, not demonic deception. In Jewish literature of the Second Temple period both these explanations for unbelief may be found.[49] In the NT the apostle Paul also advances both explanations in his letters (cf. Rom 1:18-32; 5:12-21 with 2 Cor 4:4; 11:3; 1 Tim 2:14). The story is true to life in that not all fish in the Sea of Galilee are edible; scavengers are routinely discarded. The note of final separation and judgment is clearly present in the parables of the weeds and wheat and of the dragnet and runs "against the grain" of our modern, nonjudgmental culture. This is one of many instances where Jesus is definitely countercultural.

The new scribes in the kingdom. The last parable makes an important observation about the content of the kingdom and those authorized to pass on the new traditions. Jesus' disciples are likened to a professional class of first-century Judaism called "scribes." The Pharisaic and Sadducean scribes were legal experts who passed along rulings on matters of halakah—that is, correct behavior and worship for their respective parties. They were the guardians of "the tradition of the elders" (see Mk 7:3). The Qumran community, probably the Essenes, also had an equivalent, the overseers (see 1QS 9:7; CD-A 13:7-19). In my view, Jesus did not institute a professional class of "Christian scribes." Rather, every Christian, soundly instructed, was expected to be able to transmit the traditions of the kingdom. Jesus' introductory question speaks to each generation: "Have you understood all this" (Mt 13:51)?

The central point of the parable, however, is the stress on content. It is a combination of "what is new and what is old" (Mt 13:52). In light of Jesus' assertion that he came to fulfill the law and the prophets (Mt 5:17), we can safely infer that the "old" refers to the OT Scriptures. The "new," accordingly, refers to the good news of the kingdom as taught by Jesus. Thus, the primary qualification of a Christian scribe is the ability to demonstrate the unity of God's revelation in both old and new covenants.[50]

---

[48]"Dragnets . . . were much larger than the fishing nets employed in 4:18. It is thought that floats and sinkers were attached to keep one part of the wide end of the net at the surface while the other part dragged below" (Craig S. Keener, *The IVP Bible Background Commentary: New Testament* [Downers Grove, Ill.: InterVarsity Press, 1993], p. 84).

[49]See, for example, *1 Enoch* 1—36; CD-A 2:7-8; 4:13-15.

[50]"The Christian Torah scholar or 'scribe' is one trained in the mysteries of the kingdom who

THE GOD OF THE KINGDOM

Although Jesus' message focuses on the kingdom of God, pride of place belongs to the God of the kingdom.[51] So what was Jesus' view of God? This is theology at its most fundamental, and Jesus held a fundamentally different view from that of his coreligionists. This is not to say that they shared no common ground; after all, the OT was the taproot for all reflection about God in the Second Temple period, and Jesus was heir to this as well.

Common ground. Virtually all Jews of this era were committed to ethical monotheism. Although this monotheism might occasionally be expressed in a way implying more than one divine being exercising sovereignty over creation, none of the surviving sources seriously suggests that ethical monotheism was being challenged by alternatives. Philo Judaeus, the Alexandrian philosopher, speaks of a plurality of powers emanating from the one true God (the Logos, Wisdom, the great archangel of many names, etc.).[52] These "powers" are not, however, true hypostases (separate persons); rather, they are personifications of divine attributes. The twice-daily utterance of the Shema and the matchless cadences of Deutero-Isaiah form the bedrock of Second Temple Judaism: "Hear, O Israel: The LORD is our God, the LORD alone [or, 'the LORD is one']" (Deut 6:4); "I am the first and I am the last; besides me there is no god" (Is 44:6; cf. 43:10-11; also, e.g., 43:13; 44:8; 45:6).

As a faithful son of Israel, Jesus firmly adheres to this theological confession (Mk 12:28-29). Likewise, he affirms that this one true and living God created everything (Mk 10:6; 13:19). The God of creation is also the God of revelation. He revealed himself to the patriarchs (Mk 12:26; Mt 22:32) and entered into covenant with the nation of Israel (implied in Mk 13:24 pars.) in the days of Moses (see Jn 1:17). He revealed his will supremely in the law (see Lk 10:25-26). At the very heart of the law stand the Ten Commandments, obligatory upon every Jew (Lk 16:17; Mk 10:3-5). God

---

is able to maintain a balance between the continuity and discontinuity existing between the era inaugurated by Jesus and that of the past. It is remarkable the extent to which NT theology is characterized by just this tension between the old and the new" (Hagner, *Matthew 1-13*, p. 402).

[51]In T. W. Manson's words, "The fact with which we have to reckon at all times is that in the teaching of Jesus his conception of God determines everything, including the conceptions of the Kingdom and the messiah" (*The Teaching of Jesus: Studies of Its Form and Content* [Cambridge: Cambridge University Press, 1935], p. 211). Larry Hurtado notes, "Though the Gospels are undeniably christological narratives, they are also deeply God-centered. Their whole thrust is that the one whose story they narrate represents God's new overture of revelations, fulfillment and salvation" ("God," *DJG* 270).

[52]Larry R. Helyer, *Exploring Jewish Literature of the Second Temple Period: A Guide for New Testament Students* (Downers Grove, Ill.: InterVarsity Press, 2002), p. 327.

raised up David and Solomon to reign over Israel and promised a future Davidic king, the Messiah, preceded by Elijah (Mk 2:25; Mt 12:3; Lk 6:3; Mt
12:42; Lk 11:31; Mk 11:10; 12:35-37; 9:11-12). God is bringing all history
to a climactic moment of judgment. This is likened to the days preceding
the great flood in the time of Noah (Mt 24:37-38; Lk 17:26-27). At that
time, the righteous are vindicated (see Lk 16:22) and resurrected to new
life, like the angels (Mt 12:25), while the wicked are set apart for everlasting punishment (Mt 25:46). With the exception of the Sadducees' denial
of bodily resurrection and life after death (Mk 12:18 pars.), nearly all the
aforementioned tenets were affirmed by Jews of all stripes in Jesus' time;
they formed the core convictions of Israel.[53]

The changed perspective of Second Temple Judaism. The view of God
found in the literature of the Second Temple period reflects a slightly different perspective from that of the OT. Because of the crisis of the exile and
the continued dispersion of most Jews from their ancient homeland, there
was a widespread conviction that God had withdrawn from Israel and was
waiting for signs of heartfelt repentance on the part of all Jews. What precisely should be done to regain God's favor was at least in part a cause for
the rise of diversity in Second Temple Judaism. Pharisees had one agenda,
while Sadducees, Essenes and other sects had their own agendas. On some
points these stood in direct opposition and generated considerable strife
and hostility. Common to the various sects, however, was the notion that
certain ritual and legal requirements must be rigorously kept in order for
God to grant forgiveness and restoration to the nation. The upshot of such
a conviction is a certain distancing of God from the political fortunes, if
not the individual fortunes, of the Jewish people. He is a waiting God.

JESUS' NEW PERSPECTIVE ON GOD

The seeking and inviting God. Jesus' conception of God differs from that
of his contemporaries on a couple of crucial points. God is not passively
waiting for Israel to repent so that he can then bestow his blessing; rather,
he is actively seeking out sinners now, promising blessing in this life and the
next. Perhaps no section of the Gospels makes this point as eloquently as
Luke 15, with its three parables of lost things: the lost sheep, the lost coin
and the lost sons. These parables are paradigmatic for Jesus' view of God.

The setting for all three parables is the negative reaction of the Pharisees
and their legal experts, the scribes, to Jesus' habit not only of preaching

---

[53]See E. P. Sanders, *Judaism: Practice and Belief, 63 BCE-66 CE* (Philadelphia: Trinity Press
International, 1992), pp. 241-78.

to tax collectors and "sinners" but also of practicing table fellowship with them (Lk 15:1-2). Tax collectors were individuals who contracted with the Roman government to raise so much tax revenue from a certain region or district. These tax farmers had a reputation for gouging people in order to supplement their contracted "cut" with the Roman authorities. In the eyes of most Jews, tax collectors were greedy, dishonest traitors.[54] The group identified as "sinners" encompassed people with a range of perceived short-comings, but regularly it included prostitutes and Jews who failed to live by the halakic rulings of the "in group," in this case, the Pharisees.[55]

Here is my précis of the parable of the lost sons.[56] The younger of two sons wants to leave home. We are not told why he wants to leave, but we may infer that he is already alienated from his father and older brother. This inference is based upon an unheard of, shocking request. He asks for his inheritance *before* his father's death. This flies in the face of expected behavior by a dutiful son. Even more shocking to the assumed audience is the father's response. Contrary to all expectation, he grants the request. The hearers would have murmured their sharp disapproval. In their opinion, this boy deserved a whipping! The fact that the father permits his younger son to have his share of the inheritance and leave the family dwelling already tells us something important about this father.

The younger son takes his money and leaves for "a distant country," where an unfortunate but not unexpected sequence of events unfolds. In short, he squanders his money and falls into abject poverty. He hits bottom in the pathetic scene of a young Jewish man groveling in a pigpen and longing to fill his belly with carob pods.

This is the turning point of the parable. The young man "came to himself" (Lk 15:17). He realizes his folly and remembers what he had back home with father. He prepares a speech of apology and seeks to pay off his debt by working for his father as a hired hand. This speech is essential to understanding what the parable is all about; it is the Pharisaic solution to the Jewish dilemma. In short, Pharisaism enjoins repentance defined by a determination to fulfill all legal and ritual obligations owed God. The prodigal is prepared to do exactly that.

Now comes the dramatic climax to the story, another totally unexpected occurrence. As the young man trudges down the familiar lane leading home, the waiting father sees him coming. The father casts aside all social

---

[54]See T. E. Schmidt, "Taxes," *DJG* 804-7.
[55]See M. J. Wilkins," Sinner," *DJG* 757-60.
[56]For what follows, I am indebted to Kenneth E. Bailey, *Poet and Peasant: A Literary Cultural Approach to the Parables in Luke* (Grand Rapids: Eerdmans, 1976).

convention and runs to his son, enfolding him in a loving embrace. The son begins his rehearsed speech but is only able to get out the words expressing his guilt. His father will not let him finish. Instead, he restores the contrite son to his place in the family, bypassing any suggestion of being a hired hand, and orders a sumptuous celebration.

What is the point? God is the waiting *and welcoming* Father. The surprise—Jesus' parables typically include something quite unexpected—is that the father accepts his wayward son without requiring full repayment. In other words, acceptance into the family—that is, the kingdom of God—is a matter of grace, not legal obligation. The compassionate, merciful father had already forgiven his wayward son as soon as he acknowledged his guilt. Such a view of God is unparalleled in Second Temple Judaism, where God was indeed waiting, but he was waiting for certain requirements to be met, a repayment schedule. Then, and only then, would God act in compassion and forgiveness.

The sequel confirms that we are on the right track. The elder son demands satisfaction. He wants his younger brother to repay the debt and keep all obligations as a precondition for acceptance in the family. Surely, we overhear the Pharisaic response to Jesus' teaching in the elder son's tirade against his father. Remarkably, the father shows the same compassion for his elder son as he had for the younger. We realize that in fact this is a story about *two* lost sons. One is openly such; the other is oblivious to the fact, beguiled as he is by legalistic righteousness. The genius of this parable is heightened by its open-ended nature. Jesus does not tell us whether the elder son genuinely repented and accepted his father's grace or not. The reader is forced to decide how it turned out and to make a similar decision for his or her own life. Given the total context of the Gospels, one can only conclude, sadly, that most Pharisees sided with the elder brother. In this, however, they have had lots of company within Christendom, where various forms of legalist righteousness have also flourished.

Another parable, using the imagery of a wedding banquet, casts a new light on the nature of God. In Matthew 22:1-10 God is portrayed as a king sending out invitations to a wedding banquet for his son (Jesus). Two different sets of slaves are delegated to dispatch the invitations, probably the first being the OT prophets and the second being Christian apostles and prophets. In both instances, however, the invitations are spurned, and the second group of messengers is murdered. The king responds by avenging the murders and burning the city (Jerusalem). Behind this story lies a sad reality: the majority of Jews reject Jesus' message about the kingdom. Now the king makes a renewed effort to invite guests to the wedding. This time everyone who is found is invited, "both good and bad" (Mt 22:10). In light of the neighboring parable of the wicked tenants (Mt 21:33-44), we conclude that this "mixed bag" is made up of Gentiles. Luke provides a different version of the parable of the wedding invitations. The climactic moment is the master's order "Go out into the roads and lanes, and *compel* people to come in, so that my house may be filled" (Lk 14:23 [my italics]). The point is that God is not passively waiting for repentance; rather, he is actively seeking out sinners.

Of course, the suggestion that Gentiles were now welcome at the same banquet table came as a shock to most Jews in the first century.[57] Luke anticipates this reversal of fortunes with his programmatic story of Jesus' visit to his hometown synagogue at Nazareth (Lk 4:16-30). Jesus capped

Table 4.2. Jesus and Judaism on Reconciliation.

Judaism (Pharisees, Sadducees, Essenes)	Jesus
People repent and repay their debt by performance ("deeds of the law")	God summons and invites sinners to accept forgiveness in the new covenant community
God forgives and accepts them into the covenant community	They respond out of gratitude and love with obedience ("good deeds")

his sermon there by retelling two OT stories about God's grace to Gentiles, one about the widow of Zarephath, the other about Naaman the Syrian (Lk 4:24-27). The Jewish response was visceral and violent (Lk 4:28-29).

Table 4.2 contrasts Jesus' view of reconciliation with that of his religious contemporaries.

God as heavenly father. Just as remarkable for its new perspective is Jesus' view of God as heavenly Father. Even the highly skeptical Jesus Seminar prints the word *Father* in red, affirming its authenticity as something that Jesus actually said. In Aramaic this is *'abbā'*, a term of endearment that Jewish children used (and still do) for their fathers. In English, perhaps the closest equivalent is the word *daddy*.[58] Joachim Jeremias claimed that Jesus' use of *'abbā'* ("Father") for God was unparalleled in Palestin-

---

[57]On the differing Jewish views of the fate of Gentiles in the end times, see David S. Russell, *The Method and Message of Jewish Apocalyptic, 200 BC-AD 100* (OTL; Philadelphia: Westminster Press, 1964), pp. 297-303.

[58]James Dunn objects to the translation "daddy" ("an early conclusion which Jeremias soon qualified, but which has come back to haunt the study of the Gospel traditions ever since" ["Prayer," *DJG* 617]). For a defense of Jeremias's original conclusion, see Stein, *Method and Message*, pp. 82-87.

ian Judaism.[59] Evidence from extant Jewish prayers, as found in the OT, Apocrypha, Pseudepigrapha, Dead Sea Scrolls, rabbinic literature, *Shemoneh Esreh* and *Kaddish*, suggests that ʾabbāʾ would have been considered too intimate and familiar, not appropriate for the awesome God of the universe. All the more remarkable, then, that Jesus not only used it in his prayer language (Mk 14:36) but also enjoined it upon his followers as the preferred address to God (Mt 6:9), so that it became a hallmark of the Jesus movement.[60] The fact that Greek-speaking Christians actually used the Aramaic word ʾabbāʾ in prayer (see Rom 8:15; Gal 4:6) makes sense only if we assume that the practice goes back to Jesus himself and was imitated by his earliest followers.[61]

This practice of Jesus is an important piece of evidence in the search to understand Jesus' self-consciousness. Jesus viewed God as his heavenly Father in a unique sense. Several passages draw attention to this unique relationship. At the conclusion of the Sermon on the Mount Jesus solemnly warns his audience that a confession of his lordship is a prerequisite for entrance into the eschatological kingdom. However, profession must be validated by practice conforming to God's will, the God whom Jesus calls "my Father in heaven" (Mt 7:21). Jesus' extraordinary juxtaposition of his role and that of the Father at the final assize goes far beyond what could be predicated of mere mortals and clearly implies Jesus' divinity. Equally dramatic is Matthew 10:32, in which acknowledgment of Jesus is a prerequisite for acknowledgment by the Father, again referred to as "my Father." Of similar import is the parable of the sheep and goats, in which the Son of Man performs the actual separation and announces to the faithful, "Come, you that are blessed by my Father, inherit the kingdom prepared for you from the foundation of the world" (Mt 25:34). The celebrated "Johannine thunderbolt" (Mt 11:25) elevates Jesus to a position of unrivaled sonship, indeed, from Matthew's perspective, divine sonship, with all attendant rights and privileges (see Mt 1:23; 3:17; 17:5; 28:19-20). Jesus prophesies that after his death he will return as the Son of Man, "in the glory of his

---

[59]Joachim Jeremias, *The Prayers of Jesus* (SBT 6; Naperville, Ill.: Allenson, 1967), pp. 15-29, 57-65.

[60]Gottlob Schrenk observes, "The new thing in the usage is that an everyday infant sound is applied without inhibition to God. To Jewish sensibility this is too familiar. For Jesus it is the simplest and sincerest conceivable term to express God's attitude and it also implies a rejection of all religious pretension. Hence ʾabba is a basic word of faith in the revelations of Jesus and the confession of His community. Yet it does not imply a banal self-assurance which takes things for granted" ("πατήρ," *TDNT* 5:985).

[61]James Dunn agrees with this conclusion ("Prayer," *DJG* 618-19). See also Stein, *Method and Message*, pp. 80-87; Schrenk, "πατήρ," *TDNT* 5:984-85.

Father," rendering judgment on all humanity (Mt 16:27). Jesus assures his disciples that agreement in prayer, by as few as two disciples, secures an answer from his Father (Mt 18:19-20). This is mediated by his spiritual presence among them, once again assuming a status that can only be described as divine. Nor can one leave out of reckoning the moving prayer of Gethsemane, highlighting the unique role of the Son in redemption: "My Father, if it is possible, let this cup pass from me; yet not what I want but what you want" (Mt 26:39). In the Markan version, as we noted, the term for "Father" is the Aramaic ʾabbā̓ (Mk 14:36).

Jesus taught that God the heavenly Father embraces those who embrace the kingdom. Although never sharing his exclusive relationship with the Father (see Jn 20:17), Jesus did teach believers to call upon God as their heavenly Father (Mt 6:9). This new relationship affords unparalleled privileges and power. Believers are urged to entreat their Father for all their needs, for he not only knows their needs but also delights in taking care of their needs (Mt 6:25-34; 7:7-11; Lk 12:30-31). He cares for, protects, and avenges his little children (Mt 10:29-31; 18:10-14). Among the many good gifts of the Father, none is more precious than the ministry of the Holy Spirit in their lives (Mt 10:20; Lk 11:13; 24:49). Believers are the recipients of divine revelation concerning this unprecedented new phase of redemptive history now unfolding (Mt 16:17; Lk 10:22-24). Both now and at the consummation the Father lavishly bestows upon his children authority, dominion and glory (Mt 20:23; 25:34; Lk 9:26; 12:32; 22:29).

This new relationship carries with it, however, heavy responsibility and should not be taken lightly. Being members of the family of God requires an entirely new *modus vivendi*. Grudges and offenses cannot be ignored or stored; they must be dealt with by means of forgiveness (Mt 6:14-15; 18:21-35). A failure to do so may indicate false paternity! Life together in the family of God mandates the unique fatherhood of God (Mt 23:9). No human teacher or leader ought ever to usurp God's role as the one and only heavenly Father. Furthermore, this confession involves a truly radical idea: "The greatest among you will be your servant" (Mt 23:11). How antithetical this kingdom principle stands over against the reality of "sacred politics" from Jesus' day to our own!

Jesus' understanding of God as his heavenly Father is unparalleled in Jewish sources. It shapes the entire character of the Jesus movement and was a decisive factor in the parting of the ways between church and synagogue. For mainstream Judaism, the divine sonship of Jesus undermines monotheism. Christianity reaffirms monotheism but reformulates it in such a way as to account for the indisputable sense of divine sonship experienced and expressed by Jesus.[62] I will have much more to say about this when we investigate Johannine theology.

God as righteous judge. Jesus' religious contemporaries criticized his view of God as resulting in "cheap grace." The story of the sinful woman in Luke 7:36-50 clearly implies this. Does not God take sin seriously? The answer, of course, is yes, he does. Jesus maintains a careful balance in this regard. God does not downplay sin; it remains an affront to his holiness that must be dealt with. The Disciples' Prayer dispels any notion that God is like a doting father who nods and winks at the transgressions of his kids. "Hallowed be your name" (Mt 6:9). God is holy love, and holy love does not traffic in wishy-washy sentimentality.

The fact that God is a seeking God creates another reality. Jesus' teaching repeatedly stresses that God holds people accountable for their deeds, and that there is a day of reckoning. In a most uncomfortable saying Jesus assures his listeners, "On the day of judgment you will have to give an account for every careless word you utter; for by your words you will be justified, and by your words you will be condemned" (Mt 12:36-37). God does not ignore violations of his will as the seeking God. In fact, he is simultaneously the demanding God. What he demands is an immediate response to his overture of grace and forgiveness; to spurn this incredible offer is to take one's chances on the day of judgment and "hope for the best." And there can be little doubt what the "best" might be.

God's retributive justice rings out loud and clear in Jesus' teaching. At the conclusion of the healing miracle of the centurion's servant, Jesus warned his listeners that "many will come from east and west" to the great eschatological feast, "while the heirs of the kingdom will be thrown into the outer darkness, where there will be weeping and gnashing of teeth" (Mt 8:11-12; cf. Lk 13:28-29). Six times in Matthew's Gospel this place of separation is described by the phrase "weeping and gnashing of teeth" (Mt 8:12; 13:42, 50; 22:13; 24:51; 25:30). Clearly, the seeking God is also a separating God. There is no maudlin sentimentality here. In seemingly contradictory imagery, this dark place of exclusion is also described as a place of fire and burning, a truly terrifying prospect. Jesus warns that even calling someone a fool makes one liable to "the hell [Gehenna] of fire" (Mt 5:22). In Gehenna the fire "never goes out" (Mk 9:43), it "is not quenched" (Mk 9:48); it is eternal in duration.[63]

Dealing with the doctrine of everlasting punishment is one of the

---

[62]See Larry W. Hurtado, *One God, One Lord: Early Christian Devotion and Ancient Jewish Monotheism* (Philadelphia: Fortress, 1988).

[63]For background on Gehenna, see Joachim Jeremias, "γέεννα," *TDNT* 1:657-58.

most difficult issues that evangelicals currently face and is a source of contentious debate. We all react with unease at the notion of God inflicting everlasting torment on unbelievers, even the notoriously wicked. It somehow seems beneath him to resort to such draconian measures. Why not rather simply annihilate them? Several prominent evangelicals have cautiously urged reconsideration of this position.[64] Already in the second century A.D. Origen argued for restorationism, the teaching that the wicked, even Satan, are ultimately purged and welcomed into everlasting felicity. Jesus' teaching on Gehenna can hardly be squared with this idea. Although the concept of annihilation versus everlasting punishment is appealing, it too is hard to reconcile with Scripture and the predominant stance of historic orthodoxy on this issue. The precise nature of hell, however, should be left an open question, given the metaphorical descriptions. We are on safer ground simply to assert that those not genuinely responding to God's gracious invitation experience exclusion from the Father's glory.[65]

From the standpoint of Jesus' contemporaries, what was radical in his teaching was not that he believed in the reality of Gehenna, since most affirmed this, but rather that he believed that many Jewish people, including respected religious leaders (see Mt 23:15, 33), would end up there. Perhaps just as shocking was the notion that many Gentiles would escape its flames. Although Jewish opinion varied in the Second Temple period, and some Jewish thinkers, following the lead of the OT (see Is 19:25; 45:20, 22; 51:5; 56:7; 60:11; Zech 8:23; 14:16), envisioned a great conversion of Gentiles in the end times (*1 En.* 10:21; *Sib. Or.* 3:195, 716, 725, 772, 740; *T. Benj.* 9:2; 10:5, 9; *T. Levi* 18:9; *T. Naph.* 8:3), others unreservedly consigned many, most or all of them to the torments of Gehenna (*1 En.* 90:18; 91:12, 14; *Pss. Sol.* 17:17, 32; *Jub.* 15:31; *T. Mos.* 10:7-10; *2 Bar.* 72:2-6). Among the Jewish people, only apostates and renegades were consigned to Gehenna. On this particular point Jesus' view was actually closer to that of the Essenes, who also predicted the torments of Gehenna for rebellious fellow Jews. In light of the sectarian literature as a whole, this included virtually all Jews

---

[64]Thus, for example, John R. W. Stott, "Judgment and Hell," in *Evangelical Essentials: A Liberal-Evangelical Dialogue*, by David L. Lawrence, with response from John Stott (Downers Grove, Ill.: InterVarsity Press, 1988), pp. 312-29; Clark H. Pinnock, "The Conditional View," in *Four Views on Hell*, ed. William Crockett (Counterpoints; Grand Rapids: Zondervan, 1992), pp. 135-67; idem, *A Wideness in God's Mercy: The Finality of Jesus Christ in a World of Religions* (Grand Rapids: Zondervan, 1992); Edward W. Fudge, *The Fire That Consumes: A Biblical and Historical Study of the Doctrine of Final Punishment* (Lincoln, Nebr.: iUniverse.com, 2001).
[65]See Timothy R. Phillips, "Hell," *EDBT* 338-40; P. S. Johnstone, "Hell," *NDBT* 542-44.

who did not adhere to the tenets of their sect.[66]

I conclude by noting that Jesus also pronounced historical judgment upon his contemporaries who rejected his preaching of the kingdom. There is every indication that Jesus believed that God himself authorized these historical judgments (Mk 13:20, 32). While being led to his execution, Jesus warns the women who were bewailing his fate, "Daughters of Jerusalem, do not weep for me, but weep for yourselves and for your children" (Lk 23:28). He goes on to prophesy a devastating judgment upon the city (Lk 23:29-31), literally fulfilled some forty years later in the siege and destruction of Jerusalem (A.D. 68-70). The siege of Jerusalem was also prophesied, according to Luke, during Jesus' journey to Jerusalem (Lk 13:34-35), on the day of his triumphal entry into Jerusalem (Lk 19:41-44), and again during his last week in Jerusalem (Lk 21:5-24 = Mk 13:2, 14-23; Mt 24:2, 15-28 [the Olivet discourse]) in the vicinity of the temple. These passages either intimate or depict in detail the enormous suffering and tragedy to befall that generation ("For at that time there will be great suffering, such as has not been from the beginning of the world until now, no, and never will be" [Mt 24:21 = Mk 13:19]).

Drawing Jesus' particular condemnation were the cities nearest his base of operations along the Sea of Galilee. On the judgment day Chorazin, Bethsaida and Capernaum will all fare worse than predominantly Gentile cities, such as Tyre and Sidon, and that very epitome of evil, the ancient city of Sodom (Mt 11:20-24). Jesus, like the OT prophets, probably telescoped the near and far dimensions of the Day of the Lord into one, unified picture. Thus the impending historical destruction of these cities during the First Jewish Revolt (A.D. 66-73) foreshadows eschatological judgment at the great day.

Jesus' conception of God marks him off from the various streams of Judaism in the first century. This unique God of the kingdom necessarily yields a unique kingdom of God. And since one's understanding of God greatly influences one's understanding of ethics, we are not surprised that here too significant differences surface between Jesus and his coreligionists. This is our next stop.

APPENDIX: WAS JESUS UNIQUE IN ADDRESSING GOD AS "ABBA"?

James Dunn thinks that Joachim Jeremias overstated his case and adduces several passages in which the Greek *patēr* ("father") is used in direct address to God (Wis 14:3; Sir 23:1, 4; 51:10; 3 Macc 6:3, 8; *m. Ta'an.* 3:8),

---

[66]See 1QS 4:11-14, the translation in Michael O. Wise, *The Dead Sea Scrolls: A New Translation* (San Francisco: HarperSanFrancisco, 1996), pp. 130-31. For further discussion, see Martin G. Abegg Jr., "Retribution," *EDSS* 2:767-70.

presumably with the same familial and emotional connotations as *'abbā'*. Dunn could have added Wisdom 2:16; Tobit 13:4 from the Apocrypha, *Jubilees* 1:14, 28; 19:29; 3 Maccabees 5:7; *Testament of Levi* 18:6; *Testament of Judah* 24:2 from the Pseudepigrapha (though the last two may be Christian interpolations), and 1QHᵃ 9:35 from the Dead Sea Scrolls (= 1QHᵃ 17:35 in some editions of the Dead Sea Scrolls). In reply, three points should be made. First, it is unlikely that *patēr* and *'abbā'* convey precisely the same nuance. Second, unfortunately, we do not possess the Hebrew text for any of the Sirach passages cited above, which, by the way, is the only Palestinian text cited; the others are from Diaspora works.[67] Third, in 1QHᵃ 9:35 (= 17:35) God is not addressed as "Father" but rather is likened to a father, and the word is *'ab*, not *'abbā'*. Nor does the text of *Mishnah Taʿanit* 3:8 use the word *'abbā'* to address God. Rabbi Honi simply likens himself to a son or member of God's family. The passage goes as follows: "Lord of the world! Your children have turned to me, for before you I am like a member of the family. . . . [Simeon ben Sheṭaḥ says to Honi] For you importune before the Omnipresent, so he does what you want, like a son who importunes his father *['ab]*, so he does what he wants." Note the more formal address actually used. In short, I think that Jeremias was correct.

For Further Discussion

1. What is it about the "noneschatological" view of the kingdom of God that makes it so attractive to modern, rationalistic readers of the Gospels?

2. What understanding of Jesus provided the "consistent eschatological" view a powerful argument against the noneschatological view?

3. Is the "realized eschatological" view of C. H. Dodd a return to Adolf von Harnack's position? Why or why not?

4. How does "inaugurated eschatology" attempt to make sense of all the data? Does it succeed?

5. Summarize the various understandings of the kingdom of God. Which of these options makes the best sense of the biblical data?

For Further Reading

Beasley-Murray, G. R. *Jesus and the Kingdom of God.* Grand Rapids: Eerdmans, 1986.

---

[67]For discussion and translation into English of the surviving fragments from Qumran and Masada, see *The Dead Sea Scrolls Bible*, trans. Martin Abegg Jr., Peter Flint and Eugene Ulrich (San Francisco: HaperSanFrancisco, 1999), pp. 597-606.

Caragounis, C. C. "Kingdom of God/Heaven." *DJG* 417-30.

Chilton, Bruce, and J. I. H. McDonald. *Jesus and the Ethics of the Kingdom*. Grand Rapids: Eerdmans, 1987.

Duling, Dennis C. "Kingdom of God, Kingdom of Heaven." *ABD* 4:50-69.

Evans, O. E. "Kingdom of God." *IDB* 3:17-24.

France, R. T. "Kingdom of God." *DTIB* 420-22.

Goldsworthy, G. "Kingdom of God." *NDBT* 615-20.

Guthrie, D. "Jesus Christ." *ZPEB* 3:560-72.

Hurst, L. D. "Ethics of Jesus." *DJG* 210-22.

Ladd, George E. *Jesus and the Kingdom: The Eschatology of Biblical Realism*. New York: Harper & Row, 1964.

———. "Kingdom of God." *ISBE* 3:23-29.

———. *The Presence of the Future: The Eschatology of Biblical Realism*. Grand Rapids: Eerdmans, 1974.

———. *A Theology of the New Testament*, edited by Donald A. Hagner, pp. 31-245. Rev. ed. Grand Rapids: Eerdmans, 1993.

Marshall, I. H. "Kingdom of God, of Heaven." *ZPEB* 3:801-9.

Ridderbos, Herman. *The Coming of the Kingdom*, translated by H. de Jongste, edited by Raymond O. Zorn. Philadelphia: P & R Publishing, 1962.

———. "Kingdom of God, Kingdom of Heaven." In *The New Bible Dictionary*, ed. F. F. Bruce et al., pp. 693-97. Leicester, U.K.: Inter-Varsity Press, 1962.

Riesner, R. "Teacher." *DJG* 807-11.

Scaer, David P. "Beatitudes." *EDBT* 53-55.

———. "Sermon on the Mount." *EDBT* 723-25.

Snodgrass, K. R. "Parable." *DJG* 591-601.

Stanton, G. N. "Sermon on the Mount/Plain." *DJG* 735-44.

Stein, Robert H. "Kingdom of God." *EDBT* 451-54.

———. *The Method and Message of Jesus' Teachings*. Philadelphia: Westminster Press, 1978.

White, R. E. O. "Ethics." *EDBT* 213-16.

Willis, Wendell, ed. *The Kingdom of God in 20th-Century Interpretation*. Peabody, Mass.: Hendrickson, 1987.

5

The Ethics of Jesus

A man's ethical behavior should be based effectually on sympathy, education, and social ties; no religious basis is necessary. Man would indeed be in a poor way if he had to be restrained by fear of punishment and hope of reward after death.

Albert Einstein

Christianity has not been tried and found wanting. It has been found difficult and left untried.

G. K. Chesterton

ETHICS HAS TO DO WITH THE "OUGHTNESS" OF LIFE; that is, how ought we live? What is the right thing to do in a given situation? Even more fundamentally, how does one determine what is right and what is wrong? These are crucially important questions. Jesus of Nazareth has been acclaimed by many as the greatest ethical teacher in human history, and that alone is sufficient reason to carefully examine his teaching. To those, however, who have committed their lives to him as Savior and Lord, Jesus ethics involve much more than an intellectual appreciation; it entails obedience to a way of life (Mt 7:21, 24; 1 Pet 2:21). Significantly, the Jesus movement was first called "the Way" (Acts 9:2). This chapter seeks to summarize what Jesus believed "the Way" should look like in terms of attitudes and actions on the part of those who commit to the kingdom of God.

Laying out the ethics of Jesus is not a straightforward task. Even assuming the essential reliability of the Gospels, evangelical biblical theologians must negotiate difficulties. Chief among these is the fact that Jesus himself did not provide a systematic discussion of ethics.[1] One must extract his ethical teachings from the diverse sayings recorded by the evangelists. We lack the luxury of a carefully structured discourse on ethics such as Aristotle's *Nicomachean Ethics*. Furthermore, given that Jesus' sayings are set in the context of a mission announcing the long-expected kingdom of God to a first-century Palestinian-Jewish audience, not surprisingly, Jesus' ethics are relatively limited in scope. Numerous modern ethical questions and dilemmas are simply not addressed in the Gospel traditions. In addition, Jesus' teaching involves apparent contradictions, impossibly high standards, and, at the very least, instances of figurative speech and hyperbole designed to make a dramatic point. Having said all that, I still believe it possible to synthesize a body of material foundational to any discussion of ethics. The ethical teaching of Jesus has stood the test of time and will continue to influence the lives of individuals and societies in the new millennium.

In order to summarize Jesus' teaching on ethics, I select one of Matthew's five discourses, the Sermon on the Mount. This offers a concise summary of Jesus' ethics and will be supplemented by a few related texts.[2]

INTRODUCTORY ISSUES RELATING TO THE SERMON ON THE MOUNT

The unity and authenticity of the discourse. Matthew's Gospel consists of five major discourses inserted into the narrative of Jesus' birth, ministry, and passion (Mt 5:1-7:27; 10:5-42; 13:1-52; 18:1-35; 24:3-25:46). I follow the majority view of NT scholars in assuming that Matthew makes use of Mark as his basic document. In fact, Matthew incorporates about 76 percent of Mark's material. To this Matthew adds Q material (sayings common to Matthew and Luke but not found in Mark) and his own, unique material designated as M.[3]

The first discourse, the Sermon on the Mount, probably owes its present shape to the editorial work of Matthew. That is, these three chapters condense and topically arrange material Jesus delivered on numerous occasions. In short, Matthew provides a digest of Jesus' teaching that directly

---

[1]For a brief overview of the problem, see Robert H. Stein, *The Method and Message of Jesus' Teachings* (Philadelphia: Westminster Press, 1978), pp. 88-89.

[2]G. N. Stanton rightly reminds us that "important ethical sayings of Jesus . . . are not included in Matthew's Sermon, and not all the traditions in these chapters [Mt 5—7] are ethical" ("Sermon on the Mount/Plain," *DJG* 736).

[3]For a succinct summary, see R. H. Stein, "Synoptic Problem," *DJG* 784-92.

addresses the issue of how one ought to live in the kingdom. The similarity to Luke 6:20-49, the so-called Sermon on the Plain, is probably best explained as reflecting a Lukan version of the same basic material found in Matthew. Each evangelist shapes the traditions in keeping with his own concerns and audience.

The nature of the Sermon. The placement of the Sermon on the Mount assists us in determining the purpose of the discourse. Following a genealogy delineating Jesus' Davidic descent (Mt 1:1-17), a birth narrative (Mt 1:18-25), a visit by astrologers from the east (Mt 2:1-12), an escape to Egypt no more than two years after his birth (Mt 2:13-18) and a return to Nazareth (Mt 2:19-23), Matthew picks up the familiar Markan narrative. This includes the preliminary preaching of John the Baptist (Mt 3:1-12), Jesus' baptism (Mt 3:13-17), his temptation by Satan (Mt 4:1-11), and the arrest of John and withdrawal of Jesus to Galilee (Mt 4:12-17). This latter section is capped by this announcement: "From that time Jesus began to proclaim, 'Repent, for the kingdom of heaven has come near'" (Mt 4:17). Then follows the Sermon on the Mount, Jesus' first extended discussion about the kingdom of God. As such, it assumes programmatic importance.

Very important for understanding the nature of the discourse is recognizing the identity of the initial audience. According to Matthew 5:1-2, after withdrawing from the crowds, Jesus addresses his disciples. This suggests that the discourse is primarily intended for those who have already committed to the kingdom. A survey of the contents confirms that most of the instruction is aimed at Jesus' followers. The sermon is thus not so much kerygma (evangelistic preaching) as it is didache (ethical instruction and exhortation). By design, it teaches disciples how to live in the kingdom.

On the other hand, how the sermon ends merits attention: the two ways (Mt 7:13-14), false prophets (Mt 7:15-20), false professors (Mt 7:21-23) and two foundations (Mt 7:24-27) evidence an evangelistic thrust. Although the initial audience was comprised only of disciples, by the time Jesus finishes, some who are noncommitted have joined the crowd of listeners. It is to this latter group that the conclusion of the sermon is directed. They must make a decision for or against the kingdom.

The structure of the Sermon. I think that a good description of the sermon is the "Charter of the Kingdom."[4] Here are standards and guidelines for life in the kingdom. The following is an outline of the sermon reflecting this understanding:

---

[4]For this formulation, I am indebted to Stanley Ellison, unpublished notes from "Survey of the New Testament," Western Baptist Seminary, Portland, Oregon, 1966.

- The Character of Kingdom Citizens (Mt 5:3-12)
- The Calling of Kingdom Citizens (Mt 5:13-16)
- The Conduct of Kingdom Citizens (Mt 5:17—7:12)
- The Challenge of Kingdom Citizenship (Mt 7:13-27)

The background of the Sermon. Halakah refers to the Jewish oral laws that supplement and explain the 613 laws found in the Pentateuch and forms the core of the Mishnah. In a somewhat analogous way, Jesus' sermon elaborates his own distinctive halakah. The sermon breathes the atmosphere of Second Temple Judaism, with many parallels in theme, diction and style. Gerald Friedlander has shown that virtually all the statements in Mt 5—7 can be paralleled in the Talmud and other Jewish sources.[5] And yet, at the same time, the sermon stands in striking contrast to Jewish halakic discussions as exemplified in the Mishnah and the Talmud.[6] As George Ladd aptly observes, "To read a passage from the Mishnah is a different experience from reading the Sermon on the Mount."[7] The uniqueness and genius of Jesus as an ethical teacher come to expression in his sagacious selection of moral precepts, his rejection of legalistic encumbrance, and his emphasis upon God's grace and love as the heart of true religion. But perhaps even more remarkable is his implicit claim to embody and bestow true righteousness.[8]

SUMMARY OF THE SERMON

The character of kingdom citizens (Mt 5:3-12). The Beatitudes find their roots in the sapiential and hymnic literature of the OT (e.g., Ps 1:1; 32:1-2; 144:15; Prov 3:13; Dan 12:12).[9] In the OT one never finds more than two Beatitudes bunched together, but an interesting parallel in the Qumran literature exists in which we have a text containing five Beatitudes (4Q525). The beginning of this text has been lost, and there may actually have been more than five. The wording of the individual Beatitudes displays several parallels to those of Jesus.[10] Matthew 5:3-12 consists of eight beatitudes in third-person singular with an expansion of the eighth in second-person

---

[5]See Gerald Friedlander, *The Jewish Sources of the Sermon on the Mount* (1911; reprint, New York: KTAV, 1969).

[6]For examples, see Brad H. Young, *Jesus the Jewish Theologian* (Peabody, Mass.: Hendrickson, 1995), pp. 49-126.

[7]George E. Ladd, *A Theology of the New Testament*, ed. Donald A. Hagner (rev. ed.; Grand Rapids: Eerdmans, 1993), p. 126.

[8]For a helpful discussion of this point, see Stein, *Method and Message*, pp. 109-11.

[9]See Raymond F. Collins, "Beatitudes," *ABD* 1:629-31.

[10]See Benedict T. Viviano, "Beatitudes," *EDSS* 1:89-90.

singular. Also, the first and the eighth are cast in the present tense, while the second through seventh are in the future tense.

Theologically, the Beatitudes raise an important question: Are these entrance requirements or eschatological blessings bestowed upon the righteous? In other words, do they spell out the conditions that must be met before one can enter the kingdom, or do they describe the blessedness of the righteous both now and at the consummation of the kingdom? A close reading of the text provides an answer that coheres with the message of Jesus as a whole. The first thing to notice is the echo of Isaiah 61:1-3 in our text. There, in a passage having strong affinities to the four Servant Songs of Isaiah 42; 49; 50; 52—53, we have eschatological blessings bestowed on the righteous both in the "year of the LORD's favor and "the day of vengeance of our God" (Is 61:2). The language recalls the OT Day of the Lord. Significantly, Jesus' Beatitudes strike a similar chord. Second, Matthew constructs the passage using the technique of inclusio—that is, the envelope or sandwich technique using an A-B-A pattern. As we noted above, the first and last Beatitudes are couched in the present tense; all the inner Beatitudes are in future tense. The significance of this lies in its connection to Jesus' teaching on the kingdom. There is both a "now but not yet" character to these Beatitudes. The first and last describe the "now"; the second through seventh describe the "not yet." By their very phrasing, the Beatitudes express the essential nature of the kingdom. Already those who commit themselves to Jesus are in the kingdom (first Beatitude). That kingdom necessarily entails suffering and persecution (eighth Beatitude and its expansion). Whereas the righteous may already have a small foretaste of comfort, righteousness and mercy, they have hardly experienced what it means to inherit the earth and see God. These are eschatological blessings bestowed at the consummation of the kingdom. Thus I conclude that the Beatitudes, by their very construction and phrasing, point to the "now but not yet" character of the kingdom as taught by Jesus. As such, the Beatitudes are not entrance requirements, though they are essential attitudes that should increasingly characterize kingdom citizens. Manifestations of these attitudes in this present age are harbingers of life together in the world to come.

What follows is a brief description of attitudes characterizing kingdom citizens. In each instance the person possessing this attitude is said to be "blessed." The Greek word *makarios* denotes a "nearly incomprehensible happiness . . . a deep inner joy."[11] This state of blessedness and happiness

---

[11]Donald A. Hagner, *Matthew 1—13* (WBC 33A; Dallas: Word, 1993), p. 88.

has its source in the heavenly Father and is a by-product of being in the kingdom.[12] The Beatitudes are fundamental for understanding Jesus' ethics. Just as the Ten Commandments stand at the very center of the great law code of Moses, so the Beatitudes constitute the heart of kingdom life and behavior.

"Blessed are the poor in spirit." Kingdom citizens recognize their spiritual poverty. This is another way of expressing true humility. A fundamental difference between Jesus and the Pharisees emerges at precisely this point (cf. Lk 18:9-14). The righteous realize that they have nothing to offer God. Like beggars, they hold out empty hands and receive the Father's totally undeserved mercy and grace. Possessing the kingdom is like the simple trust of a child (Mk 10:13-16; Mt 18:1-5). Luke's version of this beatitude, by the omission of the phrase "in spirit," seems to refer to literal poverty (Lk 6:20). Matthew stresses the spiritual dimension. There is a close connection in the OT, Second Temple Judaism and the NT between literal and spiritual poverty; in actuality, they often overlap.[13] Those who have nothing in this world are more apt to realize their shortcomings for the world to come (Mt 19:23-26; Lk 16:19-31). Jesus' ministry, patterned after that of the Servant of the Lord in Isaiah (Is 53:2-3; 61:1-3), was noteworthy for its constant concern for the poor and downtrodden masses (Mt 9:36; 15:32). On the other hand, Jesus by no means consigns all who are rich in worldly goods to Gehenna. After all, a few of Jesus' followers, though perhaps not wealthy by modern standards, were rather well off (see Lk 19:1-10). Jesus does, however, warn against the seduction of wealth and the false sense of security that it provides (Mt 6:24; 16:26).[14]

"Blessed are those who mourn." Kingdom citizens express sorrow over their unfaithfulness and moral failures; they exhibit genuine penitence. At no point does the kingdom citizen "arrive" while living in the "now" phase of the kingdom. Only at the consummation, the "not yet," do the righteous receive that ultimate comfort, glorification. Only then will they have no occasion to grieve their heavenly Father, since they will reflect his righteousness. In the "now" they do have this consolation: their Father in heaven forgives their trespasses and gives grace leading to increasing conformity to his high expectations. As with the first beatitude, however, one should not construe this attitude in strictly spiritual terms; mourning is often oc-

---

[12]Friedrich Hauck says that "it refers overwhelmingly to the distinctive religious joy which accrues to man from his share in the salvation of the kingdom of God" ("μακάριος," *TDNT* 4:367).

[13]See Ernst Bammel, "πτωχός, πτωχεία, πτωχεύω," *TDNT* 6:899-901.

[14]See P. H. Davids, "Rich and Poor," *DJG* 701-10.

casioned by the inevitable tragedies and sufferings of this life. Kingdom citizens must steel themselves to a grim reality: suffering is still very much a part of the "now" phase of the kingdom.[15] In the face of such mourning, the hope of everlasting comfort sustains the righteous.

"Blessed are the meek." Kingdom citizens do not demand their rights. This is the essential meaning of "meek" (Greek *praÿs;* Hebrew *ʿānāwîm*). Rather than resort to intimidation and violence, the meek entrust their cause to their heavenly Father; he is their gracious defender and righteous judge. An extended description of the meek is found in Matthew 5:38-42, summarized in the notion of nonretaliation. This attitude, so challenging and countercultural, is embodied in Jesus' own life and ministry—"I am gentle and humble in heart" (Mt 11:29)—most notably during his trial and passion (Mt 26:51-54, 62-63; 27:14; Lk 23:34). His entire ministry fulfills the messianic prophecies of the Servant of the Lord and the royal son of David, both of whom are portrayed as demonstrating remarkable meekness (Is 42:2-3; Zech 9:9). Once again, the peasants of Palestine, by virtue of their nearly powerless position, resonated with this startling reversal of fortune, the prospect of inheriting the land.[16] The beatitude echoes Psalm 37:11: "But the meek shall inherit the land." In its original context "the land" referred to the historic land of Israel. Jesus seems to enlarge the referent to include the entire earth. The promise is eschatological and looks to the consummation of the kingdom.

"Blessed are those who hunger and thirst for righteousness." This beatitude stands as the centerpiece of the Beatitudes. The first three Beatitudes lead inevitably to this one, and the next four Beatitudes are natural consequences flowing out of it. Thus, besides inclusio (a framing or bracketing device whereby the opening and closing ideas match), there is also chiasm (an arrangement of parallel members of a literary unit forming an A-B-B-A pattern) in the Beatitudes. A deep-seated desire for God's righteousness drives the kingdom citizen; it is a passion likened to the strongest drives in human nature, the need for water and food. As seen in the following sections of the sermon, the true nature of righteousness is of central importance to the entire sermon. In fact, Matthew 5:20—7:12 unpacks the meaning of righteousness; it is both a relationship, being rightly related to God, and behavior, doing that which accords with God's will.

---

[15]Rudolf Bultmann holds in balance both aspects of the mourning here described ("πένθος, πενθέω," *TDNT* 6:42-43). This theological truth must be steadfastly maintained in the face of certain versions of the gospel that promise wealth, health and happiness to all who truly exercise faith in Jesus. Such perversions show how powerful wishful thinking can be.

[16]See Friedrich Hauck and Siegfried Schulz, "πραΰς, πραΰτης," *TDNT* 6:649.

"Blessed are the merciful." Those who are merciful recognize and re-spond to the deep need of others, whether spiritual or physical. They are not content to bemoan and berate; they accept the needy as persons worthy of respect and seek to alleviate their misery. The merciful treat the needy the same way the heavenly Father treats them (Mt 5:14-15; Lk 6:41-42)—a point memorably made in the parable of the unmerciful servant (Mt 18:23-25). The merciful, having experienced God's mercy, are choice can-didates for proclaiming the good news to others (Mk 5:19-20).

"Blessed are the pure in heart." In this context purity refers primarily to "undivided loyalty."[17] It is akin to being single-minded, and its antith-esis is being double-minded. Jesus warned his disciples, "No one can serve two masters" (Mt 5:24). James, the half-brother of Jesus, also picks up on this and describes the serious failings of the double-minded: they are "unstable in every way" and "must not expect to receive anything from the Lord" (Jas 1:8). The pure in heart, then, are characterized by an unalloyed and unfeigned sincerity in their commitment to the king and his kingdom. Chastity, sometimes thought to be the sole focus of this beatitude, is but one aspect of a much larger scope.

"Blessed are the peacemakers." If, on the one hand, kingdom citizens are characterized by not insisting on their own rights, they also, on the other hand, manifest a deep-seated desire to protect the rights of others. Since *shalom* is a by-product of being in the kingdom, this sense of well-being, wholeness and harmony is a goal to be achieved everywhere. Dis-ciples ought to be healing agents in a world wracked by disharmony and conflict. Whether on an interpersonal, societal or even global level, king-dom citizens attempt to achieve "now" the state of affairs that will obtain "then" (i.e., when the kingdom comes in all its glory). For this reason, reconciliation among members of the new community of faith is a high priority (Mt 5:23-26; 18:15-22).[18]

"Blessed are those who are persecuted for righteousness sake." Those who live out the fifth, sixth and seventh Beatitudes inevitably experience the eighth. Fellowship in the kingdom, like the "fellowship of the ring," forges a bond between members, a bond strengthened by opposition and persecution. Ironically, the reason for resistance resides principally in the concept of righteousness, being in right relationship to God. As we have

---

[17]"It consists in full and unreserved self-offering to God which renews the heart and rules out any acceptance of what is against God. Those who are pure in heart in this way are called to participate in the kingdom of God, Mt. 5:8" (Friedrich Hauck, "καθαρός," *TDNT* 3:425).

[18]See Werner Foerster, "εἰρήνη, εἰρηνοποιέω," *TDNT* 2:419.

noted, this is a leading theme of the entire sermon. The various expressions of Judaism in the first century had quite different understandings of what righteousness entails. Jesus elicited intense hostility, especially from the Pharisees, because he criticized their understanding of righteousness. As Jesus warned his followers, they too can expect fierce attacks (see Mt 10:16-31; 23:34-35; 24:9-14). As the gospel spread beyond Palestine, pagan religious systems also reacted against this new message. Incredulity, derision and slander gave way to violent persecution. The church of the second and third centuries A.D. would contribute a lengthy list of martyrs before Constantine declared Christianity as the official religion of the empire in the fourth century. Persecution, however, has been a persistent feature of Christianity to this very day. Believers must look beyond this hostility and consider the blessedness and privilege of belonging to the company of the redeemed. Like the prophets of Israel, one must count the cost of discovering a right relationship with God through grace alone and weather the resistance of those who refuse to accept the good news (see Jer 8:18—9:6).

The calling of kingdom citizens (Mt 5:13-16). Jesus employs two metaphors to describe the job of kingdom citizens. The first fastens on a common necessity of first-century life. Salt served as a preservative in a time before refrigeration was invented. Just as salt is essential for preserving food, especially meat products, so disciples are essential for preserving a just and compassionate society. This is accomplished by upholding the moral and ethical values of the kingdom. Without the godly influence of kingdom citizens, society tends toward moral anarchy. The story of how Christianity transformed Western civilization does not generally receive the recognition that it deserves.

The second metaphor, light, emphasizes illumination and truth. Kingdom citizens bear witness to the true light that entered the world in the person of the Son of God (Jn 1:1-18). Jesus seems to stress not merely a verbal witness, but also a witness of deeds. Actions often speak louder than words.

The conduct of kingdom citizens (Mt 5:17—7:12). The central section of the sermon explains the nature of true righteousness, in which Jesus lays out a new standard of righteousness (Mt 5:17-48). In Judaism, law and righteousness are inextricable, and thus a key issue immediately surfaces: Jesus' view of the law.

Jesus and the law of Moses (Mt 5:17-20). This pericope raises nettlesome theological questions. These include the relationship between the Testaments, the problem of law and grace, and the question of consistency in

Jesus' view—that is, harmonizing this passage with other texts in which
he seems to abrogate at least portions of the OT law (Mk 7:19; cf. Acts
10—11; Heb 7:9-10).

I zero in on Jesus' statement that he came "not to abolish but to fulfill"
(Mt 5:17). What, precisely, did he mean by "fulfill"? Several different views
may be distinguished.

Not a few writers, especially Jewish scholars, take the Greek verb in
question, *plēroō*, to be the translational equivalent of the Aramaic *qûm*,
meaning "validate" or "confirm." Understood in this sense, Jesus is saying
that he has come to validate the law by perfectly observing its requirements.
In fact, there is no indisputable evidence in the Gospels that Jesus ever did
violate the OT laws.

The problem, however, is that Matthew 5 focuses on the relation of the
Law and the Prophets—that is, the sacred Scriptures of Israel—to Jesus'
teaching, not his actions. If in fact Jesus is referring to his actions and not
his teaching, then the early church seems to have misunderstood him, and
this is hard to explain. Furthermore, the LXX never uses *plēroō* to render
qûm or its cognates. Rather, in the LXX *plēroō* renders the Hebrew *mālē'*,
meaning "fulfill." In OT usage this characteristically refers to the "filling
up" of volume or time, meanings that also appear in the NT (e.g., Acts
24:17; Rom 15:19).

Another view, discernible only as early as Thomas Aquinas (thirteenth
century A.D.) but quite influential in the church, understands Jesus to be
referring to the moral law only; the civil and ceremonial statutes are abolished in that they were signs and symbols of Christ's work on the cross
and thus no longer normative. This view is still popular among many
conservative Christian theologians. This tripartite distinction, however,
of moral, civil and ceremonial laws is never explicitly articulated in either
the OT or the NT. Furthermore, Matthew 5:18 would seem to militate
against such an interpretation ("Not one letter, not one stroke of a letter,
will pass from the law until all is accomplished"). On the other hand, it
must be admitted that Jesus does recognize what he calls "the weightier
matters of the law" (Mt 23:23). Whether, however, this can be extended
to refer to a distinction between moral, civil and ceremonial divisions of
the law is problematic.

Some say that Jesus "fills up" the law by providing its full, intended
meaning. In my opinion, this has more merit than the previous suggestions.
The full, intended meaning is often connected to the double command to
love God and neighbor, "the law of Christ" or "royal law" (Gal 6:2; cf.
Gal 5:14; 1 Cor 9:21; see also Jn 13:34; Jas 2:8). This view is not, however,

problem-free, since an extended meaning of the Greek word *plēroō* must be assumed.[19]

A starting point for determining the meaning of *plēroo* is Matthew's employment of fourteen formula quotations in which prophetic texts in the OT find their "fulfillment" in specific events of Jesus' life and ministry (in these Matthew uses the aorist passive of *plēroo*). These "fulfillments" are understood from a promise-fulfillment, typological and redemptive-history standpoint (Mt 1:22-23; 2:5-6, 15, 17-18, 23; 3:3; 4:14-16; 8:17; 12:17-21; 13:14-15, 35; 21:4-5; 26:56; 27:9-10). At the very least, Matthew views Jesus' life, ministry, death and resurrection as the fulfillment and climactic moment of redemptive history. Thus the law and prophets point to him; he fulfills them. There is a real sense in which Jesus' life recapitulates that of ancient Israel because he is the true Israel.

But all has not been said. The following six antitheses (Mt 5:21-48) must somehow be incorporated into our understanding. Here Jesus counters prevalent interpretations of the law ("You have heard that it was said") with his own, authoritative interpretation ("But I say to you"). On the one hand, Jesus radicalizes the OT law (Mt 5:22, 28, 39-42, 44). In this sense, there is truth to the view that Jesus brings out the true and intended meaning of the law. But Jesus goes beyond this. He actually annuls the legislation of the Torah in two, possibly three, cases (Mt 5:31, 34, 39). Needless to say, this placed him in opposition to virtually every Jewish sect known to exist in the first century. Although the law points to Jesus and he fulfills the redemptive promises contained in it, and in that sense it has eternal validity, Jesus nonetheless stands above the law and even revises it for his new kingdom community. He is a new and greater Moses. There is now a new law, "the law of Christ." This new law, however, fundamentally rests upon the same foundation on which the old law of Sinai was built: love for God and love for neighbor (see Mt 22:34-40; Rom 13:8-10; Gal 5:14, 22-23). Paradoxically, both continuity and discontinuity characterize Jesus' relationship to the law.

Matthew presents Jesus as the climactic figure in redemptive history, the eschatological goal of the OT. But he is also the supreme interpreter of the sacred Scriptures. His authoritative interpretation even entails rescinding some aspects of the old Torah without thereby denying its continuing validity for salvation history. The only way this can be reconciled is by seeing

---

[19]See Don Carson, *Matthew, Mark, Luke* (EBC 8; Grand Rapids: Zondervan, 1984), p. 143; Johannes P. Louw and Eugene A. Nida, "πληρόω," *Greek-English Lexicon of the New Testament Based on Semantic Domains* (2nd ed.; 2 vols.; New York: United Bible Societies, 1988-1989), 1:405 (§33.144).

that he is greater than Moses; indeed, he is the "Lord of the law." As such, he sets out a new Torah for a new Israel.

The new righteousness illustrated (Mt 5:21-48). In what follows, the famous six "antitheses," Jesus illustrates his understanding of righteousness over against that of the Pharisees (Mt 5:21-48).

Jesus first warns his disciples about anger, hatred and unforgiveness (Mt 5:21-26). These are the taproot of the violence so endemic in society. The antidotes to these societal cancers are the Beatitudes of humility, meekness and mercy. Only fellowship in the kingdom can bring about this new society; it is imperative, therefore, that believers model kingdom life now and aggressively recruit new citizens. The call to be salt and light in the world requires that culture be made captive to Christ.

Jesus' followers must be on constant alert against lust (Mt 5:27-30). Only those who truly hunger for righteousness and purity may withstand its enticements. In an age of easily accessible pornography, Christians need to take this with utmost seriousness. A passion to be righteous must withstand and triumph over all competing passions.

In Matthew's Gospel divorce is permitted only in the case of infidelity (Mt 19:9). In Mark 10:2-12 and Luke 16:18 Jesus' saying on divorce is absolute, with no exception clause. Paul apparently follows the Lukan tradition (1 Cor 7:10-11). The exegetical issues are complex and vigorously debated.[20] Perhaps the Matthean exception clause addresses invalid marriages that ought not to have been contracted in the first place (i.e., incestuous relationships as detailed in Lev 18). The infamous episode involving Herod Antipas (Mk 6:18) may illustrate the point. If this is the case, such unions should be terminated. One is reminded here of Paul's uncompromising dictum on incest at Corinth: "Drive out the wicked person from among you" (1 Cor 5:13). What seems clear is Jesus' displeasure with divorce. Kingdom citizens are required to keep their marriage vows. His teaching goes beyond the strictest standards of Pharisaism. Only the Essenes had a marriage standard as rigorous (see 11Q19 57:17-19; CD-A 4:20-21). The literature on this question is enormous, and I refer the reader to some helpful studies.[21]

---

[20]For a helpful overview, see Robert W. Wall, "Divorce," *ABD* 2:217-19; A. D. Verhey, "Divorce," *ISBE* 1:976-78; Joseph A. Fitzmyer, "Marriage and Divorce," *EDSS* 1:511-14; David Instone-Brewer, *Divorce and Remarriage in the Bible: The Social and Literary Context* (Grand Rapids: Eerdmans, 2002).

[21]In addition to sources listed in the preceding note, see Ralph H. Alexander, "Divorce," *EDBT* 183-85; William A. Heth and Gordon J. Wenham, *Jesus and Divorce: The Problem with the Evangelical Consensus* (Nashville: Nelson, 1984); L. D. Hurst, "Ethics of Jesus," *DJG* 219; Craig S. Keener, *And Marries Another: Divorce and Remarriage in the Teaching*

Kingdom citizens are called upon to renounce oaths (Mt 5:33-37). Positively, Jesus demands unwavering integrity.[22] Matthew 15:1-9 illustrates the casuistry into which some Pharisees fell. There was a sliding scale dictating which oaths were binding and which were nonbinding. Over against that, Jesus calls for complete truthfulness and honesty. One should not have to take an oath ensuring truthfulness; one always tells the truth. As David Garland puts it, "Disciples are to speak the truth as a matter of course because they are inwardly pure in heart, not because it has been imposed by external necessity."[23] The prohibition of oaths creates problems inasmuch as believers are occasionally called upon to swear an oath in the performance of civic duties. Although not all agree, most modern Christians believe that such circumstances do not violate the intent of Jesus' prohibition.

Retaliation is forbidden (Mt 5:38-42). Once again enormous difficulties arise if this is taken literally.[24] At the very least, Jesus seems to be insisting that for individuals, retaliation is incompatible with kingdom principles. Instead, one combines meekness with peacemaking. Patient endurance in the face of personal insult is demanded. The majority position in Christendom does not extend Jesus' prohibition to include personal assault and injury. Self-defense is considered permissible when no other option exists. The majority position also understands Jesus to be dealing on the individual level, not the societal or national level. Thus pacifism, though widely held in certain circles, has not generally characterized Christianity.[25]

Love is enjoined for one's enemies (Mt 5:43-47). This extraordinary commandment goes well beyond what Jewish or pagan teachers, before and after Jesus, have required. Although the OT is not devoid of compassion toward enemies, the examples that Jesus gives to illustrate what he means are unparalleled and seem quite unrealistic. It only makes sense in

---

of the New Testament (Peabody, Mass.: Hendrickson, 1991); J. Carl Laney, *The Divorce Myth* (Minneapolis: Bethany House, 1981); J. Murray, *Divorce* (Philadelphia: Committee on Christian Education, Orthodox Presbyterian Church, 1953); Robert Stein, "Divorce," *DJG* 192-99.

[22]"Jesus therefore uses a prohibition of swearing in order to fight against lying" (H.-G. Link, "Swear," *NIDNTT* 3:741).

[23]David Garland, "Oaths and Swearing," *DJG* 578.

[24]As Dan Reid observes, "Any consideration of the question of divine and human violence in the Bible must begin by admitting that the issue resists easy resolution, for violence (in its many dimensions) involves a seemingly impenetrable mystery" ("Violence," *NDBT* 835).

[25]For a sampling of views on pacifism, see Richard B. Hays, *The Moral Vision of the New Testament: Community, Cross, New Creation* (San Francisco: HarperSanFrancisco, 1996) (pacifist); J. Daryl Charles, *Between Pacifism and Jihad: Just War and Christian Tradition* (Downers Grove, Ill.: InterVarsity Press, 2005) (just war).

light of Jesus' teaching that kingdom citizens must reflect the characteristics of their heavenly Father. Although unattainable in this present age, it is nonetheless the kingdom standard because the kingdom is already present. Thus the central section ends with this startling commandment: "Be perfect, therefore, as your heavenly Father is perfect" (Mt 5:48).

The new piety demonstrated (Mt 6:1—7:12). This section of the sermon is very practical and demonstrates how kingdom righteousness actually embodies the new ethic of love. Piety has to do with religious devotion and reverence for God. Once again, we note how very Jewish the piety depicted herein is. Nothing more epitomized the life of religious Jews than matters such as almsgiving, prayer and fasting.

Kingdom citizens demonstrate righteousness by generosity, particularly in meeting the needs of the poor. Love for neighbor requires tangible expression, and the early followers of Jesus were known for their unstinting sharing (see Acts 2:43-47; 4:32-37; 12-16; 2 Cor 8:1-7).

Prayer is the religious lifeblood of OT and Second Temple Judaism and, consequently, is also a central expression of piety in the Jesus movement. The sermon sharply contrasts the prayer practices of some Pharisees and prayer as Jesus envisions it. According to Jesus, ostentatious performance and mindless repetition eviscerate effectual prayer. One prays best in the privacy of the Father's presence.

The gem in this section is the pericope called the Lord's Prayer, the most widely known prayer in all of human history and a masterpiece of condensed theology. Countless books have been written in an effort to plumb the depths of this short model prayer. I can offer only an inadequate summary of the leading ideas.

This prayer, better identified as the Disciples' Prayer, provides a pattern for prayer. Jesus did not give it primarily to be repeated verbatim in a corporate or private setting, though Christian experience abundantly testifies to the spiritual value of such an exercise; rather, it serves as a guideline for both corporate and private prayer. As such, it outlines an approach to the heavenly Father that at the same time reorders one's theological understandings. Like all portions of the Sermon on the Mount, this prayer breathes the atmosphere of Second Temple Judaism. One thinks of the Jewish *Kaddish,* a prayer that punctuates a Jewish service and signals the end of a major section. Here is how it begins: "Glorified and sanctified be God's great name throughout the world which He has created according to His will. May He establish His kingdom in your lifetime and during your days, and within the life of the entire house of Israel, speedily and soon; and say, Amen." The similarity to the first section of the Lord's Prayer is readily apparent.

The Lord's Prayer is divided into six petitions, three focusing on God, three on ourselves and our neighbors. In this regard it reflects the basic pattern of the Ten Commandments, in which the first four relate to God and the last six to one's neighbor. Jesus' summary of the law and prophets in terms of the twofold commandments to love God and neighbor (Mt 22:32-40) expresses the very essence of biblical religion. One must be, so to speak, vertically related before being horizontally related.

Prayer is addressed to the Father. Much has been written on the background of this concept. Was Jesus' invocation an innovation in Judaism? Although not a central theme of OT theology, the notion of the God of Israel as Father does occur (see Deut 32:6; Ps 103:13; Is 63:16; Mal 2:10), and the people of Israel are metaphorically styled as Yahweh's "firstborn son" (Ex 4:22). Nowhere in the OT, however, does a prayer directly address God as "Father." In Jewish literature of the Second Temple period one does find a few references to God as "Father" in prayer (Wis 14:3; Sir 23:1, 4; 51:10; 3 Macc 6:3, 8; *m. Taʿan.* 3:8), but in each case the Hebrew word either used or lying behind the Greek translation is *'ab* or *'abinû*. On the other hand, behind the Greek word in Matthew 6:9, *patēr*, lies the Aramaic *'abbāʾ*, a child's expression considered too intimate as an address to the king of the universe *(melek hāʿôlām)*.[26] Jesus "applies to God a term which must have sounded familiar and disrespectful to His contemporaries because used in the everyday life of the family. In other words, He uses the simple 'speech of the child to its father.'"[27] The English word *daddy* comes closest to conveying the degree of familiarity connoted by "Abba." The significance of this lies in the remarkable degree of personal closeness and intimacy implied by such a word choice. It is the word that Jesus uttered from the cross (Mk 14:36) and that he taught his disciples to use in prayer, as can be seen in the NT letters (Gal 4:6; Rom 8:15).

The Father addressed is "in the heavens." The word usually translated "heaven" is plural in the Greek *(ouranois)* and translates the Aramaic *šĕmayyāʾ*, likewise plural. The plural form reflects the Jewish understanding of a multiplicity of heavens. "Heaven" could be used, firstly, of the

---

[26]Joachim Jeremias, *The Prayers of Jesus* (Naperville, Ill.: Allenson, 1967); idem, *New Testament Theology: The Proclamation of Jesus* (New York: Scribner, 1971), pp. 178-203. There are no clear examples outside of Jesus and the Jesus movement in which "Abba" is used as a direct address in prayer to God the Father. For further evidence, see, in the present volume, appendix to chapter 4.

[27]Gerhard Kittel, "ἀββά," *TDNT* 1:6. The quotation at the end of the sentence is from Gustaf Dalman, *The Words of Jesus Considered in the Light of Post-Biblical Jewish Writings and the Aramaic Language*, vol. 1, *Introduction and Fundamental Ideas*, trans. D. M. McKay (Edinburgh: T & T Clark, 1902), p. 157.

atmosphere above where the birds fly and the clouds float (see Mt 26:64). It could also be used in some contexts to refer to the supraterrestrial sphere where the sun, moon and stars hold forth (see Mt 5:18; Lk 1:78). Finally, it could refer to that transcendent realm where God Most High dwells and rules over his vast creation, surrounded by the angelic hosts (see, e.g., Mt 18:10). Judaism of the Second Temple period employed the expression "third heaven" for this majestic place, as does Paul in 2 Corinthians 12:2. In fact, given Jewish sensibilities about uttering the divine name of God, the Hebrew expression *hammāqôm,* "the place," is still used as a circumlocution for the divine name. The theological significance of the expression "in the heavens" lies in its assumption of God's sovereignty. Prayer makes sense only if directed to the one who indeed controls the universe. Jewish prayers still typically begin with this phrase: *ʾādōnāy ʾĕlōhênû melek hāʿôlām,* "Lord our God, King of the universe." Prayer changes things because it is offered to the one who makes changes, and very often those changes occur in the hearts of those who pray.

Each of the six petitions is couched in the imperative mood. The imperative mood here conveys a request, a strong desire that something be granted.[28] In the first petition the disciple entreats God that his name be treated with special sanctity and reverence. Names in the OT and Second Temple Judaism are not mere monikers; rather, they are markers pointing to the essence of a person. God's name reveals who he is. The fourth commandment is the taproot of this petition: "You shall not make wrongful use of the name of the LORD your God, for the LORD will not acquit anyone who misuses his name" (Ex 20:7) (cf. Lev 22:32: "You shall not profane my holy name, that I may be sanctified among the people of Israel"). This is essentially a request for divine assistance in order that personal attitudes and behavior, becoming to the Father, be manifest. "Help me, O Lord, display your glory." Second, it entreats that others might also come to revere and honor God. "May the nations, O LORD, proclaim your glory." The petition thus involves a mission to the world. There is an analogy to the saying about removing the speck in our own eye before removing the beam in the eye of another (Mt 7:3-5). Sanctifying God's name begins first on the personal level. Only then can it become societal.

In rabbinic Judaism the phrase "sanctify the name" takes on a distinctive nuance. During the Middle Ages, Jews frequently were forced to make a stark choice: convert to Christianity or die. Many chose to die. In so doing, they "sanctified the name." The expression became a technical term

---

[28]On this use of the imperative, see Daniel B. Wallace, *Greek Grammar Beyond the Basics* (Grand Rapids: Zondervan, 1996), pp. 487-88.

for choosing martyrdom rather than renouncing one's ancestral faith and was even occasionally used of suicide as an act of desperation to avoid converting.[29] This tragic story remains largely unknown by most Christians. My point in bringing it up here is to challenge Christians with a degree of commitment comparable to that of the Jewish martyrs. Presently there are hundreds of thousands of Christians facing the same dilemma that Jews have faced repeatedly: to sanctify God's name even at the cost of one's life. Some of the most powerful testimonies to the gospel occur under precisely these conditions.

"Your kingdom come." The petition basically asks two things: that God's rule would extend over the earth now as people submit to the Great King, and that the consummation of the kingdom would soon appear.

"Your will be done." God's will includes both his righteous demands (Mt 7:21) and his determination to bring about certain events in salvation history (Mt 18:14; 26:42). Since it is certain that God intends to create a great messianic kingdom ruling over the entire earth, the disciple has unshakable confidence in the outcome and robust assurance that one can make a difference in this regard. One cannot sincerely make this request without at the same time committing unreservedly to the agenda.

"Give us this day our daily bread." Having established a vertical relationship with the heavenly Father, the disciple now turns to personal and social needs. The reference to bread is probably an instance of synecdoche—that is, a figure of speech in which a part represents a larger whole. In this case, bread represents a wide array of personal needs. These include, but do not exhaust, physical needs, most notably, food, clothing and shelter. Jesus elaborates on these necessities in Matthew 6:25-34. Grammatically, the first three, vertical petitions stand as independent units. The last four, however, are joined by the Greek connective word *kai* ("and"). Perhaps this illustrates Jesus' observation, borne out of his own intense struggle with the devil (Mt 4:1-4; cf. Deut 8:3), that one does not live by bread alone. The spiritual dimension always has priority. This priority, however, does not mean that the physical has no importance. The disciple asks the heavenly Father for those things necessary to sustain and enrich life in order faithfully and effectively to serve him. To understand the petition in terms of a beggar's allowance calls into question the abundant generosity of the Father (see Mt 7:7-11).

The petition for "our daily bread" raises a disturbing question. How much is enough? And what if we have a lot more than is needed daily?

---

[29]For background on this, see Haim Hillel Ben-Sasson, "Kiddush ha-Shem and Hillul ha-Shem," *Encyclopaedia Judaica CD-ROM Edition* (Jerusalem: Keter, 1997), n.p.

The Gospels indicate that few of Jesus' followers possessed much of this world's goods. Many lived on subsistence diets (see Mt 15:32). Most North American and European Christians and many in Asia live in a land of abundance buoyed by a consumer-driven economy. Much of the developing world, however, lives precariously on the threshold of starvation. In light of this, what does it mean to ask for "our daily bread"? How should we live as "rich Christians in an age of hunger"?[30] I have no easy answers. The Scriptures clearly teach that believers should contribute to the needs of others. The OT and Jewish texts of the Second Temple period underscore the virtue of generous giving. The NT follows suit. Beyond this, there are some thoughtful treatments that discuss specific things Christians can do with their resources. These merit prayerful consideration.[31]

"And forgive us our debts, as we also have forgiven our debtors." The debts owed here are moral in nature; that is, they are sins. Since this is a disciple's prayer, it is talking not about the doctrine of justification but rather about the believer's daily confession of sin. There are no grounds for assuming that believers attain sinless perfection in this life. The confession of sins gives tangible evidence of the second characteristic of kingdom citizens: penitence (Mt 5:4). More difficulty attaches to the second phrase. Does Jesus mean to say that we are forgiven only if we forgive others? Or does he mean that those who entreat their heavenly Father for the forgiveness of sins will, as a matter of course, forgive those who sin against them? Perhaps we cannot really separate the two. At any rate, the petition reminds disciples to keep short accounts with God. Long overdue bills carry a heavy penalty fee for being late; if they are never paid, spiritual bankruptcy occurs.

Just as the climactic eighth beatitude is expanded, so too the fifth petition of the Lord's Prayer receives elaboration, thus drawing attention to its importance. Forgiveness is central to piety and true righteousness. The prerequisite for kingdom citizenship is forgiveness of sins by the heavenly Father; the hallmark of one so forgiven is a willingness to extend forgiveness to others. The motive power of piety is grace.

"And do not bring us to the time of trial, but rescue us from the evil one." The NRSV translation differs so markedly from the familiar KJV ("And lead us not into temptation, but deliver us from evil") as to require some explanation. Is it talking about a temptation or a trial? And is it talking

---

[30]This is the title of a challenging work by Ronald J. Sider, *Rich Christians in an Age of Hunger: Moving from Affluence to Generosity* (4th ed.; Dallas: Word, 1997).

[31]Besides Sider, *Rich Christians in an Age of Hunger*, see P. H. Davids, "Rich and Poor," *DJG* 701-10, including the bibliography at the end of the article.

about deliverance from evil generally or from the personal embodiment of evil, the devil? Although the cadence and phrasing of the KJV will always resonate in my heart, I give the nod to the NRSV as more faithfully rendering the Greek text. The Greek word *peirasmos* can be used in some contexts to refer to a temptation (i.e., an enticement to commit evil). On the other hand, it may denote a trial or test. If the former, then the request must be for divine assistance in the midst of temptation, since Scripture is clear that God entices no one to commit sin (Jas 1:13; cf. 1 Jn 1:5). But more likely, *peirasmos* should be rendered as "trial," and it connotes persecution. Recall that the Beatitudes conclude on a note of persecution (Mt 5:10-11). The NRSV, however, assumes that "the time of trial" refers specifically to the eschatological judgment connected with the end of the age, more popularly called the "great tribulation." This is possible, but more likely it refers to affliction in general.[32]

Finally, Jesus is probably referring to Satan as "the evil one" rather than evil in general. This comports with the general tenor of Matthew's Gospel, in which Jesus begins his public ministry with a direct confrontation with the devil and a trial of faith (Mt 4:1-11). Indeed, the Synoptic tradition generally highlights the malignant opposition of Satan to the coming of the kingdom. John's Gospel only intensifies this satanic hostility. We should be careful, however, not to attribute every instance of persecution and affliction to Satan. Much misery and oppression has its source in a fallen world system and in fallen human nature.

As majestic and memorable as the doxology is, it probably does not go back to Jesus but rather reflects a later liturgical development of Jesus' prayer. The manuscript evidence is decisively against its authenticity.[33] Certainly, however, it is an appropriate and thoroughly biblical summation.

The Lord's Prayer is a virtual compendium of Jesus' theology and ethics. This is seen in the following affirmations.

1. Jesus' ethics are rooted in the character of the heavenly Father. Rightness and wrongness derive from the essence of God and how he relates to his creation.

2. Jesus' ethics are eschatologically energized. Disciples pray now for what certainly will be. But in so praying, disciples commit to a course of thought and action that actualizes kingdom ideals, even if only partially. Because prayer directed to the heavenly Father assumes his sovereignty over all things, there is every reason to be confident. As the pioneer Baptist mis-

---

[32]Heinrich Seeseman, "πειρασμός," *TDNT* 6:30.
[33]See Bruce M. Metzer, *A Textual Commentary on the Greek New Testament* (New York: United Bible Societies, 1971), pp. 16-17.

sionary William Carey put it, "Expect great things from God. Attempt great things for God."[34]

3. Jesus' ethics demonstrate the priority of the spiritual over the material without negating or denying the importance of the latter. Putting the kingdom as the top priority in life prevents lapsing into humanistic solutions that locate the highest good in the created order. The Lord's Prayer teaches that no real, lasting good is accomplished until the one who is the source of all good is sought (see Jas 1:17).

4. Jesus' ethics require a realistic awareness of and accountability for the problem of sin. There are two dimensions to the problem. First, sin must be confessed to the heavenly Father. The most damaging impact of sin is its effect on the spiritual life. If this is impaired, there is no realistic hope for success on the horizontal dimension. Second, sin must also be forgiven on the human level. Sin is like a deadly virus in society, and only a persistent course of repentance and reconciliation can slow its contagion. This, of course, is the reason for secular humanism's failure to provide a solid ethical base for life; it has not acknowledged the true nature of the problem.

The rest of the sermon deals with various aspects of personal and corporate piety. Fasting should be done without ostentation (Mt 6:16-18); kingdom values take precedence over and provide perspective on this-worldly needs (Mt 6:19-34, esp. v. 33); hypocritical judgment of others is prohibited (Mt 7:1-5); discernment must be exercised in sharing spiritual truths with unbelievers (Mt 7:6); and believers ought always to entreat their heavenly Father for their needs (Mt 7:7-11).

The main body of the sermon is capped off by a climactic saying summarizing the entire section beginning at Matthew 5:17, where Jesus spells out the new righteousness that exceeds that of the scribes and Pharisees. According to Jesus, all the ethical pronouncements of the law and the prophets amount to this: "In everything do to others as you would have them do to you" (Mt 7:12). This so-called Golden Rule gives definition to the second most important law: "Love your neighbor as yourself" (Mt 22:39). A negative version of the Golden Rule may already be found in Tobit 4:15: "And what you hate, do not do to anyone" (ca. 200 B.C.). Some claim that Sirach 31:15, "Judge your neighbor's feelings by your own, and in every matter be thoughtful" (ca. 180 B.C.), is a positive version like the Golden Rule. The context of the saying, however, is a banquet where, Ben Sira advises, it is in one's self-interest to make a good impression on others by being sensitive to the other guests. This hardly goes as far as Jesus' prescription. The Talmud

---

[34]On the life of Carey, see Mary Drewery, *William Carey: A Biography* (Grand Rapids: Zondervan, 1979).

tells a story about Hillel, an older contemporary of Jesus, who reduced the entire Torah to the following: "What is hateful to you, do not do to your neighbor" (*b. Šabb.* 31a). Once again, this is a negative version. Jesus' version of the Golden Rule far surpasses Pharisaic standards of true righteousness and piety. It is in fact a lofty standard attainable only by divine help. As Paul and John make abundantly clear, only the gift of the Holy Spirit can enable one to live consistently on this plane.

The challenge of kingdom citizenship (Mt 7:13-27). Jesus concludes his sermon with a call for decision and moves from didache (ethics) to kerygma (proclamation). Jesus warns his listeners of their peril ("destruction") should they reject his message. In contrast to Albert Einstein's view (cited in the introduction to this chapter), Jesus believed that fear of punishment should be taken seriously. In fact, Jesus said more about punishment than reward in his teaching. Although punishment is not the primary motivation for ethical behavior, it should not be dismissed. Modern interpretations that deny the reality of final punishment jettison an essential aspect of Jesus' teaching.[35]

ATTEMPTS AT INTERPRETING JESUS' ETHICS

I now examine briefly how leading church figures and theologians have attempted to make sense of Jesus' ethics. Other texts from the dominical tradition will be brought into this discussion.

The Catholic interpretation. As early as the second century A.D. a two-level ethic begins to appear. According to this view, some of Jesus' teaching is intended only for those who completely devote their lives to the church and live exemplary lives. The reason for such a bifurcation among the people of God is the seeming impossibility for the average Christian to carry out all the demands of Jesus. The perceived difficulty was resolved by insisting that all Christians are committed to a "minimum ethic" consisting of the Ten Commandments, the Golden Rule and the love commandment (Mk 12:28-34), but only those seeking the "higher righteousness" are bound by all Jesus' requirements. Additional rewards and merit accrue to those who choose this option.

And what are the standards thought to be impossibly high? One example is the giving up of possessions, based on the story of the rich young ruler (Mk 10:21 pars.). Likewise, the sayings about foregoing marriage and family life (Mt 19:11-12; Lk 14:26 par.) seem beyond what is reasonably expected of the average Christian. The prohibition of all oaths and the

---

[35]See S. H. Travis, "Judgment," *DJG* 408-11; J. Lunde, "Heaven and Hell," *DJG* 309-12.

call for nonretaliation and not judging others are extremely difficult in the rough-and-tumble world in which most people live. The rise of monasteries and ecclesiastical institutions at least made it possible for communities to attempt such an ethic. As might be expected, such an approach results in a two-level Christian society, the laity and the clergy (and those few nonclerics who followed the higher spirituality).

The Catholic view takes seriously the remarkably high standards expected in the kingdom. Jesus was not kidding when he said, "For I tell you, unless your righteousness exceeds that of the scribes and Pharisees, you will never enter the kingdom of heaven" (Mt 5:20). On the other hand, it is hard to evade the conclusion that Jesus' ethics address all his followers, with no distinction between the few who exercise a "higher righteousness" and the majority who are content with a minimum ethic. Jesus demands total commitment from all who take up their cross and follow him (see Mk 8:34-38).

As for the rich young ruler, the point of the story is that he left that day possessing no righteousness, much less a "higher righteousness." Jesus challenges him to give up reliance on wealth for security, something that apparently he is unwilling to do. The point of the story is about where real security may be found, not necessarily about giving away all one's worldly goods, although in some cases the Lord may require precisely that. The pericope about being a eunuch for the kingdom of heaven does distinguish between two groups, those foregoing marriage, whether voluntarily or involuntarily, and those who marry, but the distinction has nothing to do with greater or lesser righteousness.

The utopian interpretation. Some hold that Jesus intended to set up a perfect society on earth; in such an understanding, the Sermon on the Mount functions as a constitution. Anabaptists, Franciscans, pietists, holiness groups, a few individuals such as Leo Tolstoy, and various others have attempted to implement an ideal society. Indiana has a historical site called New Harmony, in which a communal group, led by Johann Georg Rapp, sought to do just that in 1814. Like all such experiments, however, the attempt finally was abandoned.[36] These groups reasoned that if the Sermon on the Mount became the basic document governing human relationships, then social institutions such as the police, army, judicial system and civil authority could be discarded. In such a kingdom the law of love reigns supreme, and people love their neighbor as themselves. If only it were so!

It is easy to find fault with such an interpretation. On the other hand,

---

[36]For a brief history of the settlement and its founder, see http://www.ulib.iupui.edu/kade/newharmony/newharmony-in.html.

credit should be given for some correct assumptions. Surely the utopian view is right in insisting that the commands of Jesus are binding on all Christians. Also correct is the elevation of the love command to highest importance. Furthermore, the instinct to take Jesus' words literally is to be commended. On the other hand, some of Jesus' sayings are better understood as deliberate exaggeration for rhetorical effect—hyperbole. This candid recognition considerably alters one's interpretation of Jesus' ethics.

A fundamental problem with the utopian view is its failure to read the Sermon on the Mount in its larger context of the life and teachings of Jesus. Jesus did not initially come to inaugurate the "Great Society." In light of our earlier discussion of the kingdom of God, the present phase of the kingdom entails the sufferings of the Messiah followed at his parousia by the full glories of the age to come. The Gospels do not depict a Jesus who launches an attack against all the established social institutions. On the contrary, human government must be respected; Caesar deserves his due (see Mk 12:13-17 pars.).

Another major error of utopianism is its failure to understand how deeply flawed human nature really is. One of the tendencies of utopian thought is the notion that humanity is capable of a consistently lofty ethical standard. Jesus would not have commanded us to be perfect (Mt 5:48) if this were not possible, so the argument goes. However, this ignores quite clear teaching by Jesus to the contrary. Even his instructions on prayer contain a revealing observation about human nature: "If you then, who are evil, know how to give good gifts to your children . . . " (Mt 7:11; cf. Mk 7:21-23). Jesus warned his disciples in the Olivet discourse that the present age will be one of war and suffering (Mk 13:8 pars.). Nor does Jesus promise his followers that they will usher in a golden age; rather, they will be hated by all, and many will lose their lives in the struggle to proclaim the good news (Mk 8:34-38). The elder John flatly asserts, "The whole world lies under the power of the evil one" (1 Jn 5:19). This need not lead to resigned fatalism. Many will respond positively to the gospel, and much good will be achieved as believers perform their role as salt and light. Believers need a strong dose of realism. As Qohelet long ago said, "I saw under the sun that in the place of justice, wickedness was there, and in the place of righteousness, wickedness was there as well" (Eccles 3:16). The task of ushering in everlasting righteousness remains for the king when he comes in his glory.

Finally, the precise nuance of Jesus' climactic injunction, "Be perfect, therefore, as your heavenly Father is perfect" (Mt 5:48), requires further comment. The meaning of the Greek term *teleios* (and its Hebrew equivalent) refers not to ethical perfection or sinlessness but rather to a wholeness of attitude toward others, an utter sincerity for truth and respect for others. In fact, Luke's version provides a helpful paraphrase: "Be merciful, just as your Father is merciful" (Lk 6:36). This, rather than sinless perfection, is what Jesus enjoins upon his followers. Perfection awaits the parousia.

The Lutheran interpretation. As might be expected, the legacy of Luther casts a long shadow over modern Protestantism. In Luther's view, the Sermon on the Mount is both an uncompromising expression of God's righteous demand and God's gracious invitation to accept the gift of salvation. The righteousness demanded in the sermon is impossible of human fulfillment and thus drives sinners to their knees. To this cry God freely responds, and the sermon fulfills its intended purpose, preparing hardened hearts for God's grace. Here is a clear example of how Luther's law-gospel dialectic functions exegetically. The fact that Luther speaks of the sermon as both law and gospel created some confusion in later Lutheranism. Most interpreters stressed the law side of the sermon, but some have also emphasized the gospel aspect.[37]

On the one hand, such an interpretation coheres well with the overall thrust of Jesus' ministry, which was to reveal the true condition of human hearts and elicit a saving response to God's gracious offer in the gospel. But there is a major problem: Luther's view of the Sermon is colored by his conflict with Rome over the nature of justification. Luther reads the Sermon in the light of Pauline statements like Romans 3:20: "through the law [i.e., the Sermon] comes the knowledge of sin." From Luther's perspective, Jesus and Paul are fighting the same battle as he is against legalism. According to the Pharisees, God acted graciously in giving the Law of Moses at Mount Sinai. But now Jews must remain in this covenant relationship by faithful and meticulous observance of its commandments, augmented, of course, by the oral law, of which the Pharisees were the authoritative custodians. As Luther sees it, Rome is following the same path as the first century Pharisees: justification requires the performance of good deeds and only the magisterium infallibly interprets Scripture.

Luther has some things right. Jesus' teaching does indeed show the utter inability of human beings to save themselves and the incredible offer of grace in the good news of the kingdom. Still, one cannot escape the conclusion that he and his successors read into Jesus' message the later polemic of the Reformation regarding the doctrine of justification. Luther's own experience skews his context for reading Scripture; the law-gospel dichotomy becomes a criterion for correct interpretation. Every text of Scripture is one

---

[37]See G. N. Stanton, "Sermon on the Mount," *DJG* 738.

or the other. Forcing all Scripture into this paradigm results in a truncated message.

The most significant shortcoming of Luther's view lies in his misinterpretation of the intended audience. As David Scaer, himself a Lutheran, rightly points out, the sermon is best understood as instruction *(didachē)* intended for believers.[38] Those whom it addresses have already repented and committed themselves to the kingdom. The sermon provides guidance for life together in the kingdom; it is not primarily kerygma, as Luther and Lutheranism typically understand it.

The liberal interpretation. Liberalism has an enormous impact on the way the Bible is read today, especially in mainline denominations and in the academy. A leading figure in this movement was German church historian and theologian Adolf von Harnack (1851-1930).[39] His approach to Jesus' ethics may be summarized in the following way. He is embarrassed by the strong eschatological overtones of Jesus' teaching. These were, to put it plainly, not believable in the modern world. According to Harnack, they really are not central to Jesus' ethics anyway. Using the analogy of a piece of grain, he urges modern readers to remove the husk (the eschatological teachings) from the kernel (Jesus' pure ethics). Because liberalism abandoned historic orthodoxy's understanding of the person of Christ, one could either say that this husk either sprung from the early church, which added these features, or was a manifestation of the fact that Jesus was merely a child of his day and so these teachings should not be considered authoritative and binding. Thus, the ethical teachings of Jesus are salvaged for modernity at the expense of Jesus' full deity.

Harnack fastens on three features of Jesus' ethics that form the bedrock of a modern ethic. These are the fatherhood of God, the infinite value of the human soul and the love commandment. Harnack speaks for most liberals in rejecting the particularism of orthodox Protestantism (only the elect will be saved) and advocating univeralism (all human beings, without exception, will eventually be saved). Basically, he distills Jesus' teaching into principles involving attitudes and an inward disposition of the heart. For Harnack, the kingdom of God is essentially an interior experience, a profound sense of God's love and presence. "The kingdom of God comes by coming to the individual, by entering his soul and laying hold of it."[40] Love

---

[38]David Scaer, "Sermon on the Mount," *EDBT* 725.

[39]See H. M. Runscheidt, "Harnack, Adolf von," in *Dictionary of Major Biblical Interpreters*, ed. Donald K. McKim (Downers Grove, Ill.: InterVarsity Press, 2007), pp. 504-7.

[40]Adolf von Harnack, *What Is Christianity?* trans. Thomas Bailey Saunders (LRC; New York: Harper & Row, 1957), p. 56.

is the motive power for a grand societal transformation. As in the parable of the leaven, eventually the kingdom will change the world in which we live and will conform it to God's ideal for humanity. Harnack believes that "the Christian religion, represented in an unsurpassably pure manner in the person of Jesus and in the gospel he taught, protects human culture and civilization from secularization, barbarism and atheism."[41]

A major flaw in classic liberalism is its failure to take seriously the biblical portrait of fallen human nature. Some sayings of Jesus, such as "If you then, *who are evil*, know how to give good gifts to your children . . ." (Mt 7:11 [my italics]), and his depiction of the end of the age, with its wars, earthquakes, famines (Mk 13:8) and hatred for his followers (Mt 13:13), were simply dismissed as "Jewish eschatology."

Adolf von Harnack died in 1930. Adolf Hitler came to power in 1933, ushering in the Third Reich. Never has the world witnessed a more appalling outbreak of barbarism, making mockery of the fatherhood of God, the infinite value of the human soul and the commandment to love our neighbor as ourselves. The estimated death toll for World War II (1939-1945) is between forty and fifty million, making it the bloodiest and largest war in history. Six million Jews were murdered by the Nazis. In many respects, World War II was Hitler's personal war against the Jews.[42] Nazi ideology disfigured Jesus, casting him as an Aryan hero. Harnack's misguided attempt to blow away the Jewish husk of Jesus' teaching was followed by Hitler's demonic attempt to burn and bury anything Jewish. Classic liberalism died in the ashes of Auschwitz.

A chastened liberalism, taking much more seriously the biblical doctrine of human depravity, emerged in the postwar years, along with a return to some Reformation emphases traveling under the rubric of neo-orthodoxy, particularly in the writings of Karl Barth and Emil Brunner.[43]

The liberal interpretation of Jesus' ethics, typified by Harnack, is correct on at least one major point: Jesus never intended to create a new legalism. Rather, Jesus places emphasis on attitudes of the heart (see Mk 7:17-23; Mt 15:21-28). Furthermore, Jesus occasionally did use figurative language to make his point.

On the other hand, Harnack's understanding of Jesus' teaching introduces decided distortions. For example, it is misleading to insist that Jesus

---

[41]Ibid., p. 492.

[42]On this, see Lucy S. Dawidowicz, *The War against the Jews, 1933-1945* (New York: Bantam, 1986).

[43]On neo-orthodoxy, see C. A. Baxter, "Neo-orthodoxy," *NDT* 456-57. On Barth, see W. S. Johnson, "Barth, Karl," in *Dictionary of Major Biblical Interpreters*, ed. Donald K. McKim (Downers Grove, Ill.: InterVarsity Press, 2007), pp. 161-67.

focused on "being" to the exclusion of "doing." Far too many of Jesus' sayings testify that being and doing are inseparably linked. We act on the basis of our heart. "The good person out of the good treasure of the heart produces good, and the evil person out of evil treasure produces evil: for it is out of the abundance of the earth that the mouth speaks" (Lk 6:45; cf. Mt 7:16-20).

Harnack fastens on a text, Luke 17:21, that for him becomes programmatic: "the kingdom of God is within you" (NIV). This text provides the fundamental definition of the kingdom. The problem for Harnack's view is that it forces other texts into this straitjacket. As I argued in chapter four, the most probable meaning is not that the kingdom is located in the human heart, but rather that the kingdom is present in the person of the king himself ("the kingdom of God is among you" [NRSV]). In short, Harnack's view of the kingdom is very much truncated and one-dimensional.

Another problem with Harnack's view of Jesus' ethical teaching lies in his readiness to write off certain radical requirements as hyperbole. Without denying that Jesus does occasionally use hyperbole, one must also recognize that Jesus advocates a radical ethic. Matthew's Gospel records the stunned reaction of Jesus' disciples to his view on divorce: "If such is the case of a man with his wife, it is better not to marry" (Mt 19:10). In most cases, the reader can tell when Jesus is using hyperbole and when he is not. The saying "It is easier for a camel to go through the eye of a needle than for someone who is rich to enter the kingdom of God" (Lk 18:25) is obvious hyperbole. The prohibition against retaliation, "Do not resist an evil doer. But if anyone strikes you on the right cheek, turn the other also" (Mt 5:39), though quite challenging to carry out, does not appear to be deliberate exaggeration. Robert Stein cautions, "It may be that the specific applications of the ethical principles that Jesus gave in the first century are as timeless as the principles themselves!"[44]

The interim ethic interpretation. As we saw in chapter four, Johannes Weiss and Albert Schweitzer were leading figures who undermined classical liberalism's view of Jesus' teaching on the kingdom. According to Weiss and Schweitzer, Jewish apocalyptic shaped Jesus' thought such that the kingdom of God was imminent and about to bring human history to an end. Both Weiss and Schweitzer interpret the Beatitudes as entrance requirements for the kingdom.[45] According to Weiss, "The nearness of the

---

[44]Stein, *Method and Message*, p. 94.

[45]See, for example, Wendell Willis, "Discovery of Eschatological Jesus," in *The Kingdom of God in 20th-Century Interpretation*, ed. Wendell Willis (Peabody, Mass.: Hendrickson, 1987), pp. 4-6. Johannes Weiss puts it this way: "The righteousness of the Kingdom of God

Kingdom is the *motive* for the new morality."[46] Schweitzer agrees and says
that Jesus' ethical teachings take on the character of an emergency ethic;
they are essentially a call for drastic and heroic measures before the dissolution of all things.[47] They are not long-term guidelines for behavior; indeed,
Jesus' "emergency ethic is both impractical and impossible and must therefore be rejected."[48] As we noted earlier, Schweitzer nonetheless salvages
Jesus' ethics by a heroic commitment to the kingdom of God (in spite of
Jesus' misconceptions about it), in which one serves others. For Schweitzer,
this entailed dedicating his life through his considerable gifts and abilities
to the alleviation of human ills and challenging others to follow Jesus in
similar fashion.

Besides the fundamental flaw in Weiss's and Schweitzer's understanding
of the person of Jesus Christ, the notion of interim ethics fails on exegetical
grounds.[49] Do Jesus' ethical teachings really rest on an emergency basis?
Are they short-term standards in light of the imminent dissolution of the
cosmos? One is hard-pressed to answer in the affirmative. In fact, Jesus'
ethics are regularly anchored in the character of God, not in the transitory
character of the present age. For example, in Matthew 6:25-34 believers
are given specific guidance with regard to attitudes that they should have
toward the necessities of life. There is no mention here that the things of this
world will soon pass away; rather, it all comes down to trust in a heavenly
Father, who promises to provide those things for his children. His kingdom
and righteousness are the touchstone and foundation for life. This, rather
than eschatological expectation, shapes ethical considerations.

Sometimes Jesus appeals to God's creative order as a foundation for ethics. Such is the case with marriage and divorce. No appeal is made to an
imminent cataclysm; rather, the Genesis account of the institution of marriage serves as a basis for prohibiting, or at least greatly limiting, divorce

---

does not signify the ethical perfection which members of the Kingdom possess or achieve
in the kingdom of God, but rather the δικαιοσύνη which is the *condition for entrance into*
the Kingdom of God (Matt. 5:20). It is the result of μετάνοια" (*Jesus' Proclamation of the
Kingdom of God*, trans. and ed. Richard Hyde Hiers and David Larrimore Holland [Phila-
delphia: Fortress, 1971], p. 105).

[46]Ibid., p. 106.

[47]"If the idea of the eschatological realization of the Kingdom is the fundamental concept in
Jesus' preaching, his whole theory of ethics must come under the conception of *repentance*
as a preparation for the coming of the Kingdom. . . . *As repentance in view of the kingdom
of God, even the ethics of the Sermon on the Mount is interim-ethics*" (Albert Schweitzer,
The Mystery of the Kingdom of God: The Secret of Jesus' Messiahship and Passion, trans.
Walter Lowrie [New York: Macmillan, 1957], p. 88).

[48]Stein, *Method and Message*, p. 94.

[49]For a more detailed critique, see L. D. Hurst, "Ethics of Jesus," *DJG* 210-11.

(Mk 10:2-9; Mt 5:31-32; 19:1-12). In short, Jesus appeals to God's will as the touchstone for ethical behavior. "Not everyone who says to me, 'Lord, Lord,' will enter the kingdom of heaven, but only the one who does the will of my Father in heaven" (Mt 7:21).

Interim ethics offers an explanation for the radical nature of Jesus' ethics at the expense of scriptural authority. Heroic service in behalf of others, as commendable as it is, cannot substitute for acknowledging fully Jesus' claims for himself and his teaching as proclaimed in the Gospels. In the end, Weiss and Schweitzer do not escape the quicksand of theological liberalism.

The existentialist interpretation. Rudolf Bultmann reinterprets the NT kerygma in existential terms. Even though highly skeptical concerning what can be known about the historical Jesus, he insists that Jesus called for a decision for the kingdom. One must choose to embrace the kerygma. In fact, one continually faces a necessity: choose the kingdom, be open to the future and cast aside anxiety about the present. Decision entails response to God's gracious invitation to trust in the God who is there. "All that man can do in the face of the Reign of God now breaking in is this: Keep ready or get ready for it. Now is the *time of decision*, and Jesus' call is the *call to decision*."[50] "The Reign of God, demanding of man decision for God against every earthly tie, is the salvation to come. Hence only he is ready for this salvation who in the concrete moment decides for that demand of God which confronts him in the person of his neighbor."[51]

Jesus' ethics directly challenge Jewish legalism, particularly that of the Pharisees. Jesus' message calls for radical obedience to the will of God. Legalism is satisfied with formal obedience—that is, meeting the requirements of the letter of the law. Jesus' ethic, on the other hand, addresses heart attitudes, as seen in the antitheses (Mt 5:21-48). According to Bultmann, the fatal problem in adopting mere formal obedience as sufficient in God's sight is the pernicious conception that one can then add to this fund of formal obedience by doing works of supererogation, performance of more than is required. One seeks to acquire merit and secure God's favor. Jesus stands squarely against such a conception: "That is just what Jesus protests against—that man's relation to God is regarded as a legal one. God requires radical obedience. He claims man whole—and wholly."[52] As to the immense minutiae of the cultic and ritual laws, Jesus excludes them

---

[50]Rudolf Bultmann, *Theology of the New Testament*, trans. Kendrick Grobel (2 vols.; New York: Scribner, 1951-1955), 1:9.
[51]Ibid., 1:21.
[52]Ibid., 1:13.

from the demands of God. In so doing, Jesus "sets free the purely religious relation to God in which man stands only as one who asks and receives, hopes and trusts."[53]

What, then, is the will of God? Bultmann simply answers, "The demand for love."[54] Does not this love need concrete examples? Bultmann replies, "Jesus completely refrained from making the love-commandment concrete in specific prescriptions. . . . The demand for love needs no formulated stipulations; the example of the merciful Samaritan shows that a man can know and must know what he has to do when he sees his neighbor in need of this help."[55]

Much is right in Bultmann's presentation of the ethics of Jesus. The Gospels do portray Jesus as calling for a radical decision to embrace the kerygma of the kingdom. Jesus does attack Jewish legalism and focuses on heart attitudes as the essence of ethical behavior. The problem with Bultmann's theological synthesis is its reductive nature. Not all of Jesus' ethical teaching is a call for decision. In fact, much of it is instruction for living. In other words, it is didache, not kerygma. Bultmann's protest against Jewish legalism predisposes him to be averse to specific behavioral guidelines and, consequently, he "throws the baby out with the bath water." "Jesus did not leave his followers to decide for themselves how they should carry out their new commitment. . . . On the contrary, he gives concrete examples as to how his followers are to live."[56]

SUMMARY AND THEOLOGICAL SYNTHESIS

Each of the various modern attempts to understand and incorporate the ethics of Jesus grasps an essential element of Jesus' ethical teaching. The problem in each case, however, is the failure to deal adequately with all of the evidence. The result is distortion owing to presuppositions inimical to the authority of Scripture.

Essential for understanding Jesus' ethics are the following:

1. Ethics and eschatology are inextricable. "Now but not yet" is the master key for unlocking not only Jesus' view of the kingdom but also his ethics. In other words, the tension between the present irruption of the kingdom in the person and work of Jesus and its culmination at the parousia must be firmly grasped. Already, God's grace, forgiveness and love are experienced by those who commit to the kingdom. Already, the power of

---

[53]Ibid.
[54]Ibid., 1:19.
[55]Ibid.
[56]Stein, *Method and Message*, p. 95.

the age to come has broken in, but the gift of the Holy Spirit is still a future promise for Jesus' disciples (Jn 16:15). Full redemption awaits the Day of the Lord, a day that the church will soon designate as "the day of the Lord Jesus" (2 Cor 1:14; cf. 1 Thess 5:2, 23; 2 Thess 1:7—2:6). In the meantime, Jesus demands a new righteousness, exceeding that of the Pharisees, a righteousness going beyond mere formal compliance. In one sense, Schweitzer was right: Jesus' ethics are an interim ethic—but not in the sense that he intended. The "interim" is the period of the overlap between this age and the age to come—an era already approaching two thousand years. Believers live "between the ages." Consequently, Jesus' teachings are normative until the end of the present age. In the ages to come, when believers are "like the angels in heaven" (Mt 22:30), these standards will be perfectly realized.

2. One must distinguish between the ethical teaching of the historical Jesus and that of the postresurrection Jesus. The historical Jesus' ethical teaching was incomplete until he accomplished his redemptive mission and bestowed the Holy Spirit on his followers at Pentecost. Through the Spirit, additional insight and direction was given (Jn 16:12-15). The NT letters develop and elaborate the implications of the "law of Christ." One must respect the fact that there is a progressive unfolding of Jesus' ethics and not read back into his historical ministry the Spirit-guided instruction of the post-Pentecostal church. This is not to pit one against the other; biblical theology simply tries to understand the progressive nature of revelation without sacrificing its organic unity. The later NT writings are not independent developments of Jesus' teaching; they are based directly on it.

3. The heart of Jesus' ethics, the "law of Christ," lies in the love commandment. When challenged by a legal expert to name the most important commandment (Mk 12:28-34; Mt 22:34-40; Lk 10:25-28), Jesus said that two summarized all the others. The first, and most important, was the Shema: "Love the LORD your God with all your heart" (Deut 6:5). The second was "Love your neighbor as yourself" (Lev 19:18). According to Jesus, "There is no other commandment greater than these" (Mk 12:31). The NT often underscores the centrality of the love command (Rom 13:9-10; 1 Cor 13; 14:1; 16:14; 2 Cor 5:14; 13:11, 14; Gal 5:6, 13-14, 22; Eph 3:17-19; Jas 2:8; 1 Pet 1:22; 2:17; 3:8; 4:8; 1 John [passim]). A vertical relationship with God is inseparable from and indispensable for a healthy, horizontal relationship with our fellow human beings.[57]

If the essence of ethical behavior is love, what, specifically, is love? Certainly it is not the sentimental, uncritical feeling of affection so endemic

---

[57]See Bruce Chilton and J. I. H. McDonald, *Jesus and the Ethics of the Kingdom* (Grand Rapids: Eerdmans, 1987), pp. 1-2.

in modern culture; rather it is an active seeking and implementation of the neighbor's welfare. *Agapē* ("love") is a giving of oneself on behalf of others and is determined by the revealed will of God, not by cultural expectations. It involves the will; a decision to act must be made, or else love has not truly been evidenced.[58] Love is epitomized in the grand summary of Jesus' ethical teaching in the Sermon on the Mount, the Golden Rule: "In everything do to others as you would have them do to you; for this the law and the prophets" (Mt 7:12). Jesus' mission profoundly demonstrates love: "For the Son of Man came not to be served but to serve, and to give his life a ransom for many" (Mk 10:45; cf. Jn 3:16; 15:13; Rom 5:6-8).

So who is my neighbor? This question distinguishes Jesus' ethics from those of his contemporaries. For Jesus, the neighbor is whomever you encounter. This might be a dreaded leper (Lk 5:12-14), a Samaritan (Samaritans were despised by most Jews) (Lk 10:25-37), one's enemies (Lk 6:27-36), or prostitutes and tax collectors (Lk 7:34; 15:1-2). In short, Jesus greatly expands the definition of one's neighbor. The degree of difficulty in Jesus' ethics is considerably higher than that of the Pharisees or of any other sect of Judaism, to say nothing of other religions.

4. The motive power for implementing Jesus' ethics is, remarkably, grace. Herein lies an even more important distinctive of Jesus' theology over against that of his coreligionists. Although there was an awareness of God's grace, first-century Judaism, in its various manifestations, operated under a rewards system.[59] The motive for obedience was reward both now, in the form of the approbation of others (Mt 6:2, 5, 16), and in the age to come, in the form of resurrection for Pharisees and Essenes and of a blessed memory for Sadducees (Lk 14:15; Mt 22:23). In Jesus' view, there are rewards for believers in conjunction with the resurrection and final judgment (Lk 14:12-14; Mt 6:2-4), but these are not what determine one's standing before God.[60] No series of parables makes this point more powerfully than the parables of the lost items in Luke 15 (lost sheep, lost coin, lost sons). The heavenly Father takes the initiative and redeems the lost. The Beatitudes begin with spiritual poverty (Mt 5:3). This implicitly points to the utter necessity of receiving God's grace as a prerequisite for kingdom life. The parable of the laborers in the vineyard (Mt 20:1-16) teaches that God extends his favor and blessing (i.e., grace) to whomever he wishes. Sinners

---

[58]Ethelbert Stauffer, "ἀγαπάω," *TDNT* 1:41-48.

[59]One senses this in eloquent passages in the Thanksgiving Hymns from Qumran, written probably by the Teacher of Righteousness. See the introduction and translation by Michael Wise, Martin Abegg Jr., and Edward Cook, *Dead Sea Scrolls: A New Translation* (San Francisco: HaperSanFrancisco, 1996), pp. 84-114.

[60]See Wesley L. Gerig, "Reward," *EDBT* 685-87.

cannot obligate God by their achievements; he simply acts out of his good will. According to the Gospels, Jesus' mission is the supreme demonstration of God's grace to fallen human beings (Jn 1:14-18), since Jesus himself is the Savior who redeems his people (Mt 1:21; 9:2-8 pars.; Mk 10:45; 14:22-25 pars.). Only those who respond in obedience to Jesus' message belong to him (Mt 7:21-27).

Jesus' ethics demonstrate both continuity and discontinuity with the various manifestations of first-century Judaism. All sectors of Judaism share a common heritage in the OT. A major disjunction centers on the issue of what constitutes true righteousness. First-century Judaism generally, and Pharisaism in particular, insisted on a certain level of performance in order to maintain one's standing as part of God's elect people. For Jesus, one must first experience the transforming power of unmerited grace before responding to God's demand for righteous living. Heartfelt repentance and faith in a gracious, inviting, welcoming God provide the motive power to respond and live ethically in the kingdom. As Ethelbert Stauffer says, "Jesus alone broke free from the old foundations and ventured a radically new structure."[61] In John's Gospel the temple police give voice to this radically new structure: "Never has anyone spoken like this!" (Jn 7:46).

But that which decisively breaks from first-century Judaism is the role of Jesus himself in actualizing ethical transformation. By his atoning death (Mk 10:45), Jesus inaugurates a new covenant (Mk 14:22-25 pars.). Those who share in this new covenant cry out, like the repentant thief, "Jesus, remember me when you come into your kingdom" (Lk 23:42). The christological shape of Jesus' kingdom ethics has no parallel in Judaism. Our explorations of Paul and John will further highlight the centrality of Christology in early Christian thought.

FOR FURTHER DISCUSSION

1. How does the "now but not yet" characteristic of the kingdom of God help in answering the question of whether the Beatitudes are entrance requirements or eschatological blessings?

2. Does Jesus' ethical teaching differ from that of his coreligionists? If so, how?

3. Are Jesus' ethics really practicable, or are they just idealist standards that never were intended to be taken literally?

---

[61]Stauffer, *TDNT*, 1:44.

4. Which explanation for Jesus' relationship to the law best explains the evidence?

5. How is the Lord's Prayer best utilized in Christian worship and devotional practice?

6. Analyze the various interpretations of Jesus' ethics throughout church history. What are the strengths and weaknesses of each view?

7. Does Jesus' teaching contain an ethical system? If so, how would you explain it?

FOR FURTHER READING

Betz, Hans Dieter. "Sermon on the Mount." *ABD* 5:1106-12.

Bultmann, Rudolf. *Theology of the New Testament*, translated by Kendrick Grobel, 1:11-22. 2 vols. New York: Scribner, 1951-1955.

Chilton, Bruce, and J. I. H. McDonald. *Jesus and the Ethics of the Kingdom*, pp. 79-134. Grand Rapids: Eerdmans, 1987.

Guthrie, Donald. *New Testament Theology*, pp. 896-907. Downers Grove, Ill.: InterVarsity Press, 1981.

Hurst, L. D. "Ethics of Jesus." *DJG* 210-22.

Jeremias, Joachim. *New Testament Theology: The Proclamation of Jesus*, translated by John Bowden, pp. 203-30. New York: Scribner, 1971.

Kümmel, Werner Georg. *The Theology of the New Testament according to Its Major Witnesses: Jesus-Paul-John*, translated by John E. Steely, pp. 48-58. Nashville: Abingdon, 1973.

Ladd, George E. *A Theology of the New Testament*, edited by Donald A. Hagner, pp. 118-32. Rev. ed. Grand Rapids: Eerdmans, 1993.

Marshall, I. Howard, *New Testament Theology*, pp. 117-21. Downers Grove, Ill.: InterVarsity Press, 2004.

Michaels, J. R. "Commandment." *DJG* 132-36.

Perkins, Pheme. "Ethics (New Testament)." *ABD* 2:652-65.

Rowdon, H. H. "Ethics of Jesus." *ZPEB* 2:404-11.

Stanton, G. N. "Sermon on the Mount/Plain." *DJG* 735-44.

Stein, Robert H. *The Method and Message of Jesus' Teaching*, pp. 88-109. Philadelphia: Westminster Press, 1978.

Thielman, Frank. *Theology of the New Testament*, pp. 98-110. Grand Rapids: Zondervan, 2005.

Verhey, A. D. "Ethics: The Ethic of Jesus." *ISBE* 2:169-73.

PART THREE

THE THEOLOGY
OF PAUL

6

Putting Paul in His Place

There is not one word of Pauline Christianity in the characteristic utterances of Jesus. . . . There has really never been a more monstrous imposition perpetrated than the imposition of Paul's soul upon the soul of Jesus. . . . It is now easy to understand how the Christianity of Jesus . . . was suppressed by the police and the Church, while Paulinism overran the whole western civilized world, which was at that time the Roman Empire, and was adopted by it as its official faith.

George Bernard Shaw, *Androcles and the Lion*

Paul was the first corrupter of the doctrines of Jesus.

Thomas Jefferson, letter to William Short

If one may be allowed to speak rather pointedly, the Apostle Paul was the only Arch-Heretic known to the apostolic age.

F. C. Bauer, *Orthodoxy and Heresy in Earliest Christianity*

Paul is making me nervous,
Paul is making me scared.
Walk into this room and swaggers,
Like he's God's own messenger.
Change the name of my brother,
Change the things that he said.
Says that he speaks to him,
But he never even knew the man.

Glen Phillips, "Fly from Heaven"

TO SAY THAT PAUL HAS HIS DETRACTORS would be an understatement.[1] To say that he has unabashed admirers is a fact, and I gladly count myself as one of them. The reasons for such wildly diverse reactions to Paul are manifold. Before expounding Paul's gospel, I want to bring to the surface some twenty-first century values and presuppositions that militate against an enthusiastic reception.

Some have difficulties reading Paul because his perspectives and behavioral directives run against the grain of modern culture and sensitivities.[2] For example, radical feminist theologians are likely to be quite critical of Paul because he enjoins women to be submissive to their husbands and men in general. Many African American and liberation theologians are unhappy with passages that seem to accept the status quo with regard to first-century slavery. Those advocating gay rights deplore passages where Paul condemns homosexual and lesbian behavior. Living in a post-Holocaust world, many theologians are troubled by remarks and attitudes in Paul that could be construed as contributory to anti-Semitism. A number of liberal theologians lament the fact that Paul "ruined" the simple faith of Jesus and actually created Christianity with its "high Christology."

But the Pauline letters are a battleground in more conservative circles as well. Traditionalists, complementarians and egalitarians all appeal to Paul in the acrimonious debate over the role of women in the home and in the church. Long-standing disputes about spiritual gifts, head coverings and hair length necessarily focus on 1 Corinthians. Nor should we overlook the fine points of eschatology, especially the rapture question. Paul is a primary source for sorting out the pre-, mid- and postrapture options. And we could list a number of other modern issues and concerns that sooner or later involve the writings of Paul. Consequently, Paul has been claimed as a "star witness" by partisans of many disputes in the modern church. The upshot is that Paul is being read differently by different people. This calls for humility and patience.

A problemlatic practice of readers of Paul, whether lay, clerical or scholarly, is that of selective reading. That is, certain passages are seized upon and become a "canon within the canon" by which other passages are evaluated. The result is that other passages never get the fair hearing that they deserve; they are not allowed to disturb our easy accommodation of Paul's thought to our preformed intellectual and cultural framework. The latter, almost unconsciously, becomes a grid superimposed on Paul's letters, such

---

[1]"He is probably the most vilified Christian since Pentecost" (Leander E. Keck and Victor P. Furnish, *The Pauline Letters* [Nashville: Abingdon, 1984], p. 12).
[2]See ibid., pp. 12-15.

that he now seems to share our own presuppositions. Paul challenges readers of varied theological persuasions to a deeper commitment than one to mere cultural Christianity; he invites us to die and rise with Christ (Rom 6:11-12; Gal 2:20; Eph 2:1-6; Col 2:12, 20). Are we prepared to hear Paul on his own terms, as uncomfortable as that might be?

CRITICAL PROBLEMS IN PAULINE THEOLOGY

The sources of Paul's theology. Critical problems must be negotiated before launching into an exposition of Paul's theology. The problems are different from those faced in the theology of Jesus. In Paul's case, we have primary sources deriving from the apostle himself. Thirteen letters in the NT canon are attributed to Paul, written either to congregations that he founded or was responsible for founding (with the one exception of Romans) or to associates in his missionary team (the Pastoral Epistles). Philemon, the one letter approximating a personal letter, is written to a friend in Colossae.

Many modern scholars, however, doubt that Paul wrote all the canonical letters attributed to him. It would unnecessarily lengthen this book to go into a detailed discussion of this issue. I simply outline the arguments lodged against the genuineness of some of the Pauline letters and provide a brief response.

The first scholar to attempt a historical study of Paul's theology, the Swiss theologian Leonhard Usteri (1824), accepted all thirteen of Paul's letters as genuine and demonstrated to his own satisfaction that Paul's thought cohered with the rest of the NT.[3] This changed drastically in the work of F. C. Baur (1792-1860) and his students. Baur concluded that only Romans, Galatians and the Corinthian letters were authentic.[4] Baur's minimalist assessment has not gained acceptance by a majority of modern NT scholars. There is widespread agreement that seven of the thirteen letters attributed to Paul are genuine. Others include a few more in their list. The box below shows the variations.

So why do so many mainline scholars doubt the authenticity of some Pauline letters? The reasons basically fall into two main categories: linguistic and content. As to the first, it must be admitted that in Colossians, Ephesians and the Pastorals, there are a rather high number of *hapax le-*

---

[3]Leonhard Usteri, *Entwicklung des Paulinischen Lehrbegriffs mit Hinsicht auf die übrigen Schriften des Neuen Testaments: Ein exegetisch-dogmatischer Versuch* (Zürich, 1824), cited in Werner G. Kümmel, *The New Testament: The History of the Investigation of Its Problems*, trans. S. McLean Gilmour and Howard C. Kee (Nashville: Abingdon, 1972), pp. 95-96 n. 131.

[4]See S. J. Hafemann, "Baur, F. C.," in *Dictionary of Major Biblical Interpreters*, ed. Donald K. McKim (Downers Grove, Ill.: InterVarsity Press, 2007), p. 180.

Table 6.1. Views on the Authenticity of Paul's Letters

Traditional View (in canonical order)	Consensus Critical View	Moderately Critical
Romans	Romans	Romans
1-2 Corinthians	1-2 Corinthians	1-2 Corinthians
Galatians	Galatians	Galatians
Ephesians		(Ephesians)*
Philippians	Philippians	Philippians
Colossians		(Colossians)*
1-2 Thessalonians	1 Thessalonians	1-2 Thessalonians
1-2 Timothy		
Titus		
Philemon	Philemon	Philemon
*Some hold that a Paulinist composed these letters incorporating genuine Pauline material. Colossians and Ephesians, along with the Pastoral Epistles, are sometimes called the Deutero-Pauline letters.		

gomena (literally, "once spoken")—that is, words occurring only once in the Pauline corpus or even the entire NT. As it turns out, Ephesians has fifty-one *hapax legomena*. The Pastorals also have a relatively high number (175 for the entire NT). Furthermore, most of these *hapax legomena* appear in the writings of the postapostolic church fathers. On the basis of this, many critical scholars hold that a Paulinist of the early second century was the actual author.

Even more significantly, the style of writing in the disputed letters diverges from the genuine letters.[5] The vigorous prose encountered in the undisputed letters is lacking in Colossians and Ephesians, where a pleonastic (more full and expanded) style predominates. For example, Ephesians 1:3-14 is one long sentence in the original Greek, strung together by relative pronouns and participles. One does not find such constructions in the seven acknowledged letters.

One must be very careful, however, in using *hapax legomena* and style as a method for determining authenticity. Both are quite variable in authors, depending on subject matter, occasion, and the period in an author's life. Furthermore, there is a highly compelling reason why Colossians, Ephesians and the Pastorals differ so much from the widely recognized Paulines in terms of vocabulary and style. These letters are responding to the threat of false teaching among the churches in Asia, and the author draws upon existing traditional and confessional materials in order to counteract it.

---

[5]For specifics, see E. E. Ellis, "Pastoral Letters," *DPL* 659-60; Donald Guthrie, *New Testament Introduction* (3rd ed.; Downers Grove, Ill.: InterVarsity Press, 1977).

Hymns, benedictions, doxologies and confessions of faith are not typically written in the same style as personal letters. Furthermore, the author appears to be borrowing terminology from the false teaching at certain points in order to rebut it. Thus, if Paul (assuming he is the author) incorporated such material, this would account for the high incidence of *hapax legomena* and the more pleonastic style (characterized by redundancy and unnecessary additions), which occurs precisely in the sections utilizing traditional material.

Some scholars think that a given author unconsciously reflects certain linguistic patterns. For example, the use of the ubiquitous *kai* ("and," "even") is said to be highly predictable for a particular individual. The procedure is to examine usage patterns in the commonly accepted Paulines and compare this with the disputed letters. According to some researchers, the disputed letters are so "out of sync" with the genuine ones that authorship must be denied. There are respected linguists, however, who cast doubt on the validity of this approach. Making the issue even more problematic is the relatively small corpus of material at our disposal. There are sections in all the disputed Paulines that do conform nicely to the accepted letters. All in all, the argument from vocabulary and style is not decisive.

Denial of Pauline authorship of Colossians and Ephesians on the basis of content has to do with differing emphases and nuances as compared to the undisputed letters. For example, in Colossians and Ephesians the notion of the church as a cosmic body, with Christ as the head (Eph 1:22-23; 4:15-16; 5:23; Col 1:18; 2:19), develops the simpler idea of the church conceived as a body consisting of several parts appearing in Romans and 1 Corinthians. Ephesians is also thought to reflect a view of the apostles from a later time, long after their deaths (Eph 2:20; 3:5-6). Some think that the concept of cosmic Christology reflects a post-Pauline interpretation of the person of Christ. In every case, I think a strong counterargument can be advanced.[6] Paul was a gifted theologian who had the capacity to elaborate and extend theological propositions in a number of directions, especially in polemical contexts, where he is responding to false teaching (as in Colossians and Ephesians). Furthermore, he probably borrows and "baptizes" the terminology of his opponents as he theologizes, thus accounting for nuances not previously encountered in earlier letters.

Objections to Pauline authorship of the Pastorals with regard to content fall into three subcategories: historical, ecclesiastical and doctrinal. As to the historical argument, problems arise when one attempts to fit the

---

[6]See C. E. Arnold, "Ephesians, Letter to the," *DPL* 240-42.

background and setting of the Pastorals into the framework of Acts. The numerous allusions to persons and events in the Pastorals resist easy incorporation. Where, for example, does a ministry to Crete (Titus) fit into Acts? Many critical scholars (beginning with Friedrich Schleiermacher for Titus) assume a pseudonymous theory (i.e., the Pastorals are fictitious compositions attributed to Paul but actually dating to the second century). Some critical scholars tweak this hypothesis by identifying genuine Pauline fragments inserted by the pseudonymous author.[7]

Conservative scholars generally posit a release from Roman house arrest (Acts 28:30), with a subsequent ministry in Spain (Rom 15:22-24, 28), a return and resumption of ministry in the East and rearrest and execution under Nero (Pastorals; cf. *1 Clem.* 5; Eusebius, *Hist. eccl.* 2:22).[8] Operating with this plausible hypothesis, one can fit the Pastorals into a period of some four to six years after the book of Acts ends (ca. A.D. 62). The terminal date, in any case, would have to be June of A.D. 68, when Nero committed suicide. Church tradition is unanimous that both Paul and Peter suffered martyrdom under Nero.

The ecclesiastical argument is based on the contention that the Pastorals reflect a post-Pauline setting. The lists of qualifications and responsibilities for the offices of elder and deacon supposedly reflect a period closer to the mid-second century. Nowhere in the genuine letters is there such a detailed discussion of qualifications for the church offices of elder and deacon. One should note, however, that this argument is essentially an argument from silence. If one accepts the reliability of Acts, Paul already appoints elders on his first missionary journey (Acts 14:23). As Donald Guthrie sagely observes, "A man of such forethought as Paul can reasonably be expected to give some guidance to his immediate followers relating to ecclesiastical matters."[9] A further objection to Pauline authorship observes that Timothy and Titus were instructed to appoint elders in the various house churches, reflecting the period of the second century, with its monarchical bishops. But this supposition reads far more into the Pastorals than is warranted. Paul's temporary delegation of authority for the appointment of elders hardly demonstrates an institutionalized monarchical episcopacy.

The doctrinal objection typically carries the most weight and is decisive for those scholars who reject authenticity. Why are the leading Pauline doctrinal themes absent or recast in the Pastorals? For example, the righteous-

---

[7]For example, P. N. Harrison, *The Problem of the Pastoral Epistles* (London: Oxford University Press, 1921).
[8]See R. N. Longenecker, "Paul, the Apostle," *ZPEB* 4:654-57.
[9]Donald Guthrie, "Pastoral Epistles," *ZPEB* 4:613.

ness of God, mystical union with Christ and the indwelling of the Holy Spirit are absent from the Pastorals. Terms familiar in the recognized Pauline letters appear in the Pastorals with a different nuance. A good example is the notion of "faith" *(pistis)*. In Paul's other letters faith is almost always used in a subjective sense, referring to an attitude of belief and trust. In the Pastorals faith is objective, "the faith," referring to the content of what is believed and is synonymous with "the truth," "the good treasure," "the sound words or teaching" and the "faithful sayings." Furthermore, the Pastorals focus on church order and discipline, good works, sound teaching and heretical teaching; clearly there are differences from the undisputed Pauline letters. The spontaneity and charismatic nature of worship in the Pauline house churches, depicted in the undisputed letters, disappears from sight and is replaced in the Pastorals by a more formal, institutionalized church order and worship.

Once again, however, caution must be exercised when employing what is essentially an argument from omission. Is there enough evidence to say confidently that the formulations in the Pastorals are incompatible with Pauline authorship? What is certain is the unanimous attribution to Paul by the early church. No one disputes Pauline authorship until the rise of post-Enlightenment biblical criticism. Is the internal evidence of content sufficient to overthrow the weight of the external testimony? Given that virtually all critics acknowledge genuine Pauline fragments in the Pastorals and that many passages at least resemble Pauline thought, one must decide which is more likely: a pseudonymous Paulinist or Paul himself. Guthrie insists, "There is nothing in the doctrinal content of these epistles to which Paul could not have put his name."[10] I am inclined to agree. If so, the more straightforward, less complex hypothesis, Pauline authorship, is preferred.

Paul's letters are circumstantial, and no one of them fully expounds his thought. The Pastorals are not written to house churches, of which many members were new converts, but rather to trusted colleagues grappling with pressing church problems. One hardly expects formulations of doctrine to be the same under differing circumstances. The highly confessional, stereotyped formulations of doctrine in the Pastorals may well reflect development of set traditions used in the Pauline mission, especially in light of concern over deviant teaching that surfaces repeatedly in the Pastorals.

The assumption that pseudonymity was widespread in the first century and would not have been viewed as unethical is questionable. Christian writings were examined and found wanting precisely on the grounds of

---

[10]Ibid.

pseudonymity. Serapion, the bishop of Antioch (died ca. A.D. 211), declared, "We receive both Peter and the other apostles as Christ, but pseudepigrapha in their name we reject."[11] Integrity was a highly valued virtue in Christian circles (Rom 9:1; 2 Cor 4:2; 11:10; 13:8; Eph 4:15; 6:14; 1 Tim 2:7). Although one cannot exclude the possibility that the early church was duped in this case, I think it quite unlikely. In light of the early church fathers' grasp of the Greek language and the temporal closeness to the earliest traditions, their testimony should not be quickly dismissed in favor of rather subjective arguments relating to stylistic and conceptual matters.

Even the highly nuanced position of James Dunn, in which pseudonymity is viewed as carrying on an honored tradition, fails to persuade.[12] To argue that the well-established practice, seen in the literature of Second Temple Judaism, of writing in the name of revered figures, such as Daniel, Enoch, Moses and Baruch, was continued by Christians is misleading. Nowhere in the former literature are there letters to actual addressees attributed to a known figure in which personal remarks and updates are incorporated into the document. In fact, in Paul's earliest correspondence, the Thessalonian letters, he takes pains to authenticate his letters with his own signature and greeting precisely because of the problem of forgery (2 Thess 3:17). The same may be said for Galatians (Gal 6:11; cf. 1 Cor 16:21).

In this book I include the Pastorals as part of my exposition of Pauline theology. As a consequence, a more full-orbed theology is possible than is the case with the critical consensus of only seven genuine letters.[13]

A related issue has to do with the reliability of the book of Acts. Many modern scholars minimize the historical value of Acts; its statements are incorporated into a reconstruction of Paul's thought only when paralleled in Paul's accepted letters. This "minimalist" stance disallows independent information that might be extracted from Acts. In this book I assume that Acts is historically reliable and may be used, with due caution, as a valuable supplement to Paul's letters.

The background of Paul's thought. A key issue in synthesizing Pauline theology involves recovering his cultural background and discovering the sources of his thought. Paul moved in three worlds. First, he was a Hellenistic Jew of the Diaspora, schooled in Jerusalem, the religious center of Palestinian Judaism. Second, he was a Roman citizen who spoke

---

[11]Eusebius, *Hist. eccl.* 6.12.3.
[12]J. D. G. Dunn, "Pseudepigraphy," *DLNTD* 977-84.
[13]For a fine treatment of Pauline theology that makes use of all thirteen letters attributed to Paul, see Thomas R. Schreiner, *Paul, Apostle of God's Glory in Christ: A Pauline Theology* (Downers Grove, Ill.: InterVarsity Press, 2001).

and wrote fluently in Greek and moved comfortably in the larger Greco-Roman world. Third, he was a missionary church planter in the Jesus movement. As such, he established a network of house churches all across the northeastern quadrant of the Mediterranean consisting of believers in Jesus whom he regarded as brothers and sisters.

Which of these three is most significant for interpreting his letters? Scholarship has witnessed a swinging of the pendulum between the Greco-Roman world and the world of Judaism. Some have stressed one almost to the exclusion of the other. In my view, all three are important and must be taken into account. If, on the other hand, one asks what is foundational to Paul's thought, I have no doubt: his Jewish heritage.[14] The Greco-Roman world, however, shapes this Jewish substructure in many and varied ways. But surely that which best explains the contours of Paul's theology is his commitment to Jesus Christ, the Lord of glory.

Paul and Judaism. As a starting point, I turn to Paul's own autobiographical statements (Rom 9:2-5; 11:1; 2 Cor 11:22-33; Gal 1:11-2:14; Phil 3:3-11), where it is possible to glean a few salient facts about Paul's Jewish upbringing. He was named Saul, after the first king of Israel, and, like his namesake, was from the tribe of Benjamin (see Acts 13:21). The expression "Hebrew of Hebrews" (Phil 3:5) most likely means that his family spoke Hebrew in the home, going well beyond the ability to recite the traditional synagogue prayers and read the Torah portions.[15] This is supplemented by the book of Acts, where we learn that Paul was sent off to Jerusalem to study under the renowned Pharisaic scholar, Gamaliel I, the Elder (Acts 22:3). Here he honed his ability to read, speak and write Hebrew and Aramaic. But the primary curriculum in Jerusalem was the "traditions of the ancestors," the oral law (Gal 1:14). This, Paul committed to memory.

Paul shared with the great majority of his coreligionists three core convictions of first-century Judaism: temple, Torah and territory. These shaped Judaism then and now. The God of Israel elected this people Israel to be the recipients of divine revelation, "the oracles of God" in the Torah on Mount Sinai (Rom 3:2). This revelation imparted the will of God and was a guide for all of life (Rom 2:17-20). The God of Israel graciously bestowed the land of Canaan to the patriarchs and their descendants. It was an everlast-

---

[14]In agreement is S. J. Hafemann, "Paul and His Interpreters," *DPL* 677-78. For a more complete discussion, see W. R. Stegner, "Jew, Paul the," *DPL* 503-11. F. F. Bruce says, "More important by far in Paul's own eyes than his Tarsian birthplace and his Roman citizenship, and more important by far for our understanding of him, was his Jewish heritage" (*Paul, Apostle of the Heart Set Free* [Grand Rapids: Eerdmans, 1977], p. 41.

[15]See Jerome Murphy-O'Connor, *Paul: A Critical Life* (New York: Oxford University Press, 1997), p. 36.

ing grant (e.g., Gen 12:7; 13:15). As the crowning gift, God vouchsafed to dwell among the people of Israel, first in the tabernacle, then in the first Temple (Ex 25:8; 29:43-46; 1 Kings 5:3-5; 6:11-13; 8:1-66). Although there is no mention of the *shekinah* (the glory or presence of God) in the Second Temple period, it was thought that the God of Israel paid especial attention to the rituals and prayers offered up in that place. Jesus referred to the second temple as "my Father's house" (Lk 2:49).

The second temple, greatly enlarged and beautified by Herod the Great beginning in 19 B.C. and continuing up until just before the war against Rome in A.D. 66, was a focal point for Jews in Palestine and Diaspora.[16] It stood as a splendid monument to Israel's election as the people of God. Since Judaism was still a sacrificial religion, regular performance of sacrificial rituals maintained the covenant relationship between the Lord and his people. Even though a majority of Jews lived in the Diaspora, most hoped to make at least one pilgrimage to the second temple in their lifetime, and synagogue delegations from the Diaspora made occasional visits to the Jerusalem temple. Diaspora synagogues not only were meeting places for the study of Torah but also were substitute temples.[17]

The Torah, even more so than the temple, defined Israel. All Jews regarded Moses as the supreme lawgiver. The Torah was the Lord's special gift and charge to Israel. Possession of Torah was, for the great majority of Jews, the essence of what it meant to be Israel (see Rom 2:17-20). As we will see shortly, however, Torah was also a bone of contention in Israel. Although its authority was unquestioned, its interpretation, especially the legal and cultic sections, was by no means uniform among first-century Jews. We will return to this issue later.

The land of Israel was an unconditional grant by Yahweh to the descendants of Abraham (e.g., Gen 12:7; 13:15, 17; 15:18; 17:18; 23:18; 24:7). This modest-sized piece of real estate, about the size of New Hampshire was the place where Israel's obedience to the covenant stipulations was to be ob-

---

[16]See W. R. Stegner, "Diaspora," *DPL* 211-13.

[17]Ellis Rivkin explains, "These meeting houses became gathering places for the so-called *ma'amadot* [the various divisions into which priests were assigned for service in the second temple]. These *ma'amadot* had been established by the Pharisees to give the Jews at large a sense of participation in the temple worship. The people were divided into twenty-four *ma'amadot* to parallel the twenty-four watches of the priesthood. While representatives of the *ma'amadot* went off to Jerusalem to be present while the daily offering was being sacrificed by the particular priestly watch with which the *ma'amadot* was associated, the other members of that *ma'amadot* would gather in the synagogues and read from the first chapter of Genesis. Since the daily sacrifice offered in the morning and evening was for the entire people, it was felt that their representatives ought to be present (*m. Ta'an.* 4:1-4)" ("Pharisees," *IDBSup* 661).

served. It is important to grasp that peoplehood and land were inseparable for most Jews of the first century, as indeed is still the case today. A fervent hope for the full restoration of the twelve tribes of Israel to their ancestral homeland was nourished by an overwhelming majority of Jews, whether in Israel or in the Diaspora. The *Psalms of Solomon*, a Jewish work thought to emanate from Pharisaic circles in the first century B.C., gives voice to this expectation of national regathering and restoration (*Pss. Sol.* 17:21-46). The Passover Seder ends with the prayer "Next year in Jerusalem!"

This intense longing for national restoration and the sense of outrage at pagans trampling upon the Holy Land led to the rise of a radical group, the Zealots. They were prepared to use violence in order to expel the pagan presence and influence from the Holy Land. Eventually, this faction succeeded in plunging the nation into a disastrous war against Rome in A.D. 66-74. Although Paul was not a zealot in this sense, he was "extremely zealous for the traditions of my fathers" (Gal 1:14 NIV), not above using violence as a tool for coercion to his point of view ("How intensely I persecuted the church of God and tried to destroy it" [Gal 1:13 NIV; cf. Acts 8:3; 9:1-2; 22:4; 26:9-11; 1 Tim 1:13]).

These three essentials, then, formed the core convictions of a sizable majority of Jews in the first century B.C. Although a few apostatized and assimilated into the Greco-Roman culture, most remained committed to the core convictions that defined Israel.

Paul, however, was not simply a Jew; he was a Pharisee. He belonged to a sect of Judaism that insisted on much more than commitment to the aforementioned core convictions. Torah comprised more than the written regulations found in the Pentateuch; it also embodied the further interpretations and adaptations by the scribal experts of the Pharisaic party. This process of elaboration and expansion of Torah had been going on for some time before the first century A.D.

Two factors account for an enlarged Torah. One was a conviction arising out of the destruction of the first temple and the exile. In the aftermath, the religious leaders pondered why this calamity had befallen the elect people of God. The answer, based upon Deuteronomy and the history patterned after it (Joshua—2 Kings), as well as the writing prophets, was clear: Israel had broken its covenant obligations. The solution surely must lie in a sincere and zealous effort to comply with the covenant demands. This led in the course of time to an expedient designed to ensure compliance. If all the commandments *(miṣwôt),* both positive and negative, in the Pentateuch are counted up, the total comes to 613. Pharisaism insisted that these 613 commandments be punctiliously observed and performed. To assist in this endeavor, other sanctions were prescribed in order to prevent violations, even inadvertent, of any of the 613. This process was called "hedging the law" (m. ʾAbot 1:1-4).

Another factor involved adaptation and reinterpretation. After 586 B.C. most Jews lived outside the land of Israel. This meant that specific commandments regarding duties and actions to be taken in the land of Israel had to be adapted or modified for Jews living among the Gentiles in the Diaspora. Authoritative rulings by scribal experts supplied this need. A key component of Pharisaism lay in its determination that the ritual purity of the priesthood be transferred to the realm of home and hearth. Most of the book of Leviticus is priestly instruction concerning how to perform the rituals of ancient Israel's worship. The Pharisees sought to reapply these to all Jews. Thus each Pharisee was responsible to maintain a state of ritual purity much like the priests of the first commonwealth.

Two examples illustrate the process. The fourth commandment enjoined sanctifying the sabbath. This involved the cessation of work: "you shall not do any work" (Ex 20:10). This, however, prompted another question: What is work? This led to an exhaustive analysis of the different types and categories of work that might be possible. Eventually, the rabbis formulated thirty-nine distinct categories (called "fathers") of work, each of which was further subdivided. Among the basic categories are the actions of sewing, plowing, reaping, binding sheaves, threshing and so on (m. Šabb. 7:2). This demonstrates elaboration and expansion of the law.

Exodus 23:19b reads, "You shall not boil a kid in its mother's milk." The precise meaning of this prohibition is unclear. Many modern scholars assume that the prohibition is connected with a Canaanite ritual or a mother goddess fertility motif.[18] The rabbis, however, understood it to require that meat and dairy products never be eaten together. Today, observant Jews in the Orthodox tradition still follow the kashrut system (i.e., what is suitable or acceptable), which entails, among many other things, the requirement that one have separate dishes for meat and dairy products. This demonstrates reinterpretation of the law.

These examples illustrate a long process of hedging, adapting and reinterpreting the Pentateuchal legislation for new times and places. One may wonder how such extrabiblical legislation gained legitimacy with the rank-and-file populace. The answer: rabbinic tradition claimed that, on Mount Sinai, in addition to the written law, Moses received supplemental

---

[18]See W. J. Houston, "Foods, Clean and Unclean," in Dictionary of the Old Testament: Pentateuch, ed. T. Desmond Alexander and David W. Baker (Downers Grove, Ill.: InterVarsity Press, 2003), pp. 333-34.

legislation orally. This additional legislation became known as the "oral Torah" *(tôrâ bĕ ʿāl peh* [literally, "Torah by means of mouth"]). The Gospel of Mark refers to this as "the tradition of the elders" (Mk 7:3), and Paul makes reference to "the traditions of my fathers" (Gal 1:14 NIV). A tractate in the Mishnah claims that the oral Torah was passed down from Moses to Joshua, from Joshua to the seventy elders (Ex 24:1), from the elders to the judges, from the judges to the prophets, from the prophets to Haggai, Zechariah and Malachi, and from them to the Men of the Great Assembly (*m. ʾAbot* 1:1; cf. *ʾAbot R. Nat.* 1:7-16). This tradition goes back probably to the first century A.D. or even earlier. Thus the oral Torah, memorized and passed on orally to each succeeding generation of scholars, was as authoritative and binding as the written law, though the two were clearly distinguished. Furthermore, the Pharisees insisted upon the right to sit on "the seat of Moses" and adjudicate behavioral standards and practices (see Mt 23:2). The essence of Pharisaism was a fervent defense of the twofold Torah, written *(tôrâ kātûb)* and oral *(tôrâ bĕ ʿāl peh).*

By the first century A.D., Pharisaism was divided into two competing parties, the House of Hillel and the House of Shammai, two eminent teachers of the twofold Torah of the first century B.C. Gamaliel the Elder, a contemporary of Jesus and grandson of Hillel, taught a more accommodating approach to halakah than that of the generally stricter House of Shammai. The brief cameo appearance of Gamaliel in Acts portrays him as a man of moderation and caution (Acts 5:33-39). Young Saul of Tarsus, however, bursts on the scene in Acts as a firebrand (Acts 7:58—8:3; 9:1-2). One should not, on this account, call into question the reliability of Acts. After all, more than a few fledgling scholars deliberately stake out positions contrary to their mentors. Saul seems by temperament to be an activist. Convinced that only wholehearted observance of Torah by all Jews could bring about national salvation, he resisted any notion of "wait and see" toward the Jesus movement. He sprang into action determined to crush it (1 Cor 15:9; Gal 1:13-14; Phil 3:6).

Paul's Pharisaic heritage is often reflected in his theology as an apostle of Jesus Christ. Not least in this regard is his pronounced apocalyptic worldview. Like Jesus, Paul modifies the traditional Jewish apocalyptic notion of the "two ages," in that already the powers of the coming age are operative in the present evil age. We thus see continuity with the teaching of Jesus on the kingdom of God. Like Jesus, Paul shares with the Pharisees several points of continuity with regard to eschatological views, most notably the doctrine of bodily resurrection for believers (1 Cor 15).

Paul also stresses holiness and purity, so important to Pharisaism. The difference is that Paul, as a Christian, transforms ritual purity into moral purity. One still sees the influence of boundaries and markers in Pauline ethics. Sexual ethics in the Pauline letters unmistakably continue the high standards of Pharisaism—indeed, even higher than Pharisaism regarding divorce (1 Cor 7:10-11). Individual and corporate purity are hallmarks of Pauline parenesis (1 Cor 5:1-5; 6:12-20; 7:1-7; 1 Thess 4: 1-7).

A contentious issue concerns Paul's view of the Torah. Although Paul can maintain that "the law is holy, and the commandment is holy and just and good" and "the law is spiritual" (Rom 7:12, 14), he can also assert that "now we are discharged from the law, dead to that which held us captive" (Rom 7:6). Sorting this out is not easy. I reserve a separate section for a more extended discussion of this debated point. I can at least say here, however, that Paul the Christian still has high regard for the law of Israel and sees its fulfillment in the life of a Spirit-filled believer (Rom 8:4).

A more esoteric aspect of first-century Pharisaism may also be reflected in Paul's thought: *merkabah* mysticism. The Hebrew word *merkābâ* refers to the divine throne chariot of the Lord. According to 1 Chronicles 28:18, David planned the construction of a golden chariot for the cherubim surmounting the ark of the covenant. But the taproot of this notion occurs in Ezekiel's visions (Ezek 1; 10). Ezekiel sees the mobile throne chariot of Yahweh surrounded by four living creatures, fire and lightning, and gleaming amber, crystal and sapphire (see also 2 Kings 2:11-12; 6:17). In the medieval period an entire mystical literature and movement focused on the throne chariot. There is some evidence, however, that elite members of the Pharisees cultivated spiritual experiences relating to visionary ascents to the divine throne chariot. There is a famous story in the Talmud (*b. Ḥag.* 14b) that recounts an ascent to the throne room by four rabbis, of whom only one, Rabbi Akiba, survived (he died in A.D.135). The Mishnah indicates that publicly expounding upon the throne chariot was discouraged: "They do not expound upon the laws of prohibited relationships [Lev 18] before three persons, the works of creation [Gen 1] before two, or the Chariot [Ezek 1] before one" (*b. Ḥag.* 2:1). Although Paul does not mention visionary ascents as part of his Pharisaic past, he does relate an experience, after his conversion, in which he ascended to the throne of God, called "the third heaven" or "paradise" (2 Cor 12:1-10). The cosmology and terminology of this event finds numerous parallels in Second Temple texts. What is fascinating is that Paul introduces his account by speaking of "visions and revelations of the Lord" (2 Cor 12:1b). The book of Acts narrates several instances when Jesus appeared to him subsequent to his conversion (Acts 9:12; 16:9-10; 18:9-11; 22:17-21; 23:11; 27:23-24). Whether or not Paul had visionary experiences as a Pharisee remains unclear; what we can affirm is that he, as a believer in Jesus, had many visionary experiences and, at least on one occasion, was caught up to the very throne room of God.[19]

Paul and the Greco-Roman world. Paul was born in Tarsus of Cilicia, home to a university of some reputation (Acts 21:39). Even though his family identified with Pharisaism and thus would have shunned some aspects of Greco-Roman society (e.g., pagan temples, the gymnasiums and athletic contests, the public baths, the meat markets), he nonetheless benefited from its manifold contributions and institutions, not least of which was the network of roads and waterways linking the vast empire together.[20] As it turned out, Paul's Roman citizenship also served him well in his missionary enterprise. Several times he is spared life-threatening situations because of it.[21]

The most obvious example of Greco-Roman influence is Paul's letters themselves, written to predominantly Gentile Christian congregations. Paul writes fluent, polished Greek and occasionally produces elegant Greek prose (e.g., Paul's great celebration of love in 1 Cor 13). Furthermore, the Bible that Paul uses as a missionary to the Gentiles is the Septuagint (LXX), the Greek translation of the Hebrew Bible. Most of the OT quotations in Paul's letters are, understandably, from the LXX.[22]

Sprinkled throughout Paul's letters are indicators of the prevailing Greco-Roman culture. Paul shows acquaintance with Stoic thought, which should not surprise us, given the prominence of this philosophic school at Tarsus and a general awareness of its tenets even in the religiously conservative city of Jerusalem.[23] There are two certain citations from classical authors in Paul's letters: Menander's play *Thais* (1 Cor 15:33) and Epimendes' *De oraculis* (Tit 1:12). In addition, Luke places a third citation in Paul's mouth on Mars Hill: Aratus's *Phaenomena* 5 (Acts 17:28). Although this is not a lot and the quotations may well have been widely known in Greco-Roman society, it does illustrate that Paul is generally aware of the "great tradition." Paul easily incorporates various genres and literary features into his letters. For example, he adapts the diatribe style in order to outline and

---

[19]According to J. Laansma, "It could be that Paul had earlier practiced a kind of mysticism such as we encounter in these traditions—this might explain the various parallels between his writings in general and the Merkabah texts—but that experience of the thorn had effected the shift in evaluation that he now encourages the Corinthians to accept" ("Mysticism," *DNTB* 733).

[20]See L. J. Kreitzer, "Travel in the Roman World," *DPL* 945-46.

[21]See M. Reasoner, "Citizenship, Roman and Heavenly," *DPL* 139-41.

[22]For a full discussion, see M. Silva, "Old Testament in Paul," *DPL* 630-35.

[23]See T. Paige, "Philosophy," *DPL* 717.

defend his gospel in Romans 1—11,[24] and he adapts the standard letter format of the first-century world for his missionary correspondence.[25]

Beyond this, however, Paul's letters reflect the ambient Greco-Roman culture at point after point. One runs across various Greco-Roman customs in matters such as marriage and divorce (Rom 7:1-3), the patronage system (Gal 3:19-20; 1 Tim 2:5),[26] slavery (1 Cor 7:21; Eph 6:5-9; Col 3:22-4:1; Philemon; 1 Tim 6:1-2), and child tutors (Gal 3:24—4:3). Greco-Roman values and traditions such as honor and shame, status, rhetorical eloquence, intellectual abstraction and elitism repeatedly surface, most notably in the Corinthian correspondence.

From a close reading of Paul's letters, one realizes that the first readers were situated in urban settings.[27] Various images from a Greco-Roman city drift past our consciousness: marketplaces, temples and temple dining rooms, forums, courts, jails, theaters, stadiums and gymnasiums with their athletic training and contests. These were the visually impressive edifices of Greco-Roman culture at its best. But there was also a dark side, and we frequently catch glimpses of this aspect as well: Paul's reaction to idolatry, hostility, sexual perversion and callousness so prevalent in that day (Rom 1:21-32; Eph 2:1-3, 12; Phil 2:15; 1 Thess 4:5). A general sense of fear, isolation, despair and indifference hung in the air like a pall over these great cities, where the average life expectancy at birth was well under thirty years of age. Fire, epidemics and crime stalked the streets. Overcrowding, unsafe housing with inadequate heating and cooling and no water, and a lack of sanitation and sewage created a hellhole for most inhabitants. Thankfully, we cannot detect the olfactory dimension to Greco-Roman cities in Paul's letters. As Rodney Stark reminds us, these cities could be smelled from several miles away—the stench was that bad.[28] As for the wealthy, "no wonder they were so fond of incense"[29] in their more accommodating residences!

---

[24]See D. F. Watson, "Diatribe," *DPL* 213-14.

[25]See P. T. O'Brien, "Letters, Letter Forms," *DPL* 550-53.

[26]"Patron-client relations permeated the whole of ancient Mediterranean society" (John J. Pilch and Bruce J. Malina, eds., *Biblical Social Values and Their Meaning: A Handbook* [Peabody, Mass.: Hendrickson, 1993], p. 135). See also David deSilva, *Honor, Patronage, Kinship and Purity: Unlocking New Testament Culture* (Downers Grove, Ill.: InterVarsity Press, 2000).

[27]See Wayne A. Meeks, *The First Urban Christians: The Social World of the Apostle Paul* (New Haven: Yale University Press, 1983).

[28]Rodney Stark, *The Rise of Christianity: How the Obscure, Marginal Jesus Movement Became the Dominant Religious Force in the Western World in a Few Centuries* (San Francisco: HarperSanFrancisco, 1997), p. 154. Chapter 7 in Stark's book demolishes any romantic ideas that one may harbor with regard to Greco-Roman cities!

[29]Ibid.

Yet it was the Greco-Roman city that proved to be such a fertile ground for the Pauline mission and was the setting of his canonical letters.

Paul was a consummate cross-cultural missionary. Of the many examples that could be selected to illustrate the point, I choose the athletic metaphors in Paul's letters. Saul the Pharisee would not have frequented the gymnasium or stadium before his conversion. Among other impediments was the fact that participants in athletic contests competed in the nude. This offended the piety and morals of Pharisees. As a matter of fact, there is no proof that Paul the Christian attended athletic competitions. What we do see reflected in his letters, however, is an awareness of the importance of sport to the general culture. As a missionary to the Gentiles, Paul skillfully employed or alluded to athletic images to convey spiritual truths.

The most extended application of athletics to the Christian life occurs in 1 Corinthians. Corinth was the location for the celebrated biennial Isthmian Games, in which athletes from across the Mediterranean came to compete. In 1 Corinthians 9:24-27 Paul provides a brief glimpse of the Isthmian Games. He describes two contestants: one is a runner, probably a sprinter, and the other is a boxer or competitor in the *pankration*. The *pankration* was an event in which the contestants are permitted to strike opponents with any number of blows, whether a slap, kick, punch or chop. The only thing disallowed was biting! Several details in the passage demonstrate that Paul is fairly well acquainted with the specifics of the competition. He knows, for example, that one cannot compete without certifying that a certain training regimen has been followed for a prescribed time ("Athletes exercise self-control in all things" [1 Cor 9:25a]; "I punish my body and enslave it" [1 Cor 9:27]). He also knows what award the winner receives ("a perishable garland" [1 Cor 9:25b]). We know from other sources that this wreath was withered celery. He also is aware that judges could disqualify a competitor (1 Cor 9:27). Paul aptly employs the extended metaphor to illustrate the commitment and training needed to be an effective missionary for Christ and adds the nice touch that Christians receive "an imperishable" reward (1 Cor 9:25). He exhorts his Christian readers to exercise an even greater dedication to the cause of Christ.

Paul the Christian missionary. Paul was heir to the Christian tradition. He did not become a follower of Christ until three to five years after the crucifixion. Prior to Paul's conversion, according to Acts (Acts 1:15; 2:41, 47; 4:4, 33; 5:14), the Jesus movement grew rapidly in the very heartland of Judaism. In contrast to some scholars who attribute Christianity to the inventive genius of Paul, I hold that under the guidance of the Holy Spirit, the central features of what would later be called "Christian" theology were already taking shape (see Jn 16:4b-15). This is not to deny that Paul's thought represents a significant development of truths that were only latent in the earliest apostolic preaching of the gospel, but rather to affirm that Paul's theology stands in continuity with that message. This "Hebrew of Hebrews" was a choice instrument, possessing an acute theological mind honed in the Pharisaic school of Gamaliel and animated by zeal for the traditions of the fathers. This Pharisaic legacy, which, in and of itself, he later considered mere rubbish (Phil 3:8), was transformed by the renewing of his mind when he encountered the Lord Jesus (Rom 12:2). According to Paul's own words and the book of Acts, his gospel, not received from a human source, nor taught to him (Gal 1:12), was in fundamental accord with the gospel preached by the Jerusalem leadership (Gal 2:6-10; cf. Acts 15). In short, Paul was not so much an innovator as a herald of the apostolic preaching of the cross (1 Tim 2:7; 2 Tim 1:11).

On the other hand, Paul's letters bear witness to a substantial network of coworkers in his church-planting ministry. Some of these were believers before Paul came to faith (e.g., Barnabas [Acts 4:36-37; 9:27] and Andronicus and Junia [Rom 16:7]). Each doubtless contributed to the life and ministry of Paul. An intriguing question is this: How much of Paul's preaching and teaching was learned from other Christians such as Ananias, who, according to Luke, was instrumental in his baptism (Acts 9:10-19)? One can imagine the late-night sessions during which Paul plied Ananias for more information about Jesus of Nazareth. Surely Paul does not mean that Jesus Christ revealed all these details to him during the experience on the road to Damascus. Paul's letters give evidence that he was indeed indebted to the earliest followers of Jesus for basic affirmations of faith. Certain passages betray a formulaic character reflecting confessional statements. Paul uses the expressions "received" and "passed on" to describe some of these. In rabbinic literature similar expressions are used for the transmission of oral traditions. In all likelihood, Paul learned from other Christians (such as Ananias) the basic traditions about Jesus and passed them on to his converts (Rom 16:7; 1 Cor 11:2, 23; 15:1-3).[30]

One may identify at least seven elements of early Christian tradition that Paul received and incorporated into his gospel:[31]

1. the apostolic kerygma (1 Cor 15:1-7)

---

[30]See M. B. Thompson, "Tradition," DPL 943-45.
[31]See Archibald M. Hunter, The Gospel According to St. Paul (rev. ed.; Philadelphia: Westminster Press, 1966), pp. 11-12; Thompson, "Tradition," DPL 943-45.

2. the confession of Jesus as Messiah, Lord and Son of God (Rom 1:1-6; 10:9-10; Phil 2:11)

3. the gift of the Holy Spirit (Gal 3:2-5; 1 Thess 1:5-6; 4:8)

4. the meaning of Christian baptism (Rom 6:1-4; 1 Cor 10:1-5; 12:11)

5. the institution and meaning of the Lord's Supper (1 Cor 11:23-26)

6. the "words of the Lord" (dominical tradition) (Rom 12:14; 14:9; 16:19; 1 Cor 7:10; 9:14; 13:2)

7. the hope of Jesus' return (1 Thess 4:14)

Before leaving this topic, however, I must emphasize that the essential gospel that Paul preached had its origin in a personal encounter with the risen Christ. On this point he is adamant (1 Cor 15:8-11; Gal 1:1, 11-12, 15-24; 2:6-10; 1 Thess 2:4). This was the defining moment in Paul's life.[32] The raging persecutor of "the Way" is stopped dead in his tracks by the *shekinah* (Acts 9:3). Saul's question "Who are you, Lord?" elicits an answer totally reorienting his world: "I am Jesus whom you are persecuting" (Acts 9:5). Several core convictions suddenly became clear:

1. Jesus of Nazareth is alive and well (the age of resurrection has begun).

2. Jesus is the Christ and the exalted Lord (he is God's unique Son).

3. The cross is the place where God reveals himself (redemptive history has reached its climax).

4. Salvation is a divine initiative and an act of sheer grace (sinners are incapable of rendering meritorious works).

5. Jesus Christ indwells his people (sinners are reconciled to God).

These form the nucleus of Paul's gospel and the core of his theology. Just as the Pentateuch forms the basis of Jewish thought, so these five historical-theological truths are foundational for Paul's theology. This will become more evident as we delve more deeply into Paul's thought.

Jesus and Paul. One more question must be raised about the background of Paul's thought: How much continuity is there between Jesus and Paul? That is, are the introductory quotations for this chapter correct? Was Paul the virtual founder of Christianity? The short answer is no.

Although it is true that there are only a few passages in which Paul directly quotes a dominical saying (1 Cor 7:10; 9:14; 11:23; 1 Thess 4:15), this is misleading because there are a number of passages that allude to the

---

[32]See J. M. Everts, "Conversion and Call of Paul," *DPL* 156-63; Seyoon Kim, *The Origin of Paul's Gospel* (Grand Rapids: Eerdmans, 1982).

teaching of Jesus (e.g., Rom 12—14; 1 Thess 4). Beyond this, however, a careful perusal of Paul's letters shows that if one penetrates to the fundamental structures of Pauline thought, there exists a remarkable coherence with Jesus' proclamation of the kingdom.[33] In the words of Herman Ridderbos, "It is plain that . . . Paul's preaching is materially altogether in harmony with the great theme of Jesus' preaching of the coming of the kingdom of heaven."[34] This is not to deny considerable difference of perspective between the two. How could it be otherwise? Paul's letters are generated out of a mission aimed primarily at Gentiles in the northeastern quadrant of the Mediterranean. This is a completely different setting from that of Jesus' mission to Palestinian Jews. But even more important than an ethnic-geographical difference are the respective settings in the framework of salvation history. Paul's perspective must perforce be different from that of Jesus in that Jesus, during his earthly ministry, looks forward to the cross, whereas Paul looks back to the cross. With the aid of hindsight and the Holy Spirit, Paul now grasps the big picture of redemptive history. There is no denying that Paul elaborated and extended the teaching of Jesus. The point is, however, that it was the teaching of his master that he developed. There is a demonstrable, organic connection between the teaching of Jesus and Paul's gospel. This chimes in with Paul's firm conviction that as an apostle, he had "the mind of Christ" (1 Cor 2:16).

METHODOLOGICAL PROBLEMS IN EXTRACTING PAULINE THEOLOGY

The nature of the sources. We are confronted with several methodological problems as soon as we set about trying to reconstruct Paul's theology. For example, how do we synthesize Pauline theology from occasional letters? By "occasional" is meant that each letter is addressed to a particular house church or to several house churches. The biblical theologian must be acutely aware of the circumstantial nature of the Pauline letters. In each case, Paul has specific pastoral, missionary objectives: resolve congregational disputes and crises (Romans, 1 Corinthians, Philippians), counter false teachers and teaching, whether actual (2 Corinthians, Galatians) or potential (Ephesians, Colossians), clear up misunderstandings (2 Corinthians, 2 Thessalonians), exhort and encourage in Christian discipleship (1 Thessalonians), give thanks for assistance (Philippians), solicit financial support (Romans) and so forth. As noted, there are usually

---

[33]See J. M. G. Barclay, "Jesus and Paul," *DPL* 492-503; David Wenham, *Paul: Follower of Jesus or Founder of Christianity?* (Grand Rapids: Eerdmans, 1995); Hunter, *The Gospel According to St. Paul,* pp. 76-88.

[34]Herman Ridderbos, *Paul: An Outline of His Theology,* trans. John Richard De Witt (Grand Rapids: Eerdmans, 1975), p. 48.

multiple purposes in each letter. What this means is that one must infer the theological substructure that informs the specific argument or application in a given letter.

Inferring Paul's theology is no easy task. Historical distance not infrequently prevents us from grasping all the nuances of Paul's remarks. We are, as it were, listening in on a two-way conversation in which we hear only one party, Paul. There are times when Paul mentions things about which modern readers are totally in the dark because it is information shared only between him and his listeners/readers. We must frankly admit that some passages are simply opaque (e.g., 1 Cor 11:10; 15:29; 2 Thess 2:6-7). How wonderful it would be if we could call Paul on a cell phone and ask for clarification![35] But since we lack that option, our only alternative is a patient reading and rereading of Paul's correspondence in light of any new insight available from the background and thought world of the first-century A.D. Mediterranean. Fortunately, however, using an array of historical and literary approaches, we can extract a reasonably reliable understanding of Paul's theology.

The limited corpus. A second difficulty lies in an inescapable limitation: Paul's theology obviously was broader and deeper than what is conveyed in the extant letters. Once again, how helpful it would be if we could discover additional genuine Pauline writings with which to augment our canonical collection. It is worth noting at this point that we would never have known that Pauline churches celebrated the Lord's Supper were it not for a problem in this regard that prompted Paul to make some extended comments to the Corinthian congregation on the form and meaning of this central Christian ritual (1 Cor 11). The upshot is that we must be careful in framing Pauline theology lest we give the impression that we have a complete summary in hand. In fact, we have but a selective digest. Still, this digest has been instrumental in shaping Christian thought for centuries and will continue to do so until, in Paul's words, we "see face to face" and "know fully" (1 Cor 13:12).

I include a diagram to illustrate the selectivity involved in synthesizing Pauline theology (see figure 6.1 on p. 218). The smaller concentric circles, representing a particular biblical theologian's synthesis of Paul's theology

---

[35]Some years ago, during a class session on the Pauline Epistles, two of my students decided to "lighten up" the class. One of them, on the pretense of having a coughing fit, excused himself from the room. Not long thereafter, the other received a call on his cell phone. He said it was for me and was from the apostle Paul! Going along with the gag, I proceeded to engage "Paul" (whose voice sounded vaguely familiar!) in a long dialogue about some of my unresolved questions stemming from his letters. Unfortunately, "Paul" provided very vague responses or kept changing the subject! I have not had any calls from Paul since.

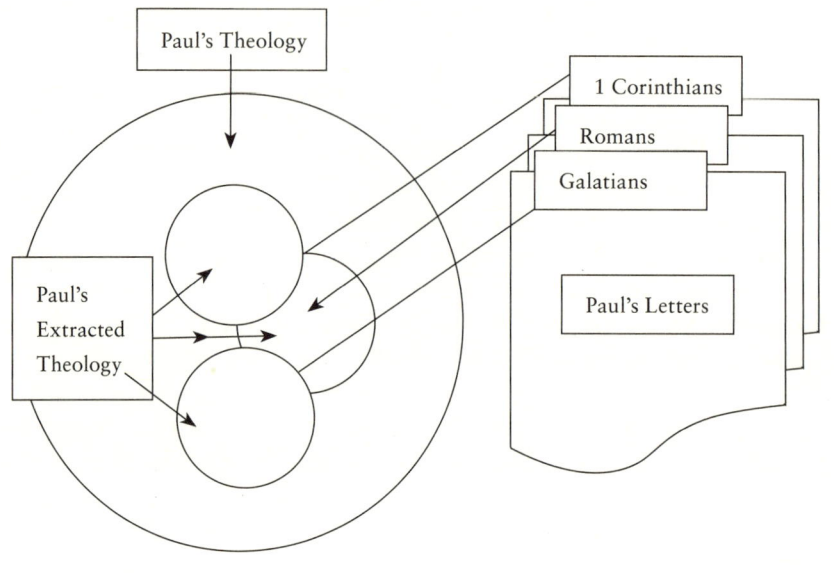

Figure 6.1. Synthesizing Paul's theology

as extracted from his occasional letters, fits within the larger circle of Paul's entire theology.

The problem of consistency and development. A third methodological problem has to do with the question of whether Paul was consistent. Did he change his mind on certain issues? Two examples quickly come to mind. Does Paul have a consistent position on the law of Moses and its continuing validity under the new covenant? Selected passages from Galatians, 2 Corinthians and Romans seemingly offer differing answers (e.g., Gal 2:19; 3:6—4:10, 4:21—5:12; 2 Cor 3; Rom 3:21-31; 6:14; 7:1-13). (We will investigate this issue more fully later.) Does Paul have a consistent position on the role of women in the church? One can easily collate verses that seem at face value to stand in tension or even contradiction (1 Cor 11:5; 14:34; 1 Tim 2:12). Related to the consistency issue is the question of development in Paul's thought. Does his theology evolve over time? How does one reconcile Paul's advice on marriage in 1 Corinthians 7:25-38 with his advice to young widows in 1 Timothy 5:11-15? Paul clearly seems to view his own participation in the parousia differently in 1 Thessalonians 4 and 2 Timothy 4. Furthermore, a case can be made that Paul changed his view of the nature and timing of the resurrection (1 Thess 4:13-18; 1 Cor 15:50-57; 2 Cor 5:1-10).

Appealing too quickly to the doctrine of inspiration may foreclose on a genuine understanding of a particular Pauline passage. Ralph Waldo Emerson's aphorism bears repeating here: "A foolish consistency is the hobgoblin of small minds." The issue is really quite complex. Determining inconsistency is not at all straightforward. Definitions become very important. Development of thought does not necessarily involve inconsistency or contradiction; it may only entail elaboration or specification. Direct contradiction would, of course, be a serious challenge to the orthodox understanding of inspiration. But here again one must distinguish what Scripture affirms and teaches from what it contains. All are agreed that Scripture contains errors but teaches none. As an obvious example, the Bible records lies and falsehoods by various personalities, beginning with the serpent in Genesis 3. The reader understands intuitively that Scripture does not endorse all that is said in it. In the case of Paul's letters, perspective is crucial. The context must be carefully scrutinized so that the various propositions are interpreted from the perspective of the writer's intention and that of the assumed readers. Many alleged contradictions may be satisfactorily harmonized in this manner, a perfectly acceptable practice in reputable historical investigation. Benefit of doubt ought to be accorded any writer with regard to alleged inconsistency. If, however, after careful investigation, one encounters evidence of contradiction, the best procedure is to acknowledge the difficulty and not forcibly harmonize the text. Our confidence in the trustworthiness of Scripture is not undermined by "problem passages" and what Gerhard Maier calls "minor imperfections." There are times when we should, as the rabbis counseled, put our hand over our mouth and frankly acknowledge, "I don't know." Most exegetes have certain passages that they set aside, like a dog buries a bone, only to retrieve them from time to time and chew on them a bit more.

The problem of identifying a center of Pauline theology. A final methodological problem has to do with determining whether there is a center to Pauline theology. In other words, is there one concept that unifies and integrates all Paul's thought? Numerous suggestions have been proffered.[36]

As we already saw in chapter 2, Martin Luther and the Reformers latched upon the notion of justification by faith. In Reformed circles this is still championed as the master key to Pauline theology. Other modern scholars, such as Rudolf Bultmann, Ernst Käsemann and Peter Stuhlmacher,

---

[36]For further discussion, see James D. G. Dunn, *The Theology of Paul the Apostle* (Grand Rapids: Eerdmans, 1998), pp. 19-23; Gerhard Hasel, *New Testament Theology: Basic Issues in the Current Debate* (Grand Rapids: Eerdmans, 1978); R. P. Martin, "Center of Paul's Theology," *DPL* 92-95; D. Moo, "Paul," *NDBT* 137-40; Stanley E. Porter, "Is There a Center to Paul's Theology? An Introduction to the Study of Paul and His Theology," in *Paul and His Theology*, ed. Stanley E. Porter (PS 3; Leiden: Brill, 2006), 1-20.

have also singled out justification by faith as the center. One should note the German Lutheran heritage shared by the three aforementioned theologians. But scholars from other theological traditions defend this option as well.[37] The problem is that justification by faith is prominent only in polemical contexts where Paul is combating Judaizers. Although the notion is mentioned (e.g., Eph 2:8-9; 2 Tim 1:9; Tit 3:5) or assumed in other passages (Phil 3:2-11), one wonders if this is truly the central notion of Pauline thought, given the number of diverse metaphors that he employs to portray salvation.

Albert Schweitzer totally rejected the centrality of justification by faith, insisting that it is a mere subsidiary crater on the edge of a much more massive one: the notion of mystical communion with Christ. At the very least, his analogy is helpful in addressing the question of center. What crater includes all the others? Similar in some respects is the position of E. P. Sanders, in which participation in Christ becomes the master key to unlocking the apostle's thought.[38] Sanders's version has much to commend it, and one cannot deny that union with Christ lies very close to the heart of Paul's message. Still, union with Christ or participation with him presupposes something even more fundamental. One must posit something else first.

Ralph Martin has ably argued that reconciliation is as close to being the center of Paul's theology as any other concept.[39] While admitting that reconciliation vocabulary is relatively infrequent in Paul, Martin still maintains that the concept is broad enough to encompass Paul's thought; indeed, it has cosmic dimensions. Martin's proposal has not, however, gained many adherents. Thomas Schreiner's objection that choosing a center such as justification, reconciliation or even something as broad as salvation exalts the gift at the expense of the giver.[40]

Other scholars, such as Werner Kümmel, Hermann Ridderbos and George Ladd, highlight redemptive history as the master key that unifies all other themes in Paul. I have already argued for the importance of this concept for the unity of the Bible. That it is important cannot be denied; that it constitutes the center of Paul's thought is debatable. Here Douglas Moo makes a good point: "Salvation history is not a 'centre' for Paul's

---

[37]Mark A. Seifrid, *Christ Our Righteousness: Paul's Theology of Justification* (NSBT 9; Downers Grove, Ill.: InterVarsity Press, 2001). Seifrid avoids calling justification by faith "the center" of Paul's theology, but he is "happy to name it the basis, foundation and most comprehensive expression of his gospel" (personal communication).

[38]See Moo, "Paul," *NDBT* 138.

[39]Ralph P. Martin, *Reconciliation: A Study of Paul's Theology* (rev. ed.; Grand Rapids: Zondervan, 1989); idem, "Center of Paul's Theology," *DPL* 92-95.

[40]Schreiner, *Paul*, p. 18.

thought in the true sense of the word, for it denotes a framework of thinking rather than a dominating idea. But a correct interpretation of Paul's theology demands recognition of the conceptual approach called 'salvation history.'"[41]

Related to the foregoing is J. Christiaan Beker's proposal that the center of Pauline theology should be determined by a model that maintains dialectical tension between coherence and contingency. That is, there is a unifying thread in Paul's thought, but this is accessible only through a contingent medium: occasional missionary letters. For Beker, that which provides coherence is the apocalyptic triumph of God.[42] This carefully thought-out proposal warrants consideration, and James Dunn is quite sympathetic with Beker on this point.[43] Still, I think that Schreiner has a point when he argues that God in Christ must be addressed before one can speak meaningfully of what has been achieved. To put it another way, the person of God is the foundation for the work of Christ.

The kingdom of God still garners support as a viable center for Paul's thought. Although such terminology is infrequent in Paul's letters, one can argue that this is the primary theological substructure that gives coherence to Paul's thought as expressed in his missionary correspondence. In regard to a leading theme that ties the entire Bible together, I have already spoken in favor of "the kingdom of God." However, a theme is not the same thing as a center. Moo's stricture about salvation history applies equally with regard to the kingdom of God. Thus I am inclined to agree with Schreiner that when it comes to inquiring about the center of Paul's thought, we can scarcely avoid looking at the central actor in the drama of the coming kingdom: God as revealed in his Son, Jesus Christ.

Schreiner sets forth his case that the glory of God in Christ must be chosen as the center. He claims that an inductive study of the Pauline letters leads to this conclusion. There is much to be said in favor of this proposal. On the other hand, Ralph Martin voices a cogent objection against themes such as Schreiner's highlighting the person of God or, in this case, the glory of God in Christ: it is too broad to be really helpful. He has a good point. If this is so, where does that leave us?

The difficulty in deciding on one center for Paul's thought has led Gerhard Hasel to conclude that no one theme or idea is equal to the task. The best approach, therefore, is to opt for a multiplex center. That is, a cluster

---

[41]Moo, "Paul," *NDBT* 138.

[42]J. Christiaan Beker, *Paul the Apostle: The Triumph of God in Life and Thought* (Philadelphia: Fortress, 1980).

[43]Dunn, *Theology of Paul*, p. 23.

of ideas must be invoked before justice is done to the complex "task theology" of Paul. All the aforementioned options deserve consideration to belong to an enlarged center. There is a pragmatic advantage to this proposal: we can capitalize on the efforts of many to distill Pauline theology into a central controlling idea by incorporating several of them into an enlarged center. On the other hand, have we foreclosed too soon? Is there, after all, one major idea providing coherence for the whole? This remains one of the elusive questions of Pauline theology.

The foregoing discussion ends on a less than satisfying note. The quest for a center continues to be the subject of animated discussion and disagreement. I am inclined to accept Hasel's multiplex approach as a default position, but with a slight tweak. Perhaps an analogy from atomic theory can assist us. Within the nucleus of an atom are a number of elementary particles. Revolving around this nucleus are electrons. On this view, Paul's thought consists of several elementary notions around which themes and ideas orbit. What are these elementary notions? Returning to our earlier discussion of Paul's conversion on the way to Damascus, I suggest that those five insights, a "Pauline Pentatuech," admirably serve as the "nucleus" of Paul's theology. As such, they hold in orbit the various themes and concepts collectively labeled as Paul's theology. With this as a working model, I propose to examine some of the leading themes in Paul.

THE CONTRIBUTION OF PAULINE THEOLOGY

Before doing so, however, I want to pay tribute to the apostle Paul. I join the many who gladly acknowledge him as "the greatest mind in the New Testament to interpret the meaning of the person and work of Jesus."[44] Three-fifths of the epistolary documents in the NT stem from Paul. The placement of his letters in the canon indirectly testifies to their importance. The impact of Pauline theology on Christian theology and Western civilization in general can scarcely be overestimated. One stands in wonder at the volume of works devoted to Paul over the centuries, and with no abatement in sight. I wish to briefly summarize his place in Christian church history in the following statements.

First, he was the missionary/church planter par excellence of the early church. Larry Kreitzer estimates that Paul traveled some 6,200 miles in the course of his missionary journeys.[45] By the end of his missionary career of about thirty years, scores of house churches established by Paul and

---

[44]George E. Ladd, *A Theology of the New Testament*, ed. Donald A. Hagner (rev. ed.; Grand Rapids: Eerdmans, 1993), p. 398.
[45]Kreitzer, "Travel in the Roman World," *DPL* 945.

his missionary team dotted the Mediterranean, like little specks of light, from Syria to Spain. Though difficult to quantify, the number of believers converted under Paul's ministry must have been in the thousands.[46] It was probably the greatest single achievement in the spread of Christianity. Paul was always mindful to whom credit was due: "But by the grace of God I am what I am, and his grace toward me has not been in vain. On the contrary, I worked harder than any of them—though it was not I, but the grace of God that is with me" (1 Cor 15:10; cf. 2 Cor 11:23).

Second, he was the first theological thinker of the early church. Augustine, Martin Luther, John Calvin, John Knox, John Wesley, Jonathan Edwards, George Whitefield, Karl Barth and a host of other theological luminaries all drank deeply at the well of Pauline theology. I hasten to add, however, that he was essentially a task theologian, not a systematic or biblical theologian, though he had the requisite skills and knowledge to be both. His task, in short, was to preach Christ to those who had never heard (Rom 15:20-21). This was the driving force behind all his theologizing. Nonetheless, the Pauline doctrines of God, sin, Christ, salvation, the church and eschatology have been the source of ongoing theological reflection. But perhaps even more importantly, Paul's writings have not been the private preserve of scholars and ecclesiastics; they have been deeply cherished by rank-and-file Christians down through the ages. "Being dead, Paul continues to speak."[47]

Third, there is something about Paul the man that continues to attract. Whether or not one agrees with all that he taught, the depth of his commitment to Christ and the church is remarkable. Here is a man in whom Christ truly lived and worked (Rom 14:8; Gal 2:20; 5:24; 6:14). One cannot but be impressed by his sensitive, caring attitude toward his converts.[48] Like a nurse and a loving father, he nourished and exhorted the faithful (1 Thess 2:7, 11-12). The Corinthian correspondence testifies to the depth of his personal involvement in the lives of his flock at great cost to him emotionally and physically: "I am under daily pressure because of my anxiety for all the churches. Who is weak, and I am not weak? Who is made to stumble, and I am not indignant?" (2 Cor 11:28-29). Paul felt

---

[46]Rodney Stark estimates that in the year A.D. 100 there were only about 7,530 Christians. I think that this estimate is too low. Among other things, Stark, following the lead of many NT scholars in the liberal tradition, considers the numbers given by Luke in the book of Acts to be inflated. Therefore, Stark's starting number (he arbitrarily chooses one thousand in A.D. 40) is much smaller than it actually was. See Stark, *The Rise of Christianity*, pp. 4-13.

[47]F. F. Bruce, "Paul in Acts and Letters," *DPL* 691.

[48]See P. Beasley-Murray, "Pastor, Paul as," *DPL* 654-58; Bruce, *Paul*, pp. 457-61.

a great responsibility to model the new life in Christ for those who had been rescued from the dregs of paganism. Sometimes in his letters he urges his converts to follow his example or imitate his behavior as he himself follows Christ (1 Cor 11:1; 1 Thess 1:6; cf. Eph 5:1; Phil 2:5). Although very much aware of his own shortcomings, he makes it his life's ambition to know Christ more personally and powerfully (Phil 3:10-14). It was his great ambition as a missionary and pastor to see his converts likewise grow to spiritual maturity—in his words, "to the measure of the full stature of Christ" (Eph 4:13). In this he continues to be a role model for all who would enter Christian ministry: "It is he whom we proclaim, warning everyone and teaching everyone in all wisdom, so that we may present everyone mature in Christ. For this I toil and struggle with all the energy that he powerfully inspires within me" (Col 1:28-29). In the end, the key to Paul the man and Paul's theology is one and the same: "Christ in you, the hope of glory" (Col 1:27).

For Further Discussion

1. What other reasons might be given either to vilify or vindicate the apostle Paul?

2. How persuasive are the arguments for limiting the genuine Pauline corpus to seven letters only?

3. What is at stake in the debate over the number of genuine letters in the Pauline corpus?

4. Why is it important at all to try to understand the background of Paul's thought?

5. What are other ways in which Paul's background in Judaism is reflected in his letters?

6. Is Paul's cross-cultural model of missions still useful for our day?

7. Is the debate over the center of Pauline theology really important? Why or why not?

For Further Reading

Betz, Hans Dieter. "Paul." *ABD* 5:186-92, 192-96.

Bruce, F. F. "Paul in Acts and Letters." *DPL* 679-92.

———. *Paul, Apostle of the Heart Set Free*, pp. 15-147, 456-74. Grand Rapids: Eerdmans, 1977.

Dunn, James D. G. *The Theology of Paul the Apostle*, pp. 1-26. Grand Rapids: Eerdmans, 1998.

Gager, John G. *Reinventing Paul*, pp. 3-75. New York: Oxford University Press, 2000.

Hafemann, Scott J. "Paul and His Interpreters." *DPL* 666-79.

Keck, Leander E., and Victor P. Furnish. *The Pauline Epistles*. Nashville: Abingdon, 1984.

Kümmel, Werner Georg. *The Theology of the New Testament according to Its Major Witnesses: Jesus-Paul-John*, translated by John E. Steely, pp. 137-41. Nashville: Abingdon, 1973.

Ladd, George E. *A Theology of the New Testament*, edited by Donald A. Hagner, pp. 397-434. Rev. ed. Grand Rapids: Eerdmans, 1993.

Longenecker, R. N. "Paul, the Apostle." *ZPEB* 4:624-34.

———. "Pauline Theology. " *ZPEB* 4:657-65.

Martin, Ralph P. *Reconciliation: A Study of Paul's Theology*, pp. 9-47, 201-33. Atlanta: John Knox Press, 1981.

McRay, John. *Paul: His Life and Teaching*, pp. 21-59, 263-93. Grand Rapids: Baker, 2003.

Moo, D. J. "Paul." *NDBT* 136-40.

Murphy-O'Connor, Jerome. *Paul: A Critical Life*, pp. 1-101. New York: Oxford University Press, 1997.

Polhill, John B. *Paul and His Letters*, pp. 5-43, 120-33. Nashville: Broadman & Holman, 1999.

Porter, Stanley E. "Is There a Center to Paul's Theology? An Introduction to the Study of Paul and His Theology." In *Paul and His Theology*, edited by Stanley E. Porter, pp. 1-20. PS 3. Leiden: Brill, 2006.

Schreiner, Thomas R. *Interpreting the Pauline Epistles*. Grand Rapids: Baker, 1990.

———. *Paul, Apostle of God's Glory in Christ: A Pauline Theology*, pp. 15-35. Downers Grove, Ill.: InterVarsity Press, 2001.

Stegner, W. R. "Jew, Paul the." *DPL* 503-11.

Yamauchi, E. M. "Hellenism." *DPL* 383-88.

Yarbrough, Robert W. "Paul the Apostle." *EDBT* 590-97.

7

Paul's Gospel

PAUL'S GOSPEL IS GOOD NEWS TO THOSE who are being saved and bad news for those who are perishing (2 Cor 2:15-16). But why is it such good news on the one hand and such bad news on the other? In short, humanity outside Christ is utterly lost, with absolutely no hope of salvation. Thus a prerequisite for sketching Paul's gospel is a brief foray into his teaching considering fallen human beings.[1]

THE PLIGHT OF HUMANKIND OUTSIDE OF CHRIST

Paul's view of sin is complex and multilayered. In fact, a close reading of Paul's letters, especially Romans, suggests that three fundamental realities exist, which, for the sake of clarity, may be depicted as levels. These levels stand in relation to each other in terms of causation. The first, or surface, level is inexplicable without understanding what underlies and produces it. Likewise, in order to understand what causes the second level, one must ultimately expose the ground level of sin. Without forcing the analogy, one might liken this to depth psychology, in which an assumption is made that beneath conscious behavior lies an unconscious realm that ultimately "explains" the conscious or surface level of behavior.

All human beings are guilty of individual or personal sin. The first level is the uncontestable fact that everyone who is honest and rational admits to having done wrong, having failed to uphold commonly accepted moral standards. Paul argues in Romans that Gentiles, not possessing God's law, nonetheless have a conscience convicting them of wrongdoing (Rom

---

[1]Donald Guthrie says, "Undoubtedly of all the NT writers, Paul approaches nearest to working out what might be called a theology of sin" (*New Testament Theology* [Downers Grove, Ill.: InterVarsity Press, 1981], p. 200).

2:14-15). The bottom line for Paul is this: "All have sinned and fall short of the glory of God" (Rom 3:23). One thing is quite certain: Paul believed in the universality of sin. In this he maintains continuity with the received tradition in the OT and Second Temple Judaism (Gen 6:5; 8:21; 1 Kings 8:46; 2 Chron 6:36; Job 4:17; Ps 51:5; Prov 20:9; Eccles 7:20; Jer 17:9; Sir 17:11—18:14; *4 Ezra* 3:21-26; *2 Bar.* 48:42-43; 54:14, 19). Indeed, the notion that all humans are sinners goes back nearly to the dawn of literacy. A Sumerian text, which has affinities with the book of Job, includes this proverbial saying: "Never has a sinless child been born to its mother . . . a sinless *workman* has not existed from of old."[2] Paul relentlessly pursues his thesis in Romans 1—3: all are guilty of personal sin, consisting of either wrong actions or wrong attitudes. He makes the case that both Jew and Gentile stand on the same ground of disadvantage, namely, condemnation—there is no difference or distinction (Rom 3:9, 22).

In Romans 1:18-32 Paul sketches what might be called "the spiral of depravity." This is an appalling description of humanity outside Christ that should itself probably be read on two levels. That is, as Paul looks out his window from his workshop in Corinth, he observes the passing throngs. Corinth is a microcosm of the Greco-Roman world. Life in "sin city" is not a pretty picture. As such, it represents "the good, the bad and the ugly," with heavy emphasis on the latter two! But that is not the only story in Romans 1; there is a second, underlying story drawn from Genesis 3, the story of the fall in the Garden of Eden. When Romans 1:18-32 is read this way, both stories inform each other. Paul probably sees a direct connection between the two stories.[3]

Paul's indictment begins with the taproot of all individual sin: the failure to acknowledge God as the source of all goodness and alone worthy of worship. This failure manifests itself as ingratitude ("they did not honor him as God or give thanks to him" [Rom 1:21]). Here is the story of Adam's sin in the Garden of Eden, but also it is the story of each and every individual, exemplified in the pagans who pass by Paul's shop.[4] As *2 Baruch* 54:19 tersely

---

[2]"Man and His God," trans. S. N. Kramer (in *Ancient Near Eastern Texts Relating to the Old Testament*, ed. J. B. Pritchard [3rd ed.; Princeton, N.J.: Princeton University Press], p. 590). The word in italics indicates a doubtful translation. This text probably dates to the third millennium B.C.

[3]For further development of this idea of two levels, see James D. G. Dunn, *The Theology of Paul the Apostle* (Grand Rapids: Eerdmans, 1998), pp. 91-92.

[4]Walter Grundmann says, "This [failure to acknowledge God] is the original sin. In this respect the sin of man in general corresponds to the sin of Adam" ("ἁμαρτάνω," *TDNT* 1:310). Dunn says, "Lurking behind this [Rom 1:21] we should probably see the figure of Adam, the archetypal human who deliberately refused to give God his due, by refusing to obey God's one command (Gen. 2.17). But in Rom 1.22 the echo becomes stronger" (*Theology of Paul*, p. 91).

expresses it, "Each of us has become our own Adam." At the very least, each person follows the example of Adam and fails to acknowledge God as Creator and Lord. But in Romans 5:12-21 Paul draws an even tighter connection between the sin of Adam and the multitudinous sins of his offspring; he explains why human beings spiral downwards into a vortex of sinful behavior.

According to Paul, failure to acknowledge God has intellectual consequences; that is, thought processes are impaired. This was first manifested in utterly irrational behavior: the invention of idolatry, that ultimate foolishness. Substitute gods, made in the image of created beings, supplanted the true and living God. Corinth was a contemporary example of this madness; the city was studded with temples and shrines to the "many gods and many lords" (1 Cor 8:5). At this point in his argument Paul delivers the first of three ominous declarations: "God gave them up" (Rom 1:24; cf. 1:26, 28). God allows sinners to sink and wallow in their self-chosen, forbidden desires. Idolatry spawns an evil brood; immorality is an inevitable offspring of idolatry. Substitute gods are mere projections of base human desires onto a cosmic screen. As a reading of literature from idolatrous cultures abundantly testifies, the gods of antiquity are selfish, immoral beings, quite indifferent to the needs and concerns of mortals. Small wonder those who worship them follow suit.

Once immorality has free reign in the human heart, the only limiting factor is imagination. Like water swirling down a toilet, sinners descend into ever-deeper levels of iniquity. The second divine giving over, in Romans 1:26, leads to what Paul considers a prime example of the distortion sin creates: homosexual and lesbian relationships (Rom 1:26-27). Paul is opposed to same-sex relationships because they are contrary to the created order; they are unnatural.[5]

This leads to Paul's third and final mention of God's reprobation (Rom 1:28). The consequence of a debased mind intent on fulfilling its own desires is a bumper crop of sinful attitudes and actions. Though not exhaustive, the list provides a summary of "every kind of wickedness" (Rom 1:29). What is particularly damning is Paul's concluding indictment: culpability is matched by defiant approval (Rom 1:32). The theological term used to

---

[5]See D. F. Wright, "Sexuality, Sexual Ethics," *DPL* 871-75; Richard B. Hays, *The Moral Vision of the New Testament: Community, Cross, New Creation* (San Francisco: HarperSanFrancisco, 1996); Thomas R. Schreiner, *Paul, Apostle of God's Glory in Christ: A Pauline Theology* (Downers Grove, Ill.: InterVarsity Press, 2001), pp. 317-20. Probably no Pauline stricture draws more ire in Western culture today than his proscription of same-sex relations. Exegetical attempts to rehabilitate same-sex relationships in modern times are disingenuous.

describe the fallen human condition is *depravity*, meaning moral corruption. All aspects of personhood and life are affected by sin; in that sense, depravity is total—there is no secure site or safe place where sin does not intrude and molest. Several passages from Paul's letters support the point so powerfully made in Romans 1—3: human beings outside Christ are evildoers who stand under God's condemnation (Rom 3:9, 10-11, 19, 23; cf. Gal 3:22; Eph 2:1-3; Col 3:21; 2 Tim 1:9; Tit 3:5).[6]

All human beings possess indwelling or inherited sin. But why do all follow Adam in rebellion and transgress God's moral law? Why does Paul adamantly insist that "no one will be justified by works of the law" (Gal 2:16)? Does he believe that human beings are incapable of living a morally impeccable life? The short answer is yes, that is precisely what he believes. Paul takes us to a deeper level of human existence. In short, he demonstrates that sin, conceived as a personal force, actually takes up residence in the human heart and dominates it. Sometimes he likens it to the very atmosphere in which people live and move: "How can we who died to sin go on living *in* it?" (Rom 6:2 [my italics]). The reason why human beings commit personal sin is that they are under the malign influence of sin. This requires further analysis.

Paul views sin as an alien intruder that takes charge of the moral clearinghouse of the human psyche. In fact, sin is personified as a slave master or tyrant in several passages (Rom 6:6, 12, 15-23; 7:9-11, 14-24).[7] This, of course, raises the question of whether individuals are responsible for this state of affairs. Some verses in Romans 7 might suggest that they are not (Rom 7:13, 17-24). When read in light of the larger context of Paul's letters, however, there can be little doubt that Paul assumes everyone is held accountable for his or her sinful condition (Rom 1:19-20; 3:19). Clearly, God did not create humans that way, nor does Paul ever indicate or imply that God implanted an evil tendency in Adam, which was passed along to all his descendants, as the rabbis held. Rather, Paul speaks of "your former way of life, your old self, corrupt and deluded by its lusts" (Eph 4:22; cf. Col 3:7-10) and describes sin as exercising "dominion in your mortal bodies" (Rom 6:12).

A distinctive Pauline expression brings us to the heart of the matter. Paul speaks of "the flesh" as the sphere in which human beings outside

---

[6]Archibald Hunter says, "'Original sin, the corruption of man's heart' was the major premise from which Paul started. He held a doctrine of general, though not total, human depravity. Sin was a state, not simply an incident without antecedents and consequences" (*The Gospel According to St. Paul* [rev. ed.; Philadelphia: Westminster Press, 1966], p. 91).

[7]Charles A. A. Scott speaks of sin as "a power invading, attacking, subjugating men from without" (*Christianity According to St. Paul* [Cambridge: Cambridge University Press, 1932], p. 47).

Christ live and act. The Greek word *sarx,* translated as "flesh," has several nuances in Paul's letters. It can refer to the substance of which our bodies are made; it can refer to what it means to be human, with all its inherent limitations and weaknesses; or it can denote the source of sin in human beings. It is this latter, ethical sense that is crucial for assessing the human plight outside Christ. Paul, on occasion, uses *sarx* to refer to the whole person standing in opposition to God and his will (Rom 7:5, 18, 25; 8:3-13; Gal 5:13-19, 24; Col 2:11, 13). Sinners are alienated from God and have within them a bias against doing God's will. They choose to live for self and determine their own destiny. This bias dominates the life of fallen human beings. Christian theology uses the expression "the sin nature" or "the lower nature" to describe this reality. One should not, however, think in material or substantive terms, for the real locus of "flesh" in an ethical sense is the inner self, the seat of personhood. To put it simply: all human beings commit personal sin *because* they are sinners—they are dominated by an invariable bent or bias toward sin and thus are hostile toward God and his will (Rom 5:10; 8:7-8). In Paul's words, we were, before coming to Christ, "*by nature* children of wrath" (Eph 2:3 [my italics]).

More questions arise. When does this takeover occur? Do we all, at a certain moment in our lives, presumably quite early, face a similar temptation as Adam? Must we then decide whether to obey God's will? In connection with this, is there a certain age of accountability after which every person is responsible for her or his own sin? Paul does not explicitly say. In the Jewish tradition, at the age of twelve or thirteen a young boy becomes a *bar mitzvah* ("son of the law") and personally responsible for his own actions.[8] On the other hand, given Paul's rootedness in the OT Scriptures, he likely holds that a condition of sinfulness existed from birth. The psalmist said, "Indeed, I was born guilty, a sinner when my mother conceived me" (Ps 51:5; cf. Gen 8:21; Job 5:7; Ps 58:3). In short, this corruption must be passed on by ordinary generation. "All of us once lived among them [the disobedient—i.e., sinners] in the passions of our flesh, following the desires of flesh and senses, and *we were by nature* children of wrath, like everyone else" (Eph 2:3 [my italics]). In some mysterious fashion, in addition to the genetic codes received from parents, the bias toward evil is passed along and becomes a fundamental part of humanity's inner being. No wonder we are in such a desperate way!

All are held accountable for Adam's transgression: imputed sin. In

---

[8]Robert Gundry sees an allusion to the age of accountability in Paul's remarks in Romans 7:9-10a ("The Moral Frustration of Paul before His Conversion: Sexual Lust in Romans 7:7-25," in *Pauline Studies: Essays Presented to Professor F. F. Bruce on His 70th Birthday,* ed. D. A. Hagner and M. J. Harris [Grand Rapids: Eerdmans, 1980], pp. 228-45).

one passage, Romans 5:12-21, Paul traces the origin of human sin back to Adam. Paul sees an indissoluble connection between Adam's sin and the sinfulness of all humanity. This appears to be the reason why humans are bedeviled with a sin nature. Although the topic is much debated and contested in theology, I think that it comes down to this: Adam's act of rebellion was our act, and we are held accountable for it. Of course, no one is conscious of this act, because we did not exist then as individuals. Many modern theologians and readers of Paul therefore flatly reject such an idea as inconceivable and unjust. Still, a patient reading of Paul challenges our modern individualistic assumptions. Paul holds to the notion of corporate solidarity, the many in the one, an idea firmly rooted in OT and Semitic backgrounds. Adam and Christ determine the conditions under which one lives and the destiny of all those who belong to them, both individually and corporately. They represent, then, the two, and only two, kinds of humanity. There are those who are "in Adam" and those who are "in Christ." The former die because of sin, and the latter will be made alive (1 Cor 15:22).

How, precisely, did Adam's sin become our sin? It is best to admit that Paul does not explicitly say in Romans 5:12-21 (or elsewhere). In terms of biblical theology, the most that can be said is that Paul holds to the corporate involvement of all human beings in Adam's sin and its consequences. Anything beyond that is speculation.[9]

Let me summarize. All human beings follow the example of Adam and commit sin. Individual sin, however, is an inevitable by-product of indwelling sin, which finds the flesh to be a willing accomplice. Sinners are liable for this corruption of nature. But in the final analysis, indwelling sin is a direct consequence of Adam's one act of disobedience in Genesis 3. God, the righteous judge, imputes Adam's sin to all his descendants. His fall is our fall; his guilt is our guilt. Using a baseball analogy, we can say that every human being has three called strikes: individual sin, inherited sin, imputed sin. And, just like in baseball, "Three strikes and you're out!"

Paul's view of the human plight is far more pessimistic than anything found in his Jewish heritage. Nothing as dire may be discerned in the extant literature of Second Temple Judaism. The only source that comes close is in *4 Ezra* (coming in the aftermath of the great disaster of the Jewish

---

[9]Systematic theology attempts to go further and understand the precise relationship between Adam's sin and its consequences for all his descendants. Two explanations, both taking seriously the Hebraic notion of corporate solidarity, vie for acceptance. The first comes under the rubric of "federal" headship, as discussed earlier in chapter 3. The second view, "realistic or seminal" headship, holds that Adam actually was the human race at that point and therefore his choice was humanity's choice. See Henri Blocher, "Original Sin," *DTIB* 553-54.

revolt and the destruction of Jerusalem and the second temple), and even there the case is not quite as hopeless as that sketched by Paul.

Rabbinic Judaism holds that God initially created Adam with two tendencies, one toward good and one toward evil (the *yēṣer haṭṭôb* and the *yēṣer hārāʿ*). These two inclinations are in equal proportions, allowing the individual to decide which dominates. Torah is present to assist and provide guidance. If the desire is there, Torah can be kept and the evil tendency subdued. No one perfectly obeys Torah; but with determination one's good deeds can outweigh one's evil deeds come judgment day. Obviously, such a view of human nature is much more sanguine about what is possible than Paul's.

THE WORLD

According to Paul, the overall plight of sinners is even more wretched. Two additional factors compound the misery, making an impossible situation even more hopeless. The first of these has to do with the notion of "the world." The Greek word *kosmos* has several crucially important nuances.[10] On the one hand, *kosmos* may simply denote the totality of creation with no intended negative connotations (Rom 1:20; 1 Cor 3:22; Eph 1:4). Paul held that God's creation was good, and sin was not owing to some cosmic limitation or flaw in matter itself (1 Tim 4:4). He quotes with approval Psalm 24:1: "The earth is the Lord's and all that is in it, the world, and those who live in it" (1 Cor 10:26). Sometimes, Paul uses *kosmos* to describe the realm in which humans live out their earthly existence (Rom 4:13; 1 Cor 5:10b; 1 Tim 1:15; 6:7). On the other hand, one encounters passages in which *kosmos* definitely carries negative connotations and refers to humanity alienated from God and working at purposes counter to his will. Since humanity operates within a web of relationships, institutions, traditions and conventions, this total complex may be thought of as a world system. As such, the world system actually serves to blind people to what is ultimately real and most important. The world system acts as a substitute for what only God and his perfect will can supply. If hope is placed in this world system as a source of deliverance and ultimate satisfaction, the result will be bitter disappointment. Interestingly, in these passages, *kosmos* is almost personified, like sin and flesh (1 Cor 2:12; 3:19; 7:29-31; 11:32; Gal 4:3; Col 2:8). Paul follows Jesus' teaching in this regard (e.g., Mk 8:36 pars.; Lk 12:30; 16:8; Mt 18:7; Jn 7:7; 8:23; 9:39).[11]

---

[10]See Hermann Sasse, "κόσμος," *TDNT* 3:883-95.

[11]See George E. Ladd, *A Theology of the New Testament*, ed. Donald A. Hagner (rev. ed.; Grand Rapids: Eerdmans, 1993), pp. 436-39; J. Painter, "World, Cosmology," *DPL* 979-82; H. Sasse, "κοσμέω, κόσμος," *TDNT* 3:868-95.

EVIL SPIRITUAL POWERS

Worse than our worst nightmare, there is an unseen evil realm inhabited by hostile personalities, headed up by the archvillain, Satan. Although largely ditched or demythologized in existential, psychological or political-economic terms by modern liberal theology, and spoofed by Hollywood films such as *Ghostbusters*, Paul takes seriously, as does Jesus and orthodox Christianity, the realm of personal, evil spiritual beings.[12] Paul mentions angels and rulers as agents with the potential to separate human beings from God's love (Rom 8:38). Although he does not locate original sin in an angelic revolt, as we find in some Jewish apocalyptic sources of the Second Temple period (e.g., the Enoch traditions), he does make passing references to these malignant beings and warns of their destructive intent with regard to believers and unbelievers alike. Thus he likens the Christian life to warfare carried on against these unseen, spiritual beings: "For our struggle is not against enemies of blood and flesh, but against the rulers, against the authorities, against the cosmic powers of this present darkness, against the spiritual forces of evil in the heavenly places" (Eph 6:12).

These malevolent beings are headed up by the devil (Eph 6:10), the evil one (Eph 6:16). Paul takes seriously the role of the devil in the temptation of Eve (2 Cor 11:3) and recalls a Jewish tradition in which Satan disguises himself as an angel when he approaches Eve (2 Cor 11:14; cf. *L.A.E.* 9:1). He warns believers of Satan's continuous activity in soliciting for evil purposes (Eph 6:16). Other names that Paul ascribes to the head of evil forces are "Satan" (Rom 16:20; 1 Cor 5:5), "god of this world" (2 Cor 4:4), "ruler of the power of the air" (Eph 2:2), and "Beliar" (2 Cor 6:15). The last title is familiar from Second Temple Judaism (e.g., *Jub.* 1:20; *Mart. Ascen. Isa.* 2:4; *Testaments of the Twelve Patriarchs* passim [e.g., *T. Reu.* 2:2]; CD-A 4:13, 15; 5:18). The Ephesians passage reminds us of the Johannine text in which Jesus describes the devil as "the ruler of this world" (Jn 12:31). The devil and his minions actively resist and oppose the preaching of the gospel through various means: inciting civil authorities against the preaching of the gospel (1 Thess 2:18), creating divisions and ill will among believers (1 Cor 2:11), false teaching (2 Cor 11:14; 1 Tim 1:20; 5:15?), illnesses (2 Cor 12:7) and especially tempting believers to sin (1 Cor 7:5; 1 Tim 5:15?). Particularly noteworthy in Paul's correspondence is the connection between sexual promiscuity and demonic activity (1 Cor 5:5; 7:5). Paul proscribes attendance of Christians at temple meals because of the influence of de-

---

[12]See D. G. Reid, "Angels, Archangels," *DPL* 20-23; idem, "Elements/Elemental Spirits of the World," *DPL* 229-33; idem, "Principalities and Powers," *DPL* 746-52; idem, "Satan, Devil," *DPL* 862-67.

mons in precisely those settings in which sexual promiscuity was so prone to occur (1 Cor 10:14-22).

Especially in Colossians and Ephesians one encounters a listing of these evil intelligences, the "thrones or dominions or rulers or powers" (Col 1:16), the "rulers and authorities" (Col 2:15), "all rule and authority and power and dominion, and . . . every name that is named" (Eph 1:21). As the book of Acts testifies, the province of Asia was a hotbed of occult powers and magic (Acts 19:11-20). Not surprisingly, in letters written to this region Paul emphasizes the sovereignty and victory of Christ over these hostile beings.

In spite of these beings "who seek to do us woe," Paul is confident that believers can resist the demonic onslaught and overcome. In one passage, dubbed "the Pauline Apocalypse" (2 Thess 2:1-12), Paul anticipates Satan's most determined effort to thwart the kingdom of God. This is the celebrated description of the "man of lawlessness," who is energized by Satan and works "all powers, signs, lying wonders" (2 Thess 2:9). Paul looks forward to the coming of the Lord Jesus, who vanquishes Satan and his hordes in fulfillment of the prophecy of Genesis 3:15 (Rom 16:20; cf. 2 Thess 2:8). But for those outside Christ "the god of this world has blinded [their] minds . . . to keep them from seeing the light of the gospel of the glory of Christ, who is the image of God" (2 Cor 4:4). The upshot is that unbelievers "believe what is false" (2 Thess 2:11), with disastrous consequences. They are spiritually dead and follow the course of this world and the ruler of the power of the air (Eph 2:1) so that they are disobedient. Counterfeit and delusion are the stock in trade of Satan and his demons. Behind the barrage of falsehoods deluging our digital age lies an evil personage who promotes narcissistic preoccupation and spiritual rebellion.

SUMMARY

Paul's depiction of sinners outside Christ is utter gloom and doom. In the words of Jonathan Edwards, American theologian and revivalist of the pre–Revolutionary War era, those outside Christ are "sinners in the hands of an angry God."[13] This ominous circumstance forms the backdrop for Paul's gospel. How can sinners ever find themselves in the hands of a pardoning God?

---

[13]This was the title of a sermon that Edwards preached July 8, 1741, in Enfield, Connecticut, during a violent thunderstorm. As lightning flashed and thunder roared, he described in graphic detail sinners being held over the flames of hell. No wonder the sermon sparked a revival!

THE DIVINE SOLUTION: PAUL'S DOCTRINE OF SALVATION IN CHRIST

Paul's picture of salvation is a stunning mosaic. Many pieces of different hues and shapes combine to depict an image of profound richness and variety.[14] The finished composition is breathtaking. According to Paul, "sin increased, [but] grace abounded all the more" (Rom 5:20). I can only sketch some of the features of this abounding grace by focusing on a few Pauline metaphors highlighting the variegated dimensions of salvation in Christ.[15] These varied metaphors are aspects of one fundamental divine event: the death, resurrection and ascension of Jesus Christ.[16] However salvation in the NT is portrayed, the effectual basis remains the work of Christ on the cross, the central symbol for this event and its effects. In Paul's words, "May I never boast of anything except the cross of our Lord Jesus Christ, by which the world has been crucified to me, and I to the world" (Gal 6:14).

SALVATION AS SACRIFICE

Words related to sacrifice. As one would expect, given Paul's OT heritage, the language of sacrifice plays a significant role in his view of salvation.[17] Jesus' death was atoning and fulfilled what was typified by the OT cult. Words belonging to the semantic field of offering and sacrifice, occurring in Paul's letters, include the following: *prosphora* ("offering, sacrifice"), *thyō* ("slaughter an animal in a ritual manner as a sacrifice to deity"), *thysia* ("that which is offered as a sacrifice"), *hierothytos* ("that which has been sacrificed to a deity"), *aparchē* ("first portion of something set aside and offered to God before the rest of the substance or objects can be used") and *spendō* ("pour out an offering as an act of worship or ritual").[18]

---

[14]Herman Ridderbos says that Paul's gospel "is like a multi-colored spectrum" (*Paul: An Outline of His Theology*, trans. John Richard De Witt [Grand Rapids: Eerdmans, 1975], p. 159).

[15]Jürgen Becker comments, "Paul . . . employs various semantic word fields . . . because none seems to him sufficient in itself to represent the entire way of salvation" (*Paul, Apostle to the Gentiles*, trans. O. C. Dean Jr. [Louisville: Westminster John Knox, 1993], p. 407).

[16]"Clearly, the death of Christ occupies center stage in Paul's theology. . . . The cross of Christ lies at the intersection of the major avenues of his theology and of his understanding of faithful living before Christ returns" (J. B. Green, "Death of Christ," *DPL* 209 [the entire article, pp. 201-9, repays careful reading]). Dunn likewise says, "There can be no doubt as to where the centre of gravity of Paul's theology is to be found. It lies in the death and resurrection of Jesus" (*Theology of Paul*, p. 208).

[17]"One of the most powerful images used by Paul to explicate the significance of Christ's death is that of the cultic sacrifice, or more precisely the 'sin offering' which could be offered up by individuals or groups in the Jerusalem temple (Leviticus 4) and the annual Day of Atonement sacrifices (Lev. 16.11-19)" (Dunn, *Theology of Paul*, p. 212).

[18]Johannes P. Louw and Eugene A. Nida, eds., *Greek-English Lexicon of the New Testa-*

Christ as passover lamb. In several instances Paul uses sacrificial language metaphorically to refer to concepts other than Christ's death on behalf of sinners (e.g., Rom 11:16; 1 Cor 10:28; Phil 2:17; 2 Tim 4:6), but in 1 Corinthians Paul identifies Jesus' death with the Passover lamb: "For our paschal lamb *[pascha],* Christ, has been sacrificed *[etythē]*" (1 Cor 5:7b). The typological linkage between the paschal lamb and Jesus' death is significant because in the former the blood of the animal, daubed on the doorframes of Hebrew homes, averted the plague of the destroying angel (Ex 12:13, 29). Although Paul does not make an explicit connection, the immediate context of 1 Corinthians 5:5 ("hand this man over to Satan for the destruction of the flesh") implies that, analogously, the blood of Jesus averts the wrath of God against sinners. Of course in 1 Corinthians 5 Paul primarily appropriates the Passover story as a paradigm for Christian living. Yeast serves as a metaphor for sin (in this case, egregious sin) that must be thrown out and burned ("clean out the old yeast" [1 Cor 5:7a]). The Christian life should now be seen as a perpetual feast of unleavened bread, characterized by "sincerity and truth" (1 Cor 5:8c). The fact that the paschal lamb was eaten by the Israelites is also not without significance in that later on Paul emphasizes the spiritual meaning of the Lord's Supper (1 Cor 11), a meal having its roots in the ancient Passover meal. As we have already noted, Paul's reference to the Lord's Supper is another instance of traditional material taken over from the earliest followers of Jesus who heard the words of institution: "This is my body that is for you" and "This cup is the new covenant in my blood" (1 Cor 11:24-25; cf. Mt 26:26-29 pars.). The sacrificial imagery of the Lord's Supper is indelibly etched on Christian consciousness, reinforced every time this simple memorial meal is shared by believers.

Christ as mercy seat or propitiatory sacrifice. In perhaps the most significant and profound theologizing on the cross in his letters, Paul describes the death of Jesus "as a sacrifice of atonement by his blood, effective through faith" (Rom 3:25). This passage stands right at the beginning of the second main section in the letter, namely, the remedy for sin—the righteousness of God imputed and imparted (Rom 3:21—8:39). Several points need to be made. First, the NRSV translation "sacrifice of atonement" for the Greek *hilastērion* is deficient. Increasingly, exegetes are favoring the rendering "mercy seat" or "place of expiation," rightly drawing attention to the OT background of the tabernacle and temple.[19] The mercy seat, "the

---

ment Based on Semantic Domains (2nd ed.; 2 vols.; New York: United Bible Societies, 1988-1989).

[19]In defense of the rendering "mercy seat," see Schreiner, *Paul,* pp. 234-36; J. M. Gundry-Volf, "Expiation, Propitiation, Mercy Seat," *DPL* 279-84.

most important cult object in the most holy place," was the gold covering on the ark of the covenant, on which sat two cherubim.[20] There the blood was sprinkled seven times by the high priest on the Day of Atonement (Lev 16). This was the moment when the holy of holies was purged on account of sins committed by the congregation of Israel. Paul's point appears to be that in contrast to the OT ritual, conducted behind a curtain and accessible only once a year by one individual, the high priest, Jesus' atoning death is a public event and accessible to all. "Thus Good Friday has become the great Day of Atonement."[21]

Second, the rendering "atonement" or "expiation" fails to capture precisely Paul's thought; a better translation is "propitiation." This focuses upon appeasing God's righteous wrath directed at sinners. This relates to the paschal imagery just discussed. Post-Enlightenment theology often considers such a notion incompatible with modern sensibilities. Nonetheless, it is difficult to be faithful to Paul's intended meaning without adhering to some idea of propitiation.[22] As I argued above, God has good reasons for his wrath against sin.

Third, the meaning of "by his blood" must be clarified. Interpretations that see in this the notion of life released must be rejected.[23] Rather, the meaning of the shedding of blood is the violent taking of life. Jesus' death entailed giving up of his own life on behalf of others.[24]

The fourth and crucial point is the notion of "on behalf of" and "in place of." Jesus died vicariously for his people and as a substitute for each one of them. The linkage between the Day of Atonement ritual, with its two goats, one a sin offering, the other a scapegoat that carried the sins of Israel away into the wilderness (Lev 16), and the suffering Servant of Isaiah 53:4-6, 8, 10-12 seems secure. Although his self-giving love demonstrated on the cross is a powerful example and assurance of God's love (Rom 5:8),

---

[20]J. Roloff, "ἱλαστήριον," *EDNT* 2:186.

[21]Ibid.

[22]See Leon Morris, *The Apostolic Preaching of the Cross* (3rd ed.; Grand Rapids: Eerdmans, 1965), pp. 144-213; Schreiner, *Paul*, pp. 234-36; R. W. Yarbrough, "Atonement," *NDBT* 390-91.

[23]So Yarbrough, "Atonement," *NDBT* 391; Guthrie, *New Testament Theology*, p. 433.

[24]On the other hand, George Ladd responds to condemnations of *Today's English Version* because it consistently translates "the blood of Jesus" as "the death of Jesus": "A moment's reflection suggests that such references are not primarily concerned with the actual physical blood of Jesus, for, as a matter of fact, Jesus shed very little of his material blood. The idea of shed blood refers to the slaughter of the sacrificial lamb, whose throat was cut and whose blood gushed forth. Nothing like this happened to Jesus. The blood and water (Jn 19:34) that came from Jesus' side did so after he had expired. In the New Testament, blood means life violently taken away, life offered in sacrifice" (*Theology of the New Testament*, p. 467).

one has not fully grasped Paul's understanding of the cross apart from the notion of substitution: "For the love of Christ urges us on, because we are convinced that one has died for all; therefore all have died. And he died for all, so that those who live might live no longer for themselves, but for him who died and was raised for them" (2 Cor 5:14-15). Whether one is speaking of pre-Pauline tradition (1 Cor 15:3) or of Paul's own interpretation of the cross (Rom 5:9; Eph 1:7, 2:13; Col 1:20), his letters uniformly speak of Christ's saving act "for us" (Rom 4:25; 5:8; 8:3; Gal 1:4; 2:20; Tit 2:14). These many passages must be read in both vicarious and substitutionary terms.[25] As James Dunn aptly concludes, "This was the good news of Paul's gospel: those who identified with Christ in his death were saved from dying their own death as the outcome of their subservience to sin."[26]

Christ as victim and priest. Ephesians 5:2 offers further insight into Christ's death as a sacrifice. In a parenetic context, Paul urges believers to "live in love, as Christ loved us and gave himself up for us, a fragrant offering and sacrifice to God." Here we have a combination of two terms from the Israelite cult, "offering" (Greek *prosphora*) and "sacrifice" (Greek *thysia*). The former probably refers to nonbloody sacrifices (i.e., from the produce of the ground [Hebrew *minḥâ*]), and the latter to bloody sacrifices (Hebrew *ʿōlâ*). A striking feature here is the fusion of two images: victim and priest. Christ represents the gift of life itself now offered up to God the source of life and every good gift. Christ gives what the sinner is obligated to give but cannot give (Rom 8:3). On the other hand, Christ is also a priest who is authorized to offer such gifts and sacrifices to God. The voluntary nature of this priestly action, an act of love, becomes the ground for Christian living. Followers of Christ live lives of self-giving love and thus replicate the unique saving act of Jesus' sacrifice. This is made explicit in Romans 12:2, where "Paul sees the Christian life as a sacrifice."[27]

SALVATION AS REDEMPTION

Words denoting redemption. Another word group in Paul's letters directs our attention to a different but related aspect of the salvation accomplished by the cross: redemption. Words such as *lytroō, apolytrōsis* and *antilytron* denote, respectively, (1) the act of setting free, redeeming or liberating; (2) the action or result of setting free, thus redemption, liberation and deliverance; (3) the means by which release is accomplished, namely, a ransom. To

---

[25]For a discussion of the Greek preposition *hyper* and its usage in Paul in both representational and substitutionary senses, see M. J. Harris, "ὑπέρ," *NIDNTT* 3:1196-97.
[26]Dunn, *Theology of Paul*, p. 223.
[27]C. Brown, "Sacrifice," *NIDNTT* 3:432.

this should be added words such as *agorazō* and *exagorazō* ("buy," but in the NT used figuratively to mean "release by means of paying a price"—i.e., to liberate someone who is a slave).[28]

Background of redemption language

First-century slavery. The relevance of this for the first century can scarcely be overemphasized. In the Roman Empire slaves comprised approximately one-fifth of the total population, with the ratio as high as one-third in Rome itself.[29] Many of these became enslaved through wars. Aristotle took it for granted that prisoners became slaves: "The one who is taken in war belongs to the conqueror" (*Politica* 1.6.1255 6-7). Subjugated peoples were routinely forced to serve as slaves to wealthy, upper-class Romans. Debt slavery was also widely practiced. Probably a majority of slaves during the era of the empire were simply born into servitude. Children born to slaves were personal property, just as the parents were. Paul mentions slaves and slavery in several of his letters; in fact, a number of his converts were slaves, and some were slave owners (1 Cor 7:20-24; Eph 6:5-8; Col 3:22-25; Philem; 1 Tim 6:1; Tit 2:9-10).

Slaves, however, might gain their freedom. "Persons in slavery under Roman law in the lst cent. A.D. could generally count on being set free by age thirty."[30] A comment by Cicero implies that a slave might be expected to wait seven years before being allowed his freedom (*Orationes philippicae* 8.32). The OT allows kinsmen to free any of their family who have fallen into servitude (Lev 25:25). Papyrii of the Greco-Roman era reveal that pagans too could redeem family members. For example, a papyrus records that a certain Cyrinus "paid fifty solidi to deliver his son."[31] Among Greeks and Romans there was a process called manumission, whereby slaves might become freemen. Manumission (from Latin *manumittere*, "release from one's hand") took two forms: formal and informal. The former was usually testamentary (*per testamentum*; i.e., the owner stipulated in his will that a designated slave [or slaves] be freed when he died). Another formal procedure, later preferred by Roman policy, required that slaves eligible (i.e., having faithfully served a sufficient time and having acquired sufficient funds

---

[28]See Louw and Nida, *Greek-English Lexicon*, 1:488 (§37.128, 130, 131).

[29]See S. Scott Bartchy, "Slavery," *ISBE* 4:543-46; idem, "Slavery (New Testament)," *ABD* 6:65-73; Keith R. Bradley, "Slavery," *OCD* 1415-16; W. G. Rollins, "Slavery in the NT," *IDBSup* 830-32; A. A. Rupprecht, "Slave, Slavery: II. Slavery in the NT," *ZPEB* 5:458-60; idem, "Slave, Slavery," *DPL* 881-83.

[30]Bartchy, "Slavery," *ISBE* 4:545; idem, "Slavery (New Testament)," *ABD* 6:71. As a matter of fact, there is inscriptional evidence that up to 50 percent of slaves manumitted were younger than thirty years of age.

[31]Ceslas Spicq, "λύτρον," *TLNT* 2:425.

to reimburse the owner for the purchase price, called a *peculium* [Latin "small savings"]) be brought before a local magistrate. If the magistrate concurred, the slave was symbolically touched by a rod—hence the name for this procedure, *per vindictam* (Latin "with a rod"). There was a 5 percent tax assessed for this service accruing to the state treasury. Informally, the owner might simply invite family and friends of the slave as witnesses to his oral declaration of freedom (*inter amicos*), or write a letter declaring his intention *(per epistulam)* or invite the slave to dine with him, a symbolic gesture indicating the dignity befitting a free man *(per mensam)*, or request his prospective heir to free the slave when he, the owner, died *(fidei commissum)*. The advantage of the informal procedure was avoidance of the manumission tax; the disadvantage was lack of an official record. Most opted for the formal procedure. Once freed, the slave was not liable to recapture and could integrate into society with all the rights and privileges of other freedmen. As a matter of fact, many persons of note had at one time been slaves. The apostle Paul stood before the procurator Marcus Antonius Felix, a former slave (see Acts 23:24—24:27). Factors that encouraged manumission were the declining birthrate of Roman citizens, with a consequent need for soldiers to serve in the military, and the increasing burden of supplying slaves with sufficient food.

My interest in this topic focuses on Paul's incorporation of slavery imagery into his doctrine of salvation. In 1 Corinthians 6:9-20 Paul's discussion of the body and sexuality is capped off by this statement: "For you were bought with a price; therefore glorify God in your body" (1 Cor 6:20), an unmistakable allusion to the institution of slavery. Paul reminds his listeners that they have now become the slaves of Christ. He has purchased them from the slave market of sin (Rom 6:1-14) or from bondage to the law (Rom 6:15-22; 7:4-6; Gal 3:13), and now they belong to him, body and spirit. The new obligations for them, as slaves of Christ, proscribe sexual unchastity, which, according to Paul, affects both body and spirit (1 Cor 6:16-18). In this analogy the purchase price is probably the blood (i.e., death) of Christ. This is confirmed by Ephesians 1:7: "In him we have redemption [*apolytrōsis*] through his blood." And in 1 Timothy 2:6, citing a creedal statement, Paul says that Christ "gave himself a ransom [*antilytron*] for all—this was attested at the right time." The latter phrase recalls the public nature of a formal declaration of liberation in the manumission process. Perhaps the Lord's Supper also reminded believers of their informal manumission from sin, since now they were invited to dine at their master's table as free men and women. At any rate, Paul's use of redemption language clearly emphasizes the cost of redemption and the sense of rescue and true freedom in Christ (Rom 6:17-19a), both of which spoke loudly and clearly to his audience.

Old Testament background. The Roman institution of slavery and the process of manumission doubtless throw light on Paul's redemption language, but another important piece of background requires mention. Israel began its national history with a miraculous liberation from state slavery. Pharaoh owned the Israelites lock, stock and barrel. They were his personal chattel. On their backs he built the infrastructure of the Egyptian Empire. The God of Abraham, Isaac and Jacob commissioned Moses, the adopted son of Pharaoh, to liberate Israel from slavery. Israel became Yahweh's own, unique people. The story, of course, is narrated in Exodus and thereafter referred to by historical, prophetic and liturgical texts; it was the equivalent of the modern American Fourth of July (e.g., Josh 24:5-7; 1 Sam 12:8; 2 Sam 7:6; 1 Kings 6:1; 8:9, 16, 21; 17:7; Ps 105:23-38; 106:6-12; 135:8; 136:10-15; Amos 3:1; Hos 11:1; Is 11:11; Jer 2:6).

This epic deliverance finds echoes in NT thought. One Pauline text in particular suggests a typological allusion to the exodus, highlighting the much greater liberation of the new people of God achieved by Christ on the cross. Colossians 1:13-14 says, "He has rescued us from the power of darkness and transferred us into the kingdom of his beloved Son, in whom we have redemption *[apolytrōsis],* the forgiveness of sins" (cf. Gal 1:4). Believers, like the children of Israel long ago, are enslaved to sin, the unrelenting taskmaster (cf. Ex 1:11-22 with Rom 7:5-6, 23-24; 8:2-3). The world and the demonic powers add to the enslavement. Because of this thralldom, Christ "gave himself for our sins to set us free from the present evil age" (Gal 1:4; cf. Tit 2:14). As we will see shortly, this rescue from servitude involves divine conflict with the demonic powers and their utter defeat— just like Pharoah of old (cf. Ex 15:1-10; Col 2:15). Those so redeemed become, paradoxically, slaves of Christ (Rom 7:22). On the other hand, they also become sons and daughters, possessing full rights and privileges (Gal 3:25—4:7; Rom 8:14-17). As sons and daughters, believers now fully share the inheritance of the firstborn son, Jesus Christ (Rom 8:17, 29), the very status conferred on ancient Israel in the story of the exodus (Ex 4:22). The condition of this new servitude, however, is genuine freedom (i.e., the ability to do what one ought). Liberation in Christ amounts to life as it was meant to be, producing the fruit of the Spirit in abundance (Gal 5:22-23). Although Ephesians 2:1-10 describes salvation primarily in terms of a resurrection and ascension, one also hears echoes of the exodus experience. The thralldom of Israel in Egypt under the tyrannical domination of Pharaoh finds its antitype in the tyranny of the "ruler of the power of the air"

(Eph 2:2). Certainly the gracious initiative of God in Christ, who exerts his power to bring the spiritually dead to life and lift them up to the heavenly realms, bespeaks a new and greater exodus than in the days of Moses (Ex 2:25; 3:7-10; 15:1-18; Deut 7:7-11).

SALVATION AS RECONCILIATION

Basic meanings of word group. Another important word group in Paul's writings employs the metaphor of relationships to convey what Christ has done through the cross. Among these words are the following: *katallassō* ("reestablish proper friendly interpersonal relations after these have been disrupted or broken"), *katallagē* ("restoration of original friendly relations"), *apokatallassō* (same as *katallassō* and found only in Paul; in fact, it may have been coined by him), *eirēnopoieō* ("cause a state of peace or reconciliation between persons, make peace, make things right") and *mesitēs* ("a person who acts as a mediator in bringing about reconciliation").[32] The key idea in all these words has to do with reconciliation.

Background. The assumption behind this image is a state of enmity and alienation. This hostility has several dimensions. The fundamental alienation underlying all others is that between God and humanity. In Paul's language, before coming to Christ, sinners are "enemies" (Rom 5:10), "who live according to the flesh" (Rom 8:5), are "hostile to God" and do not "submit to God's law—indeed . . . cannot please God" (Rom 8:7-8). This estrangement of sinners from God results in disharmony in all relationships of life.

Although Paul makes no direct reference to Genesis 3 in theological passages employing reconciliation language, the story of the fall is just below the surface. This is not surprising, given that Romans alludes to the story of Adam at several key junctures (Rom 1; 5; 7; 8). The point of Genesis 3 can be crisply stated: disharmony now poisons all relationships; society is characterized by estrangement. Adam and Eve were estranged from God ("Where are you?" [Gen 3:9]), from each other ("The woman whom you gave to be with me, she gave me fruit from the tree, and I ate" [Gen 3:12]) and from their environment ("Cursed is the ground because of you" [Gen 3:17]). Life is now lived "east of Eden," bedeviled by alienation and estrangement—self rules. The vignettes in Genesis 4—11 tragically underscore this sad reality. Because of this universal human experience, Paul's gospel of reconciliation has a powerful appeal.

Pauline use of reconciliation language. I begin with a passage using the

---

[32]Louw and Nida, *Greek-English Lexicon*, 1:502-3 (§40.1, 4, 6).

idea of reconciliation, but not in a theological sense. In dealing with the difficult matter of divorce in 1 Corinthians 7, Paul directs that if a woman separates from her husband, she should either "remain unmarried or else be reconciled to her husband" (1 Cor 7:11). In other words, separated couples have two options: they can live apart and let their estrangement continue, or they can take steps to restore a peaceful, harmonious relationship. In short, they can be friends again. This provides a helpful analogy for understanding salvation; there are, however, some important differences.

Romans 5:10 presents reconciliation as an accomplished fact: "For if while we were enemies, we were reconciled to God through the death of his Son, much more surely, having been reconciled, will we be saved by his life." This new status vis-à-vis God exists as a present ongoing experience: "But more than that, we even boast in God through our Lord Jesus Christ, through whom we have now received reconciliation" (Rom 5:11). Note that reconciliation is more than a subjective experience; it has an objective basis in what God has done for us in Christ: he made us his friends through the cross. Also striking is the close association with the notion of justification. Both concepts result in a new relationship, which can be described as "peace" (Rom 5:1; Col 1:20).

Sinners do nothing to reconcile themselves; God takes the initiative and is the one who effects a change in relationship through the death of Christ ("by his blood").[33] Furthermore, in Paul's explicit statements sinners are reconciled to God, never God to sinners. This, however, should not force us to conclude that God is in no sense reconciled to sinners by the death of Christ. As Leon Morris reminds us, "The argument from silence is always precarious, and doubly so when, as here, there are a few passages in question."[34] After examining the words "enemy" and "enmity" in Paul and in the wider biblical context of the wrath of God, Morris concludes, "Scripture is insistent that God reacts in the strongest possible way to man's sin. . . . There is a very real hostility on the part of God to all that is evil, and . . . this hostility is not incompatible with a deep love of God for sinners."[35] What we can say with certainty, however, is that the initiative in reconciliation belongs entirely to God. This is made explicit in 2 Corinthians 5:18-19: "All this is from God, who reconciled us to himself through Christ . . . in Christ God was reconciling the world to him-

---

[33]"Paul is the first attested Greek author to speak of the offended party (God) initiating reconciliation, using the active voice form of the verb" (S. E. Porter, "Peace, Reconciliation," *DPL* 695).

[34]Morris, *Apostolic Preaching*, p. 220.

[35]Ibid., pp. 224-25.

self, not counting their trespasses against them."[36]

This is in marked contrast to paganism, where the devotee performs certain acts or rituals in order to secure a "safe" relationship, and nowhere in paganism do the devotee and the deity have what could be called a "friendly" relationship.[37] Danger always threatens the devotee because the deity can never be relied on.

In Judaism reconciliation requires repentance and performance of the obligations of Torah. Performance of the commandments is a necessary precondition for *shalom* to exist between God and the worshiper. This is reflected in a couple of passages from the Midrash. According to a saying of Rabbi Isaac, Moses reconciled God and Israel after the episode of the golden calf "through the second Tables" (*Deut. Rab.* 3:15). This presupposes that Israel committed itself to keeping these commandments and thereby achieved reconciliation with an offended God. In another passage, Moses was able to effect reconciliation by fashioning the tabernacle. According to Rabbi Berkiah, "Formerly there was hostility between Me and My children, there was enmity between Me and My children. Now, however, that this Tabernacle has been made there will be love between Me and My children, there will be peace between Me and My children" (*Num. Rab.* 12:1). The difference from Paul is palpable.

Paul urges individuals, "Be reconciled to God" (2 Cor 5:20). This imperative, however, assumes an indicative: "God, who reconciled us" (2 Cor 5:18). Reconciliation is entirely a gift of God's grace. The sinner responds not by "doing" but rather by "receiving" (i.e., appropriating the gift by faith). Paul even describes himself as an ambassador, personally delivering his gracious sovereign's overture of peace: "So we are ambassadors for Christ, since God is making his appeal through us" (2 Cor 5:20). This state of being reconciled to God is maintained by ongoing trust and commitment, as Paul pointedly warns the Colossians: "provided that you continue securely established and steadfast in faith, without shifting from the hope promised by the gospel that you heard" (Col 1:23). Saints must persevere, not presume.[38]

Reconciliation to God is an eschatological event. This new relationship

---

[36]"These data lead us to one inescapable conclusion, which must be strongly emphasized: whatever else the doctrine involves, it is God who has both initiated and in Christ accomplished reconciliation" (Ladd, *Theology of the New Testament*, p. 493).

[37]"The relation between divinity and humanity does not have this personal nearness" (F. Büchsel, "καταλλάσσω," *TDNT* 1:254).

[38]"Only the one who believes in Christ can know assurance of final salvation (Col. 1:22-23). Perseverance is not automatic" (J. M. Gundry-Volf, "Apostasy, Falling Away, Perseverance," *DPL* 39-45).

of peace and friendship is part of the new age that has broken in with the coming of Christ. To partake of its benefits projects one into the coming age; it is nothing less than a new creation: "So if anyone is in Christ, there is a new creation . . . everything has become new!" (2 Cor 5:17). This verse involves much more than just the subjective experience of personal conversion; nothing less than a new era of salvation history has begun. Believers have been swept up in the dawning of the coming age. For this reason, reconciliation is more comprehensive than the idea of justification (see below). Far more than guilt is under consideration.[39]

There is a horizontal dimension to Christ's reconciling work; Christ's death reconciles alienated people and people groups to one another. Just as the Ten Commandments can be summed up in two—love for God and love for neighbor (Mk 12:28-31 pars.)—so also Paul's gospel addresses both dimensions. God in Christ reconciles us to himself through the cross and pours out his love into our hearts—the vertical dimension (Rom 5:5; 2 Cor 5:14). This love, in turn, breaks down the walls that separate us from our fellow human beings—the horizontal dimension. The vertical is, of course, prior to and indispensable for the horizontal.

One letter in particular, Ephesians, draws attention to the horizontal aspect of reconciliation. No wall of separation was more evident in the first century than the one between Jews and Gentiles. The literature of this era, whether from pagan or Jewish sources, reflects mutual suspicion and hostility. Jewish-Gentile hostility, however, was hardly the only social barrier that fractured first-century society. Other stress lines included the barrier between slave and free, nobility and commoner, Roman citizen and noncitizen, barbarian (i.e., those outside the Greco-Roman world) and Romanized, and male and female (1 Cor 12:13; Gal 3:28; Col 3:11). Paul had a mandate to preach the gospel to all who had not heard (Rom 15:18-21; 2 Cor 10:13-18; Gal 1:15-16; cf. Acts 9:15; 26:17-18; 22:21). But how do these "all" come together as the body of Christ in a specific locality? This is the burden of Ephesians, a masterpiece of pastoral theology highlighting the unity of the church in all its diversity.

Paul holds that the work of Christ creates a new humanity, one that no longer allows cultural and societal barriers to dictate fellowship. Addressing the long-standing barrier that kept Gentiles from the commonwealth of Israel (Eph 2:12), epitomized by the Mosaic law, Paul insists that Gentiles are now part of the household of God (Eph 2:11-21). In Christ, the new Adam, "the dividing wall" has come down (Eph 2:14). This, says Paul, is

---

[39]See Ladd, *Theology of the New Testament*, pp. 522-53.

what the gospel of Christ requires. This passage probably contains an allusion to the Jerusalem temple balustrade ("the dividing wall"), a three-foot-high barrier (the *soreg*), forbidding Gentiles from entering the central courtyard (the *azarah*), on pain of death. There were thirteen entrances through the *soreg*, each of which had an inscription nearby, written in Greek and Latin, warning Gentiles not to enter (Josephus, *J.W.* 5.193; 6.125; *Ant.* 15.417; Philo, *Embassy* 212). Two of these marker stones have been recovered, translated thus: "No man of another nation to enter within the fence and enclosure round the temple. And whoever is caught will have himself to blame that his death ensues."[40] According to Acts, the reason why Paul was arrested at Jerusalem and eventually wound up in Rome as a prisoner was the false accusation against him that he had brought a Gentile, Trophimus of Ephesus, into the sacred precincts (Acts 21:27-29). As Paul wrote to the Ephesians, that episode surely crossed his mind, and the irony of it did not escape him.

But the *soreg* serves as a metaphor; it is symptomatic of a deeper problem: the law of Moses and its many ritual requirements. What is especially harmful in Paul's view is the imposition of these regulations on Gentiles who come to faith in Jesus Christ. Functionally, the boundary markers of circumcision, sabbath and *kashrut* served to keep Jews and Gentiles separate. But this is not what God ultimately intends. The eternal plan of God decrees an eventual coming together and unity of all disparate ethnic and social groups into one holy family (Eph 1:3-14). Paul's argument rests on a radical new understanding of salvation history. The age of Torah has given way to the new age of the Spirit, inaugurated by Christ's redemptive and reconciling work on the cross and culminating in cosmic unity (Eph 1:10). There is no place for two peoples of God or two temples in the new age—just one people (Eph 2:11-19) and one temple (Eph 2:20-22), the body of Christ (Eph 4:4-6, 13, 15-16, 5:23, 25-27), consisting of Jew and Gentile on equal footing (Eph 3:1-6).

This message was radical then and is radical today. Faithfulness to Paul's gospel requires a sincere effort to provide a model community for the unbelieving world. The challenge is to show now what the new redeemed and reconciled humanity looks like at the consummation of the kingdom. Racism, sexism, nationalism and ethnic superiority militate against this ultimate goal. All too often the visible church has failed miserably to break down the barriers. The church urgently needs "to make everyone see what is the plan of the mystery hidden for ages in God who created all things; so

---

[40]C. K. Barrett, ed., *The New Testament Background: Selected Documents* (rev. ed.; San Francisco: Harper & Row, 1987), p. 53.

that through the church the wisdom of God in its rich variety might now be made known to the rulers and authorities in the heavenly places" (Eph 3:9-10). Whenever and wherever the church catches this vision, unity and peace prevail.

The preceding discussion touches on another important aspect of the doctrine of reconciliation. In Paul's exposition of God's great redemptive plan, several times he speaks in cosmic terms (the world, all things, etc.). How literally did he intend this? Are these examples of hyperbole, or did he really envision a cosmic reconciliation? Paul was heir to apocalyptic Judaism, in which visions of cosmic renewal regularly appear. Judging from his missionary correspondence, we see that Paul the Christian harbors similar hopes. So how extensive is Paul's scope of cosmic reconciliation? At face value, Romans 8:19-22 speaks of a liberation and renewal of "the whole creation." Paul's language alludes to Genesis 3 and the curse upon the earth. Christ's work of reconciliation is nothing less than a lifting of the primal curse at Eden. Although the word *reconciliation* is not used, the redemption metaphor implies a transformation at the parousia. There is an overlap between the semantic fields of liberation and reconciliation. Colossians explicitly employs the term *reconciliation* to describe the effects of Christ's death on the cross upon the cosmos: "Through him [Christ] God was pleased to reconcile to himself all things, whether on earth or in heaven, by making peace through the blood of his cross" (Col 1:20). Linking Colossians 1:20 with Romans 8:19-22, I infer that Paul expected the entire cosmos to experience a transformation at the eschaton.

Not all agree with my interpretation, however. Friedrich Büchsel, for example, limits the scope of reconciliation to conscious beings. His argument is that the last phrase of Colossians 1:20, "making peace through the blood of his cross," elucidates what reconciliation means in the first part of the verse, and that this is confirmed by the other two uses of *apokatallassō* in Colossians 1:22 ("And you . . . he has now reconciled") and Ephesians 2:16 ("and might reconcile both groups to God").[41] But limitation to the human sphere is hardly what Paul means in Colossians 1:20 by the expression "all things."[42] As Colin Brown points out, "The passage presupposes a cosmic catastrophe caused by the powers of evil. He, who is the creator and sustainer of all, is he who has triumphed over the powers of evil on the cross and is therefore the reconciler of all."[43] Furthermore, why would

---

[41]Büchsel, "ἀποκαταλλάσσω," *TDNT* 1:259.

[42]"That cosmic reconciliation is in view (and not just human creation) is implied by the thematic *ta panta* ('all things')" (Dunn, *Theology of Paul*, p. 230 n. 132).

[43]C. Brown, "Reconciliation," *NIDNTT* 3:172.

Paul's scope of salvation be less than that envisioned by the OT prophets (Is 11:6-9; 65:17; 66:22; Ezek 47:1-12; Amos 9:11-15; Zech 14:6-11) and the visionaries of apocalyptic Judaism (*As. Mos.* 10:1-40; *Sib. Or.* 767—808; *2 Bar.* 25—30)? Paul does not elaborate on what precisely might be entailed in this cosmic reconciliation, but that he held out hope for a removal of evil from the entire cosmos seems certain.

Does cosmic reconciliation as depicted in Ephesians and Colossians amount to universalism (i.e., the teaching that all, without exception, will eventually be saved)? Although that position was championed by Origen in the third century A.D., the nearly unanimous position of the church, up until the Enlightenment, stands opposed. Today, most in the liberal tradition advocate it and find support in Paul. The charge of bigotry and intolerance is difficult to bear. But the ultimate question must always be: What does Scripture teach? And in this case, what did Paul teach?

When the passages speaking of cosmic reconciliation are read in the context of the entire letters to the Ephesians and the Colossians, and of the entire Pauline corpus, the answer is apparent: Paul believed that only the elect would be saved, and the elect are defined as those who put their trust in Christ as Savior and Lord. When Colossians speaks of "all things, whether on earth or in heaven" being reconciled to God (Col 1:20), carefully note that this confessional passage (Col 1:15-20) is immediately followed by Paul's application to his readers, where he says, "And *you* who were once estranged and hostile in mind, doing evil deeds, he has now reconciled" (Col 1:21-22 [my italics]). Paul then goes on to warn his readers (the "you") against shifting from the faith, here equated with "the gospel that you heard," implying that they would thereby forfeit their reconciled status (Col 1:23). Furthermore, Paul warns his readers even more severely in Colossians 3:6: "On account of these [evil deeds] the wrath of God is coming on those who are disobedient." This speaks against universalism. One must also reckon with the likelihood that Paul uses the term *reconciliation* with differing nuances, depending on the object. The hostile powers are not reconciled to God in the same sense that repentant sinners are; indeed, we probably should think in terms of pacification of the demonic powers.

Other texts (e.g., Rom 5:15-19; 1 Cor 15:22; 2 Cor 5:14; Phil 2:10-11; 1 Tim 2:4, 6) have also been appealed to in support of universalism. In each case, contextual considerations and consistency in Paul's thought argue against such a stance. I marshal a few summary statements synthesizing Paul's teaching on the scope of salvation.[44]

---

[44]Here I am indebted to the fine treatment in Schreiner, *Paul,* pp. 182-88.

1. A number of Pauline passages clearly teach the reality of condemnation, judgment and death for those outside Christ (e.g., Rom 2:5-16; 5:9; 9:3, 6-7, 13, 18, 21-22, 31-33; 10:2-4; 11:7-10, 20-23, 28; Phil 3:19; 1 Thess 1:10; 2 Thess 1:8-9).

2. Paul's urgency and enormous commitment to preaching the gospel are hard to square with a doctrine of universalism (2 Cor 5:11-15). The personal cost for Paul (see 1 Cor 4:9-13; 2 Cor 11:22-33; Col 1:24; 1:29—2:1) and his associates to proclaim the gospel hardly seems worth it if everyone will be saved in the end anyway, regardless of whether they respond positively to the preaching of the gospel.

3. In Romans 5:15-19 the gift of righteousness is conditioned by receiving it (Rom 5:17). But clearly not all do receive it; only those who believe the message are justified. Paul's prayer for nonbelieving Jews was "that they may be saved" (Rom 10:1). His great concern was that unless they believed the gospel, "there will be anguish and distress for everyone who does evil, the Jew first . . ." (Rom 2:9). His great confidence was in the gospel, "the power of God for salvation to everyone who has faith, to the Jew first . . ." (Rom 1:16). If those to whom the very oracles of God had been granted (Rom 3:2) were saved only by believing the gospel, how much more true it is of Gentiles who were "dead through . . . trespasses and sins" (Eph 2:1).

4. The use of "all" language by Paul must be viewed in context. In texts such as 1 Timothy 2:4, 6—"who desires everyone [literally, 'all men'] to be saved" and "who gave himself a ransom for all"—what Paul means is all people without distinction, not all people without exception. On the other hand, the motif of the two Adams in Paul's thought does indeed entail a universalism (i.e., literally all those in the first Adam die; literally all those in the second Adam live [1 Cor 15:22]). Therefore, a person must be joined to the second Adam in order to experience the benefits and become a new creation (2 Cor 5:17). This occurs when one believes the gospel: "We entreat you on behalf of Christ, be reconciled to God" (2 Cor 5:20).

SUMMARY

Paul's doctrine of reconciliation speaks of salvation in terms of a restored relationship with the Creator. Sinners have alienated themselves from the source of every good gift; they need desperately to be friends with God, not enemies. God takes the initiative. In Christ, the "one mediator between God and humankind" (1 Tim 2:5), God acts to restore friendly relations. The fact that it is by means of Christ's death shows that reconciliation takes seriously God's anger at sin. By means of the cross, God in Christ achieves peace at the cost of the death of his Son. Reconciliation is not, however, automatic, as in some gnostic systems; sinners must respond to the gracious overture and receive it in faith. Having received it, they must continue in it. This new status is available to all peoples and groups. In Christ, the second Adam, there is a new humanity no longer recognizing ethnic and social distinctions or the religious requirements of ritual boundary markers. The only boundary marker that now counts is a new creation (2 Cor 5:17; Gal 6:15) demonstrated by God's love poured out into human hearts (Rom 5:5) and sealed by the Holy Spirit (2 Cor 1:22; Eph 1:13; 4:30; cf. 2 Tim 2:19). Furthermore, this act of reconciliation is in some mysterious way altering the entire cosmos. When the day of redemption arrives in its fullness, the Holy Spirit, now a pledge and down payment on the final installment, will act decisively to effect a cosmic transformation in which all evil will be banished and the curse of Genesis 3 lifted. Perhaps no other term in Paul's salvation inventory has such scope as *reconciliation*.[45] No wonder some have selected the notion of reconciliation as the central idea in Paul's multifaceted mosaic of salvation.

SALVATION AS DEFEAT OF THE COSMIC POWERS

A fascinating text, Colossians 2:15, depicts a cosmic conflict between Christ and the demonic powers. This text occurs in the section where Paul launches his attack on the false teaching threatening the congregation at Colossae (Col 2:8-23). At Colossians 2:13 Paul reviews how God brought dead sinners to life in Christ and forgave their trespasses, likened to an IOU nailed to the cross (Col 2:14).[46] This vivid imagery draws attention to the condemning nature of the Mosaic law and the resulting record of indebtedness on everyone's account (cf. Gal 3:10-14; Eph 2:15).[47] Immediately thereafter, Paul proceeds to describe a divine conflict with the "rulers and authorities": "He disarmed the rulers and authorities and made a public example of them, triumphing over them in it" (Col 2:15). Several questions arise: Who are these "rulers and authorities"? Who does the disarming: God, Christ or both? When does this conflict and public triumph occur? What actually happens, and what is the outcome?

The rulers and authorities almost certainly are spiritual beings hostile to God and his kingdom. Second Temple Judaism and paganism believed

---

[45]For a concise summary of reconciliation, see Ceslas Spicq, "καταλλαγή, καταλλάσσω," *TLNT* 2:265-66.

[46]See Eduard Lohse, "χειρόγραφον," *TDNT* 9:435-36; Ceslas Spicq, "χειρόγραφον," *TLNT* 3:508-10; N. Walther, "χειρόγραφον," *EDNT* 3:464.

[47]So Peter T. O'Brien, *Colossians, Philemon* (WBC 44; Waco, TX: Word, 1982), pp. 124-25.

in a wide array of semidivine, angelic beings, good and evil, with various ranks and orders. In apocalyptic Judaism the evil angels, following a ringleader, variously named Belial, Mastema, Satan, Semyaza and Yequn, participated in a revolt against God's will. The notion of an angelic revolt may be seen in the literature ascribed to the antediluvian patriarch Enoch (see *1 En.* 6—10; 41:9; 68—69; esp. 61:10), *Jubilees* 2:2, *Testament of Levi* 3:7-8, and some of the sectarian writings at Qumran, such as *Rule of the Community*, *Songs of the Sage War Scroll* and *Hodayot* (*Thanksgiving Hymns*). One also finds similar ideas in the Greek Magical Papyri.[48] The NT takes over this terminology and conception, though with this important modification: all these beings are under the ultimate sovereignty of Christ, who is their creator and Lord.

The subject of the action in Colossians 2:15 is moot. The NRSV supplies the proper name "God" as the subject of the verb "made alive" in Colossians 2:13, since God is the subject of the immediately preceding clause in Colossians 2:12, "who [God] raised him [Christ] from the dead." The succeeding participles and verbs in Colossians 2:13-15 are then understood as referring to God.

A majority of English versions translate accordingly (RSV, ESV, HCSB, KJV, NIV, NAB, NLB); with a minority implying or explicitly indicating that Christ is the subject (GNB, NET, NASB, NJB). A key issue here is how to translate the Greek participle *apekdysamenos* ("stripped off, disarmed" [active voice] or "divested himself" [middle voice]). If one translates it as a middle, then Christ must be the subject. The form itself is clearly middle; what is unclear is whether it functions as a middle or an active. Commentators are divided on the issue.[49] There is not a lot at stake here because, according to Paul, God was in Christ reconciling the world to himself (2 Cor 5:19). Thus the actions attributed to the Father are often attributed to the Son. There is a fundamental unity in the redemptive plan.

More important are questions of when and what. There can be little doubt that Paul has the crucifixion in mind. The problem is that none of the Gospels depict anything like this dramatic encounter. The Gospel nar-

---

[48]For specific references, see Clinton Arnold, "Principalities and Powers," *ABD* 5:476.

[49]Dan Reid prefers the middle voice, "to strip or divest oneself of" ("Triumph," *DPL* 949), as does J. B. Lightfoot (*Saint Paul's Epistles to the Colossians and to Philemon* [3rd ed.; New York: Macmillan, 1879], pp. 187-89). Understanding the middle in an active sense are A. Oepke, "ἀπεκδύω," *TDNT* 2:318-19; F. Blass and A. Debrunner, *A Greek Grammar of the New Testament and Other Early Christian Literature*, trans. and rev. R. W. Funk (Chicago: University of Chicago Press, 1961), §316[1]; Murray J. Harris, *Colossians and Philemon* (EGGNT; Grand Rapids: Eerdmans, 1991), p. 110; Schreiner, *Paul*, p. 234.

ratives simply portray another grim and grisly Roman execution.[50] Paul seemingly pulls back the curtain and allows us to see what was actually happening in the spiritual realm. Beyond what the naked eye could see on Good Friday was a clash of spiritual forces. The cross in some way led to the defeat, at least in principle, of the "rulers and authorities" that exercise a malevolent hold over fallen human beings. In this regard, two extremes ought to be avoided: either dismiss the text as mere literary embellishment with no historical basis or construct elaborate deception schemes in which Christ dupes the demons, as happened in gnostic and medieval theology.[51]

The key for unpacking the meaning of our text lies in a deftly inserted literary allusion. At the end of Colossians 2:15 Paul says that God (or Christ) was triumphing over the rulers and authorities in the cross. The word translated "triumphing" (Greek *thriambeuō*, "lead in a triumphal procession") is a technical term denoting a Roman victory parade.[52] When the victorious legions returned from a successful campaign, it was customary to stage an elaborate processional march.[53] The victorious general leads the way, followed by the legionnaires in their finest dress parade attire. Sometimes the procession takes on the character of a pageant, complete with floats with live performers depicting various stages of the campaign. Following the army are the spoils of war destined to enrich the coffers of the empire. At the tail end of the procession come the prisoners of war, shackled in chains and subjected to the jeers and abuse of the onlookers. Doomed prisoners could only expect public execution, death in the arena by wild animals, crucifixion, or a short and wretched life as a state slave in the salt mines or imperial galleys. In Paul's analogy, God or Christ leads the victory parade while the defeated rulers and authorities bring up the rear, subjected to humiliation and facing certain death. A vivid and memorable metaphor like this surely would have resonated with his readers at Colossae.

What is the theological significance of Colossians 2:15? By Christ's atoning death on the cross, the liability of sin is paid in full. Sin, the principle of rebellion against God's rule, is the opening that grants access by the evil spiritual beings. Once sin is dealt with and pardon is actually applied to individuals, these evil personages lose their hold—at least in principle. The indwelling Christ provides a new dynamic for living a life oriented toward God (Col 3:1-3). In short, the kingdom of Christ (Col 1:13) now holds sway

---

[50]For details on this mode of execution, see J. B. Green, "Crucifixion," *DPL* 197-99.

[51]For a brief description of such theories, see L. L. Morris, "Atonement," *NDT* 55-56.

[52]BDAG, p. 363. See also Reid, "Triumph," *DPL* 946-54; S. J. Hafemann, "Roman Triumph," *DNTB* 1004-18.

[53]For a contemporary description of the Romans' great triumphal procession after the Jewish revolt, see Josephus, *J.W.* 7.132-157.

over its repentant subjects. They have broken with their past ("the ways you also once followed" [Col 3:7]), described by Paul in his letter to the Galatians as a time "when you did not know God, you were enslaved to beings that by nature are not gods" (Gal 4:8). Therefore, the Colossians should not give heed to any so-called philosophy that is "according to the elemental spirits of the universe, and not according to Christ" (Col 2:8). And, what is of immediate relevance for the issue at hand, the Colossians should not kowtow to the purveyors of this ersatz gospel by observing its many rituals (Col 2:16) and regulations: "Do not handle, Do not taste, Do not touch" (Col 2:21). The reason is both simple and profound: you died with Christ to the elemental spirits; you must live in accordance with the new traditions of Christ (Col 2:20; cf. 2:6-7). The rituals and regulations of the false cult are mere "shadow," whereas the apostolic teaching is "substance" (Col 2:17). Already believers in Christ are raised up with him and are seated at the right hand of God (Col 3:1); the false teaching cannot deliver what it promises (Col 2:22-23). In short, the gospel of Christ is the great mystery of Christ—that is, Christ, the fullness of God (Col 1:19) and wisdom of God (Col 2:3), dwelling in every believer (Col 1:27). The message of Colossians is timeless: in Christ we have all we really need.

SALVATION AS JUSTIFICATION

Words relating to justification. I conclude this selective treatment of Pauline soteriology by examining what many, especially those in the Lutheran and Reformed traditions, consider the most important aspect of salvation: justification. Unfortunately, it is also one of the most contested aspects of Pauline theology.[54] In brief, the debate centers around the precise meaning of words that Paul uses in connection with justification, the Greek *dik-* word group: *dikaios* ("upright, just, righteous"), *dikaiosynē* ("uprightness, justice, righteousness"), *dikaioō* ("show justice, do justice, justify, acquit, vindicate"), *dikaiōma* ("regulation, requirement, commandment, righteous deed"), *dikaiōs* ("justly, in a just manner, uprightly") and *dikaiōsis* ("justification, vindication, acquittal"). The secondary literature is enormous, so I have provided a separate bibliography as an entry point into this contested area.

Background of justification language. Paul uses the Greek *dik-* word group in essentially the same way the LXX translates the Hebrew equivalents in the OT. The corresponding Hebrew word group consists of *ṣaddîq* ("just,

---

[54]"We enter . . . upon one of the most vigorous debates in current NT studies, all the more important because of its central significance for formulating the gospel, testing theology, and reappraising Christianity's Jewish roots and heritage" (Dunn, *Theology of Paul*, p. 340).

righteous, correct"), ṣedeq ("rightness, righteousness"), ṣĕdāqâ ("righteousness, righteous acts, justice"), ṣādēq and ṣādôq in Qal, ("be just, righteous"),
Piel ("justify"), Niphil ("be put right, be justified") and especially Hiphil
(hiṣdîq, "do justice, declare righteous, justify, vindicate, make righteous"),
along with the related words mišpaṭ ("justice") and ḥesed ("steadfast love,
covenant faithfulness").

The first contested issue is this: does the root idea of ṣdq signify a norm
for behavior, or does it imply a relationship (i.e., the fulfillment of the obligations of a relationship, more specifically, a covenant relationship, whether
with God or humans)?[55] In short, is the fundamental idea ethical or relational? A second question concerns whether righteousness is fundamentally
forensic (i.e., involving a legal procedure in a courtroom—a declaration
of guilt or innocence) or refers essentially to God's saving activity and the
consequent benefits to those who are its recipients.

In my opinion, a careful study of these words in context demonstrates
that the aforementioned alternatives are false antitheses. To be sure, righteousness and justification language must be understood within the overarching context of Yahweh's covenant with Israel and is thus relational in
orientation. But the ancient Near Eastern background suggests a fundamental notion of conformity to a norm or standard, and the OT assumes
this ultimate norm to be the very character of God himself.[56] "The Lord is
righteous [ṣaddîq] in all his ways and loving [ḥāsîd] toward all he has made"
(Ps 145:17 NIV). Furthermore, justification language is not restricted to the
covenant with Israel; there are texts that employ the righteousness word
group in reference to all creation—for example, Isaiah 45:8: "Shower, O
heavens, from above and let the skies rain down righteousness [ṣedeq]; let
the earth open, that salvation may spring up, and let it cause righteousness
[ṣĕdāqâ] to sprout up also; I the LORD have created it." In this larger venue,
righteousness has to do with reestablishing God's order in a fallen world;
sin necessitates a setting right of that which is out of order or in a state of
disorder. "This saving action by God in the context of divine world rule
provides the setting for references to proper comportment."[57] There are, of
course, many passages in which a forensic idea involving a declaration of
guilt or acquittal is center stage, in which ṣedeq and ṣĕdāqâ refer to the action of a judge (i.e., appeal is made to a norm or standard)—for example,

---

[55]Defending the former is Harold G. Stigers, "צדק," TWOT 2:752-53; David J. Reimer,
"צדק," NIDOTTE 3:744-66; defending the latter is Elizabeth Achtemeier, "Righteousness
in the OT," IDB 4:80-85.
[56]Stigers, TWOT, 2:752.
[57]John Reumann, "Righteousness in the NT," ABD 5:748.

Leviticus 19:15: "You shall not render an unjust judgment; you shall not be partial to the poor or defer to the poor or defer to the great: with justice *[ṣedeq]* you shall judge your neighbor."

In a majority of cases, *ṣedeq/ṣĕdāqâ* refers to God's saving action on behalf of his people and becomes closely associated with salvation and vindication. This usage is particularly pronounced in the psalms and the prophets—for example, "The LORD has made known his victory *[yĕšûʿâ]*; he has revealed his vindication *[ṣĕdāqâ]* in the sight of the nations" (Ps 98:2); "The LORD works vindication *[ṣĕdāqâ]* and justice *[mišpaṭ]* for all who are oppressed" (Ps 103:6); "I bring near my deliverance *[ṣĕdāqâ]*, it is not far off, and my salvation *[tĕšûʿâ]* will not tarry; I will put salvation *[tĕšûʿâ]* in Zion, for Israel my glory" (Is 46:13); "I will bring near my deliverance *[ṣedeq]* swiftly, my salvation *[yēšaʿ]* has gone out and my arms will rule the peoples" (Is 51:5). Still, one cannot miss the forensic imagery of the courtroom in these passages as well. Yahweh is faithful to Israel and rules in their favor; he vindicates them and thereby delivers them. "Your people shall all be righteous *[ṣāddîqîm]*; they shall possess the land forever" (Is 60:21).

According to the story line in the OT, Yahweh, the God of Israel, chose Israel as his unique people in order to bring blessing to all peoples. This is the essence of the great Abrahamic covenant (Gen 12:1-3, 7; 15; 17; 22:15-19). In other words, God's intention from the beginning was to include the Gentiles, indeed the entire created world, in his redemptive plan. Israel was his missionary people through whom this message was to be proclaimed. Even though Israel proved to be unfaithful, this did not nullify God's faithfulness and determination to bless all nations through the faith of Abraham (cf. Rom 3:3-6). This message shines through repeatedly in Isaiah 40—66.

The great problem of the story of Israel was their unfaithfulness and consequent punishment by exile. Throughout the latter part of the OT we hear repeated prayers that God would come to the aid of Israel and vindicate them over against the pagan neighbors who oppressed them (see Ps 74; 79; 137; Hab 1). This leads to an important observation. The covenant relationship between Yahweh and Israel occasionally invokes courtroom imagery. Two different courtroom scenarios emerge. Sometimes it involves Yahweh, "the Judge of all the earth" (Gen 18:25), being called upon by Israel for vindication against the accusations and oppression of surrounding nations. Israel appeals to Yahweh's faithfulness to his covenant promise—that is, his righteousness (Ps 74; 79; 89). At other times, Yahweh lodges a complaint against his own people Israel for covenant unfaithfulness and disloyalty. Now he is plaintiff as well as judge. He is represented by his messengers the prophets, who function as prosecuting attorneys (Is 1:2-20; Amos 3:1-8; Hos 4:1-3; Mic 6:1-8). The background here is the nature of the Sinai covenant as a variation of the suzerainty treaties of the second millennium B.C. in which a powerful overlord (suzerain) bound a weaker neighbor (vassal) to himself by means of a written agreement and solemn oath of obedience. The overlord would bring charges against his vassal if the latter acted disloyally. At Mount Sinai, Yahweh demanded total allegiance of Israel. No other gods were to be worshiped (Ex 20:2-6). In fact, Yahweh had provided his vassal with a complete list of regulations for all of life (Ex 20—23), at the core of which stood the Decalogue (Ex 20:1-17). These were the covenant stipulations. The obvious problem, then, was massive noncompliance on the part of Israel, hence the need for a showdown in the court of the great overlord and judge.

The problem in a nutshell was this: how could Yahweh vindicate his disobedient people against their pagan oppressors and at the same time use Israel to reach the pagans with the message of his mercy and forgiveness? The divine solution centers on the dramatic story of the suffering Servant in the book of Isaiah. In five brief vignettes (Is 42:1-9; 49:1-6; 50:4-11; 52:13—53:12; 61:1-7) a faithful Israelite arises who serves as the instrument and channel of God's grace for all peoples. There can be no doubt that Jesus understood himself as and his earliest followers confessed him as the servant-redeemer (see Acts 8:30-35). The Lord himself became the sin offering and broke the bondage to sin and death. He was not only faithful Israel; he was also the second Adam, who through his obedient life, death and resurrection creates a new humanity. Those who respond to the gracious invitation to accept his atoning work on their behalf and in their stead are granted new standing and status. They are vindicated and shown to be the true people of God. The sign of their new status is faith in the crucified one. They are now righteous (i.e., God declares them to be in relationship to him as his true people). This declaration is not something achieved by them; rather, it was granted to them as a gift on the merits of another, the sinless one, Messiah Jesus, corresponding to the lamb without blemish.

Pauline understanding of righteousness and justification. Paul's understanding of righteousness displays the same contours sketched out for the OT. God's saving activity and covenant faithfulness are cosmic in scope. God will set right the entire creation and set it "free from its bondage to decay" (Rom 8:21). There are passages where courtroom imagery clearly appears. These texts picture God the righteous judge acquitting guilty sinners who cast themselves on his mercy and love, demonstrated in the death of his Son on their behalf (Rom 5:8). Acquittal comes simply by reaching out in faith to accept the proffered pardon (Rom 3:21-31; 4:2-4, 16; 9:16; 11:6; Gal 2:16; Eph 2:8-9). On this basis, God the heavenly Father acquits all who accept his pardon. Not to be missed in all this is the fact that the great impediment separating sinners from God has in principle been removed. In this regard, recall the parable of the lost sons (Lk 15). The father was prepared to forgive both rebellious sons, but only the younger son responded to the gracious overture and accepted full reinstatement. All that is needed by sinners is sincere repentance and acceptance, by faith, of God's pardon. By faith, sinners experience atonement, redemption, reconciliation, deliverance from demonic powers, pardon and forgiveness. I have deliberately incorporated the word pictures previously examined in order to illustrate the semantic overlap and to emphasize the initial metaphor that began this discussion of Paul's doctrine of salvation: a beautiful mosaic consisting of many individual pieces.

Delving more deeply, I raise a key question: what is the precise meaning of the thematic phrase "the righteousness of God" in Romans 1:17: "For in it [the gospel] the righteousness of God *[dikaiosynē theou]* is revealed through faith for faith; as it is written, 'The one who is righteous *[dikaios]* will live by faith'" (cf. Rom 3:21-22; 10:3; Phil 3:9). Does "righteousness" here refer to an attribute of God (i.e., his character as upright and just), or does it refer to his saving activity, being virtually synonymous with salvation, described as "the power of God" (Rom 1:16)? If the latter, does it refer to his activity in acquitting the ungodly (forensic), or does it refer more generally to his faithfulness to his covenant promises and include the entire created order? On the other hand, is righteousness something bestowed by God on repentant sinners? Is it a standing or quality either imputed or imparted to believers? Once again debate is joined, and adherents may be found for each of the aforementioned choices or for combinations.[58] One can easily locate OT passages in support of the different options.

I think it best to admit that the precise nuance of what is meant by "God's righteousness" in any given passage depends upon the context and

---

[58]For a helpful chart of the various positions, see N. T. Wright, *What Saint Paul Really Said: Was Paul of Tarsus the Real Founder of Christianity?* (Grand Rapids: Eerdmans, 1997), p. 101.

is in some instances ambiguous.[59] My own tentative conclusions in this debate are as follows.

1. It can refer both to the character of God and to his saving activity toward his creation—"the divine rectitude that rectifies (makes right) the relation between the Creator and the unrighteous person who believes the gospel."[60] Such a definition combines the ethical and relational dimensions of the phrase. It does, however, emphasize God's covenant faithfulness; he faithfully and steadfastly fulfills his covenant promises. In Romans Paul understands the righteousness of God to be his saving activity and covenant faithfulness. "He did this to show his righteousness [dikaiosynē], because in his divine forbearance he had passed over the sins previously committed; it was to prove at the present time that he himself is righteous [dikaios] and that he justifies [dikaioō] the one who has faith in Jesus" (Rom 3:25-26). This usage shows indebtedness to the OT notion of covenant faithfulness. God is righteous because he upholds his obligations to his covenant people.

2. It can also refer to a status graciously bestowed on repentant sinners (i.e., they are declared to be in a right relationship with God and thereby vindicated as truly belonging to the new Israel [Gal 6:18]). In such contexts forensic imagery is to the forefront and is particularly evident where Paul is arguing against the Judaizing position (Galatians) or defending and clarifying his gospel over against objections (Romans). Paul thus views righteousness as a right relationship with God reckoned to one who repents and believes that God has made this status possible through Christ's atoning death. "Therefore, since we are justified [dikaioō] by faith, we have peace with God through our Lord Jesus Christ, through whom we have obtained access to this grace in which we stand; and we boast in our hope of sharing the glory of God" (Rom 5:1-2); "Since all have sinned and fall short of the glory of God; they are now justified [dikaioō] by his grace as a gift, through

---

[59]E. C. Blackman comments in this regard, "The actual word δικαιοσύνη in Paul's usage, especially in Romans, is not free from ambiguity. Strictly speaking, three senses can be distinguished—the theological, the forensic, and the ethical. But the way Paul's mind moves from one to the other is often confusing, and the precise meaning of a particular passage may be difficult to determine. Paul is not a precise writer, even when handling terms which are fundamental to his argument" ("Justification," IDB 2:1029). Peter Stuhlmacher makes a similar point in connection with the dispute over whether the righteousness of God refers to God's gift or God's saving activity: "According to our reflections concerning the history and meaning of the concept, one should not establish a false alternative between the two. The expression incorporates both, and it must de determined from passage to passage where Paul places the accent" (Paul's Letter to the Romans, trans. Scott J. Hafemann [Louisville: Westminster John Knox, 1994], pp. 31-32).

[60]Here I borrow the felicitous phrasing of Leander E. Keck, The HarperCollins Study Bible: New Revised Standard Version, ed. Wayne A. Meeks (New York: HarperCollins, 1993), p. 2117, note on Romans 1:17.

the redemption that is in Christ Jesus" (Rom 3:23-24; cf. Gal 2:15—4:31). The passive voice of the key verbs—"are justified"—draws attention to the divine initiative involved in justification. God declares his verdict on behalf of his people. Sinners are not rectified by any action on their part; rather, they are the recipients of a ruling in their favor by the divine judge. This divine declaration is received simply by repentance and faith (i.e., both by acknowledging rebellion and guilt and by trusting in the gracious, saving activity of the judge). The saving activity is the atoning, redeeming, reconciling death of his Son, Jesus Christ, on behalf of sinners.

3. It is a standard or norm of behavior reflecting the character of God and embodied in his moral law. Paul expects it to be reproduced in the covenant people, who are required to uphold their covenant obligations to both God and neighbor. In this endeavor the Holy Spirit provides the motive power ("so that the just requirement *[dikaiōma]* of the law might be fulfilled in us, who walk not according to the flesh but according to the Spirit" (Rom 8:4). In such contexts the ethical aspect of righteousness is center stage: "For the kingdom of God is not food and drink but righteousness *[dikaiosynē]* and peace and joy in the Holy Spirit" (Rom 14:17); "Having produced the harvest of righteousness *[dikaiosynē]* that comes through Jesus Christ for the glory and praise of God" (Phil 1:11); "For the fruit of the light is found in all that is good and right *[dikaiosynē]* and true" (Eph 5:9). This sense is particularly marked in the Pastoral Epistles (see 1 Tim 6:11; 2 Tim 3:16; 4:8). Paul rejects efforts to establish one's own righteous behavior on the basis of human deeds and rituals. As a Pharisee, he thought this attainable (Phil 3:6: "as to righteousness *[dikaiosynē]* under the law, blameless"; cf. Rom 6:15—7:6; Gal 4:1-7; 5:1-15). This kind of righteousness, "under the law," Paul considers to be mere rubbish because it is self-manufactured and is in fact unobtainable by mere human effort (Phil 3:8; cf. Rom 3:21; 9:30-33; Gal 2:16, 21; 3:10-14).

The temptation to force the *dik-* word group into one conceptual straitjacket must be resisted.[61] Paul's language exhibits flexibility. This is not to deny that one can make assertions about "what Paul really said" but rather to forewarn about the temptation to reductionism. Almost all researchers agree that Paul's thought on righteousness and justification shows indebtedness to the OT. A majority would concur that the larger context of Paul's discussion is that of creation and covenant. The Lord is faithful to his creation and his covenant people. He graciously acts to redeem and restore both and thereby uphold his covenant promises. At times, this

---

[61]Reumann calls attention to this tendency ("Righteousness in the NT," *ABD* 5:746).

background is colored by forensic imagery drawn from the courtroom, recalling the judicial procedure of the OT and the covenant lawsuit patterned after the suzerainty treaty. On the other hand, one cannot completely rule out the ordinary meaning of the *dik-* word group in Classical and Koine Greek, a meaning shared to some extent with the corresponding *ṣdq* word group in the Hebrew Bible, namely, a norm or standard.[62] Those who are "rightwised"[63] are expected to conform to a standard having its norm in the very character of God himself. We thus find instances where Pauline parenesis is anchored in the exhortation to imitate one's heavenly Father or Christ: "Therefore be imitators of God, as beloved children" (Eph 5:1; cf. Eph 5:25; Rom 15:7; 1 Cor 11:1).

It is debatable whether Paul thinks in terms of imparted and transformative righteousness (i.e., an actual making righteous). Some hold that Paul does not really distinguish between these two ideas.[64] Others insist that justification in Paul is strictly forensic. The precise nature of justification was, of course, a major issue in the Protestant Reformation, and the legacy of that bitter contention still lingers.[65] To be sure, Paul prescribes righteous behavior for believers, but this presupposes a prior divine verdict in their favor and a consequent work of transformation by the Holy Spirit. Typically, we find instances of imperatives based upon an indicative: "Be what you are" (Eph 4:20-32; Col 3:6-10). Many would argue, however, that this is really an aspect of Paul's doctrine of sanctification, not justification. Justification, in its forensic sense, is both logically and temporally prior to sanctification; nonetheless, there is an inseparable link between the

---

[62]Stigers, "צֶדֶק," *TWOT* 2:752.

[63]This obsolete English verb shows the relationship of the verb *justify* to the words *right*, *righteous* and *righteousness*. Modern English (following Latin) uses two word groups (*just*, *justice*, *justify*, *justification* and *right*, *righteous*, *righteousness*) to convey what in both Greek and Hebrew (and French, German and Spanish) is expressed by a single word group (Hebrew *ṣdq*; Greek *dik-*). Kendrick Grobel (in his translation of Bultmann's *Theology of the New Testament*) and E. P. Sanders (*Paul and Palestinian Judaism*) tried using the old English verb "rightwise" to demonstrate the linkage, but it has not caught on. For further discussion, see Reumann, "Righteousness in the NT," *ABD* 5:746.

[64]Thus, for example, Stuhlmacher asserts, "According to biblical thought, justification is a legal act of the creator God and therefore at the same time an act of new creation, by virtue of which those who are justified participate in the glory and righteousness which exist in God's presence. Hence, the dogmatic distinction which arose in the history of the church between a justification which is first only reckoned legally (forensic-imputed) and a justification which is creatively at work (effective) is, measured by the examples just named [2 Cor 5:14-21; Rom 3:23-26; 5:1-11; cf. 1 Cor 6:11; Rom 8:30], an unbiblical abstraction" (*Paul's Letter to the Romans*, pp. 63-64). Likewise, Dunn asserts, "So once again the answer is not one or the other but both" (*Theology of Paul*, p. 344).

[65]See Ted M. Dorman, "The Joint Declaration on the Doctrine of Justification: Retrospect and Prospects," *JETS* 44 (2001): 421-34.

two—one cannot exist without the other. On this there is consensus within Christendom.

Finally, justification for Paul is eschatological in orientation.[66] Already the divine verdict of the heavenly assize rings in the ear of the repentant sinner (Rom 5:1). But no one has as yet stood before the judgment seat of God; that takes place on the last day (cf. 1 Cor 4:5). How can this be? Once again we see how essential it is to grasp the notion of inaugurated eschatology. The "now but not yet" dimension of salvation characterizes not only justification but also each of the word pictures for salvation that I have selected for study. We are already rescued and redeemed (Gal 1:4; cf. Gal 3:13-14; Col 1:13), but our full redemption takes place only when Christ returns (Rom 8:19-23; cf. Phil 3:20-21). We are already reconciled (Rom 5:11; 2 Cor 5:18; Col 1:22), but have not yet witnessed the reconciliation of all things (Col 1:20; cf. Rom 11:15). We have in some sense already overcome the powers of this age (Col 2:20), but we are presently engaged in struggle with them (Eph 6:12) and look forward to their final judgment (1 Cor 6:3). In like manner, repentant sinners have already been justified (i.e., declared righteous, in right relationship to God and vindicated as the true people of God [Rom 5:1]), but they are also being vindicated now, in the heat of battle, against the forces of the world, the flesh and the devil. Last of all, at "the day" (i.e., the day of judgment [see Rom 2:5, 16; 13:12; 1 Cor 1:7-8; 3:13; 5:5; 2 Cor 1:14), God the righteous judge will issue his definitive statement: "Not guilty" and "These are my people." And so, God's saving activity has already begun in this present, fallen age. Salvation therefore is a process. It has temporal dimensions such that a believer can rightly say, "I have been saved, I am being saved, and I will be saved." This has good Pauline precedent. In Romans 5:1-2 he nicely brings together all three temporal aspects: "Therefore, since *we are justified* by faith, *we have peace* with God through our Lord Jesus Christ, through whom *we have obtained access* to this grace in which *we stand*; and *we boast in our hope* of sharing the glory of God" (my italics).

This way of formulating the matter may strike some as unsettling. A popular slogan says, "Once saved, always saved." There, is of course, an element of truth in this: the number of God's elect is fixed and certain because they are foreknown and predestined from eternity to obtain final salvation (i.e., glorification [see Rom 8:28-30; Eph 1:3-14). On the other hand, exact knowledge of who the elect are belongs to God alone (cf. Deut

---

[66]Ridderbos says that "for the proper understanding of the great theme of justification by faith it is necessary above all to obtain an insight into the manner in which it is connected with the basic eschatological-christological structure of Paul's preaching" (*Paul*, p. 161).

29:29). The individual believer is warned against making premature judgments in this regard (1 Cor 4:5), simply to make his or her election sure by persistence in faith (Col 1:22-23; cf. 2 Pet 1:10). One need not live in constant anxiety about this, however, since the Spirit witnesses with our spirit, giving assurance that we are the children of God, heirs of God and joint heirs with Christ (Rom 8:14-17). Where the slogan can be misleading is in the tendency to think that some outward show of commitment, such as raising one's hand, going forward in an evangelistic service, signing a decision card and the like, forever seals one's eternal destiny, there being nothing capable of altering the unalterable. Such an view ignores the necessity of continuing in faith (Col 1:23). Paul insists that "the only thing that counts is faith *working* through love" (Gal 5:6 [my italics]). Decisions not matched by discipleship are deceitful. They presume that one may secure salvation on one's own terms, and such presumption is precarious.

Justification and the Law. As if the problem were not already steeped in enough controversy, we add more fuel to the fire. How does Paul's view of the Mosaic law figure into this discussion?[67] Since Paul argues strenuously that "a person is justified not by the works of the law but through faith in Jesus Christ [or the faithfulness of Jesus Christ]" (Gal 2:16), does this mean the believer now has no continuing obligation to the law? Once again, theological traditions collide. As we have already seen in the discussion of Jesus and the law, the topic of Paul and the law elicits contradictory views. The discussion of justification has already touched on some aspects of this question. Owing to space limitations, I briefly synthesize my understanding of Paul and the law.

1. Paul uses the Greek word *nomos* in at least three distinct senses. Most often Paul refers to that collection of legal and ritual requirements found in Exodus, Leviticus, and Numbers and reiterated and adapted in Deuteronomy (e.g., Rom 2:12-29; 4:15; 7:7-12; Gal 3:2, 10-29; 4:4-5; 6:13). The law (consisting of several collections in Ex 21—23; Lev 17—26; Deut 12—26) functioned as the covenant obligations and stipulations laid upon Israel as a way of life. The traditions of Israel trace the taproot of these various law codes back to Yahweh's revelation to Moses on Mount Sinai. It is of great importance to emphasize that the law was not given to Israel as a way of salvation; that had already been secured by God's saving action on their behalf, made visible in the events of the exodus.

---

[67]Colin Kruse is right when he observes, "Anyone who seeks to understand Paul's approach to the law and justification encounters many problems. Not least of these is the fact that none of Paul's letters provides a systematic presentation of his views on the subject" (*Paul, the Law, and Justification* [Peabody, Mass.: Hendrickson, 1996], p. 287).

Sometimes Paul conjoins "the law" *(nomos)* and "the prophets" with the resulting meaning of "Scripture." In other words, Paul, following the precedent of other Jews during the Second Temple period, refers to the sacred Scriptures of Israel by the designation of its two leading sections: the Law or Torah (the first five books of Moses) and the Prophets (consisting of the former and latter prophets, and possibly even including portions of what later became a clearly recognized third section, the Writings [see prologue of Sirach; Lk 24:27, 44]). Paul argues that the law and the prophets (i.e., Scripture) testify to the principle of salvation by faith alone (Rom 3:21-22; cf. Rom 1:2, 17; Gal 3:8; cf. 1 Cor 14:21 with Is 28:11-12 and Rom 3:10-18).

In a couple of instances Paul uses *nomos* in a clearly attested Koine nuance to refer to a principle. "So I find it to be a law *[nomos]* that when I want to do what is good, evil lies close at hand. . . . I see in my members another law *[nomos]* at war with the law *[nomos]* of my mind" (Rom 7:21, 23; cf. 7:25; 8:2).[68] Some would also include Romans 3:27, but this is debated.[69]

In my opinion, and this is contested, Paul never uses *nomos* in his letters to signify legalism—that is, the attempt to gain merit or standing on the basis of one's deeds.[70] He does, of course, argue strenuously against such an endeavor, but I do not think that he ever uses the term *nomos*, by itself, or in combination with other words, to denote legalism.

2. A major issue centers on precisely what Paul is attacking in his polemic against "works of the law." Did first-century Judaism, or some sect within the larger umbrella of Judaism, really affirm that one was saved by "works of the law"? Here we should note briefly the so-called New Perspective on Paul. In 1977 E. P. Sanders published *Paul and Palestinian Judaism: A Comparison of Patterns of Religion*,[71] in which he argues that Luther and the later Reformation, followed by the Protestant tradition generally, read Paul against the backdrop of Judaism as

---

[68]"νόμος," BDAG, p. 542.

[69]For a detailed discussion, see Stephen Westerholm, *Israel's Law and the Church's Faith: Paul and His Recent Interpreters* (Grand Rapids: Eerdmans, 1988), pp. 122-26.

[70]As argued by Daniel Fuller, *Gospel and Law: Contrast or Continuum? The Hermeneutics of Dispensationalism and Covenant Theology* (Grand Rapids: Eerdmans, 1980), pp. 65-120. See Schreiner's reply to Fuller's view, *The Law and Its Fulfillment: A Pauline Theology of the Law* (Grand Rapids: Baker, 1993), pp. 58-59; also Douglas Moo, "The Law of Christ as the Fulfillment of the Law of Moses: A Modified Lutheran View," in *The Law, The Gospel, and the Modern Christian: Five Views*, by Willem A. VanGemeren at al. (Grand Rapids: Zondervan, 1993), pp. 332-33.

[71]E. P. Sanders, *Paul and Palestinian Judaism: A Comparison of Patterns of Religion* (Minneapolis: Fortress, 1977).

a religion of works. This, says Sanders, and I think correctly, is simply wrong. Judaism was very much aware that salvation was first and foremost by grace. He goes to great lengths to demonstrate this from the extant literature of the Second Temple. He also describes the role of the law in Judaism as the means whereby one maintained status within the covenant relationship with God. To put it another way, the law was not about "getting in" but rather about "staying in." This pattern Sanders dubbed "covenantal nomism."

Sanders argues that Paul was convinced by his experience on the road to Damascus that salvation was realized only in relationship to Jesus as Messiah and Lord. This being so, Paul must have reasoned backwards (i.e., from solution to plight). The problem with the law is that it cannot provide life; only Christ can. In controversy with Judaizers, however, Paul finds other arguments against the continuing validity of the law, such as the claim that it required perfect obedience in order to be saved. Since this was humanly impossible, the law in reality led to a curse—a point that Paul could make by quoting, out of context, the law itself (Gal 3:10; cf. Deut 27:26). This line of argumentation, of course, would have been vehemently rejected by his Judaizing opponents. According to Sanders's interpretation of Paul, the only thing wrong with the law is that it is not based on the atoning death and resurrection of Jesus Christ. Paul, then, is the one who creates the antithesis between law and grace in his polemic against the Judaizers. In short, Paul's stated arguments obscure the real objection.

James Dunn takes the argument further by reconstructing what happened at Syrian Antioch.[72] The specific issue that ignited the debate centered on entrance requirements for Gentiles. The Judaizers insisted that the "boundary markers" that demarcated Jews from Gentiles still had to be observed by the new covenant community. These boundary markers, or "badges," were rituals such as circumcision, sabbath observance and dietary laws (see Gal 2:1-14; 4:10; 5:2-6; 6:11-16). For Dunn, Paul's argument in Galatians is not directed at the entire edifice of the law but rather at the imposition of boundary markers; Paul opposes the boundary markers only because they impede the conversion of Gentiles.

In my opinion, Sanders and Dunn do a disservice to Paul's thought. That is, Paul uses the Antioch incident (Gal 2:11-14) to argue a larger point: how is one put right with God? Are works the basis of salvation or not? Paul

---

[72]James D. G. Dunn, "The New Perspective on Paul," *BJRL* 65 (1983): 94-122; "The Incident at Antioch (Gal 2:11-18)," *JSNT* 18 (1983): 3-57; "Works of the Law and the Curse of the Law (Gal. 3.10-14)," in *Jesus, Paul and the Law: Studies in Mark and Galatians* (Louisville: Westminster Press, 1990), pp. 215-41; *Theology of Paul*, pp. 334-89.

vigorously argues that they are not, and he concludes that the Sinaitic legislation is now passé.

According to Sanders, Dunn and N. T. Wright, Luther and his successors misread what the conflict was really all about. In the process, the Reformers branded Judaism in its entirety as a religion of works and saw its contemporary reincarnation in the medieval Roman Catholic Church. Furthermore, this stereotype persists, even in our own time. There is much truth in their critique. One should hesitate, however, to accept their thesis entirely. In my opinion, they overlook or incorrectly interpret clear indications that legalism had cast its blight on Judaism in its many manifestations.[73] New evidence from the Dead Sea Scrolls shows that the Qumran community could fairly be described as legalistic within a context of covenantal nomism.[74] It is not that they denied the initiating grace of God; rather, they also held that keeping "the works of the law" was essential to attain final salvation. A similar form of nomistic legalism is discernible in Second Temple literature and clearly appears in rabbinic literature. It is this "extra" against which Paul contends in Galatians, Romans, 2 Corinthians and Philippians.[75]

3. Stated positively, Paul held that the law served a vital purpose in salvation history: it defined and condemned sin (Rom 3:20; 4:15; 5:13; 7:7, 21-23). The law also, unintentionally, became a tool of sin inasmuch as prohibitions incite disobedience in sinful human beings (Rom 5:20; 6:14; 7:7-12). Paul sees clearly that the law was never given as a means of salvation (Rom 4:15; cf. 1:18); it was always by faith in God's promise, as his exposition of Abraham demonstrates (Rom 4; Gal 3:6-9). Further, even if one tried, human inability makes it impossible to keep the law as a means of salvation (Rom 2:17-24; Gal 3:10-14). Even seemingly "blameless" observance of the law is vitiated by pride and arrogance, thus falling short of

---

[73]For examples, see Larry R. Helyer, *Exploring Jewish Literature of the Second Temple Period: A Guide for New Testament Students* (Downers Grove, Ill.: InterVarsity Press, 2002), pp. 39, 232-33, 464-66. See also Ladd, *Theology of the New Testament*, pp. 541-45; F. Thielman, "Law," *DPL* 532-34.

[74]I am referring particularly to the publication of 4QMMT. Here we find the Hebrew equivalent of Paul's *erga nomou* in the phrase *māʿăśêy hattôrâ*. For a discussion, see M. G. Abegg Jr., "*Miqṣat Maʿaśey Ha-Torah* (4QMMT)," *DNTB* 709-711.

[75]Donald Hagner makes an important observation about Paul's position: "Paul opposes within Judaism what must be described as a legalistic righteousness, that is, a righteousness established by doing the works of the Law. But how is this to be reconciled with the understanding of Judaism as a covenantal nomism? In my opinion, the answer lies in a discrepancy between Judaism as ideally (and correctly) conceived and as generally lived out on a day-to-day basis" ("Paul's Quarrel with Judaism," in *Anti-Semitism and Early Christianity: Issues of Polemic and Faith*, ed. Craig A. Evans and Donald A. Hagner [Minneapolis: Fortress, 1993], pp. 138-39). See also Schreiner, *The Law and Its Fulfillment*, pp. 93-121.

the standard of divine righteousness (Phil 3:4-11). Finally, the imposition of
the Mosaic law as a way of life was a temporary measure until the promise
to Abraham was fulfilled in Christ (Gal 3:15—4:7).

4. This brings us then to Paul's view of the relationship between the
believer and the law of Moses. In my opinion, Paul holds that the entire
law, understood in the sense of the Sinaitic legislation, is no longer binding
on the conscience of Christians.[76] However, since the Ten Commandments
find their norm in the character of the unchangeable God, the moral principles enshrined there are, of course, reiterated in the new covenant under
the rubric of the law of Christ or the law of love. For example, murder,
adultery, theft and covetousness are always wrong. But the Ten Commandments (Ex 20:1-17; Deut 5:6-21), by their very wording, show that God's
moral principles have been embedded in a culturally specific document that
is no longer binding, in its specific formulation, for new covenant members.
The historical prologue to the Decalogue specifies the parties involved:
Yahweh and Israel. The occasion that constituted this relationship was the
exodus from Egypt (Ex 20:2). On the other hand, the new covenant, with
the new Israel, consisting of both Jew and Gentile, was inaugurated by the
cross and resurrection. The fifth commandment promises long life in the
land (i.e., the land of Canaan) if obeyed. But believers are to inherit the
world, not the land of Canaan (1 Cor 3:21-23; 6:2; cf. Mt 5:5). It is true, of
course, that all but one of the Ten Commandments is reiterated in the NT.
The one omission, the sabbath commandment, is instructive, however. In
the new covenant the sabbath is no longer a day but rather is an entire era—
the "now" phase of redemptive history (see Heb 4). Paul leaves the matter
of sabbath observance to individual conscience—a remarkable change for
a former Pharisee (Rom 14:5-6; Col 2:16). Rather than try to distinguish
between moral, civil and ceremonial laws, we are better advised to consider
the entire legislation as having come to an end (Rom 10:4). The fundamental, moral intent of the law is now fulfilled by those who walk in the Spirit.
NT believers are said to "fulfill" the law but never are enjoined to "do" the
law. Such a position is supported by the following four arguments.

First, Paul says that whereas the Jew is "under the law" (1 Cor 9:20),
the believer in Christ is "not under law" (Rom 6:14-15; 1 Cor 9:20; Gal
5:18). Paul says that believers have "died to the law," have been "crucified
with Christ" and now "live by faith in the Son of God" (Rom 7:4; Gal
2:19-20). This hardly seems compatible with the notion that Christians are
still bound by the specific stipulations of the Sinaitic or Mosaic law.

---

[76]In this controversial area I highly recommend Westerholm, *Israel's Law and the Church's
Faith*. For a thoughtful response, see Schreiner, *The Law and Its Fulfillment*, pp. 145-78.

Second, Paul speaks of the law as having run its course. In redemptive history, the law served a temporary purpose and has now given way to the new era of promise, an era stemming from and fulfilling the initial promise to Abraham (Gal 3—4). The wife whose husband died is free to remarry another (Christ); she is no longer bound by her former husband (the law) (Rom 7). The era of the new covenant, the time of the unveiled face, has displaced the former era of the old covenant, the time of Moses' veiled face, a ministry of death and condemnation (2 Cor 3—4). Paul's intricate argument in Galatians 3:19—4:5 underscores the temporal limitations of the law. Once the promise comes, once faith in Christ arrives, the old covenant is no longer in force. Believers are now adults who freely inherit the blessings of the promise and are no longer under the supervision of the law. "Therefore the law was our disciplinarian until Christ came, so that we might be justified by faith. But now that faith has come, we are no longer subject to a disciplinarian" (Gal 3:24-25).

Third, Paul appeals to the Spirit as the moral governor of the Christian life. He can even say, "The whole law is summed up in a single commandment, 'You shall love your neighbor as yourself'" (Gal 5:14), and, "The one who loves another has fulfilled the law. The commandments, 'You shall not commit adultery; You shall not murder; You shall not steal: You shall not covet'; and any other commandment, are summed up in this word, 'Love your neighbor as yourself.' Love does no wrong to a neighbor; therefore, love is the fulfilling of the law" (Rom 13:8-10). To those horrified at the prospect that Gentile converts will run amuck without the constraint of the law, Paul confidently counters, "Live by the Spirit, I say, and do not gratify the desires of the flesh" (Gal 5:16), and "there is no law against" the fruit of the Spirit (Gal 5:22). Paul insists that believers are not lawless, without any moral norms or guidelines; they are now under the new law of Christ, the law of love (1 Cor 9:21; Gal 6:2), a law that embodies the fundamental moral principles of the law of Moses but also includes a new motive power enabling a way of life even more in conformity to God's will than ever was possible under the old covenant (Gal 5:22-23). "For God has done what the law, weakened by the flesh, could not do: by sending his own Son in the likeness of sinful flesh, and to deal with sin, he condemned sin in the flesh, so that the just requirement of the law might be fulfilled in us, who walk not according to the flesh but according to the Spirit" (Rom 8:3-4). To this Paul adds that the new covenant has a "greater glory" than the old Sinai covenant (2 Cor 3:10). This greater glory consists of a steady progression that ends with perfect conformity to the image of Christ (2 Cor 3:18; cf. Rom 8:28-30). All this is the result of the work of the Holy Spirit: "Now the Lord is the Spirit, and where the Spirit of the Lord is, there is freedom" (2 Cor 3:17)—a keynote of Pauline soteriology.

Fourth, Paul occasionally does appeal to the law for guidance in certain disputed matters (1 Cor 9:8-9; 14:21, 34; 2 Cor 8:15; 13:1). After all, Paul holds that "whatever was written in former days was written for our instruction, so that by steadfastness and by the encouragement of the scriptures we might have hope" (Rom 15:4; cf. 1 Cor 10:6).[77] But he never appeals to the law as the final arbiter of moral matters, which is precisely the opposite of what we would expect if he viewed the law as still exercising a normative role.[78] For Paul, the new covenant operates under a new law, the law of Christ, the law of love, which, while embodying underlying moral principles of the old Mosaic legislation, should not be strictly identified with it.

CONCLUSION

Paul's gospel is a "message about the cross" (1 Cor 1:18), the "cross of Christ" (1 Cor 1:17; Gal 6:12, 14; Phil 3:18). But how can Jesus Christ accomplish all these multifaceted dimensions of salvation on the cross? Who, after all, is Jesus Christ? That question requires a survey of Pauline Christology. And although the outcome of salvation has already been touched upon in this chapter, we need to delve more deeply into Pauline eschatology to see how the various threads of his theology come together in the consummation of the kingdom. That is our mission in the next chapter.

FOR FURTHER DISCUSSION

1. Is Paul's depiction of the human plight credible today?

2. Does God hold human beings accountable for Adam and Eve's sin?

3. How does modern society account for the moral evil in humanity? Is this an improvement or impoverishment compared to Paul's analysis?

4. Is Paul's understanding of the spiritual powers necessary in the twenty-first century?

5. Is sacrificial language still important to convey the meaning of Christ's death today?

6. Which Pauline metaphor for salvation has the most appeal for mod-

---

[77]As Colin Kruse notes, "While believers are free from the law as a regulatory norm, nevertheless they still have much to learn from it" (*Paul, the Law, and Justification,* p. 284).

[78]Colin Kruse summarizes the issue by saying that "while believers were not obliged to carry out all the demands of the Mosaic law, they could nevertheless draw from the OT, read paradigmatically, lessons for Christian living" ("Law," *NDBT* 636).

ern Western culture? Which has more appeal for cultures in developing countries?

7. What is your own view on the relationship of the Mosaic law to Christians today?

FOR FURTHER READING

The Human Condition Outside Christ

Blocher, Henri. "Original Sin." *DTIB* 553-54.

Bruce, F. F. *Paul, Apostle of the Heart Set Free*, pp. 203-6. Grand Rapids: Eerdmans, 1977.

Bultmann, Rudolf. *Theology of the New Testament*, translated by Kendrick Grobel, 1:232-69. 2 vols. New York: Scribner, 1951-1955.

Dunn, James D. G. *The Theology of Paul the Apostle*, pp. 79-127. Grand Rapids: Eerdmans, 1998.

Grundmann, Walter. "ἁμαρτάνω." *TDNT* 1:308-13

Guthrie, Donald. *New Testament Theology*, pp. 200-18. Downers Grove, Ill.: InterVarsity Press, 1981.

Johnson, S. Lewis, Jr. "Romans 5:12—An Exercise in Exegesis and Theology." In *New Dimensions in New Testament Study*, edited by Richard N. Longenecker and Merrill C. Tenney, pp. 298-316. Grand Rapids: Zondervan, 1974.

Kreitzer, L. J. "Adam and Christ." *DPL* 9-15.

Kümmel, Werner Georg. *The Theology of the New Testament according to Its Major Witnesses: Jesus-Paul-John*, translated by John E. Steely, pp. 172-85. Nashville: Abingdon, 1973.

Ladd, George E. *A Theology of the New Testament*, edited by Donald A. Hagner, pp. 435-47. Rev. ed. Grand Rapids: Eerdmans, 1993.

Marshall, I. Howard. *New Testament Theology*, pp. 432-35. Downers Grove, Ill.: InterVarsity Press, 2004.

Morris, L. "Sin, Guilt." *DPL* 877-81.

Ridderbos, Herman. *Paul: An Outline of His Theology*, translated by John Richard De Witt, pp. 91-158. Grand Rapids: Eerdmans, 1975.

Schreiner, Thomas R. *Paul, Apostle of God's Glory in Christ: A Pauline Theology*, pp. 127-50. Downers Grove, Ill.: InterVarsity Press, 2001.

Thiselton, A. C. "Flesh." *NIDNTT* 1:671-82.

The Divine Solution

Becker, Jürgen. *Paul, Apostle to the Gentiles*, translated by O. C. Dean Jr., pp. 399-411. Louisville: Westminster/John Knox, 1993.

Brown, Colin. "Sacrifice." *NIDNTT* 3:417-36.

Büchsel, Friedrich. "καταλλάσσω, κτλ." *TDNT* 1:251-59.

Bultmann, Rudolf. *Theology of the New Testament*, translated by Kendrick Grobel, 1:270-306. 2 vols. New York: Scribner, 1951-1955.

Cousar, Charles B. *A Theology of the Cross: The Death of Jesus in the Pauline Letters*. Minneapolis: Fortress, 1990.

Dunn, James D. G. *The Theology of Paul the Apostle*, pp. 208-33. Grand Rapids; Eerdmans, 1998.

Fitzmyer, Joseph A. *Pauline Theology*, pp. 43-52. Englewood Cliffs, N.J.: Prentice-Hall, 1967.

Green, J. B. "Death of Christ." *DPL* 201-9.

Gundry-Volf, J. M. "Expiation, Propitiation, Mercy Seat." *DPL* 279-84.

Guthrie, Donald. *New Testament Theology*, pp. 431-36, 463-71. Downers Grove, Ill.: InterVarsity Press, 1981.

Kümmel, Werner Georg. *The Theology of the New Testament according to Its Major Witnesses: Jesus-Paul-John*, translated by John E. Steely, pp. 185-205. Nashville: Abingdon, 1973.

Ladd, George E. *A Theology of the New Testament*, edited by Donald A. Hagner, pp. 464-98. Rev. ed. Grand Rapids: Eerdmans, 1993.

Link, H.-G., with C. Brown and H. Vorländer. "Reconciliation." *NIDNTT* 3:145-76.

Martin, Ralph P. *Reconciliation: A Study of Paul's Theology*, pp. 79-198. Atlanta: John Knox Press, 1981.

Morris, Leon. *The Apostolic Preaching of the Cross*. 3rd ed. Grand Rapids: Eerdmans, 1965.

———. *New Testament Theology*, pp. 66-75. Grand Rapids: Zondervan, 1986.

———. "Redemption." *DPL* 784-86.

———. "Salvation." *DPL* 858-62.

Mundle, W., with C. Brown and J. Schneider. "Redemption." *NIDNTT* 3:177-223.

Ridderbos, Herman. *Paul: An Outline of His Theology*, pp. 159-204. Grand Rapids: Eerdmans, 1975.

Schreiner, Thomas. *Paul, Apostle of God's Glory in Christ: A Pauline Theology*, pp. 189-249. Downers Grove, Ill.: InterVarsity Press, 2001.

Salvation as Justification

Achtemeier, E. R. "Righteousness in the OT." *IDB* 4:80-85.

Achtemeier, P. J. "Righteousness in the NT." *IDB* 4:91-99.

Bultmann, Rudolf. *Theology of the New Testament*, translated by Kendrick Grobel, 1:270-85. 2 vols. New York: Scribner, 1951-1955.

Cronbach, Abraham. "Righteousness in Jewish Literature—200 B.C.-A.D. 100." *IDB* 4:85-91.

Dunn, James D. G. *The Theology of Paul the Apostle*, pp. 317-89. Grand Rapids; Eerdmans, 1998.

Guthrie, Donald. *New Testament Theology*, pp. 492-504. Downers Grove, Ill.: InterVarsity Press, 1981.

Hays, Richard B. "Justification." *ABD* 3:1129-33.

Kümmel, Werner Georg. *The Theology of the New Testament according to Its Major Witnesses: Jesus-Paul-John*, translated by John E. Steely, pp. 193-203. Nashville: Abingdon, 1973.

Ladd, George E. *A Theology of the New Testament*, edited by Donald A. Hagner, pp. 478-91. Rev. ed. Grand Rapids: Eerdmans, 1993.

McGrath, A. E. "Justification." *DPL* 517-23.

Onesti K. L., and M. T. Brauch. "Righteousness, Righteousness of God." *DPL* 827-37.

Petersen, L. M. "Justification." *ZPEB* 3:764-73.

Reumann, John. "Righteousness." *ABD* 5:724-73.

Ridderbos, Herman. *Paul: An Outline of His Theology*, pp. 159-81. Grand Rapids: Eerdmans, 1975.

Quell, Gottfried, and Gottlob Schrenk. "δίκη." *TDNT* 2:174-225.

Schreiner, Thomas. *Paul, Apostle of God's Glory in Christ: A Pauline Theology*, pp. 189-217. Downers Grove, Ill.: InterVarsity Press, 2001.

Seebass, Horst, and Colin Brown. "Righteousness." *NIDNTT* 3:352-77.

Seifrid, Mark A. *Christ Our Righteousness: Paul's Theology of Justification*. NSBT 9. Grand Rapids: Eerdmans, 2000.

———. "Righteousness, Justice and Justification." *NDBT* 740-45.

Spicq, Ceslas. "δίκαιος." *TLNT* 1:318-47.

Toon, Peter. "Righteousness." *EDBT* 678-89.

Wright, N. T. *What Saint Paul Really Said: Was Paul of Tarsus the Real Founder of Christianity?* pp. 95-133. Grand Rapids: Eerdmans, 1997.

Justification and the Law

Dunn, James D. G. *The Theology of Paul the Apostle*, pp. 128-61. Grand Rapids: Eerdmans, 1998.

Esser, H. H. "Law." *NIDNTT* 2:438-51.

Hübner, H. "νόμος." *EDNT* 2:471-77.

Koperski, Veronica. *What Are They Saying about Paul and the Law?* New York: Paulist Press, 2001.

Kruse, Colin G. *Paul, the Law, and Justification*. Peabody, Mass.: Hendrickson, 1996.

Ladd, George E. *A Theology of the New Testament*, edited by Donald A. Hagner, pp. 538-54. Rev. ed. Grand Rapids: Eerdmans, 1993.

Schreiner, Thomas. R. *The Law and Its Fulfillment: A Pauline Theology of Law*. Grand Rapids: Baker, 1993.

———. "Law of Christ." *DPL* 542-44.

———. *Paul, Apostle of God's Glory in Christ: A Pauline Theology*, pp. 103-25. Downers Grove, Ill.: InterVarsity Press, 2001.

———. "Works of the Law." *DPL* 975-79.

Sprinkle, Joe M. "Law." *EDBT* 467-71.

Thielman, F. "Law." *DPL* 529-42.

VanGemeren, Willem, et al. *The Law, the Gospel, and the Modern Christian: Five Views*. Grand Rapids: Zondervan, 1993.

Westerholm, Stephen. *Israel's Law and the Church's Faith: Paul and His Recent Interpreters*. Grand Rapids: Eerdmans, 1988.

———. *Perspectives Old and New on Paul: The "Lutheran" Paul and His Critics*. Grand Rapids: Eerdmans, 2004.

Wright, N. T. *What Saint Paul Really Said: Was Paul of Tarsus the Real Founder of Christianity?* pp. 113-33. Grand Rapids: Eerdmans, 1997.

8

Pauline Christology
and Eschatology

He who formerly had been the bearer of the message was drawn into it and became its essential content. The proclaimer became the proclaimed—but the central question is: In what sense?

Rudolf Bultmann

PAUL'S EXPERIENCE ON THE ROAD TO DAMASCUS implodes his prior Pharisaic notions of the promised Messiah and the end times. The reconstruction is breathtaking. Before long, nothing less than cosmic Christology majestically rises out of the ashes of nationalistic messianism. Paul's cosmic Christology is matched by his cosmic eschatology, a grand culmination of the kingdom of God in which all things are finally unified in Christ. To these twin peaks of Pauline theology we now turn.

PAULINE CHRISTOLOGY

Pharisaism probably did not maintain a uniform view of the Messiah, but certainly a leading version focused on a great descendant of David (see Lk 1:32-33; 18:38; 20:41) and his mission to defeat the enemies of Israel and restore the nation to greatness (see Lk 1:68-73). The *Psalms of Solomon*, a pseudepigraphic work dating to the first century B.C. and perhaps emanating from Pharisaic circles, affords a window into messianic expectations at the time of Jesus and Paul. There we read of a Davidic descendant who

fulfills the ancient covenant promises to David and rules over all Israel as
well as the nations. He ushers in an ideal age and actualizes Israel's destiny
(*Pss. Sol.* 17:4, 21-46). This hope was founded, of course, on the numerous
prophecies of national restoration in the Hebrew prophets. In some of these
passages a royal scion emerges who reigns in justice and righteousness (Is
9:6-7; 11:1-9; 32:1-8; Jer 23:5-6; 33:14-18; Ezek 34:20-31; Amos 9:11; Mic
5:2-5; Zech 6:12-13). This hope was nurtured and amplified in apocalyptic
thought of the Second Temple period.

In his letter to the Romans Paul announces his primary topic: the gospel
of God (Rom 1:1). Included in this good news is the long-cherished promise
of a "Son, who was descended from David according to the flesh" (Rom
1:3; cf. Rom 9:5; 2 Tim 2:8). What jarred his coreligionists was the notion
that this Son, Jesus of Nazareth, was uniquely the Son of God, having been
put to death on the cross as a sin offering, resurrected from the dead and
having inaugurated the age to come. He was none other than the "Lord," a
name used for the God of Israel in the OT. Especially galling was the notion
that this risen Lord Jesus Christ was calling Gentiles into a newly constituted Israel. This radical transformation in Paul's messianic beliefs put him
at odds with the great majority of his fellow Jews and was the fundamental
point that separated them.[1]

Son of God. Paul calls Jesus "the Son of God." What he means by this title,
however, goes well beyond anything previously understood within Judaism.
In what may be his earliest letter and, for that matter, the earliest Christian
document of any kind, 1 Thessalonians, Paul summarizes his gospel. The
first part is characteristically Jewish: turning away from idols to the true and
living God (1 Thess 1:9). The second part is distinctively Christian: waiting
for the return from heaven of God's Son, Jesus (1 Thess 1:10). Jesus' work is
narrowly and circumstantially described as rescue from the coming wrath of
God. In the other candidate for Paul's earliest letter, Galatians, Paul gives this
personal testimony: "I have been crucified with Christ; and it is no longer I
who live, but it is Christ who lives in me. And the life I now live in the flesh I
live by faith in the Son of God, who loved me and gave himself for me" (Gal
2:19-20). Here divine sonship and salvation are inextricably linked. But what
precisely did Paul mean by calling Jesus "the son of God?"

In the OT the expression "son(s) of God" can be used in several ways.
The people of Israel were designated, collectively, as the firstborn son of
Yahweh (Ex 4:22; cf. Jer 31:9; Hos 11:1). The latter expression is clearly

---

[1] "It was at this one point that Paul parted company with Judaism, at the valuation of Jesus of
Nazareth as the Messiah with all this implied" (W. D. Davies, *Paul and Rabbinic Judaism*
[London: SPCK, 1948], p. 324).

metaphorical and stresses the special privilege and responsibility attaching to this new people of God. By no means did the expression imply pagan, mythological notions whereby a particular god physically begat a people group. There are also several references to angelic or spiritual beings styled as "sons of God" (Gen 6:2; Job 1:6; 2:1; 38:7; Ps 29:1). The point seems to be that these beings share a common attribute: a spiritual nature. Or, perhaps the significance lies in the notion of a sender (God) and the ones sent (angels viewed as his "sons").

Of more importance are those few times in which the relationship between a Hebrew king and Yahweh is expressed in the adoptive terms of father and son. Thus we read in Psalm 2:7, "He said to me, 'You are my son; today I have begotten you.'" In 2 Samuel 7:14 Yahweh promises David, "I will be a father to him [David's heir], and he shall be a son to me." This, however, is formulaic not mythological language. The king of Israel stood in a special relationship to Yahweh, not a physical one. Israel's neighbors, on the other hand, held either that their kings either were the actual incarnation of a national deity (Egyptian ideology) or acquired divine or semidivine attributes at their coronation (Mesopotamian and Canaanite ideology).[2] One sees this satirized in Ezekiel 28:2. Israel never officially subscribed to this ideology of "divine kingship," but they did borrow the language and imagery. Thus the king was "born" of God at his coronation. But the relationship is an adoptive one, not a physical begetting. This seems to be the significance of royal psalm texts such as Psalm 2:7; 45:6; 72:1; 89:27, based upon the Davidic covenant (2 Sam 7:14-16; cf. 1 Chron 17:13; 22:10; 28:6).

During Second Temple times passages such as Psalm 2:7 and 2 Samuel 7:14 were interpreted as messianic.[3] We know, for example, that the Qumran community viewed both texts as messianic references (4Q174 3:10-13, 18-19). That is, the Messiah was endowed by God with extraordinary, though not divine, capabilities. Jewish messianism tended to enlarge and embellish messianic attributes (e.g., *Similitudes of Enoch*), especially in the era after the destruction of the Second Temple (e.g., *4 Ezra* 12:31; 13:26, 32; *2 Bar.* 27—30; 36—50; 53—76), but never did it elevate the Messiah to the status of full deity. The apostle Paul did, and he was not the first to do so. The evidence points to the earliest Palestinian followers of Jesus in the immediate aftermath of Jesus' resurrection (Acts 2:34-36). Paul uses the title "Son of God" to describe Jesus' unique relationship to God, as is dem-

---

[2]See Jarl Fossum, "Son of God," *ABD* 6:129.

[3]"Sometime in the third or second century BCE, messiah takes on this eschatological nuance" (Craig A. Evans, "Messiahs," *EDSS* 1:538).

onstrated by the fact that he "repeatedly and strikingly brackets God and Jesus together in one phrase" (cf. Rom 1:7: Grace to you and peace from God our Father and the Lord Jesus Christ).[4] Paul's letters already witness to an emergent doctrine of the deity of Christ.

In the Thessalonian correspondence Paul uses the full title "Lord Jesus Christ" some eleven times (e.g., 1 Thess 1:1, 3), and in his other letters approximately another 195 times. Many have assumed that "Christ," originally a title ("the anointed one or messiah") and occasionally so used by Paul (Rom 9:5), is most often used by Paul simply as Jesus' full name. But more likely Paul regularly employed it as a title.[5] "Messiah Jesus" is a better rendition in conveying what Paul intended. He believed that Jesus was the fulfillment of the prophetic hope centering on a great Davidic king who would rescue and restore Israel.

Lord. With the addition of the title "Lord," however, Paul elevates messiahship to an entirely new level.[6] The Greek term *kyrios* is the regular translation of the Hebrew *Yahweh* in the LXX.[7] Many scholars concur that by the first century, Greek-speaking Jews referred to God reverentially using the word *kyrios*.[8] Paul's letters, the earliest extant Christian literature, display a remarkable fact: "Paul applies *kyrios* to Jesus without explanation or justification, suggesting that his readers already were familiar with the term and its connotation."[9] Accordingly, Paul's denominating Jesus as Lord constitutes an acclamation of astounding proportions. Among these many instances in Paul's letters, none is more impressive than Philippians 2:10-11: "So that at the name of Jesus every knee should bend, in heaven and on earth and under the earth, and every tongue should confess that Jesus Christ is Lord, to the glory of God the Father." Jesus shares the "name" of God—that is, "Lord." "The passage thus refers to a status and endow-

---

[4]David Wenham, *Paul: Follower of Jesus or Founder of Christianity?* (Grand Rapids: Eerdmans, 1995), pp. 120-21.

[5]N. T. Wright, *What Saint Paul Really Said: Was Paul of Tarsus the Real Founder of Christianity?* (Grand Rapids: Eerdmans, 1997), pp. 51-55; Wenham, *Paul,* pp. 120-21.

[6]Wenham observes, "If one had to identify Paul's favorite way of describing Jesus, 'the Lord' would probably win" (*Paul,* p. 121).

[7]"The word κύριος, "lord," as a name for God in the LXX is a strict translation only in cases where it is used for אֲדוֹן or אֲדֹנָי (in the *ketīb*). As a rule, however, it is used as an expository equivalent for the divine name יהוה. It is thus meant to express what the name, or the use of the name, signifies in the original" (Gottfried Quell, "κύριος," *TDNT* 3:1058). According to Quell, it is used some 6,156 times for the proper name of the God of Israel (ibid., p. 1059).

[8]See L. W. Hurtado, "Lord," *DPL* 560-63. For a thorough defense of this view, see Gordon D. Fee, *Pauline Christology* (Peabody, Mass.: Hendrickson, 2007), pp. 20-27, 41-55, 127-34, 406-10, 631-38.

[9]Ibid, p. 562.

ment given to Christ that can be compared only with God's status and attributes."[10] Jesus of Nazareth is thus identified with and yet distinguished from the covenant-keeping God of Abraham, Isaac and Jacob, who appeared to Moses in the burning bush, revealed the Torah on Mount Sinai, intervened in Israel's history and commissioned the prophets. But even more mind-boggling is that in two passages Paul affirms that the Lord Jesus Christ is the one through whom all things are created and sustained, and the one who guides all things to their appointed end (1 Cor 8:6; Col 1:15-17; cf. Rom 11:36; Eph 1:3-10). We are thus beholding cosmic Christology in all its grandeur.

Cosmic Christology. The classic Pauline text exhibiting cosmic Christology is the justly famous Colossians 1:15-20. Paul wrote Colossians to a house church that he did not personally establish (Col 2:1). Epaphras, one of Paul's disciples, apparently was the church planter (Col 1:7-8). The occasion prompting the letter is the presence of false teaching, disdainfully described by Paul as "philosophy and empty deceit, according to human tradition, according to the elemental spirits of the universe, and not according to Christ" (Col 2:8). Epaphras apparently sought Paul's counsel in dealing with this deviant teaching, and the letter to the Colossians constitutes his response.

Most exegetes agree that Colossians 1:15-20 serves as Paul's platform from which he levels his criticisms at the aberrant teaching. The first explicit mention of false teaching occurs at Colossians 2:8, but, in retrospect, Paul prefaces his direct attack on the system by passing under review the basic affirmations of belief in Christ. It seems justified to assume that the human tradition is fundamentally flawed because of its defective Christology. Christ has been displaced as the central datum of belief. In all likelihood, this passage asserts the centrality of Christ in cosmic proportions precisely because the false teachers placed considerable importance on the elemental spirits of the universe and alleged ascents to the heavenly throne room (Col 2:8, 18). As we noted earlier, the circumstantial nature of Paul's missionary correspondence must always be reckoned with in reconstructing Pauline theology. We may be grateful in one sense for the Colossian heresy in that it elicited dimensions of Pauline Christology that otherwise we would only have been able to infer from a few scattered references elsewhere.

Structure and background. Colossians 1:15-20 is widely recognized as a preexisting piece inserted by Paul as the foundation for his attack on the Colossian error.[11] Many consider it to be an early Christian hymn; others

---

[10]Ibid., p. 564.

[11]For a full discussion of the various exegetical and theological issues for this passage, see

identify it as a confession or creed. A few prefer to view it as a freely composed passage by Paul drawing upon earlier confessional and creedal statements. All are agreed that the passage exhibits the earmarks of deliberate composition, clearly demarcated from its immediate context. This is best seen in the switch from predominantly first- and second-person plural referents ("we" and "you") before and after the section (Col 1:9-14, 21-23) to a consistently third-person singular perspective in the passage itself ("he"). Add to this the presence of four *hapax legomena*, exalted language, repetition of key words and carefully arranged lines, and one has a presumptive case for a hymnic or confessional poem. We should also note that, like other assumed hymnic passages, this one begins with the relative pronoun *hos* ("who" [cf. Phil 2:6; 1 Tim 3:16]). As for the intended strophic arrangement, there are varied suggestions. I think that there are at least two stanzas as indicated thus:

hos estin eikōn tou theou . . .	*hos estin archē tou sōmatos*
who is the image of God . . .	who is the head of the body [the church]
prōtotokos pasēs ktiseōs	*prōtotokos ek tōn nekrōn*
firstborn of [or over] all creation	firstborn from the dead
hoti en autō . . . di' autou	*hoti en autō . . . di' autou . . .*
for in him . . . through him	For in him . . . through him . . .
kai eis auton	*eis auton*
and for him	for him

Note the matching "who is" lines, the matching "firstborn" predications, and the matching clauses "for in, through and for" in the two stanzas. My own view is that Paul is the author of this carefully crafted confession. I am inclined to the notion, first advanced by C. F. Burney in 1925, that Paul offers a midrashic exposition on Genesis 1:1 by means of Proverbs 8:22-23, 30.[12] Employing the technique of *gezera shawa* (literally, "an equivalent regulation"—i.e., an analogy), Paul explains one passage (Gen 1:1) by another (Prov 8:22) on the basis of the similar words and phrases found in each.

Larry R. Helyer, "Colossians 1:15-20: Pre-Pauline or Pauline?" *JETS* 26 (1983): 167-79; idem, "Arius Revisited: The Firstborn over All Creation (Col 1:15)," *JETS* 31 (1988): 59-67; idem, "Recent Research on Col 1:15-20," *GTJ* 12 (1992): 51-67; idem, "Cosmic Christology and Col 1:15-20," *JETS* 37 (1994): 235-46.

[12]C. F. Burney, "Christ as the ARXH of Creation: Pr 8, 22, Col 1, 15.18, Rev 3, 14," *JTS* 27 (1925-1926): 160-77.

The argument goes as follows: Paul expounded the meaning of the opening phrase of Genesis 1:1, "In the beginning" *(běrē'šît)*, by means of Proverbs 8:22: "The LORD created me at the beginning *[rē'šît]* of his work."[13] Paul elaborates his description of Christ in terms of the primary meanings of the word *rē'šît* and the several meanings of the Hebrew preposition *bě*. The Hebrew word *rē'šît* has at least four meanings or nuances: (1) "firstfruits" (a cognate word in Akkadian, a related language, has the meaning "firstborn"),[14] (2) "first, best, or supreme"), (3) "head or chief"), (4) "beginning or starting point." Observe how these various nuances are predicated of Christ in this passage. He is "the firstborn of all creation" (Col 1:15), "before all things" (Col 1:17), "the head of the body" (Col 1:18), "the beginning" (Col 1:18), "the firstborn from the dead" (Col 1:18), "first place in everything" (Col 1:18). The Hebrew preposition *bě* has as its principal meanings "in, by, for." These meanings are employed in both stanzas, as can be seen in the stanza comparison above. We should also note that the argument works even if Paul was interpreting Genesis 1:1 by Proverbs 8:22 using the LXX version, where the key term is *archē*, having the various nuances "beginning," "first" (in time), "origin," "first cause," "authority" and "rule." The Greek preposition *en* also bears the meanings "in" (location) and "by" (instrument or agency), besides other shades of meaning approximating the Hebrew *bě*.

Accordingly, the taproot of the hymn should be traced back to the OT creation narrative in Genesis 1 and the portrait of personified Wisdom in Proverbs 8. Whereas in Genesis 1:26 humankind is created "as" (literal translation versus "in") God's image, in Colossians 1:15 the Son "is" the very "image of the invisible God." In the book of Proverbs Woman Wisdom beckons young men to harken to her advice. Proverbs 8:22-31 takes this personification even further, portraying Wisdom as preexistent and actively involved in creation. This reminds us of Jewish wisdom speculation in which personified Wisdom, equated with the Torah (Sir 24:1-34; Bar 3:9—4:4; Wis 7:15—8:1; *Gen. Rab.* 1:1), is both preexistent and involved in creation. In my opinion, Paul has adapted this Jewish understanding of Wisdom. The result is stunning.

Affirmations. So what does this passage affirm about the "beloved Son"? Fundamentally, Christ is the mediator of both creations, old and new. Identifying him with the figure of Wisdom in the OT and Jewish literature of the Second Temple, this passage attributes all things to his

---

[13]On *gezerah shawa*, see Larry R. Helyer, *Exploring Jewish Literature of the Second Temple Period: A Guide for New Testament Students* (Downers Grove, Ill.: InterVarsity Press, 2002), pp. 454-57.

[14]Bill T. Arnold, "ראשׁית," *NIDOTTE* 3:1025.

workmanship. But the opening predication, *eikōn tou theou tou aoratou* ("the image of the invisible God"), goes well beyond the OT figure of Wisdom and actually places Christ on the same plane as God. The term *eikōn* ("image") denotes that which partakes of the same reality and nature as the original. What God is, Christ is, as the confession clearly states: "For in him all the fullness of God was pleased to dwell" (Col 1:19).[15] If anyone objects that Colossians 1:19 may be a pre-Pauline composition, we should note that Paul himself draws out the theological significance of the confession for his readers in Colossians 2:9, where he says, "For in him the whole fullness of deity dwells bodily." A clearer affirmation of the deity of Christ could hardly be formulated.

The term *prōtotokos* is used twice in the hymn, with a slightly different nuance in the two occurrences. With regard to the first creation, Christ is the ruler or sovereign over creation in that he is its maker and sustainer. In this first stanza *prōtotokos* is not used in a strict temporal sense such that Christ is the first created being, but rather the emphasis falls on his position relative to creation. As mediator through whom creation came into existence, he is superior to and sovereign over it.[16] As the firstborn, he is "heir of all things" (Heb 1:2), the meaning of *prōtotokos* in Colossians 1:15. Not only is he the agent of creation, but also he is the one who sustains it, who literally "holds it together" (Col 1:17; cf. Heb 1:3: "he sustains all things by his powerful word").

The second stanza focuses on Christ and the new creation, of which the church is the centerpiece, employing "firstborn" *(prōtotokos)* in its temporal sense. Thus Christ is the first in time to experience resurrection (cf. Rom 8:29). But precisely in this role he is also the second Adam, the beginning of a new race (Rom 5:12-21; 1 Cor 15:20-28). On this understanding, *prōtotokos* in Colossians 1:18 bears both nuances of temporal priority and superiority of position and privilege. As the firstborn, Christ is the head of the church, depicted as a cosmic entity (cf. Eph 1:22-23; 3:10). He possesses "all the fullness of God" and reconciles "all things, whether on earth or in heaven" (Col 1:20). This surely implies that he is fully divine and is the agent who accomplishes cosmic reconciliation ("making peace through the blood of the cross"). In short, God in Christ brings about a new creation—he is Lord and redeemer of all creation. On the basis of texts such as Colos-

---

[15]"Image is not to be understood as a magnitude which is alien to the reality and present only in the consciousness. It has a share in the reality. Indeed, it is the reality. Thus εἰκών does not imply a weakening or a feeble copy of something. It implies the illumination of its inner core and essence" (H. Kleinknecht, "εἰκών," *TDNT* 2:389).

[16]So also H. Langkammer, "πρωτότοκος," *EDNT* 3:190.

sians 1:15-20, the church fathers developed the trinitarian theology that appears in the great creeds of the fourth and fifth centuries.[17]

The scope of cosmic Christology. The preceding summary represents traditional, orthodox Christology until the post-Enlightenment and modern eras. Today this conception of Christ has undergone significant modification within the liberal wing of the church. The impact of a scientific worldview has resulted in nuanced presentations of cosmic Christology or the outright rejection of the category as a meaningful one. Many modern scholars downplay or deny that Paul intended a truly cosmic Christology. In their view, what Paul was really describing had to do with the salvation of human beings, not the actual cosmos in its immensity. Thus one must scale back cosmic language to anthropological referents; the cosmic imagery provides merely the trappings for what is of real importance: salvation from the impersonal forces that enslave and engender guilt and anxiety. Rudolf Bulmann gave classic expression to this approach to Paul's cosmic Christology, and many others have followed him.[18]

A closely related approach simply shrugs off the cosmic language as incidental to Paul's thought as a whole. Paul's adoption of such language is highly circumstantial in nature and consists of an ad hoc response to the Colossian errorists, who were advocating, among other things, astrological and cosmological doctrines. Were it not for this aberrant teaching, cosmic Christology would never have been part of Paul's theologizing at all.[19]

Still another approach insists that in order to hear Paul correctly in our day, we must recognize that he, like other NT Christians, was groping for ways to explain the significance of Christ. He naturally had recourse to the language of mythology in order to convey this meaning. Paul was trying to

---

[17]Evangelical biblical theologians acknowledge that the doctrine of the Trinity is a post-NT development. This admission does not call in question the correctness of the later development; it simply recognizes that what is implicit in the NT is made explicit by later theological reflection. Gordon Fee's comments in connection with 1 Corinthians 8:6 bear repeating: "Although Paul does not here call Christ God, the formula is so constructed that only the most obdurate would deny its Trinitarian implications" (*The First Epistle to the Corinthians* [NICNT; Grand Rapids: Eerdmans, 1987], p. 375).

[18]Bultmann, *Theology of the New Testament*, 1:227-32, 254-59. T. E. Pollard claims that "the cosmology, if it is cosmology, is totally subservient to soteriology, and by making it thus Paul runs true to form" ("Colossians 1.12-20: A Reconsideration," *New Testament Studies* 27 [1981]: 573).

[19]Representative of this view is Friedrich Wilhelm Eltester: "In Col 1:15 the original, cosmological motif appears in the foreground. Paul has no interest in it: he employs the conception of the Image of God in order to express the fact that Christ is the revelation and representation of God" (*Eikon im Neuen Testament* [BZNW 23; Berlin: Töpelmann, 1958], p. 149 [my translation]). Very similar is the approach of Jürgen Becker, *Paul: Apostle to the Gentiles* (Louisville: Westminster John Knox, 1993), p. 380.

assert that God was truly at work in the man Jesus, and that God's ultimate intention for creation, especially human beings, could be discerned in the person and work of Christ. Cosmic Christology is thus a pointer to the salvific intentions of God—intentions that, of course, preexisted the original creation and are adumbrated in the new creation in Christ (see 2 Cor 5:17; Rom 8:16-25, 32). This may be styled an ideal cosmic Christology.

In my opinion, the attempt to redefine cosmic Christology or relegate it to the periphery of Paul's theology fails exegetically. Virtually all modern students of Paul acknowledge the ad hoc nature of his letters, which provide at best a truncated view of his theology. I have already acknowledged that Colossians 1:15-20 is Paul's pastoral response to the Colossian heresy. It is quite a different matter, however, to claim that he simply improvised cosmic Christology. There are, in fact, contexts where polemic against false teaching involving the created order is not in view and yet one discerns passing references implying cosmic Christology. These texts either assume preexistence, a corollary of cosmic Christology, or, in one case, refer to his mediatorship in creation (Rom 8:3; 1 Cor 1:30; 2:7; 8:6; 10:1-5[?];Gal 4:4-5; Phil 2:6-11; 1 Tim 1:15). All but one of these references predate Colossians.

The trajectory of cosmic Christology. How did Paul arrive at this tremendous confession? Was cosmic eschatology uniquely a Pauline creation, or did he reformulate an already existing belief? This was the problem that Bultmann posed. How did the Galilean proclaimer of the kingdom of God become the content of the proclamation by the early Christians and Paul in particular?[20] This question must be squarely faced. Bultmann's solution involves a Hellenizing of the earliest, primitive kerygma. He traces a trajectory of gradual divinization whereby the Galilean Jesus, who cannot really be recovered through historical investigation, becomes transmuted into a divine being, the *kyrios.*[21] To this end, Bultmann assumes the presence and availability already in the first century A.D. of gnostic myths and motifs that are clearly demonstrable only in the later second century A.D.

Is this, however, what really happened? Let us revisit the question and see if we can reconstruct belief in Jesus Christ as cosmic Lord without re-

---

[20]More recently Hendrikus Boers has reiterated this supposed problem: "The fundamental problem of a Christology of the NT . . . was that the view of Jesus found in NT Christology was not historically true of Jesus himself" ("Jesus and the Christian Faith: New Testament Christology since Bousset's *Kyrios Christos," Journal of Biblical Literature* 89 [1979]: 452).

[21]Bultmann and others in the liberal tradition assume evolutionary models analogous to Darwinian evolution in the biological sciences. For a rejection of such "evolutionary Christologies," see C. F. D. Moule, *The Origin of Christology* (Cambridge: Cambridge University Press, 1977), pp. 1-10.

sorting to the demythologizing program of Bultmann or the ideal cosmic Christology of Dunn. In this exercise I make a concession to historical criticism: I eliminate at the outset any appeal to the Gospel of John, since it comes from near the end of the first century. Having set aside John's Gospel, can we infer a Christology from the Synoptic Gospels that prepares the way for Paul's cosmic Christology?

As a starting point, I call attention to pericopes in which Jesus acts with an unprecedented degree of authority. For example, his assumed authority to pronounce forgiveness of sins stunned and enraged Pharisaic scribes (see Lk 5:21) who witnessed it. In Mark's account of the healing of the paralytic in Capernaum, they respond to Jesus' absolution with these accusing questions: "Why does this fellow speak in this way? It is blasphemy! Who can forgive sins but God alone?" (Mk 2:7) Precisely! Jesus dared to speak on behalf of God. Another powerful story makes the same point: the sinful woman at Simon the Pharisee's house. The punch line comes when Jesus says to the woman, "Your sins are forgiven" (Lk 7:48). Once again the reaction of the guests is outrage: "Who is this who even forgives sins?" (Lk 7:49). Clearly, the evangelists portray Jesus exercising an authority that pious Jews believed to be the possession of God alone.

Jesus' authority vis-à-vis Torah and temple likewise jarred religious sensibilities. His occasional willingness to modify or even abrogate portions of Torah engendered intense hostility. How could this Galilean prophet be so presumptuous as to tamper with the very oracles of God delivered on Mount Sinai (whether written or oral)? And yet this is precisely what Jesus did. One thinks of Jesus' famous "But I say to you . . . " statements in the six antitheses of the Sermon on the Mount (Mt 5:21-48). Such authoritative statements in connection with Torah were unheard of in first-century Judaism. Furthermore, Jesus' symbolic action of cleansing the temple and likening it to a "den of robbers" (cf. Jer 7:1-11) not only alienated him from the Sadducees and high priests but also was a decisive factor leading to his arrest and execution. His prediction of the second temple's destruction (Mk 13:2 pars.), with an apparent prophecy that he would raise it up anew, struck at the very heart of Jewish piety (Mk 14:58; cf. Mk 11:15-16; 15:29 pars.; Mt 26:61; Jn 2:19-21). No wonder the old wineskins and old garments were incompatible with Jesus' gospel of the kingdom (Mk 2:21-22)!

Even more telling are those places where Jesus implies that one's eternal salvation depends on faith in him. The Sermon on the Mount concludes with exhortations and warnings: "Not everyone who says to *me*, 'Lord, Lord,' will enter the kingdom of heaven, but only the one who does the will of my Father in heaven" (Mt 7:21 [my italics]); "Everyone then who hears these words of *mine* and acts on them will be like a wise man who built his house on rock" (Mt 7:24 [my italics]). Nothing like this exists in the extant sources of first-century Judaism. At the very least, here is a messenger who speaks with God's own authority—in short, God's personal *shaliach* (emissary or agent).[22]

But there is more to be said. What about the miracles? The Synoptics record a wide variety of healing miracles. These testify that Jesus of Nazareth possessed an extraordinary power. As impressive as the healing miracles are, however, they still fall well short of cosmic Christology. What must be taken into account is a subset of miracles, the so-called nature miracles. These are instances in which Jesus does something contrary to the known laws of nature: changing water into wine, stilling a storm, walking on water, and multiplying food. These deal with the realm of creation and providence. Of course, many modern scholars deny that such miracles actually occurred, preferring instead to attribute them to the early church's piety and apologetic interests. But if one embraces supernaturalism and assumes the essential reliability and authority of the Gospel tradition, the nature miracles provide a key building block of cosmic Christology. On a face-value reading, Jesus Christ possessed power over the created order.

To the nature miracles we append another piece. The transfiguration of Jesus, recorded by all three Synoptics, depicts Jesus' radiance like the *shekinah* glory of the God of Israel (Mk 9:2-8; Mt 17:1-13; Lk 9:28-36). At the very least, the evangelists believed that Jesus was more than a mere mortal; he was also divine.

Finally, we add the piece that makes all the difference: the resurrection. Here we have the grand demonstration and vindication of the Son of God (cf. Rom 1:3). Three times in the Gospel of Mark Jesus predicts the death of the Son of Man at the hands of the elders, chief priest and scribes, followed by his rising again (Mk 8:31; 9:31; 10:33-34). This threefold repetition is also included by Matthew and Luke (Mt 16:21; 17:22-23; 20:18-19; Lk 9:22, 44; 18:31-33). To be sure, the Synoptic Gospels do not explicitly attribute the resurrection to Jesus' own inherent power. In particular, Matthew's use of the passive voice implies that God the Father raises the Son of Man to life. Even though John's Gospel portrays the Son as possessing the power to come back from the dead (Jn 10:18), this is not an independent act. The Synoptics, however, are quite sufficient to make the point: Jesus Christ is a unique individual standing in a unique category. In Paul's later creedal formulations he is the "one mediator between God and humankind,

---

[22]On this point, see Ben Witherington III, *The Christology of Jesus* (Minneapolis: Fortress, 1990), pp. 132-37.

Christ Jesus, himself human" (1 Tim 2:5), the one "who abolished death and brought life and immortality to light through the gospel" (2 Tim 1:10). According to the book of Acts, the earliest post-Easter church affirmed Jesus as Lord (Acts 2:32-36; cf. Rom 10:9; 1 Cor 12:3;), the unique Son of God, possessing the power of life and death (Acts 2:24). With the resurrection of Jesus, the earliest community of believers confessed his lordship in terms of victory over death and vindication by God. In keeping with their Jewish heritage, the followers of Jesus also confessed that the God of Israel was the "Sovereign Lord, who made the heaven and the earth, the sea, and everything in them" (Acts 4:24). But as we have already seen, Jesus was also invoked as Lord *(kyrios).* By an inexorable logic, the confession and experience of Jesus as Lord prompted the primitive community to understand this lordship in terms transcending soteriology and eschatology; it involved nothing less than a relationship to the entire created order, comparable to that of the *kyrios* of the OT. This is reflected in, for example, Romans 10:13; Philippians 2:10 and Hebrews 1:8, 10, where quotations from the OT referring to Yahweh are applied to Christ (Rom 10:13 [Joel 2:32]; Phil 2:10 [Is 45:23; cf. Ps 95:6]; Heb 1:8 [Ps 45:6-7], 10 [Ps 102:25-27]). In brief, cosmic Christology was implicit from the very beginning of the primitive church.[23]

When Paul wrote the Colossian letter in the early 60s, he included a confessional statement that either was already known to the readers (whether pre-Pauline or Pauline) or was composed by Paul as an ad hoc response to the Colossian error. If the former, we have no way of knowing precisely when and by whom this creed was composed. What seems quite certain is that Paul agreed with its formulations. If the latter, it is possible that the cosmic Christology of Colossians 1:15-20 owes its formulation to Saul of Tarsus. On the other hand, as early as the mid 50s Paul uses creedal language that certainly implies cosmic Christology: "one Lord, Jesus Christ, through whom are all things and through whom we exist" (1 Cor 8:6). In other words, the notion of cosmic Christology may well go back even earlier, but on the basis of available sources, we cannot be sure. What we can say is that Paul's letters already attest such a belief by the mid 50s.

Summary. Here is how I think this all came together. Paul's experience on the road to Damascus, reinforced by worship of the Lord Jesus Christ

---

[23]See Moule, *The Origin of Christology,* pp. 35-46. He notes, "I am inclined to believe that a good case could be made for the ingredients for such conclusions [cosmic Christology] being present immediately in the experience of the risen Christ" (p. 44). Wenham says, "Bultmann's 'proclaimer becoming the proclaimed' will not do: Jesus saw himself as having a vital role in the coming kingdom; he was himself proclaimer and proclaimed" (*Paul,* p. 124 n. 57).

with fellow believers, was the taproot of his cosmic Christology. The wisdom tradition of ancient Israel and Second Temple Judaism then provided Paul with a category conducive to cosmic Christology. Especially important were passages from Sirach and Wisdom of Solomon. A key passage is Wisdom 7:22—8:1, a text rightly considered "the climax of all Jewish writing on wisdom."[24] This text comes quite close to hypostatizing Wisdom—that is, ascribing material existence to an abstract idea. Wisdom is thus viewed as a distinct person alongside God and involved in creation and providence. There are significant similarities in phrasing to 1 Corinthians 1:30; 8:6; 2 Corinthians 4:4; Philippians 2:6-11 and Colossians 1:15-20 (cf. Jn 1:1-3, 10, 14; Heb 1:1-3).

The keen mind of the apostle Paul almost certainly was steeped in this background. How could he have studied at Jerusalem and not known this work? Striking parallels between Wisdom of Solomon and Paul's letters exist beyond Colossians 1:15-20. Basically, Paul transferred to Jesus Christ the attributes and role of personified Wisdom. The fundamental difference—making all the difference!—lies in the fact that Paul does not merely personify Christ as Wisdom; rather, he incarnates Christ as Wisdom. Like Wisdom, the Lord Christ preexisted, was mediator of all creation, sustains all creation and guides all creation to its appointed end. Unlike Wisdom, the Lord Christ became the Lord *Jesus* Christ; that is, he assumed true humanity (see Phil 2:6). The attributes of wisdom were taken up and incorporated into cosmic Christology but were dramatically transcended.

To this should be added Paul's "second Adam" Christology. The "image of the invisible God" predication in the first stanza of Colossians 1:15-20 evokes the creation narrative in which Adam is created as God's image. The "firstborn from the dead" predication in the second stanza of Colossians 1:15-20 finds an echo in "Christ the first fruits" (1 Cor 15:23), a context in which Christ is explicitly designated "the last Adam" (1 Cor 15:45) and "the second man" (1 Cor 15:47). Christ is thus a new Adam, heading up a new humanity created in his image (see Col 3:10). As the second Adam, he is the first *(prōtotokos)* to experience bodily resurrection. Paul's diction thus displays a melding of Wisdom and second-Adam motifs. As we have already noted, the actual structure of Colossians 1:15-20 may be indebted to a midrashic exposition of Genesis 1:1 by means of Proverbs 8:22 using the technique of *gezera shawa*.

However one explains the composition of Colossians 1:15-20, the fin-

---

[24]Donald Hagner, "Wisdom of Solomon," *ZPEB* 5:948. But see Fee, *Pauline Christology*, pp. 595-630, for a vehement denial that Paul was indebted to the Wisdom tradition for his Christology.

ished product is a magnificent confession, celebrating the cosmic significance of Jesus Christ, awe-inspiring in its scope. In the man Jesus of Nazareth we have the incarnation of the eternal Son of God, the one in, through
and for whom all things were created in the beginning, and who, by means
of the cross and resurrection, brings into existence a new creation. May
"the Messiah, who is over all, God blessed forever" be praised![25]

Corporate Christology. One more important concept, the distinctly Pau-
line formulation "in Christ," requires discussion, a notion overlapping with
Pauline ecclesiology. The "in Christ" formulation grows seamlessly out of
Paul's idea of Christ as the second Adam. As already seen in Paul's doctrine
of sin, all people are either in Adam or in Christ, the second Adam. There
are two, and only two, humanities recognized by God. In Paul's words,
"For as all die in Adam, so all will be made alive in Christ" (1 Cor 15:22).
One is transferred from the first Adam to the second Adam through an act
of faith in Christ (Col 1:13), summarized in the earliest Christian confession: Jesus is Lord (Rom 10:9; 1 Cor 12:3). This confession is closely linked
to an accompanying outward rite: water baptism.

For Paul, baptism visibly signifies the union of a believer with the risen
Lord. When one is baptized, he or she calls upon the name of the Lord
(Rom 10:9) and is submerged beneath the water, a powerful symbol of dying with Christ. Being raised up from the baptismal waters speaks of sharing in Christ's resurrection (Rom 6:1-4). This has a "now but not yet" character; that is, already the power of Christ through the Spirit is present to
assist the believer in the struggle against the world, the flesh and the devil,
but the final and full installment of power and transformation occurs at the
parousia (1 Cor 15:20-28; Phil 3:20-21; Col 3:1-4; 1 Thess 4:13-18).

Two misleading explanations of Paul's formulation require comment.
Some scholars continue to speak, much like Albert Schweitzer did earlier, of
Paul's "Christ mysticism."[26] This refers to a subjective experience of union
with Christ. As we noted earlier, Schweitzer saw this as the real center of
Paul's theology. Other scholars, following in the train of Rudolf Bultmann
and heavily influenced by history of religions research, link Paul's mysticism
with the various mystery religions of the first century A.D. On this understanding, the initiate is actually joined to Christ.[27] Mystery religions spon-

---

[25]For a defense of Colossians 1:15-20 as affirming the full deity of Jesus Christ, see Murray
J. Harris, *Jesus as God: The New Testament Use of Theos in Reference to Jesus* (Grand
Rapids: Baker, 1992).

[26]See, for example, Alan F. Segal, *Paul the Convert: The Apostolate and Apostasy of Saul the
Pharisee* (New Haven: Yale University Press, 1990), pp. 34-71. See also Albert Schweitzer,
The Mysticism of Paul the Apostle (New York: Henry Holt, 1931), pp. 219-26.

[27]Some early scholars of the history of religion, such as Adolf Deissmann, thought that the

sored secret rituals and ceremonies, involving baptisms and sacred meals, promising eternal life to the devotees. According to Bultmann, Paul's view of baptism involves an actual participation in the death and resurrection of Christ (see Rom 6:1-4) but clearly is a secondary addition to the earlier, essentially Jewish, understanding of baptism among Jesus' followers.[28]

In regard to the subjective interpretation, instead of saying that Paul's theology is based on mystical experiences, one must speak instead of an objective reality. The indwelling Christ actually accomplishes God's saving purpose for his people through his atoning death, resurrection, exaltation and heavenly intercession, and he actually indwells his people by means of the Holy Spirit. With regard to Bultmann's contention that participation in the death of Christ is a secondary, Hellenistic addition to the original meaning of Christian baptism, recent scholarship has cast considerable doubt on his correlation with the mystery religions. The parallels are more apparent than real and rely on sources later (sometimes much later) than the first century A.D.[29]

But how does one actually make sense of this? How can many individuals be said to live "in" a solitary person? How can the one person Jesus Christ transcend his individuality such that all who believe in him as Savior and Lord are joined organically to him and constitute a corporate entity? Here is a new version of a very old problem: the problem of the one and the many. C. F. D. Moule is not alone in expressing puzzlement about the intelligibility of this doctrine.[30] And yet, as Moule patiently argues, this seems to be precisely what Paul affirms.

The fact is this affirmation points in the same direction as cosmic Christology. Only by allowing that Jesus shares the status and attributes ascribed to God the Father does corporate Christology make sense. Only a person capable of transcending his own individuality, without thereby ceasing to be an individual, meets the requirements assumed by Paul's corporate Christology. What is patently clear from Paul and other NT writers is the experience of being united with Christ. This is what distinguishes true believers; they are now "in Christ," and the Spirit witnesses to them that this is so. Paul's pastoral parenesis at point after point simply takes this for

---

"in Christ" formula was based on a conception in which "the glorified Christ was understood to be a light ethereal substance, like air, [that] could infill the believer and in which the believer had his or her existence" (Ladd, *Theology of the New Testament*, p. 400). See Adolf Deissmann, *Paul: A Study in Social and Religious History* (London: Hodder & Stoughton, 1926), pp. 137-49.

[28]Bultmann, *Theology of the New Testament*, 1:140.

[29]See G. R. Beasley-Murray, "Baptism," *DPL* 60-66.

[30]Moule, *The Origin of Christology*, pp. 57-54, especially p. 51.

granted. The brief sketches of the early church in Jerusalem (Acts 1—5) highlight this overwhelming sense of being one with him.

I conclude that the experience of the risen Christ necessarily entails the "high Christology" later enshrined in ecumenical creeds. Each believer is individually indwelt by the Spirit of Jesus, and, correlatively, each believer exists in Christ. One may properly speak of a corporate entity: the body of Christ. Corporate Christology has its genesis in the immediate aftermath of Easter and Pentecost.[31] In Paul's words, the Lord Jesus Christ has "all the fullness of God" dwelling in him (Col 1:19; 2:9), and therefore all believers "have come to fullness in him" (Col 2:10), have been gathered up in him (Eph 1:10), and corporately have the "fullness of him who fills all in all" (Eph 1:23) and are "filled with all the fullness of God" (Eph 3:19). Such affirmations cannot be empirically substantiated or rationally demonstrated; only faith takes hold of the sweeping ramifications of being "in Christ." In Paul's words, "We walk by faith, not by sight" (2 Cor 5:7).

PAULINE ESCHATOLOGY

As has frequently been observed, virtually all Pauline theology is eschatology. This is because his theology stands under the shadow of the "now but not yet," a distinctly Christian modification of the traditional "two ages" framework of Second Temple Judaism, a modification going back to Jesus himself. Consequently, all Pauline theology stands beneath this overarching structure.[32] Having said that, one must recognize that the end times will come to a climax at the second coming of Jesus Christ (1 Cor 15:23-24; cf. 1 Tim 4:1; 2 Tim 3:1). In several passages Paul describes this grand consummation, besides alluding to it on numerous occasions.

The Day of the Lord. As we noted earlier, one of the major concepts of the OT prophets was the notion of Yahweh's final and decisive intervention in human history. Paul was heir to this notion and especially its elaboration in the Jewish traditions of Second Temple Judaism. In fact, already on the day of Pentecost, the book of Acts reports Peter as proclaiming that "the last days" have begun leading up to the Day of the Lord (Acts 2:17, 20). Peter, like the OT prophets before him, calls for repentance in anticipation of this awesome day. He also makes it abundantly clear that Jesus of Nazareth is none other than the Lord himself (Acts 2:36). A perusal of Paul's letters makes it evident that he too identifies Jesus as the Lord who acts on that

---

[31]Ibid.

[32]In the view of Thomas Schreiner, "We could include every topic under Paul's eschatology" (*Paul, Apostle of God's Glory in Christ: A Pauline Theology* [Downers Grove, Ill.: InterVarsity Press, 2001], p. 454).

great day, the Day of the Lord Jesus Christ (1 Cor 1:7).

Like the Pharisees, Saul of Tarsus understands the Day of the Lord to be supremely a day of deliverance and vindication for Israel. Certainly a majority position among Pharisees, if not a unanimous one, envisions a Davidic messiah playing a leading role in this vindication. Typically this involves a messianic war against the hostile Gentile nations, liberating and exalting the land of Israel. The centerpiece, of course, in this national restoration is the temple and its environs. Ezekiel inspired the dreams of many with a grand vision of a new, imposing edifice situated in a transformed environment on the site of the first temple (Ezek 40—48). The visions of Isaiah (Is 2:1-5), Jeremiah (Jer 31:38-40) and Zechariah (Zech 14:3-21) likewise encouraged pious Jews to expect Jerusalem to be the capital of the world and a magnet of world pilgrimage by repentant Gentiles in the halcyon days following the Day of the Lord. As a Christian, the apostle Paul transposes these received traditions in distinctive ways, modifications that invite careful reflection.

The return of Christ. I begin with Paul's doctrine of the return of Christ, a constellation of beliefs centered on his conviction that Jesus of Nazareth is the promised Messiah of Israel, the unique and preexistent Son of God, and the Lord of the OT. The risen Lord Jesus Christ, exalted to the right hand of God, is now, by his Spirit, calling out a new people of God, the church, the new Israel. From heaven Jesus will soon return, visibly and bodily, to reward the righteous, punish the wicked, and establish his worldwide rule over the cosmos.

Paul's earliest extant missionary correspondence, the two letters to Thessalonica (ca. A.D. 50/51), provides the fullest discussion of this doctrine. The reason for this, as is characteristic of all of Paul's writings, is entirely circumstantial in nature. Paul addresses the issue because of certain misunderstandings on the part of the Thessalonian believers; to these misapprehensions he applies specific correctives and instruction.

The first misunderstanding, a focal point of 1 Thessalonians, concerns believers who die before the return of Christ. Apparently, several had passed away in the brief interval since Paul established the church and was forced to leave town (Acts 17:1-9; cf. 1 Thess 2:17-18). The Thessalonian Christians apparently assume that the deceased suffer a severe disadvantage in not living until Christ returned. Possibly, some Thessalonians harbor misgivings about the genuine salvation of the deceased, whose deaths are interpreted as a sign of divine judgment and disbarment from the kingdom. More likely, however, in view of what Paul actually says by way of correction, they are deeply grieved that their loved ones will miss out on the glories and vindication of Christ's return. I personally think that they also expect to share in Christ's visible reign on earth, hence their distress over those who failed to survive until the glorious return of Christ.

Paul's pastoral response to this misunderstanding is fascinating. We may organize it in terms of four primary questions: What actually happens? What is the origin of this teaching? When will it happen? What is the significance?

The sequence of events. The most important corrective that Paul makes is stated in 1 Thessalonians 4:14. In language sounding almost like a creed ("For since we believe that . . . "), Paul affirms that believers who have died will accompany Christ at his return. In a nutshell, this addresses the misunderstanding and alleviates the grief; believers will not miss out on the second advent. Paul supports his claim by an appeal to "the word of the Lord" (1 Thess 4:15), the source of which is debatable.[33] Suggestions include (1) a saying of Jesus found in the Gospels;[34] (2) a genuine saying of Jesus not recorded in the canonical Gospels (an *agraphon* [see Acts 20:35]); (3) a word stemming from a Christian apocalyptic source no longer extant; (4) a prophetic oracle revealed to Paul by the Lord or to some other anonymous Christian prophet.[35] Whatever the precise source, Paul sketches a sequence of events that transpire virtually simultaneously.

Three audible occurrences announce the descent of Christ: a cry of command from the Lord himself, the archangel's call and a trumpet blast. Perhaps these three discrete items are really one: the Lord's cry of command is a trumpet blast blown by an archangel. In any case, Paul's description of Jesus' descent is depicted as a tangible, visible, public event originating in

---

[33]"The tradition of the Jerusalem Church is at least in substance behind the 'word of the Lord' on the parousia and resurrection in 1 Thess. 4:15-17, though it is not certain whether Paul is here quoting a traditionally transmitted saying or whether he is appealing to a revelation accorded to him by the exalted Lord" (Bultmann, *Theology of the New Testament*, 1:188-89).

[34]Robert Gundry argues that Paul is referring to a saying lying behind John 11:25-26 ("The Hellenization of Dominical Tradition and Christianization of Jewish Tradition in the Eschatology of 1-2 Thessalonians," *New Testament Studies* 33 [1987]: 164-66). For other suggestions from the canonical Gospels, see Wenham, *Paul*, pp. 332-33. Actually, no dominical saying in the canonical Gospels conforms to the Pauline formulation. One must assume that Paul paraphrases the saying(s) of Jesus and adapts it (them) to the specific issue causing concern at Thessalonica.

[35]James Dunn argues that the word of the Lord was "an inspired utterance or prophecy given to Paul (privately or in the Christian assembly, perhaps drawing on earlier Jesus tradition) as he meditated prayerfully on the Thessalonians' distress" (*The Theology of Paul the Apostle* [Grand Rapids: Eerdmans, 1998], p. 303). In a footnote on this passage he muses, "Perhaps it is unfamiliarity with the phenomenon of (inspired) prophetic utterance which has made this less obvious or attractive as an option for so many commentators. But neither Paul nor the Thessalonians were strangers to the experience of prophecy" (ibid., n. 45).

the heavenly realms and terminating in the air above the earth. Since the dead in Christ are said to rise first, we must envision a situation in which the disembodied spirits of the deceased, accompanying Christ, are suddenly clothed with their new, resurrection bodies. Immediately thereafter, living believers are caught up to meet the Lord in the air, joining the newly resurrected. Although not explicitly stated, this implies a spiritual transformation of their bodies, since they are now capable of what is impossible for ordinary, physical bodies.[36] The instantaneous and transformational nature of the event is explicitly stated in a parallel passage, written to the Corinthians, where Paul describes in some detail the resurrection body (1 Cor 15:35-53).[37]

Paul's description of the Lord's return in 1 Thessalonians 4 advances just beyond the climax in 1 Corinthians 15 and thereby provides an appropriate pastoral word to the distressed believers at Thessalonica: "and so we will be with the Lord forever" (1 Thess 4:17). At this point, he breaks off his portrayal of the so-called rapture of the church and concludes with exhortations to spiritual preparedness and words of encouragement (1 Thess 4:18—5:11).

Background. Paul bases his depiction on a word of the Lord. Are we to assume, then, that this teaching was an innovation of Jesus himself? As I have argued repeatedly, the taproot of both Jesus and Paul's thought lies in the OT and its elaboration in Second Temple Judaism. It is no different here. The OT provides the point of origin, especially passages describing theophanies (appearances of God).

Two prime candidates are the theophany at Mount Sinai and the theophany associated with the Day of the Lord. A number of significant verbal and conceptual parallels exist between Paul's description of Christ's descent in 1 Thessalonians 4 and the narratives describing Yahweh's descent on Mount Sinai (Ex 19:9-20; cf. Is 64:1; Mic 1:3).[38] Common elements include announcement by a trumpet blast, descent of the Lord in fire and clouds, and ascent of Moses, as representative of the people, to the very presence of the Lord. To these features the Day of the Lord adds cosmic,

---

[36]The Greek word is ἀλλάσσω, meaning "change, alter." "Paul writes that Christians who are still living at the time of the parousia must be changed, i.e., transformed, since flesh and blood cannot inherit the kingdom of God; mortality must be transformed into immortality" (H. Merkel, "ἀλλάσσω," *EDNT* 1:62).

[37]In 1 Corinthians 15:52 Paul says that the transformation will take place "in the twinkling of an eye." The blinking (twinkling) of an eye, the quickest reaction in the human body, is timed by Bell Laboratories at 1/29th of a second!

[38]For a listing of these elements and the textual support, see T. Francis Glasson, "Theophany and Parousia," *NTS* 34 (1988): 259-62.

celestial phenomena, accompaniment of angels, regathering and resurrection of the righteous, and final judgment on the wicked (e.g., Is 13:9-13; 25:6-10; 27:12-13; Joel 2:30-32; Zeph 1:14-18; Zech 14:4-5; Dan 7:9-10, 13-14; 12:1-3).

Yet this is not the last word on the subject. As Max Wilcox reminds us, we are really dealing with "the Old Testament understood in the light of the accepted exegetical traditions."[39] The early followers of Jesus read the OT through the lenses of the inherited traditions of a multifaceted Judaism. One of these facets was apocalyptic Judaism, with its hope pinned on an imminent coming of the Lord to conclude this present evil age and inaugurate the glorious age to come. A number of stock features in apocalyptic descriptions of the Lord's coming on the last day also appear in 1 Thessalonians 4:16, such as the trumpet (*4 Ezra* 6:23), the clouds (*2 En.* 3:1) and the archangel (*4 Ezra* 4:36). Surprisingly, however, nowhere in extant apocalyptic literature do we read of a messianic descent to the earth.[40] On the other hand, as we have already seen, early Christians identified Jesus as the Lord, whom they readily saw fulfilling those prophecies in which Yahweh comes down to earth to effect deliverance and execute judgment. Still, there are some noteworthy differences between Paul's description in 1 Thessalonians 4:15-17 and the theophany at Sinai. The "cloud" (singular) at Sinai covered Yahweh's presence, whereas Paul says that the "clouds" (plural) convey believers into the Lord's presence. More importantly, the people of Israel stood at the foot of the mountain, whereas, according to Paul, believers are snatched up into the air. Clearly, there is a conceptual advance in Paul.

This advance is probably the result of Paul's adaptation, a feature of Greco-Roman society: a royal visit to a Hellenistic city. The technical term for such a visit by a high-ranking dignitary is *parousia*. The word itself has the meanings of "presence, arrival, or coming."[41] Paul uses the word six times to refer to an individual's presence or coming, whether his own or someone else's (1 Cor 16:17; 2 Cor 7:6, 7; 10:10; Phil 1:26; 2:12). Most often, however, he refers to the coming and presence of Jesus Christ at the Day of the Lord. A careful reading of our passage in 1 Thessalonians 4 reveals that Paul skillfully portrays the coming of Jesus in terms of a royal parousia. Accordingly, I use this technical term to refer to the second coming.[42]

---

[39]Max Wilcox, "On Investigating the Use of the Old Testament in the New Testament," in *Text and Tradition: Studies in the New Testament Presented to Matthew Black*, ed. E. Best and R. McL. Wilson (Cambridge: Cambridge University Press, 1979), p. 235.

[40]As noted by Eduard Schweizer, "The Son of Man Again," *NTS* 10 (1963): 260; Glasson, "Theophany and Parousia," p. 262.

[41]On παρουσία *(parousia)*, see BDAG, p. 780; W. Radl, *EDNT* 3:43-44; A. Oepke, *TDNT* 5:858-71; Ceslas Spicq, *TLNT* 53-55.

[42]The expression *second coming* is not used in the NT. Hebrews 9:28, however, does say that

Paul deftly transposes several features of a royal parousia into a new key, or better yet, onto a new plane.[43] A parousia placed enormous burdens on a Hellenistic city. If the emperor was to visit a city, extensive preparations were mandatory. General sprucing up and provision for adequate transportation, including new roads, were typical. New coins commemorating the event might be minted to celebrate the special occasion. Other frills included public orations, special banquets, lavish gifts and ornate decorations. Because of the close connection between royal visits and the "presence" of patron gods, the occasion took on religious as well as political significance and thus entailed any number of religious rituals and ceremonies. Of prime importance was the necessity of forming a welcoming committee to meet the royal figure and his accompanying entourage, well outside the city limits, and escort him into the city. This welcoming delegation would, of course, be composed of officials and leading citizens. Typically, a parousia terminated at the *bēma* ("judgment seat"), where the royal dignitary took his seat and decided certain cases that were pending or appealed to the highest tribunal (see Acts 25:10). With this brief reconstruction of a parousia, note how several features suddenly come into focus when we identify the royal figure with Jesus Christ.

The most important transposition, of course, has to do with the axis of our word picture. Instead of a horizontal axis, think of it vertically. In other words, King Jesus, in his parousia, descends. The entourage accompanying Jesus consists of believers who die before the parousia and are present with him (1 Thess 4:14). And certainly the welcoming delegation is there to meet him well outside the city limits, now located "in the clouds" and "in the air" (1 Thess 4:17). Who is this welcoming committee? There can be little doubt it consists of those "who are alive, who are left" (1 Thess 4:17). Paul breaks off his exposition right after mentioning the reunion in the air and does not continue his analogy, since the problem prompting it in the first place was now answered. Comparing other Pauline texts, I infer that had he continued the analogy, the sequel would have featured the Lord Jesus, accompanied by the newly resurrected and transformed saints, descending to earth and taking his place on the judgment seat (Rom 2:16; 14:9-10; 1 Cor 4:5; 2 Cor 5:10). I think that Paul also would have proceeded to speak of Christ's earthly reign and the participation of the saints in this triumphant phase of the kingdom (1 Cor 6:2-3).

Related expressions. Other related words or phrases fill out Paul's

---

Christ "will appear a second time." Apparently, the first Christian theologian to use the expression *second coming* is Justin Martyr in the second century A.D.

[43]See Gundry, "The Hellenization of Dominical Tradition," pp. 161-78.

conception of Jesus' return to earth. Four times he employs the noun *apokalypsis,* meaning "unveiling" or "disclosure" (Rom 2:5; 8:19; 1 Cor 1:7; 2 Thess 1:7). Christ's lordship now remains hidden and veiled at the right hand of God (see Col 3:3-4); at the second advent it will be visibly and publicly unveiled with great glory. Another term in the same semantic field is *epiphaneia,* meaning "appearing" or "appearance." Paul uses the word five times to refer to Jesus' second coming (2 Thess 2:8; 1 Tim 6:14; 2 Tim 4:1, 8; Tit 2:13) and once to refer to his first advent (2 Tim 1:10). In the first century A.D. it was a religious technical term referring to a "visible manifestation of a hidden deity either in the form of a personal appearance, or by some deed of power by which its presence is made known."[44] Paul nicely adapts it to Christ's return. In Colossians 3:4 Paul uses the passive voice of *phaneroō* ("reveal, make known, show") to depict this moment of self-disclosure. As we have already noted, Paul also uses various forms of the OT expression "Day of the Lord" to refer to this grand arrival (e.g., Phil 1:6; 1 Thess 5:2; 2 Thess 1:10; 2:2). As can be seen, this prominent theme is richly ornamented in Pauline diction.

Timing. The question of timing, while more easily answered, leaves us somewhat disappointed: in short, we do not know when the parousia will occur. Paul apparently had instructed the Thessalonian believers about the parousia during his brief time there ("You do not need to have anything written to you. For you yourselves know very well . . . " [1 Thess 5:1-2]). But equally apparent, Paul never set a calendar date, because such information is privy to God alone. Unfortunately, many well-meaning individuals have attempted to supply what both Jesus and Paul refused to provide. Paul assumes that it will be soon, but nowhere does he say when. When it does occur, it will be sudden (1 Thess 5:3), like the blink of an eye (1 Cor 15:52); it will also be unexpected, like a thief in the night (1 Thess 5:2). And, given that Paul seems to include himself among those who are still alive at the parousia ("we who are alive, who are left until the coming of the Lord" [1 Thess 4:15; cf. 1 Cor 15:51]), he must have thought it would be in his lifetime, when he wrote this letter. Later in his career, it became increasingly evident that he would not live to see the Lord's coming (2 Cor 5:1-5; 2 Tim 4:6-8).

On the other hand, Paul's second letter to Thessalonica indicates that certain signs precede the parousia. This leads to a hotly debated question: will the rapture precede, be in the midst of or follow the so-called great tribulation? These three options are generally designated as the pretribula-

---

[44]BAGD, p. 304.

tion, midtribulation and posttribulation rapture views. More than a little emotional energy has been invested in this question. Let us examine the "Pauline Apocalypse" (2 Thess 2:1-15) more closely for an answer.

Paul's second letter to the Thessalonians was prompted primarily by another eschatological misunderstanding: the impression that the Day of the Lord had already arrived ("We beg you, brothers and sisters, not to be quickly shaken in mind or alarmed, either by spirit or by word or by letter, as though from us, to the effect that the day of the Lord is already here" [2 Thess 2:1b-2]). To this Paul replies that it cannot now be present, nor can it be in the immediate future, since two preliminary signs must take place first: the rebellion and the revelation of the lawless one. Both signs require unpacking, but I frankly confess that a more opaque passage in Paul can scarcely be found.

What, precisely, does Paul mean by "the rebellion" (2 Thess 2:3)? The Greek word is *apostasia*. In the Bible this term refers to religious apostasy, as illustrated in three LXX occurrences (Josh 22:22; 2 Chron 29:19; Jer 2:19; see also 2 Chron 28:19; 33:19 *[apostasis]*). In 1 Maccabees 2:15 is recounted a moment of truth for Mattathias and his sons: Antiochus IV Epiphanes dispatches his officers to the town of Modein. The officers are charged with "enforcing the apostasy," consisting of participation in a pagan sacrifice by all citizens. In the above cases, the nature of the rebellion or apostasy is religious.[45]

Probably the most helpful cross-references are found in Paul's letters to Timothy. In 1 Timothy 4:1 Paul reports the Spirit saying that "in later times some will renounce the faith." The context suggests that those doing so are professing Christians. Again, in 2 Timothy 3:1, Paul warns that "in the last days distressing times will come." He speaks of those "holding to the outward form of godliness but denying its power" (2 Tim 3:5). Both passages likely are indebted to Jesus' Olivet discourse, in which he warns his disciples that before the Son of Man comes, "Many will fall away, and they will betray one another and hate one another. And many false prophets will arise and lead many astray. And because of the increase of lawlessness, the love of many will grow cold" (Mt 24:10-12). Paul probably has this crisis in mind in 2 Thessalonians 2:3. Before Christ returns, professing Christians commit wholesale apostasy.

The options for identifying the "restrainer" are numerous, with few exegetes willing to express certitude. The fact that Paul uses both the masculine and neuter genders to refer to the restrainer complicates matters (2 Thess

---

[45]Josephus uses *apostasia* to refer to political rebellion (*J.W.* 7.82, 164; *Life* 43).

2:6: "what is now restraining" *[to katechon]*; 2 Thess 2:7: "the one who now restrains" *[ho katechōn]*). Interpreters seek to identify a candidate for which both genders are appropriate. Options include the Roman emperor as the embodiment of the Roman Empire; the principal of human government and its titular head or personification; the Holy Spirit (*pneuma* ["spirit"] is neuter in Greek, but masculine pronouns are used for the Holy Spirit); the apostle Paul and his missionary preaching; an archangel or similar angelic being; Satan; or God himself.[46] My preference is the archangel Michael, who functions in Daniel and other Second Temple literature in a somewhat analogous role (Dan 11:13, 21; 12:1), but perhaps it is best to say that God alone knows.

Thankfully, the identity of the lawless one is less obscure. Most exegetes see this as a reference to the antichrist mentioned in 1 John 2:18; 4:3 and the "beast rising out of the sea" in Revelation 13. This was the majority opinion in the ancient and medieval church, and most modern scholars concur. The lawless one declares himself to be God when he "takes his seat in the temple of God" (2 Thess 2:4). This action is analogous to the sacrilege perpetrated by Antiochus IV Epiphanes in 167 B.C. and nearly repeated by Caligula in 41 B.C. The "temple of God," at face value, refers to the second temple in Jerusalem, still standing when Paul wrote these lines. Admittedly, many modern exegetes interpret the expression in metaphorical terms to refer to Christendom or some such notion.

In my opinion, Paul's letters offer scant support for a pretribulation rapture. Exegetically, a mid- or posttribulation view is preferable.[47] The admonition of Revelation is clear: one must choose Christ or antichrist; there can be no compromise (Rev 13; 14:12; 20:4). Christians living during those days of distress must be prepared to stand up and be counted. Only after a brief but intense period of persecution will the Lord return to gather his people to himself.

Did Paul's eschatological views change? Some scholars maintain that Paul's views changed over time, and that this change can be tracked in his letters. All agree that Paul did come to realize in the course of his career that he would not live until the parousia. In that sense he did change his mind, but we should note that although he assumed that he would be alive when Christ returned, he never presented that as a teaching. It is quite another thing, however, to claim that Paul changed his mind on the nature and timing of the resurrection body. Three texts are put forward to demon-

---

[46]See L. Morris, "Man of Lawlessness and Restraining Power," *DPL* 592-94.

[47]For a convenient overview of the three major rapture views, see Gleason L. Archer, ed., *Three Views on the Rapture: Pre-, Mid-, or Post-Tribulation?* (Grand Rapids: Zondervan, 1996).

strate this alleged change in viewpoint: 1 Thessalonians 4:13-18; 1 Corinthians 15:20-28, 50-56; 2 Corinthians 5:1-10. First Thessalonians may be Paul's earliest letter (indeed, the earliest Christian document that we possess), dated to about A.D. 50/51, 1 Corinthians may be placed at about A.D. 54, and 2 Corinthians would fall somewhere between A.D. 54 and 56. The following chart illustrates the supposed development in Paul's thought:

Table 8.1. Alleged Development in Paul's Eschatology

1 Thess 4:14-18	1 Cor 15:20-28, 50-56	2 Cor 5:1-10
Resurrected physical body	Transformed spiritual body	Transformed spiritual body
Received at parousia (the Day of the Lord)	Received at parousia (Day of the Lord)	Received at death

Note the two alleged changes in Paul's conception of the resurrection of believers. First, in regard to 1 Thessalonians 4:14-18, it is claimed that Paul adheres to the Pharisaic notion whereby the resurrection body is a restored physical body not essentially different from its predecessor. However, in 1 Corinthians and 2 Corinthians Paul now conceives of the resurrection body as radically different, so much so that he calls it a "spiritual" body (1 Cor 15:44). The second change has to do with the time when the believer receives a spiritual body. In both 1 Thessalonians and 1 Corinthians Paul follows the traditional Pharisaic view that the resurrection occurs on the Day of the Lord, but in 2 Corinthians 5:1, so it is claimed, he advances the notion that a believer receives the resurrection body at death: "For we know that if the earthly tent we live in is destroyed, we *have . . .* a house not made with hands, eternal in the heavens" (my italics). Why Paul changes his mind on this point is not certain, but a common conjecture is that Paul had a near-death experience, probably in Ephesus. This causes him to reflect more deeply about life after death, leading to a more Hellenized perspective in which the physical/material body is of little or no importance (cf. 2 Cor 1:8-10; 1 Cor 15:30-32).

In my opinion, this supposed change in Paul's perspective is dubious. In the first place, 1 Thessalonians 4:13-18, like 1 Corinthians 15:50-53, assumes a transformation of the physical bodies of both the resurrected and the raptured at the parousia. This is clear from Paul's description. Deceased saints receive their resurrection bodies in their descent to earth ("the dead in Christ shall rise first" [1 Thess 4:16]), and living believers are caught up to meet them in instantaneously transformed bodies that are capable of flight. This is hardly a merely resuscitated, physical body Paul is talking about! In 1 Corinthians 15 Paul simply elaborates on what is implicit in 1 Thessalonians 4.[48]

The problemmatic text is 2 Corinthians 5:1-10. This text, however, coheres nicely with the first two when we unpack what is actually described. In order to do this, I lay out in chart form the essential points that Paul makes in this passage:

Table 8.2. Paul and the Intermediate State

This Life	Death	The "Intermediate State"[a]	The "Life to Come"
"we groan, longing to be clothed with our heavenly dwelling" (v. 2); "at home in the body" (v. 6); "away from the Lord" (vv. 6, 9)	"if the earthly tent we live in is destroyed" (v. 1); "to be unclothed" (v. 4)	"be found naked" (v. 3); "unclothed" (v. 4); "away from the body and at home with the Lord" (v. 8)	"a building from God, a house not made with hands, eternal in the heavens" (v. 1); "our heavenly dwelling" (v. 2); "to be further clothed" (v. 4); "swallowed up by life" (v. 4); "for all of us must appear before the judgment seat of Christ" (v. 10)

[a]Otherwise called "the third heaven" (2 Cor 12:2) or "paradise" (2 Cor 12:4) or "Abraham's bosom" (Lk 16:22-23 NRSV margin).

Paul actually describes four possible states that a believer may experience. The first is life in physical bodies marked by frailty and mortality. The image of a tent effectively portrays this condition. The experience of death, the second possibility, is alluded to under the metaphors of the tent being destroyed or of suddenly being without clothes. The grim reality behind the metaphors is separation of spirit and body at death. What is not so clear, but I think is essential for grasping Paul's thought, is a fleeting reference to the third possibility: an intermediate state, a disembodied existence after death and before the parousia. Paul uses the metaphor of nakedness to make the point. Finally, he describes the fourth possibility: the grand consummation of redemptive history, resurrection life in the age to come, where what is mortal is "swallowed up by life."

In short, Paul does not teach that a believer receives the resurrection body at death. But he is so sure that believers will receive a new body at the parousia that he uses the present tense "we have" *[echomen])* in 2 Cor-

---

[48]Joseph Plevnik criticizes exegetes for putting too much weight on the "silence" of 1 Thessalonians 4 with regard to the transformation of the body and not recognizing that the rapture language of Paul requires and assumes a transformation of mere mortal bodies ("Paul's Eschatology," *Toronto Journal of Theology* 6 [1990]: 86-99).

inthians 5:1. This is a futuristic use of the present tense, a usage common to both Greek and English. At death, one is away from the body—that is, in the intermediate state. On the one hand, Paul much prefers this state to being in the body because it is "at home with the Lord" (2 Cor 5:8). To this we compare Philippians 1:23, where he says that "to depart and be with the Christ . . . is far better." On the other hand, this is not the final state. Paul most desires to be with Christ in his heavenly house (i.e., possessing a resurrection body). In keeping with Paul's Hebraic heritage, God's ultimate purpose for human beings involves corporeal existence. The resurrection body is an imperishable, glorious, powerful, spiritual and heavenly body—an enormous advance over a mere physical body—but it is still a very concrete and real body.

Final judgment. The Day of the Lord is portrayed in the OT prophets primarily as a time of judgment. The judgment scene in Daniel 7, with its books and ledgers, becomes a standard feature of Pharisaic belief that lives on in rabbinic Judaism. Rabbinic Judaism places increasing emphasis on individual judgment and the factors determining human destiny. This notion reappears in Paul's thought with, of course, significant christological modification.[49] In particular, apocalyptic streams of Second Temple Judaism considerably elaborate on the fate of the righteous and the wicked. Although no uniform scenario emerges from the available written sources, standard features include diametrically opposed destinies of the righteous in paradise and the wicked in Gehenna. Pharisaism eventually develops the notion of a "treasury of merit"—that is, a reservoir of good deeds performed by such righteous stalwarts as Abraham and Moses. From this surplus of the "merits of the fathers" God the righteous judge graciously makes transfers to the account of those whose good deeds are precariously balanced by their bad deeds and who thus teeter on the brink between paradise and Gehenna. This combination of grace and good works is the inherited tradition of Saul of Tarsus.

Paul, the servant of Christ, however, significantly modifies this inherited tradition. To be sure, everyone, believer or not, will stand before the *bēma* ("judgment seat") of God or Christ—these are synonymous expressions in Paul (Rom 14:10; 2 Cor 5:10).[50] But Paul associates final judgment with the

---

[49]According to Larry Kreitzer, Paul "creatively integrates this OT hope with his own developing Christology, effectively transforming the 'day of the Lord (Yahweh)' into the 'Day of the Lord *Jesus Christ*.' This creativity stands as one of the most important contributions within Pauline eschatology" ("Eschatology," *DPL* 259).

[50]See Donald Guthrie, *New Testament Theology* (Downers Grove, Ill.: InterVarsity Press, 1981), pp. 856-63; Larry Kreitzer, *Jesus and God in Paul's Eschatology* (JSNTSup 19; Sheffield: JSOT Press, 1987), pp. 99-112; Schreiner, *Paul*, pp. 467-69; S. H. Travis, "Judg-

parousia of Jesus Christ (1 Thess 3:13; 2 Thess 1:6-10). Nor did he, as a follower of Jesus, accept the Pharisaic notion of a "treasury of merit" that accrues to the benefit of others who were marginal. Rather, Paul believes in salvation by grace through faith in Christ and in judgment on the basis of works.

At first glance this may seem contradictory, but on closer examination, Paul's view is consistent. God in Christ graciously provides a complete and totally sufficient salvation appropriated by faith alone (Rom 3:21-31; Gal 2:15-21; Eph 2:8-9). This does not mean, however, that judgment is no longer relevant for a believer in Christ. A faith that saves is also a faith that works (Eph 2:10; Tit 2:14), and good works validate saving faith on the day of judgment (Rom 2:6-10; 1 Cor 7:19; Gal 5:6). For true believers, the outcome is not in doubt; their good works demonstrate saving faith.[51]

Although some have denied it, Paul does seem to envisage degrees of reward in the life to come based upon the quality, not quantity, of good works.[52] In his discussion of the day of judgment Paul affirms that "the work of each builder will become visible, for the Day will disclose it, because it will be revealed with fire, and the fire will test what sort of work each has done. If what has been built on the foundation survives, the builder will receive a reward. If the work is burned up, the builder will suffer loss; the builder will be saved, but only as through fire" (1 Cor 3:13-17). Since good works are the result of the Holy Spirit working in and through the believer (Gal 5:22-23; Eph 4:11-16; 5:18-20), they are an occasion not for boasting but rather for glorifying God, the source of all good things (1 Cor 15:10-11; 2 Cor 10:13-18). The point of this teaching rests in the notion of responsibility. The Christian life is one of submission to the lordship of Christ, the paradigm for which is that of a "bondservant" or "slave" (Rom 6:12-14). Those who fail to live responsibly under the yoke of Christ and thus fail to reproduce the fruit of the Spirit forfeit rewards in the consummated kingdom. Precisely what these rewards might be is never directly discussed by Paul. He simply speaks of "commendation from God" (1 Cor 4:5), "the prize" (Phil 3:14), "an imperishable [wreath]" (1 Cor 9:25), a "crown" (Phil 4:1; 1 Thess 2:19), and "a crown of righteousness" (2 Tim 4:8). Most likely, he followed the dominical tradition pointing to differ-

---

ment," *DPL* 516-17.

[51]See Thomas R. Schreiner, "Did Paul Believe in Justification by Works? Another Look at Romans 2," *BBR* 31 (1993): 131-58.

[52]S. H. Travis holds that "these tantalizingly unspecific texts [he is referring to 1 Cor 3:14-15; 2 Cor 5:10] are an uncertain basis for such a doctrine" ("Judgment," *DPL* 517). On the other hand, R. M. Fuller concludes that "rewards . . . play a most important role in encouraging Christ's followers to be faithful and diligent in the ministries to which each is called" ("Rewards," *DPL* 820).

ent degrees of responsibility and leadership in the future kingdom (see Mt 25:14-30).

Only hints surface from Paul's letters concerning the final state of the righteous. Paul speaks of glorification as the ultimate experience of believers (Rom 8:29).[53] This is crisply stated in Colossians 1:27 as "Christ in you, the hope of glory." The glory to which Paul refers recalls the *shekinah* glory of the OT—that brilliant radiance associated with the presence of the Lord. To this should be compared Jesus' statement that at the resurrection believers will be "like angels in heaven" (Mt 22:30). Paul even speaks of the resurrection body as "raised in glory" (1 Cor 15:43) and assures the Corinthians that "just as we have borne the image of the man of dust, we will also bear the image of the man of heaven" (1 Cor 15:49). Likewise, he encourages the Philippians that Jesus Christ "will transform [their] lowly bodies so that they will be like his glorious body" (Phil 3:21 NIV). More fundamentally, "glory" connotes the moral perfection of Christ as the ultimate pattern after which believers are conformed (Rom 8:29). Typically, Paul grounds his imperative ("Do not lie to one another" [Col 3:9]) in the indicative by reminding his readers that they "have clothed [themselves] with the new nature, which is being renewed in knowledge according to the image of its creator" (Col 3:10). In keeping with Paul's fundamental understanding of the "now but not yet" character of the kingdom, he already sees the process of glorification at work in the lives of believers: "And we, who with unveiled faces all reflect the Lord's glory, are being transformed into his likeness with ever-increasing glory, which comes from the Lord, who is the Spirit" (2 Cor 3:18 NIV). In two vivid metaphors, Paul likens believers, corporately, to a gigantic temple or to a cosmic body that finally rises "to the measure of the full stature of Christ" (Eph 2:21; 4:13-16).

Paul teaches that unbelievers stand at the final judgment and suffer everlasting exclusion from the presence of God, described as "eternal destruction" (2 Thess 1:5-10; cf. Rom 2:8; Phil 3:19). Quite in contrast to apocalyptic Judaism, Paul never elaborates on the fate of the condemned; a veil of silence shrouds this tragic outcome. We do well to respect that.

APPENDIX: A RESPONSE TO JAMES DUNN'S IDEAL COSMIC CHRISTOLOGY

The most challenging modern alternative to traditional Christology is ideal Christology, represented in the work of James D. G. Dunn.[54] While can-

---

[53]See R. B. Gaffin Jr., "Glory, Glorification," *DPL* 348-50.
[54]Dunn, *The Theology of Paul the Apostle*, pp. 182-293.

didly acknowledging that a face-value reading of Paul yields a Christology involving preexistence, mediatorship in creation and incarnation, he questions whether this was really what Paul intended to say. Dunn canvasses the OT and the literature of Second Temple Judaism in order to place Paul's cosmic Christology in its proper context.

His main arguments are as follows. (1) Passages employing "sending" language (Rom 1:3; 8:3; Gal 4:4) are best regarded as indebted to the messenger motif of the OT whereby the prophet was an emissary of Yahweh. Preexistence is not really in view. (2) On closer reading, Paul's language is circumstantially conditioned such that preexistence is not really the point at all. In Galatians 4:4, for example, the emphasis is on soteriology, not Christology. The point is that Jesus, the son of God, and Israel, the firstborn son of God, both had to live under the restraints of the law. In 1 Corinthians 1:24, 30 Paul's description of Christ as God's wisdom derives from "the wayward elitism of the Corinthian 'gnostic' faction,"[55] not any notion of preexistent wisdom. (3) It is scarcely credible that Paul believed in and expected his readers to assume that Christ preexisted, since this would have been such a radical notion at the time. Paul, in accord with Second Temple Judaism, was firmly committed to monotheism, as may be seen in 1 Corinthians 15:27-28, where Jesus is subordinated to God the Father. Dunn posits a developmental theory of the doctrines of preexistence and incarnation in which a bona fide doctrine of incarnation first appears in the prologue of John's Gospel, dated near the end of the first century.[56]

First, Dunn's reconstruction of Pauline cosmic Christology concedes too much to the presuppositions of liberal historical-critical scholarship: (1) he eliminates John's Gospel as a source for ascertaining Jesus' self-understanding; (2) he dismisses the transfiguration narrative in Mark as a literary creation designed to anticipate the resurrection; (3) he nowhere discusses the nature miracles in the Synoptics, suggesting that he does not view them as historical. Each of these methodological moves betrays a failure of nerve.

Second, Dunn's contention that Paul never actually affirmed that the exalted Lord Jesus personally preexisted and had an active role in creation is simply unconvincing. Equating the "sending" language used of Christ with that of OT emissaries of Yahweh diminishes the NT emphasis on the superiority and finality of Christ. He is not simply *primus inter pares* ("first among equals"); he is unique (Rom 9:5; Phil 2:6-11; Col 2:2-3, 9-10; cf. Tit

---

[55]Ibid., pp. 178-79.

[56]I concur with Schreiner's assessment: "Dunn's work is seriously flawed, however, in restricting the notion of preexistence to John. It is fair to say that most scholars have not been convinced by such a thesis" (*Paul*, p. 155).

2:13; Heb 1:1-2; 3:1-6; Mt 5:21-48; 7:21-27; 22:41-46). To be sure, Paul is always careful to affirm monotheism as foundational for his converts (see 1 Cor 8:6; Eph 4:6). But when Dunn admits that cosmic Christology is a plausible interpretation of Paul's affirmations, only to insist that this is not the probable meaning because it would undermine Jewish monotheism, something has misfired.[57] Is there not something new, even unheard of, in Paul's depiction of Christ (see Rom 16:25-27; 1 Cor 1:20-25; 2:6-16; 8:6; 2 Cor 5:16-21; 8:9; Phil 3:7-11; Col 1:25-27; cf. Eph 3:7-13; 1 Tim 3:16)?[58]

Third, is it credible that the one whom many consider to be the greatest interpreter of the significance of Christ never affirmed cosmic Christology because he lived in a time not yet ready intellectually and spiritually to take the next step?[59] Dunn's attempt to reconstruct a trajectory of developing cosmic Christology owes more to speculation than substantiation.

The problem with Dunn's explication of Paul's cosmic Christology in Colossians 1:15-20 lies not in what he affirms but rather in what he fails to affirm. To say that God intended from the beginning that Jesus should embody all that humanity was meant to be surely reflects a biblical emphasis. It just does not say enough. Dunn's hypothesis constricts the meaning of Paul's cosmic Christology by a dubious assumption concerning what Paul would have been able to believe as a committed Jewish Christian monotheist living before the (also dubious) remarkable intellectual breakthrough during the last quarter of the first century A.D.

FOR FURTHER DISCUSSION

1. Why is the affirmation that Jesus is Lord central to Christianity?

2. Why is cosmic Christology embarrassing for many modern theologians?

3. Is trinitarian theology really implicit in Paul's letters?

4. Can Christianity and Judaism find common ground on the question of Christology?

5. Why is the "rapture" so contentious an issue in evangelical circles?

---

[57]In my view, Larry Hurtado, *Lord Jesus Christ: Devotion to Jesus in Earliest Christianity* (Grand Rapids: Eerdmans, 2003), does more justice to the evidence.

[58]See Oscar Cullmann, *The Christology of the New Testament* (rev. ed.; Philadelphia: Westminster Press, 1963), p. 5; Hurtado, *Lord Jesus Christ*.

[59]Martin Hengel is a more reliable guide on this point: "One is tempted to say that more happened in this period of less than two decades (30s and 40s) than in the whole of the next seven centuries, up to the time when the doctrine of the early church was completed" (*The Son of God: The Origin of Christology and the History of Jewish-Hellenistic Religion*, trans. John Bowden [London: SCM Press, 1976], p. 2).

6. Does Paul's teaching on judgment by works compromise salvation by faith alone?

7. Is Paul's position on the fate of the wicked consistent with his view of God's mercy?

For Further Reading

Pauline Christology

Bruce, F. F. *Paul, Apostle of the Heart Set Free*, pp. 95-125. Grand Rapids: Eerdmans, 1977.

Cole, R. A. "Son of God." *ZPEB* 5:48-85.

Dunn, James D. G. *The Theology of Paul the Apostle*, pp. 182-293. Grand Rapids: Eerdmans, 1998.

Fee, Gordon D. *Pauline Christology*. Peabody, Mass.: Hendrickson, 2007.

Guthrie, Donald. *New Testament Theology*, pp. 248, 295-99, 317-19, 333-39, 343-60. Downers Grove, Ill.: InterVarsity Press, 1981.

Ladd, George E. *A Theology of the New Testament*, edited by Donald A. Hagner, pp. 448-63. Rev. ed. Grand Rapids: Eerdmans, 1993.

Hurtado, Larry W. *One God, One Lord: Early Christian Devotion and Ancient Jewish Monotheism*. Philadelphia: Fortress, 1988.

———. "Lord. " *DPL* 560-69.

———. "Son of God." *DPL* 900-906.

———. *Lord Jesus Christ: Devotion to Jesus in Earliest Christianity*. Grand Rapids: Eerdmans, 2003.

Machen, J. Gresham. *The Origin of Paul's Religion*, pp. 120-36. Grand Rapids: Eerdmans, 1947.

Marshall, I. Howard. *The Origins of New Testament Christology*. Downers Grove, Ill.: InterVarsity Press, 1976.

———. *New Testament Theology*, pp. 425-29, 459-60. Downers Grove, Ill.: InterVarsity Press, 2004.

Morris, Leon. *New Testament Theology*, pp. 39-55. Grand Rapids: Zondervan, 1986.

Moule, C. F. D. *The Origin of Christology*. Cambridge: Cambridge University Press, 1977.

Schnelle, Udo. *Apostle Paul: His Life and Theology*, translated by M. Eugene Boring, pp. 410-77. Grand Rapids: Baker, 2005.

Schreiner, Thomas R. *Paul, Apostle of God's Glory in Christ: A Pauline Theology*, pp. 151-88. Downers Grove, Ill.: InterVarsity Press, 2001.

Thielman, Frank. *Theology of the New Testament*, pp. 452-62, 375-81. Grand Rapids: Zondervan, 2005.

Wenham, David. *Paul: Follower of Jesus or Founder of Christianity?* pp. 116-24. Grand Rapids: Eerdmans, 1995.

Witherington, Ben, III. "Christology." *DPL* 100-115.

Pauline Eschatology

Dunn, James D. G. *The Theology of Paul the Apostle*, pp. 294-315. Grand Rapids: Eerdmans, 1998.

Guthrie, Donald. *New Testament Theology*, pp. 803-10; 828-40; 856-63; 879-82; 890-91. Downers Grove, Ill.: InterVarsity Press, 1981.

Kreitzer, L. J. "Eschatology." *DPL* 253-69.

————. "Intermediate State." *DPL* 438-41.

————. "Resurrection." *DPL* 805-12.

Ladd, George E. *A Theology of the New Testament*, edited by Donald A. Hagner, pp. 595-614. Rev. ed. Grand Rapids: Eerdmans, 1993.

Morris, L. "Man of Lawlessness and Restraining Power." *DPL* 592-94.

Ridderbos, Herman. *Paul: An Outline of His Theology*, pp. 487-562. Grand Rapids: Eerdmans, 1975.

Schnelle, Udo. *Apostle Paul: His Life and Theology*, translated by M. Eugene Boring, pp. 577-97. Grand Rapids: Baker, 2005.

Schreiner, Thomas R. *Paul, Apostle of God's Glory in Christ*, pp. 453-84. Downers Grove, Ill.: InterVarsity Press, 2001.

Wenham, David. *Paul: Follower of Jesus or Founder of Christianity?* pp. 289-337. Grand Rapids: Eerdmans, 1995.

Witherington, Ben, III. *Jesus, Paul, and the End of the World.* Downers Grove, Ill.: InterVarsity Press, 1992.

PART FOUR

THE THEOLOGY OF JOHN

9

The Johannine Portrayal
of the Person
and Work of Christ

*I have spent many years in the study of the fourth Gospel
and have reached the highly unoriginal conclusion that it is a
complex and difficult book.*

Leon Morris

*John's Gospel, together with the letter to the Romans, can
justifiably be called "the Mount Everest of NT theology."*

Andreas Köstenberger

*The Johannine writings constitute a microcosm of early
Christianity, and a microcosm of the final defining documents of biblical theology.*

D. A. Carson

*More than any other New Testament writer, John offers the
material for a total picture of what the Christian revelation means. Only he has given us both a Gospel and a set
of teaching epistles, probably in addition to the prophecy of
Revelation. Thus we can gain from him not only a profound
and impressive portrait of Jesus of Nazareth but an almost
full-orbed view of the Christian life.*

J. Ramsey Michaels

MY THIRD AND FINAL WITNESS TO THE THEOLOGY of the NT is the apostle
John. According to early church tradition, John was the longest-surviving
member of the twelve apostles (Eusebius *Hist. eccl.* 3.23).[1] I think it fitting
that he, the last of that privileged circle who "looked at and touched with
[their] hands . . . the word of life" (1 Jn 1:1), should have the last word. With
his passing, we enter the postapostolic age. But John's significance transcends being merely the last witness; his theological contribution is enormous. No other apostle provides so comprehensive a presentation of the
gospel: "faith in the Gospel, love in the Epistles, hope in the Apocalypse."[2]
Considered by itself, "the Fourth Gospel is by common consent one of the
most important books that has ever been written. Its influence in the Christian church and beyond it has been incalculable."[3]

THE PROBLEM OF AUTHORSHIP

Once again, critical problems confront the reader.[4] In the first place, who
is John? Traditions as early as the second century identify the "disciple
whom Jesus loved" (Jn 13:23; 19:26; 20:2; 21:7, 20) as John the son of
Zebedee, one of the twelve apostles. By the fourth century, the Western
church is nearly unanimous that he wrote the Gospel of John, 1-3 John
and Revelation.[5] This tradition has, however, with few exceptions, been
rejected by modern critical scholarship.[6] Although many conservative
scholars still attribute all five documents to John the son of Zebedee,
some express doubts about Revelation. Although many critical scholars
acknowledge that John's Gospel and 1 John demonstrate enough similar-

---

[1]A tradition perhaps inferred from the epilogue to John's Gospel (Jn 21:20-23) correcting
the false rumor that the beloved disciple would survive until Jesus' return.

[2]A. Schlatter, *Die Briefe und die Offenbarung des Johannes* (Stuttgart: Calwer, 1950), p.
127, cited in Donald Guthrie, *New Testament Introduction* (Downers Grove, Ill.: InterVarsity Press, 1974), p. 949 n. 1.

[3]Leon Morris, *New Testament Theology* (Grand Rapids: Zondervan, 1986), p. 225.

[4]"In this 'child of sorrow of New Testament scholarship' just about everything is disputed"
(Eduard Schweizer, *A Theological Introduction to the New Testament*, trans. O. C. Dean
Jr. [Nashville: Abingdon, 1991], p. 149).

[5]See *Barnabus* 5:9-11; Justin Martyr (ca. A.D. 100-165), *Dialogue with Trypho* 81; Clement
of Alexandria (A.D. 155-220) as cited in Eusebius (A.D. 260-340), *Historia ecclesiastica*
6.14.7; Irenaeus (ca. A.D. 135-202), *Against Heresies* 1.8.5; 1.16.3; 2.22.5; 3.1.1; 3.3.4;
3.16.5, 8; Muratorian Canon (a list of twenty-two books accepted by the churches as canonical in about A.D. 200 [some scholars date it to A.D. 400]); Origen (ca. A.D. 185-254)
as cited in Eusebius, *Historia ecclesiastica* 6.25. For a summary of the ecclesiastical traditions about John, see Raymond F. Collins, who nevertheless concludes that John the son of
Zebedee probably did not write any of them ("John [Disciple]," *ABD* 3:885-86).

[6]John A. T. Robinson, hardly a conservative theologian, bucks the trend and presents a good
case for the traditional view in *Redating the New Testament* (Philadelphia: Westminster
Press, 1976), pp. 254-311.

ity to emanate from a common background or milieu, they prefer a "Johannine school" rather than a single author.[7] Very few critical scholars include Revelation as a work of this school.[8]

There is insufficient space here for a full treatment of the problem of authorship, an issue intertwined in the related questions of provenance, sources and purpose. I can only summarize the situation. The modern critical rejection of the traditional view boils down to two basic objections. (1) How could a Palestinian Jew, an "uneducated and ordinary" man (Acts 4:13), write the Gospel and letters that now bear the name of John?[9] And how could the same author write Revelation, given that it is so very different in language and outlook? (2) Does it seem likely that the apostle John would refer to himself as "the one whom Jesus loved"?[10] To be sure, other arguments against the traditional view are advanced: the Fourth Gospel itself is anonymous; theological differences between the Gospel and the letters are said to be pronounced; 2 John and 3 John are in fact attributed to "the elder" and are so similar to 1 John in language, literary style and ideas that all three should be attributed to this anonymous individual or the community represented by him. None of these additional objections, however, carries quite the weight of the first two.

Nonetheless, a credible case can be argued for the traditional authorship of all five documents on the grounds of both internal and external evidence. In short, the internal evidence, though not without problems, does not overturn the traditional ascription, especially if one nuances the notion of apostolic authorship.[11] As already indicated, the external evidence, the

---

[7]See Robert Kysar, "Community and Gospel: Vectors in Fourth Gospel Criticism," in *Interpreting the Gospels*, ed. James L. Mays (Philadelphia: Fortress, 1981), p. 277.

[8]"It is one of the most certain results of New Testament scholarship, however, that Revelation cannot come from the same author as the four other writings handed down under the name of John (cf. the introductions to the New Testament)" (Werner G. Kümmel, *The Theology of the New Testament according to Its Major Witnesses: Jesus-Paul-John*, trans. John E. Steely [Nashville: Abingdon, 1973], p. 255).

[9]Kümmel argues, "Acts 4:13 reports that Peter and John were ἄνθρωποι ἀγράμματοι ('illiterate men'); yet Jn is written in Greek that is good, though semitizing. The authorship of Jn by John the son of Zebedee is thus out of the question" (*Theology of the New Testament*, p. 245). But Robinson rightly points out that "the lack of education attributed to John and Peter . . . need indicate no more than that in their professional eyes these were 'untrained laymen' (NEB), a view shared by the authorities both of Jesus (John 7.15; cf. 9.29) and of Paul (Acts 21.37f.). The astonishment was that *despite* this they showed themselves so articulate" (*Redating the New Testament*, pp. 300-301).

[10]"Perhaps the most frequently advanced reason for denying that the beloved disciple is the evangelist lies in the expression 'beloved disciple' itself. It is argued that no Christian would call him- or herself 'the disciple whom Jesus loved'" (D. A. Carson and Douglas J. Moo, *Introduction to the New Testament* [Grand Rapids: Zondervan], p. 241).

[11]"There are no irrefutable historical grounds for rejecting the identification of the beloved

earliest traditions dating to the second century A.D., attributes authorship to John the apostle. I assume the traditional view. The interested reader may pursue the detailed arguments elsewhere.[12]

JOHANNINE CHRISTOLOGY

To use a space-age analogy, John's Christology takes orbit. We gaze in wonder at a majestic portrait filling the "big screen." A kaleidoscope of images meld together: the eternal Logos, the light and life of the world, apart from whom nothing has been made; the Son who proceeds from the Father, reveals the Father, and incorporates his own into the Father; the Lamb of God who takes away the sin of the world; the good shepherd who gives his life for the sheep and embodies the meaning of love; the water of life who quenches all spiritual thirst, the bread of life who satisfies all spiritual longings; the Alpha and Omega who transcends all conceivable limitations and inhabits an eternal now. The great cosmocrater stands unveiled before us. No wonder the writings of John are perennial favorites. With deceptive simplicity they lead us away from the shoreline only to drop us into the depths of theological reflection.[13]

In what follows, the perceptive reader will observe that my treatment blurs the person and work of Christ in John's Gospel. This is almost unavoidable because John, more than any other Gospel writer, refuses to make a sharp distinction. In other words, it is a hallmark of Johannine thought that *who Jesus is* is discerned by *what Jesus does*.[14] The "I am"

---

disciple as John the son of Zebedee" (Guthrie, *New Testament Introduction*, p. 249), and "no argument has ever been advanced to show the *impossibility* of the author being John the Apostle" (Gary Burge, *Interpreting the Gospel of John* [Grand Rapids: Baker, 1992], p. 45).

[12]For the case against John the apostle as author, see Werner G. Kümmel, *Introduction to the New Testament*, trans. Howard Clark Kee (rev. ed.; Nashville: Abingdon, 1975), pp. 188-246, 442-45, 469-74; M. M. Thompson, "John, Gospel of," *DJG* 368-70; Richard Bauckham, *Jesus and the Eyewitnesses: The Gospels as Eyewitness Testimony* (Grand Rapids: Eerdmans, 2006), pp. 358-471. For a thorough defense of the traditional view, see B. F. Westcott, *Commentary on the Gospel According to St. John* (1882; reprint, Grand Rapids: Eerdmans, 1958); Guthrie, *New Testament Introduction*, pp. 237-335, 864-69, 876-83, 884-90, 934-49; Carson and Moo, *Introduction to the New Testament*, pp. 229-54, 670-75, 700-707.

[13]Archibald Hunter puts it this way: "His Gospel still speaks to the condition of sage and simple, serving at once as 'the text-book of the parish priest' and a divine philosophy for a Wordsworth or a Westcott" (*Introducing New Testament Theology* [Philadelphia: Westminster Press, 1957], p. 125).

[14]Larry Kreitzer insists, "It is crucial that we do not set what God *does* and who he *is* at odds with each other in this regard" (*The Gospel According to John* [RSG 1; Oxford: Regent's Park College, 1990], p. 10). See also G. Kittel, "λέγω," *TDNT* 4:129; Bultmann, *Theology of the New Testament*, 2:60.

sayings found in John's Gospel make the point. The bread of life (Jn 6:35, 41, 48), the light of the world (Jn 8:12), the door of the sheep (Jn 10:7, 9), the good shepherd (Jn 10:11, 14), the resurrection and the life (Jn 11:25), the way and the truth and the life (Jn 14:6), and the vine (Jn 15:1, 5) combine inseparably Christ's person and mission. They resist neat compartmentalization into the categories of Christology and soteriology. Jesus is a missionary on a mission.

The Johannine writings along with Paul's prison letters present the highest Christology of the NT. Throughout appear the lineaments of a divine-human being who sits comfortably alongside God and shares his attributes. The familiar outline of preexistence, active role in creation and sovereignty over all creation, already sketched in Paul, reappears in the Gospel of John—indeed, in an even clearer and unambiguous manner. Evidences of this high Christology also surface in 1 John and Revelation.

The polemical tone of Johannine Christology. John's Christology bears the earmarks of having been formulated in response to aberrations from apostolic norms. One gets the impression that the implied readers are embroiled in controversy and John is refuting what he considers defective teaching. At the heart of the controversy lies the true nature and identity of Jesus; individuals and groups fail to grasp who he is. The prologue of John's Gospel already anticipates this failure: "He was in the world, and the world came into being through him; yet the world did not know him. He came to what was his own, and his own people did not accept him" (Jn 1:10-11).

The Gospel of John, though sharing a few familiar landmarks with the Synoptics, narrates the story of Jesus in such a way that one can scarcely fail to detect counterblasts here and there aimed at rival viewpoints. John's first letter speaks of those who "went out from us, but they did not belong to us" (1 Jn 2:19). John's second letter warns true believers about "deceivers" who must not be welcomed and shown hospitality (2 Jn 7-10). In Revelation we hear of factions called the "Nicolaitans" (Rev 2:6, 15), those "who hold to the teaching of Balaam" (Rev 2:14), a prophetess called Jezebel who has a number of followers (Rev 2:20-23) and stinging denunciation of self-styled Jews who are called "a synagogue of Satan" (Rev 2:9; 3:9). Clearly, the end of the first Christian century already manifests signs of doctrinal controversies and deviations so characteristic of subsequent Christian church history. These aberrant currents require sorting out.

Incipient Gnosticism. Although the matter is still disputed and scholars interpret the evidence differently, John's writings probably contain a polemic against incipient Gnosticism. At the very least, a majority of scholars detect in John's Gospel and 1 John a polemic against Docetism. Docetism is an early Christian heresy that denies the reality of Jesus' human nature. Docetics (the Greek verb *dokeō* means "seem, appear") rejected the orthodox view of an actual, literal incarnation of the Son of God, arguing that Jesus only "appeared" to be God fully incarnate. Docetism was an essential part of the later full-blown systems of Gnosticism. The Johannine corpus suggests a counterblast against an early form of Gnosticism, an incipient Gnosticism.

John's first letter, because it is more like a doctrinal treatise, best enables us to appreciate the polemical nature of John's Christology. The opening lines establish a point that appears to be contested: a true incarnation of the Son Jesus Christ ("what we have heard, what we have seen with our eyes, what we have looked at and touched with our hands" [1 Jn 1:1-3]). This is made explicit in 1 John 4:2-3a: "By this you know the Spirit of God: every spirit that confesses that Jesus Christ has come in the flesh is from God, and every spirit that does not confess Jesus is not from God." Failure to confess the incarnation carried with it a radical implication: denial of the reality of Jesus' sacrifice on the cross for sin (1 Jn 1:7; 2:2; 3:16; 4:10; 5:6). In fact, it appears that the false teachers made exaggerated claims of moral perfection, claims that John emphatically denies (1 Jn 1:6—2:11; 3:4-10; 5:2-3); indeed, he pointedly condemns those who advance such claims and places them beyond the pale of grace and forgiveness (1 Jn 5:16-17).

Interestingly, the features of the heresy that 1 John combats show some similarity to second-century gnostic teaching. For this reason, many NT scholars have argued that an incipient form of Gnosticism was already taking shape at the end of the first Christian century. The Johannine writings make good sense against such a backdrop.[15]

The Gospel of John contains passages seemingly directed against "gnosticizing" tendencies. The prologue immediately comes to mind. The climax of this amazing passage, which some have labeled a "Logos hymn," comes in John 1:14: "And the Word became flesh and lived among us, and we have seen his glory, the glory as of a father's only son, full of grace and truth."[16] The Greek word rendered "flesh" *(sarx)* draws attention to the very material, weak and limited nature of what it means to be human. John uses *sarx* in his Gospel several times in opposition to that which is divine (Jn 3:6;

---

[15]See D. M. Scholer, "Gnosis, Gnosticism," *DLNTD* 400-412.

[16]On the form and function of the prologue, see G. R. Beasley-Murray, *John* (2nd ed.; WBC 36; Dallas: Word, 1999), pp. 3-4; Ernst Käsemann, "The Structure and Purpose of the Prologue to John's Gospel," in *New Testament Questions of Today* (Philadelphia: Fortress, 1969), pp. 138-67. For the intriguing suggestion that all or part of the prologue was an actual hymn sung by early Asian Christians mentioned by Pliny the Younger, see Michaels, *The New Testament Speaks*, p. 390.

6:63; 8:15). This ringing affirmation of the real humanity of the Son probably does not just come "out of the blue." Given what we already saw in 1 John, this statement seems directed at those who reject a real incarnation—in short, Docetics. James Dunn describes John's assertion as "shocking," "scandalous," "needlessly offensive," and "deliberately and provocatively directed against any docetic spiritualization of Jesus' humanity, *an attempt to exclude docetism by emphasizing the reality of the incarnation in all its offensiveness.*"[17]

A careful examination of John's Gospel for other clues strengthens this claim. The narrative of the Samaritan woman in John 4 is a case in point. Jesus is "tired out by his journey" and requests a drink of water (Jn 4:6-7). The divine Christ shares in the limitations of all human beings. Another well-known text, the shortest verse in the Bible, John 11:35, speaks volumes, despite its brevity, about the human condition: "Jesus began to weep." John alone among the evangelists records Jesus saying from the cross, "I am thirsty" (Jn 19:28).

But especially in passages where the implied author inserts commentary, a polemical thrust against Docetism becomes apparent. The dramatic scene at the foot of the cross makes the point loudly and clearly: "But when they came to Jesus and saw that he was already dead, they did not break his legs. Instead, one of the soldiers pierced his side with a spear, and at once blood and water came out. (He who saw this has testified so that you also may believe. His testimony is true, and he knows that he tells the truth.)" (Jn 19:33-35). One could hardly be more emphatic that a real death occurred. Docetics held that the divine Christ did not really suffer and die on the cross; the Gospel of John resolutely refutes this.[18] Another uniquely Johannine episode makes the same point. "Doubting" Thomas refuses to believe until he can "see the mark of the nails in his hands, and put [his] finger in the mark of the nails and put [his] hand in his side" (Jn 20:25). A week later, he is bidden to do precisely that (Jn 20:27), and this leads to the climax of the book and the exalted confession "My Lord and my God!" (Jn 20:28). To these passages another should be added: the postresurrection appearance narrated in the epilogue. On that occasion (Jn 21:1-14), Jesus breakfasts with seven of his disciples along the shore of the Sea of Tiberias. The narrator mentions explicitly that Jesus ate with them (Jn 21:13). No

---

[17]James D. G. Dunn, *Unity and Diversity in the New Testament* (London: SCM Press, 1977), pp. 300-301. See also E. Schweizer, "σάρξ," *TDNT* 7:139; Everett F. Harrison, "A Study of John 1:14," in *Unity and Diversity in New Testament Theology: Essays in Honor of George E. Ladd*, ed. Robert A. Guelich (Grand Rapids: Eerdmans, 1978), p. 26.
[18]See D. F. Wright, "Docetism," *DLNTD* 306-9.

mere phantom here! The evidence clearly points to a refutation of a docetic or gnostic faction as one purpose of John's Gospel.

Polemic against a John the Baptist sect. Another, perhaps related, polemic in the Gospel of John surrounds the figure of John the Baptist. The Synoptics give a brief account of his ministry, but in the Gospel of John the Baptist plays a distinctly different and more expansive role. He now becomes the first confessor of Jesus as the Messiah (Jn 1:6-9) and personally testifies to his own subservient role not once, but twice (Jn 1:19-34; 3:22-36). Why such emphasis upon the Baptist denying that he is the Messiah unless there were those who thought he was? Some evidence from the NT and extrabiblical sources suggest that a rival group continued for some time to maintain a messianic status for John the Baptist. Two Gospel passages seem to reflect disgruntled feelings on the part of the Baptist's disciples (Jn 4:1-2; Mk 2:18 pars.). According to Acts, Paul encounters disciples of John the Baptist in Ephesus on his third missionary journey (Acts 19:1-7). A Jewish Christian source from the fourth century A.D. claims that there was a group that proclaimed John the Baptist as the Messiah.[19] There is still a gnostic sect of some fifteen thousand followers in Iraq and Iran today, the Mandaeans, who revere John the Baptist as one of their prophets or priests. Whether there is any direct connection between a first-century Baptist sect and the Mandaeans, however, is uncertain.[20]

Polemic against the synagogue. There can be little doubt, however, that a major debate centers on Jesus' relationship to Judaism.[21] Already annunciated in the prologue, Jesus transcends the legacy and traditions derived from Moses: "The law indeed was given through Moses; grace and truth came through Jesus Christ" (Jn 1:17). As Everett Harrison points out, "John is introducing the λόγος as the one who transcends the Torah, for he is God's final Word to men, one who not only declares the truth with authority and finality but who exhibits it in his life. . . . The adulation of the Torah is a well-known feature of late Judaism. It is strikingly evident that John's statements regarding the λόγος are couched in such a way as to

---

[19] "Yea, some even of the disciples of John, who seemed to be great ones, have separated themselves from the people, and proclaimed their own master as the Christ. But all these schisms have been prepared, that by means of them the faith of Christ and baptism might be hindered" (*Recognitions of Clement* 1.54).

[20] See E. M. Yamauchi, "Mandaeism," *IBDSup* 563; Kurt Rudolph, Mandaeism," *ABD* 4:500-502.

[21] "The Gospel is primarily concerned with the interaction between Jesus and Judaism, particularly as represented by the Jewish leader, the priests and the Pharisees" (I. Howard Marshall, *New Testament Theology* [Downers Grove, Ill.: InterVarsity Press, 2004], p. 512).

point to the extravagant claims of the Jews for the Torah, as though to say that these exaggerated claims should now be laid aside."[22]

John's portrait of Jesus.

Jesus the prophet. During Second Temple times an expectation existed of a great prophet like Moses who would arise and be involved in the final restoration of Israel. Several passages in John's Gospel refer to an eschatological figure called "the prophet." This expectation apparently derives from Deuteronomy 18:15: "The LORD your God will raise up for you a prophet like me from among your own people; you shall heed such a prophet." In some circles this prophet was identified with Elijah *redivivus* ("come back to life") (Mal 3:1-4; 4:5-6; Sir 48:10; 1 Macc 14:41; 1QS 9:11; 4Q175; 4Q521). The delegation dispatched from Jerusalem wants to know if John the Baptist claims to be the Messiah, Elijah or "the prophet" (Jn 1:21, 25). The Samaritan woman thinks that Jesus is a prophet; indeed, she wonders if he is "the Messiah" (Jn 4:29).[23] Jesus seems to include himself within the class of prophets in the saying "A prophet has no honor in the prophet's own country" (Jn 4:44), perhaps drawn from the Q source (Mt 13:57; Lk 4:24). After the miracle of the feeding of the five thousand, the crowd exclaims, "This is indeed the prophet who is to come into the world" (Jn 6:14). At the climax of the Festival of Booths, Jesus dramatically invited those who were thirsty to come to him (Jn 7:37). At this, some cried out, "This is really the prophet" (Jn 7:40), though others were convinced that he was the Messiah (Jn 7:41). Finally, the man born blind, whom Jesus healed, when asked who he thought Jesus was, offered this assessment: "He is a prophet" (Jn 9:17). What is clear in John's presentation is that Jesus certainly possesses prophetic gifts and properly stands within the great prophetic tradition of Israel, but he is much more than a prophet; indeed, he is much more than even the luminaries Moses and Elijah—he transcends these traditional categories.[24] It is this "much more" that constitutes a challenge to Judaism.

Such a direct challenge to the very foundation of Judaism highlights a major purpose of John's Gospel. The first of Jesus' seven signs performed

---

[22]Harrison, "A Study of John 1:14," p. 35.

[23]Samaritan eschatology expected a messianic figure, the Taheb, or "restorer," obviously a non-Davidide, functioned much like a Moses *redivivus*. See Dietmar Neufeld, "'And When That One Comes': Aspects of Johannine Messianism," in *Eschatology, Messianism, and the Dead Sea Scrolls*, ed. Craig A. Evans and Peter W. Flint (Grand Rapids: Eerdmans, 1997), pp. 132-33; R. T. Anderson, "Samaritans," *ISBE* 4:307; idem, "Samaritans," *ABD* 5:946.

[24]See M. M. Thompson, "John, Gospel of," *DJG* 378-79.

in John's Gospel, changing of water to wine (Jn 2:1-11), symbolically implies the inferiority of first-century Judaism to the new message of Jesus. The cleansing of the temple strongly suggests that Jesus himself replaces the temple, the central monument of Judaism (Jn 2:21). Nicodemus, a Pharisee and "leader of the Jews" (Jn 3:1), and a "teacher of Israel" (Jn 3:10), fails to comprehend Jesus' new teaching about being reborn "from above" (Jn 3:4, 7). The encounter with the Samaritan woman, while emphatically rejecting Samaritan claims to religious superiority vis-à-vis Judaism (Jn 4:22), equally emphatically indicates that both are superseded in a new way of approaching God. Many more examples in John's Gospel make the same point.

Jesus the Messiah of Israel. But that is not all. John's portrait of Jesus radically revises another belief of first-century Judaism. In the prologue we are told that "grace and truth came through Jesus Christ" (Jn 1:17). As we have already noted, "Christ" initially was a title meaning "anointed one," and in Second Temple Judaism generally it referred to the long-expected Davidic scion. Right at the beginning of his Gospel John identifies Jesus of Nazareth as that figure. Near the end of his gospel John declares that his purpose all along has been "that you may come to believe that Jesus is the Messiah, the Son of God, and that through believing you may have life in his name" (Jn 20:31). John here singles out two titles and places them side by side. But as his Gospel narrative makes clear, these traditional titles undergo drastic transformation.[25] Here I will summarize how John accomplishes this.

Following the prologue, the narrative of John's Gospel begins with an emphatic denial by John the Baptist that he is the Christ (Jn 1:20). On the other hand, he refers, somewhat enigmatically, to a person who can scarcely be other than the expected Messiah: "Among you stands one whom you do not know, the one who is coming after me; I am not worthy to untie the thong of his sandal" (Jn 1:26-27). The very next day, to an unspecified group, he explicitly identifies Jesus as the Lamb of God and as "he of whom I said, 'After me comes a man who ranks ahead of me because he was before me'" (Jn 1:29-30). Thus, the opening narrative makes it quite clear who the Messiah is, even if Jesus himself says nothing. This picks up on a statement in the prologue: "He was in the world, and the world came into being through him; yet the world did not know him" (Jn 1:10). John the Baptist's mission was to introduce him to the world, and that he does.

The rest of John's Gospel comes back to this claim again and again.

---

[25]Larry Hurtado speaks about "the profound redefinition of messiahship in early Christianity . . . nowhere more evident than in John" ("Christ," *DJG* 114).

I briefly mention a few episodes to underscore the point. After John the Baptist's dramatic announcement that Jesus is the Lamb of God, Andrew, having spent some time listening to Rabbi Jesus, rushes to find his brother Peter and enthusiastically proclaims, "We have found the Messiah" (Jn 1:41). The following day, Philip assures Nathanael that Jesus is the one "about whom Moses in the law and also the prophets wrote" (Jn 1:45). Nathanael then identifies Jesus as "the Son of God" and "the King of Israel," messianic titles during the Second Temple period (Jn 1:48).[26] To this, Jesus replies that Nathanael will see the "angels of God ascending and descending upon the Son of Man" (Jn 1:51). This latter statement seems to conflate Jacob's vision of the ladder reaching to heaven (Gen 28:12) and Daniel's mysterious vision of "one like a human being" who receives everlasting dominion and worship (Dan 7:13-14). John is demonstrating how Jesus fulfills messianic prophecies of the OT.[27]

Jesus' cleansing of the temple (Jn 2:12-25) probably had messianic connotations.[28] In his encounter with the Samaritan woman (Jn 4:1-42) we have the only recorded instance in which he explicitly told anyone that he was the Messiah ("I am he, the one who is speaking to you" [Jn 4:26]), with the exception perhaps of his trial before the high priest (Mk 14:62; cf. Mt 26:64; Lk 22:70). As we noted earlier, Jesus avoided this title with Jewish audiences because of its political and nationalistic connotations. In John 5 Jesus, after healing an ill man at the pool at Beth-zatha (NIV: Bethesda), engages his critics in a lengthy defense and concludes with this significant condemnation: "You search the scriptures because you think that in them you have eternal life; and it is *they that testify on my behalf*" (Jn 5:39 [my italics]); "If you believed Moses, you would believe me, *for he wrote about me*" (Jn 5:46 [my italics]). This can scarcely be understood as anything less than a messianic claim, harking back to Philip's excited announcement to Nathanael (Jn 1:45). The miracle of the feeding of the five thousand has clear messianic overtones. The multitudes wanted to "take him by force to make him king" (Jn 6:15). As Leon Morris reminds us, "There was a

---

[26]R. S. Anderson notes that "Son of God" is not a common title for the Messiah in pre-Christian Judaism. "One exception is the messianic expectation at Qumran based on Ps 2:7 and 2 Sam 7:14 (4QFlor; cf. 1QSa 2:11f.; 4QPs Dan A)" ("Son of God," *ISBE* 4:572). See also the Synoptic trial accounts, in which the high priest equates the title "Messiah" with "Son of the Blessed One" (Mk 14:61) or "Son of God" (Mt 26:63; Lk 22:67-70). See R. Bauer, "Son of God," *DJG* 769-75, and bibliography cited there.

[27]See Morris, *New Testament Theology*, p. 228. Second Temple texts interpret Daniel 7:13-14 as messianic (*1 En.* 46:1; 48:10; *4 Ezra* 13; cf. *b. Sanh.* 98a).

[28]Edwyn Hoskyns claims that this act is "not merely that of a Jewish reformer; it is a sign of the advent of the Messiah" (*The Fourth Gospel*, ed. F. N. Davey [London: Faber & Faber, 1947], p. 194).

Jewish expectation that when the Messiah would come, the miracle of the manna would be renewed."[29]

In John 7 messianic speculation about Jesus is rife among the Jerusalem pilgrims. As John repeatedly points out in his Gospel, there is a sharp division of opinion about this Galilean prophet. The specific point of contention in John 7 has to do with the origin of the Messiah. Apparently, there were conflicting traditions. Some held that the Messiah must be a Bethlehemite (Jn 7:41-42; see Mic 5:2; cf. Mt 2:4-5), a problem for them because they think that Jesus was born in Nazareth. Others held that his origin would be unknown and his appearance totally unexpected (Jn 7:27). As Morris observes, "Had these objectors really known Jesus' origin as they said they did, they would have had the refutation of their objection. They thought he was just a man from Nazareth."[30]

Other passages in which the question of Jesus' messianic status is prominent include the following: Jesus' claim to be "the light of the world" (Jn 8:12);[31] the mention of excommunication from the synagogues for those who believed that Jesus was the Messiah (Jn 9:22); a pointed demand issued to Jesus by the religious leaders: "How long will you keep us in suspense? If you are the Messiah, tell us plainly" (Jn 10:24); Martha's confession, "I believe that you are the Messiah, the Son of God, the one coming into the world" (Jn 11:27); and to this incomplete listing I add the puzzled response of the crowd to Jesus' announcement about the "lifting up" of the Son of Man: "We have heard from the law that the Messiah remains forever. How can you say that the Son of Man must be lifted up? Who is this Son of Man?" (Jn 12:31-34). Morris nicely summarizes the evidence:

> In every chapter of this Gospel that deals with Jesus' public ministry, the subject of messiahship comes up. A claim may be made or denied, or events may show who Jesus is. But John never lets his readers go for long without some aspect of messiahship coming forward. This is by no means John's only category for interpreting Jesus, but it is a very

---

[29]Morris, *New Testament Theology*, p. 229. Morris cites *2 Baruch* 29:8 as evidence. This early second-century work probably incorporates a tradition that goes back to the first century. See Larry R. Helyer, *Exploring Jewish Literature of the Second Temple Period: A Guide for New Testament Students* (Downers Grove, Ill.: InterVarsity Press, 2002), pp. 422-29.

[30]Morris, *New Testament Theology*, p. 230. This is a clear example of John's intentional irony in his Gospel, something that I will elaborate on below.

[31]A rabbinic source says that "light" is a name of the Messiah (*Echah Rabbathi*, fol. 68.4, cited in John Lightfoot, *A Commentary on the New Testament from the Talmud and Hebraica*, vol. 3, *Luke-John* [1859; reprint, Peabody, Mass.: Hendrickson, 1995], pp. 330-31).

important one. We cannot understand what his Gospel is aiming at unless we see this.[32]

Jesus the Son of God. But John clearly wants his readership to realize that Jewish messianism is quite inadequate to account for who Jesus really is. He is the Messiah, but a Messiah who transcends traditional categories. The primary focus of Johannine Christology is the presentation of Jesus as "the Son of God," or more simply and most often, "the Son." Filial relationship between Jesus and his heavenly Father is a Johannine hallmark.[33] A quick glance at word usage statistics bears this out. In the Synoptics the word *patēr* ("father"), as used of God, occurs four times in Mark, eight or nine times in Q, and twenty-three times in Matthew. By contrast, in John's Gospel we find 106 occurrences. In the entire NT the title "Son of God" occurs eighty times, referring to Jesus. In the Gospel of John alone, however, the title "Son of God" or simply "the Son" occurs twenty-seven times, as compared to seventeen times in the entire Pauline corpus. In addition, Jesus calls himself "the Son of Man" thirteen times in John's Gospel. The absolute phrase "the Son" (ὁ υἱός, *ho huios*) occurs twenty-five times in the Johannine writings in comparison to nine in the Synoptics, one in Paul, and six in Hebrews.[34]

What does John intend to convey by this usage? Jesus' sonship is unique.[35] Only he stands in this special filial relationship to God the Father. Already in the prologue this point is made by the use of *monogenēs,* "only (one of its kind), unique." John uses this term five times in his writings to designate Jesus' relationship to God (Jn 1:14; 18; 3:16, 18; 1 Jn 4:9). To be sure, John calls believers "children," but he does not call them "sons," and of course he uses "only Son" for no one but Jesus (Jn 1:12, 13; 13:33; 1 Jn 3:1-2, 10; 4:4; 5:2, 19). After his resurrection, Jesus says to Mary Magdalene, "I am ascending to my Father and your Father, to my God and your God" (Jn 20:17). Note the careful distinction. Believers are part of God's family, but they do not partake of the unique filial relationship between Father and Son. In short, believers do not become "gods" as in Mormonism. By identifying Jesus as both "the Word" and the "only Son" (Jn 1:14), John makes

---

[32]Morris, *New Testament Theology,* p. 232.

[33]"There are more than a hundred occasions on which Jesus speaks of God as Father, distributed throughout the public ministry and not confined to any particular type of audience. . . . This indeed is the dominant feature in John's Christology and distinguishes it from that of the synoptic gospels" (Guthrie, *New Testament Theology,* p. 312).

[34]F. Hahn, "υἱός," *EDNT* 3:381-87.

[35]See C. F. D. Moule, *The Origin of Christology* (Cambridge: Cambridge University Press, 1977), pp. 22-31; I. Howard Marshall, *The Origins of New Testament Christology* (Downers Grove, Ill.: InterVarsity Press, 1976), pp. 111-25.

it clear that only Jesus truly reveals the Father and his will (see Jn 14:6). There can be little doubt that John views Jesus as truly divine. Quite apart from the mind-boggling prologue, the great high priestly prayer of Jesus places us on "holy ground": "So now, Father, glorify me in your own presence with the glory that I had in your presence before the world existed" (Jn 17:5).[36]

John's first letter is particularly focused on this notion of Jesus as the Son of God. In five short chapters we find no fewer than twenty-one mentions of the Son. The sonship of Jesus is the "central confession expected of believers" (1 Jn 2:22-23; 3:23; 4:15; 5:5, 10, 12-13). As in John's Gospel, so too in 1 John, believers experience fellowship with both the Father and his Son (Jn 17:21-23; 1 Jn 1:3). This fellowship is made possible by the work of the Son, whose blood "cleanses us from all sin" (1 Jn 1:7). Reminding us very much of John's Gospel (Jn 3:16), 1 John 4:9 depicts the mission of the Son as the one sent by the Father: "God sent his only Son into the world so that we might live through him." Just as John the Baptist exclaims in John's Gospel, "the Lamb of God who takes away the sin of the world" (Jn 1:29), so in 1 John this can be stated declaratively: "God . . . sent his Son to be the atoning sacrifice for our sins" (1 Jn 4:10), a sacrifice availing "not for ours only but also for the sins of the whole world" (1 Jn 2:2). According to 1 John, one of the primary purposes of the Son's mission to overcome the evil one (1 Jn 3:8), a point made with dramatic effect in John's Gospel (Jn 12:31; 13:27-30; 14:30-31). As so often occurs in John's Gospel, where we see disputes with the religious leadership in Jerusalem focusing on Jesus' authority to speak and act as he did (Jn 5; 7; 8; 10), so too in 1 John we see emphasis on the Father's testimony validating his Son's mission (1 Jn 5:9-12). Both John's Gospel and 1 John conclude with a clearly stated purpose that strikes the same note: "I write these things to you who believe in the name of the Son of God, so that you may know that you have eternal life" (1 Jn 5:13; cf. Jn 20:31).

Not surprisingly, given its quite different genre and life setting, the title "Son of God" is not prominent in Revelation. But it bears mentioning that the church at Thyatira is addressed by "the Son of God, who has eyes like a flame of fire, and whose feet are like burnished bronze" (Rev 2:18). The descriptive language recalls the inaugural vision of the risen Lord in which Jesus is designated "one like the Son of Man" (Rev 1:13), a title that is functionally very similar in Revelation to "Son of God."

John's presentation of Jesus as the unique Son of God should not be

---

[36]"Nowhere else in the gospels is the mind of Jesus in his filial consciousness so vividly presented" (Guthrie, *New Testament Theology*, p. 315).

diluted in order to be "politically correct" or avoid "the scandal of particularity." Some have attempted to diminish John's high Christology by arguing that "Son of God" conveyed no more than a sense of closeness and fellowship, such as any godly person might experience in his or her relationship to God. This runs counter to the clear intent of John's Gospel. Nowhere in his Gospel does John use "Son" in reference to anyone else but Jesus. And a quick survey of how the title functions in John's Gospel is decisive. As Morris notes, "In a variety of ways John gives expression to the thought that the Father and the Son are so intimately related that what anyone does (or does not do) to the one he does (or fails to do) to the other."[37] One must, for example, believe in the name of the only Son of God in order to be saved (Jn 3:16-18, 36). All things have been placed in the hands of the Son (Jn 3:35). The Son is so intimately connected with the Father that he does "nothing on his own," and "whatever the Father does, the Son does likewise" (Jn 5:19), and "the Father shows him all that he himself is doing" (Jn 5:20). "Anyone who does not honor the Son does not honor the Father who sent him" (Jn 5:23). The oneness that exists between Father and Son is dramatically stated in two affirmations: "The Father and I are one" (Jn 10:30), and "Whoever has seen me has seen the Father" (Jn 14:9). This can be expressed in the form of a crucial question: "Do you not believe that I am in the Father and the Father is in me?" (Jn 14:10). John's Gospel leads us inexorably to the climactic confession, placed on the lips of "doubting" Thomas: "My Lord and my God!" (Jn 20:28).

With few exceptions, the religious leaders of Israel reject the messianic claims of Jesus. Even more adamantly, they refuse to accept him as the unique Son of God: "For this reason the Jews were seeking all the more to kill him, because he was not only breaking the sabbath, but was also calling God his own Father, thereby making himself equal to God" (Jn 5:18; cf. Jn 10:30-33). Nowhere is this refusal more dramatically and ironically portrayed than in the aftermath of the raising of Lazarus: "If we let him go on like this, everyone will believe in him. . . . It is better . . . to have one man die for the people than to have the whole nation destroyed. . . . So from that day on they planned to put him to death" (Jn 11:48-53).

John narrates episodes that pit Jesus against the religious leadership centered in Jerusalem. A series of disputations unfold, focusing on the question of Jesus' authority to say what he was saying and do what he was doing (Jn 5:16-47; 6:41-71; 7:14-52; 8:12-59; 10:22-42). There can be little doubt that

---

[37]Morris, *New Testament Theology*, p. 233.

Excursus: John's Gospel and Anti-Semitism

The negative portrayal of "the Jews" in John's Gospel has brought it center stage in our post-Holocaust world. The reason is obvious: many modern scholars detect in it a strong anti-Judaic, even anti-Semitic, polemic. One cannot deny that John's Gospel has provided anti-Semites grist for their mill. This comes about from several distinctive features. First, there is the frequently occurring designation of Jesus' opponents as "the Jews." This group, persistently refusing to believe, seems to be distinguished from Jesus and his followers. One might even get the impression that Jesus and his disciples were not Jewish. Such an inference would, of course, be quite mistaken. We have already had occasion to note the very Jewish character of John's Gospel in the introductory chapter. Nonetheless, the disparaging way in which "the Jews" are depicted in John's Gospel has provided anti-Semites an appeal to a sacred text in order to denigrate the Jewish people in modern times.

Second, the portrayal of Jews in John's Gospel as children of the devil has been particularly devastating, fueling anti-Semitic attitudes throughout church history and in the modern era. "You are from your father the devil, and you choose to do your father's desires. He was a murderer from the beginning and does not stand in the truth, because there is no truth in him" (Jn 8:44). During the Middle Ages, for example, it was common for Jews to be depicted in both Christian art and graffiti as having horns and tails. The awful venom directed against Jews throughout their history has often been justified by this appalling stereotype. No wonder modern scholars have brought serious charges against the Gospel of John as being a contributor to modern anti-Semitism. How should Christians respond to such accusations?

First, we must acknowledge that not only has John's Gospel been wrongly appropriated by anti-Semites, but also it has the potential to cause great harm if not carefully handled in the church. Second, such an admission should be accompanied by a twofold response: (1) a firm and forceful denunciation of anti-Semitism in all its mutations and perverse attempts at justification; (2) a careful and sensitive use of John's Gospel in church liturgy and instruction. Hearing and teaching John in its historical context is essential if we are to head off false, potentially anti-Semitic attitudes.

This involves close attention to the historical and rhetorical features of John's Gospel that require explanation for a modern audience. When we give such attention, we discover that the Gospel of John views as defective the various expressions of Judaism as these existed in the first century. Whether the Judaism of the masses, Pharisaism, Sadduceanism or a circle associated with John the Baptist, these all fall under the same condemnation: "The light has come into the world, and people loved darkness rather than light because their deeds were evil" (Jn 3:19). Though not directly mentioned in John's Gospel, the Essenes and similar eschatological movements would also certainly receive the same indictment.

But—and this is crucial—John's message is ultimately directed beyond the various sects of Judaism: all people who refuse the gospel stand under the shadow of the evil one, for Jesus is "the light of all people" (Jn 1:4), "the true light, which enlightens everyone" (Jn 1:9). All unbelievers now stand under condemnation (Jn 3:18-20; 1 Jn 2:2). The finality of Jesus Christ shows that anti-Judaism is not what really drives the Gospel of John. The "scandal of particularity" so evident in John is of one accord with the entire NT. In reality, the "problem" of John's Gospel is much greater than anti-Judaism; it is anti-*anything* that rejects the "way, and the truth, and the life" (Jn 14:6; cf. 1 Jn 5:11-12).

Furthermore, we need to remember that the Gospel of John uses rhetoric to denounce opponents that had a long prehistory. That is to say, the OT prophets used harsh, even abusive, language to upbraid their contemporaries for covenant violations (see Is 1:4, 10, 21; 5:18-24; Jer 3:6-10; Ezek 16; 23). The Gospel of John continues this tradition of prophetic critique; it does not mince words. At Qumran the rhetoric of dissent was also shrill. In the *Thanksgiving Hymns* the Teacher of Righteousness refers to his opponents with the following diction: "Violent men have sought after my life because I have clung to Thy Covenant. For they, an assembly of deceit, and a horde of Satan, know not that my stand is maintained by Thee" (1QH[a] 2:21-22 [= 10:21-22]). In 1QH[a] 7:34 (= 15:34) he refers to "the congregation of Vanity" and "the council of the cunning."*

My point is not to justify the use of such rhetoric but rather simply to be aware of the highly charged historical context that produced it. One must, above all, realize that in both the Gospel of John and the Qumran sectarian writings what we see is an internecine debate: Jews accusing other Jews of failing to be the true Israel. For modern Christians to brand Jews with such epithets is quite a different matter. To do so is simply unchristian and deplorable. The teaching of Jesus and his apostles is clear: one must love one's neighbor, even one's enemy (Rom 13:8-10; Gal 5:14; Jas 2:8; 1 Pet 3:13-17), and afford respect for all because all are created in the likeness of God (Rom 13:7; Jas 3:9). Paul insists that Christians "must get rid of all such things—anger, wrath, malice, slander, and abusive language from your mouth" (Col 3:8; cf. Eph 4:29).

In short, great pains must be taken with John's Gospel so that it can be heard in its proper historical setting. Explicit and repeated warnings need to be voiced from pulpit and lectern against transferring the harsh language and lurid imagery of John's Gospel either to the Jewish people as a group or to individual Jews. Once we have done our homework, we discover that John's Gospel is not anti-Semitic; on the contrary, it is a Jewish writing that proclaims a Jewish Messiah as the embodiment of true Israel and the savior of the entire world.[†]

I am fully aware that my position will still be viewed by those in the liberal tradition as anti-Judaic at the very least, if not anti-Semitic. The finality of Christ, the "scandal of particularity," is a burden that evangelicals must bear if we are to remain faithful to the truth revealed in Scripture. Only by a denial of the authority of Scripture can one abandon the uniqueness and finality of Christ. What I want my liberal friends to appreciate is that holding to the finality of Christ neither necessitates nor inevitably facilitates anti-Semitism. I do not deny that there is latent anti-Semitism among some evangelicals. But liberal Christianity's record on this score is not much better. Both wings of Christendom need to close ranks on this issue and address ways of eradicating anti-Semitism in our respective circles.

---

*Translation by Geza Vermes, *The Dead Sea Scrolls in English* (4th ed.; New York: Penguin, 1995), pp. 194, 213.

[†]For further discussion, see J. A. Weatherly, "Anti-Semitism," *DJG* 13-17; Robert Kysar, "Anti-Semitism and the Gospel of John," in *Anti-Semitism and Early Christianity: Issues of Polemic and Faith*, ed. Craig A. Evans and Donald A. Hagner (Minneapolis: Fortress, 1993), pp. 113-27.

John narrates his story with an eye to the increasingly tense and confronta-
tional situation existing between church and synagogue at the end of the first
century, especially in the province of Asia (the Roman province located in
modern western Turkey). Only John tells us, for example, that the Jerusalem
religious authorities threatened expulsion from the synagogue for those who
believed in Jesus of Nazareth as the Messiah (Jn 9:22; 12:42; 16:2). In fact,
tense relations between the two daughter faiths are reflected in Revelation,
where the churches at Smyrna and Philadelphia (in Asia Minor) obviously
are engaged in bitter dispute with neighboring synagogues. At Smyrna John
delivers a prophetic oracle from the risen Lord accusing unbelieving Jews of
slander and describing them as "those who say that they are Jews and are not,
but are a synagogue of Satan" (Rev 2:9). At Philadelphia the oracle prophesies that unbelieving Jews will be humbled in the presence of Christians (Rev
3:9). One still detects tension between unbelieving Jews and Christians in the
letter of Ignatius to Philadelphia (Ign. *Phld.* 6:1 [ca. A.D. 110]).

I conclude that John's presentation of Jesus as the Messiah of Israel,
the one greater than Moses and Elijah, the one who transcends Torah and
temple, the one who is the unique Son of God, forcefully challenges the
beliefs of Jews living at the end of the first century. John's approach is
deliberate and direct. The Johannine community found itself in sharp controversy with a powerful, long-established Jewish community in the major
cities of Asia Minor. John's transformation of the Jesus traditions in his
Gospel clearly reflects this tension and responds to it. But there is still hope
that "his own people" (Jn 1:11), people such as John the Baptist (Jn 1:34),
Andrew (Jn 1:40), Simon Peter (Jn 1:42), Philip (Jn 1:45), Nathanael (Jn
1:49), Martha (Jn 11:27) and many other sons and daughters of Israel,
"may come to believe that Jesus is the Messiah, the Son of God" and "have
life in his name" (Jn 20:31).

The paradoxical shape of Johannine Christology. John's presentation
of Jesus is also distinctive for its emphasis on paradox. A paradox is a
statement that is seemingly false but may nonetheless be true. It refers to
that which is contrary to normal expectations and received opinion. The
Gospel of John abounds in paradox, as do, to a lesser extent, the Johannine Epistles and Revelation. Of course, the prologue of John's Gospel
confronts us immediately with a paradox of immense proportions. How
can a divine being become a human being? This seems self-contradictory.
John unabashedly proclaims its truth. It is precisely in the incarnation, says
John, where the supreme revelation of the glory of God occurs. As has often
been pointed out, in John 1:14 John uses a word, *skēnoō* (literally, "live in
a tent"), that harks back to the tent or tabernacle in which God's visible

presence accompanied the people Israel in their wilderness wanderings (Ex 25:8; 29:45-46). We could render John 1:14 literally as "And the Word became flesh and tabernacled among us." Paradoxically, the glory of God, the *shekinah*, reappears in a human being, Jesus of Nazareth. Rudolf Bultmann nicely captures the significance of this: "This is the paradox which runs through the whole gospel: the 'doxa' ['glory'] is not to be seen *alongside* the 'sarx' ['flesh'], nor *through* the 'sarx' as through a window; it is to be seen *in* the 'sarx' and nowhere else."[38] In short, "the flesh of the Word prohibits recognition of the Word made flesh."[39]

By means of his narrative structure, John highlights the paradoxical nature of Jesus and his mission. Observing the narrative suture lines is the first step in unpacking this uniquely Johannine theological emphasis. John's Gospel falls into four discernible sections: (1) a prologue (Jn 1:1-18), masterfully setting out the leading theme and ideas; (2) a book of signs (Jn 1:19—12:50), unfolding seven signs or pointers that unveil the mystery of Jesus' person and mission; (3) a book of glory (Jn 13:1—20:31), narrating the supreme moment when the glory of the Son is manifested; (4) an epilogue (Jn 21:1-25), narrating a postresurrection appearance, the reinstatement of Peter, and a validation of John's testimony as an eyewitness. On closer inspection, we discern that the book of signs describes a public ministry and corresponds to this statement in the prologue: "He came to what was his own, and his own people did not accept him" (Jn 1:11). By the close of the book of signs, Jesus' rejection is evident: "Although he had performed so many signs in their presence, they did not believe in him" (Jn 12:37). The book of glory, however, is a private ministry directed to the little flock who believe in him and corresponds to this statement in the prologue: "But to all who received him, who believed in his name, he gave power to become children of God" (Jn 1:12). John 13—16, often called the "farewell discourse," is set in the movement from the upper room to the Garden of Gethsemane. John 17 is the Lord's high priestly prayer in the garden, in many ways the "holy ground" of the entire Gospel. John 18—20 then narrates Jesus' arrest, trial and execution, with John 20 bringing both the book of signs and the book of glory to a conclusion in the resurrection appearances.[40]

So much is fairly straightforward. What we need to appreciate, however,

---

[38]Rudolf Bultmann, *The Gospel of John*, trans. G. R. Beasley-Murray (Oxford: Blackwell, 1971), p. 63.

[39]Paul J. Achtemeier, Joel B. Green and Marianne Meye Thompson, *Introducing the New Testament: Its Literature and Theology* (Grand Rapids: Eerdmans, 2001), p. 191.

[40]For a more detailed literary examination of the shape of John's Gospel, see Burge, *Interpreting the Gospel of John*, pp. 57-83.

is how this narrative sequence is actually structured to draw attention to a wonderful paradox. Running throughout the narrative is a thematic device: the "hour of his glory." Viewed in linear fashion, John's Gospel leads us to expect a climactic moment when at last the full glory of the Son of God is unveiled, much like a public unveiling of an official portrait of a famous figure. The book of signs thus functions as a technique whereby we are brought ever closer to the grand moment of disclosure. John sets this up with the very first sign. "Jesus did this, the first of his signs, in Cana of Galilee, and revealed his glory; and his disciples believed in him" (Jn 2:11). Of course, we are expecting that at some point in the narrative there will be a dramatic full disclosure of his glory, a spectacular epiphany, and this not just to a limited circle but rather to the entire world.

The temporal element "my hour" is important in the progression. To his mother's urgent request to help out in an embarrassing social situation Jesus replies, "My hour has not yet come" (Jn 2:4). In other words, there is a divinely determined moment for him to display his glory, and no one may alter or accelerate its occurrence. The reader is thus led to anticipate when this will be. Two times after the miracle at Cana there is a postponement: the hour is not yet come (Jn 7:30; 8:20). Suddenly, at the conclusion of the book of signs, we have the dramatic announcement: "The hour has come for the Son of Man to be glorified" (Jn 12:23). So what happens? Jesus seems to have second thoughts. Should he go through with it (Jn 12:27)? Momentary indecision and inner struggle (very human traits) are followed by determined resolve: "No, it is for this reason that I have come to this hour. Father, glorify your name" (Jn 12:27-28). And what happens next? A voice from heaven, the Father himself, audibly speaks and reassures Jesus that he has and will again glorify his own name, presumably at Jesus' "hour," which now has come (Jn 12:28). But many in the crowd interpret the "voice" as thunder, while others think that perhaps an angel spoke to him (Jn 12:29). As so often happens in John's Gospel, the real meaning of what is happening escapes the listeners. His own simply fail to "get it." The question still remains: when does the "hour" come? The narrative proceeds to narrate a private teaching ministry directed at Jesus' disciples just before Passover. In other words, other than a sound from heaven, variously interpreted by those who heard it, nothing dramatic or spectacular happened.

There is more. The book of glory nowhere explicitly tells us, "And then the Son of Man was glorified." What the reader must do is carefully reread the narrative and look for the moment. The clues are there and can scarcely be missed. The conclusion of the book of signs tells us when the destined moment occurs. It is a moment fraught with paradox and irony. "'And I, when I am lifted up from the earth, will draw all people to myself.' He said this to indicate the kind of death he was to die" (Jn 12:32-33). The moment of glory is the crucifixion, the cross. The execution itself is recounted in John 19:16-42. This is a most unlikely moment for the glory of the Son of Man to be revealed. And yet, what could be more glorious? Both Father and Son are glorified by the mystery of atonement (cf. Jn 12:23 with Jn 12:27-28). The Lamb of God takes away the sin of the world. In retrospect, we see how significant was John the Baptist's testimony (Jn 1:29). This is the central moment of redemptive history, and John has portrayed it with an exquisite sense of paradox. From a human perspective, the cross is gory; from a divine perspective, it is glory. John agrees with Paul that "God's foolishness is wiser than human wisdom" (1 Cor 1:25). If nothing else, Mel Gibson's film *The Passion of the Christ* certainly brought home the gory part. I wish that the film had placed more emphasis on the glory.

What irony that being "lifted up from the earth" conveys a double meaning of exaltation and humiliation.[41] What irony that cynical Caiaphas sarcastically declares, "You do not understand that it is better for you to have one man die for the people than to have the whole nation destroyed" (Jn 11:50). What irony that the only time Jesus is anointed in John's Gospel is in preparation for his burial, not his enthronement (Jn 12:3, 7). What irony that the *titulus* above his head reads, "Jesus of Nazareth, the King of the Jews" (Jn 19:19). Indeed he was, but much more than that. The "King of kings and Lord of lords" (Rev 19:16) reigns from his cross and draws an innumerable multitude into fellowship with himself and the Father (Jn 17). "The way of the cross is the way to the throne of the world."[42] Around the great throne these "drawn ones" cast their crowns at his feet and sing his praises (Rev 7:9-10). And what supreme irony that "the one who alone has the power to grant eternal life . . . must himself die!"[43] Only the eyes of faith penetrate beyond this miscarriage of human justice and wanton cruelty to see a divine "hour" that is the means for taking away the sins of the world. The last word from the cross, pregnant with irony and paradox, says it all: "It is finished" (Jn 19:30). John is a master of paradox, and his portrayal of Jesus' saving work in his Gospel is a literary and theological masterpiece.[44]

---

[41]"There could be no vainer controversy than the dispute whether in these passages the crucifixion or the exaltation is meant. The death is the exaltation" (Vincent Taylor, *The Atonement in New Testament Teaching* [2nd ed.; London: Epworth, 1945], p. 147).

[42]These are the apt words of George Barker Stevens, *The Theology of the New Testament* (New York: Scribner, 1910), p. 200.

[43]Ibid., p. 406.

[44]"John has himself sensed the inevitability of the cross and has skillfully traced the undevi-

Nor does John confine paradox to his Gospel. The genre of apocalyptic is uniquely suited to display the paradoxical nature of Jesus' person and work, and John makes full use of it in Revelation. Nowhere is this more apparent than in the vision of the throne room in Revelation 4—5. Immediately after John's rapture to the heavenly throne room, he begins describing what he sees (quite in contrast to Paul, who was forbidden to do so [2 Cor 12:4]). What John sees is a series of concentric circles surrounding a throne on which sit "the one who lives forever and ever" (Rev 4:10). Arrayed around the throne in these concentric circles are various ranks and orders of angelic beings extending out to "every creature in heaven and on earth and under the earth and in the sea, and all that is in them" (Rev 5:13). In short, the universe revolves around the throne of God—a stunning visual portrayal of God's sovereignty.

Into this scene of worship and adoration John injects a moment of seeming crisis. In the right hand of the one seated on the throne is a mysterious scroll so laden with information that it is written on front and back (in technical language, the recto and verso sides) and sealed with seven seals. The crisis arises when a mighty angel asks, "Who is worthy to open the scroll and break its seals?" (Rev 5:2). The scroll apparently needs to be opened, or else the final destiny of the universe will never be realized. The scroll is a last will and testament, listing the heirs (i.e., the book of life [Rev 3:5; 13:8; 17:8; 20:12, 15]) and describing the inheritance, the climactic phase of the kingdom of God, the new heaven, new earth and new Jerusalem (Rev 21—22). But it also is a sort of doomsday book, narrating end time events leading up to the last judgment (Rev 6—19). Only if the scroll is opened can the kingdom of God fully come (cf. Mt 6:10). But "no one in heaven or on earth or under the earth was able to open the scroll or to look into it," and so John weeps bitterly (Rev 5:3-4). Can it be that the kingdom of God, in which he has so fervently believed and for which he has ministered so long and suffered so much, will never be fully realized on earth? An angelic being, one of the twenty-four elders, assures him that there is one who is worthy to open the scroll: "Do not weep. See, the Lion of the tribe of Judah, the Root of David, has conquered, so that he can open the scroll and its seven seals" (Rev 5:5).

This sets up a moment of supreme irony and paradox. Surely the reader/ listener is prepared for the blare of trumpets, the clash of symbols, the roar of multitudes and a grand entrance the likes of which no Roman emperor could ever imagine or orchestrate. In our contemporary setting we might

---

ating movement of Jesus toward that goal" (Guthrie, *New Testament Theology*, p. 450).

well envision strobe lights, deafening music generated by computers and synthesizers, smoke and mirrors, and writhing masses of screaming partisans. What John delivers is a theological masterstroke. The spotlight falls on the throne. Standing right next to the throne, closer than anyone or anything in the universe, is "a Lamb standing as if it had been slaughtered" (Rev 5:6). The Lion is a Lamb—and a sacrificial lamb at that—displaying the telltale sign of having had its throat slit.[45]

Condensed into this compact scene is an entire theology of redemption. Once again we see Johannine paradox. Where is the moment of glory and grandeur? Is it found in those places the world looks for so vainly, the quest for self-fulfillment, the will to power? The answer lies before us in utter simplicity: the key to the reconciliation of the world lies in a majestic person who lays aside kingly prerogatives and raw power and humbly and sacrificially gives of himself for others.[46] The one who is the "Son of Man" (Rev 1:13), "the first and the last, and the living one (Rev 1:17-18)," "the Alpha and the Omega, the first and the last, the beginning and the end" (Rev 22:13), the Word of God, who was with God and was God in the beginning and through whom all things were made (Jn 1:1), and who brings salvation history to its glorious culmination (Rev 19:13) embodies love (1 Jn 4:16).

Love triumphs over the will to power. There is no "Rambo theology" or "Terminator theology" in John. The cross is not about retaliation and revenge, about smiting one's enemies and casting them down to the dust. To be sure, the cross involves judgment. Those who refuse the gospel invitation already stand under judgment (Jn 3:17-21; 12:31). And the risen Christ will indeed confront the forces of evil with overpowering force at his triumphant return, at which time he will administer retributive justice (Jn 5:27; Rev 18:11-21; 20:9-10). But forgiveness is offered before force is exerted. Love, the motive force that achieves salvation (Jn 3:16), overcomes hate and fear (Jn 3:20; 15:18, 24-25; 1 Jn 2:9, 11; 4:18). Love must necessarily be the *modus operandi* of those who belong to Christ, symbolized by the lowly towel (Jn 13:1-20; 1 Jn 2:3-6; 3:16-24). "Do you know what I have done to you? . . . I have set you an example, that you also should do

---

[45]One thinks here of the well-known altarpiece at Ghent by Jan van Eyck, "Adoration of the Lamb." The flow of blood from the throat of the lamb into a chalice makes vivid the imagery of John.

[46]Charles Ringma extends this countercultural phenomenon to the entire Bible: "The Bible turns our world upside down. Forgiveness, not self-seeking power is the way to life. Servanthood, not exploitation is the way to serve others. Greatness is humility. Transformation comes through a cross, not through might and splendor" (*Whispers from the Edge of Eternity: Reflections on Life and Faith in a Precarious World* [Vancouver: Regent College Publishing, 2005], p. 122).

as I have done to you" (Jn 13:12, 15). In 1 John the love commandment is a leitmotif tying the whole treatise together (1 Jn 2:1-17; 3:11-24; 4:7—5:5). John and Paul are on the same page here (cf. 1 Cor 13; Gal 6:2; Phil 2:5-11; Col 3:12-14; 1 Thess 4:9-10).

J. K. Rowling, in a memorable scene from her novel *Harry Potter and the Half-Blood Prince*, captures at least a glimpse of this profound paradox:

> "But I haven't got uncommon skill and power," said Harry, before he could stop himself.
>
> "Yes, you have," said Dumbledore firmly. "You have a power that Voldemort has never had. You can—"
>
> "I know!" said Harry impatiently. "I can love!" It was only with difficulty that he stopped himself adding, "Big deal!"
>
> "Yes, Harry, you can love," said Dumbledore, who looked as though he knew perfectly well what Harry had just refrained from saying. "Which, given everything that has happened to you, is a great and remarkable thing. You are still too young to understand how unusual you are, Harry."
>
> "So, when the prophecy says that I'll have 'power the Dark Lord knows not,' it just means—love?" asked Harry, feeling a little let down.
>
> "Yes—just love," said Dumbledore.[47]

The primacy of the Word. I conclude my remarks on Johannine Christology with a few words about "the Word." Occurring only in John, this title obviously is a distinctive contribution to NT thought. It has, however, also been a battleground in NT scholarship. Disagreements have arisen about its background and function. Here I briefly survey the issue and attempt to summarize a vast secondary literature.

Background of Logos. The Greek term *logos* occurs in all eras of Greek literature with a wide variety of meanings.[48] Usage includes meanings such as "counting, "reckoning," "calculation," "account," "narrative," "word" and "speech." The last three nuances occur as early as Homer and become very important among the Greek philosophers.[49] For them, the term embodied the principle of rationality that they discerned in the totality of the universe.[50] As Morris observes, "They thought of a Logos, a Word, that

---

[47]J. K. Rowling, *Harry Potter and the Half-Blood Prince* (New York: Scholastic Books, 2005), p. 509.

[48]See Thomas H. Tobin, "Logos," *ABD* 4:348; H. Kleinknecht, "λέγω," *TDNT* 4:77.

[49]For particulars, see A. Debrunner, "λέγω," *TDNT* 4:73-75; Kleinknecht, "λέγω," *TDNT* 4:77-91.

[50]"Although little used in epic, λόγος achieved a comprehensive and varied significance with

runs right through the universe, something like a 'world soul.'"[51]

At first glance, one might think that this is precisely what John has in mind in the prologue to his Gospel. As we noted in the preceding chapter, interpreters in the nineteenth and the first half of the twentieth centuries tended to view John through a Hellenistic lens. John's Gospel, in the words of Adolf von Harnack, evidenced "acute hellenization."[52] It is true that in Heraclitus one finds the idea that individuals are incapable of understanding this Logos, and that in Stoicism the Logos is conceived as an immanent, sustaining "world-reason," but nowhere do we find the notion of the Logos as personal and as resisted by the world of humanity as is so clearly enunciated in John's prologue. Recent scholarship has rather substantially dismissed indebtedness to Greek philosophy, owing in considerable measure to the discoveries at Qumran.[53]

The biblical context of John's prologue once again points back to the OT and its interpretation in Second Temple Judaism. As we already saw in the theology of Paul, the OT personifies the wisdom of God and attributes to it a role in creation, providence and judgment (see Prov 8:22-30). Second Temple literature, most notably in Sirach 24; Baruch 3:9—4:4; Wisdom 7:1—8:21, elaborates on this. Also in the OT appears the more pervasive concept of the word of God, the *dābār* of prophetic revelation that comes to a particular prophet (Jer 1:2, 4; Ezek 1:3; Hos 1:1). This word of God can be portrayed in a highly dynamic, almost personal way: "So shall my word be that goes out from my mouth; it shall not return to me empty, but it shall accomplish that which I purpose, and succeed in the thing for which I sent it" (Is 55:11). But more relevant yet is a passage actually portraying creation by this dynamic word of the Lord: "By the word of the LORD the heavens were made, and all their host by the breath of his mouth" (Ps 33:6).[54] This

---

the process of rationalization which characterized the Greek spirit. Indeed, in its manifold historical application one might almost call it symbolic of the Greek understanding of the world and existence" (Kleinknecht, "λέγω," *TDNT* 4:77).

[51]Morris, *New Testament Theology*, p. 225. Cicero (106-43 B.C.) made this well-known statement about the Logos: "The Logos is the soul of the world, it pervades the universe as honey fills the honeycomb, and links time with eternity" (*De natura deorum* 2.20).

[52]Adolf von Harnack, *Outlines of the History of Dogma*, trans. Edwin Knox Mitchell (Boston: Starr King, 1957), pp. 48-60 (reprint of *History of Dogma* [Boston: Little, Brown, 1902]).

[53]See G. A. Turner, "John, Gospel of," *ZPEB* 3:668; D. M. Smith, "John, Gospel of," *IDBSup* 484; B. Klappert, "Word," *NIDNTT* 3:1116; H. Ritt, "λόγος," *EDNT* 2:357; Kleinknecht, "λέγω," *TDNT* 4:90-91.

[54]T. W. Manson went so far as to say, "It is, I think, indisputable that the roots of the doctrine are in the Old Testament and that its main stem is the dᵉbar Yahweh, the creative and revealing Word of God, by which the heavens and earth were made and the prophets inspired" (*Studies in the Gospels and Epistles* [Philadelphia: Westminster Press, 1962], p. 118).

text clearly is based on the creation account, with its sevenfold "And God said" (Gen 1:3, 6, 9, 14, 20, 24, 26). John begins his prologue, "In the beginning." An allusion to Genesis 1:1 is unmistakable. "The historical figure of Jesus [is identified] with the Word of the divine Creator."[55] Just as God originally spoke creation into existence (Gen 1:3—2:3), so in John's prologue the word of God is the agent through whom creation comes into being: "All things came into being through him, and without him not one thing came into being. What has come into being in him was life, and the life was the light of all people" (Jn 1:3-4).

What is missing, however, in both the OT portrayal of creation by the word of God (Gen 1; Ps 33:6; 147:15-18) and the personification of Woman Wisdom in Jewish wisdom speculation is any notion of personal agency. They speak of an abstraction or personification of God's attribute of wisdom, not a true hypostasis or person. The same may be said for the designation of the creative word of God as *mêmrā'* ("word") in the Targumim (Aramaic paraphrases of the Hebrew Bible) and later rabbinic reflections on Torah.[56] Furthermore, and perhaps decisively, wisdom is expressly said to have been created by the Lord "at the beginning of his work" (Prov 8:22). This falls considerably short of John's astounding declaration "He was in the beginning with God" (Jn 1:2), and even more so of his assertion "the Word was God" (Jn 1:1). The most that can be said is that there is indirect wisdom influence on the prologue.

Some scholars hold that the Logos concept derives from Gnostic circles. According to Bultmann, "The figure of Jesus in John is portrayed in the forms offered by the Gnostic Redeemer-myth which had already influenced the Christological thinking of Hellenistic Christianity before Paul and then influenced him."[57] This hypothesis suffers from two serious objections. First, the full-blown gnostic redeemer myth cannot be dated with certainty earlier than the second century A.D. It looks like Gnosticism was influenced by Christianity on this point, not vice versa. Second, the whole notion of the Logos in John is antithetical to Gnosticism, with its abhorrence of the "flesh."[58]

---

[55]Kittel, "λέγω," *TDNT* 4:131.

[56]The Targumim were handed down orally and not committed to writing until the beginning of the third century A.D. For further discussion of these and the rabbinic comments, see Klappert, "Word," *NIDNTT* 3:1116; Kittel, "λέγω," *TDNT* 4:134-36.

[57]Bultmann, *Theology of the New Testament*, 2:12-13.

[58]See Klappert, "Word," *NIDNTT* 3:1116. Bultmann is aware, of course, that John's presentation of Jesus does not follow the gnostic myth in all details: "It is true that the cosmological motifs of the myth are missing in John, especially the idea that the redemption with which the 'Ambassador' brings is the release of the pre-existent sparks of light which

Some find in Philo of Alexandria a probable source for John's Logos concept.[59] The reason is that a number of characteristics and attributes affirmed of various figures in Hellenistic Judaism are melded by Philo into one being, the Logos. For example, he identifies Jewish wisdom with the Logos, who exercises certain divine prerogatives. Three specific parallels between Philo's Logos concept and the Johannine prologue stand out. First, both authors describe the Logos as an intermediary between God and the cosmos. Second, both distinguish between an eternal Logos and a temporal creation. Third, both employ the same prepositions in order to convey the notion of the Logos as the agent of creation.[60] If one locates John's Gospel and 1 John in the Roman province of Asia toward the end of the first century, perhaps that would explain why he, alone among NT writers, adapted this title for Christ; he was very much aware of the general intellectual milieu.

Still, a word of caution is in order. Despite similarities, significant differences exist between Philo's Logos and John's Logos. "The Philonic Logos is sometimes hypostatized and personified, but it is never personalized. . . . Philo's Logos concept is employed in the interests of a dualistic cosmology that removes God from immediate contact with creation, whereas John uses the Logos concept to bring God in Christ directly into his creation."[61] Furthermore, John's identification of Jesus with the Logos is not the result of his speculation on the prior notions current in Second Temple Judaism such as wisdom, Torah, the primal man and so forth. Nor does it arise from mysticism or even theological reflection on the Synoptic preaching of Jesus as "the word of God." Rather, John arrives at his statement on the basis of a first-hand experience with the Word made flesh. John says, "We have seen his glory" (Jn 1:14). Even more dramatically, and linking the opening of 1 John directly to the prologue of John's Gospel, is the startling announcement "We declare to you what was from the beginning, what we have heard, what we have seen with our eyes, what we have looked at and touched with our hands, concerning the word of life" (1 Jn 1:1).

---

are held captive in this world below by demonic powers"; nonetheless, he maintains that "Gnostic terminology places its stamp mainly on the words and discourses of Jesus" (*Theology of the New Testament*, 2:13).

[59]Klappert avers, "Philo's Logos-doctrine provides the strongest contacts with the Johannine Logos concept. . . . In the question of the origin of the Logos-concept, pre-eminent significance is therefore to be attributed to Hellenistic Judaism" ("Word," *NIDNTT* 3:1116-17). See Craig A. Evans, *Noncanonical Writings and New Testament Interpretation* (Peabody, MA: Hendricksons, 1992), pp. 83-84; Helyer, *Exploring Jewish Literature*, pp. 326-28.

[60]G. E. Sterling, "Philo," *DNTB* 792-93.

[61]George E. Ladd, *A Theology of the New Testament*, ed. Donald A. Hagner (rev. ed.; Grand Rapids: Eerdmans, 1993), p. 277.

An even more important caveat must be registered: John's theological
use of Logos moves in a significantly different direction, which brings us to
the most important part of the discussion: what does John intend to convey
theologically by designating Jesus as the Logos? Several observations are
in order.

1. John employs the Logos title to affirm Christ's preexistence (Jn 1:1-2).
As we already noted, the opening sentence of both John's Gospel and
1 John alludes to the opening sentence of the creation account in Genesis
1: "In the beginning." But John goes well beyond the personification of
Wisdom in Proverbs, since there Wisdom is the first created being (Prov
8:22). The prologue "points behind creation, for the Logos was the agent
of creation."[62] Three other passages in John's Gospel either affirm or imply Jesus' preexistence: (1) "Then what if you were to see the Son of Man
ascending to where he was before?" (Jn 6:62); (2) "Before Abraham was,
I am" (Jn 8:58; cf. Ex 3:14; Deut 32:39); (3) "So now, Father, glorify me
in your own presence with the glory that I had in your presence before
the world existed" (Jn 17:5). The link between Son of Man and Logos is
striking in view of *1 Enoch*, which speaks of a heavenly Son of Man who
is also preexistent (*1 En.* 39:7-8; 48:6; 62:7). Though debated, a good case
can be argued that this section of *1 Enoch*, called the "Similitudes" (*1 En.*
37—71), is pre-Christian.[63] The point is that within apocalyptic Judaism of
the first century there was the notion of a preexistent heavenly being who
descends to earth to establish the kingdom of God. That Jesus preferred
for himself the title "Son of Man" is highly significant and reinforces the
argument that the Logos title likewise carries with it the theological claim
of Jesus' preexistence.[64]

2. John uses the Logos title to affirm Jesus' deity (Jn 1:1). When he says,
"the Word was with God *[ho logos ēn pros ton theon],*" he means "in God's
presence, implying movement toward God and yet distinct from God: it expresses perpetual intercommunication or fellowship."[65] He then goes on to
say, "and the Word was God *[kai theos ēn ho logos].*" A more explicit claim
to deity could scarcely be formulated. The Word possesses the same essence
or nature as God himself. The grammar here is important. A translation
following the precise word order of the Greek reads thus: "and God was the

---

[62]Ibid.

[63]So J. J. Collins, "Enoch, Books of," *DNTB* 316; Helyer, *Exploring Jewish Literature*, pp.
383-86.

[64]"The Johannine use of 'the Son of Man' is distinctive, as compared with that of the Synop-
tists, and, in particular, it adds the dimension of preexistence (3:13, 6:62) which is lacking
in the Synoptic tradition" (Moule, *The Origin of Christology*, p. 18).

[65]G. E. Turner, "Logos," *ZPEB* 3:957.

Word." This is not an accurate translation, however, because it is not what the sentence really means. In Greek there is no article before "God," but there is one before "Word." In English we usually distinguish between the subject and its predicate nominative by word order. In Greek this is usually determined by the presence or absence of the definite article. Since here *theos* is anarthrous (without the definite article), "God" is the predicate nominative even though it precedes the verb; hence the reversed word order in English translations.[66] The significance of the construction is this: "the predicate nominative describes the class to which the subject belongs."[67] The upshot is that "God is more inclusive than the *logos* while the Godhead is not limited to *logos*. The relationship to God is as intimate as language can describe it and still retain individual identity."[68] "If John had used the definite article also with *theos,* he would have said that all that God is, the Logos is: an exclusive identity. As it is, he said that all the Word is, God is; but he implies that God is more than the Word."[69]

3. John affirms that the Logos was the agent of creation: "All things came into being *through* him, and without him not one thing came into being" (Jn 1:3 [my italics]). The preposition used is *dia* ("through, by"), not *ek* ("from, out of"). The former, in certain contexts, is used to denote personal agency or an intermediary; the latter, in certain contexts, denotes the source, origin or cause of something. God the Father is the source of all things; the Word is the personal agent through whom all things came into existence. "It is astonishing that the first-generation Christians who had known Jesus of Nazareth 'after the flesh' could have become convinced that He was also the One who had caused the universe itself to have come into existence."[70] Once again, we see how John and Paul are on the same page theologically (cf. 1 Cor 8:6; Col 1:16).

4. John affirms that the Word became flesh (Jn 1:14). This preexistent divine being who had intimate fellowship with God and possessed a similar nature took on a new nature, human nature. He became a real flesh-and-blood person. This astounding teaching "would amaze and refute all Hellenistic philosophical and Gnostic dualisms that separated God from his

---

[66]This is now called "Colwell's Rule." See E. C. Colwell, "A Definite Rule for the Use of the Article in the Greek New Testament," *JBL* 52 (1933): 12-21. For a lengthy and technical discussion of the proper interpretation of Colwell's Rule, see Daniel B. Wallace, *Greek Grammar Beyond the Basics* (Grand Rapids: Zondervan, 1996), pp. 256-70.

[67]Wallace, *Greek Grammar*, p. 41.

[68]Turner, "Logos," p. 957. See also Wallace, *Greek Grammar*, p. 269.

[69]Ladd, *Theology of the New Testament*, p. 278.

[70]Turner, "Logos," p. 957.

world."[71] John's Logos doctrine is thus fundamentally distinct from that of Philo. For Philo, God is utterly transcendent, the source of the Platonic "ideas," but having no real contact with the material, created order. The latter was brought into existence by the Logos, a second, lesser deity. John, on the other hand, insists that the Word not only created all things but also actually entered into the material world by becoming a real human being.

5. John employs the Logos title to convey the fact that Jesus reveals the true and living God. "No one has ever seen God. It is God the only Son, who is close to the Father's heart, who has made him known" (Jn 1:18; cf. Jn 1:14). This fact, writ large across John's Gospel, prompted Bultmann to declare it as the primary motif.[72] Jesus is the Revealer. Throughout John's Gospel Jesus reveals hidden truths that must be grasped if one is to pass from death to life (e.g., Jn 1:51; 3:3-15; 4:23-24; 5:25-29; 6:26-40). But if one inquires into the specific content of this revelation, a striking truth emerges: fundamentally he reveals himself. He is the supreme revelation of God. The one who sees, hears and obeys Jesus actually sees, hears and obeys God. "Whoever has seen me has seen the Father" (Jn 14:9). God confronts us in Jesus. Bultmann says,

> The astonishing thing . . . is that Jesus' words never convey anything specific or concrete that he has seen with the Father. Not once does he communicate matters or events to which he had been a witness by either eye or ear. Never is the heavenly world the theme of his words. Nor does he communicate cosmogonic or soteriological mysteries like the Gnostic Redeemer. His theme is always just this one thing: that the Father sent him . . . [and] in him the Revelation of God is once for all given to the world, and this Revelation is inexhaustible.[73]

Summary. In a striking and unique way, John invests the Greek word *logos* with new content. In so doing, he makes use of a concept that has meaning and relevance for Hellenistic readers. A more appropriate word choice can scarcely be imagined. By identifying Jesus as the Logos, John masterfully melds the notions of preexistence, creation, providence, revelation and truth. This Logos is personal and most often identified simply as "the Son." And yet, paradoxically, the Son is also flesh, a real human being.

---

[71]Ibid.

[72]Bultmann, *Theology of the New Testament*, 2:11-14. He doesn't go far enough, however, when he claims, "Jesus as the Revealer of God *reveals nothing but that he is the Revealer*" (ibid., 2:66).

[73]Ibid., 2:62-63.

THE WORK OF CHRIST: JESUS' DEATH AS ATONEMENT

My treatment of the person and work of Christ tends to blur the lines of distinction between them. A key issue relating to Johannine soteriology, however, requires separate treatment. Bultmann contends, "In John, Jesus' death has no preeminent importance for salvation, but is the accomplishment of the 'work' which began with the incarnation. . . . The common Christian interpretation of Jesus' death as an atonement for sins is not, therefore, what determines John's view of it."[74] For those who have read John's Gospel, this is a bit jarring. What are we to make of John 3:16 and similar texts in John's writings?

First of all, Bultmann, for all his brilliance, has a distinctive interpretive grid by which he reads the text. Certain Johannine themes and concepts are quite congenial to his existentialist framework, and these he integrates into his theology. Because he is convinced that the gnostic redeemer myth shaped John's presentation, he latches on to themes and motifs that have a gnostic ring. No one quarrels with Bultmann that John casts his Gospel in language that is, at points, compatible with gnostic ideology (I refer the reader back to earlier comments on the polemical nature of John's theology). This, however, is far from proving John's indebtedness to Gnosticism for his basic message. In fact, Gnostics probably borrowed from early Christianity the descent-ascent motif, the "sending" of the Son, the heavenly Redeemer, rather than vice versa.

But what about Bultmann's contention that atonement theology plays little or no part in John's theological understanding? Will this bear up under close scrutiny? In order to maintain his stance, Bultmann resorts to a highly questionable procedure. He admits that there are texts that clearly articulate the early Christian view of the death of Christ as a sacrifice on behalf of others. What he does, however, is dismiss them as John's way of "adapting" himself to early Christian tradition or assign them to an ecclesiastical editor—they are interpolations, not genuine Johannine theology. He then confidently concludes, "Whatever may be the origin of these passages, the thought of Jesus' death as an atonement for sin has no place in John, and if it should turn out that he took it over from the tradition of the Church, it would still be a foreign element in his work."[75] This looks very much like a case of making the evidence fit the theory.[76]

---

[74]Ibid., 2:52-53.

[75]Ibid., 2:54. See further his treatment of the various passages on pp. 53-55.

[76]Marshall observes, "The view of Bultmann that in effect Jesus reveals nothing more than that he is the revealer is superficially plausible but breaks down on closer inspection" (*New Testament Theology*, p. 520).

Taken at face value, John's writings do indeed depict Jesus' death in harmony with the earliest kerygma. Near the beginning of John's Gospel, the Baptist introduces Jesus as the Lamb of God who takes away the sin of the world (Jn 1:29). Like an A-B-A pattern, the scene at the cross returns once again to the initial theme of Jesus' death as a paschal lamb: "These things occurred so that the scripture might be fulfilled, 'None of his bones shall be broken'" (Jn 19:36). Although the classic text John 3:16 ("he gave his only Son") does not explicitly use sacrificial language, it surely echoes the near-sacrifice of Isaac (Gen 22) and thus requires a sacrificial background for comprehension.[77] The saying about Jesus' flesh being "true food" and his blood being "true drink" (Jn 6:51-58), though evoking the Lord's Supper, primarily directs attention to Jesus' death as an atoning sacrifice.[78] Another saying, in John 12:24, also points toward Jesus' death as a sacrifice and does so with characteristically Johannine paradox: "Very truly, I tell you, unless a grain of wheat falls into the earth and dies, it remains just a single grain; but if it dies, it bears much fruit." "The saying . . . carries unmistakable sacrificial implications. There can be no doubt that Jesus was referring to himself under the figure of the seed. He recognized the need for his own approaching death, but he also saw death as a means of multiplication."[79] Although John's Gospel may not highlight Jesus' saving activity in terms of sacrifice, it certainly does include this dimension.

In 1 John three passages clearly depict Jesus' work as an atoning sacrifice. According to 1 John 2:2, Jesus Christ is "the atoning sacrifice for our sins and not for ours only, but also for the sins of the whole world." The Greek word rendered "atoning sacrifice" is *hilasmos,* "a noun of action which generally describes the actions through which atonement is accomplished."[80] The background of this term is rooted in the OT Day of Atonement (Lev 16). Similar is 1 John 4:10: "In this is love, not that we loved God but that he loved us and sent his Son to be the atoning sacrifice *[hilasmos]* for our sins." Especially noteworthy is the divine motive for this action. "This is a remarkable case of God providing the propitiation, a reinterpretation of

---

[77]Kümmel comments, "One may not limit the 'giving' of the Son by the Father to the sending of the Son. Instead, the 'giving up' of the Son to death must also be heard in these words, particularly since just before this (3:14-15), the lifting-up of the Son of Man on the cross and into heaven is identified as the precondition for the reception of eternal life" (*Theology of the New Testament,* p. 298).

[78]"Many see this as a reference to the Christian sacrament, but this is certainly not its primary meaning" (Guthrie, *New Testament Theology,* pp. 452-53).

[79]Ibid.

[80]J. Roloff, "ἱλασμός," *EDNT* 2:186.

the idea which totally transforms it."[81] It is 1 John 1:7, however, that most directly ties the death of Christ with the action of atonement: "The blood of Jesus his Son cleanses us from all sin." Donald Guthrie observes that "the 'blood' must mean the 'death' in common with other NT usage."[82] But we should also be aware that "one cannot . . . simply substitute the death of Christ for the blood of Christ. 'The blood of Christ means more than this. It stresses the close links between the death of Jesus and both his life and his triumph in his resurrection and exaltation.'"[83] To these references should be added 1 John 3:16: "He laid down his life for us." The expression "laid down his life" most likely goes back to the suffering Servant of Isaiah 53:10, a text lying behind the Q saying in Mark 10:45 = Matthew 20:28: "to give his life a ransom for many." The phrase "for us" (the Greek preposition is *hyper*) in 1 John also strongly suggests the notion of substitution.[84]

The book of Revelation, by means of its evocative imagery and symbols, resonates with the idea of Jesus' death as an atoning sacrifice. John's image of Jesus as the "Lamb standing as if it had been slaughtered" (Rev 5:6) is the most dramatic, but by no means only, such reference.[85] In fact, the theme frames and punctuates the entire book. Already, the introductory salutation praises Jesus as the one "who loves us and freed us from our sins by his blood" (Rev 1:5). Right after the Lamb takes the scroll from the one seated on the throne, the twenty-four elders praise the Lamb: "You were slaughtered and by your blood you ransomed for God saints from every . . . people and nation" (Rev 5:9). Revelation 7, the vision of the redeemed safely gathered around the throne, depicts the saints as those who "have washed their robes and made them white in the blood of the Lamb" (Rev 7:14), another striking instance of John's irony. Revelation 12, a vision compressing the entire redemptive drama into a compact vignette, climaxes with a heavenly victory proclamation (Rev 12:10-12). Those who share in the Messiah's victory over the dragon overcome "by the blood of

---

[81]Guthrie, *New Testament Theology*, p. 475.

[82]Ibid.

[83]F. Laubach, "Blood," *NIDNTT* 1:224 (Laubach is quoting H.-J. Iwand, in *Religion in Geschichte und Gegenwart*, ed. K. Galling [3rd ed.; 7 vols.; Tübingen: Mohr Siebeck, 1957-1965], 1:1330).

[84]Stephen Smalley comments, "John's understanding of the 'surrender' of Jesus 'for us' in this v (with its probable echo of the good shepherd in John 10 who lays down his life for the sheep) has a strongly piacular significance. Jesus is presented not only as the shepherd, but also as the servant, of God; his life is surrendered for others and in their place" (*1, 2, 3 John* [WBC 51; Waco, Tex.: Word, 1984], p. 193).

[85]"Astonishingly the title is used twenty-six times of him in the book . . . [and] evokes a powerful image of sacrifice" (Marshall, *New Testament Theology*, p. 561).

the Lamb" and, in imitation of the Savior, do not "cling to life even in the face of death" (Rev 12:11). The grim warning in Revelation 13 about the extent of the beast's authority during his brief reign of terror indicates that all but the elect come under his malign sway. The book of life records the names of the elect, those who belong "to the Lamb that was slain from the creation of the world" (Rev 13:8 NIV). In the climactic vision of Revelation 19, when Jesus Christ, the Word of God, returns victoriously to the planet, his parousia includes this graphic piece of imagery: "He is clothed in a robe dipped in blood" (Rev 19:13).

Revelation thus chimes in nicely with John's Gospel and 1 John in depicting Jesus' saving work as a sacrifice. The following piece of Christian liturgy, *Victimae Paschali Laudes*, poetically captures the point.

> May you praise the Paschal Victim,
> immolated for Christians.
> The Lamb redeemed the sheep;
> Christ, the innocent one,
> has reconciled sinners to the Father.
> A wonderful duel to behold,
> as death and life struggle;
> The Prince of life dead,
> now reigns alive.

The distinctive idea in John is that believers in Jesus Christ have eternal life *now*. For John, the presence of the future has invaded history, and believers are in a real sense already living in the end times. How, then, does this strong note of realized eschatology impact John's teaching on the Christian life? That is the focus of the next chapter.

FOR FURTHER DISCUSSION

1. Is the question of authorship really important for Johannine theology?

2. Does John's Christology advance beyond Paul's thought? If so, how?

3. Is John's Christology polemical? Why or why not?

4. Is John's Gospel anti-Semitic? Why or why not?

5. Why is John's prologue so important to the Christian faith?

6. Discuss the significance of John's adaptation of the Logos idea for Christology.

7. Discuss whether John, in his writings, views Jesus' death as a sacrifice for others.

For Further Reading

Barker, Glenn W., William L. Lane, and J. Ramsey Michaels. *The New Testament Speaks*, pp. 385-93; 402-8. New York: Harper & Row, 1969.

Burge, Gary M. "John, Theology of." *EDBT* 423-25.

Bultmann, Rudolf. *Theology of the New Testament*, translated by Kendrick Grobel, 2:33-69. 2 vols. New York: Scribner, 1951-1955.

Caird, G. B. *New Testament Theology,* completed and edited by L. D. Hurst, pp. 279-334. Oxford: Clarendon, 1994.

Guthrie, Donald. *New Testament Theology*, pp. 222-24, 243-45, 263, 282-90, 293, 312-16, 321-29, 330-33, 338, 425-27, 449-60. Downers Grove, Ill.: InterVarsity Press, 1981.

Harrison, Everett F. "A Study of John 1:14." In *Unity and Diversity in New Testament Theology: Essays in Honor of George E. Ladd*, edited by Robert A. Guelich, pp. 23-36. Grand Rapids: Eerdmans, 1978.

Hunter, Archibald M. *Introducing New Testament Theology*, pp. 145-51. Philadelphia: Westminster Press, 1957.

Hurtado, L. W. "Christ." *DJG* 114-17.

Kreitzer, Larry. *The Gospel According to John*, pp. 1-14; 87-98; 99-109. RSG. Oxford: Regent's Park College, 1990.

Kümmel, Werner Georg. *The Theology of the New Testament according to Its Major Witnesses: Jesus-Paul-John*, translated by John E. Steely, pp. 266-321. Nashville: Abingdon, 1973.

Ladd, George E. *A Theology of the New Testament*, edited by Donald A. Hagner, pp. 273-89. Rev. ed. Grand Rapids: Eerdmans, 1974.

Marshall, I. Howard. *New Testament Theology*, pp. 512-17. Downers Grove, Ill.: InterVarsity Press, 2004.

Morris, Leon. *New Testament Theology*, pp. 225-55. Grand Rapids: Zondervan, 1986.

Thielman, Frank. *Theology of the New Testament*, pp. 150-62. Grand Rapids: Zondervan, 2005.

Thompson, M. M. "John, Gospel of," *DJG* 376-79.

10

Johannine Eschatology and Ecclesiology

JOHANNINE ESCHATOLOGY

Johannine thought stands apart from the rest of the NT in its pronounced "realized eschatology." John stresses the "already" or "now" dimension of Christian eschatology more than any other NT author. Only Ephesians and Colossians strike a comparable note. One must be careful, however, not to so emphasize John's realized eschatology that futuristic eschatology is completely lost from view. But before showing that futuristic eschatology is "alive and well" in John, I set out the abundant evidence stressing the presence of the future in the here and now.

Realized eschatology in John's Gospel. As we have already noted, the familiar Synoptic focus on the kingdom of God nearly disappears in John and is replaced by the notion of eternal life. Furthermore, John's teaching on eternal life is distinctive, as George Ladd notes: "While eternal life is eschatological, the central emphasis of the Fourth Gospel is not to show people the way of life in the Age to Come but to bring to them a present experience of this future life. Here is a teaching that is not found in any explicit form in the Synoptics, that the life of the Age to Come is already imparted to the believer."[1]

The prologue to John's Gospel sets the agenda for the entire book. John stresses how the Word of God "shines" in the darkness and "enlightens" those "who believed" on his name (Jn 1:5, 9, 12), but he also says that we "have all received" grace upon grace, and that Jesus Christ "has

---

[1]George E. Ladd, *A Theology of the New Testament*, ed. Donald A. Hagner (rev. ed.; Grand Rapids: Eerdmans, 1993), p. 293.

made . . . known" the Father (Jn 1:16, 18). The aorist tense in the last two examples signifies that the actions (receiving and making known) are viewed as complete; that is, they have taken place already. The collocation of present and aorist tenses in the prologue results in a decided emphasis upon the present experience of illumination, grace and revelation for those who receive the Word.

After the motif is initially sounded, echoes recur throughout John's Gospel, as in a Mozart piano concerto. For example, in the theological commentary by the evangelist following Jesus' conversation with Nicodemus, we read these startling words: "Those who believe in him are not condemned; but those who do not believe are condemned *already*, because they have not believed in the name of the only Son of God" (Jn 3:18 [my italics]). For contemporary Jews, this must have sounded odd. In most streams of first-century Judaism there was a common expectation of a future assize in which all render an account of their deeds before the divine judge. He in turn would issue a verdict of either acquittal or guilt. Final judgment, already declared in the present and determined by one's belief or unbelief in Jesus, must have seemed a decidedly dangerous innovation. How could one be sure now what the verdict would be then? And why should the verdict hang on belief "in the name of the only Son of God" (Jn 3:18)? John's answer is simply an assertion: "Those who do what is true come to the light, *so that it may be clearly seen that their deeds have been done in God*" (Jn 3:21 [my italics]). God's verdict of acquittal is already manifest in the lives of those who respond to the light. Conversely, God's verdict of judgment is already manifest in the lives of those who reject the light. Deeds that are true—that is, acceptable to God—spring not from human effort (Jn 1:13; 3:21) but rather from an encounter with the light, embodied in the person of Jesus Christ.

This requires further discussion. A pronounced determinism pervades John's Gospel. Much like the theology of Qumran, John maintains an ethical dualism. One is either in the light or the darkness. There are no shades of gray in Johannine theology. Like Qumran, John provides a theological explanation why some believe and others do not. John's Jesus states that no one can come to him "unless drawn by the Father" (Jn 6:44) or "unless it is granted by the Father" (Jn 6:65). "And I, when I am lifted up from the earth, will draw all people to myself" (Jn 12:32). One's choice to believe is subsequent to an antecedent choice: "You did not choose me but I chose you" (Jn 15:16; cf. Jn 15:19). The Son bestows eternal life on those given him by the Father (Jn 17:2, 6). There is no question about the initiative belonging to God. On the other hand, invitations are freely offered to all to avail themselves of the life-giving water (Jn 7:37) and the food that endures for eternal life (Jn 6:27). Furthermore, the invitation extends to all: "Everything that the Father gives me will come to me, and *anyone* who comes to me I will never drive away" (Jn 6:37 [my italics]). The "everyone who believes" (Jn 3:16-17) and "all people" (Jn 12:32) should be taken seriously (cf. Jn 6:45).[2]

At Qumran the explanation why some believe and others do not lies in a particular kind of divine determinism: the children of darkness are created with an evil spirit; the children of light, a good spirit.[3] In short, a divine decree inexorably dictates the outcome. There is seemingly little room for "free will."[4] Evangelical theologians in the Reformed tradition, following the theology of John Calvin, adhere to a doctrine of election *functionally* similar. Those who feel more kinship with the theology of Jacob Arminius and John Wesley have recourse to God's saving decree predicated on foreseen faith.[5] Parties in both sides of the debate appeal to the apostle John for proof texts. Since John nowhere resolves the issue or even seems aware of any tension, the soundest course is to affirm both divine initiative and authentic human freedom, being content to let this perennial antinomy stand without resolving it in favor of one pole or the other.[6] In this regard, John and Paul are, once again, on the same page.

Other examples of realized eschatology can be documented in John's Gospel. In the narrative of the Samaritan woman, Jesus says to her, "But the hour is coming, and is *now here*, when the true worshipers will worship the Father in spirit and truth " (Jn 4:23 [my italics]). With reference to

---

[2]Rudolf Bultmann insists that "the Father's 'drawing' does not precede the believer's 'coming' to Jesus—in other words, does not take place before the decision of faith" (*Theology of the New Testament*, trans. Kendrick Grobel [2 vols.; New York: Scribner, 1951-1955], 2:23).

[3]1QS 3:15-17 makes this point quite clear: "All that is now and ever shall be originates with the God of knowledge. Before things come to be, He has ordered all their designs, so that when they do come to exist—at their appointed times as ordained by His glorious plan— they fulfill their destiny, a destiny impossible to change. He controls the laws governing all things, and He provides for all their pursuits" (trans. by Michael O. Wise, in *The Dead Sea Scrolls: A New Translation* [San Francisco: HarperSanFrancisco, 1996], p. 129).

[4]For a detailed discussion of Qumran dualism as compared to Johannine dualism, see James H. Charlesworth, "A Critical Comparison of the Dualism of 1QS 3:13–4:26 and the 'Dualism' Contained in the Gospel of John," in *John and the Dead Sea Scrolls*, ed. James H. Charlesworth (New York: Crossroad, 1991), pp. 76-106.

[5]See W. R. Godfrey, "Predestination," *NDT* 528-30; D. M. MacKay, "Determinism," *NDT* 195.

[6]"John makes no effort to reconcile systematically these sayings about divine predestination and moral responsibility. He sees no contradiction that faith is the free decision of a person's will and at the same time the gift of God's grace" (Ladd, *Theology of the New Testament*, p. 313).

the ripening grain fields, Jesus informs his disciples, "The reaper is *already* receiving wages and is gathering fruit for eternal life, so that sower and reaper may rejoice together" (Jn 4:36 [my italics]). Even more dramatic are Jesus' words to the Jews in Jerusalem after his healing the invalid: "Very truly, I tell you, the hour is coming, and is *now here*, when the dead will hear the voice of the Son of God, and those who hear will live" (Jn 5:25 [my italics]). But perhaps the most dramatic instance of realized eschatology in John's Gospel occurs in John 12, the climax of Jesus' public ministry. As already sketched out in the preceding chapter, this is the point at which Jesus finally says, "The hour has come for the Son of Man to be glorified" (Jn 12:23). A heavenly voice, like a clap of thunder, punctuates Jesus' request that the Father be glorified by this impending hour (Jn 12:28). The thunderclap of realized eschatology reverberates in Jesus response: "*Now* is the judgment of this world; *now* the ruler of this world will be driven out" (Jn 12:31 [my italics]). Jewish apocalyptic works occasionally depict the demise of this world ruler, variously styled Azazel (*1 En.* 13:1), Beelzeboul (*T. Sol.* 6), Beliar (*Jub.* 1:20; *T. Dan* 6:1), Mastema (1QM 13:4; *Jub.* 10:8), the devil (Wis 2:24), Satanail (*2 En.* 18:3), Sammael (*Mart. Ascen. Isa.* 1:8), Semyaz (*1 En.* 6:3) or Satan (*T. Gad* 4:7), at the end of the age (cf. *1 En.* 54:6). In John's Gospel Jesus announces final judgment upon Satan because the "ruler of this world" is already being driven out by the saving work and word of Jesus. Finally, we note Jesus' high priestly prayer, in which he announces, "Father, the hour has come" (Jn 17:1). The hour is specified as the time when the Son grants eternal life to all those given by the Father. Eternal life is defined as knowing "the only true God, and Jesus Christ whom you have sent" (Jn 17:3). The present possession of this eternal life is verified in the experience of those who believe: "Now they know" (Jn 17:7).

Realized eschatology in the Johannine epistles. Likewise, 1 John emphasizes the present dimension of eternal life. John says that "the darkness is passing away and the true light is *already* shining" (1 Jn 2:8b [my italics]). The world, synonymous with darkness, is also passing away, "but those who do the will of God live forever" (1 Jn 2:17). Eternal life is concomitant with the present possession of knowledge (1 Jn 2:20; cf. 2 Jn 1-2), a knowledge based on what was heard in the beginning: the word of life embodied in Jesus Christ (1 Jn 2:24; cf. 1 Jn 1:1-2; 5:20). This sure knowledge of eternal life is verified in the life of the believer by the manifestation of love for others: "We know that we have passed from death to life because we love one another" (1 Jn 3:14). The believer thus has a robust assurance of belonging to God's family: "Beloved, we are God's children *now*" (1 Jn 3:2 [my italics]; cf. 1 Jn 5:19). This assurance is anchored in the apostolic testimony: "God

gave us eternal life, and this life is in his Son. Whoever has the Son has
life; whoever does not have the Son of God does not have life. I write these
things to you who believe in the name of the Son of God, so that you may
know that you have eternal life" (1 Jn 5:11-13). The entire treatise assumes
realized eschatology.

Realized eschatology in Revelation. Revelation, owing to its genre, is
oriented toward futuristic eschatology. Accordingly, one does not hear the
echoes of realized eschatology here in quite the same way as in John's
Gospel and 1 John. Rather, everything moves inexorably to the climactic
denouement of redemptive history: the triumphant return of Christ and his
victorious reign in the new Jerusalem. Nonetheless, realized eschatology,
in muted tones, may still be overheard throughout the composition. The
opening salutation includes a doxology praising Jesus Christ as the one
who has already "freed us from our sins" and "made us to be a kingdom,
priests serving his God and Father" (Rev 1:5b-6a). The inaugural vision
of the risen Christ draws attention to the fact that he has triumphed over
Death and Hades (Rev 1:18 NIV). The churches are reminded of this repeatedly. Christ offers life now even if believers face the very real prospect
of death. This is especially noteworthy in Revelation 13, where the reign of
the beast is depicted. In spite of death at the hands of this tyrant, believers
are exhorted to be faithful unto death: "Here is a call for the endurance
and faith of the saints" (Rev 13:10). This is reinforced by the second of
seven Beatitudes sprinkled throughout the book: "Blessed are the dead
who . . . die in the Lord . . . for their deeds follow them" (Rev 14:13). One
detects strains of realized eschatology in the letters to the seven churches.
The risen Lord addresses each congregation as the one "who holds the
seven stars in his right hand, who walks among the seven golden lamp-
stands" (Rev 2:1). This image emphasizes his continuing presence in their
midst. Each church hears these words confirming his real presence: "I
know your works [etc.]" (Rev 2:2, 9, 13, 19; 3:1, 8, 15). The living one is
in their midst, and those who know him live with him, even in the midst
of death (Rev 2:9, 13; 3:4, 12, 20). But nowhere do we hear the notes of
realized eschatology in Revelation so clearly as in the central vision of the
woman, child and dragon in Revelation 12. After the dragon is cast out
of heaven following the ascension of the Christ child, the angelic hosts
proclaim victory: "*Now* have come the salvation and the power and the
kingdom of our God and the authority of his Messiah" (Rev 12:10 [my
italics]). This strikes the same note as John's Gospel in John 12:31. Already
the Messiah reigns in his kingdom, and his saints reign with him. That this
is not the final consummation of the kingdom is clear from the last line of

Revelation 12:12: "the devil . . . knows that his time is short!"

We briefly look at 2 John. In this short letter we hear both realized and futuristic eschatology. Already, says the elder, the truth abides in those who confess that Jesus Christ has come in the flesh (2 Jn 2, 7). But this selfsame truth "will be with us forever" (2 Jn 2) and will involve "a full reward" (2 Jn 8). Though not spelled out, this full reward almost certainly refers to the eschatological consummation of redemptive history, since the elder had just warned against the antichrist (2 Jn 7) and issued a warning ("Be on your guard" [2 Jn 8]) echoing that of Jesus in the Olivet discourse (Mk 13:23).[7]

We thus have abundant evidence that John's writings, across all four genres employed, resonate with realized eschatology to a degree unmatched in the rest of the NT. This needs to be counterbalanced, however, with a sampling of his futuristic eschatology; the "not yet" dimension of the kingdom has by no means fallen off the radar.

Futuristic eschatology in John's Gospel. George Ladd reminds us that in the Fourth Gospel "life still retains its eschatological character."[8] In support of this he cites what he believes is the clearest example in John's Gospel: "Those who love their life lose it, and those who hate their life *in this world* will keep it for eternal life" (Jn 12:25 [my italics]). The italicized words draw attention to the by now familiar idiom of the "two ages" doctrine of Second Temple Judaism and the Synoptic Gospels. Furthermore, the Johannine saying "more clearly sets forth the antithetical structure of the two ages than the sayings in the Synoptic Gospel where the similar thought occurs (Mk 8:35; Mt 10:39; 16:25; Lk 9:24; 17:33)."[9] Rudolf Bultmann's attempt to divest John 12:25 of its traditional Jewish eschatology and reinterpret it as a vision of future unending glory is unconvincing.[10] Even he admits that John 5:28-29; 6:39-40, 44; 6:51-56; 12:48 do in fact evidence Jewish and early Christian eschatology. As one might expect, however, he dismisses them as redactional interpolations and thus not genuine Johannine passages.[11]

---

[7]"The warning of Jesus to his disciples was given in an eschatological context; they were to be vigilant in view of the approaching end. The elder's admonition here implies an equally eschatological dimension. Self-protection is necessary since the end-time (heralded by "the deceiver and the antichrist," v 7) is imminent (Stephen S. Smalley, *1, 2, 3 John* [WBC 51; Waco, Tex.: Word, 1984], p. 330).

[8]Ladd, *Theology of the New Testament*, p. 292.

[9]Ibid., p. 293.

[10]"The promises in the future tense do not refer to a later eschatological future but to the moment of decision when confronted by the Word" (Rudolf Bultmann, "ζάω," *TDNT* 2:870).

[11]"If we do not regard it as possible to interpret these passages in harmony with the others, and thus to achieve the union of both streams in a common view, we shall have to ascribe

I backtrack momentarily in order to highlight instances of futuristic eschatology still plainly manifest in John's Gospel. The narrative about the call of the first disciples concludes with a solemn asseveration by Jesus: "Very truly, I tell you, you will see heaven opened and the angels of God ascending and descending upon the Son of Man" (Jn 1:51). George Beasley-Murray probably is correct in seeing here the entire drama of Christ's saving activity, from his baptism to his triumphant parousia, compressed in the fascinating vision of Jacob's ladder.[12] I think it worth considering that Jacob's vision, according to the Genesis text, culminates with Jacob crying out in wonder, "Surely the LORD is in this place—and I did not know it!" (Gen 28:12-17). Is this allusion another instance of John's masterful use of irony? At any rate, the eschatological dimension of this saying should be neither minimized nor eliminated.

As we have noted, futuristic eschatology, quite in keeping with traditional Jewish eschatology, appears in the reference to the resurrection of both "those who have done good" and "those who have done evil" in John 5:28-29. This is the same eschatology as in the Synoptics. Again, although the miracle of the feeding of five thousand stresses the realized dimension of Jesus' saving activity in the present possession of eternal life, not to be overlooked is the clear reference to the future bodily resurrection "on the last day" (Jn 6:39, 40, 44, 54).[13] And consider also Jesus' promise in John 14:2-3: "In my Father's house there are many dwelling places. If it were not so, would I have told you that I go to prepare a place for you? And if I go and prepare a place for you, I will come again and will take you to myself, so that where I am, there you may be also." This probably refers to the parousia, not to the coming of Jesus at the death of a believer or to the descent of the Holy Spirit at Pentecost. Donald Guthrie emphasizes that "all Jesus' sayings in John about his Parousia are capable of another interpretation, but there seem to be insufficient grounds for excluding the possibility that a future coming of an apocalyptic type is intended."[14] I conclude

---

the second group to a redaction of the Gospel which tries to bring it into line with traditional eschatology; cf. also 1 Jn 2:28f.; 3:2; 4:17" (Bultmann, "ζάω," TDNT 2:879-71). C. K. Barrett rightly objects to Bultmann's removal of traditional eschatology from consideration in John's Gospel by "the use of quite uncritical scissors" ("The Place of Eschatology in the Fourth Gospel," ExpTim 59 [1947-1948]: 302).

[12]George R. Beasley-Murray, John (2nd ed.; WBC 36; Waco, Tex.: Word, 1999), p. 28.

[13]Frank Thielman is correct, however, that John reverses the traditional order: "resurrection at the last day and subsequent eternal life" (Theology of the New Testament [Grand Rapids: Zondervan, 2005], p. 172).

[14]Donald Guthrie, New Testament Theology (Downers Grove, Ill.: InterVarsity Press, 1981), p. 801. Guthrie cites Aune's observation that second-person plural pronouns are used in this section. This does not accord well with an "individualized parousia" (ibid., n. 41, cit-

that futuristic eschatology has not disappeared from John's Gospel; rather, analogous to John's juxtaposition of vertical and horizontal dualism, realized eschatology has been superimposed upon a fundamental horizontal eschatology of the "now but not yet" variety found in Jesus and Paul.

Futuristic eschatology in the Johannine epistles. Like the Gospel of John, 1 John contains vestiges of futuristic eschatology. Two texts speak unambiguously about the parousia and are set in an eschatological context signaled by 1 John 2:18, where the elder exclaims, "Children, it is the last hour!" This assertion is confirmed by the appearance of schismatics (1 Jn 2:19), styled by John as "antichrists," who have withdrawn from the community over Christology (1 Jn 2:22). As already discussed, the issue appears to involve a denial of a genuine incarnation. These antichrists, however, merely anticipate the appearance of the final antichrist (1 Jn 2:18). The antichrist referred to most likely is the lawless one whom Paul describes in 2 Thessalonians 2:3-12, appearing just prior to Jesus' parousia. Jesus does not mention him specifically in the Olivet discourse, but Jesus probably does refer to his sacrilegious activity when "the end" comes (Mk 13:14; Mt 24:15; cf. 2 Thess 2:4). Revelation depicts this same individual under the figure of the beast from the sea (Rev 13).

The two texts speaking about the parousia focus on the significance of this event for believers. In 1 John 2:28 believers who continue to abide in Christ and confess that Jesus is the Christ will have no occasion for shame: they will confidently stand before the revealed Christ at his parousia. This seems to presuppose some sort of judgment involving reward or lack thereof and is reminiscent of Paul's teaching in this regard (cf. 1 Cor 3:11-15). The second text, 1 John 3:2-3, already examined in connection with its clear realized eschatology, also manifests futuristic eschatology: "But we know that when he appears, we shall be like him, for we shall see him as he is. Everyone who has this hope in him purifies himself, just as he is pure" (NIV). John seems to be describing the same event that Paul does in the Thessalonian correspondence: the rapture of the church at Jesus' parousia. To be sure, John does not actually speak of a rapture, but he does imply a transformation into the likeness of Jesus. This transformation would seem to be the glorification of believers that Paul mentions several times in his letters and that is connected with Jesus' parousia (Rom 8:18-21, 29-30; 1 Cor 15:42-44, 49, 51-54; 1 Thess 2:19; 3:13; 4:13-18; 5:23; 2 Thess 1:10). Thus 1-2 John still maintain futuristic eschatology, even if it is somewhat muted.

---

ing D. E. Aune, *The Cultic Setting of Realized Eschatology in Early Christianity* [NovTSup 28; Leiden: Brill, 1972], p. 129).

The futuristic eschatology of Revelation.

Exegetical and interpretive issues in Revelation. Revelation, more than
the other Johannine writings, focuses on futuristic eschatology. Unfortunately, our investigation runs into several exegetical snags. How should
one interpret this most unusual writing, which incorporates at least three
distinct genres? Sharp differences of opinion quickly emerge. Is the book
of Revelation a symbolic or idealistic view of the perennial struggle between good and evil, Christ and Satan? Or is it essentially about the
struggle of the church with imperial Rome and pagan culture at the end
of the first Christian century? This latter approach, known as the preterist interpretation (i.e., describing what is in the past), views the book on
a par with other Jewish apocalyptic works of roughly the same era. Or is
it rather a forecast of Christian church history leading up to final judgment and reward? The Reformers preferred this approach, known as the
historicist interpretation. Or is it primarily a description of the events
transpiring during the last seven years of earth history, the "great tribulation," and having to do primarily with Israel following the rapture of
the church at Revelation 4:1 ("Come up here, and I will show you what
must take place after this.")? Dispensationalists champion this approach,
the futuristic interpretation. A variation on this is the moderately futuristic view, in which the sharp distinction between Israel and the church
is dropped and the church is seen undergoing intense persecution by the
antichrist throughout most of the tribulation period. Rather than entering further into the strengths and weaknesses of each view, I will simply
set out my stance. The reader may investigate the various options in more
depth elsewhere.[15]

I adopt a moderately futuristic approach to the book of Revelation. That
is, I hold that the inaugural vision (Rev 1:9-20), the letters to the seven
churches (Rev 2:1—3:22), and John's rapture to the throne room (Rev
4:1—5:14) are set in the time of the seer himself, the end of the first Christian century. The remaining chapters (Rev 6—22), for the most part, are
yet future, taken up with the events leading up to and including the return
of Jesus and the grand culmination of the kingdom of God. An exception
is the first five seals (Rev 6:1-11), which depict the course of the present age
up to the sixth seal, the Day of the Lord, "the great ordeal" (NRSV) or "the
great tribulation" (Rev 7:14 NIV). Most of the rest of Revelation 7—19 describes events that will unfold during this time of travail. A few exceptions
occur as flashbacks that survey earlier tracts of redemptive history (e.g.,

---

[15]See Merrill C. Tenney, *Interpreting Revelation* (Grand Rapids: Eerdmans, 1957); idem,
"Revelation, Book of," *ZPEB* 5:95-98.

Rev 12). Revelation 20—22 concludes by giving a glimpse of the millennial reign of Christ and the new Jerusalem.

What should be noted, however, is that these visions of the future are painted in the hues of first-century imperial Rome. There is an element of truth in the preterist view. The trappings of Rome do appear in the portrait of this future demonic state. So one is obliged to pay attention to this background in one's interpretation. Imperial Rome is the lens through which "Babylon the Great" is projected onto the screen. But in my opinion, John refers to the final form of this satanic system, not literal first-century Rome. We are dealing with genuine prophecy and not wishful thinking like that found in outwardly similar Jewish apocalypses such as *4 Ezra* and *2 Baruch*. In Ladd's words, "The elaborate symbolism of Jewish apocalyptic literature was employed in the interests of a prophetic forecast of the consummation of God's redemptive purpose."[16]

There are probably as many outlines of Revelation as commentators. Here is my simplified outline, designed to bring out a few salient points of John's eschatology:

Theme: "Your kingdom come, your will be done, on earth as it is in heaven" (Mt 6:10; cf. Rev 1:5, 6; 2:26; 3:21; 7:10; 11:15; 12:10; 15:3-4; 17:14; 19:6-8; 20:4).

A. The Inaugural Vision: The Risen and Reigning Christ (ch. 1)
> B. Messages to the Seven Churches: The Church Militant (chs.
> > 2—3): What is the present prospect and promise for the church?
> > > C. Vision of the Throne Room (chs. 4—5): Who is in charge?
> > > > D. Visions of the War for the Throne (chs. 6—16):
> > > > The Wrath of the Lamb
> > > > > 1. Seven Seals
> > > > > 2. Seven Trumpets
> > > > > 3. Seven Bowls
> > > C'. Vision of Babylon the Great (chs. 17—18): Who will lose charge?
> > B'. Vision of the King and His Kingdom: The Church Triumphant (chs. 19—21): What is the future prospect and fulfillment for the church?
A' The Final Vision: The Returning and Rewarding Christ (ch. 22)

The chiastic structure draws attention to the careful design and focus of the book. Each main section answers to its counterpart. Seen from this

---

[16]Ladd, *Theology of the New Testament*, p. 672.

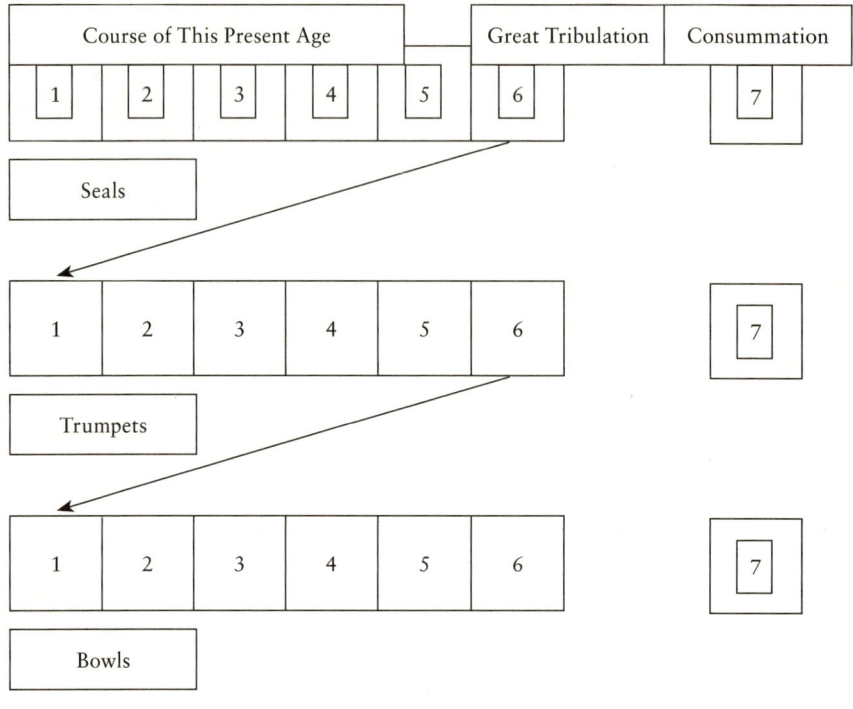

Figure 10.1. Relationship of seals, trumpets and bowls

angle, Revelation is really an unveiling of Christ and his kingdom. The struggle between Christ and Satan for control of planet Earth is the backdrop for this cosmic drama. The outcome is never in doubt. The purpose for this writing is therefore quite transparent: to encourage readers to hold on to the testimony of Jesus whatever the cost. The reward for faithfulness is really beyond description: a walk in the new Jerusalem.

Perhaps the key exegetical decision after deciding on whether to adopt an idealist, preterist, historicist or futuristic approach is how to interpret the three sequences of seals, trumpets and bowls. In other words, are these three series parallel, successive or telescopic (i.e., the trumpets occur during the seventh seal and the bowls occur during the seventh trumpet)? Once again the scholarly literature is voluminous. My own view combines the successive and telescopic. That is, the seventh seal, trumpet and bowl terminate at the same point, the grand finale of redemptive history. The five seals depict the course of the present age from the time of Jesus until the events of the Day of the Lord, just preceding the second advent; they are chronologically prior to the trumpets and bowls.[17] The six trumpets and six bowls transpire within the sixth seal, also called "the great tribulation," but the six bowls follow the six trumpets chronologically. The six bowls are more extensive and intensive than the six trumpets and culminate God's wrath on the beast and his followers. The diagram on page 354 attempts to depict the relationship.

On this view, John does an interesting thing. Just as in his Gospel, he structures his visions in such a way as to create suspense by means of delay (recall the use of "my hour is not yet come" in John's Gospel). Instead of describing the consummation when the seventh seal is broken, the text greets us with silence (Rev 8:1). John then starts a new sequence of judgments with the trumpets. When the seventh trumpet is blown, a preliminary indication that Christ will commence his visible reign occurs (Rev 11:15-18), but once again John delays (Rev 11:19) with another interlude (Rev 12—14). Even after the seventh bowl is poured out, Jesus does not immediately return. Instead, an interlude depicting the great whore, Babylon, takes up two chapters (Rev 17—18). Finally, John describes the victorious return of Jesus on the white horse. By delaying the parousia, John not only sustains suspense but also adds further details clarifying end time events. The comparable literary technique in John's Gospel and Revelation is striking.

Leading themes in revelation. The prologue, introductory salutation and inaugural vision of the risen Christ establish the keynotes echoed throughout the book. Thus the opening words tell us the primary content of the book: "The revelation of Jesus Christ" (Rev 1:1). Rather than being a calendar of eschatological events, the book is primarily a portrait of a person, the central figure of redemptive history. The descriptive imagery applied to Christ is freighted with theological meaning. For example, the message of the book is compressed in the three descriptive titles given to Jesus Christ in Revelation 1:5: "the faithful witness, the firstborn of the dead, and the ruler of the kings of the earth." These titles are fraught with futuristic eschatology.

Being a faithful witness *(martys)* of Jesus Christ and bearing faithful witness to him *(martyria)* are part of the special vocabulary of Revelation.[18] The beleaguered church of Smyrna is commended because they hold fast to Jesus' name and have not denied their faith in him "even in the days of An-

---

[17]"In the breaking of the five seals are disclosed the agencies God uses before the end to lead up to the fulfillment of salvation and judgment: the preaching of the gospel and the evils of war, death, famine, and martyrdom. These are, as it were, anticipations of the consummated salvation and judgment that are contained within the sealed book" (ibid., p. 674).

[18]See J. Beutler, "μαρτυρία," *EDNT* 2:392-93.

tipas my witness, my faithful one, who was killed among you, where Satan lives" (Rev 2:13). The lukewarm church of Laodicea is reminded that the risen Lord is "the faithful and true witness" (Rev 3:14), a truth they failed to emulate ("For you say, 'I am rich. . . .' [but] You do not realize that you are wretched, pitiable, poor" [Rev 3:17]). In Revelation 11 two witnesses, perhaps symbolic of a larger group, bear witness to their Lord, who was crucified (Rev 11:8). This witness is placed in the turbulent era just before Christ's parousia. In Revelation 17 we are informed that the great whore, Babylon, has executed many witnesses to Jesus (Rev 17:6). Just as Jesus was a faithful witness unto death, so his followers must be prepared to do the same, as Revelation 6:9-11; 12:17; 20:4 make ominously clear ("slaughtered for the word of God and for the testimony they had given"; "beheaded for their testimony to Jesus and for the word of God"). The time of the end runs red with the blood of martyrs (Rev 16:6; 17:6; 18:24).

The second descriptive title, "firstborn of the dead," is closely connected to the previous idea of witness. Jesus Christ is the victor over death and promises that those who put their trust in him will likewise overcome death. Whereas the realized dimension of this promise is emphasized in the messages to the seven churches (Rev 2:7, 10; 3:5, 12), in the rest of Revelation John directs attention to the consummation of redemptive history, when death will be cast into the lake of fire and a blessed immortality for the faithful begins (Rev 20:4-6, 13-15). Resurrection hope serves as a primary motivation for perseverance (Rev 7:14-17; 12:10-11; 13:9-10; 14:13). Faithful unto death is the watchword.

The third title, "ruler of the kings of the earth," looms even larger over the apocalyptic landscape of Revelation. In many respects, the throne room scene is decisive for understanding what is going on. God the Father has the book of destiny, and only the Lamb can open it. As he breaks the seals, certain events happen on earth. Quite in keeping with the Olivet discourse, the things mentioned in the first five seals characterize human history from the first century until the present (cf. Mt 13:3-14). In other words, none of them is an indicator in itself of Jesus' return. They are simply aspects of human existence that recur with tragic regularity. This prompts the following observation: the precise time of Jesus' return cannot be calculated. Agreeing with the Synoptic traditions and Paul, John does not set a date for Jesus' parousia. The people of God, however, will have a general idea once the sixth seal is opened. That ushers in the Day of the Lord or the great tribulation. The things that happen during this brief era, apparently seven years in duration (cf. Dan 7:25; 9:27: 12:6-7; Rev 11:2; 12:14; 13:5), have no precedent. With the opening of the sixth seal, the Day of the Lord quickly runs its course. My view of the end times does not incorporate a pretribulation rapture. The saints will not be rescued from the wrath of the antichrist; they will, however, be spared the wrath of the Lamb (Rev 3:10; 7:3, 14; 9:4; cf. 1 Thess 5:9). In this connection, Jesus' high priestly prayer is relevant: "I am not asking you to take them out of the world, but I ask you to protect them from the evil one" (Jn 17:15). The people of God are reminded that all history is in the hands of the Lamb. Nothing that overtakes them is outside his control. Since he holds the book of destiny, they can be assured that his purposes will ultimately be achieved. The book of Revelation is in many ways a "tract for hard times." The question "Who is in charge?" must be answered confidently by the saints: "The Lamb on the throne, who is Lord of lords and King of kings" (Rev 17:14). The sovereignty of God and the Lamb is the linchpin of Christian assurance and confidence.

As already indicated, Revelation 6:12, the opening of the sixth seal, inaugurates the great day of the wrath of God and the Lamb (Rev 6:16-17); in other words, we have come to what the OT calls "the Day of the LORD" (cf. Is 2:11-22; Jer 17:16-18; Ezek 30:3; Joel 1:15; Amos 5:18-20). This will be an unparalleled period of human suffering and natural catastrophe. Behind this upheaval lies a power struggle. In keeping with an apocalyptic worldview, John traces the taproot of evil to an evil supernatural being, Satan. The natural realm reels in response to this titanic showdown in the spiritual realm. The Day of the Lord is the next-to-last attempt by this prince of demons to maintain control of planet Earth (for his last-ditch effort, see Rev 20:7-10). To this end, he unveils his most cunning and cruel counterfeit, a false messiah of incredible power and charisma (Rev 13). In response, God and the Lamb unleash an arsenal of "weapons of mass destruction" that defy imagination, symbolized by the trumpet and bowl judgments (Rev 8—9; 16).

John's explanation for the problem of evil is characteristic of apocalyptic: evil is more than simply human sin, whether individual or corporate; there are cosmic and supernatural roots. Jewish apocalypses trace it back to the angels who sinned by cohabiting with women (Gen 6). The NT shares an apocalyptic worldview and, while stressing individual responsibility, acknowledges a demonic cause of sin in the world. Revelation makes this abundantly clear.

Satan desires to hold on to his claim as "ruler of this world" (cf. Jn 14:30). With Jesus' death, resurrection, ascension and bestowal of the Spirit, however, the powers of darkness are being steadily pushed back. Many switch allegiance and become followers of the Lamb. The great tribulation is Satan's last stand. Similar to the Battle of the Bulge in World War II, in which the German *Wehrmacht* attempted to throw back the steadily advancing Allied forces by an all-out counterattack, Satan launches a desperate counteroffensive. Or, to use an analogy from the movie world, "the Empire strikes back." The entire planet is engulfed in a global conflict.

All of this is epitomized in Revelation 12. Pausing the action momentarily, after the seventh trumpet has sounded, John sketches a dramatic episode, a vignette, that provides an understanding for what is going on in the entire series of seals, trumpets and bowls. This he does masterfully by sketching a sweeping canvas of redemptive history, revolving around three leading *dramatis personae*: a woman, a male child and a fierce red dragon. The woman probably is the true people of God, believing Israelites and the church; the male child, "who is to rule all the nations" (Rev 12:5), clearly is Christ; and the fierce red dragon is explicitly identified as Satan (Rev 12:9).

Here is the significance of this portent: the incarnation of Christ marks a major invasion of the dragon's turf. The latter responds with an attempt to kill the infant Messiah. Matthew recounts the same murderous episode from the perspective of the visible world. That is, behind the paranoia of Herod the Great, prompting the massacre of the innocents at Bethlehem, are the machinations of the dragon (Mt 2:1-18). The entire ministry and death of Christ is passed over in the vision in order to focus on the aftermath of Christ's ascension. "And war broke out in heaven" (Rev 12:7). The powers of darkness, reminiscent of Paul's description of Christ's death in Colossians 2:15, are ousted from heaven. That leads Satan to launch an all-out assault upon the woman and her children, those who "hold the testimony of Jesus" (Rev 12:17). The point is clear and ominous: the Jewish people and the church are under demonic attack until Christ returns. This is the ultimate explanation for unrelenting anti-Semitism and persistent persecution of Christianity. No other reason is sufficient to account for the extent and intensity of these phenomena.

Revelation 13 carries the action forward. Since Satan's repeated assault upon the church fails to stall the kingdom's advance, he resorts to draconian measures. He counterfeits the incarnation of Christ. A powerful human figure, energized by the dragon's immense power, is brought on the scene in an effort to smash the kingdom of God on earth. Under the image of a terrifying beast from the sea, the antichrist arises. Not only is there a counterfeit incarnation, but also, even more chilling, the dragon conjures a counterfeit resurrection (Rev 13:3, 12). The impact upon the unbelieving world is enormous. The dragon achieves a moment of glory: "They worshiped the dragon" (Rev 13:4; cf. Mt 4:9). A reign of terror ensues once the beast is securely in control of the entire world. The church is mercilessly persecuted, and one gets the impression that the number of martyrs far exceeds that of any other period (Rev 13:5-10). The dragon spawns another blasphemous counterfeit. On the scene arises another beast, a parody of the Lamb, who serves as a kind of minister of propaganda and high priest (Rev 13:11-18). Not to be overlooked is the creation of an unholy trinity (dragon = Satan, beast from the sea = antichrist, beast from the earth = false prophet [Rev 19:20]) that mocks the triune God. Seemingly, the triumph of evil is complete.

But the Lamb will not allow it. Revelation 14 is a blessed interlude, a word of encouragement and hope for the beleaguered church. Arrayed around the Lamb, the saints, the entire redeemed people of God, portrayed as pure virgins, "sing a new song before the throne" (Rev 14:3). The last battle is about to begin, and announcements of impending judgment ring out from heaven. John, with a significant shift of terminology, reports that the "Son of Man" now orders the final assault (Rev 14:14-20).

The bowl judgments are horrific. Great Babylon, a fitting image of godless culture and society, collapses under the onslaught. Shockingly, the wicked curse God to the bitter end. John once again postpones the dramatic arrival of the Lamb by sketching more fully the nature of "Babylon the Great, mother of whores and of earth's abominations." It is a foul portrait, with the stench of depravity and death oozing from the canvas. Once again imperial Rome serves as the template (see esp. Rev 17:9-10), but Babylon is hardly to be pigeonholed into a particular time. This is an eschatological portrait possessing a timeless quality. Abuse of power, self-aggrandizement, oppression, injustice and exploitation are common denominators in the history of human government. Babylon the Great embodies the mindset of that first defiant generation at the tower of Babel ("Come, let us build ourselves a city, and a tower with its top in the heavens, and let us make a name for ourselves" [Gen 11:4]) and all its subsequent manifestations in human civilization, until its final demise at the Day of the Lord. The only reason given by those who lament the fall of Babylon is economic. Those who trafficked with her and were made wealthy bewail her fate (Rev 18:1-24). They love her for what she provided materially (cf. Mt 6:19-24). It is sobering to ask whether modern civilization, and North American culture in particular, is any different. John's prophetic appeal to Christians of his day is as relevant today as then: "Come out of her, my people, so that you do not take part in her sins, and so that you do not share in her plagues; for her sins are heaped high as heaven, and God had remembered her iniquities" (Rev 18:4-5; cf. Is 48:20; Jer 51:45).

John depicts the parousia of Christ in terms appropriate to apocalyptic. He arrives on a white horse and arrayed in a robe dipped in blood and bearing an inscribed name that only he knows. The imagery is an amalgam of OT and Second Temple Judaism texts depicting either God or the Messiah as a divine warrior who triumphs over his enemies.[19] In addition, the passage incorporates imagery drawn from a Roman triumph. In short, Christ leads his army like an all-conquering Caesar.[20] The "armies of heaven, wearing fine linen, white and pure" (Rev 19:14) almost certainly are angels, not redeemed saints, the significance being that saints do not actually engage in violent warfare against unbelievers. The destruction meted out derives from divine and angelic agency, not human.[21] Adoption of militarism by Christians in support of dubious nationalistic and political agendas has greatly hindered the advance of the kingdom throughout history; thankfully, God's kingdom moves forward in spite of grievous misinterpretations of kingdom policy (see, e.g., Mt 26:51-54).

Two suppers of radically different character occur at the parousia and frame Revelation 19: the first is the marriage supper of the Lamb, a glorious celebration of Christ and his church (Rev 19:7-10); the second is a grisly supper of death and destruction visited upon the beast and his followers (Rev 19:17-21). John is indebted to two sources for this feature. Already in the OT we have the imagery of a grand banquet for the redeemed in the aftermath of the Day of the Lord (Is 25:6). Jesus himself used this imagery to describe the future manifestation of the kingdom of God (Mt 8:11; 22:1-14; Lk 13:29; 14:15-24; 22:16). The second source is Ezekiel's vision of Gog's defeat at the end of days (Ezek 39:4, 17-20), in which "the slaughter of those who dared oppose God and oppress his people is regarded as a sacrifice to God's glory."[22] These two suppers illustrate the black-and-white ethical dualism of John; one is either for or against Christ. The final separation of the righteous and the wicked is starkly presented and reminds us of Jesus' parables of the weeds and wheat and

---

[19]See Exodus 15:1-18; Deuteronomy 33:1-3, 26-29; Judges 5:4-5; Isaiah 26:20—27:5; 59:15b-20; 63:1-6; Habakkuk 3:2-16; Zechariah 14:1-5; *Testament of Moses* 10:3-7; Wisdom 18:15; *Targum Neofiti* Genesis 49:11.

[20]See David E. Aune, *Revelation* (WBC 52C; Dallas: Word, 1998), pp. 1050-51.

[21]Ibid. This contrasts with the Qumran literature, in which we have the notion of active participation in the battles of the end times in which the "Sons of Light" eventually annihilate the "Sons of Darkness." See the *War Scroll* (1QM) for particulars, and discussion by Lester L. Grabbe, "Warfare: Eschatological Warfare," *EDSS* 2:963-65; Philip R. Davies, "War of the Sons of Light against the Sons of Darkness," *EDSS* 2:965-68.

[22]Victor R. Gold and William L. Holladay, *The New Oxford Annotated Bible: New Revised Standard Version* (New York: Oxford University Press, 1991), p. OT 1110, note on Ezekiel 39:1-20.

of the good and bad fish (Mt 13:24-30, 36-43, 47-50).

This brings us to an intensely debated feature of John's eschatology: the millennial kingdom. In my opinion, John, in agreement with Paul, believed that after the parousia Christ would reign visibly on the earth with his saints. The length of this intermediate kingdom is said to be one thousand years (six times in seven verses). This may be a symbolic number simply conveying the idea of a long time, but that is not the real issue in dispute. The more substantial question is whether the reign of Christ is literal. Many argue that the one thousand years refers to a spiritual reign of Christ throughout this age until his parousia. Thus both deceased and living saints are now part of this "millennial reign." This view, as we already saw in chapter 3, is somewhat inappropriately labeled "amillennialism."

The arguments for taking the passage literally are as follows. First, this is the meaning of the text at face value. The recapitulation theory—the one thousand years are symbolic and function as a retrospective view of the entire church age—seems forced.[23] For example, it is difficult to interpret Revelation 20:3, in which Satan is locked and sealed in the pit and rendered unable to deceive the nations during the one thousand years, as applying to the church age. Satanic deception has been the order of the day. Second, the key sentence at the end of Revelation 20:4, "They came to life and reigned with Christ a thousand years," can only with great difficulty be construed as a spiritual resurrection. The verb "came to life" *(ezēsan)*, in this context, refers "to dead persons who return to life."[24] Third, the notion of a temporary, intermediate, messianic kingdom, compatible with statements of both Jesus and Paul, also appears in Jewish apocalyptic works such as *4 Ezra* and *2 Baruch* and possibly in *1-2 Enoch*, all either contemporaneous with or prior to Revelation. It also occurs in later rabbinic traditions.[25] And fourth, this was the prevailing view in the second and third Christian centuries. Church fathers such as Papias, Irenaeus, Justin Martyr, Tertullian, Commodianus, Victorinus and Lactantius adhered to a literal reign of Christ on earth for one thousand years.[26] To be sure, there were dissenters,

---

[23]J. W. Montgomery claims that "only a literal interpretation of Rev. 20 fulfills the basic hermeneutic rule that a passage of Scripture must be taken in its natural sense unless contextual considerations force a nonliteral rendering. (The burden of proof thus falls upon the opponent of premillennialism to show that such considerations do in fact exist.)" ("Millennium," *ISBE* 3:361).

[24]BDAG, p. 336.

[25]For specific references and discussion, see Larry R. Helyer, "The Necessity, Problems, and Promise of Second Temple Judaism for Discussions of New Testament Eschatology," *JETS* 47 (2004): 597-615.

[26]For specific texts, see ibid., p. 609.

as Justin Martyr admits, who held a nonchiliastic view of the kingdom.[27] But it was the influence of Augustine's amillennial interpretation in the fourth century that carried the day and eventually eclipsed the literal understanding, though the latter never entirely disappeared. Nonetheless, it is fair to say that a majority of evangelicals today agree with the earlier view of the premillennial church fathers. One should, of course, decide exegetical and theological issues on the basis neither of historical priority nor personal preference but rather always on the basis of the meaning of the text itself. In that regard, the plain meaning of the text—a temporary earthly reign—commends itself over a figurative or spiritualized meaning.

But what theological significance should be attached to this doctrine of the millennial reign of Christ? What purpose does it serve in the larger context of redemptive history? A couple of observations may be offered. The temporal kingdom is consonant with the entire kingdom program initiated in the call of Abram. God's kingdom has been in the process of coming for over four thousand years now. Promises have been given that the Lord himself will reign over his people and establish his capital in Jerusalem. The nations will flow to this spiritual capital of the world (Is 2:1-5; Joel 3:17). The nations will bring their glory to this place and pledge their allegiance to the God of Jacob, and the enemies of God will be punished (Zech 14:16-21). The Lord's saving purposes through his servant Israel and its continuation in the church will be publicly vindicated (Is 42—44; Eph 3). In short, the millennial kingdom will be a dramatic, visible confirmation of God's intention to reclaim planet Earth and install his people as stewards over its vast resources. Ladd nicely captures the rationale for an interim kingdom:

> Christ is now reigning as Lord and King, but his reign is veiled, unseen and unrecognized by the world. The glory that is now his is known only by people of faith. So far as the world is concerned, Christ's reign is only potential and unrealized. Nevertheless, contrary to appearances, he is reigning and "he must reign until he has put all his enemies under his feet" (1 Cor 15:25). Then his reign must become public in power and glory and his Lordship universally recognized (Phil 2:10-11).[28]

A further theological significance of the millennium revolves around the issue of theodicy. Is God just, righteous and holy if, in the end, he consigns

---

[27]See, for example, Charles E. Hill, *Regnum Caelorum: Patterns of Millennial Thought in Early Christianity* (Grand Rapids: Eerdmans, 2001), pp. 249-71.
[28]Ladd, *Theology of the New Testament*, p. 680.

to hell those who reject his saving grace? Does the punishment fit the crime? Some may argue that if their situation in life had been different or better, they would have responded positively. The implication of this view is that the playing field has not been equal throughout redemptive history, and that God is to blame for this inequity. But is there a positive correlation between the quality of life that one experiences and a saving response to the gospel? The millennial age demonstrates just the opposite, and thus the objection that God is ultimately to blame for unbelief is baseless. After an era of unparalleled peace and prosperity, righteousness and justice, Satan is released from his prison, and he deceives the nations and mobilizes a force " as numerous as the sands of the sea" to besiege the beloved city (Rev 20:7-8). This shocking rebellion against the righteous rule of Christ demonstrates beyond dispute the incorrigibility of human nature. No one can plead his or her case on the ground of extenuating circumstances. If, under the very best of circumstances, human beings defy God's will, then his righteous judgment against all sinners of all eras is vindicated and "every mouth . . . silenced, and the whole world . . . held accountable" (Rom 3:19).[29]

John concludes his apocalypse with a breathtaking vision of the eternal state (Rev 21—22). He leads us on a guided tour of the new Jerusalem in all its splendor, complete with bejeweled walls, gates and foundations, agleam with the glory of God and the Lamb. The depiction of the twelve gates named after the twelve tribes of Israel and the twelve foundations named after the twelve apostles of the Lamb (Rev 21:12-14) emphasizes the unity of God's people and, by inference, the unity of his plan of salvation. From beginning to end the Bible locates redemptive history on *terra firma*. The kingdom of God unfolds on earth, and it is on earth that it achieves its ultimate expression—a fact not always realized by modern Christians. As surely as believers anticipate a resurrection body, so also they should look forward to a renewed environment (Rev 21:1). The prophets caught glimpses of a renewed earth that surpassed anything ever experienced (Is 11:6-9; Joel 3:18; Amos 9:13-15). In fact, in Isaiah we read of new heavens and a new earth (Is 65:17; 66:22). These Isaianic passages, however, pose a theological problem. Though wonderful in description, they nonetheless depict death (Is 65:20). How can we account for this, especially in comparison with John's vision of the new earth, where "death will be no more"

---

[29] "The millennial reign of righteousness is the backdrop for the last judgment, that when the final terrible doom of the wicked is pronounced, God may be justified in his acts and his righteousness vindicated in his judgments" (ibid., p. 681). See also David A. Hubbard, *The Second Coming: What Will Happen When Jesus Returns?* (Downers Grove, Ill.: InterVarsity Press, 1984), pp. 83-91.

(Rev 21:4)? Some attempt to harmonize this by supposing that Revelation 21:1-8 describes the eternal state, whereas Revelation 21:9—22:5 reverts back to the millennial era. They then suggest that Isaiah 65:17-25; 66:22-24 also describe the millennial era, even though proleptically called the new heavens and new earth. This seems unnecessary. It is better to take Revelation 21—22 as portraying the eternal state and to recognize that Isaiah's vision is limited by its location in redemptive history. The NT advances the Isaianic prophecy by unveiling the *complete* abolition of suffering, pain and death (Rev 21:4; cf. 2 Tim 1:10). Revelation 21—22 conveys this perfection by means of symbolism, most notably in its portrayal of the new Jerusalem, a cube perfect in all dimensions, where sin is forever banished (Rev 20:10-15) and God makes all things new (Rev 21:5).

Not to be overlooked is the continuance into the eternal state of distinct ethnic and political entities (Rev 21:24-26; 22:2). God did not decree a homogeneous culture for the final phase of the kingdom; rather, he created diversity and celebrates it everlastingly. To be sure, in our own day multiculturalism is sometimes hijacked and enlisted to support practical atheism, but cultural diversity per se is an eternal value that should be cherished. Contemplating the incredibly rich cultural and physical environment planned for the people of God in the ages to come is exhilarating.

JOHANNINE ECCLESIOLOGY

The community of light. One of the primary metaphors in the Johannine corpus is light. As we have already noted, John's writings evidence a sharp polemic against Docetism and incipient Gnosticism. In gnostic theosophy the Most High God dwells in light, and true believers are conceived as sparks of light broken off from their source and trapped in darkness. John counters this heresy by taking over some of their key terms and concepts and infusing them with apostolic content. At face value, 1 John 1:5 sounds quite gnostic: "This is the message we have heard from him and proclaim to you, that God is light and in him there is no darkness." But the context of the entire document, is clearly anti-gnostic and argues a point quite different from those who "went out from us, but they did not belong to us" (1 Jn 2:19a).[30]

The Gnostics were not the first to employ the metaphor of light in a religious context.[31] The imagery of light and darkness is an obvious way of

---

[30]Hans Conzelmann points out the fundamental distinction between John's Gospel and Gnosticism in that the former contains no metaphysical and cosmological speculation about light ("φῶς," *TDNT* 9:350).

[31]"'Light' is one of the most widely attested of the 'primal words' in the phenomenology of

contrasting religious truth and error, as seen in, for example, the OT (e.g., Ps 104:2) and its development in Second Temple Judaism (Ps 43:3; 97:11; 112:4; Prov 4:18; Eccles 2:13-14; Is 5:20; Bar 3:14; 2 Esd 7:97; 14:20). The Qumran sectarians well before Jesus made much of the light/darkness contrast in order to explain and justify their own self-understanding. They were preeminently "the sons of light," and all who disagreed or opposed them were "sons of darkness" (1QS 1:9-11; 3:13). An important plank in their eschatological platform involved a final battle in which, by divine assistance, the sectarians, the "sons of light" fight a successful battle against the forces of Belial, the "sons of darkness" (1QM 3:6-9; 13:14-16; 14:16-18; 15—19).[32]

The Gospels also present Jesus making use of this imagery in his proclamation of the kingdom. In this regard, John's Gospel takes pride of place. The prologue immediately sets the agenda by depicting Christ as "the light of all people" (Jn 1:4), "the true light, which enlightens everyone" (Jn 1:9). The apostolic testimony affirms, "We have seen his glory, the glory as of a father's only son, full of grace and truth" (Jn 1:14), and this son "is God the only Son, who is close to the Father's heart" (Jn 1:18). At the Festival of Booths, during which the golden lamps in the temple court were lit, Jesus dramatically testifies to his role as the light bearer: "I am the light of the world. Whoever follows me will never walk in darkness but will have the light of life" (Jn 8:12). Rejection of this testimony places the unbeliever in a condition of culpable judgment: "And this is the judgment, that the light has come into the world, and people loved darkness rather than light because their deeds were evil" (Jn 3:19). By contrast, believers come to the light and demonstrate their true nature as "children of light" (Jn 12:36). The Gospel of John contains urgent appeals not to reject this witness of the true light but rather to receive it now while it is available and walk in its illumination: "The light is with you for a little longer. Walk while you have the light, so that the darkness may not overtake you" (Jn 12:35; cf. Jn 9:4-5; 11:9-10; 12:44-46).

The notion of fellowship in the light as a primary metaphor to depict the new community of faith takes center stage in 1 John.[33] Those who believe the apostolic testimony about Jesus "walk in the light" and thus have "fellowship one with another" (1 Jn 1:7). Belief and behavior are so

---

religion that address the archetypal human yearning for God" (H. Ritt, "φῶς," *EDNT* 3:447).

[32]See L. Morris, "Light," *ISBE* 3:134-36; and Jean Duhaime, "Light and Darkness," *EDSS* 1:495-96.

[33]Otto Piper refers to John's "rather elaborate theology of light" ("Light, Light and Darkness," *IDB* 3:132).

inextricably linked in Johannine theology that one can begin at either pole
to demonstrate the reality of the other. Those who genuinely believe in Jesus Christ sincerely love their brothers and sisters in Christ, and those who
sincerely love their brothers and sisters in Christ genuinely believe in Jesus
Christ. This kind of dialectic permeates 1 John and serves as litmus tests
for discerning genuine faith.[34]

The flock of God. Another metaphor illuminating Johannine ecclesiology is that of shepherd and sheep. Once again the OT is a primary source
for this conception. OT historical narratives occasionally employ the shep-
herd/sheep relationship in depicting Israelite kingship (2 Sam 5:2; 7:7; cf.
1 Kings 22:17; Ps 78:71). The consoling cadences of the Psalter, supremely
in Psalm 23, portray the Lord as a good shepherd and his people as his
sheep (Ps 23:1; 28:9; 80:1; 79:13; 100:3). And on several occasions prophets incorporate the theme in oracles both of judgment and of salvation (Is
13:14; 40:11; 53:6-7; Jer 23:1; 50:6; Ezek 34:6-31; Mic 2:12). In short, the
Hebrew Scriptures resonate with this evocative metaphor, and so it is no
surprise that it appears in Jesus' message.

John 10 is the focal point of this metaphor. Ezekiel 34 and Psalm 118:19-20
provide indispensable background for unpacking the narrative world in this
parabolic discourse, with its true-to-life details about shepherding in Palestine. Common themes include the depiction of faithless shepherds who
pillage and plunder, the Lord's purpose to gather and provide for his sheep,
and the Lord as a gate through which his people must enter. Several important theological points emerge from the parable of the good shepherd. First,
only those sheep that respond in faith and obedience are truly part of the
flock of God. The fact that shepherd and sheep know each other intimately
is especially emphatic: "I know my own and my own know me" (Jn 10:14).
In the parable Jesus is portrayed both as the shepherd who leads the flock
out to pasture and as the gate through which the sheep may enter the fold.
Both figures emphasize the finality of Christ; he is the exclusive means or
agent of salvation. Second, the sheepfold represents Israel. Note, however,
that thieves and robbers and hireling shepherds have access to the fold. The
Jewish religious establishment clearly falls under indictment. Furthermore,
there are other flocks that the good shepherd desires to bring into the fold.
Like the Greeks who desired to see Jesus at the Passover (Jn 12:20-21),
these represent the Gentiles. John, like Paul, has no brief for two peoples of
God; Jews and Gentiles together form one flock. Third, Jesus is the good
shepherd who saves his sheep by dying for them. One thinks of the young

---

[34]See Glenn W. Barker, William L. Lane and J. Ramsey Michaels, *The New Testament
Speaks* (New York: Harper & Row, 1969), pp. 414-23.

David when brought before King Saul after he had volunteered to fight the giant Goliath. David informed the king, "Whenever a lion or a bear came, and took a lamb from the flock, I went after it and struck it down, rescuing the lamb from its mouth; and if it turned against me, I would catch it by the jaw, strike it down, and kill it" (1 Sam 17:34-35). Like David, Jesus rescues his lambs. Unlike David, however, Jesus does not resort to a violent assault upon evil or evildoers. He does something quite extraordinary: he lays down his life to save his sheep. The vicarious nature of this sacrifice is extraordinary and stands in stark contrast to Jewish militarism that led to two failed attempts at national liberation from Rome (A.D. 66-73, 132-135). Fourth, Jesus' voluntary sacrifice is followed by his return to life. Death does not end the story; it simply makes possible the fulfillment of his ultimate promise: "I came that they may have life, and have it abundantly" (Jn 10:10). Eternal life is grounded in self-giving love by the one who is the very source of life itself. Once again, we stand amazed in the presence of Johannine paradox.

The True Vine. John places the allegory of the vine and the branches (Jn 15) in the narrative framework leading up to Jesus' arrest. The Last Supper is the setting for the discourses in John 13—14. Right at the end of John 14 comes a word of command from Jesus, "Rise, let us be on our way" (Jn 14:31), immediately followed by the parable of the vine (Jn 15:1-11). Discourse material occupies the rest of John 15 and all of John 16. John 17 is devoted to Jesus' high priestly prayer. Only at John 18:1 do we resume narrative movement to the Garden of Gethsemane, where Jesus' arrest unfolds. In light of this narrative framework, I suggest something that may have prompted the allegory of the vine. If one were walking from the traditional site of the upper room, on what is today called Mount Zion, a more-or-less direct route to Gethsemane crosses either the bridge spanning the Tyropeon Valley and the Temple Mount (the Kingsway Bridge) or, more to the south, a great arched stairway, today called Robinson's Arch. Either entrance to the Temple Mount permitted one to circle around the *azarah* (the sacred courtyard area surrounding the temple itself) and proceed to the eastern gate of the Temple Mount, from which one could then descend into the Kidron Valley below. As Jesus and his disciples traversed the southern and eastern boundaries of the *azarah*, they would have been able to see, illuminated by huge golden lamps, a portion of the magnificent decoration above the massive door to the temple itself, a rendition of a golden grape vine with its branches trailing gracefully down the door jambs. Perhaps Jesus paused, admiring this golden vine, and delivered the allegory of the vine. Josephus's description of the temple includes a detail that explains how Jesus and his disciples could have clearly seen the golden grape vine: "The middle [where the sanctuary was] was much higher . . . [and thus was] visible to those that dwelt in the country for a great many furlongs, but chiefly to such as lived over against them *and those that approached to them*" (*Ant.* 15.394 [my italics]).

The image of a vine representing Israel is deeply rooted in the Hebrew Bible. One thinks of the famous "song of the vineyard" in Isaiah 5:1-7, in which Yahweh expends tender, loving care on the preparation and planting of a vineyard, only to be bitterly disappointed in the result: "wild grapes." A similar point is made in Hosea 10:1; Jeremiah 2:21, Ezekiel 19:10-14; Psalm 80:8-13. Psalm 80:14-17, however, is a prayer that God would come to the rescue of the vine that his own right hand has planted. The imagery of a vine representing Israel frequently appears on Jewish coins of the Second Temple period and in religious texts (*Lev. Rab.* 36 [133a]).[35] Thus Jesus' allegory taps into an important metaphor depicting Israel as it was meant to be: a fruitful vine, a source of blessing and joy to all the earth (cf. Gen 49:11, 22); and in fact he incorporates it regularly in his teaching (Mt 20:1-7; 21:28; Mk 12:1-11; Lk 13:6-7).[36]

The main point of the allegory seems transparent: one must be united with Christ in order to be fruitful. Unless the individual branches partake of the sap supplied by the main trunk of the vine plant, there can be no life and hence no fruit. Branches that are broken off are worthless and are thrown into the fire to be burned. Analogously, believers are totally dependent upon their mystical union with Christ by faith for spiritual life and fruit. The key verb in this passage as it relates to the responsibility of believers is *menō* ("remain, continue, stay, abide"). The fundamental idea of the term in this context is the lasting nature of an immanent and intimate relationship between Christ and his people.[37] There is a correlative relationship between the mutual indwelling of Father and Son and that of the Father and Son in believers: Jesus prays, "that they may all be one. As you, Father, are in me and I am in you, may they also be in us. . . . I in them and you in me, that they may become completely one " (Jn 17:21, 23). In these words we hear a similar idea to Paul's "in Christ" formulations. The notion of incorporation and participation is common ground to both the Pauline and Johannine formulations.[38]

---

[35]For discussion and examples, see H. Hamburger, "Money," *IDB* 3:427-35.
[36]See J. Behm, "ἄμπελος," *TDNT* 1:342. Also helpful are the comments of Gary M. Burge, *John* (NIVAC; Grand Rapids: Zondervan, 2000), pp. 414-19.
[37]See F. Hauck, "μένω," *TDNT* 4:576.
[38]See Ladd, *Theology of the New Testament*, pp. 313-14.

Also central to the allegory is the tender, loving care with which the Father, the vinekeeper, seeks to improve productivity through careful pruning (cf. Is 5:4). Suckers and diseased tendrils are regularly removed in order to stimulate new growth, which is where new grape clusters form each season. The Greek word *airō* is occasionally given a different meaning than "remove, prune." Since the most frequent meaning of *airō* is simply "lift," it has been suggested that the verb be so translated here.[39] The idea is not that of placing the branches on a trellis or fence such as is done in the vineyards of France, Italy and California. Rather, in Palestine a hefty rock is placed under the main trunk of the vine after it turns and grows horizontally to the ground. This "lifting up" of the trunk tends to keep the branches from lying on the surface of the ground and thus prevents mold and other diseases. When transferred to the disciples, the analogous meaning is that God continually "lifts up"—sustains, supports and protects—believers so they may bear fruit. Though not impossible, this nuance seems unlikely. First, *airō* is used in this passage alongside *kathairō* ("purify, cleanse"), the latter in the sense of cutting off useless sprouts. The two words are thus used here in a manner comparable to synonymous parallelism or Semitic word pairs, which makes the notion of "lifting up" for *airō* less likely. Second, even though Palestinians who raise grapes on the Judean hills today may place a rock under the main trunk, many of the branches nonetheless still spread out on the ground. As a Palestinian tour guide once explained to me, by leaving the branches on the stony soil, the grapes actually absorb more sunlight and hence achieve a higher temperature than if they were trained to climb a trellis. The resulting grapes have a higher sugar content and thus are sweeter than those on trellises. Thus, on both linguistic and cultural grounds, a translation such as "cuts off," "removes" or "prunes" is preferable.[40]

Related to the foregoing is the notion of purity. "It is a basic thesis that the disciples of Jesus are clean (15:3; 13:10)."[41] The agency of cleansing is Jesus' "word," further described as "my words" and "my commandments" (Jn 15:7, 10). This reference to being clean picks up on the upper room and the foot washing. There Jesus also says, "You [plural] are clean" (Jn

---

[39]See, for example, A. W. Pink, *Exposition of the Gospel of John* (3 vols.; Cleveland: Cleveland Bible Truth Depot, 1929), 3:337; James Montgomery Boice, *The Gospel of John* (5 vols.; Grand Rapids: Zondervan, 1978), 4:228; Earl D. Radmacher, "The Word as Truth: Its Authority," in *Celebrating the Word* (Portland, Ore.: Multnomah Press, 1987), pp. 22-23.

[40]See W. Radl, "αἴρω," *EDNT* 1:41; J. Carl Laney, "Abiding Is Believing: The Analogy of the Vine in John 15: 1-6," *BSac* 146 (1989): 58-60.

[41]F. Hauck, "καθαρός," *TDNT* 3:426.

13:10). In that passage there is no explicit reference to Jesus' word; rather, the state of being clean is predicated on an act of cleansing by Jesus that results in participation: "Unless I wash you, you have no share with me" (Jn 13:8). But if we move ahead in the narrative to the high priestly prayer, we hear Jesus petitioning the Father, "Sanctify them in truth; your word is truth" (Jn 17:17). Clearly, Jesus' teaching, equated with the truth, functions as the cleansing agent. One cannot neatly separate who Jesus is from what he teaches—a point made also in 1 John. Trust in and love for Jesus occur when his word is taken seriously and obeyed (Jn 14:21; 15:10; 1 Jn 2:3; 3:22, 24; 5:2-3).

The section John 15:18-25 further develops an important aspect of purity. This has to do with the relationship of the believer to the world. Just as the OT ritual purity laws served as a barrier protecting ancient Israel from pagan influence, so too Jesus' word involves separation from the world. The "world" *(kosmos)* refers to the present world as created by God but now alienated from him and ruled by the evil one (Jn 14:30). The disciples should not be surprised at the hostility and venom directed at them by the world; to belong to Jesus necessarily means to experience with him this fundamental antagonism (Jn 15:18). Jesus' word cleanses his disciples and liberates them from the bondage of error and impurity emanating from the world (see Jn 8:31-36).

Three essential truths about the new community of faith emerge from this extended metaphor of the vine and branches. First, vital union with Christ by faith is absolutely essential. Only true believers are beneficiaries of the Father's "TLC," steadily improving in terms of spiritual health and productivity. This is in harmony with the notion of progressive sanctification.[42] Second, believers must avail themselves of the means of grace. Acting on Jesus' word and invoking Jesus' name for assistance ("If you abide in me, and my words abide in you, ask for whatever you wish, and it will be done for you. . . . The Father will give you whatever you ask him in my name" [Jn 15:7, 16]) are the instrumental means whereby pruning and cleansing occurs. Third, the end result, bearing much fruit and being a disciple, brings glory to the Father (Jn 15:8). As to the nature of this fruit, Ladd probably is correct: "The fruit is love—the supreme evidence of the Christian life in John."[43] This seems securely based in the immediately following section, John 15:12-25. There, Jesus reiterates his primary commandment: "Love one another as I have loved you" (Jn 15:12). The primary example of this

---

[42]See Klaus Bockmuehl, "Sanctification," *NDT* 613-16.
[43]Ladd, *Theology of the New Testament*, p. 319.

love is Jesus' own action in laying down his life for his "friends" (Jn 15:14-15). This kind of self-giving love is the hallmark of Christians.[44]

The Holy Spirit. Finally, we turn to John's most distinctive contribution to ecclesiology: his doctrine of the Holy Spirit. No other evangelist develops this to the extent that John does. Absolutely essential to the ongoing life of the new community is the ministry of the Spirit. Right at the end of the teaching on the vine, Jesus promises the coming of the "Advocate" or "Helper" *(paraklētos),*[45] "the Spirit of truth who comes from the Father" and who testifies on Jesus' behalf (Jn 15:26). What role does the Spirit play in the formation and continuance of the community of light?

In harmony with the Synoptics, John's Gospel emphasizes the importance of Jesus' baptism as the moment in which the Holy Spirit endowed Jesus with divine power for his ministry, a ministry of bestowing that same Spirit on others (Jn 1:32-33). Significantly, John the Baptist says that the Spirit "remained" on Jesus (Jn 1:32). In the Gospel of John there is no mention, as in Luke (Lk 4:1, 14, 18; 10:21), about Jesus being filled with the Spirit; rather, he is a constant source of the Spirit and can pour out this Spirit on those who believe in him.

Jesus confounds Nicodemus with his teaching on the necessity of being "born from above" by the Spirit in order to see or enter the kingdom of God (Jn 3:3, 5). This birth from above is as mysterious as the blowing of the wind.[46] One cannot "see" it; one can only experience its profound impact (Jn 3:8). Jesus intrigues the Samaritan woman with his offer of "living water," water that "will become . . . a spring of water gushing up to eternal life" (Jn 4:10, 14). Jesus probably alludes to the Holy Spirit in this figure.[47] At any rate, there can be little doubt that in John 7:37-38 Jesus presents himself as the one who pours out the Holy Spirit on those who believe in him. The setting for Jesus' dramatic announcement probably was the climactic seventh day of the Festival of Booths. This day featured a ritual in

---

[44]W. Feneberg notes that "election makes φίλοι from δοῦλοι (a contrasting pair), though fulfillment of Jesus' commission becomes the criterion of his friendship" ("φίλος," *EDNT* 3:428).

[45]Sometimes this Greek noun is simply transliterated as "Paraclete." A very literal rendering of the Greek verb παρακαλέω, from which the noun is derived, is "call to the side of." Hence English translations variously render the noun παράκλητος as "Comforter," "Counselor," "Helper" or "Advocate."

[46]There is a play on words here, as as the Greek word πνεῦμα has a literal meaning "wind" or "breath" as well as a transferred meaning of "spirit" or "Holy Spirit" See J. Kremer, "πνεῦμα," *EDNT* 3:117-22; F. Baumgärtel, "πνεῦμα," *TDNT* 6:359-67.

[47]Beasley-Murray comments, "It is evident that 'living water' has a variety of nuances that must be taken into account; chiefly it appears to denote *the life mediated by the Spirit sent from the (crucified and exalted) Revealer-Redeemer*" (*John*, p. 60).

which a golden pitcher with water from the Pool of Siloam was brought up to the temple and poured out as a drink offering on the altar.[48] There is no OT text containing the precise words here uttered by Jesus; rather, it appears to be an allusion to several OT passages (see Ex 17:1-6; Ps 78:15-16; 105:40-41; Ezek 47:1-11; Zech 14:8). Lest the reader miss the allusion, John editorializes: "Now he said this about the Spirit, which believers in him were to receive; for as yet there was no Spirit, because Jesus was not yet glorified" (Jn 7:39).

Of theological importance is the necessary link between Jesus' saving work and the gift of the Spirit. This linkage becomes the centerpiece of the five Paraclete sayings in the upper room discourse. In John 13:33 Jesus informs the disciples that he is going away. This, understandably, prompts an anxious question from Peter, "Lord, where are you going?" (Jn 13:36), and a confused and equally anxious question from Thomas, "Lord, we do not know where you are going. How can we know the way?" (Jn 14:5). In response to the disciples' anxiety and confusion, Jesus assures them that it is essential for him to return to his Father. But he promises, "I will not leave you orphaned; I am coming to you" (Jn 14:18). That is where the Paraclete sayings come into play.

The first saying (Jn 14:16-17) makes the point that by means of the Advocate (Spirit), both Jesus and the Father will be not only with the disciples but also in them. The Spirit mediates the presence of both Father and Son in the heart of the believer. This indwelling presence, the "Spirit of truth," is known only to believers and conveys an assurance of a true knowledge of God, thus answering the nagging question of religious certainty.

The second saying (Jn 14:26) highlights the teaching role of the Spirit. The Spirit assists the apostles to recall accurately and interpret correctly Jesus' teachings, thus guaranteeing the authority and reliability of apostolic teaching. This teaching function of the Spirit seems to anticipate the process of inspiration whereby the NT writings eventually become part of the Christian canon. The Spirit ensures the truthfulness of apostolic teaching.

The third Paraclete saying (Jn 15:26-27) highlights the role of the Spirit in witnessing to unbelievers. The Spirit's task is to argue the case for Christ in an unbelieving world. Unbelievers will not be won over unless and until the Spirit mysteriously works upon and woos their hearts.[49] Evangelism is

---

[48]For details, see Alfred Edersheim, *The Temple: Its Ministry and Services as They Were at the Time of Jesus Christ* (Grand Rapids: Eerdmans, 1950). For an illustrated article on the newly discovered location of the Pool of Siloam in Jesus' time, see Hershel Shanks, "The Siloam Pool: Where Jesus Cured the Blind Man," *BAR* 31, no. 5 (2005): 16-23.

[49]"It takes a work of the Holy Spirit in our hearts for us to see ourselves for what we really are—sinners, people who have broken God's law and are guilty before him, those who

carried out in reliance on the Spirit in a twofold sense: the believer is led by the Spirit to testify on behalf of Jesus, and the unbeliever is acted upon by the Spirit to respond to the testimony. Viewed from this perspective, evangelism will not fall prey to gimmickry and pressure. "The [Spirit] blows where it chooses" (Jn 3:8).

The fourth Paraclete saying (Jn 16:7-11) stresses the convicting role of the Holy Spirit. He proves the world wrong about sin (or "convicts the world of sin," as in the NRSV alternate translation), righteousness and judgment. The three items listed seem to involve the following points: by failing to believe in Jesus as the true revelation of God the Father, the unbelieving world is guilty of sin in its most fundamental sense, missing the mark; by means of the resurrection and exaltation of Jesus, the world's false verdict against Jesus is reversed and he is vindicated (i.e., shown to be "in the right"); by its wrongful judgment against Jesus, the unbelieving world now shares Satan's just condemnation as claimant to be world ruler.[50]

The fifth Paraclete saying reemphasizes the teaching ministry of the Holy Spirit in the lives of apostles (Jn 16:12-14). The connection to the preceding saying seems to be this: the Holy Spirit does not operate as an independent prosecutor; rather, his convicting ministry occurs by means of the witnessing community. The Holy Spirit thus promotes the glory of the Son, not himself. Furthermore, the Spirit guides the apostles into "all the truth," herein defined as the teaching belonging to the Father and Son ("All that the Father has is mine" [Jn 16:15]). There is no license for independent, esoteric teaching that breaks entirely new ground and supposedly relies on the Holy Spirit for its source. The relevance of this for the Johannine churches beset by incipient Gnosticism is obvious, but it also serves as a salutary reminder in our own time when the "new" and "exciting" are much in vogue. Teaching that claims to be Christian but is not christocentric is defective. This reminds us of the Colossian heresy that Paul combats and should warn our present generation against subtly substituting "spiritual experiences" for truth about Jesus.[51]

There is one more reference to the Holy Spirit in John's Gospel (Jn 20:22), a rather perplexing one. At face value, it suggests that the disciples

---

must say, 'We have left undone what we ought to have done and done what we ought not to have done'" (Leon Morris, *New Testament Theology* [Grand Rapids: Zondervan, 1986], p. 262).

[50]See M. M. B. Turner, "Holy Spirit," *DJG* 350. Morris draws attention to a connection with Pauline thought: "The language of justification, with its emphasis on righteousness, is typically Pauline; but this passage shows that Jesus used it during his earthly ministry" (*New Testament Theology*, p. 262).

[51]On the contemporary significance of this section in John, see the perceptive comments in Burge, *John*, pp. 405-13, 448-56.

received the Holy Spirit on the evening of resurrection Sunday. This, of course, does not square with Luke's account in Acts, where the pouring out of the Spirit clearly occurs on the day of Pentecost (Acts 2:1-4). Probably we are to understand Jesus' action in John 20:22 as proleptic—that is, a symbolic action anticipating what would happen forty days hence. Several times in Jesus' public and private ministry he performed symbolic actions in the mold of well-known OT prophetic figures (Isaiah, Jeremiah, Ezekiel). One thinks of the cleansing of the temple, the changing of water to wine, the cursing of the fig tree and especially the Last Supper. To these should be added this Johannine passage in which the breath of Jesus symbolizes the Spirit. To put it another way, the Spirit is the alter ego of Jesus. By means of the Spirit, Jesus himself is now present in all believers as is the Father (Jn 17:21). Mystical union is the essence of what it means to be part of the new community.

The other puzzling feature of this saying in John's Gospel is this promise: "If you forgive the sins of any, they are forgiven them; if you retain the sins of any, they are retained" (Jn 20:23). The meaning seems to be that the church is authorized to announce the terms whereby sinners may be forgiven and incorporated into the new community of faith. The church not only may announce the terms of forgiveness, but also may assure those who sincerely respond to the gospel invitation (cf. Mt 16:19; 18:18). The actual authority to carry out such a vital role is here linked with reception of the Spirit. Only by means of the leading and empowerment of the Holy Spirit may the church so act as the very mouthpiece of God.

Likewise, 1 John highlights the role of the Holy Spirit in providing the ground of religious certainty and the means of sanctification. Thus the Spirit assures believers of their status as children of God as they obey Christ's commandments (1 Jn 3:24). And both obedience to the great love commandment and confession of Christ's incarnation are enabled by the Holy Spirit and are evidence of his presence in one's life (1 Jn 4:1-6). Praxis and doctrine are intimately joined in Johannine theology, just as they are in Jesus and Paul. Assurance of one's faith in Jesus Christ comes up for discussion one more time in 1 John 5:6-12. Here is an interesting correlation of historical fact and the reality of the Spirit's presence. John mentions three witnesses whose testimonies to Christ converge: "the Spirit and the water and the blood" (1 Jn 5:8). The water apparently refers to Jesus' baptism and recalls the divine voice that authenticated Jesus' sonship (see Jn 3:29-34). The blood refers the cross. In 1 John we have a polemic against Docetics, who were denying a real incarnation and thus a real death on the part of the divine Christ. John therefore insists on the unity of the divine Christ and human Jesus in these two historical events. For John, they are foundational for salvation. The Spirit testifies to their reality and significance in the lives of those who embrace the truth (i.e., the gospel).

Revelation presents a portrait of the Holy Spirit from its own distinctive perspective, although, I believe, still in harmony with Johannine thought. The book is marked by a fourfold occurrence of the phrase "in the Spirit" (Rev 1:10; 4:2; 17:3; 21:10). These markers roughly divide the book into larger blocks of material corresponding more or less to the words of the risen Christ at Revelation 1:19: "Now write what you have seen, what is, and what is to take place after this." The inaugural vision, on the Lord's day (i.e., Sunday), corresponds to "what you have seen." Although John is not said to be in the Spirit in the section describing "what is," the Spirit speaks to the seven congregations and challenges them to faith and commitment ("Let anyone who has an ear listen to what the Spirit is saying to the churches" [Rev 2:7, 11, 17, 29; 3:6, 13, 22]). The section corresponding to "what must take place after this" (Rev 4:1) is marked by John's possession by the Spirit and translation to the heavenly realms (Rev 4:2). This begins the long central section detailing the protracted struggle for control of planet Earth. A "tale of two women," two antithetical visions that John beholds under the influence of the Spirit, summarizes the outcome of this titanic struggle. The first describes the degenerate world system styled "Babylon the Great, mother of whores and of earth's abominations" (Rev 17:5). The second describes the glorious bride, "the wife of the Lamb" (Rev 21:9). In short, the entire book claims to be a Spirit-inspired account of visionary experiences. This is in keeping with another NT work, 2 Peter, in which we have this programmatic statement: "First of all you must understand this, that no prophecy of scripture is a matter of one's own interpretation, because no prophecy ever came by human will, but men and women moved by the Holy Spirit spoke from God" (2 Pet 1:20-21).

Revelation shows a strong kinship with the ancient Hebrew prophets; in fact, allusions to virtually every prophetic book in the OT are peppered throughout its contents.[52] This reminds us of the role of the Holy Spirit in John's Gospel, whereby the apostles are promised that the Spirit will assist them in the proclamation of the truth. The selfsame Spirit who inspired the OT prophets comes alongside John the seer and inspires him. No wonder the resultant work is a virtual tapestry of OT allusions—the same composer and conductor is at work. In fact, the book of Revelation explicitly asserts that the proclamation of Jesus is the very essence of prophecy (Rev

---

[52]See the "Index of Allusions and Verbal Parallels" in Barbara Aland et al., eds., *The Greek New Testament* (4th ed.; Stuttgart: United Bible Societies, 1993), pp. 896-900.

19:10). Here again we see the NT conviction, springing from Jesus himself, that the OT must be read christologically if its true intent be grasped. Revelation is at one with our primary witnesses.

Two other references to the Holy Spirit in Revelation deserve mention. In both, the Spirit utters words of consolation and exhortation, reminding us of Paul's comment that the gift of prophecy functions for the "upbuilding and encouragement and consolation" of believers (1 Cor 14:3). The first is a word of consolation for the martyrs. Those who have not denied their faith under the onslaught of the antichrist are promised rest and reward (Rev 14:13). One recalls words of the Master: "The one who endures to the end will be saved" (Mk 13:13; Mt 24:13; cf. Lk 21:19). Paul and John likewise reinforce the necessity of perseverance (1 Cor 15:2; Gal 5:2-6; 6:7-9; Col 1:23; 1 Thess 3:2-5; Jn 15:6; 17:14-15).

The last direct address from the Spirit in the canon is a word of encouragement for those who long for the consummation of the kingdom. "The Spirit and the bride say, 'Come.' And let everyone who hears say, 'Come'" (Rev 22:17). The Spirit longs to finish the work of redemption, and the redeemed long to be finished! Perhaps we hear an echo of Jesus' words recorded by Luke: "I have come to bring fire on the earth, and how I wish it were already kindled! But I have a baptism to undergo, and how distressed I am until it is completed!" (Lk 12:49-50 NIV). Here I leave it to John to speak the last word, appropriately, a word from the cross: "When Jesus had received the wine, he said, 'It is finished.' Then he bowed his head and gave up his spirit" (Jn 19:30). Surely we hear an echo of this in Revelation when the risen Christ, seated on the throne, triumphantly proclaims, "It is done!" (Rev 21:6). The "not yet" is no more.

FOR FURTHER DISCUSSION

1. Why do the Johannine writings place such emphasis on realized eschatology?

2. Why is it important to insist that futuristic eschatology occurs in John?

3. What do common eschatological themes in Jesus, Paul and John tell us about early Christian preaching?

4. In what ways does Revelation culminate redemptive history?

5. How does one reconcile God's grace and wrath as depicted in Revelation?

6. How do John's metaphors for community complement Paul's?

7. Why is the Johannine teaching on the Holy Spirit so important for Christianity?

FOR FURTHER READING

Allison, Dale, Jr. "Eschatology." *DJG* 209.

Beale, G. K. "Eschatology." *DLNTD* 335-41.

Burge, Gary M. "John, Theology of." *EDBT* 425-27.

———. "John, Letters of." *DLNTD* 593-95.

———. *John*, pp. 361-480. NIVAC. Grand Rapids: Zondervan, 2000.

Guthrie, Donald. "Johannine Theology." *ZPEB* 3:632-36.

———. *New Testament Theology*, pp. 526-35, 720-31, 785-87, 798-801, 812-17, 823-26. Downers Grove, Ill.: InterVarsity Press, 1981.

Kümmel, Werner Georg. *The Theology of the New Testament according to Its Major Witnesses: Jesus-Paul-John*, translated by John E. Steely pp. 312-21. Nashville: Abingdon, 1973.

Kysar, Robert. "John, Epistles of." *ABD* 3:910-12.

———. "John, Gospel of." *ABD* 3:928-30.

Ladd, George E. *A Theology of the New Testament*, edited by Donald A. Hagner, pp. 306-44. Rev. ed. Grand Rapids: Eerdmans, 1993.

Marshall, I. Howard. "Johannine Theology." *ISBE* 2:1089-91.

———. *New Testament Theology*, pp. 522-24. Downers Grove, Ill.: InterVarsity Press, 2004.

Morris, Leon. *New Testament Theology*, pp. 256-65, 289-91, 292-97. Grand Rapids: Zondervan, 1986.

Beasley-Murray, G. R. "Revelation, Book of." *DLNTD* 1025-38.

Thielman, Frank. *Theology of the New Testament*, pp. 172-80, 551-55, 620-50. Grand Rapids: Zondervan, 2005.

Thompson, M. M. "John, Gospel of." *DJG* 382-83.

Turner, M. M. B. "Holy Spirit." *DJG* 347-51.

PART FIVE

THREE WITNESSES, ONE MESSAGE

11

Jesus, Paul and John

Putting It All Together

*Historical-critical exegesis of the NT writings forces us to
conclude that they . . . do not develop a unified teaching but
offer different theological presentations.*

E. Lohse

*There is a real unity in the New Testament presentation of
the Christian religion under all its diversity, in its view of
God, of his revelation, of salvation, of the finality and abso-
luteness of Christ.*

F. C. Grant

AT THE END OF THE DAY, CAN ONE RECOGNIZE in our three major witnesses—Jesus, Paul, John—a common message? Mainline scholarship in
general is wary of confident pronouncements in this regard.[1] In contrast to
this reticence, my concluding chapter argues that there is indeed a remarkable unity displayed in our three primary witnesses. Despite obvious differences in emphasis, style and diction, a profound unity ties them together in
what we can rightly call the central message of the NT. What are some of
these common threads?

---

[1]For a convenient and concise survey of leading scholars and their approach to this issue, see
D. A. Carson, "New Testament Theology," *DLNTD* 796-814.

A UNIFYING THEME

I begin by drawing attention, once again, to a leading theme that ties our three major witnesses together; indeed, it binds together the entire Christian Bible. There is one great message proclaimed from Genesis to Revelation: the coming of the kingdom of God.

As was discussed extensively in connection with the message and mission of Jesus, the announcement of the imminent arrival of the kingdom of God is the keynote of his preaching. The fundamental notion of the "now but not yet" in Jesus' message must be grasped in order to make sense of his various pronouncements and word pictures about the kingdom. Jesus believed that already the kingdom of God was present in his ministry, the powers of darkness were being pushed back, individuals must make a total commitment to its message, and it will ultimately issue in a glorious and triumphant climax to salvation history. This is the very heart of Jesus' theology.

Although the actual phrase "kingdom of God," or a variant thereof, occurs relatively infrequently in Paul's missionary correspondence, I have argued that in fact the notion is one of the fundamental substructures of Pauline thought without which one fails to grasp his indebtedness to the theology of Jesus as well as his own unique contribution to its theological elaboration. The reason for the low frequency resides in the circumstantial nature of his letters. Most of his correspondence is taken up with pressing pastoral concerns and crises; they are not polished theological essays.

Still, as Paul brings his theological convictions to bear on these varied circumstances, kingdom theology surfaces as crucial points in the argument. A good example occurs in Colossians 1:13, where, in a lead up to the majestic confessional statement (Col 1:15-20), the platform from which the "Colossian heresy" is critiqued, Paul asserts, "He has rescued us from the power of darkness and transferred us into the kingdom of his beloved Son, in whom we have redemption, the forgiveness of sins." Or, in a context dealing with tensions over dietary and calendrical disputes, Paul redirects the discussion by reminding his readers that "the kingdom of God is not food and drink but righteousness and peace and joy in the Holy Spirit" (Rom 14:17). Similar occurrences of this phrase punctuate Paul's parenesis and point to its underlying theological importance for Christian praxis (1 Cor 4:20; 6:9, 10; Gal 5:21; 1 Thess 2:12; 2 Thess 1:4). In two eschatological contexts (1 Cor 15:24, 50; 2 Tim 4:1, 18) Paul expects a grand consummation of the kingdom of God at the parousia.

Another line of argumentation in this regard is to recall the importance of the "now but not yet" rubric for grasping Pauline theology. Paul was not the originator of this notion; it derives from the Master himself. Several times Paul indicates his indebtedness to Christian tradition (Rom 1:3-4; 1 Cor 11:2, 23-26; 15:1-8). Paul's parenesis makes sense in terms of his belief that the kingdom of God was already present and yet had a future dimension.[2] In short, Paul's theological thought reflects his belief in the kingdom of God as a major construct. Its importance for Pauline theology is more substantial than its mere textual occurrences might otherwise suggest.

With regard to John, I readily admit that "kingdom of God" terminology almost disappears, although, significantly, at the terminal points of Jesus' ministry, as narrated by John, we see important occurrences (Jn 3:3, 5; 18:36). What must be recognized, however, is the presence of the kingdom of God clothed in different terminology and metaphors. Metaphors such as "light," "truth," "love," "knowledge" and "life" portray essentially the same notion as the kingdom of God. In addition, a vertical dualism ("above and below") overshadows, but by no means eliminates, the familiar horizontal dualism of the Synoptic tradition ("now but not yet"). Once again, circumstances dictated this terminological shift. John deliberately borrows terminology from his gnosticizing opponents and recasts the Master's teaching in order to effectively counteract this false teaching. The light, truth and knowledge of the Johannine Gospel and Epistles function just like the message of the kingdom of God in the Synoptics, expelling the powers of darkness and quelling rebellious hearts. Nor should instances in the Synoptics be forgotten where eternal life equates to life in the kingdom (Mk 10:17-27; 9:43, 45, 47; Mt 19:16, 29; 25:46; Lk 16:9; 18:30). Beneath Johannine metaphors, glimpses of kingdom theology appear. The concept of "now but not yet" is patently woven into the fabric of Johannine theology. The predominant stress on realized eschatology by no means eliminates the "not yet" dimension of the kingdom. For John, salvation in the present is incomplete; the believer still awaits the final expulsion of the ruler of this world.

In short, there is a fundamental thematic unity in the thought of Jesus, Paul and John. At the very center of this unity stands the kingdom of God. This major theme shapes the respective theological thought of our major witnesses. Priority, of course, goes to Jesus, the fountainhead of this teaching. Taking up the OT teaching about the kingdom of God and fundamentally redefining it, Jesus produces "new wine in new wineskins." Paul and John simply elaborate what is found in Jesus.

---

[2]Werner Kümmel nicely captures this perspective: "Paul also sees the present as the combination of the time of salvation and the hope of the consummation of salvation, both bound to the concrete Christ event and hence provisional and oriented to the consummation" (*The Theology of the New Testament According to Its Major Witnesses: Jesus-Paul-John*, trans. John E. Steely [Nashville: Abingdon, 1973], p. 327).

A UNIFYING STRUCTURE

Closely related to the "kingdom of God" theme is the issue of structure. Our primary witnesses display a common narrative substructure. Assumed throughout is a basic story line: the culmination of God's saving activity in Israel now supremely and finally revealed through the sinless life, atoning death, bodily resurrection and heavenly session of his beloved Son on behalf of his elect people (Mk 10:45; Jn 3:16; Rom 3:23-25; Gal 4:4-5; 1 Tim 2:5-6; 1 Jn 2:1-2; cf. Heb 1:1-4). Redemptive history best describes this narrative substructure and links the Testaments in one grand metanarrative. The NT story of Jesus' saving activity organically connects with OT salvation history. The Christ event climaxes a long series of saving deeds begun in the Garden of Eden (Gen 3:15) and culminating in the new Jerusalem (Rev 22:1-5).

This narrative underpinning of NT thought is essential for correct interpretation. At every point the interpreter must be sensitive to the fact that NT authors interpret the OT from the vantage point of Jesus Christ. Christological interpretation goes back to the Master (Lk 24:25-27). Christ is the fulfillment of the story of Israel (Mt 5:17); he and his followers constitute the new Israel (Rom 2:29; Gal 3:29; 6:16; Phil 3:3). The OT is a rich depository of evocative narratives, images, metaphors and symbols. Jesus, Paul and John creatively employ them in order to explicate the meaning of the kingdom of God and redemptive history. Inasmuch as the story of Jesus is an integral and culminating chapter in the larger story of God's dealings with Israel, one must always be alert to this context when reading specific texts. A continuing legacy of Oscar Cullmann is the attention now given to narrative theology for grasping the meaning of NT texts.[3] Among evangelical biblical theologians, following in the train of George Ladd, redemptive history remains a valued approach in affirming the unity of the entire Bible. In addition to the OT, one must also take into account interpretive traditions deriving from Second Temple Judaism that influenced the way NT authors read their sacred Scriptures.[4]

A FOCAL POINT

Is there a center or focal point in the three primary witnesses whom we

---

[3]See, for example, Richard B. Hays, *Echoes of Scripture in the Letters of Paul* (New Haven: Yale University Press, 1989); N. T. Wright, *The Climax of the Covenant: Christ and the Law in Pauline Theology* (Edinburgh: T & T Clark, 1991); idem, *Jesus and the Victory of God* (Minneapolis: Fortress, 1996).

[4]See further discussion in Larry R. Helyer, "The Necessity, Problems, and Promise of Second Temple Judaism for Discussions of New Testament Eschatology," *JETS* 47 (2004): 597-601.

have interrogated? I think so. The very heart of their message is Christ and the cross. Christology and soteriology, the person and work of Christ, are intertwined at the very center of NT proclamation, especially in our three witnesses. One cannot speak of one without the other. As Richard Longenecker says, "The earliest Christian theology was almost exclusively Christology. . . . What concerned them, and that which they centered upon, was the redemptive activity of God in the person and work of Jesus of Nazareth. No other consideration loomed so large in their thinking."[5] And, on a most encouraging note, there is significant agreement among biblical theologians across the theological spectrum that this is the case.[6]

In this context, I refer not to the cross as the actual instrument of torture used to crucify Jesus but rather to the theological significance of the cross. Much more is involved than the grisly execution of an innocent man, something that occurred rather often under the Roman occupation of Israel. The cross constitutes the supreme moment of redemptive history. God's saving work on behalf of fallen human beings uniquely comes to expression in this particular event.

How do our three witnesses express this? A problem immediately surfaces: Jesus says very little about the cross. If the cross is so important to NT theology, why does Jesus not say more about it? The concept of progressive revelation must be taken into account. Owing to the understandable limitations in his disciples' comprehension, Jesus did not, during his earthly ministry, devote extensive teaching to this doctrine. Sound pedagogy requires that one begin where students are and take them where they need to go. What Jesus does is warn his disciples of his impending death, although it appears that they had great difficulty grasping what was actually going to happen and why it was necessary (Mk 8:32; 9:30-32; 10:32-34; Lk 18:31-34). They do not make the connection between Jesus, the Son of Man and the suffering Servant of Isaiah 53. Only in the post-Easter era, with the personal instruction of the risen Christ (Acts 1:3) and the aid of the Holy Spirit (Jn 15:26-27; 16:7-15), do all the pieces in the puzzle come together

---

[5]R. Longenecker, "New Testament Theology," *ZPEB* 4:431.

[6]See G. B. Caird, *New Testament Theology*, compl. and ed. L. D. Hurst (Oxford: Clarendon, 1994), pp. 409-12. Ferdinand Hahn recently published the most ambitious and comprehensive NT theology yet. Hahn holds that "the NT writings express . . . themes differently, and that there are tensions and even contradictions among them. . . . Nevertheless, there is a remarkable agreement and convergence among the NT writings in regard to God's revelatory activity in Christ" (*Theologie des Neuen Testaments* [2 vols.; Tübingen: Mohr Siebeck, 2002], 2:803-5, summarized and cited in Frank J. Matera, "New Testament Theology: History, Method, and Identity," *CBQ* 67 [2005]: 14). From an explicitly evangelical perspective, I commend to the reader the fine summaries by Leon Morris, David Wenham and Frank Thielman (see the bibliography at the end of the present chapter).

for them. Then the cross is seen in all its glory.

Despite this paucity of teaching on the cross during Jesus' earthly ministry, a few highly significant sayings point to this central idea. Mark places an important announcement of Jesus' death right at the hinge point of his work, the confession of Peter at Caesarea Philippi (Mk 8:29). Immediately after Peter's confession, Jesus predicts what will happen to the Son of Man (Mk 8:31-33). This so unnerves Peter that he rebukes Jesus, only to receive a stinging reproach in return. Then follows this dramatic and challenging invitation from Jesus: "If any want to become my followers, let them deny themselves and take up their cross and follow me."

The context of this saying suggests that the Son of Man's death is paradigmatic for discipleship; that is, disciples imitate their Lord by complete commitment to him and his teaching. Since for Jesus' audience a Roman cross was an instrument of barbaric torture and not a pretty piece of jewelry to be worn around one's neck, carrying one's cross to a place of execution is a call for total commitment—the willingness, if need be, to give up one's life for Christ's sake. Losing one's life in order to gain it is a tall order (Mk 8:35), the kind of commitment that only a few willingly embrace. In short, this saying draws attention to the cross as a symbol of unwavering allegiance and devotion. As Mark's Gospel makes clear, Jesus of Nazareth gives his life as a ransom for many (Mk 10:45) and pours out his blood for many (Mk 14:24). The vicarious and substitutionary nature of Jesus' death is vividly implied in these sayings. Although Jesus does not explicitly link the cross with the ransom, Mark certainly understands it this way, as do the other NT writers.

Yet for the original audience, much remains unexplained and enigmatic: why must the Son of Man undergo great suffering, and precisely who is the Son of Man? Jesus only adds to their bewilderment when he speaks of the Son of Man rising from the dead (Mk 9:9) and reveals that his sufferings and betrayal are prophesied in Scripture (Mk 9:12; 14:17-21; Lk 18:31-34). Of course, Mark's Christian readers already know the answer because they know the story and have embraced its message. Those hearing and reading for the first time, however, must count the cost and make a weighty decision. Will the "many" for whom Jesus died demonstrate what the cross signifies?

I go a step further. The Jesus tradition conveys the message of the cross indirectly. Kenneth Bailey's treatment of Jesus' parables demonstrates how the message of the cross is unobtrusively imbedded in these stories drawn from everyday life.[7] For example, in the parable of the lost sons, the actions

---

[7]See Kenneth E. Bailey, *Poet and Peasant: A Literary Cultural Approach to the Parables in Luke* (Grand Rapids: Eerdmans, 1976); idem, *Through Peasant Eyes: More Lucan Para-*

of the leading figure, the waiting father, foreshadow the cross. The father, ignoring convention and custom, lays aside his dignity and displays an unprecedented measure of grace to an undeserving, rebellious son. Surely the message of Golgotha resonates in that memorable story. The stories of the sinful woman (Lk 7:36-50) and the dishonest manager (Lk 16:1-9) likewise convey unforgettable word pictures of the cross. The taproot of the doctrine of the cross is rooted in the teaching of Jesus.

In Paul, the full light of theological reflection on the cross bursts forth. He is supremely a theologian of the cross. Paul's solemn vow says it all: "May I never boast of anything except the cross of our Lord Jesus Christ, by which the world has been crucified to me, and I to the world" (Gal 6:14). Although *cross* is a word that Paul does not use frequently in his letters (ten times), the concept of the cross runs through his correspondence like a scarlet thread. Abstracting the cross as a symbol and summary for God's saving activity revealed in Christ, Paul employs an assortment of metaphors conveying its deep significance: sacrifice, redemption, reconciliation, justification and divine combat against the powers of darkness. These and others contribute to a rich montage demonstrating the undeserved grace and unfathomable love of God in Christ. Sometimes Paul speaks of the death of Christ (Rom 5:10; 6:5, 10; 1 Cor 11:26; 2 Cor 4:10; Phil 2:8; 3:10) or the blood of Christ (Rom 3:25; 5:9; 1 Cor 10:16; Eph 1:7; 2:13; Col 1:20), but these are essentially variations on the same reality. Underlying all these varied expressions is a central Pauline affirmation shared by John and, for that matter, all the NT witnesses: "God was in Christ reconciling the world to Himself" (2 Cor 5:19 NASB). The cross did not pit Father against Son; at the cross, Father and Son acted in concert to accomplish the salvation of all who believe. C. A. Dinsmore has it right: "There was a cross in the heart of God before there was one planted on the green hill outside Jerusalem."[8]

To those enamored with Greek thought, for whom the notion of the cross was scandalous and foolish (1 Cor 1:18), Paul hammers home its centrality for new life in Christ. Paul's pastoral directives to an "out of control" congregation in Corinth amount to an urgent summons to implement the theological significance of the cross for life together in the church. In place of rhetoric, worldly wisdom, status, selfishness, pride and honor, Paul urges a cruciform lifestyle—that is, a life conforming to the self-giving love displayed by Jesus Christ on the cross. The magnificent portrait of love

---

bles, Their Culture and Style (Grand Rapids: Eerdmans, 1980).

[8]C. A. Dinsmore, *Atonement in Literature and Life* (London: Constable, 1906), p. 232, cited in D. M. Baillie, *God Was in Christ: An Essay on Incarnation and Atonement* (New York: Scribner, 1948), p. 194.

(1 Cor 13) "matches both his understanding of God's love as disclosed in Christ (Rom 5.6, 8; 15.3, 7-8; 2 Cor 8.9; Phil 2.6-11) and his understanding of what constitutes appropriate conduct for those who are in Christ (10.24, 32-33; Rom 15.1-2; 2 Cor 5.14-15; Phil 2.3-4)."[9]

Paul's second letter to the Corinthians responds to personal attacks and denials of his apostolic authority by turning his opponents' argument on its head. Instead of asserting his rights and reciting his impressive credentials, recommendations and achievements (something that his opponents relied on [see 2 Cor 3:1; 10:12-17; 11:12-13, 16-23]), he resorts to a "fool's" speech. The underlying argument of this clever rhetorical move is simply this: a true apostle demonstrates a cruciform life and ministry; his detractors fail to measure up. Self-giving love and suffering (2 Cor 11:23-33) are the primary credentials for apostleship. The shadow of the cross falls heavily upon this portrait of a genuine apostle even though the word *cross* occurs not even once![10]

Much more could be said in this regard, but I dare not conclude without drawing attention to the scope of the cross according to Paul. Far from being merely an existential encounter, as important as that is, the cross literally, not mythologically, conveys cosmic implications. Christ's death on the cross is much more than martyrdom, the memory of which motivates followers to more resolve, as important as that is. We must go beyond ourselves and reckon with this stupendous truth: the death of Christ on the cross reconciled fallen and rebellious humanity to God. In some way, beyond our present ability to fathom, the entire cosmos will be renewed because of that once-for-all event (Rom 8:18-25; Col 1:20). No wonder Paul insists, "In Christ, there is a new creation: everything old has passed away; see, everything has become new!" (2 Cor 5:17).

As we noted earlier, John deliberately structures his Gospel so that the climactic moment, the moment when the glory of the Son is supremely unveiled, occurs precisely at the cross (Jn 12:23-26). There the king of glory reigns, and from there he draws all people to himself into a fellowship of the cross (Jn 12:32). Revelation likewise employs supreme irony in its depiction of the great lion of the tribe of Judah suddenly portrayed as a lamb "standing as if it had been slaughtered" (Rev 5:6). John's writings, more than any other in the NT, emphasize the love of God poured out on

---

[9]Victor Paul Furnish, "1 Corinthians," in *The HarperCollins Study Bible: New Revised Standard Version*, ed. Wayne A. Meeks (New York: HarperCollins, 1993), p. 2158, note on 1 Corinthians 13:4-7.

[10]For a good discussion of the notion of cruciform in Paul's thought, see Michael J. Gorman, *Apostle of the Crucified Lord: A Theological Introduction to Paul and His Letters* (Grand Rapids: Eerdmans, 2004), pp. 115-23.

his redeemed people. It is the cross that displays the Father's unfathomable love for a lost world (Jn 3:16), and it is this love flowing from the cross that transforms the lives of those who stand in its shadow (1 Jn 1:7; 2:1-6; 3:1-3, 16; 4:7-12). "See what love the Father has given us, that we should be called the children of God; and that is what we are. . . . For this is the message you have heard from the beginning, that we should love one another" (1 Jn 3:1, 11).

HUMAN PLIGHT

The three witnesses converge in their understanding of the human condition outside the kingdom. They sketch a completely hopeless situation. There is a desperate need for divine intervention, without which none can be rescued. The human heart is rebellious and intractable. The world system in which humanity lives runs counter to kingdom values and exerts a powerful pull away from God and his kingdom. Standing behind the entire world system and manipulating it to great effect, lurks the "Dark Lord," the prince of this world, the archdeceiver, the devil. He and his demonic denizens exert a malign influence through all aspects of human life and culture and constantly seek to remake people in his own misshapen, self-centered, loveless image. The consequences for fallen humanity are predictable and dire; the verdict is unanimous: all stand condemned and deserving of divine punishment (Rom 3:23).

Once again the teaching of Jesus is foundational. The Pauline and Johannine portraits of the human condition go back to the teaching of the Master. Jesus describes the human situation in desperate terms. Several parables starkly depict the condition of fallen humanity (Mt 13:10-15; 13:37-42; 13:49-50; 23:1-39). Mark's Gospel is well known for its portrayal of the disciples as dull and lacking faith (Mk 4:13; 7:18; 8:17, 21; 9:32). Within the inner circle of the Twelve stands Judas the betrayer (Mk 3:19). Jesus' family members do not believe in him and think that he has suffered a mental breakdown (Mk 3:21). He characterizes his own followers as those who are evil (Mt 7:11). He warns his listeners of eternal punishment and seems to imply that those who suffer this fate are not few but rather many (Mt 7:14; Lk 13:23-24). This is not a pretty picture.

Jesus warns against trusting anything in this world for security and salvation (Mt 6:19-34). Riches not only fail to provide real spiritual security but also are a serious threat to the soul's health (Mk 10:23-25 pars.; Lk 6:24; 16:13-15; 18:24). Only trust in the heavenly Father and grasping hold of Jesus' teaching can offer any real sense of security in a fallen world (Mt 6:32-34; 7:24-27).

Human beings are under assault from the "Dark Lord," Satan. So Jesus teaches (Lk 13:16). In spite of modern embarrassment about this, Jesus' theology takes seriously the reality of the devil and demons. Jesus' ministry of exorcism is not some spectacular sideshow; it lies at the very heart of his mission (Lk 11:20). Jesus teaches that there is an ongoing struggle for control of the planet and the human heart. He personally launches the final and decisive offensive against the evil empire (Mt 16:18). But the war is fierce and Satan is not easily dislodged. The campaign lasts until the parousia (Mt 8:29; 25:41). For now, the tide of battle ebbs and flows; Satan notches his victories before his final defeat at the end of the age (Mk 4:15 pars.; Mt 13:39; Lk 22:3). Until then, believers must be vigilant and cognizant of his tactics (Mk 8:33 par.; Lk 22:31).

Turning to Paul, one readily sees that his description of the human plight matches that of the Master. Whether speaking of the individual, the world or Satan, he sketches the same stark situation. In fact, Paul goes into more detail about aspects that are only rudimentary in Jesus' teaching. In Paul we find the most developed anthropology and hamartiology in the entire NT. His analysis of sinful humanity probes deep beneath the surface of sinful attitudes and actions into the well springs of the human heart (the flesh) and reaches back into the mists of antiquity to the very genesis of sin in Adam's act of disobedience (Rom 5:12-21). There is in Paul a more developed reflection on the seductiveness of the world system for believers (Rom 12:2; 1 Cor 1:20-21, 27-28; 2:12; 3:19; 5:10; 2 Cor 10:2-4; 11:18; Gal 4:3; 6:14; Eph 2:2, 12; 6:12; Col 2:8, 20; 2 Tim 4:10). And in Paul we have a more developed sense of the demonic dimension of evil. We read of hostile rulers, authorities, powers of this dark world and spiritual forces of evil in the heavenly realms, against whom believers must arm themselves and exercise unceasing vigilance (Gal 4:3, 8; Eph 6:10-18; Col 2:8, 10, 15). Paul's understanding of the human condition clearly has common ground in the thought of Jesus. Both, of course, are indebted to the OT Scriptures and Second Temple Judaism.

The same can be said of John. He too portrays an evil axis of human sin, the world system and Satan. Though couched in a somewhat different idiom, John's view of the human plight fundamentally agrees with that of Jesus and Paul. According to John, darkness, a metaphor for the fallen human condition, lies over the world of human beings, who have not "understood" the light (Jn 1:5 NIV), who love darkness rather than light (Jn 3:19). Over this dark kingdom reigns the Dark Lord, the "ruler of this world" (Jn 12:31; 14:30). Even Jesus' own people "did not accept him" (Jn 1:11), and after Judas the betrayer leaves the upper room, we read the ominously freighted words "And it was night" (13:30).

First John employs the same imagery depicting the human plight. Darkness and light represent fundamentally opposed existential states and salvific outcomes. For John, it is intolerable that false teachers blatantly disregard the ontological impossibility of claiming to be in the light while yet living a life having all the earmarks of darkness. No greater tension exists than to claim to be in the light and yet not love one's brothers and sisters. Praxis for John is inseparably linked to theological purity. The confession of Jesus Christ come in the flesh must be joined to obedience to Christ's great commandment: love one another. This can be stated in terms of a test for true discipleship: "Whoever says, 'I abide in him,' ought to walk just as he walked" (1 Jn 2:6). According to John, the hallmark of believers is that they overcome the evil one (1 Jn 2:13-14) and his agents in the world (1 Jn 4:4) by means of their faith in Christ (1 Jn 5:4). The book of Revelation dramatically portrays the intensity of this spiritual conflict by styling believers as those who overcome (Rev 2:7, 11, 17, 26; 3:5, 12, 21; 21:7). John's second two letters testify to the ongoing struggles of believers still beset by darkness, their own hearts and false teaching (2 Jn 7-11; 3 Jn 9-11).

In Revelation the most graphic portrayal of rebellious human nature found anywhere in the NT confronts us. The world system, viewed through the lens of imperial Rome, displays its dark underside (Rev 17—18). The evil triumvirate, the unholy trinity—the dragon, the beast and the false prophet—show their true colors by unveiling their inveterate hatred for the sons of Adam and daughters of Eve (Rev 13). The response of sinners to being justly punished (Rev 16:7), "They did not repent and give [God] glory" (Rev 16:9; cf. Rev 16:11, 21), is a shocking commentary on the unregenerate human heart. The fate of the wicked in Revelation matches that described by Jesus and Paul (Mt 5:22; 18:9; 25:41; Rom 9:22; Phil 3:19; 1 Thess 5:3; 2 Thess 1:8-9).

ECCLESIOLOGY: THE NEW COVENANT COMMUNITY

All three of our witnesses, each in his own distinctive way, affirms the creation of a new people of God, centered in a new covenant arrangement and called to mutual obligations to maintain this covenant relationship.[11]

The Jesus tradition attributes to him actions and sayings that shed light on the new covenant community. First, it is highly significant that Jesus chose twelve disciples to form a sort of inner circle around him (Mk

---

[11]For this section, I am indebted to the fine treatment by Petrus J. Gräbe, *New Covenant, New Community: The Significance of Biblical and Patristic Covenant Theology for Contemporary Understanding* (Waynesboro, Ga.; Paternoster, 2006).

3:13-19 pars.). The number "twelve" can hardly be a coincidence. It recalls the twelve-tribe federation of ancient Israel as recounted in the Pentateuch and Prophets (Former and Latter). Given the prophecies of a regathered and renewed Israel in the latter days (Is 2:1-4; 11:1-16; 60:1-14; Ezek 34:11-31; 36:16-38; Hos 2:14-23; Amos 9:11-15), Jesus' selection of twelve apostles conveys the deep-seated conviction that they constitute the righteous remnant, the new Israel.[12] In this light, Jesus' ministry was a reform movement. Israel is not abandoned; Israel is reconstituted.

Jesus' itinerant ministry, as recorded in the Synoptics, consists of preaching, teaching and healing primarily in the synagogues and countryside of Galilee, with brief forays into Judea and also into neighboring provinces and districts that were predominantly Gentile. Jesus invites listeners to join his movement. The circle of disciples is much broader than the Twelve. The relationship of Jesus to his followers bears some similarity to that of recognized Jewish teachers and their pupils in the first century. Jesus' ministry, however, because of its itinerant nature and "on-the-job training," is not generally typical of the time. Definitely atypical is the inclusion of women disciples who accompany and support him financially (Mt 14:21; Mk 15:41; Lk 8:2-3; 23:49, 55; 24:22).

What was the purpose of this activity? Did Jesus consciously intend to create the church? Many modern scholars doubt it because the kingdom of God dominates Jesus' preaching, not the church that arose later.[13] As Howard Marshall rightly reminds us, we should not hastily identify the kingdom of God with the empirical church—after all, only Matthew uses the Greek word *ekklēsia*, the primary term used for the body of believers in the NT letters (Mt 16:18; 18:17); nonetheless, this should not obscure the fact that "there is a community of people who own God as king (however imperfectly they may obey him) and in whom his gracious power is at work."[14] Jesus describes this community in various ways. He can address his disciples as a "little flock" (Lk 12:32) or liken them to "a city built on a hill" (Mt 5:14). Several parables assume that followers are like servants (Mt 20:1-16; 25:14-30) or managers and renters working on a large estate (Lk 16:1-8); indeed, the estate itself can sometimes imply the idea of this new community ("his field" [Mt 13:24]). On other occasions Jesus employs the

---

[12]Ibid., p. 86. See also E. P. Sanders, *Jesus and Judaism* (Philadelphia: Fortress, 1985), pp. 95-106; Wright, *Jesus and the Victory of God*, p. 300; John P. Meier, "Jesus, the Twelve and the Restoration of Israel," in *Restoration: Old Testament, Jewish, and Christian Perspectives*, ed. James M. Scott (JSJSup 72; Leiden: Brill, 2001), pp. 365-404.

[13]For a helpful discussion, see George E. Ladd, *A Theology of the New Testament*, ed. Donald A. Hagner (rev. ed.; Grand Rapids: Eerdmans, 1993), pp. 103-17.

[14]I. H. Marshall, "Church," *DJG* 123.

word picture of a wedding party (Mk 2:19; Mt 22:1-14; 25:1-13). A particularly important image is that of family. A striking saying implies that Jesus' followers are incorporated into a new family: "'Who are my mother and my brothers?' And looking at those who sat around him, he said, 'Here are my mothers and my brothers! Whoever does the will of God is my brother and sister and mother'" (Mk 3:33-35). The upshot of this is that the unique Matthean material, putting into the mouth of Jesus his intention to raise up a community of believers designated as "my church," should not be hastily dismissed as anachronistic. There is good reason to believe that this was Jesus' intention from the beginning.[15]

The account of the Last Supper should be read in connection with the new people of God. Jesus clearly speaks of a new covenant to be established on the basis of his death (Mk 14:24; Mt 26:28; Lk 22:20). As is well known, Jeremiah and Ezekiel prophesied that in the future the Lord would make a new covenant with Israel and Judah (Jer 31:31-33; 32:40; Ezek 16:60-62; 34:25-26). This new covenant must have been what Jesus was referring to the evening before his death. The connection of this meal with the Passover is also significant because of its covenantal context. Jesus' twelve disciples constituted a renewed Israel in fulfillment of the prophetic promises. But are the "many" for whom Jesus' blood is poured out confined to repentant Jews only? There are indications, especially in Matthew's Gospel, that Gentiles are also incorporated into this new people of God.[16] Here I will lay out the essential elements of the Pauline and Johannine notion of the church consisting of both Jew and Gentile.

The summons to be part of this new covenant community takes a distinctive form in Jesus' preaching. Simply stated, he called individuals to "deny themselves and take up their cross and follow me" (Mk 8:34 pars.). As we already noted, this involves the notion of dying to self and living for Christ. An important outward sign of willingness to accept this challenge consists of table fellowship with the Master and his disciples. Such table fellowship serves as an acted parable portraying the expected eschatological banquet of the messianic kingdom (Lk 14:15). This stands in stark contrast to the practice of exclusive and hierarchical table fellowship practiced by the Pharisees, Jewish sectarianism and, indeed, Mediterranean culture in general during the first century. Jesus' practice is "radically open" (Lk 5:30 pars.; cf. Lk 14:23-24). Breaking bread together in a new community

---

[15]Ibid., p. 124. For a more detailed argument in agreement with Marshall, see Ben Witherington III, *Jesus, Paul and the End of the World* (Downers Grove, Ill.: InterVarsity Press, 1992), pp. 84-92.

[16]See S. McKnight, "Gentile," *DJG* 259-63.

composed of people who cross traditional boundary lines earmarks the Jesus movement.[17] A saying of Jesus highlights this break with tradition: "Many will come from east and west and will eat with Abraham, Isaac and Jacob in the kingdom of heaven" (Mt 8:11; cf. Lk 13:29). The essence of discipleship in the ministry of Jesus involves the twin ideas of incorporation and participation. The notion of a new covenant community bound to the person and teachings of Jesus of Nazareth sums it up nicely. The followers of Jesus, both Jews and Gentiles, constitute the new Israel living under the new covenant.

Turning to Paul, one is surprised that, like the term *kingdom of God*, the word *covenant (diathēkē)* is infrequent in his letters (ten times). This should not, however, lead to the inference that the idea of a new covenant community is of little or no importance to him. On the contrary, there are numerous indications that Paul's theology assumes this concept as a fundamental substructure.[18]

Although the word *covenant* occurs but twice in Romans, one appearance carries great weight. Paul is struggling with a personally wrenching question: why are the Jewish people, by and large, rejecting the gospel (Rom 9—11)? As he brings his reflections to a close, he reveals a mystery (the partial and temporary hardening of Israel [Rom 11:25]) and voices his certain conviction that "all Israel will be saved" (Rom 11:26). This is supported by an appeal to prophetic Scripture, in this case a conflation of texts from Isaiah and Jeremiah (Is 59:20-21; 27:9; Jer 31:33-34). The last part of the quotation reads, "And this is my covenant with them, when I take away their sins" (Rom 11:27). Note especially that this text recalls the new covenant prophecy of Jeremiah and was alluded to by Jesus at the Last Supper. The bottom line is this: Paul believes that a majority of the Jewish people will at last (apparently in connection with the parousia) come to Christ because of the new covenant prophecies. Although Gentiles are now entering and experiencing the blessings of the new covenant (Rom 11:17, 25), the Jewish people will repent and be grafted back into the olive tree (a metaphor for the people of God [Rom 11:23-24, 26-29]).

This core conviction surfaces explicitly at other places in Paul's letters. For example, in 2 Corinthians 3:1-18, a highly polemical section, Paul

---

[17]"One goal of Jesus' strategy of inclusive table fellowship was presenting himself and his followers as a living parable of how a renewed Israel could indeed live together from God's abundance" (S. Bartschy, "Table Fellowship," *DJG* 799 [see the entire article, pp. 796-800]).

[18]See W. S. Campbell, "Covenant and New Covenant," *DPL* 179-83.

seems to be responding to critics who are denying his apostolic status and denouncing his gospel. His argument in this extraordinary passage contrasts the greater glory of the new covenant, of which he is a minister, to the inferior covenant of Mount Sinai, administered by Moses. Paul assumes in his argument that believers, Jew and Gentile, are now part of a more glorious, new covenant.

In another illuminating passage, also highly polemical, Paul contrasts two covenants. The covenant of promise first established with Abraham and his heirs is stylized both as a free woman and her son, Sarah and Isaac, and as a city, the Jerusalem above. The other covenant, made on Mount Sinai, is stylized as the slave woman and her son, Hagar and Ishmael, and corresponds to the present Jerusalem, which likewise is in (spiritual) slavery with her children (i.e., the Judaizers). Although Paul is arguing a different point than 2 Corinthians 3, underlying both arguments is a core conviction: the true people of God stand in a new covenant relationship promised to Abraham and his heirs through faith in Jesus Christ.

This conviction is strengthened in numerous ways in passages not using explicit new covenant terminology. For example, in 1 Corinthians 10:1-13 Paul, by recounting the story of the wilderness wanderings, warns the congregation about being involved in pagan temple sacrifices. What is fascinating is his easy assumption that the ancient Israelites are "our ancestors" (1 Cor 10:1). The predominantly Gentile Christians at Corinth are connected to the ancient people of Israel. The lessons of that era are directly applicable to the Corinthians. In short, Paul assumes that they are the continuation of Israel, the people of God. This could be multiplied many times over. Like Jesus, Paul uses family language to describe the new relationship that believers now enjoy. God is heavenly Father, and believers are sons and daughters (Rom 8:16-17; Eph 5:1: Phil 2:15) who look to Jesus as the firstborn son. Indeed, they anticipate being conformed into his image (Rom 8:29). The most frequent designation for believers is the expression "brothers and sisters" (NRSV, TNIV). Paul also regularly calls believers "God's people" (Rom 12:13; 1 Cor 16:1; 2 Cor 9:12; Eph 2:19; 3:8; 4:12; 5:3; Col 3:12; 2 Thess 1:10). He also uses agricultural and architectural metaphors to make the same point, likening believers to a field (1 Cor 3:9; cf. Mt 13:38) or a great temple rising to the sky (1 Cor 3:9; Eph 2:21). Particularly worth noting are those occasions when he refers to Gentile believers as "the circumcision" in a spiritual sense (Rom 2:28-29; Phil 3:3; Col 2:11). The importance of circumcision as the sign of the covenant relationship between God and the Jewish people makes these references all the more remarkable.

I conclude with a highly significant appellation that Paul applies to the

Galatian believers. Having summarized his argument in one climactic statement, "Neither circumcision nor uncircumcision is anything; but a new
creation is everything!" (Gal 6:15), Paul pronounces a benediction upon all
who concur with this affirmation: "As for those who will follow this rule—
peace be upon them, and mercy, and upon the Israel of God" (Gal 6:16).
This benediction, very similar to synagogue benedictions, seems to refer
to all Christians, whether Jewish or Gentile, as the Israel of God. If this
interpretation is correct, one could scarcely find a more striking declaration
that Gentiles are now incorporated into Israel and that this new Israel is the
new covenant community.

So how does Paul typically summon individuals to be part of this new
covenant community? Proclaiming the gospel after the cross and resurrection, Paul appeals to his readers to die and rise with Christ. The notions of
incorporation and participation are front and center. Paul himself testifies
that he has "been crucified with Christ" and now lives in the flesh "by faith
in the Son of God" (Gal 2:19b-20). He pointedly reminds the Romans that
"our self was crucified with him," and that they "will certainly be united
with him in a resurrection like his." These two moments of individual salvation history are dramatically symbolized by the rite of baptism by im-
mersion (Rom 6:1-11). The "in Christ" motif permeates Pauline parenesis.
Although this is verbally dissimilar from Jesus' call for discipleship, the
organic connection can scarcely be missed.

Only one time does the word *covenant* occur in the Johannine corpus,
at Revelation 11:19, a reference to the archetypal, heavenly ark of the covenant. Surely, one would think, covenant theology has no place in Johannine
thought. But once again, such an admission would be premature because
John, employing different metaphors, conveys the essential ideas of covenant: incorporation and participation.[19]

Using dualistic terminology, John speaks of two spiritual realities: light
and darkness. Those who respond to the light, walk in the light (1 Jn 1:7).
There is a mutual exclusivity between these two realms (Jn 3:19-21; 1 Jn
2:8-10). One participates in the "fruit" of these two realms or states (Jn
11:9-10; 1 Jn 1:6-10) (Paul makes a similar point in Rom 7:4-6).

Well known from John is the image of Jesus' followers as a flock of sheep
that enters a sheepfold at night and goes out to pasture the next day (Jn
10:1-6). Jesus is likened to a gate through which the sheep enter (Jn 10:2,
7-10) and the good shepherd who leads them in and out (Jn 10:2-4), knows

---

[19]"Although one cannot detect a covenant theology in the Johannine literature in the narrow
sense of the word since the term does not appear in John, one can still speak of a reflection
of the new covenant notion" (Gräbe, *New Covenant, New Community*, p. 149).

each sheep intimately (10:3-6, 14), and lays down his life for them (Jn 10:11, 15, 17-18). Essentially, this is covenant theology, with its twin ideas of incorporation and participation, under a different image. In Revelation believers are not explicitly called "sheep," but the image of the Lamb surrounded by his adoring people stands out in bold relief. Highly significant is the affirmation that Jesus Christ is the shepherd who "is seated on the throne" (Rev 7:15) and is "at the center of the throne" (Rev 7:17). As such, he "will be their shepherd, and he will guide them to springs of the water of life" (Rev 7:17).

Besides speaking of walking in the light, John's Gospel and 1 John strike a keynote of abiding (remaining [NIV]) in fellowship with Christ (Jn 15:4, 6-7, 9-10; 1 Jn 2:24, 27; cf. Rev 2:13; 14:12). This is the typical Johannine summons to discipleship. For example, Christ is the vine, believers are the branches, and God the Father is the vineyard owner (Jn 15:1-11). Incorporation and participation lie just below the surface of this metaphor. Only as one continues to abide in Christ and observe his teaching is fruitfulness possible; indeed, spiritual life of any kind is contingent upon continuance in his word. Although couched in different terms, the essence of covenant theology is present. This becomes clear when we examine the occurrence of the notion of a "new commandment" in John (Jn 12:50; 13:34; 15:12, 14, 17; 1 Jn 2:7-8; 3:23; 4:21; 2 Jn 5-6; cf. Rev 3:10). This new commandment is actually equivalent to the prophesied new covenant of Jeremiah and Ezekiel and is summarized in the love commandment.

ESCHATOLOGY

My last category demonstrating fundamental unity among the three primary witnesses is eschatology. All three are on the same page in terms of their understanding of the climax of the kingdom of God. In my view, this is because Paul and John, theologians in their own right, elaborate Jesus' eschatological teaching. But is it possible to crystallize this expanded teaching into a single motif? Probably not. The eschatological teaching of Jesus and his apostles is simply too variegated to be reduced to a single idea. But perhaps there is a concept that comes close to including the manifold truths of the eschatological dénouement. I offer the related ideas of restoration and new creation.[20]

---

[20]"The New Testament writings are united in the conviction that the eschatological restoration both of Israel and of all things has dawned with the coming of Christ Jesus" (Frank Thielman, *Theology of the New Testament* [Grand Rapids: Zondervan, 2005], p. 724). See also Greg Beale, "The Eschatological Conception of New Testament Theology," in *Eschatology in Bible and Theology: Evangelical Essays at the Dawn of the New Millenium*,

Jesus understood his ministry in terms of the inbreaking of the kingdom of God. The kingdom of God possesses a "now but not yet" character. But in what terms did he see the "not yet" dimension? What follows is a brief summary of a number of texts that sketch a partial answer.

Easily documented are standard items of Jewish belief that Jesus continued to affirm. Among them are final judgment (Mt 7:21-23; Lk 17:30-35), the resurrection of both the righteous and wicked (Mk 12:18-27 pars.; 9:43, 45, 47 par.), and everlasting reward for the righteous and punishment for the wicked (Mt 13:38; 25:31-46). Going well beyond the belief of his contemporaries, however, are those passages in which Jesus appears as a witness for or against the accused (Mt 10:32-33); in others, he actually presides as judge (Mt 7:21-23; 16:27).

Jesus, like other first-century Jews, believes that Daniel's "one like a human being" (Dan 7:13 [see NRSV margin: "one like a son of man"]) will come from heaven and reign forever (Dan 7:14; cf. *1 En.* 37—71). What distinguishes him from his compatriots is his claim that he himself is that particular human being, the Son of Man (Mk 14:62). In regard to the timing, he only gives general indicators of the course of this age, such as war, famines, earthquakes, persecution (Mk 13:4-9; Mt 24:3-13) and one objective that must be fulfilled before his coming: preaching the gospel of the kingdom throughout the world (Mk 13:10; Mt 24:14). In my opinion, there is one, definite, preliminary event preceding his coming: a "desolating sacrilege." Even though the Synoptic tradition does not identify who perpetrates this sacrilege, I think that it can be inferred that Jesus expected the appearance of the antichrist, whose character and deeds are reminiscent of the Jews' archenemy, Antiochus IV Epiphanes (Mk 13:14; Mt 24:15; cf. Dan 9:27; 11:31; 12:11; 1 Macc 1:54; 2 Macc 8:17). In connection with the appearance of the antichrist, there will be a time of intense persecution and affliction (Mk 13:19-23; Mt 24:16-22). Jesus refers to an unspecified "sign of the Son of Man" appearing in heaven just before his actual return (Mt 24:29-30; cf. Mk 13:26, where no sign is mentioned). Following this, he gathers his elect from the entire earth—an indication of the gospel proclamation's amazing success (Mt 24:31).

Although his actual coming is sudden and the exact day and hour unknown (Mk 13:32; Mt 24:36), spiritually prepared believers will have some indication of its general timing ("you know that summer is near" [Mt 24:32-35]). As a warning to those tempted to become indifferent and spiritually lax, Jesus uses the apt analogy of a thief in the night to describe his

---

ed. Kent E. Brower and Mark W. Elliott (Downers Grove, Ill.: InterVarsity Press, 1997), pp. 11-52.

arrival (Mt 24:43). Several parables emphasize the necessity of using one's God-given talents and abilities for the kingdom and the peril of not living according to kingdom values and standards in the interim (Mt 24:45-51; 25:1-13, 14-30, 31-46). These teachings about his coming are items that the apostles Paul and John elaborate and adapt.

Jesus conceived of his circle of twelve disciples as the nucleus of a new Israel. He commissioned his apostles to undertake a mission to call "the lost sheep of the house of Israel" (Mt 10:5-15, 23) and promised that his "assembly" (i.e., church, *ekklēsia* [Mt 16:18-20]) would triumph against all opposition: "Truly I tell you, at the renewal of all things, when the Son of Man is seated on the throne of his glory, you who have followed me will also sit on twelve thrones, judging the twelve tribes of Israel" (Mt 19:28; cf. Mt 20:20-23). But there are also indications, especially in Matthew's Gospel, that this renewed Israel incorporates Gentile believers (Mt 2:1-12; 13:38; 15:21-28; 21:41, 43; 22:9-10; 24:14, 31; 25:31-46; 28:19-20).[21]

One senses a definite tension between Jewish particularism and universalism in Jesus' kingdom preaching. Is the ultimate form of the kingdom conceived in strictly nationalistic terms—that is, a restoration of the glorious Davidic empire consisting of righteous Jews and perhaps some converted Gentiles? Or is nationalism transcended by a universalism in the sense that Gentiles who believe in Jesus will also be part of this new Israel? In addition to the texts cited above, indicating that Gentiles do indeed have a significant part in the kingdom, there are two easily overlooked sayings that throw light on this question and point us in what I think is the right direction. In Matthew 5:5 we have the beatitude on meekness: "they will inherit the earth *[hē gē]*." In Matthew 5:13 Jesus describes his followers as "the salt of the earth *[hē gē]*." In this context "the earth" indicated more than merely the historic land of Israel.[22] It refers to the entire planet. In the eschaton God's kingdom matches the extent foreseen by the prophets in which "all the nations shall stream" to Zion (Is 2:2-4; Mic 4:1-3: Zech 14:9, 16-19). I think that we have enough evidence in Jesus' own teaching to conclude that Gentiles were indeed included in his purview, even if it was necessary during his earthly ministry to confine, for the most part, his ministry to the house of Israel.

I leave aside the controversial question of whether a restored Israel also

---

[21]"For the most part it appears that the practice of Jesus was confined to Jews. Yet the three Evangelists are aware [that] the gospel is to be preached to all nations. Gentiles will come into the kingdom" (I. Howard Marshall, *New Testament Theology* [Downers Grove, Ill.: InterVarsity Press, 2004], p. 721).

[22]See A. Kretzer, "γῆ," *EDNT* 1:246.

involves distinctive national privileges for the Jewish people during a millennial age. In other words, how literally should the prophetic texts be interpreted that speak of Israel's future restoration? What can be affirmed is a truly worldwide reign of Christ in which his people, Jew and Gentile, participate. This, I think, was a fundamental tenet of the Master.

But can we say more about the "renewal of all things" mentioned by Jesus? The prophets spoke of a renewal that extended to the entire created order. Isaiah 65:17-25 envisions nothing short of a new heaven and earth for the redeemed. Given the wide currency of the notion of cosmic renewal in apocalyptic Judaism, I think that Peter Trummer is correct when he says, "the context in Matthew connects [*palingenesia*, "renewal"] primarily with the Son of man and his final revelation and judgment, and *implies hopes for the future that point beyond individual, personal, or purely spiritual dimensions*"[23] In short, Jesus promises to usher in an entirely new order when the kingdom comes in all its fullness. Latent in his teaching is a cosmic soteriology, the "renewal of all things."

David Wenham ably demonstrates Paul's indebtedness to Jesus' eschatology.[24] A careful comparison of the Olivet discourse and Paul's eschatological teaching, primarily in the Thessalonian and Corinthian correspondence, illustrates numerous eschatological parallels. Most of the standard features of Pharisaic eschatology, and even some features of apocalyptic Judaism, find counterparts in Paul's letters. He believes in an assize at the judgment seat of Christ (or God) at which time all must render an account of their deeds. Believers' works will be judged, though clearly they are saved not by their works but by the grace and merit of Christ. Paul adheres to the doctrine of bodily resurrection, in keeping with his Pharisaic training. He elaborates on the nature of the resurrection body, developing more fully hints of a glorious spiritual body found in the sayings of Jesus. Like Jesus, Paul believes that the parousia will be sudden and unexpected, and that "the lawless one," the antichrist, will arise and attempt to usurp God's place. At his glorious coming, Jesus annihilates the antichrist and shares his victorious reign over the world with all the saints.

Like Jesus, Paul believes a new world order is coming. He speaks of a "newness of life" (Rom 6:4) and insists that already "if anyone is in Christ, there is a new creation: everything has . . . become new!" (2 Cor 5:17), and that this "new creation is everything!" (Gal 6:15). This newness involves creating a new people of God consisting of Jew and Gentile on equal footing

---

[23]P. Trummer, "παλιγγενεσία," *EDNT* 3:8 (my italics).

[24]David Wenham, *Paul: Follower of Jesus or Founder of Christianity?* (Grand Rapids: Eerdmans, 1995), pp. 289-337.

(Eph 2:15). But the scope of this new order transcends anthropology; according to Paul, it is cosmic. He anticipates a time when creation itself will be set free from bondage to decay and "obtain the freedom of the glory of the children of God" (Rom 8:20-21, 23). "Just as humanity's forfeited glory will be restored (3.25; 5.2), so creation's original status will be restored."[25] The cosmic scope of redemption in Christ is also implied in Philippians 3:21, where Paul adds that Christ's power to transform a believer's body at the parousia "also enables him to make all things subject to himself." This reminds us of Paul's discourse on the resurrection body in 1 Corinthians 15, where he details the sequence of resurrections (1 Cor 15:22-28). There, Paul speaks of a time "when all things are subjected" to Christ (1 Cor 15:27-28). As Larry Kreitzer observes, "Once again the transformation of humankind and the subjection of the cosmos are interconnected ideas."[26] But it is supremely the Colossian letter that highlights cosmic soteriology. In some mysterious way, the cross reconciles to God "all things, whether on earth or in heaven" (Col 1:20). Finally, Paul's climactic pronouncement in Ephesians rhapsodizes on God's saving plan "as a plan for the fullness

Table 11.1. The Unity of the Three Witnesses

Category	Jesus	Paul	John
Unifying Theme	Kingdom of God	Kingdom of God	Kingdom of God (under rubrics of "light," "truth," "knowledge" and "love")
Organizing Structure	Redemptive History	Redemptive History	Redemptive History (disguised by vertical dualism)
Focal Point	Christ and the Cross	Christ and the Cross	Christ and the Cross
Human Plight	Sin/World/Devil	Sin/World/Devil	Sin/World/Devil
Ecclesiology	"Take up your cross and follow me" (incorporation and participation)	Die and rise with Christ (incorporation and participation)	Believe and abide in Christ (incorporation and participation)
Eschatology	Renewal of all things	New humanity and new creation	New birth and new creation

---

[25]Leander E. Keck, "Romans," *The HarperCollins Study Bible: New Revised Standard Version*, ed. Wayne A. Meeks (New York: HarperCollins, 1989), p. 2127, note on Romans 8:21.

[26]L. J. Kreitzer, "Eschatology," *DPL* 264.

of time, to gather up all things in him, things in heaven and things on earth" (Eph 1:10).[27] Without doing injustice to Paul's thought, the category of restoration or new creation nicely captures his eschatological vision of the future.

John chimes in with Jesus and Paul in terms of his eschatological expectations. Easily verified is John's belief in the bodily resurrection of believers (Jn 5:29; 6:39-40, 44, 54; 11:23-25). Though not explicitly mentioned, the resurrection is implied in the parousia saying of John 14:1-3. The parallel between the seven seals (Rev 6:1—8:1), Jesus' Olivet discourse (Mt 24:3-31), and Paul's "Little Apocalypse" (2 Thess 2:1-15) has already been noted. If Jesus can speak of the "desolating sacrilege" (Mt 14:15) of the end times and Paul characterizes the perpetrator as "the lawless one" (2 Thess 2:3, 8-9), John is the first Christian writer to call him the "antichrist" (1 Jn 2:18). John is aware, as were Jesus and Paul, that precursors precede the antichrist (see Mt 24:4-5, 11-12, 23-25; 2 Thess 2:3, 7) whom John also labels as "antichrists" (1 Jn 2:18, 22; 4:3; 2 Jn 7). The most detailed portrait of the antichrist figure occurs in Revelation 13. Melding the ancient mythological imagery of Leviathan (see Ps 74:13-14; Is 27:1) with the trappings of imperial Rome, John depicts the rise of a demonically inspired person and his tyrannical oppression of the entire earth, especially his vicious persecution of the church.

What receives special billing in Revelation, however, is the relatively lengthy description of the new Jerusalem, the resplendent crown jewel of the new earth (Rev 21:1—22:5). Especially noteworthy is the use of the word *new* (*kainos* [nine times]), stressing the quality of newness.[28] Believers receive a new name (Rev 2:17; 3:12), sing a new song (Rev 5:9; 14:3), inhabit a new earth (Rev 21:1) and dwell in a new city, the new Jerusalem (Rev 21:2), capped off with the glorious declaration by the one who sits on the throne: "See, I am making all things new" (Rev 21:5).

This newness can be expressed in different ways. The Johannine Gospel and Epistles are well known for the expression "born again" or "born from above" (Jn 1:13; 3:3-8; 1 Jn 2:29; 3:9; 4:7: 5:1, 4, 18). This mysterious work of the Spirit of God is the divine side of believing in Jesus. This new birth ushers one into the kingdom of God; it is the "now" phase for the individual. But in a sense, the entire cosmos must also be "born

---

[27]Kreitzer comments, "The author of Ephesians . . . includes an unusual verb *(anakephalaiō-sasthai)* to denote the ultimate goal of this plan as it is fulfilled in Christ. This verb carries with it a strongly eschatological note, as well as a cosmological one (it is *ta panta,* 'all things,' which is said to be 'summed up' in Christ)" (ibid).

[28]J. Behm, "καινός," *TDNT* 3:447-50.

again" or "from above." Does not John's description of the new heaven and new earth really amount to a new birth for the cosmos? Note, for example, that the new Jerusalem comes "down out of heaven from God" (Rev 21:2). This is very close to Paul's language. "We know that the whole creation has been groaning in labor pains until now" (Rom 8:22). Creation too must be "set free from its bondage to decay and . . . obtain the freedom of the glory of the children of God" (Rom 8:21). "Everything has become new!" (2 Cor 5:17). This strikes precisely the same keynote as John.

CONCLUSION

Much more could be and ought to be said about the unity of our three primary witnesses. Enough, however, has been said to counteract the lopsided insistence that diversity and contradiction drown out any meaningful sense of unity and harmony. I think that this modest introduction to three star witnesses demonstrates a remarkable unity of message. In this I am not alone; a sizable cadre of biblical scholars, holding a high view of Scripture, are laboring to make the same essential point: in spite of the varied viewpoints and differing circumstances, one hears a symphony, not a cacophony. The divine conductor, the Holy Spirit, has orchestrated a most remarkable composition. In these "27 documents that changed the world" we hear the Master's voice.[29] Whether through evangelists who faithfully transmit the sayings and deeds of Jesus or through apostolic letters and tracts, before us lies one coherent message. Jesus Christ, Son of God, Savior,[30] has become one with us in order to redeem and recreate a fallen humanity and world. His saving death on the cross and triumphant resurrection from the grave are the basis of "so great a salvation" (Heb 2:3)—indeed, "eternal salvation for all who obey him" (Heb 5:9). It is the privilege and responsibility of evangelical biblical theology to make sure that this message is heard "loud and clear" until he comes.

Soli Deo gloria!

FOR FURTHER DISCUSSION

1. Is a fundamental unity in the NT message necessary? Why?

---

[29]For this phraseology, I am indebted to William C. Tremmel, *The Twenty-Seven Books That Changed the World: A Guide to Reading the New Testament* (Orlando, Fla.: Holt, Rinehart & Winston, 1981).

[30]I borrowed an early acronym for Christianity: ΙΧΘΥΣ *(ichthys)*, the Greek word for "fish." The individual letters correspond as follows: Ι = ΙΗΣΟΥΣ (Jesus); Χ = ΧΡΙΣΤΟΣ (Christ); Θ = ΘΕΟΥ ([of] God); Υ = ΥΙΟΣ (son); Σ = ΣΩΤΗΡ (savior).

2. What other ways, besides the ones discussed in this chapter, demonstrate unity?

3. How much diversity is acceptable before one compromises essential unity?

4. Why are the OT and Second Temple Judaism important factors in this discussion?

5. How may the church more effectively proclaim scriptural unity in diversity?

6. Are some themes more effective than others for presenting the gospel today?

FOR FURTHER READING

Bultmann, Rudolf. *Theology of the New Testament*, translated by Kendrick Grobel, 2:155-202. 2 vols. New York: Scribner, 1951-1955.

Caird, G. B. *New Testament Theology*, completed and edited by L. D. Hurst, pp. 409-25. Oxford: Clarendon, 1994.

Carson, D. A. "New Testament Theology." *DLNT* 796-814.

Grant, Frederick C. *An Introduction to New Testament Thought*, pp. 29-62. Nashville: Abingdon, 1950.

Guthrie, Donald. *New Testament Theology*, pp. 49-59. Downers Grove, Ill.: InterVarsity Press, 1981.

Hasel, Gerhard. *New Testament Theology: Basic Issues in the Current Debate*, pp. 140-70. Grand Rapids: Eerdmans, 1978.

Hunter, Archibald M. *Introducing New Testament Theology*. Philadelphia: Westminster Press, 1957.

Kümmel, Werner Georg. *The Theology of the New Testament According to Its Major Witnesses: Jesus-Paul-John*, translated by John E. Steely, pp. 322-33. Nashville: Abingdon, 1973.

Longenecker, R. N. "New Testament Theology." *ZPEB* 4:428-34.

Marshall, I. Howard. *New Testament Theology*, pp. 707-32. Downers Grove, Ill.: InterVarsity Press, 2004.

Matera, Frank J. "New Testament Theology: History, Method, and Identity." *CBQ* 67 (2005): 1-21.

Morris, Leon. *New Testament Theology*, pp. 325-33. Grand Rapids: Zondervan, 1986.

Rosner, Brian S. "Salvation, History of." *DTIB* 714-17.

Thielman, Frank. *Theology of the New Testament*, pp. 681-725. Grand Rapids: Zondervan, 2005.

Treier, Daniel J. "Scripture, Unity of." *DTIB* 731-34.

Wenham, David. "Appendix: Unity and Diversity in the New Testament." In George E. Ladd, *A Theology of the New Testament*, edited by Donald A. Hagner, pp. 684-719. Rev. ed. Grand Rapids: Eerdmans, 1993.

Author Index

Subject Index

Scripture Index